ORGANIZATIONAL BEHAVIOR

Second Edition

Don Hellriegel
Texas A&M University

John W. Slocum, Jr.
Southern Methodist University

WEST PUBLISHING COMPANY

St. Paul ▲ New York ▲ Los Angeles ▲ San Francisco

To our children,
Jill, Kim, and Lori
and
Christopher, Bradley, and Jonathan

Copyright © 1976, 1979 by West Publishing Co.
50 West Kellogg Boulevard / P.O. Box 3526 / St. Paul, Minnesota 55165

Library of Congress Cataloging in Publication Data

Hellriegel, Don.
  Organizational behavior.

  (The West series in management)
  Bibliography: p.
  Includes index.
  1. Organizational behavior. 2. Management.
I. Slocum, John W., joint author. II. Title.
HD58.7.H44 1979   658.4   78–27090
ISBN 0–8299–0195–7

3rd Reprint—1980

ORGANIZATIONAL BEHAVIOR

Second Edition

THE WEST SERIES IN MANAGEMENT

Consulting Editors:
Don Hellriegel and John W. Slocum, Jr.

Contents

III   INDIVIDUAL DIFFERENCES

5. The Perceptual Process   139

6. Managing Behavior Through Learning and Reinforcement   165

7. Personality and Problem Solving   217

8. Interpersonal Communication   241

IV   GROUP PROCESS

9. Dynamics Within Groups   279

V INDIVIDUAL, GROUP, AND ORGANIZATIONAL PROCESSES

VI ORGANIZATIONAL CHANGE

Preface

In studying chemistry, biology, or physics, the real world is carried into the laboratory. The science student need not rely on verbal explanations or pictures to describe events in the real world. If students doubt Galileo's theory, they can test the theory for themselves by rolling a ball down an inclined plane. In such settings, students can learn how to do scientific experiments, practice these skills and ultimately acquire the knowledge needed to attain a degree in science.

A major problem in teaching and studying organizational behavior is to provide an effective counterpart for the laboratory. Firsthand experience in many organizations is hard to come by. We cannot always find the factory, church, hospital, university, or other organization that will allow students to observe the behavior of its members. Therefore organizational behavior is a difficult area to study and teach, in part, because many of the concepts appear as abstractions.

To help the student better understand these concepts, we have included in the second edition of our text numerous lively, firsthand examples of problems facing managers. We have emphasized the actual behavior and analytical thinking required by managers and have not stressed abstract "principles" and theories. Research findings are integrated into the text only when they are meaningful and relevant. Brief managerial problems and discussion questions are included as parts of each chapter, and, in addition, more extensive cases are located in the last section of the book. This is not a book that you can read in a detached way. It is written to involve you with its contents.

A second major goal in preparing the revision has been to include topics and illustrations of high interest to students, professionals, and managers. The manager's job is not neatly compartmentalized into the traditional categories of leadership, motivation, decision making, and conflict resolution. Instead, almost every managerial action discussed has elements of all these.

A third major goal of the book is to help you understand why certain events and behavioral processes occur in organizations and how as a potential manager, you can best affect the behavior of subordinates. Behavior in organizations, as elsewhere, is exceedingly complex, and solutions are not simple. Cookbook approaches, while seemingly practical and easy to understand, are usually shortsighted and do not work in all situations. Many practical approaches to management look deceptively simple; if you follow certain principles, then you will be a more effective manager. The promise is that anyone can be an effective manager if he or she will only try the medicine. Some managers are continuously trying to find the best way to motivate subordinates or the best style of leadership. There is no perfect style. The kind of technology available and the kind of job being supervised will have a profound impact on what the manager can and should do. We recognize that the manager and the department are always part of a total system that includes the operations closely related to making the product or providing a service, other departments, the larger organization, and perhaps the external environment. For managers to understand the behavior of their subordinates, these interrelationships and dependencies must be understood. Managers must weigh carefully the impact of their actions and decisions on each one, and must consider the role played by various individuals and the group norms which have evolved.

Written for the introductory course in organizational behavior, this second edition of *Organizational Behavior* presents a contingency approach. This approach seeks to understand the interrelationships among the various parts of an organization. Each department, work group, or manager can be analyzed separately or as a unit related to other departments, work groups or managers. The contingency approach requires that the manager diagnose as partially unique each situation confronting him or her, and then apply as needed the concepts presented in the chapters. These concepts provide you with the knowledge you need to understand what is happening and what can be done about it.

Skill in diagnosing situations is achieved only through effort. Thus, as you go back and forth between concepts, solving managerial problems and answering the discussion questions, we hope your skills in using the ideas will develop so that you can be a more effective student of human behavior. You will learn about the theoretical knowledge now available in organizational behavior by reading the book. Ideally, this book should also help you to master the human skills necessary to apply this knowledge in practical ways within organizations.

The book is divided into six parts. In Part I, "Foundations of Organizational Behavior," we describe the nature of managerial work and some of the problems that a typical manager confronts on the job. In Chapter 1, we introduce the contingency approach and tell how environmental, individual, group, and organizational factors influence the behavior of employees in organizations. The second chapter introduces the reader to the ways in which knowledge about management and organizational behavior can be acquired.

Part II, "Organization and the Environment," contains Chapters 3 and 4. Its purpose is to develop the concepts for the design of organizations.

The first chapter focuses on how the environment affects the structure of an organization, while the second, entirely new chapter presents contingency solutions to related problems. The focus of these chapters is managing organizations; in this second edition these chapters have been rewritten to provide a clearer presentation on the design of organizations.

How "Individual Differences" affect the behavior of employees in organizations is the subject of Part III. Chapters 5–8 discuss how performance of individuals within organizations is affected by their perception, the reinforcement contingencies applied by the organization, the employees' personalities, and the system of interpersonal communications. These chapters have been entirely rewritten in this edition, and Chapter 6, "Managing Behavior Through Learning and Reinforcement," is an entirely new chapter. It is hoped that these revised chapters more clearly present how individual differences can affect an organization's effectiveness.

Part IV, "Group Processes," stresses how groups influence individuals and the organization. The history of mankind is the history of organized groups, created to obtain mutual benefits through improving the quality of life and satisfying the needs of group members. High productivity resulting from effective groups makes the development of group skills one of the most essential aspects of your managerial "tool kit." An efficient and effective group is one of the best friends a manager can ever have. We talk about desirable and undesirable functions of groups, the reasons why an individual may be attracted to a group, and ways that you can assess the effectiveness of your own work group. Part IV concludes with a discussion of relations between groups, the factors that affect intergroup conflict or harmony, and management skills to effectively handle intergroup problems.

Part V, "Individual, Group, and Organizational Processes," focuses on motivation, job design, leadership, and conflict processes. Chapter 12, "Job Design," is a new chapter, and we have entirely rewritten the other chapters in this part. Organizations distribute a large number of rewards to their members every day. Pay, promotions, fringe benefits, and symbols of status are perhaps the most obvious rewards. Because of the importance attached to rewards, the ways that they are distributed can have a profound impact on the motivational desires of employees. Individual differences in motivation stem in part from the types of experiences people have in different jobs, the leadership styles used by their manager, and basic differences in personality, life styles, values, and so forth. Obviously not all jobs are suited to all people. Some individuals prosper in routine work, while others prefer highly complex and challenging tasks; some are happier and more productive when working with a democratic leader, while others become frustrated and unhappy unless their work is structured by the leader. Our aim in this part is to discuss the interdependencies between an employee's need system and how the characteristics of the work itself, the style of supervision used by the manager, and how conflicts resolved in the work place influence the individual's adjustment to the organization.

The last section, Part VI, "Organizational Change," consists of three chapters. The first chapter has been rewritten to include the characteristics of successful and unsuccessful change attempts, and the qualifications change agents should bring with them to be effective managers of the change process. The rest of the material in this chapter has been updated and more examples have been included. The materials in Chapters 16 and 17 have been reorganized such that Chapter 16 focuses only on "people approaches to change," whereas Chapter 17 includes "structural, technological, and task approaches" to achieving organizational change. We felt that this reorganization will allow you to understand each major change strategy as a unit. We have made an effort to clarify the ways in which the approaches can be employed and the conditions under which they have a real chance for success.

A desire to avoid sexist connotations has created a few minor editorial problems in writing this revision. An attempt has been made to avoid the inference, by the use of personal pronouns such as "he," that all managers are male. Thus, we usually use terms such as "they," "leaders," "change agents," "managers," or the double pronouns "he or she."

We continue to be grateful for the intellectual stimulation and guidance provided by the reviewers for the first edition of this book. For the second edition, we would like to add our expression of deep appreciation to the following individuals for their insights leading to improvements in this second edition: Chris J. Berger, Purdue University; T. W. Bonham, Virginia Polytechnic Institute and State University; Donald D. Bowen, University of Tulsa; Patrick Connors, Oregon State University; Fred Crandall, Southern Methodist University; Thomas Cummings, University of Southern California; William J. Fisher, East Tennessee State University; Jack R. Goodwin, University of Concordia; Milton Gordon, California State University, Northridge; Phillip D. Jones, University of Cincinnati; Robert T. Keller, University of Houston; Robert Kreitner, Arizona State University; Loretta Nitschke, East Tennessee State University; F. Milton Parker, East Tennessee State University; Craig C. Pinder, University of British Columbia; John Rizzo, Western Michigan University; John Sheridan, Pennsylvania State University; and Kenneth G. Wheeler, University of Minnesota. In addition, we would like to provide our special thanks to Donald D. Bowen, University of Tulsa, for his significant help with the entire manuscript through its several phases of development.

For the cases they have written so that others might learn, we thank all the casewriters. For permission to use many of the cases in this book, we thank the President and Fellows of Harvard College and express gratitude to Professor Charles Gebhard for help in securing permissions. The authors of each case and other copyright information appears at the beginning of each case. Longer cases are located after the last chapter in the book.

For excellent support and assistance, we thank the people at West Publishing Company. In particular, we appreciate the assistance of Ernie Kohlmetz for his expertise in improving the readability and flow of the manuscript. Andrew Somogyi was responsible for designing and executing the illustrations that effectively reinforce the text. For prompt and accurate typing, we thank seven superb secretaries: Tricia Harrison, Teresa Marin, Beth Rhea, Judy Sartore, Judy Sorenson, Ildiko Takacs, Janie Taylor, and Delores White. Without them, its is doubtful that this manuscript could ever have been completed.

Appreciation is also expressed to Dean Gene Kelley and Michael Hottenstein, the Pennsylvania State University, as well as to Dean John E. Pearson, Texas A&M University, who were most helpful in providing assistance and other needed resources.

The authors would like to acknowledge the special contributions made by the following individuals for writing specific chapters in this revision.

Professor Meriann Jelinek, Chapter 4 *Organizational Design*
Professor Henry P. Sims, Jr., Chapter 6 *Managing Behavior Through Learning and Reinforcement*
Professor Denis Umstot, Chapter 12 *Job Design*
Professors Thomas Ruble and Richard A. Crosier, Chapter 14 *Conflict Processes*

D.H.
J.W.S., Jr.

College Station, Texas
University Park, Pennsylvania

PART I

INTRODUCTION

1

An Introduction to Organizational Behavior

1

LEARNING OBJECTIVES

When you have finished reading and studying this chapter, you should be able to:

▲ Describe the basic characteristics of managerial work.

▲ Compare traditional approaches to organizational behavior with the contingency approach.

▲ Explain the various contingencies confronting managers in organizations.

▲ Understand the interrelationships between the various contingencies facing managers.

THOUGHT STARTERS

▲ What do managers do?

▲ What is a typical day in the life of a manager like?

▲ What is meant by the contingency approach to management?

▲ How does a manager use the contingency approach to understanding the behavior of subordinates?

OUTLINE

BASIC CHARACTERISTICS OF MANAGERIAL WORK
  Hard Work in a Variety of Activities
  Preference for Nonroutine Tasks
  Face-to-Face Verbal Communications
  Involvement in a Series of Communication Networks
  Blend of Rights and Duties
APPROACHES TO ORGANIZATIONAL BEHAVIOR
TRADITIONAL APPROACHES
    Taylor
    Fayol
    Barnard
THE CONTINGENCY APPROACH
  Advantages of the Contingency Approach
  A Contingency Model
    Environmental Factors and Organizational Designs
    Individual Differences
    Group Properties
    Individual, Group, and Organizational Processes
    Organizational Change
SUMMARY
DISCUSSION QUESTIONS
MANAGERIAL PROBLEM
  The Case of the Missing Time
KEY WORDS
REFERENCES

Bill Handler was really angry this time. He had just finished asking Al Pfizer to skip his lunch period today (and either eat a sandwich on the job or go out later) in order to finish a rush order that Bill's boss, Shirley Carr, had especially requested to be finished by 2 P.M. The job involved reviewing a number of accident claims in one set of insurance files, and Bill knew this was "duck soup" for an old hand like Al. But Al had simply mumbled something about having to stop at the bank today and some other important personal errands and that, after working hard all morning, he really needed a lunch break—after all it was what all employees received.

Bill thought to himself how right he had been to turn down Al's request for promotion to senior claims analyst. At the time he had done it because of Al's poor attendance record even though he had to admit that Al was one of the sharpest analysts around. But promotion ought to reflect a sense of responsibility as well as ability, and once more Al had showed that he couldn't "cut it." "He just doesn't care about his reputation," thought Bill.

If only Bill could have seen the situation from Al's perspective. Al watched Bill take over as supervisor of the department two years before. At the time he was wary because Bill, unlike his predecessor, Joan Crispo, was standoffish. Bill didn't mingle much with the others in the department, never joked around, and didn't seem to like Al much at all. Al reasoned that Bill was probably concerned that someone as experienced as he was—Bill had never seen an insurance claim before taking the job—would resent a "green" supervisor. He became more sure of it after the incident with the bike took place.

Al got the flu, and it seemed to hang on for days. He got a call from Bill after his third day out asking if he couldn't come back soon because work was backing up. Al told him the doctor had said to take a full week. As luck would have it, on the fourth day he had gotten restless, and since the weather was so beautiful, he had ridden his son's bike down the street to a repair shop, all of 10 minutes away from his house, to get the gears fixed. Just as he was turning into the shop, he caught a glimpse of Bill driving by.

When he went back to work on the following Monday, he had tried to explain, but he knew that Bill didn't believe him. He found just how damaging a few weeks later when a promotion slot to senior claims analyst opened up, a job for which Al was certain he was well qualified. After he had indicated he wanted to be considered for the post, Bill told him that the job required a real sense of personal responsibility, and while Al was a long-service employee, his overall record was only fair.

Everyone in the department told Al he had been discrim-

From *How Managers Motivate: The Imperatives of Supervision* by W. Dowling & L. Sayles. Copyright © 1978 by McGraw-Hill Book Company. Used with permission McGraw-Hill Book Company.

inated against and he ought to fight it, to file a grievance, to see Ms. Carr, not take it lying down, and so on. But Al was too humiliated at being passed over. He only hoped that Bill wouldn't stay around too long. At least his friends in the department had stuck by him.

So when Bill asked him to give up lunch, Al saw red. Imagine what all the others would say about his doing favors for the boss who had kicked him in the teeth. Anyway, what would management say about working over lunch time?[1] And what would they say about his going along with management's feeling that lunch time wasn't really theirs?

Being a manager is a tough task. Look at the difficulties that Bill is having with Al. Bill is Al's boss, yet he is having difficulty getting Al to extend himself for the company. The organization expects Bill to get to know the people working for him well enough not only to maintain good day-to-day relationships but also to obtain that "extra" effort when the going gets tough. If you were Bill, what would you do to win Al over? Managers must make such decisions many times a day. The purpose of this book is to help you understand why problems like those facing Bill occur and to provide you with the means for resolving such problems.

Complete answers as to why people and organizations do not always function smoothly have yet to be found, but through a study of organizational behavior, the complexities of organizations and employees' behaviors can be better understood. Part of Bill's problem is that he has to work with people like Al. But managers cannot isolate themselves from others in the organization, especially their subordinates. Organizations are social systems. If you wish either to work in them or to manage them, you must understand how they operate. The study of *organizational behavior* is a systematic attempt to understand the behavior of people in organizations. To do this, you must achieve a sense of the organization's entirety by studying and understanding the complexity of its parts.

To assist you in understanding the behavior of Bill and Al, look at Figure 1–1. From Bill's viewpoint, trying to understand Al's behavior is analogous to looking at the tip of an iceberg and trying to guess its size. Only one-ninth of an iceberg is above water. Bill only knows one thing: Al is not working over the lunch period. The important behavioral factors influencing Al's decision remain hidden from Bill. Bill only knows the *formal aspects* of the Seven Springs Insurance Company:

1. The *goals* of the company: to make a profit; be a responsible member of the community; grow by 10 percent a year; sell quality insurance; and be a leader in the insurance field.
2. The *technology* of the company: complex computerized systems to handle the massive flow of paperwork; clerks to process salespersons' orders; and orderly systems and procedures to assist clients in their insurance adjustments.
3. The *structure* of the company: the departments—adjustments, under-

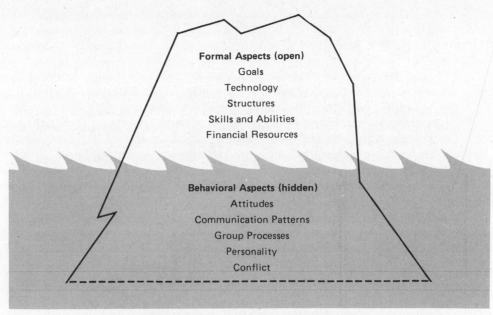

FIGURE 1–1.   Organizational Iceberg

writing, loss prevention; and division of labor—managers, sales-persons, clerks, and adjusters.

4. The *skills and abilities* of personnel: clerks need a high degree of manual dexterity; salespersons need to be aggressive, friendly, and have some degree of mathematical ability.

5. The *financial resources* of the company: rate of return on investment; cash flows; and areas of cash reserve.

Even if Bill could tell you all he knows about the Seven Springs Insurance Company, he still wouldn't know why Al refused to work over the lunch hour.

This book focuses on the behavioral and organizational problems facing a manager. The manager's job is unlike most other jobs. In other jobs, such as typists, clerks, janitors, and machinists, people are used to having clear goals that they pursue pretty much on their own. Managerial work has many different goals, some of them in conflict. Moreover, the people managers work with have different goals at different times. Some people are motivated to do first-class work, to get a sense of personal accomplishment on the job; others want to do the least amount possible and acquire as much leisure time as they can in the process; and still others want minimal risk and maximum job security. Managers need to understand not only themselves but also the other people in the organization who affect their department's work, including subordinates, other managers, and top management.

BASIC CHARACTERISTICS OF MANAGERIAL WORK

Among the thousands upon thousands of books written about managers, relatively few have been devoted to examining what managers actually do.[2] From these studies and articles, one gets the impression that managers spend most of their time reading reports in their air-conditioned offices, trying to get to the airport to catch the 5:30 plane, entertaining important customers, and solving complicated problems. Studies about chief executives suggest that they seldom stop thinking about their jobs. Four nights out of five are spent working for the company. One night is spent at the office, another entertaining business associates; on the two other "working" nights, the chief executive goes home, not to rest but to use it for a branch office. Such an approach to time management succeeds in freeing some time at work, but it creates stresses on most family situations. Tightly scheduled workdays, heavy travel, and simultaneous demands exert considerable pressures. Work weeks of 60 hours or longer are not uncommon in management positions. During a typical day, a chief executive opens 36 pieces of mail, handles five telephone calls, and attends eight meetings. A true break seldom happens. Coffee is taken during meetings, and lunchtime is often devoted to informal meetings with other managers in the company's executive dining room. When free time occurs, eager subordinates quickly try to see the manager.

One reason why managers work at such a fast pace is that managerial work is open-ended. The manager is responsible for the success or failure of the organization. There are no guidelines to say "My job is finished." While an engineer can say that the project is designed or the computer programmer can say that the system is operational, the manager's job is perpetual motion. Managerial work has five basic characteristics: (1) hard work in a variety of activities; (2) preference for nonroutine tasks; (3) face-to-face verbal communication; (4) involvement in a series of communications networks; and (5) blend of rights and duties.

Hard Work in a Variety of Activities

Many jobs require specialization and concentration. A machine operator may require 40 hours to machine a part; a computer programmer may need a month to design a system to handle the materials flow of the purchasing department; and a certified public accountant may need a month to audit the books of a large customer. But a manager's job is characterized by *variety, brevity,* and *fragmentation.* One study found that foremen averaged 583 different job problems a day (about one every 48 seconds). As a result, foremen have little time to plan. A general manager's day might include processing mail, listening to a subordinate tell him that a consumer group is boycotting their product, attending a meeting with other community leaders to discuss how to handle the energy short-age, listening to another manager complain about the lack of office space, attending a ceremonial luncheon for an employee who has been with the company for 45 years and is retiring, discussing the loss of an $8-million contract with the marketing manager, and discussing how to buy another plant so that the production facility might be more efficient. Throughout the day, the manager must confront a variety of activities. Constant inter-ruptions characterize the executive's day. The effective manager must be able to shift gears quickly and frequently. One financial vice-president told the authors "I change hats every ten minutes. I act as a tax specialist for a while, a manager for the next few minutes, then a banker, a personnel spe-cialist, and so on." The constant and seemingly endless telephone calls, sudden meetings, and personnel problems that seem designed to run the manager off schedule are always occurring.

The actions that a manager takes are also brief. Most of a man-ager's activities take less than 9 minutes. Telephone calls average about 6 minutes (brief and to the point), unscheduled meetings about 12 min-utes, while routine desk work takes about 15 minutes. Few managers do more than skim long reports and memos.

The activities that managers engage in are also fragmented. That is, there are few common patterns. Managers frequently leave meetings be-fore they are over and frequently interrupt subordinates and others to come by and chat about a problem. One study found that in 35 days a manager worked undisturbed in the office for an interval of at least 23 minutes only 12 times.

A look at the problems that confronted Stephen Spielberg, director of the film *Jaws*, might serve to highlight the variety, brevity, and frag-mentation of a manager's job.[3]

Jaws, *one of the most successful films ever produced, features a great white shark—one of nature's most efficient killing ma-chines.* Jaws *is also an efficient entertainment machine and a great box office success. In the movie, a shark terrorizes the fic-tional town of Amity by attacking swimmers. Three men, includ-ing a police chief and a professional shark killer, attempt to kill the shark. The final battle is explosive.*

Stephen Spielberg was twenty-six when he was selected to direct the film. For four years, he had directed television produc-tions, including episodes of The Psychiatrist, Columbo, *and* Mar-cus Welby. *He progressed to directing (managing) movies, in-cluding a chiller called* The Sugarland Express—*the film that got him the job of directing* Jaws. *During the filming, he managed about 150 people, including the film crew, actors, technicians, scriptwriters, and the crews of ships and boats.*

Although the movie was successful, its filming took twice as long as originally scheduled. The delay was due to a constant series of managerial problems that Spielberg had to solve.

One of the first problems was the location for shooting the movie. Martha's Vineyard, an island off the coast of Massachusetts, was picked because it closely resembled the fictional town of Amity. However, the choice was made in the winter. What Spielberg did not realize then was that in summer, when the filming was actually to take place, Martha's Vineyard is one of the most popular ports on the Atlantic coast. Literally hundreds of boats enter and leave the harbor each day.

During the filming, shots were frequently interrupted by curiosity seekers in small craft sailing too close to the cameras. How do you maintain suspense if a family of four is picnicking on a sailboat only fifty feet away from a "dramatic struggle"?

Another managerial challenge was Bruce, the mechanical shark. Actually, there were three sharks. Each weighed 1½ tons and cost about $150,000, and each was used for different movements (right-to-left, left-to-right), and different scenes. Thirteen technicians controlled the shark by means of a hundred-foot-long cable from a twelve-ton steel platform that had to be anchored to the ocean floor. The first time out, Bruce sank; the second time, the hydraulic system exploded. Only constant tinkering kept Bruce in action.

Planning and coordination were major managerial challenges. Each day, a flotilla set out to sea. One ship was for Bruce. Another was for the technicians handling the controls. Still others were for the camera crews and actors. There were even supply boats and an old ferry. The journey was made six days a week from May through October. Some days, the flotilla came back with no film at all. The failures were caused by Bruce, the weather, the small craft in the area, and a variety of other problems.

Organizing the script required constant work and tinkering. Versions were rewritten nightly before the next day's filming. Real sharks were hard to find; a dead one needed for the finale was finally flown up from Florida. It hung on the Edgartown dock for four days, creating a powerful stench. Local townsfolk retaliated by leaving dead fish on the doorsteps of the houses where the members of the cast were living.

Theft, curiosity seekers, weather, and a myriad of other problems aggravated the situation. Almost everything that could go wrong did. Spielberg had to reassure a despondent cast. Nevertheless, the daily trips continued until the last scenes were filmed in October.

Many members of the crew and cast took vacations off the island, but Spielberg never left. Although he put on a good front for the cast and crew, he was afraid that if he did leave, he would not come back. Finally, the job was done and he left the island, vowing firmly that he would never return. He has since directed Close Encounters of the Third Kind.

Preference for Nonroutine Tasks

Managers move toward the active elements in their work. Routine jobs, such as handling the mail or previewing long reports, are delegated to subordinates. Managers constantly seek new and "hot" information, which is picked up from unscheduled meetings, telephone calls, gossip, and speculation. Such hearsay forms an important part of a manager's informational diet. When the manager receives this type of information, it is given top priority.

Because of a manager's desire for the most current information, routine reports receive little, if any, serious attention. Although most managers write reports, few top managers take the time to read them. Top managers are concerned with today and tomorrow.

The avoidance of routine does not suggest that managers establish dates and deadlines that are easily missed. When an appointment is made, it is kept. An unspecified meeting time, "sometime next Friday," does not generate much interest. Unless a time is specified and written down, something else will take priority.

Managers work in a stimulus-response environment. In the Seven Springs Insurance Company, the most important thing for Bill to do is get the report out on time. How that gets done is Bill's job as a manager. Shirley, Bill's boss, does not want to hear about Bill's problem with Al. She wants the report by 2 P.M.

Face-to-Face Verbal Communications

Managers communicate in five ways: mail (documented communication), telephone (verbal), unscheduled meetings (informal person-to-person), scheduled meetings (formal person-to-person), and tours (visual). There are fundamental differences between these means of communication.

Mail requires the use of formal communication and is hampered by long delays in feedback. There is little opportunity for give-and-take and none for nonverbal gestures. Mail processing is a chore, something to be done but not enjoyed. Managers can process more than 30 pieces per hour by just skimming over inconsequential matters—solicitations, acknowledgments. Managers' treatment of mail is explained by the fact that nearly 90 percent of mail communication does not deal with "live" action. Managers prefer verbal communication. As shown in Figure 1–2, 78 percent

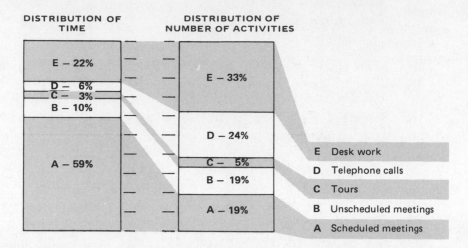

FIGURE 1–2.   Distribution of Time and Activities by Media

Adapted from Mintzberg, H., *The Nature of Managerial Work* (New York: Harper & Row, 1973), p. 39.

of all managerial time is spent using verbal communication. Telephone calls and unscheduled meetings are generally short in duration, but together account for nearly two-thirds of the executive's verbal communications. The telephone and unscheduled meetings are used when the parties know each other and have to transmit information quickly or to make a request. It is through these contacts that the manager gives or obtains a great deal of "live" information quickly. When problems suddenly arise, unscheduled meetings can be called and telephone calls can be made to "straighten" out the mess.

Scheduled meetings tend to be held when a large amount of information needs to be transmitted, when the individuals are relatively unknown to the manager, or when scheduling a meeting is the only way to bring people together.

Tours give the manager a unique opportunity to get out of the office and chat informally with employees. While it is used infrequently, managers use this time to see individuals and extend congratulations on a recent marriage, birth, graduation, or other honors.

To summarize, managers like verbal communication. Informal telephone conversations and unscheduled meetings are important to maintain "live" action. Formal, scheduled meetings are used for the delivery of communications or for events that involve a large number of people, such as ceremonies, labor management negotiations, and stockholder meetings.

The point that needs emphasis is that communication is a manager's work. Managers do not do research, admit emergency patients to the hospital, or write computer programs. Rather, managers are transmitters of information.

Involvement in a Series of Communications Networks

Not only do managers prefer verbal communications, but managers also are the center of a series of communications networks. These networks include subordinates, peers, superiors, and others outside the organization.

Usually, managers spend considerably more time with subordinates (approximately one-third to one-half their time) than with superiors. Studies of foremen indicate that only 10 percent of their time is spent with supervisors. The same percentage appears to hold true for middle and upper managers. And when a lower-level manager communicates with the boss, much of the communication is formal—status requests and formal reports.

Then who do managers spend their time communicating with? Much of their time is spent talking with other managers and others outside their department and organization. There is constant contact with other managers in other departments for information concerning planning, facilities, scheduling, customer problems, market opportunities, and people problems. Contacts outside the organization include trade associations, consultants, lawyers, underwriters, suppliers, governmental agencies, and consumer associations. Each of these groups provides specialized information to the manager. For example, the National Industrial Distributors Association keeps its members abreast of the latest legislation pending in Washington, unionization problems, and new product development.

In dealing with a large variety of outsiders, the manager acts as a "hub" in a series of communications networks. Conversations are primarily verbal and deal with information giving and receiving. Such contacts also involve managers with people over whom they have little direct control or authority.

Blend of Rights and Duties

To what extent do managers control their own time? According to Peter F. Drucker:

> The manager has the task of creating a true whole that is larger than the sum of its parts. . . . One analogy is the conductor of a symphony orchestra, through whose effort, vision, and leadership, individual parts that are so much noise by themselves become the living whole of music. But the conductor has the composer's score; he is only the interpreter. The manager is both composer and conductor.[4]

Drucker portrays the manager as one who brings order out of chaos. But there are times when managers are unable to decide on their activities. The telephone rings, the calendar pad is filled with a long list of meetings, subordinates drop in with a personal or organization problem, and unexpected problems arise. Thus managers can be depicted as either conductors or puppets, depending on how they handle their own communications.

Managers do have two important areas of freedom. *First*, managers are able to make initial decisions that define many of their own long-term commitments. For example, they can decide on whether or not to join a board of directors of a local bank, although once done, many of their activities are planned for them by others. Also, managers can develop their own information channels, and having done so, they do not need to control the day-to-day information that flows toward them. Clearly, control is exerted in terms of the "key" decisions. *Second*, managers take advantage of their obligations. When an employee retires at Standard Steel Corporation, John Fogarty, president, is provided with the opportunity for collecting information from those in attendance. Also, during the short ceremony, Fogarty is able to interject some of his values to those present. An effective manager uses the opportunity to speak to lobby for the cause, to short-circuit potential problems, and to kill stories in the rumor mill.

APPROACHES TO ORGANIZATIONAL BEHAVIOR

If most managers do tasks that are brief, fragmented, and varied, and prefer face-to-face communication to more formal impersonal communication, then what are some ways to understand their behavior? The behavior of managers and employees can partially be understood by developing frameworks from the behavioral sciences. The *behavioral sciences* represent a systematic body of knowledge from sociology, psychology, economics, and anthropology pertaining to why and how people behave as they do. A primary objective of this book is to integrate and apply behavioral science concepts to the understanding and managing of individual and group behavior within organizations. As you will discover, there are no simple cookbook recipes for understanding people. Seldom is there the "one best answer" or the "ideal organization."

A key to understanding behavior in organizations is knowing what to look at or for. You can begin by trying to see the "whole" organization, or you can begin by looking at small parts of the organization. Examples of these parts are individuals, teams, groups, and departments. Of course, focusing on a particular part of an organization only partially solves the problem. To understand the behavior of individuals in organizations, it is necessary to know something about the interrelationships between the various parts of the structure. Joe Paterno, coach of the Penn State football team, says that to gain an understanding of a football team, you need to give each unit attention. For example, on the kickoff, how far did the team get? How many times did the team have the ball within their opponent's 30-yard line and fail to score? How many punts did the team block? Only by analyzing each unit's strengths and weaknesses does the coach get a feel for the team.

One way to avoid a feeling of hopelessness in understanding behavior is to assume that explanations of behavior are simple and simply discovered. The tendency to think only in causal terms is an example of simple reasoning. The automobile accident was "caused" by the carelessness of one of the drivers, or by dangerous road conditions, or by some other single factor of the many cited as the cause of a particular automobile accident. If you drew up a long list of these single causes of automobile accidents, you might be struck by the fact that many, if not all, of the items on the list could play some causative role in any single accident you might examine.

If the single-cause assumption is inadequate, an obvious substitute is the assumption that events are caused by many forces working in complex reaction to each other. If you were interested in establishing the conditions within which the frequency of automobile accidents is reduced, then you would be well advised to study the primary factors associated with collisions and the relationships of these factors to one another. The notion of a "system" in essence assumes multiple causation and a complex interrelation of forces. Or put simply, everything is related to everything else. Organizations can be thought of as systems, such as work flows, reward structures, communications networks, and role structures. All these, functioning together, constitute what we commonly refer to as an organization. The *system approach*, which emphasizes the interrelatedness of parts and suggests the importance of interpreting an individual part only in the context of the whole, is critical to an understanding of behavior.

To be effective managers, we do not need to know *all* that can be known about every relevant system. (If this were the case, we would never get through analyzing the first problem we encountered, since everything is related to everything else in a complex chain of interdependence.) Instead, we establish who we are, our role, our competencies, and our goals. Then we choose to analyze the systems whose conditions are something we want to control or understand. Other systems whose conditions lie beyond our competence and/or control are taken into account only insofar as they affect the systems we are trying to influence.

Given the purpose of this book—to deal with behavior within organizations—we must learn about the individuals, groups, and structures that affect the behavior of people in organizations. Individual behavior in the group, the groups themselves, relationships between work groups, and groups within organization are all analyzed. The interrelationships within and among various groups in the organization are described and explained. Because the emphasis is on dealing with causes of human behavior in organizations, the structure of the organization, its technology, and job designs are all important. Individual behavior can best be understood by studying such topics as job design, motivation, leadership, group dynamics, communication, interpersonal styles, learning, and perception.

TRADITIONAL APPROACHES

Traditional approaches to organizational behavior emphasized the development of principles that were appropriate to all organizations and managerial tasks. These universal principles were generally prescriptive— there was only one way to manage organizations and employees. The founders of modern management principles, most notably Frederick Winslow Taylor, Henri Fayol, and Chester Barnard, sought to develop principles that would increase the efficiency of the corporation.[5] Using economics as their base, they were concerned with the efficiency of resource allocation and with profit-maximizing market behavior.

Taylor.   Frederick Winslow Taylor advocated the scientific management of factory production utilizing time and motion studies and the standardization of parts and processes, among other techniques. Taylor's approach was to study operations and, after careful observation and experimentation, to determine the principles by which operations could be performed optimally for management. He believed in a system of rewards and punishments geared to performance and output. He also advocated setting up a system of management controls so that supervisors would only be burdened with the exceptional problem situation and not with the moment-to-moment personal supervision of subordinates.

Fayol.   While Taylor was oriented to the management of production, Henri Fayol, a French executive and engineer, sought to systematize the whole management process. Fayol saw management's primary responsibility as planning—the setting up of formal structures for carrying out organizational activities—organizing, leadership, coordination of activities, and control. Fayol advocated several principles of management. Each manager should have only one boss to avoid conflicting demands (the principle of unity of command). Every employee must report to some boss (hierarchy of authority). Employees engaged in the same activities must be assigned identical objectives in the organization's plan (unity of direction).

Barnard.   Chester Barnard, for many years the president of New Jersey Bell Telephone Company, advanced the notion that organizations are cooperative systems in which authority is really delegated upward rather than downward. Unless employees accept the authority of management to issue orders, the right of management to issue orders is meaningless. The coal miners' strike of 1978 was an example of this principle. The president of the United States invoked the Taft-Hartley Act to get the miners back to work, but the miners disobeyed the order. Will the threat of the Taft-Hartley Act ever again intimidate strikers?

Barnard argued that an organization cannot function unless individuals within it can communicate with each other and are willing to contribute action toward achieving some shared goals. He felt that the managerial task was to specialize the work of the organization and this consisted of three principles:

1. The executive must maintain organizational communication by defining positions; by getting qualified personnel to fill these positions; and by helping to establish informal lines of communication so that formal channels of communication are seldom used.
2. The manager must secure essential services from employees by maintaining morale through incentives, controls, supervision, training, and education.
3. The manager must formulate the purposes and objectives of the organization and push these down to the organization's lowest levels.

While these principles may be applicable in some organizations, whenever they have been tested in numerous organizations, they have fallen like autumn leaves. Obviously some other approach to organizational behavior is required.

THE CONTINGENCY APPROACH

The contingency approach to organizational behavior rejects the notion that universal principles can be applied to all situations. Principles are like proverbs—they give managers insight in a vague, general way. We don't mean to derogate principles. The contingency approach uses principles when the situation calls for them.

Answer the questions in Table 1–1. If you answered all the questions as maybe/sometimes, you have grasped the meaning of the contingency approach. If your answers were more in the yes or no column, your answers can be correct depending on the situation. For example, satisfied workers are not always more productive; the satisfaction they derive from their job can come primarily from the work group, coworkers, and the ability to form friendships at work, all of which have very little to do with performance. Bureaucratic organizations, such as McDonalds, K-Mart, Burger King, Anheuser-Busch, State Farm Insurance Company, are efficient because they perform routine tasks (e.g., making Big Macs, fries, shakes) and their customers, suppliers, and regulatory bodies are relatively stable. Daily changes in McDonald's menu would make it less efficient. Not all workers wants challenging jobs. Many workers want jobs that provide good pay, require little thinking, have high security, and give them good fringe benefits (e.g., vacation time, sick days, paid holidays, and life/

TABLE 1–1. Contingency Quiz

Instructions: Answer each of the following questions by checking "YES," "NO," "MAYBE/SOMETIMES"

	Yes	No	Maybe/ Sometimes
1. Satisfied workers are more productive workers than nonsatisfied workers.			
2. Adding a piece rate pay system to a job context where the employee is already intrinsically motivated to work will be best in the long run for management.			
3. Bureaucracy is inefficient and is a bad way to organize.			
4. Workers should participate in decisions that concern them.			
5. Workers want challenging jobs			
6. Cohesive work groups are more productive than noncohesive work groups.			
7. Organizational structures should be very flexible, readily changed to achieve maximum productivity.			
8. Leaders should use styles that are person-oriented rather than task-oriented.			
9. The behavior observed in an organiaztion is the result of the total of all the personalities in it.			
10. Cohesiveness among group members will result in better group decision making than a lack of cohesiveness.			

From Pinder, C., University of British Columbia, Vancouver, British Columbia, Canada, June 1978. Used with permission of the author.

medical insurance). These workers repeatedly turn down promotions to jobs that would challenge them. Lastly, not all successful leaders are people-oriented. Woody Hayes, Bear Bryant, Vince Lombardi, noted successful football coaches, have a leadership style that would hardly be called "people-oriented."

The theme of the contingency approach is that there is *no one best way* to design organizations, lead subordinates, motivate workers, and lead group discussions. A wide variety of managerial behaviors can be appropriate in different situations. It all depends on the circumstances surrounding the manager at the time. Only after the particular situation has been properly understood by a manager can certain "management principles" be followed.

Does the contingency approach provide a panacea for solving all an organization's problems? The answer is no; this approach does not provide us with three or four or five easy steps to success in management. Cookbook approaches, while seemingly practical and easily understood, are usually short-sighted and don't work. Fundamental contingency concepts are more difficult to grasp, but they do facilitate a more thorough understanding of complex situations and increase the probability that appropriate action will be taken. According to one author, "Contingency management represents perhaps the most sophisticated approach to management yet devised."[6]

The contingency approach seeks to understand the interrelationships within, between, and among the various individuals and groups (such as departments, of an organization. Each department can be analyzed separately or as a department interacting with other departments in the organization's system. We can examine the conduct of an employee who is involved in the actual production of goods and/or analyze his behavior in relation to achieving the goals of his work group. In this instance, the individual is part of a larger system, the work group. An individual assembly-line worker who wants to work overtime is dependent upon management's willingness to offer overtime work, as well as upon the agreement of other members of his work group to work overtime, since they must provide the worker with materials, equipment, and the like. A worker's desire to work overtime is "contingent" upon others' desire to work overtime. Stated more formally, a contingency approach recognizes that individuals and groups within an organization are dependent upon each other, influence each other, and that the entire organization is dependent on the environment.

Advantages of the Contingency Approach

What are some of the advantages of using the contingency approach to understanding organizational behavior? *First*, rather than making the pretense that there is one best way to design organizations or departments, motivate employees, lead subordinates, conduct group meetings, design reward and punishment systems, the contingency approach opts for a variety of management responses based on the characteristics of the situation. In the words of two management scholars, "The beginning of administrative wisdom is the awareness that there is no optimum type of management system."[7]

According to the contingency approach, the nature of the organization's environment, its size, technology, character of its markets, its legal charter, personnel, and other factors confront the organization with opportunities as well as with problems. How the organization changes itself to solve these problems is an evolutionary process. This idea is an elaboration of the biologist's view that living forms adapted to their environment survive. For example, elephants have trunks that enable them to feed from great heights and apes have prehensile fingers and toes that enable them to swing from trees. The contingency approach to management holds that different kinds of structures, reward systems, and change strategies may be appropriate responses to different managerial problems.

Second, the contingency management approach holds that the environment of an organization is unlikely to be stable. Change is accepted as a constant in the managerial process, thus bringing pressures on organizations that heretofore relied on stability of procedures for their success. Here is perhaps the classic marketing mistake of the modern business era, the Edsel:

The Edsel, Ford's entry into the medium-priced field, was introduced for the 1958 model year. Ford Motor Company had set a goal to sell about 200,000 cars per year, which was considered by most top management people to be a conservative figure. Approximately 50 million dollars was spent for advertising and promoting the car, and another 250 million dollars in actual developmental and production costs. On the first day, more than 6,500 orders were taken, but during the next ten days, sales were only 2,751. In order to sell 200,000 cars per year, between six and seven hundred would need to be sold each day. For all of 1958 only 34,481 Edsels were sold, less than one-fifth the targeted sales. To stimulate sales, additional advertising dollars were spent, but sales continued to decline. On November 19, 1959, production was discontinued. Between 1957 and 1960, 109,466 Edsels were sold. Ford was only able to recover a small part of its original investment, leaving a nonrecoverable loss of more than a hundred million dollars.

So carefully planned, how could this happen? While complicated in its details, there appear to be several reasons. First, the Edsel was introduced during the beginning of the 1958 recession and few medium-priced cars sold well. The economists of Ford didn't foresee a recession in the economy when Ford started designing the car in 1954. Second, Consumer Reports was not overly thrilled about the Edsel. Its 800,000 subscribers found this sentence in the magazine's evaluation of the car: "The Edsel has no important basic advantage over the other brands." Third, changing consumer preferences for smaller cars had been in the wind for several years, but the marketing group ignored these changes. Disillusionment was setting in regarding large size, powerful cars. Fourth, parts did not adhere to quality standards. As a result, brakes failed, engines leaked oil, the car was besieged with rattles, and sometimes dealers could not even start them. Before these problems could be overcome, the car was labelled by the public as a "lemon."[8]

Third, contingency management rests on building blocks established in the systems approach. The management of behavior thus becomes interdependent on an understanding not only of people and people-related problems, but also of organizational design, group processes, and means to achieve change in organizations. In essence, it gives a multidimensional perspective toward understanding behavior of people in organizations. The task of management is to give a sense of purpose to all individuals and groups within the organization and to create a more viable future.

A Contingency Model

In building a contingency model for understanding behavior of employees in organizations, five major areas are stressed:

1. Environmental factors
2. Organizational designs
3. Individual differences
4. Group properties
5. Organizational change

The relationships among these areas are shown in Figure 1–3, which sets forth the themes presented in this book. The figure lists the most important dimensions in each of the major areas that will be discussed. The analysis of the areas and their key dimensions provides a pattern for understanding behavior in organizations. The relationships between these major areas are much too dynamic to allow us to set forth "laws" about their relationships. We recognize that the relationships indicated in Figure 1–3 are tentative because of the variety of events that can affect the behavior of people in organizations. For example, consider the routine characteristics of an airline flight, which suddenly change when a hijacker says, "Fly this plane to Cuba." The behavior of the flight crew and the passengers is changed; it becomes "contingent" upon the demands of the hijacker. This example highlights three important factors in applying a contingency approach to understanding behavior: environment, behavior, consequences.

First, the behavior of individuals within a system is dependent on their *environment*, which gives them a framework within which to perform their tasks. In the airliner example, the relevant environment is the plane that is being hijacked. Other environments, such as the kind of a car a person drives, the type of job she has, her home, her family life, are not relevant determiners of behavior in the present situation.

Second, the *behavior* of individuals in an environment is dependent

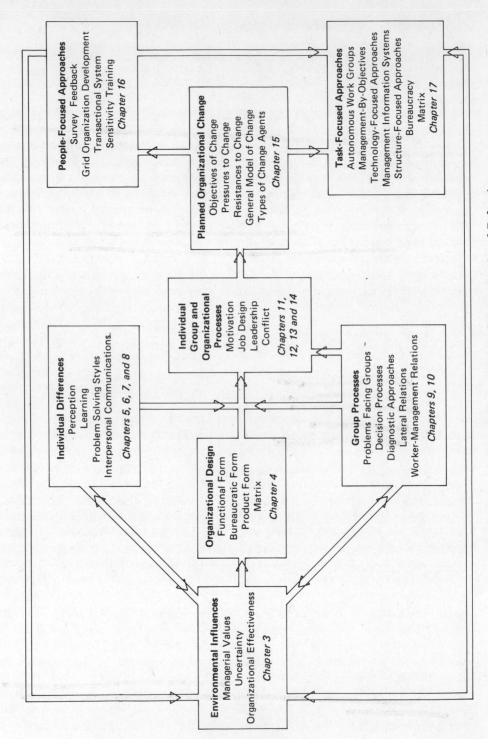

FIGURE 1–3. A Contingency Model of Organizational Behavior

on their alternatives. In the present example, most of us would sit quietly and try not to disturb the hijacker. Alternatives, such as jumping out a window, starting a riot, wrestling with the hijacker, may all result in detrimental consequences.

Third, the *consequences* of any behavior must be understood in that particular environment. Consequences are always contingent upon the behavior within the environment. In this example, the consequence of jumping out an airliner's window will probably be death, whereas the consequences of following the hijacker's orders will result in considerable personal frustration and anxiety but may not result in death.

Environmental Factors and Organizational Designs. The Edsel case showed that organizations and their environments must coexist. The organization must identify its relevant environment, for its success lies in its ability to secure resources from the environment, transform these into valuable goods and services, and then return them to the marketplace. Environments that organizations must live with include customers, suppliers, governmental bodies, competitors, and consumer groups. The environment is a source of pressure for top managers of organizations. And the environment is not immune from pressures that the organization exerts on it. Marketing activities, such as advertising campaigns, political lobbying, trade associations, diversification of activities, are organizational attempts to influence the environment.

As we saw with the Edsel, without reliable information an organization is unlikely to adapt effectively to changes in its environment. If reliable information about changes in customer preferences, governmental legislation, and the like are not available, the organization cannot plan effective responses to them. At any given time, the information coming from the environment is filtered through the managers' own value system(s) before it reaches key decision makers. If the information is reliable and important, decisions will be taken by management that can affect the organization's strategy and structure. If the organization's strategy or goals are changed, it may result in changes in the organization's structure, personnel requirements, performance-reward system, and ways of handling conflicts between departments. Chapter 3 examines some of the critical dimensions of the environment that concern decision makers. The chapter also stresses the kinds and quality of information reaching decision makers and the interpretation and use of this information by them. Chapter 4 illustrates how organizational designers attempt to match the demands of the environment with the structure of their organization. If the organization is operating in a stable environment, then a bureaucratic organization might be effective. If the organization is operating in a changing environment, then a more flexible structure, such as matrix design, should be more effective.

Individual Differences. Each of us makes assumptions about the people with whom we work, whom we supervise, or with whom we engage in leisure activities. These assumptions, to some extent, influence our be-havior toward others. Effective managers understand the psychological influences that affect their own behavior before attempting to influence the behavior of others. Chapters 5 through 8 focus on factors influencing managerial behavior. These chapters are concerned with the behavior of individuals. Each individual is also a system, comprised of a number of physiological subsystems—digestive, nervous, circulatory, reproductive—each of which can be considered as a system in its own right. This book focuses on individuals from a psychological perspective. Here the impor-tant factors are perception, learning, personality, communications, feel-ings, and values. These and other factors often hidden from others are examined.

Chapter 5 describes the basic elements in the perceptual process: se-lection, organization, interpretation, and response(s) to environmental stimuli. Two objects may be different in size, shape, and motion, but if people perceive them to be the same, they will react similarly to the objects. Thus behavior is a function of perceptions. Consider the following classic story:

> There were once four blind people who were placed near an ele-phant. Each of them was placed in a different spot and asked to describe the object. The first blind person felt the tail and said, "It's like a rope." The second blind person felt the trunk and said, "It's like a large snake." The third blind person felt the side and said, "It's like a large house or wall." The fourth blind person felt the foot and said, "It's like a trunk of a large tree."

While each of these individuals described the same object, their behavior toward the object would likely be quite different. Through each person's perceptual processes, they made an interpretation of a common stimulus.

Chapter 6 describes how people learn. Learning is so common that we often fail to recognize that it is happening. Nevertheless, one of the major premises of our approach to organizational behavior is that all im-portant managerial behaviors can be learned. Learning involves the acqui-sition of knowledge and then the translation of this knowledge into per-formance. The importance of learning in organizational settings is aptly stated:

> Every aspect of human behavior is responsive to learning experiences: knowledge, language, and skills, of course; but also attitudes, value sys-tems, and personality characteristics. All the individual's activities in the organization—loyalties, awareness of organizational goals, job perfor-mance, even safety records have been learned.[9]

The kind of learning we are interested in is operant conditioning. In operant conditioning, rewards and punishments are given as a consequence of an individual's behavior or failure to behave. Managers often fail to "motivate" workers to perform in the desired manner, as in the Seven Springs Insurance Company case, because they lack an understanding of the power of the rewards/punishments managers have and the manager's role in arranging these to increase effectiveness. As Chapter 6 indicates, in many instances managers give considerable rewards to workers even when they are not made contingent on the behavior the manager wishes to promote or stop. The necessity for arranging appropriate reinforcement contingencies is a focal point of learning.

How perception, learning, and personality combine to influence managerial problem-solving styles and abilities is the focus of Chapter 7. Problem solving and decision making are viewed in terms of the processes through which individuals organize the information they perceive in their environment and organize what they perceive. A manager's activities are bounded not only by the formal constraints of the job and the organization's structure but also by the more informal traditions and expectations that are implicit in the manager's role. Because of this, decision-making activity is initiated by and depends on the manager's environmental assessment. Consistent modes of problem solving develop through training and experience. For example, there is a strong tendency, particularly in college students and in new managers, to choose courses and professional careers that build upon their strengths. While this reinforcing pattern further develops their strengths, it perhaps also lessens the skills in which they are less confident.

How people communicate with each other is the focus of Chapter 8. Communication is the basic process through which everything between people happens in an organization. Unfortunately, communications problems plague most organizations. Communications breakdowns occur despite advances in mechanical and electronic methods of transmitting information. An illustration might highlight this problem:

Chuck Sims was the manager in charge of concessions for a football stadium. One month prior to the opening game, he made specific assignments about ordering supplies for the season. One person was to order souvenirs, one programs, one food, one beverages, and so forth. Two hours before the opening kickoff, the refreshment booths were set up to serve a crowd of more than 76,000 fans. A hungry worker accidentally discovered that the hot dog rolls were nowhere to be found in the stadium. The person in charge of ordering the hot dog rolls could only respond, "I'm sure I told the bakery the right date. It's not my fault." Chuck Sims listened to the worker and said, "It must have been a communications breakdown with the bakery. Stop cooking hot dogs and push burgers today."[10]

According to Keith Davis:

> Communication is as necessary to an organization as the bloodstream is to a person. Just as a person gets arteriosclerosis, a hardening of the arteries which impairs efficiency, so may an organization get . . . a hardening of the communication arteries which produces impaired efficiency.[11]

Not all communications are written or verbal. Nonverbal communications, such as facial gestures, eye contact, dress, are important forms of communication for managers to understand and use. The personality of the individual and the structure of the group are important contingencies affecting the quality of communications in most organizations. Giving a subordinate feedback on performance is probably one of the most important things for that person. How the feedback is given to you and how you give feedback to others are central themes developed in Chapter 8.

Group Properties.　Skills in group functioning are vital to all managers. The time managers spend in meetings (see Figure 1–2) makes up more than two-thirds of their working day. People are inherently social. It is not our nature to live alone. We are born into a group called a family and would not survive without membership in a group. Almost all our time is spent in interacting groups; we are educated in groups, we worship in groups, we play in groups. Our personal identity is derived from the way in which we are perceived and treated by other members of our groups.

Many of the goals of organizations can only be achieved with the coordination and cooperation of others. The history of organizations such as General Motors, General Electric, IBM, Westinghouse, Kodak, and RCA is the history of organized groups created to obtain mutual benefits to members and to find ways of improving the quality of life and satisfying the needs of members. The productivity resulting from effective groups makes the development of group skills one of the most essential aspects of managerial training. Membership in productive and cohesive groups is essential to maintaining psychological health throughout our lives.

To be an effective group member, you need to understand the dynamics of what happens in groups and how to increase group effectiveness. This is the focus of Chapter 9. The major contingencies affecting groups—norms, leadership, goals, communication channels, member composition—are discussed in this chapter. The model presented should give you some direction to the building of a productive group. Group members must have the skills to eliminate barriers to the accomplishment of the group's goal, to solve problems in maintaining high quality interaction among group members, and to overcome obstacles to developing a more effective group. How did you respond to questions 6 and 10 in Table 1–1? After reading Chapter 9, you might want to rethink your answers.

How groups relate to one another within organizations has considerable bearing on the effectiveness of the organization. The dynamics of intergroup relations are discussed in Chapter 10. Groups are often in conflict because of disagreement about goals, sharing of scarce resources, and attitudes of hostility. Chapter 10 examines some of the properties of intergroup relations and develops a basic set of concepts that are helpful for understanding the complex set of behaviors, emotions, and beliefs that arise when groups work together in organizations. Chapter 10 concludes by presenting ways for managing intergroup relations and discussing several behavioral science techniques that can be used to reduce the destructive effects of intergroup conflict and enhance the possibility of improving organizational life and performance.

Individual, Group, and Organizational Processes.   Each year thousands of managers participate in executive development programs for the purpose of increasing the effectiveness of their leadership style and their ability to motivate people, resolve conflict, and improve the quality of working life for employees in their firms. Like organisms, people and organizations are composed of many interrelated parts that interact with each other and with the larger environment. Chapters 11 through 14 deal with how individuals, groups, and the larger environment interact to affect job satisfactions of people and the effectiveness of the organization. For example, it would be foolish to introduce a new reward system or a new job design without adapting the work group structure, norms, and supervisor-subordinate relationships to these changes.

The impact and strategy of any reward system is contingent on the characteristics of the setting in which it is used and on the people to whom it is applied. People differ in how they perceive the world, what kinds of rewards they seek at work, what constitutes their problem-solving style, and how they communicate with others. These individual differences derive, in part, from different types of experiences, values, family and educational situations, and personalities. In short, all these individual differences interact to affect a person's job performance and the ways that the person interacts with a group.

Chapter 11 spells out the concept of and application of motivational approaches to management. The basic motivational process and the major motivations that affect individuals' behavior are examined, as are the ways organizations use rewards to motivate employees. The motivational theories of Maslow, Herzberg, McClelland, Vroom, and Porter and Lawler are evaluated in terms of whether they can explain why employees are motivated to perform in organizations.

How to design jobs so that employees meaningfully and effectively contribute to the success of the organization is the focus of Chapter 12. First, how the design of a job can affect employee satisfaction, motivation, and productivity is discussed. Then examined are factors that influence people's reactions to their work, including individual differences and organizational properties. Such factors explain why there is no such thing as a universally good design for work. Principles for enriching jobs are presented. Several special problems and opportunities encountered in attempts to carry out job enrichment are noted, and a set of guidelines for installing planned changes in jobs are developed.

Whenever two or more people join together to achieve a goal, a group structure develops. Part of the structure pertains to the way in which members influence each other. Within a group, when two or more members who depend on each other to reach the group's goal influence one another, leadership exists. The process of leadership is the focus of Chapter 13. Leadership within organizations begins with the formal role of the individual (president, vice-president, manager, worker) that defines the authority hierarchy. Because subordinates usually obey their superiors, a person with authority will influence those under him or her. The ways in which this influence process is accomplished are discussed in three approaches: trait, behavioral, and contingency.

Managements today need leaders who have the ability to integrate the goals of the employees and those of the organization. At times, this may require adapting the organization to the needs of employees, while at other times, it may require influencing employees toward the attainment of the organization's goals. While the group is the natural home of the leader, just as the organization is the natural home of the group, not every person is able to influence the group in the direction best suited for the group. In its simplest terms, effective organizational leadership depends upon the degree to which the leader's ability and style, as well as the group's situation, provide the leader with control and influence to act effectively in the situation. Despite the fact that the organization's structure is supposed to govern the way employees work and that it is shaped to some extent by technological considerations, the leader still has some latitude to influence people. The formal structure is often shaped by the ideas of the person in charge. Within any given structure, as a result of supervisory behavior or group influences, patterns of relationships emerge that are different from the relationships that the formal structure says should apply. For example, a leader with a directive, controlling nature is likely to set up structures and procedures that differ from those established by a leader with a permissive predisposition, even though both leaders are concerned with essentially the same products and technology. Of course, decisions will affect, and be affected by, the social groupings and informal norms that emerge in the group's system.

Imagine that you are part of a group that just has been given $5,000 to spend any way it wishes during the next six weeks. Your group has four members—Carla, Don, Eileen, and Mike. Carla wants to donate the money to the American Cancer Society; Don wants to throw a big party for his friends; Eileen wants to use the money for college scholarships; and Mike wants to divide it equally among the four group members. Your group is in conflict. These and other related issues form the basis of Chapter 14. Conflicts are inevitable in organizations because scarce resources (e.g., money, personnel, parking, and office space) must be allocated among the competing needs of the group's members. The potential values of conflict are also discussed in Chapter 14. If managed properly, conflict can help ensure that all members are committed to implementing the group's decision and that the group's problem-solving ability does not fall off during the decision-making process. Four different types of conflict and managerial strategies used to reduce the amount of conflict are covered in Chapter 14.

Organizational Change.   While the proceeding sections of the book emphasize particular dimensions of behavior that influence employees' behavior at work, the final section focuses on the change process and the various strategies that managers have used for bringing about change in their organizations. Change involves adapting the organization to the demands of the environment and modifying the actual behaviors of employees. If employees do not change their behaviors, then the organization cannot change. Chapter 15 examines a number of choices that must be made when organizational changes are undertaken. The choices facing a manager include: What types of pressures are being exerted on the firm to change? What kinds of resistances to change are likely to be found? Who should implement change? To assist the manager in answering these questions, a general process model of achieving organizational change is developed. Change is an inevitable part of organizational life. Shifts in attitudes of consumers, technological breakthroughs, and demands from diverse groups (Federal Drug Agency, Nader's Raiders, among a host of others) are some of the forces that underlie organizational change.

Chapters 16 and 17 present four specific strategies available to managers for achieving change:

1. People approaches: using behavioral science techniques to create atmospheres of trust and openness among organizational members.
2. Technological approaches: changing the methods by which the work is accomplished.
3. Structural approaches: rearranging authority, responsibility, and decision-making in the organization.
4. Task approaches: redesigning individuals' jobs.

The four approaches do not represent an exhaustive list, but provide one useful classification scheme.

Chapter 16 focuses on the people approaches. These approaches—survey feedback, grid organization development, transactional analysis, and sensitivity training—are aimed at changing organizations through changing the behaviors of individual members. Chapter 17 focuses on the technological, structural, and task approaches. For example, task-focused approaches include management by objectives and the formation of autonomous work units. For a manager to use the task approach, the problem is usually diagnosed as to task difficulty or task variability. Task difficulty is the degree to which the work is easily understood by the employee, whereas task variability is the number of exceptions (nonroutine activities) the employee encounters.

The essence of these last two chapters is that managers must learn to diagnose the problem(s) before making a decision on what approach to use to achieve change. Managers who see themselves as "change agents" and who know how to function effectively in this capacity are clearly among the most valuable members of the organization.

SUMMARY

The purpose of this chapter has been to describe the typical life of managers, the problems confronting them, and how they use behavioral science techniques to improve the organization's effectiveness. Five characteristics of managerial work were given: (1) hard work on a variety of activities; (2) preference for nonroutine activities; (3) face-to-face verbal communication; (4) involvement in a series of communication networks; and (5) blend of rights and duties.

After briefly reviewing three traditional approaches to organizational behavior, the contingency approach was presented in greater detail. The contingency approach does not rest upon a set of principles, but does use principles when the situation calls for it. The contingency approach looks at the interrelationships within and among the various groups within the organization. Each group or individual employee is dependent upon others. Thus, the contingency approach to understanding organizational behavior recognizes that employees are interdependent and that the organization is dependent upon its environment for developing an appropriate structure.

The contingency model has five major building blocks: (1) the environment; (2) the formal design of the organization's structure; (3) the individual; (4) the group; and (5) the necessity to change to meet the demands of the environment, employees, and work groups. Each of these building blocks represents a major section of the book.

DISCUSSION QUESTIONS

1. What kind of a manager do you think Bill Kelley of the Seven Springs Insurance Company is?

2. What is the study of organizational behavior?

3. Describe the life of a manager.

4. What is meant by the phrase, "Management is situational"?

5. If Frederick Taylor were alive today,

what do you think would be his feelings about the field of organizational behavior?

6. What is the contingency approach?

7. Give examples of the contingency approach using your own personal study habits.

8. What are the major building blocks of the contingency model presented in this chapter?

MANAGERIAL PROBLEM

THE CASE OF THE MISSING TIME*

At approximately 7:30 a.m. on Tuesday, June 23, 1959, Chet Craig, manager of the Norris Company's Central Plant, swung his car out of the driveway of his suburban home and headed toward the plant located some six miles away just inside the Midvale city limits. It was a beautiful day. The sun was shining brightly and a cool, fresh breeze was blowing. The trip to the plant took about 20 minutes and sometimes gave Chet an opportunity to think about plant problems without interruption.

The Norris Company owned and operated three quality printing plants. Norris enjoyed a nation-wide commercial business, specializing in quality color work. It was a closely held company with some 350 employees, nearly half of whom were employed at the Central Plant, the largest of the three Norris production operations. The company's main offices were also located in the Central Plant building.

Chet had started with the Norris Company as an expediter in its Eastern Plant in 1948 just after he graduated from Ohio State. After three years Chet was promoted to production supervisor and two years later was made assistant to the manager of the Eastern Plant. Early in 1957 he was transferred to the Central Plant as assistant to the plant manager and one month later was promoted to plant manager, when the former manager retired.

Chet was in fine spirits as he relaxed behind the wheel. As his car picked up speed, the hum of the tires on the newly paved highway faded into the background. Various thoughts occurred to him and he said to himself, "This is going to be the day to really get things done."

He began to run through the day's work, first one project, then another, trying to establish priorities. After a few minutes he decided that the open-end unit scheduling was probably the most important; certainly the most urgent. He frowned for a moment as he recalled that on Friday the vice president and general manager had casually asked him if he had given the project any further thought. Chet realized that he had not been giving it much thought lately. He had been meaning to get to work on this idea for over three months, but something else always seemed to crop up. "I haven't had much time to sit down and really work it out," he said to himself. "I'd better get going and hit this one today for sure." With that he be-

* All names and organizational designations have been disguised.

Northwestern University cases are reports of concrete events and behavior prepared for class discussion. They are not intended as examples of good or bad administrative or technical practices.

gan to break down the objectives, procedures, and installation steps of the project. He grinned as he reviewed the principles involved and calculated roughly the anticipated savings. "It's about time," he told himself. "This idea should have been followed up long ago." Chet remembered that he had first conceived of the open-end unit scheduling idea nearly a year and a half ago just prior to his leaving Norris's Eastern Plant. He had spoken to his boss, Jim Quince, manager of the Eastern Plant, about it then and both agreed that it was worth looking into. The idea was temporarily shelved when he was transferred to the Central Plant a month later.

A blast from a passing horn startled him but his thoughts quickly returned to other plant projects he was determined to get under way. He started to think through a procedure for simpler transport of dies to and from the Eastern Plant. Visualizing the notes on his desk he thought about the inventory analysis he needed to identify and eliminate some of the slow-moving stock items; the packing controls which needed revision; and the need to design a new special-order form. He also decided that this was the day to settle on a job printer to do the simple outside printing of office forms. There were a few other projects he couldn't recall offhand but he could tend to them after lunch if not before. "Yes sir," he said to himself, "this is the day to really get get rolling."

Chet's thoughts were interrupted as he pulled into the company parking lot. When he entered the plant Chet knew something was wrong as he met Al Noren, the stockroom foreman, who appeared troubled. "A great morning, Al," Chet greeted him cheerfully.

"Not so good, Chet; my new man isn't in this morning," Noren growled.

"Have you heard from him?" asked Chet.

"No, I haven't," replied Al.

Chet frowned as he commented, "These stock handlers assume you take it for granted that if they're not here, they're not here, and they don't have to call in and verify it. Better ask Personnel to call him."

Al hesitated for a moment before replying. "Okay, Chet, but can you find me a man? I have two cars to unload today."

As Chet turned to leave he said, "I'll call you in half an hour, Al, and let you know."

Making a mental note of the situation Chet headed for his office. He greeted the group of workers huddled around Marilyn, the office manager, who was discussing the day's work schedule with them. As the meeting broke up Marilyn picked up a few samples from the clasper, showed them to Chet, and asked if they should be shipped that way or if it would be necessary to inspect them. Before he could answer, Marilyn went on to ask if he could suggest another clerical operator for the sealing machine to replace the regular operator who was home ill. She also told him that Gene, the industrial engineer, had called and was waiting to hear from Chet.

After telling Marilyn to go ahead and ship the samples, he made a note of the need for a sealer operator for the office and then called Gene. He agreed to stop by Gene's office before lunch and started on his routine morning tour of the plant. He asked each foreman the types and volumes of orders they were running, the number of people present, how the schedules were coming along, and the orders to be run next; helped the folding-room foreman find temporary storage space for consolidating a carload shipment; discussed quality control with a pressman who had been running poor work; arranged to transfer four people temporarily to different departments, including two for Al in the stockroom, talked to the shipping foreman about pickups and special orders to be delivered that day. As he continued through the plant, he saw to it that reserve stock was moved out of the forward stock area; talked to another pressman about his requested change of vacation schedule; had a "heart-to-heart" talk with a press helper who seemed to need frequent reassurance; approved two type and one color order okays for different pressmen.

Returning to his office, Chet reviewed the production reports on the larger orders against his initial productions and found that the plant was running behind schedule. He called in the folding-room foreman and together they went over the line-up of machines and made several necessary changes.

During this discussion, the composing-room foreman stopped in to cover several type changes and the routing foreman telephoned for approval of a revised printing schedule. The stockroom foreman called twice, first to inform him that two standard, fast-moving stock items were dangerously low; later to advise him that the paper stock for the urgent Dillion job had finally arrived. Chet made the necessary subsequent calls to inform those concerned.

He then began to put delivery dates on important and difficult inquiries received from customers and salesmen. (The routine inquiries were handled by Marilyn.) While he was doing this he was interrupted twice, once by a sales correspondent calling from the West Coast to ask for a better delivery date than originally scheduled; once by the personnel vice president asking him to set a time when he could hold an initial training and induction interview with a new employee.

After dating the customer and salesmen inquiries, Chet headed for his morning conference in the Executive Offices. At this meeting he answered the sales vice president's questions in connection with "hot" orders, complaints, the status of large-volume orders and potential new orders. He then met with the general manager to discuss a few ticklish policy matters and to answer "the old man's" questions on several specific production and personnel problems. Before leaving the Executive Offices, he stopped at the office of the secretary-treasurer to inquire about delivery of cartons, paper, and boxes, and to place a new order for paper.

On the way back to his own office, Chet conferred with Gene about two current engineering projects concerning which he had called earlier. When he reached his desk, he lit a cigarette, and looked at his watch. It was 10 minutes before lunch, just time enough to make a few notes of the details he needed to check in order to answer knotty questions raised by the sales manager that morning.

NORRIS COMPANY ORGANIZATION CHART

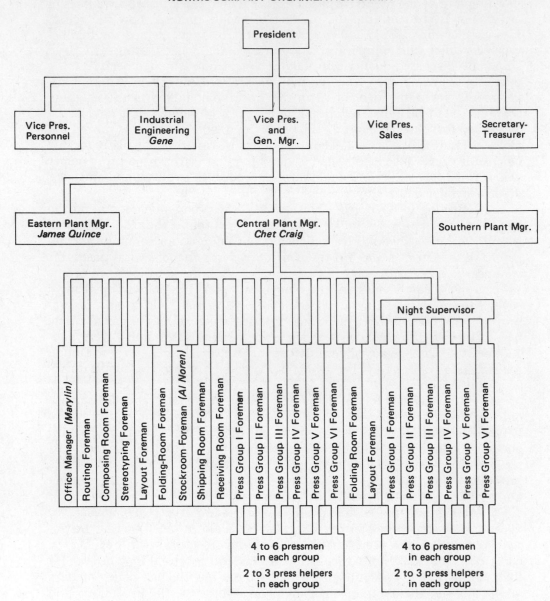

FIGURE 1–4.

After lunch Chet started again. He began by checking the previous day's production reports; did some rescheduling to get out urgent orders; placed appropriate delivery dates on new orders and inquiries received that morning; consulted with a foreman on a personal problem. He spent some

20 minutes at the TWX[1] going over mutual problems with the Eastern Plant.

By midafternoon Chet had made another tour of the plant after which he met with the personnel director to review with him a touchy personal problem raised by one of the clerical employees; the vacation schedules submitted by his foremen; and the pending job evaluation program. Following this conference, Chet hurried back to his office to complete the special statistical report for Universal Waxing Corporation, one of Norris' best customers. As he finished the report he discovered that it was ten minutes after six and he was the only one left in the office. Chet was tired. He put on his coat and headed through the plant toward the parking lot; on the way he was stopped by both the night supervisor and night layout foreman for approval of type and layout changes.

With both eyes on the traffic, Chet reviewed the day he had just completed. "Busy?" he asked himself. "Too much so—but did I accomplish anything?" His mind raced over the day's activities. "Yes and no" seemed to be the answer. "There was the usual routine, the same as any other day. The plant kept going and I think it must have been a good production day. Any creative or special project-work done?" Chet grimaced as he reluctantly answered, "No."

With a feeling of guilt, he probed further. "Am I an executive? I'm paid like one, respected like one, and have a responsible assignment with the necessary authority to carry it out. Yet one of the greatest values a company derives from an executive is his creative thinking and accomplishments. What have I done about it? An executive needs some time for thinking. Today was a typical day, just like most other days, and I did little, if any, creative work. The projects that I so enthusiastically planned to work on this morning are exactly as they were yesterday. What's more, I have no guarantee that tomorrow night or the next night will bring me any closer to their completion. This is a real problem and there must be an answer."

Chet continued, "Night work? Yes, occasionally. This is understood. But I've been doing too much of this lately. I owe my wife and family some of my time. When you come down to it, they are the people for whom I'm really working. If I am forced to spend much more time away from them, I'm not meeting my own personal objectives. What about church work? Should I eliminate that? I spend a lot of time on this, but I feel I owe God some time too. Besides, I believe I'm making a worthwhile contribution in this work. Perhaps I can squeeze a little time from my fraternal activities. But where does recreation fit in?"

Chet groped for the solution. "Maybe I'm just rationalizing because I schedule my own work poorly. But I don't think so. I've studied my work habits carefully and I think I plan intelligently and delegate authority. Do I need an assistant? Possibly, but that's a long-time project and I don't be-

---

[1] Leased private telegram communication system using teletypewriter.

lieve I could justify the additional overhead expenditure. Anyway, I doubt whether it would solve the problem."

By this time Chet had turned off the highway onto the side street leading to his home—the problem still uppermost in his mind. "I guess I really don't know the answer," he told himself as he pulled into his driveway. "This morning everything seemed so simple but now. . . ." His thoughts were interrupted as he saw his son running toward the car calling out, "Mommy, Daddy's home."

QUESTIONS

1. In terms of the five characteristics of managerial work described in this chapter, which one(s) seem to reflect Chet's day?

2. What important contingencies did Chet handle today?

3. How would you rate Chet as a manager?

4. For each of the six basic management roles below, indicate what percent of Chet's time is currently spent performing that role (1 = highest, 6 = lowest).*

% Time
Now
___3___

1) Technical Specialist:
    e.g., Performing technical operations.
        Reviewing technical proposals/plans.
        Evaluating technical operations and results.
        Performing specialized tasks (i.e., doing rather
            than managing).

___5___

2) Team Member:
    e.g., Building and maintaining working relation-
        ships with peers and/or other functions.
        Participating in an ongoing group (e.g., staff
        group, task group).

___2___

3) Leader:
    e.g., Motivating and activating others.
        Setting goals for/with others.
        Delegating authority.
        Reviewing performance.
        Counseling and disciplining.
        Orienting and training new employees.

* This has been adapted from Hershey Foods, Hershey, Pa., June 1978.

Conducting salary reviews.

Developing subordinates (e.g., merging organizational and subordinate needs).

Staffing (i.e., selecting and promoting).

Establishing a climate.

4) Company Representative:

e.g., Selling, negotiating, servicing (customers, suppliers, contractors, vendors, and others).

Maintaining other external relationships as required (community, government, educational, professional, trade, industry, etc.).

Developing a network of contacts who provide information and favors.

Transmitting information about the organization to external contacts.

Serving as an expert in the field in which the organization operates.

Seeking out current information about the environment in which the company operates.

5) Administrator:

e.g., Overseeing the allocation of all resources (e.g., scheduling own time, programming work of others, and authorizing actions before implementation).

Formulating organization strategies, plans, and budgets.

Complying with reporting requirements.

Seeking and receiving organizational information and values.

Disseminating external and internal information and organizational values to subordinates as a guide for decision making.

Handling unexpected disturbances.

Overseeing the system by which decisions are made and interrelated.

6) Entrepreneur:

e.g., Continually searching for problems and opportunities for change/improvement.

Initiating and designing improvement projects in the organization.

Monitoring progress/results of ongoing improvement projects.

KEY WORDS

Organizational behavior
Behavioral sciences
Systems approach
Traditional management approach
Contingency approach

Environment
Organizational design
Individual differences
Group properties

REFERENCES

1. From *How Managers Motivate: The Imperatives of Supervision* by W. Dowling and L. Sayles. Copyright © 1978 by McGraw-Hill Book Company. Used with permission of McGraw-Hill Book Company.

2. Much of this section is drawn from Mintzberg, H., *The Nature of Managerial Work* (New York: Harper and Row, 1973), pp. 28–52; also see, Maccoby, M., *The Gamesman: Winning and Losing the Career Game* (New York: Simon and Schuster, 1976); Lynton, S., Lawmakers lack the time to think, *Washington Post*, August 28, 1977, pp. A1.

3. Reproduced by permission from *The Modern Manager,* by Edgar Huse, copyright © 1979, West Publishing Company, all rights reserved.

4. Drucker, P., *Management: Tasks, Responsibilities, and Practices* (New York: Harper and Row, 1973), p. 398.

5. For a review of basic management principles, see Hellriegel, D., and J. Slocum, *Management: Contingency Approaches* (Reading, Mass.: Addison-Wesley, 1978), pp. 108–139.

6. Wooton, L., The mixed blessings of contingency management, *Academy of Management Review,* 1977, 2, 432; Galbraith, J., and D. Nathanson, *Strategy Implementation: The Role of Structure and Process* (St. Paul, Minn.: West Publishing, 1978), p. 55.

7. Burns, T., and G. Stalker, *The Management of Innovation* (London: Tavistock Publications, 1961), p. 125.

8. This has been abridged from Hartley, R., *Marketing Mistakes* (Columbus, Ohio: Grid, 1976), pp. 59–70.

9. Costello, T., and S. Zalkind, *Psychology in Administration* (Englewood Cliffs, N.J.: Prentice-Hall, 1963), p. 205.

10. Modified from DuBrin, A., *Fundamentals of Organizational Behavior* (Elmsford, N.Y.: Pergamon Press, 1974), p. 270.

11. Davis, K., *Human Behavior at Work* (New York: McGraw-Hill, 1972), p. 379.

2

Learning About
Organizational Behavior

2

LEARNING OBJECTIVES

When you have finished reading and studying this chapter, you should be able to:

▲ Describe how the manager-researcher can use the scientific approach in the study of individual, group, and organizational behavior.

▲ Describe the four most common research designs used in the behavioral sciences.

▲ Provide criteria for evaluating the usefulness of the various research designs.

▲ Describe the basic data collection methods.

▲ Explain the ethical obligations of the manager-researcher.

THOUGHT STARTERS

▲ What does the term *scientific approach* mean to you?

▲ Have you ever been in an experiment? If so, what happened?

▲ How many different ways can you learn about human behavior?

▲ What is the importance of ethics in conducting experiments?

OUTLINE

Psychologists, sociologists, anthropologists, political scientists, economists, and practicing managers—all study organizational behavior. Results of organizational behavior research are being supplied to managers at an increasing rate through journals, monographs, film and television documentaries, survey summaries, and executive development programs. Professionals may use different methods to focus on specific aspects of human behavior, but all attempt to use the scientific approach in studying the behavior of individuals in organizations.

Organizational behavior is to the applied behavioral sciences what medical science is to the biological and physical sciences. Organizational behavior is not a specific discipline, but a grouping of applied principles focusing on people in organizational and group settings, organizational characteristics, organizational processes, managerial styles, and the management of change.

Students and managers often ask researchers to develop simple theories because they are easy to understand, remember, and apply generally. But such simplistic prescriptions ("A satisfied worker is a productive worker") for organizational and personnel management problems are no longer justified. Researchers and practitioners in the organizational behavior field are experiencing self-criticism over fundamental issues, including whether the scientific approach is appropriate for the study of organizations and employee behavior. Because of such doubts, the question is raised: How much of organizational behavior is now ready for commercial application? The answer is that application seems unwise unless managers fully understand the methods and guidelines behind the research supporting the application.[1] Such an appreciation is also critical to a sound education. Students can and should be given an appreciation of the importance of most evaluation criteria, especially by showing them how to apply these criteria.

The scientific approach is based on the assumption that events do not occur merely by chance, but, rather, that events are linked together. For you, it may appear that effective and ineffective days in the classroom or work setting are completely random, or related as much to your horoscope or biorhythms as to anything else. A major purpose of this chapter is to give you clues so that, with practice, you may be able to discover the causes that explain why you have effective and ineffective days. Once you are able to predict effective and ineffective days in terms of cause and effect, you will be able to do something about them rather than being a victim of circumstances.

Horoscopes, tarot cards, and palm readings are just some of the unscientific attempts to establish regularity in the relationship between events—to discover the predictable laws underlying all actions. The behavior of individuals is lawful and not as chaotic as it sometimes seems. For example, drivers stop at red lights, people report to work on time, paychecks arrive when they are due. There are exceptions, of course. Occasionally, someone runs a red light, people are late to work, or the paycheck is late. But these are regarded as exceptions to the law.

Countless events take place with amazing regularity throughout a manager's working day to demonstrate the lawfulness and predictability of human behavior. Indeed, managers depend on regularity to perform their jobs effectively. The more a manager can come to know about an event, the more clearly the manager can understand the cause-effect relationship and the better the manager is able to predict future behavior.

THE SCIENTIFIC APPROACH

What good management is all about is being able to understand problems and make good predictions about employees' behavior. The key to good management is understanding the scientific approach. *The scientific approach is a method for seeking out and analyzing information in a systematic and unbiased manner.* Figure 2–1 illustrates the three basic steps of the scientific approach: observation, measurement, and prediction. These steps are so simple that most people, without even realizing it, operate on the basis of the scientific approach in their everyday living.

N.B.

Let's consider an example of the application of the scientific approach to management:

The manager of the community relations department of a large public utility needs to evaluate the performance of a new subordinate. The manager starts with observations *of the employee's behavior. How effective is he in dealing with coworkers, with subordinates, with the public? Besides observing him in the daily office routine, the manager observes him running a meeting, presenting a report to top management, and representing the company at the local Chamber of Commerce meeting. The manager carefully studies all the reports the new employee submits to her. Are they complete, accurate, to the point? After a week or so, the manager has enough data to begin* measurement *of the worker's performance. How does it measure up to company standards? To her expectations? To the performance of other workers? From these measurements, the manager can make a* prediction *as to*

EXPLANATION WITH EXAMPLES

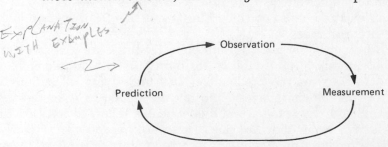

FIGURE 2–1.   The Scientific Approach

the future performance of the new employee and begin to plan for his future role in the department.

Besides illustrating the three basic steps of the scientific approach, this example illustrates some other important aspects of the scientific approach. The manager observed the employee in several different situations rather than focusing on a single example of performance. If conclusions about a person's performance are based solely on the individual's performance at one time or in one particular situation, a manager may erroneously conclude that the worker is either a high or low performer. In our example, the employee might be observed to be a poor telephone communicator, but he may be an excellent report writer and direct communicator. And the employee may have appeared to be a poor telephone communicator simply because he had a poor connection at the time of observation. The scientific approach encourages a manager to study all other events that could possibly affect the individual's performance. A thorough study—not just a one-shot observation or study of a few isolated incidents—is needed.

The scientific approach requires managers to systematically test their assumptions. If it appeared that the employee in our example was a poor telephone communicator, then the manager could have tested this assumption by having the employee convey the same message by telephone and in writing. She then would compare the results. A careful testing of the apparent problem may reveal that it is less serious than was initially assumed. The scientific approach guards against preconceptions or personal bias by requiring an assessment of the problem or issue whenever possible.

Such managerial applications of the scientific approach are not necessarily cold and clinical. Employees being evaluated can be given feedback on their performances. They can be encouraged to build on their strengths and be given advice on how to overcome their weaknesses. How they react to this feedback itself becomes a part of the ongoing scientific approach to employee evaluation.

Occasionally, researchers are criticized for being so involved in their theories that they have little to offer the practicing manager. If organizational researchers are to have an impact on managerial practices, they must offer managers a set of clear explanations for their research findings. The researcher must communicate so that managers in hospitals, banks, steel mills, automobile plants, petrochemical plants, or any other organization can use the information to understand employee behavior. If the manager and researcher both have an understanding of the scientific approach and are concerned with applying worthwhile theory to a practical problem, the research can provide the manager with something of value. The researcher needs accurate information to create theories or test models; the manager needs accurate information for taking action. An example of this process might help clarify this problem:

John Gray, manager of the computer center at a steel mill, called his subordinates together for a discussion of a time-sharing problem with a local bank. He observed that when workers had a chance to participate in the discussion, a spirit of cooperativeness and belongingness prevailed. He heard comments like "we should get together like this more often," and "now I feel like a team member." John theorized that there was a relationship between the abstract ideas of problem discussion meetings and cooperativeness. He went a step further and predicted that more meetings would produce more cooperativeness. He then decided to try out his theory. But before doing so, he contacted Professor Faust at the local university to ask him about his private theory. Faust used the information John had given him along with the knowledge he had gained from others in the field to create a model of employee participation.

The ultimate payoff for John is having Professor Faust provide him with an explanation of what's happening in his group discussion and a plan for improving the effectiveness of the computer center. Professor Faust will help solve John's problem, but he must also communicate his findings to fellow researchers, future researchers, and society in general. The benefits to John and to other researchers can only happen through an effective explanation of what the researcher believes he has found in the data.

RESEARCH DESIGNS

A research design is a plan, structure, and strategy of investigation developed to obtain answers to one or more questions.[2] The *plan* is the overall scheme or program of the research effort. It includes a list of everything the researcher will do from the start until the final analysis of the data and submission of the report. A plan should include types of data to be collected, sample populations, research instruments, tentative target completion dates, and the like. The *structure* is an outline that specifies the variables to be measured. When we draw diagrams outlining the variables and their relationships, we are building a structural schema for accomplishing the research. If we wish to examine students' learning in a class, the structure might indicate a direct relationship between student evaluation of faculty performance and academic achievement. The *strategy* represents the methods used for gathering and analyzing the data—that is, how the research objectives will be reached and how the problems encountered in the research will be resolved. The strategic issues are likely to focus on how to validly measure academic achievement and faculty performance. Other strategic questions might be: What happens if students do not sign their evaluation forms or if some students fail to fill out the forms completely? What statistical tests will be used to measure the degree of association between the two variables?

Purposes of Research Designs

A research design has two major purposes: to provide answers to questions and to provide control for nonrelevant effects that could influence the results of the study. A nonrelevant effect is anything that the researcher has little control over but that could have an impact on the results. In our student evaluation example, some nonrelevant effects might include whether half the class was absent or whether an examination was returned the day measurements were taken.

Research designs are drawn up by the researcher to obtain answers to questions as validly, objectively, accurately, and economically as possible. How does a research design help in accomplishing these aims? The design communicates, in a general sense, what observations to make, how to make them, and how to analyze them. It provides a guide to the researcher as to directions to pursue or to avoid.

Fundamentals of Research Designs

Rarely does a research design satisfy all the criteria associated with the scientific approach, but we should strive to satisfy as many as possible. If the research design is poorly conceived, the ultimate findings may be invalid or limited in applicability. If it is well conceived, the ultimate product has a greater chance of being worthy of serious attention.

Typically, the entire design of a research project has the ultimate purpose of providing for the collection of data about a hypothesis in such a way that inferences of a causal relationship between an independent (causal) variable and a dependent (effect) variable can be legitimately drawn.

N.B.

TENTATIVE

Hypothesis. A hypothesis is a statement about the relationship between two or more variables. It asserts that a particular characteristic or occurrence of one of the factors (independent variable) determines the characteristic or occurrence of another factor (dependent variable). Some examples of hypotheses are:

1. Group study for examination contributes to higher academic achievement than does studying alone.
2. Profit-sharing plans lead to reduced turnover.
3. Young college graduates are likely to experience more job dissatisfaction than older college graduates.

* Difference between a dependent & independent variable

The first hypothesis represents a relation between one variable, group study, and another variable, grade achievement. Group study is the independent variable and grade achievement is the dependent variable.

Let's consider a fourth hypothesis:

4. Business students will have more positive attitudes toward business and choose it more frequently as an occupation than will psychology students.

Here we have a relation stated between one variable, students (business and psychology), and two other variables, positive attitudes and occupational choice. The student's academic major is the independent variable and attitudes toward business and occupational choice are the dependent variables.

Researchers make a hypothesis, then investigate to determine if the facts support or disprove the hypothesis. Often, a cause-and-effect relationship is not as easy to establish as the hypothesis assumed. Yet managers informally pose hypotheses on a day-to-day basis to structure their decision-making processes. With this in mind, let us examine the basics of an experimental design.

Experimental Design.   Some types of hypotheses provide more convincing grounds for drawing causal inferences than do others.[3] The concepts of causality and experimental designs are complex; a thorough analysis of them would be far beyond the scope of this book. The discussion here will be limited to those points that seem essential to understanding the requirements for an adequate research design.

Let's suppose that the president of a company wants to test the following hypothesis:

Managers who attend training programs in human relations principles will have higher job performance that will managers who do not attend human relations programs.

In an experimental setting, the president would arrange for a number of managers to attend an executive human relations program and for a number of managers not to attend this program. The determination of who would or would not attend the program can be based on random selection or matching.

In *random selection,* each subject has an equal chance of being selected. Assigning each manager a number and then consulting the table of random numbers would be a way to randomize subjects. Or a coin may be flipped for each manager: all "heads" attend, all "tails" do not. Such a "flippant" system assures that the choices are not influenced by any preconceptions or biases of the experimenter. Each manager has the same chance as any other manager of being assigned to the program.

In *matching,* subjects must first be determined to be equal on all factors considered to be relevant to the experiment. In this example, all subjects might have to be on the same managerial level, have been with the company for five years, and be earning $25,000 a year. The subjects who fit these requirements would then be divided into two groups (quite possibly by random selection).

Accurate matching is not easy to achieve or to verify. First, a large number of subjects are needed to achieve adequate matching. Second, it is difficult to know in advance which factors are the most important to match. Third, it is difficult to match on three or more factors. Finally, it may be difficult to obtain adequate measures for all the factors. An example of the last difficulty is attempting to match subjects' past performance records when the company has not maintained consistent performance evaluation forms across departments.

Two groups are always used in an experiment. The *experimental group*—in this example managers taking the program—is exposed to the treatment or independent variable. The *control group*—managers not taking the program—is not exposed to the treatment. At the end of the training program or at some later time, the president will compare the job performance data of managers in the experimental and control groups. If the managers who attended the human relations training program perform higher on the average than those managers who did not take the training, there might be a basis for concluding that human relations training programs and managerial performance are positively related.

The use of the control group permits the president to rule out other causes for improvement in managerial job performance. Among the major ones are:

1. Natural maturing or development. Whether or not managers attend the program, day-to-day experiences that have nothing to do with training could affect performance.
2. Influence of the measurement process itself. If managers feel that they are being studied they might respond differently than if they were not being studied.
3. Contemporaneous events other than exposure of managers to the program. Events that happen during the training that are completely uncontrollable by the manager.

Whether or not managers attend the program, it is still possible for them to show an increase in their human relations skills during the period of the training program. But if this maturational process can be assumed to be the same in the experimental and control groups, and if it can be assumed that the effect of the program was not specific to any given career stage of a manager, the effects of maturation can be ruled out by comparing the two groups.

If managers feel that they are "guinea pigs" being experimented with, or if they feel that they are being "tested" and must make a good impression, the measuring process might distort the experimental results.

(Variations in experimental designs have been worked out to take account of the effects of the measuring process, but they are too complex to discuss here.)

Some contemporaneous events that may affect the outcome of the experiment that cannot be controlled for by the researcher may occur. For example, a feature story in the *Wall Street Journal* indicating that in a nationwide sample of chief executive officers, executives who are considerate of employees are in great demand by companies may lead to an increased use of human relations practices regardless of the type of training program. But as with maturational effect, if such an event affects the experimental and control group in the same way, no problem is created, since an effect common to the two groups should not be a cause of differences between them in terms of job performance.

TYPES OF RESEARCH DESIGNS

Before discussing the major types of research designs, let us explain that the discussion here is limited in scope and does not pretend to be encyclopedic. There are many types of research designs and numerous textbooks written on the subject.[4] The limited discussion here arises from the growing recognition that a basic knowledge of certain research methods is needed by present or prospective managers to understand adequately the contributions and limitations of the enormous and growing body of research in organizational behavior. In addition, this discussion should be useful in tempering a tendency to rush into cause-and-effect solutions to questions that frequently confront managers.

The researcher should be familiar with the similarities and differences among several research designs so that the most efficient design for understanding the problem at hand is selected. The researcher should select the design that will do the most complete job. The selection of a research design depends on such issues as:

1. The kinds of information it provides.
2. How clean or pure the data are—that is, how confident the researcher can be about inferences made about the findings.
3. The amount of time required and available to perform the research.
4. What kinds of resources are needed by the researcher and organization to use the design.

Instead of scientifically considering these and other issues, researchers often select a favorite research design, become comfortable with it, and apply it in situations where its usefulness is limited. Unfortunately, prior habits, experiences, and biases often play a significant role in determining the researcher's choice of research design. Instead of becoming solely interested in, say, laboratory experiments or field surveys, a researcher needs

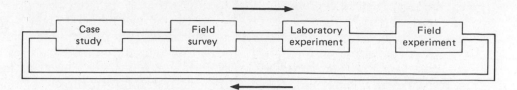

FIGURE 2–2.   Interrelationships of Research Designs

Adapted from Evan, William, *Organizational Experiments: Laboratory and Field Research* (New York: Harper & Row, 1971), p. 4. Reproduced by permission of publisher.

to understand and appreciate the usefulness of all the available research designs.

The four most common research designs used in the study of organizational behavior are the case study, the field survey, the laboratory experiment, and the field experiment. This section reviews the advantages and disadvantages of these research designs. The interrelationships of these four designs may be represented in numerous ways. One way of suggesting the relationships between the designs is by means of the diagram in Figure 2–2. Although other feedback loops are possible (for example, field survey to case study, laboratory experiment to field survey, case study to laboratory experiment, and so on), the rationale for the relationships shown in Figure 2–2 is appealing. A case study of an organization may identify one or more important variables that a researcher may then wish to investigate by means of a field survey. The major relationships uncovered in the field survey may leave unanswered questions concerning their dynamics and cause-and-effect relationships. The researcher may then pursue the problem of cause-and-effect relationships among the important variables in a laboratory experiment. If the laboratory experiment yields a relationship of general significance to theory or practice, the researcher may then wish to explore the importance of the relationship in a field experiment.

Case Study

In a case study, a researcher seeks detailed information about an individual or a group through a review of records, interviews and questionnaires, and observations. The case study is a particularly fruitful method for stimulating insights into what the problem(s) might be in relatively new areas where there is little experience to serve as a guide.[5] Several distinctive features of the case study make it an important strategy for stimulating new insights. A major one is the attitude of the researcher, which should be one of alert receptivity, of seeking rather than testing. Instead of being limited to the testing of existing hypotheses, the researcher is guided by the features of the subject being studied. A second feature is the intensity of the study. The researcher attempts to obtain sufficient information to characterize and explain the unique features of the case being studied and other cases with which it has common features. A third feature is reliance on the researcher's ability to draw together the many diverse bits of information into a unified interpretation.

If careful attention is given to these three key features, the case study can be an effective research technique for the analysis of organizational behavior. It is highly adaptable to many problems found in organizations. For example, the case study might be a useful approach for obtaining the reactions of a newcomer to an established work group. A newcomer tends to be sensitive to social customs and practices that members are likely to take for granted. For example, a six-man work group loses one member because of retirement. His or her place in the group is taken over by a newcomer to the plant. The social practices of the work group (lunch breaks, bowling league) and its production standard of no more than 100 axles per day must be communicated to this newcomer. In this case, the depth of analysis attained through the case study is its major advantage.

The limitations of the case study must also be considered by the researcher. The method's most prominent disadvantage is that it is not usually practical or logical to generalize the results of one case study to other cases. That is, only rarely does one find two cases that can meaningfully be compared in terms of essential characteristics (growth potential, number of employees, location, number of products made, levels of hierarchy, and technology used to manufacture the goods). Therefore, case studies can rarely be exactly repeated or their findings held true in other settings.

A further disadvantage is that a case study does not usually lend itself to a systematic investigation of cause-and-effect relationships. Although a case study extending over time can offer the opportunity to determine changes, the range of variations observed in the case study may be too limited for practical analysis. Hence, case studies may not afford definitive proof of a hypothesis, but they are frequently rich in clues and insights for further investigation.

Field Survey

In a field survey, data are collected through interviews or a questionnaire from a sample of people selected to represent the group under examination. Using a sample avoids the extensive and time-consuming procedure of taking a census. (A census is a complete accounting of every person in the group being studied.)

The intent of a field survey is to gather information. It is not intended to change or influence the respondents. The aim is simply to find out how things are and how people feel and think. To carry out these aims, each person in the sample is asked the same series of questions. Their answers are put together in an organized way so that conclusions can be drawn.

The content, or type of information gathered, usually concerns people's *behavior*, their *attitudes*, and their *environment*. Many organizational surveys deal with the behavior of employees. For example, the leadership strategies of executives, the client contact methods of sales personnel, the work habits of the maintenance crew. Other surveys study employee attitudes—such as job expectations, their opinion of the company or of their fellow workers or superiors. Attitudinal studies include many of the most interesting motivational studies available to the manager researcher. Finally, the manager researcher may want to know the circumstances in which employees live in order to interpret their responses to their work more accurately. This could include information about the local neighborhood, membership in groups and organizations, use of public transportation.

The field survey is not the best research design for obtaining some kinds of data. Its use is limited to data about things the subjects are consciously aware of. If the subjects' unconscious motivations are important, then an in-depth personal interview would be more productive.

A field survey requires a large number of people in its sample in order to draw valid conclusions. And of those initially selected to be sampled, many fail to respond. Typically, only 40 to 50 percent of the people who receive a questionnaire fill it out. A single firm may have too few employees to provide an adequate sample. In such circumstances, the case study would be a better approach.

Last, there remains the problem of inferring cause-and-effect relationships. A case in point would be an analysis of the relationships among job satisfaction, leadership styles, and performance. Does job satisfaction lead to higher performance and then does the leader change his or her personal style? Or is leadership related to job satisfaction, which is then associated with high performance? Because of the large number of variables typically investigated in a field survey, problems concerning the causal relationships among the variables remain unanswered.[6]

Laboratory Experiment

Compared with the case study and the field survey, the laboratory experiment increases the ability of the researcher to establish cause-and-effect relationships between variables.[7] By conducting the experiment in an artificial setting under his/her control, the researcher can create and control the exact conditions desired.

The essence of the laboratory experiment is to observe the effects of manipulating an independent variable(s) on a dependent variable(s). For example, one group of three blindfolded subjects is instructed by an autocratic leader to build a tower as high as they can with Tinker Toys. Another group of subjects is instructed by a democratic leader to perform the same task. The dependent variable is the height of the tower; the independent variable is leadership style.

There are several disadvantages in using the laboratory design. Given the practicalities of the situation, the subjects are usually college students. It is difficult to justify the use of college students as representatives of actual managers involved in decision-making processes. Students are transitory and their academic livelihood is not dependent on successful completion of a task under laboratory conditions. Therefore, to what populations and treatment variables can the laboratory results be generalized? Simulating many properties of organizational structure and process in the laboratory may increase the "realism" of the experiment, but at the cost of decreasing experimental control and precision.

Another general problem is that much of the work undertaken in the laboratory deals with phenomena that cannot be reproduced in or applied to the "real" world. A firm could not readily restructure its organizational hierarchy to fit an ideal model. Even if it found the "perfect" personnel, the changeover would result in serious morale and productivity problems. Conversely, many behavioral problems in organizations cannot be meaningfully isolated to permit their examination under lab conditions. Thus researchers tend to focus narrowly on problems that can be implemented in the laboratory setting. Nevertheless, experiments in the laboratory should derive their direction from studies in real-life situations and results should be continually checked by studies in real-life situations.

Field Experiment

A field experiment is an attempt to apply the laboratory method to ongoing real-life situations.[8] The field experiment permits the researcher to manipulate one or more independent variables in an ongoing organization. The changes in the dependent variables can be studied and the direction of causality can be inferred with some degree of confidence.

The subjects in a field experiment ordinarily know that they are under investigation, so there is a need to adopt procedures that will decrease the possibility that subjects will change their behavior simply because they are being observed. Compared to the laboratory experimenter, the field researcher has less control over the situation. The researcher must make the assumption that events are affecting both the experimental and the control groups equally and that these events will not be a major determinant of the dependent variable.

An example of a field experiment is the study discussed earlier of the effects of a human relations training program on the leadership behavior and performance of managers.[9] The purpose of the research was to answer the question: Does the job-related behavior of executives enrolled in a human relations training program change? The hypothesis was that managers who received the training would develop attitudes more sensitive to the needs of others, would more frequently structure their subordinates' work and show them consideration, and would be rated as more effective by their superiors than would managers who did not take part in the program. Forty-two managers were randomly selected from the same level in the organization. Half were randomly assigned to the experimental group that would undergo the human relations training; the remaining half became the control group.

The independent variable was the human relations training program. The training consisted of 90-minute training sessions given once a week for 28 consecutive weeks. It included materials on managerial styles, leadership, motivation, communication, and lectures on group dynamics and motivation. The dependent variables were the managers' attitudes toward themselves and others, their leadership behavior, and their performance.

Leadership style and sensitivity to the needs of others were measured by questionnaires. Performance was measured by ratings from immediate supervisors of technical knowledge, drive/aggressiveness, reliability, cooperation, and organizing ability.

The results generally supported the hypothesis. Members of the experimental group (those who had received the training) were rated as more sensitive to the needs of others, more considerate of their subordinates, and significantly more effective than the members of the control group. In fact, for managers in the control group, showing consideration to subordinates decreased.

Comparison of Research Designs

Each of the research designs just discussed has both strong and weak points. By selecting one design, the researcher must often forgo some of the advantages of alternative designs. Let's compare the major designs on a few points.

Realism   A major advantage of doing research in a natural setting, such as within an organization, is the ability to increase the level of realism. The researcher has some confidence that the subjects (managers, workers, administrators) are behaving under conditions that are natural and ongoing. While this is an advantage over the laboratory setting, which typically uses "artificial" conditions, the researcher in the field loses the ability to manipulate the independent variable(s) as freely as in the laboratory condition.

Scope   Case studies and field surveys are usually broad in scope and incorporate many variables of interest to the researcher. Laboratory experiments are by their nature the most limited in scope. A field experiment is often an expansion of a laboratory experiment.

Precision.   Research undertaken in the laboratory setting is usually more precise than research undertaken in the field setting. The intention is to measure accurately the variables under consideration. The use of multiple measures of the same variable(s) under controlled conditions allows the researcher to obtain more accurate information about the variables than with other strategies. The use of videotape, for example, permits the researcher to record the entire experiment and then to study it at a later time to examine such things as styles of behavior, motives, and gestures.

Control.   The researcher wishes to control the situation in such a way that the events under observation are sure to be related to the causes he or she thinks exist and not to some unknown events. The laboratory experiment allows the researcher to reproduce the situation over and over again. This means that he/she does not have to rely on a single observation to come to a conclusion. By replicating the study, predictions about cause-and-effect relationships are refined from "sometimes" to say, "95 times out of 100." In the laboratory experiment many factors that occur in the field (personnel changes, employees forgetting to fill out the questionnaire) over which the manager has little control are avoided. But the results drawn from ideal circumstances may not fit the real situation.

These desirable conditions—realism, scope, precision, and control—pose a constant dilemma for the researcher. All four are desirable. Yet the researcher cannot maximize all of them in any one study. A shift in a research design from a case study to a laboratory experiment will automatically increase precision and control but will probably decrease scope and perhaps realism. Thus most research designs are compromises between these conditions. Researchers must decide how much they are willing to give up in precision, scope, realism, and/or control.

Researchers must also reckon with the fact that research designs differ in their relative costs and in the kinds of resources they require. Designs vary in initial set-up costs—that is, in the time and resources needed to plan and initiate the study. They also vary in the cost per case for additional samples. For example, the laboratory experiment is relatively low in both set-up costs and costs for additional subjects. The resources required can be found in most colleges. The cost picture also suggests why field experiments and surveys tend to be carried out by large research organizations rather than by a researcher and a few assistants. In these designs, a large number of subjects are needed and computation facilities are needed to analyze the data.

No one research design is devoid of some weaknesses and none is lacking in important advantages. And there is no optimal strategy in the general case. Too much is said in the literature and in the classroom about the reasons why one strategy is weak or why one strategy is better than others. It is far more important to study how each of the various research designs differs from and is complementary to all others—to see what one gains and loses by choosing one and giving up some others. The trick is not to search for the "right" strategy to pick but to select the design that is best for your purposes and circumstances and then to use all the strengths of that research design and do whatever can be done to limit or offset its inherent weaknesses.

DATA COLLECTION METHODS

Throughout the course of a day, managers observe and gather data. Some data they reject, some they store, and some they act on. The problem with ordinary data gathering, as opposed to scientific data gathering, is that day-to-day observations of behavior are frequently unreliable or biased by personal attitudes or values. Also, the sample of behaviors observed is often limited and not truly representative of typical behavior and hence not a good basis for generalizations. Thus, erroneous conclusions are frequently drawn from observations of human behavior.

The quality of research depends not only on the adequacy of the research design but also on the adequacy of the data collection methods used. Data collection by the manager-researcher can be done in a number of ways: by interviews, by questionnaires, by observation, or by examining secondary sources. The rules for using these data to make statements about the subject matter in which one is interested may be built into the data-collecting technique or they may be developed as a supplement.

Interviews

One of the oldest and most often used devices for obtaining information is the interview. The interview relies on the willingness of people to communicate. Asking someone a direct question can save considerable time and money if the respondent is willing to talk and the answer is honest.

The interview's quality depends heavily on the mutual trust and goodwill that is established between the interviewer and the respondent. The trained interviewer will build these relationships early on in the interview so that the data will be useful. One way to build trust is to assure the respondent that all answers will be confidential. In addition, the interviewer must be a good listener to hold the attention of the respondent.

An interview may have one of three general purposes. *First*, it can be used as an exploratory device to help understand the variables in question. For example, if you are attempting to predict what jobs candidates will prefer, you might interview several candidates to find out what they are looking for in their work (salary, prestige, challenging job assignments, opportunity to continue their education). After you have discovered what job characteristics attract candidates, you might hypothesize that jobs with the desired characteristics will be more attractive to candidates than jobs without these characteristics.

Second, the interview can be used as the major research instrument.

For example, if you want to understand what causes absenteeism in a firm, you could interview employees who are frequently absent and those who are rarely absent. Comparing their responses may assist you in answering your question.

Third, the interview can be used to supplement other data-collection methods. A major strength of the interview is its ability to obtain much information in a straightforward manner. Although questions have to be carefully worded, respondents can and usually will give much information directly. Of course, the research purposes should determine the types of questions asked, their content, sequence, and wording.

There are, on the other hand, several major shortcomings in the interview method of data collection. *First*, there are certain types of information respondents may be unwilling to provide readily in a face-to-face situation. An employee may be unwilling to express negative attitudes about a superior when the interviewer is from the personnel department. It is best if the employee has never met the interviewer or has known the person only casually. To get an employee to talk openly even to an outsider and answer job, individual, and organizational questions is a difficult task because of the trust issue. Thus, the importance of establishing trust cannot be underestimated. *Second*, interviews take time, and this large investment in time costs money. *Third*, to achieve reliability, interviewers must be well trained and questions must be pretested to assure validity. Interviewers' personal biases must be eliminated, and questions must be tested for hidden biases. *Fourth*, the questions asked by the interviewer pose limitations to the kinds of answers respondents will freely give.

Questionnaires

Developing a questionnaire to learn about organizational behavior is a difficult task. It is more of an art than a science. After carefully establishing the reasons for using a questionnaire to study a particular problem, the researcher must then construct the specific questionnaire. Some useful points to consider include:

Is the question necessary?
Is the question repetitious?
Does the question contain more than one idea?
Can the respondents understand it?

Two types of questionnaires are used to acquire organizational behavior knowledge: objective and descriptive. The *objective* questionnaire presents the subjects with a question and a choice of answers. The subjects read all the answers to each question and then mark the answer to each question that is nearest to how they feel.

Figure 2–3 is an example of an objective questionnaire. It is part of

FIGURE 2–3.   An Objective Questionnaire

Instructions: We would like you to describe the "climate" of your plant. To do this, read each statement and ask yourself how descriptive this statement is of your plant. We are not asking whether you think the statement should or ought to be descriptive, rather whether it actually is descriptive.

To indicate how well each statement describes your plant, write a number in the blank beside each statement, based on the following scale.

1	2	3	4	5	6
Never true	Almost never true	Sometimes true	Frequently true	Nearly always true	Always true

_____ 1. In this plant, a manager's superior watches over him carefully to make sure he does things correctly.

_____ 2. As long as he keeps within broad limits, a manager can plan and schedule his work as he wants to.

_____ 3. A manager's boss tries to supervise him too closely here.

_____ 4. Managers here must submit frequent oral and written reports concerning what they are doing.

_____ 5. There are many close friendships among managers in this company.

_____ 6. This plant's management is sympathetic with the personal problems of its employees.

_____ 7. There are a lot of policies and standard procedures in this plant that a new manager must know before beginning a job.

_____ 8. This organization has excellent benefits for its managers.

_____ 9. The most deserving managers are the ones who get promoted.

_____ 10. This plant has a real drive to be number one.

_____ 11. Top management personnel are called by their first names.

_____ 12. Traditions are so strong here that it is difficult to modify established procedures or undertake new programs.

_____ 13. Decision-making in this organization is accomplished through shared authority (by which top and lower levels of management arrive at decisions jointly).

From Hellriegel, D. W., W. Joyce, and J. Slocum, unpublished questionnaire, Pennsylvania State University, June 1978.

a larger study conducted at Mack Trucks. This questionnaire was developed after interviewing managers at the plant. The interview step prevented the researchers from studying the organization only in terms of their own preconceptions, preconceptions that might result in an inappropriate set of questions for these employees. The questions were also developed after examining other questionnaires and from reviewing the empirical evidence of previous attempts to measure the organizational climate.

The chief advantage of objective questionnaires is that they are easy to administer and to analyze statistically. This permits much of the analysis to be performed on computers, which is an important cost consideration when hundreds of employees are surveyed.

The *descriptive* questionnaire also presents questions to the subjects, but it lets the subjects answer in their own words. However, the questions are carefully worded so that the subjects' answers focus on a specific aspect of the topic being studied. Here is how some of the objective questions given in Figure 2–3 could be transformed into descriptive questions:

2. How is a manager's work planned and scheduled?
6. How does management handle employee personal problems?
9. What criteria determine which managers get promoted?
12. What role do traditions play in this company?

A descriptive questionnaire gives subjects more leeway in answering the question than does an objective questionnaire. Sometimes a pattern of responses alerts the researchers to variables they had not originally considered.

Observations

Everyone observes the actions of others. On the basis of these observations, we infer their motivations, feelings, and intentions. A major advantage of the observation method is that it focuses attention on the behavior of individuals rather than relying on their verbal or written reports. By looking at behavior, the observer must study the entire person or group. The person's total behavior becomes the primary interest of the manager-researcher.

A major difficulty with the observation method is inherent in the observer. The researcher must digest the information derived from the observations and then make inferences about problems. Due to human fallibility, these inferences may be incorrect. Suppose, for example, a person who intensely dislikes college football observes the game, the recruiting of candidates, and the pressure to win. This individual's personal biases may well invalidate the observations and inferences he/she makes about the sport.

One method for reducing the affect of personal bias is to develop an observational form on which the observer(s) records specific conditions or acts. For example, two graduate students observed individuals approaching the ticket office of an X-rated movie in a university town. Some of the observational categories were:

1. Sex
2. Alone or with group
3. Stag group or mixed
4. How did patron pay? Fumbled around with money, quickly paid, looked to see who was around
5. Age bracket: 18 and under, college age, 25–30, over 31
6. Apparent occupation: student, businessperson, homemaker, retiree

Sitting in a car across from the theater, each observer marked a place on the form for each theater patron. If there were discrepancies between the two observers in describing the behavioral characteristics, a third observer could be used or the two observers could reach a mutually agreeable decision about the patron.

Secondary Sources

If we wish to know something about someone, instead of asking that person directly or observing them, we may turn to secondary sources for our information. Secondary sources represent data others have compiled. Company records have provided researchers with valuable data on absenteeism, turnover, grievances, performance ratings, and demographics. In some cases, this source of data may be more accurate than that obtained directly by questioning the subject. For example, company records on individual job performance may yield greater accuracy than would direct questions to the individual.

Comparison of Data Collection Methods

Figure 2–4 presents a summary of the problems and potentials for collecting data using the four major methods. This figure classifies and orders the methods according to four factors:

1. The control over the investigator's question
2. Investigator's control over the respondent's answer
3. Degree of precision
4. Breadth and depth of respondent's potential responses

In general, as more constraints are placed on the investigator and the respondent, the hidden biases of the method decrease while the precision increases. For example, if the respondents must confine themselves to a specific topic, say, pay satisfaction, and their answers must be placed in one category (highly satisfied with my pay, satisfied with my pay, dis-

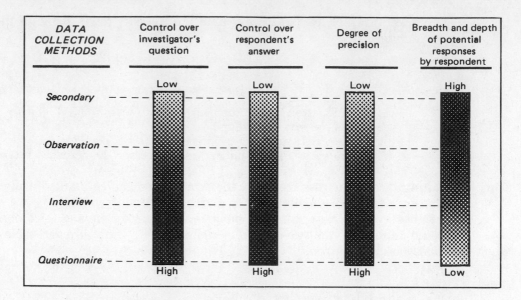

FIGURE 2–4.   Classification of Data Collection Methods

satisfied with my pay, very dissatisfied with my pay), their answers become more directly comparable one to another.

Use of a questionnaire increases the investigator's control over the question posed and the respondent's answer. But a questionnaire cannot tap the breadth of potential responses because of the limited nature of the questions asked. If the researcher wants to increase the respondent's breadth and depth of answers, using the interview method would be better. And the observation method would allow for unexpected responses. Secondary sources can only supply past responses, but they too can be valuable in formulating a complete picture.

All four methods of data collection—interviews, questionnaires, observations, and secondary sources—are currently being used by manager-researchers. Each method can be used in case studies, field surveys, laboratory experiments, and field experiments. As Figure 2–4 indicates, there is no single best method for gathering data. Methods of data gathering are not good or bad per se. Rather, some are more or less useful in answering particular questions. The important point to remember is to select a data collection method that will allow you to answer the question(s) fully and effectively.

Criteria for a Good Data Collection Method

Before any data collection method is used to measure behavior, it must meet three important requirements: reliability, validity, and practicality.

definitions of ✓

Reliability.   The reliability criterion is one of the most important characteristics of any good data collection method. *Reliability is the consistency of the data obtained.* A bathroom scale would be worthless if every time you stepped on it you got different readings. Similarly, a questionnaire would be useless if the score obtained was not consistent or stable on successive administrations. Consistently different performance scores by the same individual at different times would reflect low reliability. Before a data collection method can be used for research purposes, its reliability must be shown to be adequate.

Normally, all that is required for high reliability is control. As long as the directions are clear, the environment is comfortable, the method broad enough, and ample time is given to the subject to respond, there should be little problem with reliability. But the reliability of a data collection method can be threatened by unexpected environmental interferences. All data collection methods, except secondary sources, are affected to some degree by random changes in the subject (fatigue, distraction, emotional strain). The researcher's reliability, especially in the observation method, also can be affected by these conditions. And changes in the setting of the data collection (unexpected noises, sudden changes in weather) can also affect reliability.

Validity.   Even if a data collection method is reliable, it does not automatically follow that it is valid. *Validity is the degree to which a data collection method actually measures what it claims to measure.* The method may be reliably measuring the wrong variables. A low score on a math test may deny a job to a potential machine repairer. The test might have reliably measured the applicant's abstract math ability, but it might not be a valid measure of the applicant's skill at actually repairing machines.

The validity of many psychological tests used by firms in employee selection has recently been called into question. The Equal Employment Opportunity Commission insists that the use of tests that cannot be validated be discontinued. Tests that are not valid are worse than useless, they are misleading and dangerous. Often they have been used consciously or unwittingly to discriminate against certain social or ethnic groups. The major challenge facing the use of psychological tests in the selection process is not with reliability but with validity.

Practicality.   The importance of practicality, the final requirement of good data collection, should not be underestimated. Questionnaires, interviews, and other data collection methods should be acceptable to both management and the employees asked to fill them out. Where the employees are unionized, it is essential that the data collection method be approved by the union. This is especially true since unions have traditionally raised numerous questions about management's right to know. To ensure widespread acceptance, it is advisable to have a planning committee consisting of representatives from each management level and the unions. In this way, the viewpoints of all these groups can be taken into consideration in deciding on the data collection method. Whichever measures are chosen, they should be readily accessible and easily administered so as to save time and money and to minimize the disruption of the organization's normal operations.

Timing of Data Collection

After you have decided on your research design and on the method(s) for collecting the data, you must still decide how often you will collect these data. Frequently used methods are single-time, after-only, and before-and-after measures.

Single-time.   The single-time method collects data about the subjects' attitudes, performance, or other characteristics at only one time. A control group is usually not used. About 80 percent of the researchers in organizational behavior occasionally use this method. Thus, it is important to understand its usefulness and limitations.

The single-time method is most often used to investigate current practices and events. For example, student evaluations of professors have become popular on many campuses. The students enrolled in the class are sampled once during the semester and their perceptions are recorded. Within organizations, management uses single-time measures primarily to determine the relevance of certain practices and trends or to compare its practices against trends in the industry. This approach can also be employed to investigate relationships between two or more groups of data. If we measure an individual's job satisfaction and obtain a measure of job performance, we then can test the degree of relationship between job satisfaction and performance.

There are two limitations of the single-time measurement. First, the data do not demonstrate how the variables are related—no causal relationships can be claimed. Second, the data reported hold true only under the conditions at a specific time. In this respect, single-time measurements resemble photographs.

After-only.   As the name implies, in the after-only method the experimental and control groups are measured with respect to the dependent variable only after the experimental group has received a "treatment." The main difference between this method of data collection and the single-time method is the formation of control and experimental groups. It has been estimated that about 90 percent of the researchers and managers studying human-relations training use this method.

Perhaps the most serious weakness of this design is the researcher's assumption that the two groups were equal prior to the exposure of the experimental group to the treatment. Thus, it might be incorrectly concluded that the differences between the groups can be attributed to introduction of the treatment. Without prior measures, it is necessary to assume that both groups hold similar attitudes toward some object or that they have similar job-performance profiles. It is also necessary to assume that the groups were exposed to the same environmental and maturational processes between the time when the groups were selected and the time the measures were taken.

Before-after. The use of both experimental and control groups and before and after measurements is a reasonable design for most managers to use. This improves the ability of the researcher to conclude that changes in the experimental group were in fact a result of the "treatment," rather than the passage of time or some uncontrolled change. Two groups are selected either randomly or by matching. Before the actual experiment begins, measures of the dependent variables are made in the experimental and control groups. The experimental group is then given a "treatment," such as a human relations training program, a change in leadership style, or a modification of its task structure.

The possible effect of the treatment is subsequently evaluated by again measuring the dependent variables in both groups. The differences between the two groups after the treatment, minus the differences that may have existed before, is considered to be the effect of the treatment. Figure 2–5 presents the logic of this method. This research design is the closest organizational behavior has come to demonstrating cause and effect. This type of design is particularly important in evaluating the effectiveness of organizational change programs and may be used in any real-world setting.

Comparison of Data Collection Designs

To understand the complexity of learning about organizational behavior more clearly, Table 2–1 provides a means for comparing and con-

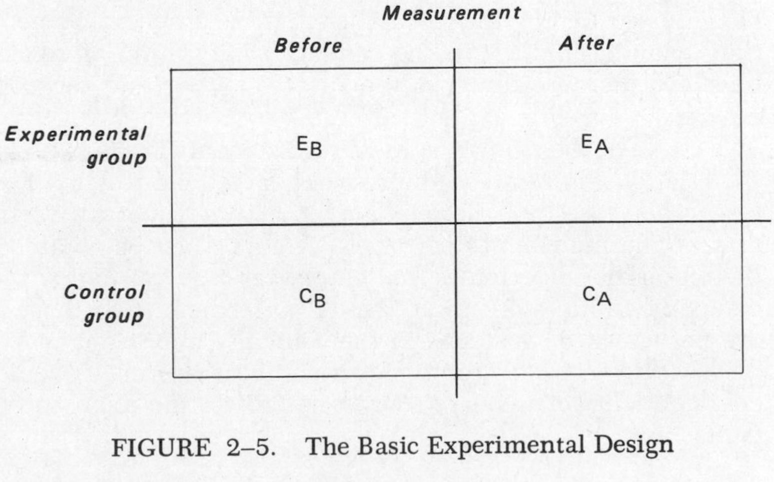

FIGURE 2–5. The Basic Experimental Design

TABLE 2–1.   Comparison of Data Collection Designs

Research design	Method of data collection	Timing of data collection
Case study	Observation Interview Secondary source	After-only Single-time
Field survey	Questionnaire Interview	Single-time
Laboratory experiment	Observation Interview Questionnaire	Before-after
Field experiment	Questionnaire Observation Interview Secondary sources	Before-after

trasting all the research designs, methods of collecting data, and timing of data collection. Each research design is described in terms of its usual procedures for collecting data and the timing of the measurement processes. The characteristics assigned represent our interpretation of the "best fit" for each strategy. Thus, there is latitude for debate and discussion on some of the characteristics assigned to certain of the designs.

ETHICS

To the extent that data are derived from the general public, students, or company employees, there arises the question of the ethical and legal obligations owed by the researcher to these subjects. Some of these obligations may be implicit in the conduct of any kind of relationship. Others have specific application to the subject matter and techniques under discussion.

One of the primary ethical requirements is the confidential nature of the relationship between the researcher and subject(s). For example, if a researcher is testing the relationship between job satisfaction and performance, the individual's performance data must be obtained. Let's assume the researcher determines that employees who are highly satisfied with the company and its policies are better performers than those employees who are not satisfied. Someone in the company may want to know which employees are in each group. However, the researcher should maintain the confidentiality of his data sources to protect the anonymity of the respondents.

By their very nature, certain types of research designs require naiveté on the part of the respondent, which is impaired under conditions of complete candor. In marketing research, for example, subjects are often asked to evaluate two samples of a product that are identical, but which are presented in different packages. Obviously, the research would be largely worthless if the respondents were informed prior to the evaluation that the contents of the packages were identical.

Similar practices are common in psychology, where false statements are presented, or true statements are attributed to false sources, in order to determine various influences of credibility. The code of ethics of the American Psychological Association requires "only when a problem is significant and can be investigated in no other way is the psychologist justified in giving misinformation to research subjects."[10] Many researchers feel an ethical obligation to inform the subjects of any falsehoods as soon as possible after the research has been terminated.

The U.S. Department of Health, Education and Welfare has issued an extensive report for the protection of human subjects.[11] To protect the respondent, objective and independent reviews of research projects and activities involving the use of human subjects are conducted by a committee. At the Pennsylvania State University, for example, the independent review committee is composed of various directors of research from the colleges within the university.[12] Each member of the review board arrives at a decision based on his/her professional judgment as to whether the research will place the participating subjects "at risk." If a majority of the review committee members feel that the procedures to be employed will not place the subject at risk, the proposal will be approved. After the proposal has been approved, each subject must sign an agreement of consent. The basic elements of informed consent include:

1. A fair explanation of the procedures to be followed, including those that are experimental
2. A description of the study
3. A description of the benefits to be expected
4. An offer to answer any inquiries concerning the procedures
5. An instruction that the subject is free to withdraw consent and to discontinue participation in the activity at any time

When the research has been completed, an abstract of the report should be made available to all interested subjects who took part in the study.

We recognize that procedures such as the ones mentioned here do not resolve all of the possible ethical issues associated with organizational behavior research. However, they do suggest some of the positive steps that should be taken to minimize risks to human subjects.

SUMMARY

This chapter reviewed the methods managers and researchers use to derive knowledge about employee behavior in organizations. These methods are all based on the scientific approach, which consists of systematic, unbiased observation, measurement, and prediction. The most commonly used research designs—case studies, field surveys, laboratory experiments, and field experiments—were analyzed. Each method has its advantages and disadvantages. Case studies provide rich insights, but they cannot be used to prove or disprove anything. Field surveys, which are the most widely used research design, enable managers to collect much information about employees, but cause-effect relationships cannot be drawn. Experimentation is superior for determining cause-effect relationships. Laboratory experiments offer the greatest control for the researcher, but this control decreases their generalizability. Field experiments sacrifice some control by the researcher but increase the generalizability of findings.

Most researchers in organizational behavior use one of four methods to collect their data: interviews, questionnaires, observations, and secondary sources. The most important point to remember is to select the most effective method for answering the research question posed. The method selected must be reliable, valid, and practical. The timing of data collection is also an important consideration. Three methods are single-time, after-only, and before-after. The ethical considerations of organizational behavior research, including establishing trust and confidentiality, were also discussed.

DISCUSSION QUESTIONS

1. What are the shortcomings of personal experience as a source of knowledge?

2. What are the purposes of a research design?

3. What are the basic features in an experimental design?

4. What is the difference between an independent and a dependent variable? Give an example of a relationship between two variables and state which one is independent and which is dependent.

5. What are some of the major research designs used by managers today?

6. Compare the research designs in terms of (a) realism, (b) scope, (c) precision, and (d) control.

7. What types of data collection methods are used by managers? Evaluate the strengths and weaknesses of each method?

8. What is reliability? What is validity? Give examples of each.

9. Why must researchers be concerned with ethics?

— confidentiality (individual results)

—

MANAGERIAL PROBLEMS

EASTCHESTER COLLEGE

Eastchester College is a small (1,500 students) private liberal arts college. For most of its history, it has operated on a conventional semester program with no classes during the summer months. In order to bring money into the college during the summer months, efforts were made by the director of continuing education to attract conferences to the campus and thereby achieve more productive use of the idle facilities during the summer. But these efforts had little success.

All administrative activities slowed down during the summer. It had become the custom to close the office at 3:30 P.M. rather than the usual hour of 5:00 P.M. The revised hours usually started immediately after commencement activities in the spring and extended through Labor Day. Approximately 75 clerks, typists, and other secretarial personnel were affected by the change. Each year, the vice-president for academic affairs notified these personnel about the new summer hours in a memo.

In January, the Board of Trustees approved a plan to switch the college to an academic quarter plan and to enroll some freshman students in both summer and fall quarters. This was done in the belief that the facilities of the college would be used more fully and that the added income would alleviate the financial strain on the college. It was also hoped that this plan would enable students to graduate more quickly because some students would attend college on a year-round basis.

Academic plans for the switch-over had been going smoothly, and Dr. Watson, business manager and vice-president for financial planning, called a staff meeting in early May to review the overall plan. During the course of the meeting, Mr. Richards, the treasurer of the college, indicated that with 300 freshman students entering the college within a month, his staff was going to have difficulty getting its work accomplished in the shortened work hours, and that he assumed that the shortened summer hours were now a thing of the past.

Dr. Kelley, the director of public administration, said that it was her understanding that the reduced summer hours would still be in effect. She further noted that many of her staff had already made plans on the basis of the traditional summer working hours. Others at the staff meeting echoed Dr. Kelley's thoughts. The vice-president for academic affairs immediately replied that no memo had gone out this year indicating that the shortened summer hours schedule would be in effect for the coming summer. He reasoned that employees should not assume that the usual changes would take place unless they received a memo from his office to that effect.

After the meeting, the word spread among the nonacademic staff that there would be no shortened work hours in the summer. During the rest of May, most administrators noticed that the morale was low, the technical quality of the work was substandard, and the problems that should have been handled by senior clerical personnel were being neglected.

QUESTIONS

1. What type of research design would you employ to study this problem? Include in your discussion your plan, structure, and strategy of investigation.
2. Explain why the research design you chose in question 1 allows you to obtain answers that would not be available if you selected any of the other designs.
3. Indicate the ethical obligations the selected research design would impose upon you.

ST. TERESA HOSPITAL

The director of management development for St. Teresa Hospital in Columbus, Ohio, had to recommend someone from the hospital for a high-level managerial position. After careful screening of all qualified employees, two names were finally selected: Jean Jarvis and Bill Franklin. After lengthy interviews with both candidates, the following information was accumulated.

Jean Jarvis had been with the hospital for three years. She had obtained a college degree in business administration and an MBA by taking evening courses at a local university. Her supervisors rated her managerial potential as promising. She was described by her peers as interested in power and status and as being dominant, optimistic, and generally intelligent. The one complaint voiced against her by her present boss, the director of community relations, was that she appeared impatient and overly ambitious. During her interview with the director of development, Jarvis indicated that promotions had not come along fast enough and that unless she received this promotion she would seek employment elsewhere.

Bill Franklin was several years older than Jarvis. Since graduating from the local university six years previously, he had been with two hospitals before joining St. Teresa's. He was rated by his superiors as steady, practical, responsible, dependable, status-oriented, very intelligent, with high mechanical aptitude. On his present job as a purchasing agent for the hospital, he felt that he had been given little opportunity to adequately display his talents. Three years ago he had turned down a more responsible position in another city citing the fact that his wife liked Columbus and was having a baby. Since that time, he had not been given another opportunity to move upward at St. Teresa's or at any other company.

QUESTIONS

1. What are some problems with the interview approach?
2. Which candidate would you recommend?
3. How did you make your selection?

KEY WORDS

Scientific approach	*Field survey*
Research design	*Laboratory experiment*
Hypothesis	*Field experiment*
Independent variable	*Reliability*
Dependent variable	*Validity*
Random selection	*Practicality*
Matching	*Single-time measurement*
Experimental group	*After-only measurement*
Control group	*Before-after measurement*
Case study	

REFERENCES

1.   Moore, L., and C. Pinder, *Managers as Consumers of Organizational Behavioral Science: The Relevance Debate* (Vancouver, B.C., Canada: University of British Columbia, working paper no. 510, November, 1977).

2.   Kerlinger, F., *Foundations of Behavioral Research* (New York: Holt, Rinehart and Winston, 1964).

3.   Campbell, D., and J. Stanley, *Experimental and Quasi-Experimental Designs for Research* (Chicago: Rand McNally, 1963). Also see Stone, E. *Research Methods in Organizational Behavior* (Santa Monica, CA: Goodyear Publishing Company, 1978).

4.   See Dunnette, M. (ed.), *Handbook of Industrial and Organizational Psychology* (Chicago: Rand McNally, 1976), Section II, Methodological foundations of industrial and organizational psychology, pp. 147–466.

5.   Yin, R., and K. Heald, Using the case survey method to analyze policy studies, *Administrative Science Quarterly*, 1975, 20, pp. 371–381.

6.   Cook, T., and D. Campbell, The design and conduct of quasi-experiments and true experiments in field settings, in M. Dunnette (ed.), *Handbook of Industrial and Organizational Psychology* (Chicago: Rand McNally, 1976), pp. 223–326.

7.   Fromkin, H., and S. Streufert, Laboratory experimentation, in M. Dunnette (ed.), *Handbook of Industrial and Organizational Psychology* (Chicago: Rand McNally, 1976), pp. 415–466.

8.   Edwards, A., *Experimental Design in Psychological Research* (New York: Holt, Rinehart and Winston, 1963).

9.   Hand, H., and J. Slocum, A longitudinal study of the effects of a human relations training program on managerial effectiveness, *Journal of Applied Psychology*, 1972, 56, pp. 412–417.

10.   Ethical standards of psychologists, *The American Psychologist*, 1963, 18, pp. 56–60.

11.   *The Institutional Guide of DHEW Policy on Protection of Human Subjects* (Washington, D.C.: Department of Health, Education and Welfare, 1971).

12.   Osborn, R., *Policy and Procedure in Research: The Pennsylvania State University* (University Park: Pennsylvania State University, 1970).

PART II

ORGANIZATION AND THE ENVIRONMENT

3

Environmental Influences

3

LEARNING OBJECTIVES

When you have finished reading and studying this chapter, you should be able to:

▲ Describe the nature and importance of values to management.

▲ Explain how values can influence the behavior of individuals and the actions of organizations.

▲ Identify three types of managerial value systems and how they are likely to lead to different ways for dealing with employees and other groups.

▲ Discuss the relationship between values and different criteria of organizational effectiveness.

▲ Describe different types of environments for organiaztions.

▲ Explain how and why organizational structures and management practices should be contingent upon the type of environment facing the organization.

THOUGHT STARTERS

▲ What type of environmental influences do you think affect organizational behavior?

▲ Are there differences between personal values and managerial values? Should there be?

Several top executives of a large urban corporation are disturbed by a community activist organization that is protesting the treatment of minority groups. The executives feel that the activists are doing more harm than good to the schools, urban renewal programs, public transportation, and retail business. The chief executive himself has expressed his fears about the activists at local business meetings. However, Charles Hines, a young official in the marketing department, thinks that the activists are on the right track. He spends many evening and weekend hours volunteering his services to the activist organization. Occasionally he is quoted in the newspaper and identified with his company.

The marketing manager of the company has come under pressure from several senior executives. They urge her to warn Hines either to stop working for the activists or resign. How should she answer them. If you were the marketing manager, which of the following possible responses would come closest to the response you would make?

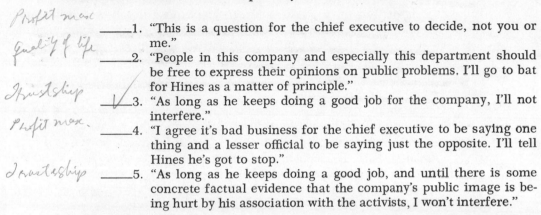

_____1. "This is a question for the chief executive to decide, not you or me."

_____2. "People in this company and especially this department should be free to express their opinions on public problems. I'll go to bat for Hines as a matter of principle."

_____3. "As long as he keeps doing a good job for the company, I'll not interfere."

_____4. "I agree it's bad business for the chief executive to be saying one thing and a lesser official to be saying just the opposite. I'll tell Hines he's got to stop."

_____5. "As long as he keeps doing a good job, and until there is some concrete factual evidence that the company's public image is being hurt by his association with the activists, I won't interfere."

Or, consider the case of James Dworkin, an electrical engineer, who has been employed by his company for more than a dozen years. Although known to be critical of many company policies, Dworkin is well liked by associates, his work has been good, and he has earned regular increases in salary. To everyone's surprise, he and his wife coauthored a novel published by a small publishing firm. While the story takes place in a fictional setting with fictional characters and events, the novel is clearly a lampoon of the company. It represents management as greedy, inflexible, and insensitive to scientific progress. Although the novel is not likely to sell many copies, the company managers are incensed.

If you were the department head to whom Dworkin reports, which of the following actions would you most likely take? (Assume no employment contract and no union.)

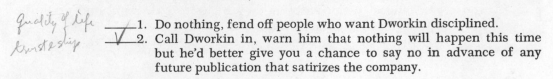

_____1. Do nothing, fend off people who want Dworkin disciplined.

_____2. Call Dworkin in, warn him that nothing will happen this time but he'd better give you a chance to say no in advance of any future publication that satirizes the company.

Profit mise. _____3. Fire Dworkin.

Profit max. _____4. Keep Dworkin on the payroll but assign him to tasks he won't like, cut any future raises, and hope he will resign after finding a job elsewhere.[1]

Take a minute or so and, on a separate sheet of paper, record how you think a representative group of managers would respond to each of the above incidents. Do this by estimating the percent of managers you think would choose each of the responses. For example, if you feel that 20 percent of the managers would choose the first alternative response, record this number. The actual findings to these questions are presented in the summary at the end of this chapter.

These two incidents highlight the close relationships between values, the organization's external environment, and managerial decision making and styles. First, in both incidents, the choices available to management involve judgments—even the decision to do nothing involves a value judgment. Second, both incidents clearly demonstrate that many important decisions are partly influenced by the values held by managers and others. Third, both incidents show the close interface between events external to the organization and how this interface can create problems (or opportunities) *within* the organization.

Throughout the 1980s, organizations are likely to continue to experience turmoil in such wide-ranging environmental areas as employee relations and working conditions, marketing and financial power and practices, consumerism, the ecology, equality of opportunity, individualism, productivity, governance, community and government relations, international operations, inflation and controls, health and safety, and the role of organizations in society.

Jerome Jacobson, senior vice-president of Bendix Corporation, has observed "In a rapidly changing economic environment, some plans are out of date in three to six months." The importance of new expectations for organizations, especially large ones, is suggested by chief executives spending more of their time on environmental influences. For example, Alonzo McDonald, Jr., a managing partner of McKinsey & Co., notes, "Just a few years ago the CEO (Chief Executive Officer) of a big company spent 10% of his time on external matters. . . . Today the figure is generally 40%."[2] But even this may be just the tip of the iceberg. Managers at all levels of organizations must confront new issues, problems, and opportunities created by the changing environment.

Within this chapter, the discussion of environmental influences is highly selective. It is impossible to deal with all the concepts and issues relevant to a complete development of the interface between environments and organizations, particularly as they relate to individual and group behavior within organizations.

The first part of this chapter focuses on values and value systems because:

1. Values provide the foundation for the legal, financial, industrial, and political parts of our culture.
2. Values provide one source of explanation for some of the actions by individuals, groups, and organizations.
3. Values represent a major part of the meaning and significance we assign to our personal lives and to the organization within which we work.
4. Values influence how we perceive wants and the actions of others.
5. Values provide a background for maintaining perspective on many of the more specific concepts and issues discussed in later chapters.

The role of values and value systems will be illustrated and made more explicit as the chapter unfolds.

The second part of the chapter is a discussion of a model that indicates how managers can assess and understand their organizational environments. The model presents the key variables and the interrelationships among them that need to be understood by managers. It is important for managers to understand their external environment because:

1. The type of environment partly determines how the organizations should be structured (highly structured versus unstructured).
2. The type of environment influences the types of relationships that should be encouraged between individuals (formal versus informal).
3. The type of environment affects the decision-making practices that should be encouraged (authoritarian versus participative decision making).

The implications of these three types of environmental influences are developed throughout the book. What happens internal to the organization is strongly influenced by the external environment. Moreover, the external environment represents a major source of uncertainty for managers. Uncertainty is a key challenge to management and the key reason for the existence of management. Without uncertainty, fewer managers would be needed, since most of the operations of the organization could be programmed and standardized. The continuous flow of uncertainties inside and outside the organization creates significant challenges, opportunities, and problems for managers.

As emphasized in Chapter 1, the definition of environment is a relative matter.[3] It depends upon the unit of analysis that is of interest (an individual, a group, a division of an organization or an organization) as well as the issues and problems being considered. For example, if we are interested in understanding and predicting the productivity of an individual employee, it might be useful to know something about the internal and external environment of the organization. Relevant variables in the internal environment of the organization might include the expectations held by fellow workers, leadership practices, and the nature of reward systems. A relevant variable in the external environment would be the value system regarding the importance attached to hard work. A second variable would be the alternative employment opportunities provided by the economic system. Thus internal and external environmental variables may influence the employee's attitude toward management's desire for higher levels of productivity. Of course, the value of hard work will only assume importance if it has been personally accepted by the employee.

Individuals, groups, and organizations not only may be acted upon by their environments but also may actively influence their environments. For example, when General Motors found itself with too few economy cars during the energy crisis, it speeded up its timetable for the introduction of new compacts. At the same time, some of the divisions, particularly Oldsmobile and Cadillac, launched major advertising campaigns promoting the safety and comfort features of larger cars. This campaign was accomplished by the claim that the additional gasoline costs to operate the larger cars, compared with those for compacts, might be less than $200 a year for the average driver. The intent in this example is not to pass judgment as to whether these actions are good or bad. Rather, it is to illustrate the possibility of individuals', groups', and organizations' being reactive as well as proactive with respect to their environments.

A *reactive orientation* is the tendency to take action as a result of being influenced by some external event or force. A *proactive orientation* is the tendency to take action as a result of ideas, goals, or perceived opportunities that are created or formulated by the individual, group, or organization. Typically, proaction is intended to create greater self-control relative to the environment and/or to influence the actions of others in the environment. For an organization to survive and be successful, it is necessary for its management to be both proactive and reactive.

VALUES AND VALUE SYSTEMS

One of the major areas that management has to react to is values and value systems that exist in the culture within which the organization operates. Since all people do not share exactly the same values within a given society (such as the United States), these differences in values create many of the significant conflicts and problems with which management must deal. Obviously, these differences also show up in various employees' holding somewhat conflicting values as groups and/or as individuals. Managements have the multiple tasks of understanding their own values and the values of other groups and individuals that can influence the organization.

Nature of Values

The definitions of value and value system set forth by Milton Rokeach substantially represent the meanings that will be assigned to the concepts in this chapter. Rokeach states:

A *value* is an enduring belief that a specific mode of conduct or end-state *← INSTRUCTOR* of existence is personally or socially preferable to an opposite or converse mode of conduct or end-state of existence. A *value system* is an enduring organization of beliefs concerning preferable modes of conduct or end states of existence along a continuum of relative importance.[4]

This definition means that values and value systems cannot simply be labeled as "good" or "bad" or "true" or "false."[5] The reason for this should become clearer as the definitions are considered more closely.

Belief   A value is a belief that does not change from day to day. But the idea of continuity in a value does not mean it is completely stable or rigid. One of the characteristics and problems of present-day industrialized societies is the increased rate of change and instability in values. In industrialized countries, there is a great probability for subgroups within the societies to possess different values that may come into conflict. The belief element in the value definition is quite complex, consisting of three distinct, yet related, components: cognitive, affective, and behavioral.

1. The *cognitive component* means the individual has a conception or knowledge of what is desirable. To suggest that an individual accepts the value of working hard is to say that, cognitively, this person knows that the appropriate way to behave on the job is to work hard.
2. The *affective component* of a value means that the individual can experience emotions or feelings about the value, both negative and positive. Someone who believes in the value of hard work may feel good about working hard, as well as experiencing resentment and even hostility toward those who don't share this belief and are low performers.
3. The *behavioral component* of the value suggests that it influences the actions of individuals. Someone who believes in hard work is more likely to translate this value into action by actually working hard.

Modes of Conduct and End-states of Existence.   Modes of conduct and end-states of existence as elements in the definition of a value are distinct, yet interrelated. *Modes of conduct* are the means for attainment of values. *End-states of existence* are the terminal or ultimate values attained. The value framework presented in this chapter is primarily concerned with modes-of-conduct values that are instruments for achieving end-states-of-existence values. Some examples of modes-of-conduct values are:

- Individualist (self-reliant, self-sufficient)
- Cooperative (working with and for the welfare of others)
- Competitive (striving to win over others)
- Loving (affectionate, tender)
- Obedient (dutiful, respectful)
- Responsible (dependable, reliable)

Ambitious (hard working, aspiring)
Honest (sincere, truthful)

By following certain modes-of-conduct values, people believe that they will achieve certain end-states of existence. For example, the Protestant ethic, which characterized a number of people in the United States at one time, holds that through hard work, frugality, and self-sacrifice here on earth (modes-of-conduct values), individuals earn their way into salvation and the kingdom of God (end-states-of-existence values).

In contemporary America, according to many scholars, the work ethic is rapidly eroding and being replaced by the rise of a consumer ethic. In the consumer ethic, earning money to consume is replacing earning money to save and invest as one of life's prime modes-of-conduct values. Organizations, especially through advertising, stimulate the value shift by reinforcing a philosophy that defines the individual's primary role in terms of consumption rather than work.[6] Such shifts in values have created new challenges for the management of employees at all levels in organizations. The specifics of many of these challenges will be addressed throughout the remainder of this book. According to Rokeach, end-states of existence might be illustrated by such values as:

Comfortable life (prosperous life)
Exciting life (stimulating, active life)
Sense of accomplishment (lasting contribution)
World of beauty (beauty of nature and the arts)
Freedom (independence, free choice)
Inner harmony (freedom from inner conflict)
Self-respect (self-esteem)[7]

Two people can share similar end-states-of-existence values but hold different and possibly conflicting modes-of-conduct values. They both may believe strongly in freedom but differ substantially over issues involving freedom, such as relative rights of workers and managers and the appropriateness of government controls over an organization's activity.

Personally or Socially Preferable.   A value is a conception of something that is personally or socially preferable. One's values are not necessarily intended to apply equally to oneself and to others. A manager, with no thought of being inconsistent, might say: "I believe in competition in our economic system because it increases efficiency" and "There are too many firms in our industry engaged in cut-throat competition—what we need is more cooperation if we are going to survive." In the one instance, the manager is applauding the modes-of-conduct value of competition, in the other, the modes-of-conduct value of cooperation. In everyday life, values are often used flexibly: they may be viewed as applicable to ourselves and not to others, or vice versa; and they may be used as a single or double standard of behavior.

Importance of Values

From the standpoint of organizational behavior, an understanding of values is extremely important because they influence the decisions and behavior of employees and managers today as well as in the future.[8] Today's values and changes in them help shape our future. One author notes, "Values are concerned in the future of every size of entity, from the individual to the groups and organization, from the nation to all homo sapiens."[9] Individual value systems, particularly of managers, are of significance because they influence:

1. The way other individuals and groups are perceived, thereby influencing interpersonal relationships.
2. The decisions and problem solutions chosen by an individual.
3. The perceptions of situations and problems an individual faces.
4. The limits for determining what is and what is not ethical behavior.
5. The extent to which an individual will accept or resist organizational goals and pressures.
6. The perception of individual and organizational success and its achievement.
7. The choice of individual and organizational goals.
8. The means chosen for managing and controlling the human resources in the organization.[10]

Relation of Values to Defining Organizational Effectiveness

The criteria of organizational effectiveness, for the entire organization or one of its units, reflect value judgments. *Effectiveness is the extent to which organizations choose the proper goals and achieve them efficiently within the constraints of limited resources.* A strategic issued faced by management is the choice of goals that will result in goods or services that are desired or wanted by individuals. The goals chosen by managers must always be based upon an underlying understanding of the values held by individuals. Since people have a variety of values, which at times may conflict with each other, many organizations often use multiple criteria or factors for evaluating their relative effectiveness. Moreover, a variety of groups (customers, employees, stockholders, managers, and government) often have a stake or interest in an organization. These groups often place different priorities or emphasis on these criteria of effectiveness. For example, stockholders may emphasize profits and rate of return on investment as the most important criteria of effectiveness, whereas employees may place relatively high emphasis on their own satisfaction in terms of good pay, secure employment, and the like.

Table 3–1 summarizes the stated goals of General Electric. A number of goals, which may come into conflict with each other, need to be sat-

TABLE 3–1.   Stated Goals of the General Electric Company

1. To carry on a diversified, growing, and profitable worldwide manufacturing business in electrical apparatus, appliances, and supplies, and in related materials, products, systems, and services for industry, commerce, agriculture, government, the community, and the home.

2. To lead in research in all fields of science and all areas of work relating to the business in order to assure a constant flow of new knowledge that will make real the Company theme, "Progress Is Our Most Important Product."

3. To operate each decentralized business venture to achieve its own customer acceptance and profitable results by taking the appropriate business risks.

4. To design, make, and market all Company products and services with good quality and with inherent customer value, at fair, competitive prices.

5. To build public confidence and friendly feeling for products and services bearing the Company's name and brands.

6. To provide good jobs, wages, working conditions, work satisfactions, stability of employment, and opportunities for advancement for employees, in return for their loyalty, initiative, skill, care, effort, attendance, and teamwork.

7. To manage the human and material resources of the enterprise for continuity and flow of progress, growth, profit, and public service in accordance with the principles of decentralization, sound organization structure, and professional management.

8. To attract and retain investor capital through attractive returns as a continuing incentive for wide investor participation and support.

9. To cooperate with suppliers, distributors, retailers, contractors, and others who facilitate the production, distribution, installation, and servicing of Company products and systems.

10. To meet the Company's social, civic, and economic responsibilities with imagination and with voluntary action which will merit the understanding and support of all concerned among the public.

isfied for General Electric to consider itself as effective. The presence of these multiple goals is a direct reflection of the variety of values that may be held by any one individual and the differences in values that are likely to be held by powerful groups or individuals that have a stake in the organization.[11]

A challenge for the management at General Electric is to maintain some type of balance between stated goals so that the organization will survive and grow. Unfortunately, much uncertainty faces managers in attempting to choose the relative blend and balance in these goals. An important factor in determining the blend and relative emphasis on various organizational goals is likely to be the profile of values held by the managers of an organization. The next section illustrates how the mix of goals of an organization are in part contingent upon the types of managerial value systems that are present in the organization.

MODELS OF MANAGERIAL VALUES

I am concerned about a society that has demonstrably lost confidence in its institutions—in the government, in the press, in the church, in the military—as well as in business.[12]

Richard C. Gerstenberg
Past President, General Motors

We are witnessing the development of a responsive corporation which . . . should be increasingly capable of handling new issues whether they be "business" or "social." They will probably have different values, as has been rather widely suggested.[13]

Raymound A. Bauer
Professor, Harvard Business School

Whether you agree with the pessimism of Gerstenberg or the optimism of Bauer, both are claiming that people are expressing decreasing concern for the value framework that managers of our major institutions, particularly business, have operated in. Depending upon one's personal value system, this changing reality is a problem or an opportunity.

For managers in organizations, it is difficult enough to function in an environment in which traditional values are being rejected with increasing frequency. The current situation is made even more complex because new values are neither well defined nor easily implemented in organizations designed to reflect earlier value systems. Managers tend to respond to the diversity in new value systems with either uncertainty or fear.[14]

To illustrate these developments, three alternative managerial value systems—profit-maximizing management, trusteeship management, and quality-of-life management—are discussed. The discussion of these three types of managerial value systems is adapted from the analysis and synthesis of R. Hay and E. Gray.[15] The systems are presented as "pure" types to emphasize differences and their possible implications, but it should not be assumed that a particular manager or the managers of a single organization can be described as representing only one of the three types.[16]

Profit-maximizing Management

The profit-maximizing managerial value system is the oldest, simplest, and most limited of the three systems. The manager's value and the value of the organization are to maximize profits. All other managerial decisions and actions should be directed toward this sole end. While this value system promotes a selfish outlook, it was advanced as a desirable and appropriate form of behavior within a particular type of economic system. It was assumed that this selfish interest would be pursued in an economic system with the following characteristics:

not true today

1. Consumers would have complete knowledge about alternatives and the characteristics of the product and services.
2. There would be so many sellers and buyers that none of them could independently control the number of items produced.
3. The suppliers would have no control over price, i.e., they would have to sell at the price established by the impersonal interaction of market forces.
4. Government would not interfere with the economic system.

While there are a number of other assumptions underlying this type of economic system, the key point is that it was assumed that the exclusive pursuit of profits would ultimately result in the lowest prices for consumers. Profit-maximizing management was thus accompanied by values such as individualism (survival of the fittest), individual property and private ownership of the major means of production, competition, and less government control and intervention into the economic system. Major changes in religious beliefs accompanied the development of profit-maximizing management. These changes started with the Protestant Reformation, which was led by Martin Luther in the early 1500s. The Protestant ethic emphasizes the importance and desirability of hard work, self-discipline, simplicity of life, sobriety, frugality, and individualism.[17] These religious values served to justify and reinforce the values in profit-maximizing management.

Effects on Managerial Behavior.   Several personal modes-of-conduct values in profit-maximizing management are important for the understanding of managerial behavior. Decisions and actions in regard to customers are likely to reflect the value of caveat emptor ("let the buyer beware"). Within the organization, employees are considered to be just another resource needed to create the firm's goods and services. These human resources should be hired, fired, demoted, and promoted only on the basis of what is considered best by the managers for the owners of the organization. Employees are only means, not ends.

Because the top managers of the firm would also typically be the owners, there should be no conflict between the interests of the owners and those of key managers. The leadership style might be one of a rugged and authoritarian individualist, which is consistent with the underlying value of survival of the fittest. Thus, the welfare of employees should be considered only from the standpoint of helping the organization to maximize its profits. Ultimately, it is assumed that the employees' welfare and that of society in general would benefit from competition between firms.

Rationale.   The rationale for the profit-maximizing manager might be somewhat as follows:

> *I have to survive in an impersonal and competitive marketplace. If my employees can do better in the labor market, it is their option to quit. If I were to start considering my employees' needs beyond what my competitors do, this would drive up my costs, eliminate all profits, and result in failure. I wouldn't survive and my employees would be out of work. So what did I accomplish? You should also remember that the plight of most of my employees is not my fault, but is a result of their own weaknesses and inability to compete. Look at me! I brought myself up by hard work and sticking to it. If they weren't so lazy, they could be much better off. Through hard work, they could have money and wealth, too. But I guess it's God's will that only some of us will make it. These radicals, who think they can change things, don't realize that the laws of nature and God control our destiny. If they would only listen . . .*

This description does not necessarily portray how all profit-maximizing managers did or do act and feel. Rather, it describes one of the three "pure" types of managerial value systems—the profit-maximizing value system—that was most often and vocally expressed in the United States in the 1800s and early 1900s. Parts or all of the profit-maximizing managerial value system are probably still accepted by various groups in the United States.

Trusteeship Management

The trusteeship management value system modified and added to profit-maximizing management beginning in the 1920s. It had become evident that the structure of the economic and social system no longer adequately mirrored the assumptions of profit-maximizing management. Instead, the economic system was increasingly characterized by large-scale, complex organizations that functioned as oligopolies, where a few suppliers provided 70 percent or more of the goods and services in a particular industry. The tire industry, which is dominated in the United States by Goodyear, Firestone, B. F. Goodrich, General Tire, Uniroyal, and Dunlop, is often considered to be an oligopolistic industry. Monopolies, such as telephone, electric, and natural gas companies were also increasing in relative size and importance.

There was a growing tendency for the ownership of these complex organizations to be distributed among thousands of stockholders and for the managerial group to control these firms, but to have little stock ownership in them. The concept of trusteeship management gained the greatest recognition among the managers of these large and complex organizations. The practical effect of this change for most stockholders was to weaken their influence. If they became dissatisfied with the management and the performance of the firm, there was little they could do but sell their shares.

Another change that accompanied the development of the trusteeship management value system was the conception of the United States as a pluralistic society. A pluralistic doctrine means "counterbalancing interests and institutions in society prevent one group or interest from achieving hegemony (dominance). Offsetting businesses are the regulatory organs of the government . . . organized labor, competing interests within business, and the legal system that affords means of redress for the average consumer or his representatives."[18] The extent to which society actually mirrors pluralism remains subject to debate and different interpretations. (A consideration of this debate is beyond the scope of this chapter.)

Pluralism implies that the power and the right to influence an organization is diffused among a number of groups with conflicting values and goals and does not reside solely in the owners. Accordingly, managers are supposed to be responsible to those groups with important stakes in the firm, particularly the workers, customers, stockholders, creditors, suppliers, and the community. With these diverse demands on the organization, management's role is to balance and reconcile the claims of the various groups. (The stated goals of General Electric in Figure 3–1 reflect a claim that they will try to satisfy the various demands on them.)

Effects on Managerial Behavior.   The value system of trusteeship management is broader and more complex than that of profit-maximizing management, for no longer is there one clear, well-defined goal serving as a guideline in managerial decision making. Questions illustrating these uncertainties might include:

1. What are the tradeoffs, if any, between improved working conditions for employees and dividends for stockholders?
2. Should we impart information about our products to customers that enables them to make more informed choices but that also reveals that there are virtually no differences as compared with lower priced products of competitors?
3. Should we pay employees at the market rate even if it barely permits subsistence?
4. If we pay employees above the market rate, how much above should it be, and does this result in lowering the profits that rightfully belong to the stockholders?

Numerous questions such as these are left to be answered by the managers and possibly by the group(s) that have the greatest relative power to affect the survival and growth of the organization. You may want to stop a moment and see if you can identify other difficult questions that are likely to face the manager under trustee management.

While trustee management created ambiguities, it also led to critical modes-of-conduct values regarding the management of employees. Employee needs are recognized as going beyond simple economic ones, including needs such as security, belonging, and recognition. Individuals in the organization are viewed as much more complex in nature. While still adhering to the importance of individualism, the trustee management value system is less likely to be accompanied by the assumptions of the inevitability of intense competition and the doctrine of survival of the fittest. There is likely to be some recognition of the value of group and individual participation in decisions. Employees are viewed as both a means and an end, as more than a resource to be hired and discarded in the impersonal labor market. Employee rights must be recognized, for if they are not, the employees have the ability and the right to form employee groups, such as unions, to focus attention on their interests.

Role of Self-interest.   Within the concept of trustee management, there is still a strong sense of self-interest and the need to earn certain targeted profit levels. Rather than profit maximization, earning a satisfactory profit level, such as 20 percent return on investment, becomes a major guide to decision making. While the necessity of government is recognized, it is one of those evils to be maintained at a minimum level of influence, particularly with regard to the economic system. There might be a strong feeling of "what's good for the company is good for the country."

The trustee management value system is probably the one most frequently expressed today by managers. Henry Ford II seems to articulate a version of the trustee management model in these words:

> There is no longer anything to reconcile—if there ever was—between the social conscience and the profit motive. The first duty of a company to society as well as to its owners is still to strive for profit . . . the difference between capital investment and social is much more a difference of degree than of kind.[19]

Quality-of-Life Management

The quality-of-life management value system represents an extension of the trustee managerial model. It is the newest of the models, having emerged in the 1960s. It probably has the fewest advocates in the management community.[20] The quality-of-life approach recognizes the need for profits, but prefers that they be rationalized in terms of social benefits, rather than just in terms of owner benefits. Profits are viewed more as a means than an end. The need for responsiveness to various groups with a stake in the organization is expanded to include the interests of society as a whole. As a corollary, there is a greater tendency to think "what is good for society is good for the company." Changes in people, both within and outside the organization, are viewed as more important than money, materialism, or technology.

Effects on Managerial Behavior. The humanistic bias of quality-of-life management means that the dignity and worth of each employee is recognized. Managers recognize that employees bring all of themselves to the work place. Jobs are designed so that they enable employees to utilize their skills and abilities. Group and individual participation in the organizing, planning, and controlling of work relevant to the job is viewed as necessary and desirable. Participation is considered necessary because it increases the probability of the organization's being successful and it is one of the primary avenues for recognizing the dignity and humanness of individuals and groups. Leadership practices are likely to be democratic, and there is likely to be much sharing of information and trust between managers and employees.

At the top executive level of the organization, managers are likely to feel that society's problems require cooperation between business and government. Business managers are likely to feel that government must and should play a leading and vigorous role in certain social areas. For the first time, the necessity of a vigorous government is seen in a favorable light.

The value system in quality-of-life management continues the shift from individualism, competition, and raw self-interest to sharing, cooperation, and enlightened self-interest. Life is seen less as "I win when you lose" and more as "I win when you win."

Whether the value system that makes up quality-of-life management will be widely accepted by managers and, more importantly, practiced by them remains an unanswered question. For example, a Japanese executive in commenting on working life in the United States versus Japan, had this to say:

> My most unpleasant experiences while I was in the U.S. were in connection with differences in thinking about the proper relationship of a person to the group. When something went wrong, where there was a fear of blame being assigned, American employees always, almost like a reflex reaction, turned to self-defense. This has to do with a different sense of responsibility. Americans tend to think of themselves as individuals, distinct from the group, and are quick to take the defensive in order to protect themselves. Japanese have a primary responsibility to their group or company, and are thinking of the best interest of the group or company rather than of themselves.[21]

When managers, given the present institutional system within the United States, should or even can adapt to quality-of-life management in all its forms also remains an unanswered question. For example, Xerox Corporation has been regarded as a "leader in providing job training to disadvantaged workers and financial and other aid to ghetto business [and] can be considered by some to be a prime example of a socially responsible

TABLE 3–2.   Summary of Models of Managerial Values

Dimensions	Profit-maximizing Management	Trusteeship Management	Quality-of-Life Management
Overall Objective	Maximize profits	Reach satisfactory profit level plus satisfy other groups	Profits of secondary importance, only a means
Primary Modes-of-Conduct Values	Individualism, competition, ambitions	Mixture	Cooperative, loving, honest
Role of Government	The less the better	Necessary evil, sometimes needed	Partner with business
View of Employees	Means, with only economic needs	Both means and ends	Ends in themselves
Leadership Practices	Authoritarian	"Velvet glove," mixture	Democratic, high participation
Role of Stockholders	Primary importance	Important, but other groups recognized as having a stake	No more important than any other group

corporation," while others consider it to represent an "immoral investment."[22] Xerox Corporation was viewed by some as an immoral investment because it does business in South Africa and thus, it is claimed, indirectly support apartheid (strict segregation between whites and blacks) and racism.

Assessment of Models of Managerial Values

Table 3–2 summarizes the three models of managerial values. All three models operate to some extent among different managers and managerial groups. No one is found in its "pure" form, nor is any one system applied exactly the same in all similar circumstances.

Radical Criticism of Managerial Value Systems.   Certain groups contend that the trusteeship and quality-of-life models are essentially propaganda and rhetoric designed to hide the true nature of the values actually being implemented by managers. These groups contend that organizational and managerial values are beyond change and must be eliminated entirely through various radical means. Their thoughts might be summarized as follows:

We should and could eliminate the nonsensical concern with profits by having the benefits of the organization shared with all the people. Private ownership should cease and these huge organizations, including big business, big unions, and big government, should be broken up to permit real decentralization to the people. The idea of pluralism is a big joke. The managers of the big institutions are cooperating and feeding off the efforts of the common working man. Only a revolution and tearing apart to start anew will bring about any meaningful changes in the values that influence the way organizations are run and the way people are treated within them.

Such views disturb, and even frighten, leading managers of American industry. The quality-of-life management value system might have obtained some impetus from those within or associated with American management who see the necessity of responding to some of the problems pointed out by radical groups. However, these spokespersons are not likely to go so far as the radicals hope to, because they believe that a revolution in the institutional system would bring more problems than cures. Regardless of one's personal beliefs as to the "right" managerial values, there will probably continue to be major concern with this area in the business community and various segments of society over the coming years. The primary purpose of this section has been to consider the outlines of the major alternatives being considered—not to prescribe an answer.

Importance of Values to Organizational Behavior. Values are extremely important in organizational behavior because they influence people's actions and decisions. The tangible relationship between managerial values and behavior can be illustrated by suggesting what top management might do about water pollution from one of the company's plants, given each value system. With profit-maximizing management, there might be a tendency to do the minimum required and to use the courts in order to delay compliance with government orders to clean up the water they use before dumping it back into the river. With the trustee management value system, there is likely to be a tendency to react positively and to work with the government agency after they have been notified of being in noncompliance. With quality-of-life management, there might be a tendency to be proactive in recognizing the need to clean up their waste water, possibly even before governmental action is implemented.

Although suggestions for coping with value changes are developed later in the book, it is important to recognize two essential points here. First, the types of changes desired by various groups in the environment of organizations are often conflicting. Some employees may desire more meaningful jobs with greater responsibility while other employees may focus on job security and be fearful of changes in jobs. Second, the means for bringing about changes that are agreed upon are often complex and not well defined. For example, Chrysler Corporation has made some efforts to enrich jobs of production workers but has encountered numerous difficulties in keeping production costs from increasing, maintaining the concept of job security, making equitable adjustments in reward systems, and revising labor management agreements. While the general goal of making the workplace more meaningful and humane is widely applauded, the means for doing so without revising other desired goals is not so clear.

The first part of this chapter emphasized the importance of value changes in society as representing a major environmental influence on organizations. The second part of this chapter shifts focus somewhat by suggesting a "mental map," or model, for diagnosing and assessing the environment of an organization. This assessment approach can be used to diagnose many environmental forces in addition to values. This discussion will primarily emphasize the types of environments managers may confront and the types of problems they have to diagnose.

ASSESSING THE ENVIRONMENT

Almost every aspect of our society appears to be in a state of crisis and to be undergoing revolutionary change. A National Conference on Public Administration identified five contemporary revolutions: the social, the technological, the political, the economic, and the administrative. One can add educational revolution, the urban revolution and many others.

The revolutions through which our society is going are not independent of one another. They reflect some very basic cultural changes: Interrelated changes in man, his environment, and how and what he thinks about both.[23]

This quote implies three key concepts that need to be kept in mind when you think about the external environment of an organization. The first key concept in discussing environmental assessment is to recognize that an organization encounters and interacts with many external subenvironments, not simply with a single environment. In a practical sense, an organization breaks down its environment into subenvironments, each of which may be primarily dealt with by different individuals or groups in the organization. Relationships between one subenvironment and organizational group may have implications for relationships with another subenvironment and organizational group. For example, a major U.S. tire manufacturer threatened to cancel about a million dollars a year in shipping business with a trucking firm when it discovered that this firm was not purchasing any of its truck tires.

A second key concept is that there are differences in these subenvironments that require differences in the ways of organizing and managing to match up with the characteristics of the particular subenvironment. For example, a research and development unit has a different environment than an assembly plant. The specific management implications of this will be developed in Chapter 4 as well as in later chapters.

Third, an organization is typically faced with demands from its sub-environments that exceed its available resources. For example, consumers may want lower prices, suppliers desire higher prices, the states want more taxes, the federal government desires more pollution control.

The variety of subenvironments that can face a single organization or different organizations is presented next.

Change-Complexity Environmental Model

The change-complexity environmental model is adapted from the work of Duncan.[24] *Environment* is defined as "the totality of physical and social factors that are taken directly into consideration in the decision-making behavior of individuals in the organization."[25] The breadth of this definition permits recognition of an internal environment within the boundaries of the organization, and external environment outside the organizational boundaries. We will be primarily concerned with the external environment. It is critical for management to have a "mental map" for diagnosing and perceiving their external environment and differences within subenvironments. The accuracy of their diagnosis should help management understand the amount and types of uncertainty facing them in the decision-making process. Moreover, an accurate diagnosis is essential for avoiding the growing trend of failing because they solved the wrong problem rather than because they used the wrong solution to the right problem. For example, management might perceive the problem of declining sales of an item as a result of a price and thus cut it. But, the real problem could be a result of poor product design.

Specific external subenvironments are likely to vary among types of organizations. The subenvironments and the relative importance of each may well differ among industrial organizations, private service organizations, government organizations, hospitals, and universities. However, managerial and individual values represent one environmental component that acts on all organizations, although the impact of values on management is not likely to be the same among all organizations. Societal changes in instrumental values may not be as relevant, in the short run, to managers of a firm located in a stable rural community (in terms of religious, political, and economic values) as they would be to managers of a firm located in a major metropolitan area with a labor force that is diverse in terms of value orientations.

In addition to the values of the population and the work force, the following subenvironments may be particularly relevant to industrial organizations: customers, suppliers, competitors, government agencies, labor unions, consumer groups, and environmental groups. Subenvironments such as these can be assessed in terms of two key dimensions: (1) the degree of complexity and (2) the degree of change. (You may want to see

Starbuck for a more complex framework of organizational environments.[26])

Degree-of-Complexity Dimension. The degree-of-complexity dimension (variable) is the extent to which an individual or group in an organizational unit must deal with few or many factors that are similar or dissimilar to one another. People in an organizational planning unit are typically confronted with a complex environment, whereas the custodial staff faces a relatively simple environment. The degree of complexity might be determined by asking employees what factors they consider in making decisions and then determining how many of the factors are located in different subenvironments.

Degree of complexity depends upon both the number of factors and the number of subenvironments in which these factors are located. Five factors in one subenvironment, such as the customer subenvironment, would not be given as high a point rating on complexity as five factors located in three subenvironments, such as customers, suppliers, and competitors.

We need to add the qualifying statement that the degree of complexity is somewhat influenced by whether decision makers perceive their environments as complex or simple. The perception of an environment as simple or complex is likely to be influenced by both the nature of the environment *and* the characteristics of the individuals perceiving the environment.

Degree-of-Change Dimension. The degree-of-change dimension is the extent to which the environmental factors considered by an individual or group in a particular work unit of the organization are in a constant process of flux or remain basically the same over time. For example, values of organizational members, while they have always been complex, are changing rather than remaining static and stable. It is also becoming increasingly necessary to get individuals who have varying and oftentimes conflicting value systems to work together. Another example is the frequency with which customers change their requests for different levels of output or different characteristics in the output for a given product. The production of an automobile is much more complex today than it was thirty years ago because of the hundreds of options that are now available to consumers.

The degree-of-change dimension is assessed by asking the individuals in a work group *how often* the environmental factors (that they had already identified as being important in their decision making) change. A related aspect of the degree-of-change dimension is the frequency with which individuals in a work group have to consider new and different factors in their decision-making process. For example, a marketing group may have to consider many classes of customers, such as automobile dealers, car rental firms, and auto supply stores.

A more general aspect of the degree-of-change dimension is the number of major changes in goals or objectives during a given period. The greater the number of changes in goals or objectives over a given period, the higher the rate of change; the lower the number, the lower the rate of change.[27]

Perceived Environment

The overall perceived environment for a specific work group or organization is dependent upon both the degree-of-complexity and the degree-of-change dimensions, as shown in Figure 3–2. The vertical axis shows the degree of change as varying along a continuum from *static* to *dynamic*. The degree-of-complexity dimension is represented on the horizontal axis as varying along a continuum from *simple* to *complex*. Each of the cells in Figure 3–1 indicates the amount of uncertainty that is likely to be associated with each of the four extreme environments, such as a static/simple environment (cell 1) and a dynamic/complex environment (cell 4).

Without going into the mechanisms for measuring uncertainty, some of the questions that might be presented to determine the amount of uncertainty for various factors include:

1. How often do you believe that the information you have about each factor (such as customer preferences) is adequate for decision making in your work unit?
2. How often is it hard to tell how each factor (such as customer preferences) will react to, or be affected by, a decision of your work unit before it is actually implemented?
3. How often do you feel that the work unit can tell if the decisions made

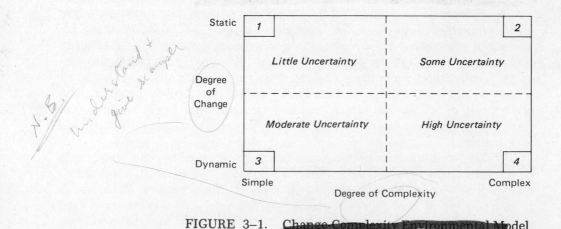

FIGURE 3–1.   Change-Complexity Environmental Model

From Duncan, R., Characteristics of Organizational Environments and Perceived Environmental Uncertainty, *Administrative Science Quarterly*, 1972, 17, pp. 313–327.

will have a positive or negative effect on its and the organization's performance?

4. How sure are you about how each factor (such as customer preference) would affect the relative success of your work unit and the organization?

Implications for Organizational Effectiveness

Characteristics of the managers and the internal organization can play an important role in determining the type of external environment that the managers perceive for the organization. If the perceived external environment is not the same as the "true" external environment, managers will make mistakes in such things as the choice of goals, priorities put on problems, allocation of scarce resources, structuring of the organization, and formal reward and motivational systems. Managers of too many organizations tend to perceive the organization's external environments as relatively static and simple when they are actually complex and dynamic. One result of this is that managers spend too much of their time in a reactive rather than in a proactive position. This dominant reactive position results in too much "fighting fires" and crisis management.

Managers may come to perceive their environments as relatively simple and stable because habits and automatic responses are developed that create a form of tunnel vision on the part of the management group. These habits may well have been useful in one environment. But, over time, these habits may actually blind the managers to recognizing changes in the external environment. As a result, management may stagnate to the point that new problems are ignored or misinterpreted and new opportunities are missed. Ultimately, the mismatch between managerial perceptions and reality may become so great that the organization begins to stagnate and a managerial atmosphere of hopelessness and futility sets in. This is obviously a much worse approach than reactive management. Starbuck and Hedburg graphically describe the organization in a stagnating environment and their proposed solutions in these terms:

Nearly all of the top management group deny the existence of hope: messages are not comprehended if they describe opportunities or if they contradict major tenets of the generally held world view; centralized controls and the lack of flexible resources drive away entrepreneurs; repeated failures discourage optimists; conflicts over what is to be done multiply until they block action and reinforce the conviction that all actions will fail. . . .

If it is to succeed, a turn-around must begin by destroying this atmosphere of hopelessness and discarding the world view that led to it. Since both are embodied in the organization's people, especially in its top management, the top management as a group must be replaced. The new group can safely retain only the deviant executives who did not accept their colleagues' world view.[28]

While this is obviously an extreme situation, it does dramatize the potential role of behavioral factors in influencing organizational effectiveness and the importance of having a reasonably close match between the perceived external environment (or subenvironments) and the "true" external environment (or subenvironments).

Since Chapter 4 discusses how managers should structure the organization (or its component parts) to deal with different types of external environments, this next section only highlights and briefly illustrates the four "pure" types of environments.

Types of Environments

Figure 3–1 shows the four "pure" types of environments or subenvironments that can face an organization or its various parts: simple/static; complex/static; simple/dynamic; complex/dynamic. Of course, the actual environment of an organization or one of its parts could be located at any place on this grid.

Simple/Static.   The simple/static environment (cell 1 in Figure 3–1) represents the easiest management situation. There are few surprises in this situation. The role of management focuses on making sure that well-established routines and procedures are consistently followed. The level of managerial skill needed in this situation is at a minimum. Little formal training is necessary; a moderate amount of on-the-job training is probably all that is needed.

The manager of a movie theater is faced with a relatively simple and static environment. The interaction of the movie theater personnel with customers is of limited scope, usually consisting of the exchange of money for admission and possibly the sale of simple and standardized snacks. The operation of a movie theater changes very little from one year to the next. The fact that some films draw more patrons than others has little effect on the local manager, with the possible exception of the hiring of a few more employees to work at the concession stand or to usher. Any major problems, such as a breakdown in the projector or air conditioning, are usually handled by calling in specialists. As long as the theater manager follows the rules and regulations set forth by top management, there will usually be few surprises or complex problems. Of course, the top management of a movie chain is faced with a much more dynamic and complex environment.

Complex/Static.   The complex/static environment (cell 2 of Figure 3–1) is likely to result in some uncertainty for managers. Many of the decision problems in this environment are characterized more by risk than uncertainty. Under conditions of risk, managers usually have a fairly good understanding of the nature of their problems and the available alternatives. The future can't be predicted, but it is possible to assign probabilities to the effects of various alternatives. This environment is relatively stable, but it may take considerable training or on-the-job experience to develop an understanding of it.

An example of a complex/static environment is that of the manager/operator of a television repair shop. Customers who call on a television repair shop are usually of one type—those with broken television sets. Moreover, the usual types of problems with black and white or color televisions are fairly standardized. But the process of diagnosing the problems associated with a single television set is not a simple matter. Quite the contrary, the diagnosis of problems and the techniques for solution can be relatively complex. This example ignores the situation confronting the television repair shop when a new technology is introduced into television sets, such as occurred when television manufacturers introduced transistor components. The initial experiences with this new technology probably resulted in the manager/operator perceiving a complex/dynamic environment and experiencing a considerable amount of uncertainty in knowing how to repair these transistor television sets.

Simple/Dynamic. The simple/dynamic environment (cell 3 of Figure 3–1) requires managers to be highly adaptable. However, there is little need for sophisticated training in conceptual and technical skills. A number of changes are taking place, but they can be managed with a reasonable level of intelligence and motivation. Management is often aided in keeping track of these changes through the use of computer-based information systems.

The manager of the grocery section of a supermarket is a good example of someone who faces a simple/dynamic environment. The types and relative amounts of goods to be stacked in the grocery section are constantly changing, as are the prices that are to be marked on these goods. In this sense, the grocery manager faces a dynamic environment. However, the techniques and decisions associated with keeping the shelves stocked and orderly are quite simple. The grocery manager usually plays a minor role in determining the more complex issues associated with the grocery section, such as prices to be charged for the goods, relative space allocated to the goods, location of the goods, and use of special displays within the grocery area.

Complex/Dynamic. The complex/dynamic environment (cell 4 of Figure 3–1) represents the most difficult management situation. It is filled with numerous uncertainties in decision making. The need for professional managers and sophisticated insight and intuition is the greatest here. While decision-making techniques can aid managers in this situation, they cannot substitute for human judgment. The problems and issues confronting managers cannot be solved through the use of standardized rules and procedures.

One of the more dramatic examples of a management team that faced a complex/dynamic environment occurred when Standard Oil of

Ohio (SOHIO) literally bet its very existence on the development of the Alaskan pipeline and the North Slope. Sohio owns a third of the Alaskan pipeline and a little more than half of the North Shore reserves. Over the past decade, it has moved from a relatively small regional refiner and marketer to the third biggest producer of crude oil in the United States and the largest owner of domestic oil reserves.

The path to achieving these ends was incredibly complex and dynamic. Starting in 1970, the company management was faced with one complex and unanticipated problem after another. There were numerous delays in the construction of the pipeline, including unforeseen technical problems, tremendous pressures from various environmental groups, and endless hassles with state and federal regulatory bodies. Costs seemed to shoot up exponentially. For the pipeline alone (which opened five years behind schedule), the costs rose tenfold over the initial estimates to $9.3 billion. Sohio wound up borrowing $4.6 billion, which is six times its assets (as of 1978) and nearly 50 times the debt it had in the late 1960s. On several occasions, the ability to borrow money nearly ran out. But Charles Spahr (the chief executive officer of Sohio) and the entire management team kept forging ahead. Spahr explains: "We, and particularly I, wanted to be remembered as men of courage and judgment, as risk takers on a grand scale—not as damn fools. There could be no in-between."[29]

As mentioned earlier, the problems and opportunities confronting most complex organizations have become more numerous and diverse, the scope of the relevant environment (subenvironments) has expanded, and the rate of change has accelerated. As one management scholar noted: "From the simple task of giving it to them in any color as long as it is (cheap and) black, defined by Henry Ford, management tasks have expanded to include global diversification, mastering the R&D monster, coping with external sociopolitical pressures, and responding to growing demands for redesign of the working environment within the firm."[30]

Some Further Implications of Types of Environments

Several implications of different levels of perceived uncertainty, which will be developed more fully in later chapters, can be briefly mentioned here. As implied in the earlier discussion of values, some individuals may experience anxieties and tensions if their work group faces a complex/dynamic environment versus a simple/static environment. Because of personality differences, other individuals may perceive the same environment more favorably. At a group level, there is often a greater need for job-related interaction and communications among peers and with their manager in a complex/dynamic environment than in a simple/static environment.

The level of skills and knowledge needed by individuals in work groups is also likely to depend somewhat on the degree of change and complexity in the external environment. Finally, the ease or difficulty in managing work groups varies somewhat, according to their external environment. Many issues, problems, and recommendations in the field of organizational behavior are partially dependent upon the character of the external environment confronting a work group or individual.

SUMMARY

At the beginning of this chapter, two incidents were presented along with lists of alternative responses that might be made by a manager. Based on usable responses from about 2,000 individuals (93 percent of whom were managers), the following distribution of responses was obtained for the first incident: 1, 5 percent; 2, 19 percent; 3, 6 percent; 4, 8 percent; 5, 62 percent. For the second incident, individuals responded as follows: 1, 41 percent; 2, 39 percent; 3, 12 percent; 4, 7 percent.

These two incidents might also be considered in terms of how individuals holding each of three managerial value systems would respond. In the first incident, profit-maximizing management would likely choose 1 or 4; trusteeship management, 3 or 5; and quality-of-life management, 2. In the second incident, responses for profit-maximizing management would likely be 3 or 4; trusteeship management, 2; and quality-of-life management, 1.

This chapter has explored some trends, issues, and approaches for assessing the environment of organizations. Although the major intent was not to be prescriptive or to make simplistic judgments about "what is right," some of this probably occurred. One bias was to consider only pressures from the environment and possible reactions by organizations. Considerable data suggest that organizations influence and are very proactive with their environment as well. A second obvious bias is simply the choice of concepts, trends, and issues presented. These choices were made to present materials that might have the greatest relevance to an understanding of individual and group behavior within organizations and that could be built upon and extended in later chapters.

DISCUSSION QUESTIONS

1. What *similarities* are there between the three managerial value systems?

2. What *differences* are there between the three managerial value systems?

3. What difficulties do you think a manager might have if he or she possessed the quality-of-life managerial value system?

4. Are there any significant relationships between values and organizational effectiveness? Explain.

5. Can an organization be faced with both a simple/static environment and a complex/dynamic subenvironment? Explain.

6. How would you describe the environment or subenvironment of an organization you have worked for?

MANAGERIAL PROBLEMS

GENERAL ELECTRIC'S ENVIRONMENTAL ASSESSMENT

For several years, the management of General Electric has been systematically studying their external environment. One concern has been to evaluate and rank the relative importance of different charges, complaints, threats, and demands from the external environment. The top management of General Electric contends that the company is faced with the traditional demands of economics—the need for the firm to be concerned with efficiency, productivity, and profits—and with the new and emerging expectations and pressures from various segments of society. Since G.E. assumes that these expectations and pressures exceed its resources and capabilities (at least in the short run), its managers are faced with several fundamental questions. What demands should they respond to? What constituencies and pressure groups should they listen to? Implicit in their approach is the desire to devote scarce resources to those issues that will yield the greatest benefit to the firm. Resources expended on an issue that is a passing fad, even if there is strong current pressure behind it, might be viewed as resources that should have been used for some other issue or some other purpose (higher salaries, bigger profits, more comfortable offices).

G.E. came up with two groupings of factors that are related to the management of human resources. One grouping of factors was concerned with the charges or complaints being levied against large business firms. The other grouping of factors identified the various demands and threats that have accompanied these charges and complaints. The specific factors in these two groupings are shown in Table 3–2.

QUESTIONS

1. Assuming you were a member of top management at General Electric, how do you think you would rank the *relative importance* of the factors presented as pressures (charges and complaints)? You should also rank the relative importance of the factors presented as demands (threats). There are 15 factors presented in each of these categories. Rank each set of factors by assigning "1" to the factor that you feel is most important and "15" to the factor you consider least important.
2. Why did you choose the three highest factors in each grouping?
3. Why did you chose the three lowest factors in each grouping?
4. What actions, if any, do you feel the management of General Electric can take in dealing with the three highest ranked factors in each grouping?

TABLE 3–2.   Presures and Demands in Employee Relations

Pressures (Charges and Complaints)	Demands (Threats)
__ 1. Authoritarian, hierarchical systems suppress individual initiative and participation in decisions affecting employees' interests.	__ 1. Deterioration in productivity of employees at all levels.
__ 2. Profit, not employee welfare, determines decisions such as layoffs.	__ 2. Alienation of blue-collar workers and, to a lesser extent, middle management and professional personnel.
__ 3. Work, whether in the plant or in the office, is monotonous, deadening, dehumanizing.	__ 3. More participatory management, employee involvement in decisions affecting their interests.
__ 4. Profit emphasis corrupts individual value systems (of managers and others) and distorts decision making.	__ 4. Job enlargement/enrichment (team and individual work in plants and offices).
__ 5. "The system" retaliates against "whistle blowers": it demands unconditional loyalty ("organization men").	__ 5. More flexible scheduling of work.
__ 6. Working conditions, especially in plants, show minimal regard for occupational health and safety.	__ 6. Greater employment security (guarantees of income or work; government as "employer of last resort"); massive.
__ 7. Management thinks only of an "adversary role" vis à vis unions' legitimate demands for better wages, benefits, and conditions.	__ 7. More attention to career development, retraining, growing obsolescence of skills at all levels.
__ 8. Business is racist, denying equal opportunity (in hiring, training, promotion) to minorities.	__ 8. More leisure time; longer vacations; earlier retirement; sabbaticals.
__ 9. Business is sexist, denying equal opportunity to women.	__ 9. Affirmative action on hiring, training, promotion of minorities and women (compliance reviews, termination of government contracts).
__10. Business is elitist, favoring "crown princes," and concentrating power in the hands of a few.	__10. Tighter enforcement of occupational health and safety standards.
__11. Business has a "brick curtain" preventing movement from shop to office.	__11. More "whistle blowing" by employees, with protection for their rights.
__12. Employees are cheated out of their pension rights through un-	__12. Strikes, sit-ins, class-action suits to enforce demands.
	__13. White-collar unionization including middle management, professionals.

___ reasonable vesting provisions or none at all.

___13. Business is no longer capable of creating and maintaining a sufficient number of jobs at all levels (blue-collar, professional, management).

___14. Corporations pay too little attention to the needs of middle management—both with respect to compensation benefits and job security and with respect to more subtle aspects of corporate life.

___15. Top management people vote themselves excessive salaries for work that has little to do with the useful, productive enterprise of producing and delivering goods and services.

___14. Restrictions on "management rights" (to limit exercise of arbitrary authority).

___15. Escalation of labor's bargaining power.

From Estes, R. M., The business-society relationship: Emerging major issues, in Steiner, G. A., *Selected Major Issues in Business Role in Modern Society* (Los Angeles: Graduate School of Management, UCLA, 1973), pp. 36–38. Used with permission.

WHAT'S REALLY WRONG AT CHRYSLER?

An article in *Fortune* entitled "What's Really Wrong at Chrysler" suggests that Chrysler is having difficulties because its management has never clearly answered three fundamental questions that confront all organizations: "What is our purpose? What are we trying to do? Whom are we trying to serve?" In the case of Chrysler, it is claimed that top management has never been able to decide the types of cars it wants to build or the types of customers it wants to serve. As a result, Chrysler is said to shift gears continuously—thereby missing out on its strengths and reinforcing its weaknesses. The author goes on to assert:

Any successful business is founded on a concept of a product it can make or a market it can serve. This idea becomes the company's central heritage. Over time it comes to dominate both the strategy and the spirit of the company, so that problems and opportunities are seen in relation to the fundamental principle. Organizations can often move beyond their original concept, but they can seldom abandon it.

QUESTIONS

1. Discuss the implications of the chapter materials in substantiating, or being at odds with, the above conclusions.
2. In what ways do you agree and/or disagree with the conclusions reached?

KEY WORDS

Reactive orientation
Proactive orientation
Value
Value system
Modes of conduct
End-states of existence
Effectiveness
Profit-maximizing management
Trusteeship management
Quality-of-life management

Pluralism
Environment
Degree of complexity
Degree of change
Perceived environment
Simple/static environment
Complex/static environment
Simple/dynamic environment
Complex/dynamic environment

REFERENCES

1. Ewing, D. W. What business thinks about employee rights, *Harvard Business Review*, 1977, 55, pp. 81–91.

2. The top man becomes Mr. Outside, *Business Week*, May 4, 1974, p. 38.

3. Moos, R. H., Conceptualizations of human environments, *American Psychologist*, 1973, 28, pp. 652–665.

4. Rokeach, M., *The Nature of Human Values* (New York: Free Press, 1973).

5. Brown, M. A., Values—A necessary but neglected ingredient of motivation on the job, *The Academy of Management Review*, 1976, 1, pp. 15–23.

6. Chamberlain, H., *Remaking American Values* (New York: Basic Books, 1977).

7. Rokeach, *Nature of Human Values*.

8. Whitley, W., and G. W. England, Managerial values as reflection of culture and the process of industrialiaztion, *Academy of Management Journal*, 1977, 20, pp. 439–453.

9. Fowles, J., The problem of values in futures research, *Futures*, 1977, 9, pp. 303–314.

10. England, G. W., O. P. Dhingra, and N. C. Agarwal, The manager and the man: A cross-cultural study of personal values, *Organization and Administrative Sciences*, 1974, 5, pp. 1–97.

11. Steers, R. M., *Organizational Effectiveness: A Behavioral View* (Santa Monica, Calif.: Goodyear Publishing, 1977).

12. Gerstenberg, R. C., *1973 Report on Progress in Areas of Public Concern*, February 8, 1973.

13. Banks, L., The mission of our business society, *Harvard Business Review*, 1975, 53, pp. 57–65.

14. Toffler, A., *Future Shock* (New York: Random House, 1970); Lodge, G. C., Business and the changing society, *Harvard Business Review*, 1974, 52, pp. 59–72.

15. Hay, R., and E. Gray, Social re-

sponsibilities of business managers, *Academy of Management Journal*, 1974, 17, pp. 135–143.

16. Behling, O., C. Schriesheim, and J. Schriesheim, Hay and Gray's phases of social responsibility: An empirical assessment, 1975, unpublished manuscript.

17. Long, J. D., The Protestant ethic reexamined, *Business Horizons*, 1972, 15, pp. 75–82.

18. Perrow, C., *The Radical Attack on Business: A Critical Analysis* (New York: Harcourt Brace Jovanovich, 1972).

19. Ford, H., II, The reduction of human misery—voluntary contributions, *Vital Speeches*, 1966, 27, pp. 278–280.

20. Richman, B. M., and K. Marcharzina, The corporation and quality of life: Part I: Typologies, *Management International Review*, 1973, 13, pp. 3–16.

21. Japanese managers tell how their system works, *Fortune*, 1977, 46, pp. 127–138.

22. Malkiel, B. G., and R. E. Quandt, Moral issues in investment policy, *Harvard Business Review*, 1971, 16, pp. 37–47; also see Carson, J., and G. A. Steiner, *Measuring Business Social Performance: The Corporate Social Audit* (New York: Committee for Economic Development, 1974).

23. Ackoff, R. L., *Redesigning the Future: A Systems Approach to Societal Problems* (New York: John Wiley and Sons, 1974).

24. Duncan, R., Characteristics of organizational environments and perceived environmental uncertainty, *Administrative Science Quarterly*, 1972, 17, pp. 313–327; Duncan, R., Multiple decision making structures in adapting to environmental uncertainty: The impact on organizational effectiveness, *Human Relations*, 1973, 26, pp. 273–291.

25. Ibid., p. 314.

26. Starbuck, W. H., Organizations and their environments, in M. Dunnette (ed.), *Handbook of Industrial and Organizational Psychology* (Chicago: Rand McNally, 1976), pp. 1125–1174.

27. Downey, H. K., D. Hellriegel, and J. W. Slocum, Jr., Environmental uncertainty: The construct and its applications, *Administrative Science Quarterly*, 1975, 20, pp. 613–629.

28. Starbuck, W. H., and B. L. T. Hedberg, Saving an organization from a stagnating environment, in H. B. Thorelli (ed.), *Strategy + Structure = Performance: The Strategic Planning Imperative* (Bloomington: Indiana University Press, 1977), pp. 249–258.

29. Morner, A., For Sohio, it was Alaskan oil—or bust, *Fortune*, 1977, 46, pp. 173–184.

30. Ansoff, H. I., The state of practice in planning systems, *Sloan Management Review*, 1977, 18, pp. 1–24.

4

Organizational Design

This Chapter Contributed by

MARIANN JELINEK

Dartmouth College

4

LEARNING OBJECTIVES

When you have finished reading and studying this chapter, you should be able to:

▲ Describe four basic ways for designing the structure of an organization.

▲ Understand the differences in the four organizational designs and the relative advantages and disadvantages of each.

▲ Identify the type of environment in which each of the four organizational designs is likely to be most effective.

▲ Increase your awareness of how different formal structures can affect organization members and influence the types of behavioral issues that are likely to develop.

THOUGHT STARTERS

▲ What do you think the term organizational design means?

▲ How can organizational structure affect employees?

▲ Why do organizations change their structures?

Organizational design is the formal system of communication, authority, and responsibility that is created by management to aid in achieving organizational goals. In the most basic sense, organizational design entails deciding on the degree and nature of the division of labor that will be used and then deciding on how employee effort will be coordinated to achieve the desired results. Stated another way, organizational design entails deciding on *who* is going to do *what* and *how* people and the tasks that they perform are going to be coordinated. Selected aspects of organizational design are also considered in later chapters. In particular, Chapter 12 zeros in on how to design the tasks that are performed in individual jobs.

Proper design is a key factor in influencing the relative efficiency and effectiveness of organizations in providing goods and services. Adam Smith, the father of the capitalist economic system, recognized the importance of one key factor in organizational design in *The Wealth of Nations*, which was published in 1776. Smith noted that the wealth of a nation could be increased if organizations used the proper division of labor in their structures. In general, Smith prescribed that the greater the division of labor used in the design of the organization, the greater the efficiency of the organization. He illustrated this principle by describing how work should be divided in a pin factory:

> One man draws out the wire, another straightens it, a third cuts it, a fourth points it, a fifth grinds it at the top for receiving the head; to make the head requires two or three distinct operations; to put it on is a peculiar business, to whiten the pins is another; it is even a trade by itself to put them into the paper.[1]

By dividing the labor in this manner, Smith calculated that ten individuals could make 48,000 pins per day or 4,800 per person. If one person had to perform all the operations, his production would be limited to maybe 20 pins per day.

Many people who followed Smith also tried to identify the key principles that should be used in designing organizations. Early writers often gave conflicting advice on the best way to design organizations and usually proclaimed that their view was the only view. One reason for this conflict was that these early writers usually considered only one or two different factors for designing an organization. While many of the early writers had some good ideas, *these ideas were good only if applied under certain conditions*. Today it is recognized that there are no simple answers or universal prescriptions for designing all organizations.

It would require an entire book to completely consider all the knowledge that has accumulated about the design of organizations. The intent of this chapter is to outline some of the major approaches to structuring organizations and to illustrate how each of these could be effective in different environments.

Chapter 3 identified four "pure" environments: simple/static, complex/static, simple/dynamic, and complex/dynamic. These four types of environments are based upon the degree-of-complexity dimension (simple to complex) and the degree-of-change dimension (static to dynamic). It is probably intuitively obvious that an organizational design that would work well in a simple/static environment, which has little uncertainty for management, would be a disaster in a complex/dynamic environment, which is characterized by high uncertainty. In sum, no single organizational form is "best" for all organizations or circumstances.

FUNCTIONAL FORM OF ORGANIZATION

An effective way of designing an organization is through the functional form of organization. Early writers on organizational design spent much time and effort attempting to develop concepts and principles for creating effective functional forms. Four of these concepts are considered here: functional division of labor, line and staff, chain of command, and span of control.

Functional Division of Labor

Division of labor is the dividing up of tasks that have to be performed to permit standardization, specialization, and the use of specialized equipment. *Functional divisions of labor* explores the various ways of dividing up the tasks that have to be performed. All the insights provided by the early thinkers on organizational design are found in practice today. Whenever knowledge of how to perform the work is beyond the ability of a single person, division of labor offers advantages. Whenever the component activities can be broken down and simplified, economies may be possible. Whenever the steps in a process differ in the skills required to carry them out, the benefits first outlined by Adam Smith may be derived.

The functional division of a typical manufacturing business might be by managerial function, such as engineering, manufacturing, shipping, sales, and finance (see Figure 4–1). A second way for dividing up work on a functional basis is by the *processes used*, such as stamping, plating, assembly, painting, and inspection. Figure 4–2 shows an organization that has departmentalized itself on the basis of both managerial function and

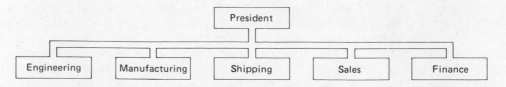

FIGURE 4–1.   Departmentation by Managerial Function

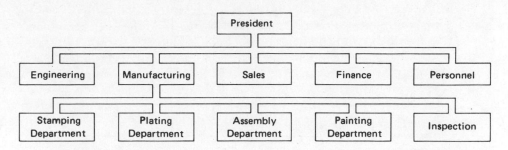

FIGURE 4–2.   Departmentation by Managerial Function and Process

process, demonstrating that several bases of functional division of labor can be used in a single organization.

Regardless of the form of the functional division of labor, a common theme of the writers on the functional form of organization was the desirability of standardizing and routinizing repetitive tasks whenever possible. Management could then concentrate on exceptions and eliminate any gaps or overlaps.

Line and Staff

Line activities are functional activities directly affecting the principal work flow in the organization. In a manufacturing firm, for instance, all activities such as engineering, stamping, assembly, painting, inspection, and shipping would be considered line activities. *Staff activities* are ancillary activities that provide service and advice to line personnel. These might include personnel, legal, and controller departments. Figure 4–3 illustrates a line and staff organization that uses several bases of departmentation.

Chain of Command

In addition to the distinction between line and staff, early writers on organizational design stressed two basic ideas about the chain of command. First, *scalar chain of command*—the idea that authority and responsibility are arranged hierarchically. They flow in a clear, unbroken line from the highest executive (who holds the maximum authority and responsibility) to the lowest worker. Clarity is at the heart of the scalar chain. Second, *unity of command*—the idea that no subordinate should receive orders from more than one superior. In modern organizations, unity of command is not always followed, but the insistence of these thinkers did rest upon important insights. They recognized that overlapping lines of authority and responsibility may make it difficult to manage or to work. Without unity of command, it is not clear who may order whom to do

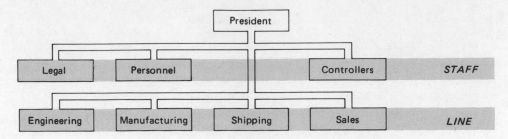

FIGURE 4–3.   Typical Line and Staff Organization

what; much must be done by persuasion or "horsetrading"—means clearly outside the early writers' notions of how an organization should be run. This forced the early writers to emphasize a relatively simple organizational design, with line activities specialized into functional departments supplemented by staff.

Span of Control

Early writers on organizational design also advocated a limited span of control. *Span of control* is the number of persons supervised by a given manager. The span of control used is a major influence on the shape and structure of an organization. Where the span of control is broad, many persons are under the authority of a single supervisor, and there are relatively few hierarchical levels between the top and the bottom of the organization. Where the span of control is narrow, each manager supervises only a few subordinates. For the same number of workers, more levels of hierarchy are required. This is illustrated in Figure 4–4.

Early writers suggested that span of control should vary with the nature of the tasks being performed. Generally, they recommended a range between two and six subordinates; except that a foreman supervising a simple and repetitive operation might have charge of twenty to thirty workers.

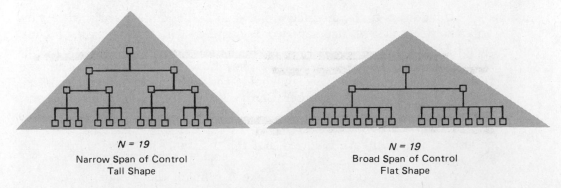

N = 19
Narrow Span of Control
Tall Shape

N = 19
Broad Span of Control
Flat Shape

FIGURE 4–4.   Span of Control and Organization Shape

This principle is still in evidence today. In a modern automobile assembly plant, supervisors have many workers reporting to them. But at higher organizational levels, the plant manager or department head may have only four or five subordinates reporting.

Advantages and Disadvantages

As with every organizational form, the functional form of organization has both advantages and disadvantages. No form is without problems. Rather, some forms are relatively better than others under certain conditions.

On the positive side, the functional form of organization permits the clear assignment and identification of responsibilities. This form of organization is easily understood. People doing similar work and facing similar problems work together, increasing the opportunity for interaction and mutual support among them. The functional form also eliminates duplication of equipment and effort. By permitting the maximum use of resources, it also encourages the use of specialists and specialized equipment. Moreover, people can be added and subtracted easily, without eliminating all expertise in a given functional area.

On the negative side, the functional form of organization encourages a limited point of view that focuses on a portion of the overall task rather than the task of the organization as a whole. *Suboptimizing*—the optimizing of the work of one department—may be less than optimum for the organization as a whole. Coordination and support across functional departments otfen becomes difficult because different departments are usually separated geographically and people come to consider problems only from their limited functional points of view. Under conditions of great change, or where many different products are involved, these coordinating difficulties may lead to the need for reorganization. The technology being used by the departments can certainly influence the tendency toward suboptimization with the functional form of organization. If the technology requires sequential interdependence between departments, it will be essential that the functional departments work closely together. *Sequential interdependence* occurs when department C cannot act before department B performs certain duties, which cannot act before department A and so on. This type of interdependence between departments is illustrated by the assembly line.

Environment for Effectiveness

The functional form of organization is likely to be effective in a simple, static environment. You will recall that there are few surprises in this environment and the role of management focuses on making sure that well-established routines and procedures are consistently followed. Organization efficiency can be maximized in a simple/static environment if there is a clear division of labor, a well-defined chain of command, and a relatively narrow span of control. The addition of specialized staff units to the functional form of organization enables the firm to deal with more complex environments. The staff units provide the line units with the expert advice that they need to make rational decisions about more complex problems.

Before discussing the next form for designing the structure of an organization, a clarification is in order. Each of the additional forms of organization being presented builds upon the preceding form(s). These forms are not mutually exclusive. Rather, they reflect the increasing complexity and shifts in emphasis that can take place when management moves from one form to another.

BUREAUCRATIC FORM OF ORGANIZATION

The bureaucratic form of organization is the next stage of complexity in choosing an organizational design. The bureaucratic form shares many features with the functional form of organization, but it is much more complex and provides more guidelines to management.

In everyday usage, the word bureaucracy often conjures up thoughts of rigidity, incompetence, red tape, inefficiency, and ridiculous rules. Max Weber, a German scholar who wrote in the early 1900s, used "bureaucratic model" as a scientific tool and frame of reference for evaluating, characterizing, and comparing all types of organizations. It is primarily in this sense that the term bureaucratic model is used here. A number of the aspects of the formal bureaucratic model are reasonable and desirable. In discussing the bureaucratic model we need to distinguish between the way it should ideally function and popular ideas of the way some large-scale organizations actually operate.

Degrees of Bureaucracy

As shown in Figure 4–5, the relative and absolute degree to which the structure of an organization emphasizes each dimension in the bureaucratic model can vary substantially.[2] Subsystems (such as an assembly plant or a research and development facility) within a single organization can also vary in these dimensions. Organization A in Figure 4–5 illustrates a relatively high level of bureaucracy across all dimensions, whereas organization B is much less of a bureaucracy and is more varied in its emphasis on each dimension. For example, organization B has a relatively high emphasis on hierarchy of authority but a very high emphasis on technical competence.

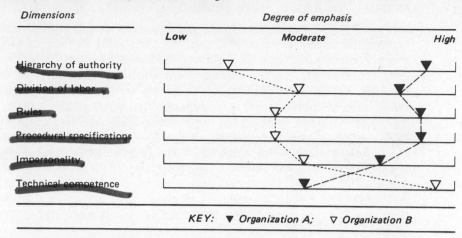

FIGURE 4–5.   Dimensions in the Bureaucratic Model

Organization A could be an automobile assembly plant and organization B could be a research and development facility. This pattern could also be found if the automobile assembly plant and the research and development facility were part of the same organization, such as General Motors, Ford, or Chrysler.

Let's briefly consider each of the dimensions of the bureaucratic model.

Hierarchy of Authority

Virtually all organizations use a *hierarchy of authority,* which is the extent to which decision making is prestructured by the organization and the degree to which participation in decision making varies in direct relation to one's position level in the hierarchy. Of course, this is virtually the same concept as the scalar chain of command that was presented in our discussion of the functional form of organization. Higher-level units or individuals assign or approve goals and budgets for lower-level units or individuals. For example, an advertising department may have considerable decision-making discretion over the form and content of the organization's advertising program, but the program is probably carried out within certain budget guidelines previously approved by top management.

The hierarchy of authority dimension is sometimes confused with centralization. *Centralization,* a relative concept, prevails when all major, and possibly many minor, decisions are made only at the top levels of the organization. In contrast, hierarchy of authority implies specification of the decisions that can be made by the employees occupying the various positions in the organization. If the advertising department has to have virtually all decisions relating to its advertising program approved by higher management, we might conclude that the organization is highly centralized relative to the advertising function. If the organization simply specifies in detail the types of decisions that can and cannot be made by the advertising manager, there exists a hierarchy of authority that could permit considerable discretion. For example, higher management might specify that 40 percent of the advertising dollars should be expanded on television, 40 percent on magazines, and 20 percent on newspapers. The timing and specific choice of television stations, magazines, and newspapers are left to the advertising department. A final implication of the hierarchy-of-authority dimension is the idea that each higher level has the authority to withdraw any authority that has been delegated to a lower level.

Division of Labor

As explained under the functional form of organization, division of labor relates to the extent to which the tasks to be performed are subdivided and carried out by different individuals and units. As will be explained in detail in the discussion of job enrichment in Chapter 12, recently there has been concern over the extremely high degree of division of labor in organizations. This is particularly true for individuals at lower organizational levels, where many employees perform simple, routine tasks that require few skills. This may have the personal consequences of boredom, indifference, low productivity, and dissatisfaction. Even though the division of labor may be carried to the point where it becomes dysfunctional for both task accomplishment and employee needs, it remains a fundamental dimension in all organizations.

A simple example of the division of labor would be a firm with three major functions: marketing, production, and finance. A greater or lesser degree of division of labor can be illustrated by examining two possibilities in the marketing function. Figure 4–6 shows two hypothetical structures for performing similar marketing functions, each with eight individuals. In the marketing function that shows "low" division of labor, each sales representative may call on three types of customers of the firm (retailers, wholesalers, and manufacturers), handle all service requests and complaints for their accounts, and be responsible for performing market research tasks. In the case where the marketing function has a "high" division of labor, some attempt has been made to divide certain tasks among several positions. Without going into a discussion of the possible pros and cons of each approach, it should be emphasized that the case showing "high" division of labor could provide challenging and meaningful positions for all the employees.

Rules

Rules are formal written statements specifying acceptable and unacceptable behaviors and decisions by organization members. One of the

'Low' division of Labor example

'High' division of Labor example

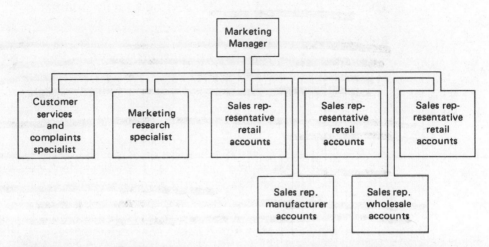

FIGURE 4–6.   "High" versus "Low" Division of Labor for a Marketing Function

ironies in the proliferation of rules that attempt to reduce individual discretion is that someone must still exercise discretion as to which rules
apply to specific situations.

Rules are often associated with negative feelings, and for good reason.

> *Several years ago, New York City was forced to make substantial
> layoffs in the police, fire, and other departments. One fireman,
> who was scheduled to be laid off at 9:00 A.M. had been called to
> fight a fire at about 8:45 A.M. A little over fifteen minutes later,
> the fireman climbed a ladder several times and carried three peo-
> ple out of the fire. As a result, he suffered burns, smoke inhala-
> tion, and other personal harm. When it was determined that this
> rescue took place after 9:00 A.M., the "bureaucracy" concluded
> that he was not, at that time, employed by the city. Thus, he had
> acted as a "civilian" and was therefore ineligible for medical and*

other benefits normally available to fire fighters injured on the job.

It is the narrow and ridiculous application of rules, such as in this case, that often results in much resentment among workers. After the news media made the fireman's plight public, the decision to deny benefits was reversed.

Good rules often go unrecognized. The rule that everyone must wear a hard hat on construction sites of high-rise buildings is likely to be universally accepted as a good and necessary rule. Rules designed to prevent or stop favoritism, or nepotism (hiring one's own relatives), and discriminating on irrelevant grounds are often viewed favorably.

The dual character of rules has been succinctly summarized:

Rules do a lot of things in organizations; they protect as well as restrict; coordinate as well as block; channel effort as well as limit it; permit universalism as well as provide sanctuary for the inept; maintain stability as well as retard change; permit diversity as well as restrict it.[3]

(Universalism is treating people on the basis of merit or achievement in performing their jobs.)

Three final points should be made with respect to organizational rules. *First,* rules viewed as "bad" today may have been desirable when first formulated. This suggests that rules often need modification to accommodate changing values, tasks, employee abilities, and other circumstances. *Second,* rules are a means to assist the organization in reaching its goals. When a rule hinders rather than helps goal achievements, it should be eliminated or changed. *Third,* we need to distinguish whether frustration concerns the need for rules covering certain behavior and decisions or the substance of the rules. It is one thing to argue that there should be no rules covering the layoff of employees; it is quite another to argue whether the rules should emphasize seniority or degree of merit as a basis for layoffs.

Procedural Specifications

Procedural specifications are the predetermined sequence of steps an employee must follow in performing tasks and dealing with problems. Procedural specifications often consist of a number of rules that are to be implemented in a particular sequence. To obtain reimbursement for expenses, for example, an employee must adhere to a well-defined set of procedures, such as (1) obtaining prior approval for the travel from a superior; (2) providing hotel and transportation receipts; (3) limiting food expenditures to $12 a day; (4) stating the purpose of the trip and listing the individuals contacted on a travel voucher form; and (5) obtaining signatures on the form from the higher levels of management and the budget officer. Since procedural specifications are substantially made up of rules, they share many of the same positive or negative features.

As with rules, procedural specifications can be carried to ridiculous extremes. Rather than serving as aids in making the organization run more efficiently, they can become excessive and cumbersome. Nowhere is this more obvious than in the bureaucracy of the federal government. For example, in the procedures that are required to fire civil service employees from the federal government, the process starts by the managers supplying a written explanation to the employee 30 days ahead of time. Employees may appeal the firing up the chain of command. If the decision is upheld, they can demand a hearing before the federal Employee Appeal Authority. If the ruling still goes against them, they can then appeal to the federal courts, which have shown increasing sympathy toward employees' claims of discrimination on grounds of race or sex.

To illustrate how cumbersome and expensive the process is, one federal manager put together a 21-foot long chart in his office illustrating one Environmental Protection Agency official's 21-month effort to fire a $9,600 a year stenographer. Various lines snaking through a maze of boxes and triangles denoted all the required memos, warnings, suspensions, and conferences. The official devoted so much time and effort to the firing that he began getting bad ratings on his own work.[4]

Figure 4–5 showed that an organization or its various departments can have a low-to-high emphasis on rules and procedures. Within a single organization or department, the use of rules and procedures can also vary substantially among task and problem areas. For example, workers on the assembly line of an automobile plant are required to adhere to well-defined rules and procedures regarding how their work is to be performed and the accompanying safety requirements. In contrast, the professionals in a research and development facility working with radioactive materials may have to adhere to safety rules and procedures that are much more elaborate than those required of the assembly-line workers. But there are likely to be fewer rules and procedures specifying the tasks the professionals are to perform.

Impersonality

Impersonality is a measure of the extent to which organizational members, as well as outsiders, are treated without regard to certain individual qualities. Of course, individual qualities are considered if they are related to predetermined and specified standards. The ability to pass a physical examination when applying for a position is usually viewed as an appropriate individual quality for assessment. On the other hand, individual qualities such as sex, race, color, creed, or national origin have been formally stated as attributes that are not to be used as bases for rejecting an applicant. Organizations, particularly government agencies, are often expected to treat "outsiders" the same, regardless of their personal wealth or position in other organizations. The public often decries the favoritism and cronyism found in and between the top officials of some bureaucracies. Max Weber, in advocating the impersonality dimension, was also concerned over the tendency of some individuals, especially those at high levels, to utilize their positions and organizations for excessive personal gain.

The following is a recent example of a breakdown in the impersonality dimension:

> A U.S. Senator appeared at the loading gate of a major airline with his family and demanded seats on the flight that was being loaded and was soon to depart from Washington, D.C. The Senator and his family did not have tickets, and the flight was already booked to capacity. Nonetheless, the airline agent gave the Senator and his family the needed seats. The airline agent knew that the Senator was a powerful member of a congressional committee responsible for legislation affecting the airline industry. Because of the ticket agent's actions, several angry passengers with confirmed tickets were left behind. Many passengers who did board the plane and observed these actions openly criticized the Senator during the flight. The news media also widely reported the incident. The Senator made a public apology and high airline executives publicly claimed it was not their policy to show such favored treatment. Presumably, the impersonality dimension for this type of situation would be widely supported by the public.

Technical Competence

Technical competence is a measure of the extent to which standards of individual skill and performance are used in the selection, retention, demotion, dismissal, or advancement of employees. To the extent that technical competence and achievement, rather than family lineage, friendships, personal loyalties, social class of the individual, and the like, are the primary determinants of one's position, the organization is regarded as "high" on that dimension.

Technical competence among a limited number of individuals may be difficult to evaluate. To reduce competitive pressures among individuals and to maintain a sense of "impersonality," seniority is often used as a substitute criterion for technical competence, on either a formal or informal basis.[5] Of course, unions are quite explicit (and often adamant) in placing a high emphasis on seniority. But the best that can be assumed is that seniority is compatible with technical competence in some cases and not in other cases.

Case Example: Seven-Eleven

This section is a personalized account of how one particular organization, the Seven-Eleven grocery chain, was perceived as fitting the bureaucratic model to a high degree. It is based on a report by a student on his experiences as a clerk in one of the Seven-Eleven grocery stores in Florida.[6]

Anecdotal accounts have limitations. In reading this account, try to apply a personalized and concrete sensitivity to the nature of the bureaucratic model in its more extreme form. Think about how some of the structural arrangements could be functional for the organization in achieving its goals of profit, control, and growth, but dysfunctional for a skilled individual at a low organizational level because of the simplicity and routinization of the job.

Becoming an Employee.   Technical competence was a key element of the hiring procedure at Seven-Eleven. A battery of standardized tests was administered. Each employee was expected to fulfill a set number of company qualifications, which varied from previous work experience to avowals of never having used hard drugs and of never having shoplifted more than twenty-five dollars' worth of merchandise during one's life. Part of the hiring procedure was a polygraph test to verify the factuality of the personal information submitted. (Research suggests that polygraphs may not be nearly as accurate as believed by some individuals.)

One's personality was a partial consideration in obtaining a clerical position, but it was evaluated as impersonally as possible through standardized tests and successful fulfillment of standard requirements. Sound personal health was assessed by a physical examination that finally determined one's fitness for a position in the Seven-Eleven organization.

In line with procedural specifications, new employees were introduced to their district supervisor. This wasted little time in acquainting employees with who the main boss would be and what the written rules of the organization were. The supervisor explained how rules would guide a clerk's job performance ("a clerk shall wear . . . a clerk shall always report on time"), and how obedience to the rules would be required in order to perform a good job.

Working in the Organization.   In fulfilling the duties of clerk, there were many applications of the bureaucratic model. Rules existed for washing the floor (including the cleaning agents to be used) and the frequency of waxing. Rules existed limiting the amount of money allowed in the register at any time, the denominations of this cash, and the denominations of bills employees were allowed to accept from customers. The effective operation of the store seemed to be determined by properly tabulating how closely the rules and procedures that were believed to lead to high profits were being met.

One example was particularly revealing of the organization's reliance on rules for meeting its goals. Once a month the store received a promotional packet from district headquarters. This package alerted the store manager to the company marketing plans and promotions for the coming month. The packet came complete with promotional banners, window displays, and other needed materials. Rather than giving the store managers the discretion to use the material as they saw fit, the packet came complete with a store diagram of the front windows, presenting the predetermined positioning of banners upon particular glass sections. In-store banners came with similar diagrams, commanding where they were to be displayed.

Besides tying into the bureaucratic model's concept of rules for limiting the behavior of employees, this example also touches on the model's concept of hierarchy. Discretion was exercised by those in power above; decisions were merely implemented by employees lower in the hierarchy.[7]

This extensive use of rules in organizing the workplace helped contribute to another concept of the bureaucratic model—the division of labor. Because the clerk position was so controlled by rules, the amount of decision making required of an individual in that position was quite low. Anyone capable of learning and following the rules would be able to perform an adequate job in the workplace. The job was reduced to a form that required no great skills or level of training. The following incident dramatically illustrates the high division of labor.

Once a week the store received its grocery order from the warehouse. Groceries came into the store prepriced, ready to be placed directly on the shelves. While this may have been done because many items were ordered in less than case quantities for each store, it also simplified the running of the store, thus dividing the otherwise required labor among more employees. Night-shift clerks were given responsibility for leaving the store clean, making a final sales reading for the day, depositing the day's receipts, and ensuring that shelves were well stocked for the following day's business. Day-shift clerks were responsible for compiling the weekly orders, checking and storing the orders as they arrived, and making price changes on items as the need arose. While these particular responsibilities were assigned according to time availability and need, they still display the clean markings of a division of labor.

Polygraph tests were used to ensure the proper enforcement of rules as well as the impersonality of the entire organization. When shortages occurred above a given level, all members of the store who could have played some part in the shortage were required to take the polygraph test. In fact, there was much talk about several managers who had lost their jobs because of their personal involvement in inventory shortages, showing the rule's universal application to all involved.

The Seven-Eleven organization had many more rules, even including how one should go about leaving the organization. The goal in describing the Seven-Eleven organization here and in relating it to the dimensions of the bureaucratic form of organization has been to give a concrete feel for how this form of organization might operate on a day-to-day basis. The advantages and disadvantages of the bureaucratic form of organization were sprinkled throughout this entire discussion. Thus, a separate section on advantages and disadvantages need not be presented here.

Environment for Effectiveness

The Seven-Eleven organization has successfully applied, with a relatively high degree of emphasis, the dimensions of the bureaucratic form of organization to its lower levels. Cases such as this, and other more systematic research studies, suggest that a relatively high degree of application of the bureaucratic model may be associated with organizational effectiveness under certain contingencies.[8] A consideration of more detailed aspects of different versions of the bureaucratic model is beyond the scope of this chapter.[9]

The bureaucratic form of organization is likely to be most effective in a complex/static environment. Managers in this environment have a fairly good understanding of the nature of their problems and the available alternatives. The complex/static environment is relatively stable (unchanging), but complicated. This complexity is partially handled by the development of numerous and detailed rules and procedures that specify how repetitive problems should be solved. But a high degree of emphasis on the bureaucratic form of organization would usually be unnecessary in a simple/static environment. Because of the simplicity and unchanging nature of this environment, there would be little need for the extensive development of rules and procedures.

A single contingency, even one as crucial as the nature of the environment, cannot fully determine the proper choice of organizational form.[10] The real world of management is never quite that simple. Some other contingencies (in addition to a complex/static environment) that are compatible with a high emphasis on the bureaucratic form of organization include:

1. Routine tasks that are not too difficult or changing.
2. Employee and management groups whose values and attitudes are compatible or neutral toward the "requirements" of the bureaucratic form of organizations.
3. A well-defined technology that can be simple (as in the Seven-Eleven stores) or somewhat more complex (as on the assembly line of an automobile plant.)

PRODUCT FORM OF ORGANIZATION

The *product form of organization* is the grouping together of activities that are necessary to create each of the outputs (products or services) of the organization. Elements of the functional and bureaucratic forms of organization are incorporated into the product form. The product form of organization is possible or necessary only if the organization has multiple products or services. For example, General Motors markets many products; separate organizational units manufacture or market each of these outputs. The product form reduces the complexity that would otherwise confront managers in the more typical functional and bureaucratic forms of organization. For example, in the functional form of organization, the marketing vice president might have to be concerned with all the products created by the organization. When sales of different products become substantial, it may be more effective to create a key marketing manager for each of the product lines. This reduces the complexity that any one manager has to handle. Moreover, it becomes an attractive alternative when the competitive environment for each product line becomes more dynamic. When these environmental changes speed up, the ability to develop and rely on extensive rules and procedures that are so much a part of the bureaucratic form of organization is reduced.

Typically, organizations that adopt the product form previously used the functional form in conjunction with the bureaucratic form. But the growth, complexity, and increasing rate of environmental change created management problems that could not be efficiently or effectively dealt with only through the functional or bureaucratic forms. The functional or bureaucratic forms are not completely tossed out. Rather, all three forms are found at different organizational levels and in different parts of the organization. For example, General Motors has product units (such as Chevrolet, Buick, and Oldsmobile) and functional units (such as Public Relations, Finance, and Legal). At the lower organizational levels of both the product and functional units, General Motors makes use of the bureaucratic form through reliance on extensive rules, procedures, and a well-defined hierarchy of authority.

Case Example: DuPont

This description of DuPont provides an example of how organizational forms used by management will and should change over time as new problems are faced.[11] It also provides an excellent example of a firm that adopted a product form of organization while retaining some elements of the functional form.

In 1902, DuPont was reorganized from a cluster of family-owned predecessor firms. Pierre and Coleman DuPont, organizers of the new firm, faced the problem of coordinating and managing these predecessor firms as a single organization. Only thus could they realize the economies of scale and the efficiencies in production and administration that would permit profitable combination of the old firms. DuPont had at that time 31 factories producing three main product lines: dynamite, black powder, and smokeless powder. These products were sufficiently different and their markets and raw materials sufficiently diverse to multiply the required coordinating effort manyfold. Production had to be standardized to ensure uniformity of outputs, inefficient plants eliminated, and duplications resolved. This could not take place without systematic, uniform information. The predecessor firms had been run with few records and little mechanism beyond the principal owner's autocracy for controlling expenditures. In the old DuPont Powder Company, Col. Henry du Pont had written all company correspondence himself in longhand! Clearly, in a firm as large as the new DuPont, no individual could comprehend and control the myriad details. Formerly, little attention had been paid to organization, or to efficiency in production, purchasing, or marketing. Frequently, plants were poorly maintained, and sales agents competed or duplicated one another's efforts. Old and inefficient production processes were used. From the firm's meager records, it was impossible to determine the worth of the various properties or even the value of the holdings in cash and securities, let alone the cost of manufacturing a given product or operating a given plant.

Because of the differences in the three products the new company was to produce, the first step was to organize three separate product divisions, one for each of the main product lines. Within each of these product divisions, a functional department structure was set up. Product division heads became part of an executive committee responsible for managing the company as a whole. This structure dealt explicitly with a new need. Not only must the activities of any given product's operating division be coordinated, but the operations of the firm as a whole also had to be directed. This was a separate task, distinct from the day-to-day operations of the three divisions.

A critical step in the reorganization of DuPont was the design of a system to provide comprehensive information on all company activities. This was necessary to evaluate performance, to set prices properly, and, most importantly perhaps, to provide the basis for allocating resources among the three product lines. Without standardized information, it would be impossible to know whether the company should continue to sell a product, expand production, or cease to manufacture it. Information was gathered on a company-wide, uniform basis. This information made comparisons among different product lines possible, on the basis of return on investment, for the first time. For the first time too, as historical records were accumulated, it became possible to delegate responsibility to the operating product divisions while retaining centralized control. This freed top management to deal with exceptions and with strategy for the firm as a whole. These controls, and the centralized monitoring they made possible, enabled the DuPont Company to survive drastic economic changes during the international financial panic of 1907–1908 because top-level management could match expenditures to forecast income. The forecast could be quickly adjusted to reflect actual experience.

After World War I, a more streamlined version of this structure, with further separation of day-to-day operating responsibility from the long-term management of the firm, permitted DuPont to concentrate on new products and markets. Since an adverse antitrust ruling had foreclosed further expansion in explosives, this new focus was essential to allow reinvestment of substantial profits from efficient wartime production of military explosives. The two basic tasks on which top-level management concentrated were allocating investment among the competing activities of the various product lines and financing new capital for expansion. The rule of thumb was no investment if the money could be put to better use in some other branch of the company's business. Return on investment was the criterion, and accurate, uniform financial information was its foundation.

DuPont's organizational design made use of product-line structure (the main product operating divisions), functional departmentalization (within the operating product departments), and staff units. In addition, top-level management activities were specialized, including a committee structure that was distinct from the operating departments, the operating hierarchy, and the staff departments that assisted in day-to-day operations and long-term problems.

Advantages and Disadvantages

Departmentation by product line eases the problems of complexity and coordination, while also making use of individual expertise and knowledge in specific areas.[12] For example, the sales effort of a particular individual may be maximized when that person is discussing nuclear power plants, solar energy units, or laser beams, each of which is best sold by an expert thoroughly familiar with the product. Product departmentation is especially useful if the firm's volume is high enough to warrant employing such experts.

Product departmentation may also enable the efficient use of highly specialized capital equipment. For example, General Electric must use highly specialized equipment in the production of nuclear turbines for the generation of electrical power. If such equipment is used to full capacity, economic gains may be realized in the manufacturing, assembling, and handling of the product. General Electric has also found that the coordination between the sales and engineering efforts in the production of these power-generation plants can easily be maintained by grouping activities by product line. Corporate headquarters of General Electric has also found that profit responsibility can be pinpointed to each vice-president. When the vice-president is required to supervise sales, engineering, service, and cost functions, headquarters can set predetermined profit goals for the management and can more intelligently evaluate the contributions of each product line to total profit.

One disadvantage of product departmentation is that a firm must have a large number of personnel with the needed managerial talent available to staff the product lines. The danger of increased costs through the duplication of activities also exists.

Environment for Effectiveness

The product form of organization is likely to be most effective in a simple/dynamic environment. The adoption of the product form often *reduces* the complexity of the environment facing any one department or manager. The unit need focus only on the environment for one product or service rather than on multiple products or services. You will recall that managers in this environment probably face somewhat greater uncertainty than managers in the complex/static environment. In the simple/dynamic environment, changes are continously taking place. Managers must be highly adaptable. Because of this constant change, it is not nearly as easy to rely on established rules and procedures as it is in the complex/static environment.

MATRIX FORM OF ORGANIZATION

The matrix form of organization represents a balance between organizing resources around product lines and functional classifications. It imposes an overall structure upon the product and/or functional structures. Organizing solely by function may neglect unique product needs. And organizing solely around products might reduce desired functional specialization. Dow Corning Corporation uses a matrix form of organization in conjunction with product units such as rubber and sealants, resins and chemicals, fluids and compounds, specialty lubricants, and consumer products.[13]

The main feature of a matrix organization is duality in authority, information, and reporting relationships and systems. The integrating (or matrix) department has an authority, information, and reporting relationship with at least one functional department and one product department. In turn, the integrating department is evaluated by both a product department and a functional department. For example, the managers of product and functional departments affect the chances for promotion and salary increases of those involved with integration. Ideally, this results in a power balance between the influence of the product department and the functional department on the integrating department.

Stages of Development

Like other structures, matrix forms develop in stages.[14] The first stage toward a matrix is a temporary task force. Composed of representatives from the various departments of divisions of the parent organization, the task force is formed to study a problem and to make recommendations. Team members retain their usual organizational affiliations (an engineer continues to report to the head of engineering; a marketing representative, to the head of marketing). But these temporary team members are also responsible for the special project.

The second stage in matrix formation is the creation of permanent teams or committees organized around specific needs or problems. Again, representatives from the various functional and/or product departments sit on this team or committee, each presenting the view of the home department.

The third stage occurs when a project manager is appointed and held responsible for coordinating the activities and input of the team or committee assignment. Project managers are responsible for the final project output. Often they must negotiate or "buy" the human resources necessary to carry out the task. With project managers, the organization is well on the way to permanent matrix structure, with the difficulties and benefits of multiple authority patterns.

Figure 4–7 shows what a fully working matrix form of organization might look like for a business school. Typical functional departments are accounting, finance, management, and marketing. In addition, the business school has four programs (or products): the undergraduate, MBA, doctoral, and executive development programs. The example in the figure also shows that faculty members in finance are evaluated by both the head of the finance department and the director of the MBA program. If a finance faculty member also taught in the undergraduate program, the input of that director would also be included in the performance evaluation.

The matrix organization form does away with the simple, straightforward, and unitary chain of command. Multiple authority relationships is a distinguishing characteristic of matrix organizations. While the traditional hierarchical structure is based on formal reward or position power, the matrix demands instead negotiation by peers of optimal solutions based on their own viewpoints.[15] Obviously, the matrix structure is complex and difficult to implement. It is a costly form of organization that may take two or three years to implement. Power balances are subtle and difficult to maintain. Thus, it should only be used in special situations.

Case Example: General Motors

General Motors has selectively applied the matrix form of organization in dealing with complex, rapidly changing demands.[16] General Motors was compelled to respond to increasing government and public pressures for better emission controls and gasoline mileage. It was apprent that smaller cars was the answer. The problem lay in redesigning the entire product line quickly in order to meet government standards and the competition of foreign imports and domestic compacts. To meet these needs, new techniques of engineering and new technology would be required, while tolerances for error and correction time would have to be minimized.

In 1974, GM adopted the project center, a method of engineering

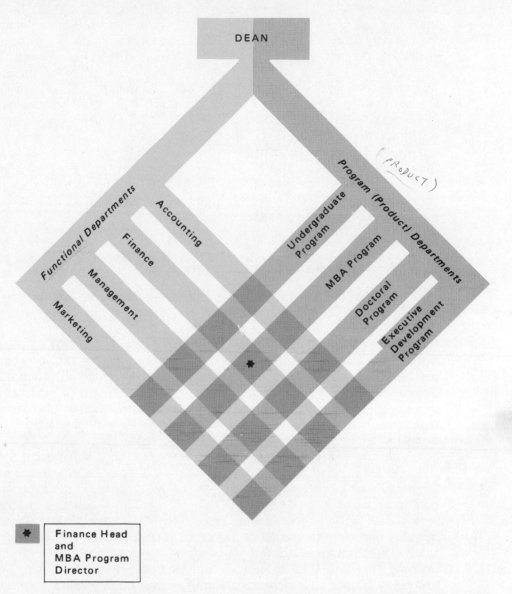

FIGURE 4-7.   Matrix Organization in a Business School

management modeled on aerospace research management at National Aeronautics and Space Administration. A GM project center, made up of engineers lent by the five automotive divisions, was devised to coordinate the efforts of the five divisions in what GM called "downsizing" the product line. The project center is a temporary group that reports to a board composed of the chief engineers from all five automotive divisions. A project center forms around a major redesign effort. The A-body center, which was responsible for 1978 intermediate-car development, ran from late 1975 until the fall of 1977. The X-body center, which started later, worked on front-wheel drive compacts for 1979. When a project center's work is completed, its personnel return to their divisions and their usual work.

Benefits of the project center for employees involved include the opportunity to work on the most important and exciting design work facing the corporation. Also, project center members come into contact with the best engineers from all divisions. The project center form puts a premium on innovation and creativity, thus encouraging intrinsic rewards for the engineers. For the organization, benefits of the project center include top-flight technical design, use of the latest techniques, and close coordination at all stages of the project among the five automotive divisions. A not inconsequential additional benefit is high motivation and enthusiasm throughout the corporation for a challenging problem.

Advantages and Disadvantages

The matrix form of organization allows multiple orientations to be maintained. A complex organization can quickly evolve new products or new responses to change of a high order of technical quality, while retaining the benefits of its product and functional forms. General management skills—negotiating, balancing, and trading off among various costs and benefits—can be developed more widely and at lower organizational levels. Often the personal rewards, motivation, and excitement of matrix participants is high. Because of the diverse "organizational homes" of matrix team members, both quality of solutions and ease of implementation are improved.

On the negative side, the matrix form demands substantial managerial overhead, particularly in the installation stages (which may take two to three years) while participants learn how to operate in the new organization. Learning may be slow because fundamental attitude changes are required of participants, who are typically used to expecting unity of command, unambiguous authority structure, and command orientation. The matrix form changes all this. It is often necessary to engage in special training programs such as team building to implement this design. To work properly, a matrix form must maintain continuing tension between participants' multiple orientations. This, in turn, requires a whole set of different interpersonal skills facilitating confrontation, conflict resolution, bargaining, and trade-offs. Matrix forms are also difficult to perceive and comprehend.

In a projection of General Electric's organization over the next ten years, its *Organization Planning Bulletin* sums up the dilemmas of the matrix form in these words:

We've highlighted matrix organization . . . not because it's a bandwagon that we want you all to jump on, but rather that it's a complex, difficult, and sometimes frustrating form of organization to live with. It's also, however, a bellwether of things to come. . . . And all of us are going to have to learn how to utilize organization to prepare managers to increasingly deal with high levels of complexity and ambiguity in situations where they have to get results from people and components not under their direct control . . . where so many complex, conflicting interests must be balanced.[17]

Environment for Effectiveness

The matrix form of organization is likely to be effective in a complex/dynamic environment. But not all complex/dynamic environments require the use of the matrix form. A number of other structural mechanisms beyond our scope of discussion can also be used for dealing with this type of environment.[18] The complex/dynamic environment is the most difficult environment to manage. Managers in a complex/dynamic environment are faced with numerous uncertainties in decision making. The organization finds itself in a sea of change for which there are no simple answers. Often a need exists to deal quickly with new and changing problems that require many types of professional judgment and expertise. The matrix form is obviously one of the means for helping management to cope with this type of environment.

Some related factors, in addition to a complex/dynamic environment, that influence the desirability and potential effectiveness of the matrix form are:

1. The need to have multiple points of view and expertise present in the consideration of problems
2. The need to achieve a high degree of coordination between different functional and product (or program) units
3. The need to respond rapidly to changes

INTEGRATION AND OVERVIEW

Four basic approaches to organizational design have been presented: functional, bureaucratic, product, and matrix. These forms can be used in combination with one another in a single organization. Brief applications of each form were presented and the environmental conditions under which they might be effectively used were noted. The treatment has tried to be consistent with the following theme expressed by Peter F. Drucker:

In designing organizations, we have to choose among different structures, each stressing a different dimension and each, therefore, with distinct costs, specific and fairly stringent requirements, and real limitations. There is no risk-free organization structure. And a design that is the

TABLE 4–1.   Relative Emphasis on Four Organizational Forms within Four Environments for Organizational Effectiveness

| | Organizational Forms | | | |
Environments	Functional	Bureaucratic	Product	Matrix
Simple/static	High	Low to Moderate	Low	Low
Complex/static	Moderate	High	Low	Low
Simple/dynamic	Low to Moderate	Moderate	High	Low
Complex/dynamic	Moderate	Low	Moderate	High

best solution for one task may be only one of a number of equally poor alternatives for another task, and just plain wrong for yet a third kind of work.[19]

Table 4–1 is a general framework for providing an integrated overview of organizational design. It also emphasizes the possible relationships between the environment of an organization and its various units. The four general types of environments identified are based on the change-complexity model presented in Chapter 3 and referred to throughout this chapter. The four design strategies are identified across the top of the figure. To develop a more integrated view of each of these strategies and the possible combined patterns of usage within a single organization (and/or unit), the figure presents the degree of utilization or emphasis on each strategy that should probably exist in the four extreme environments. The degree of emphasis is identified as varying from low to moderate to high. The pattern of emphasis on the four structural strategies in organizations (or units) with the different environments could represent effective combinations in the ways of structuring an organization.

SUMMARY

Choice among design options depends upon a variety of factors. No single form—function, product, bureaucratic, or matrix—is best for all organizations or all circumstances. Instead, the design choice must balance benefits against costs in the context of clear thinking about the organization's critical problems, ability to bear costs, and tolerance for the disadvantages of the chosen form. The designer must keep advantages and disadvantages of a given form in mind. A form that was appropriate at one time may be inappropriate at another.

The key contingency variable emphasized throughout this chapter was the nature of the environment facing the organization and its various units. The overriding theme was that organizational form should change as the environment of the organization and its units change.

Where the organization's strategy and environment bend toward quick response, the organizational form must bolster flexibility. Where the organization's strategy and environment are conservative and unchanging, predictability and stability are required. Where several product lines of different characteristics must be dealt with, some form of decentralization, allowing lower managers to focus on a given product and upper management to emphasize coordination and strategy, should probably evolve. Thus, for example, DuPont eventually developed decentralized operations with centralized coordination guiding an overall strategy. When the environment is extremely complex and dynamic, the matrix form might be selectively used within the organization.

As will be seen in a number of the following chapters, the organizational form (or combination of forms) chosen by management has a direct bearing on many behavioral processes. On a short-term basis, the organizational form creates the internal structure or content within which behavioral processes (such as motivation, leadership, communication, and conflict) take place. Over the long run, behavioral problems may provide motivation for management to change the organizational structure.

DISCUSSION QUESTIONS

1. What problems is the functional division of labor intended to solve?

2. Describe an organization in which you are presently a member in terms of the dimensions of the bureaucratic form of organization. How would you characterize the degree of emphasis placed on each of the bureaucratic dimensions?

3. Give some examples of organizational rules you have encountered that seemed to be functional and dysfunctional

from the standpoint of organizational effectiveness.

4. What are the advantages of the product form of organization, and its disadvantages? What managerial problem does it solve?

5. What are the difficulties associated with matrix organization forms? What managerial problem is it intended to solve?

6. What factors should influence the design of organizations?

MANAGERIAL PROBLEMS

MONTREAL AIRPORT*

Montreal Airport is a large international airport handling many flights from all over the world every day. Ramp crews are responsible for guiding the incoming planes into the gate, unloading the passengers and

* Adapted from: The Montreal Airport ramp crews, *The Business Quarterly*, Winter 1976. Used with permission.

their baggage, and servicing the plane. They must see that all required provisions and fuel are restocked and that the plane is moved to its takeoff position.

A scheduler monitors arriving flights and schedules crews to service the aircraft by means of a closed-circuit television screen that carries announcements to crews. For example, "Crew 5 . . . Flight 826 . . . Gate 14 . . . DC9 arriving 1400."

Supervisors, responsible for from three to five crews, receive information from the television screen. The supervisor monitors the crews' work directly, by driving to crew work locations around the airport. In a single day, a supervisor might drive as much as 100 miles in monitoring crew activities.

The lead hand of each ramp crew is responsible for watching the television screen to determine where and when the next assignment will be and what equipment will be required. Tow-bars, which vary from aircraft to aircraft, baggage carts, provision trucks, and so on, will be needed.

This system of assigning work crews worked well when the Montreal Airport was small and there were few crews. As the people involved increased to some 600 ramp crew workers, however, it became progressively less efficient. One problem was safety, of concern to both management and the union. Crews were racing from one gate to another under all weather conditions. This presented some serious hazards, particularly when runways were icy. Also, because of the wide distribution of the crews, it was difficult for supervisors to monitor crews. While the television screen told where crews were, it could not indicate whether crew members were wearing safety equipment (earmuffs to deaden noise and fluorescent clothing to make crews easily visible).

A second problem was competition over equipment, particularly at peak periods. In anticipation of their next assignment, a crew might assemble equipment ahead of time and literally stand guard over it, leaving one crew member on guard while the others went for coffee. Clearly, the system was no longer working effectively. Problems were reflected in eight to ten grievances filed daily, mostly over safety items.

Chart 1 illustrates how one crew moved from one location to another during the day. Their shift began at point 1, the Ready Room. After getting a tractor, the crew moved to their first aircraft at Gate 3, point 2 on the chart. (The chart does not show movements to collect equipment.) After completing this task, they moved to Gate 41 to handle a second aircraft (3), then back to Gate 1 (4). The crew then had lunch (5). After lunch, the crew moved to Gate 36 (6). Their next assignment was Gate 23 (7). After this, they returned to the Ready Room (8), having completed their shift.

Chart 1 shows the movements of only one team from work assignment to work assignment. Since each supervisor had three to five teams, it was clearly difficult to know where crews were at any time or to manage them safely and effectively by personal observation. Chart 2 shows the activities pattern of the teams under one supervisor during one day.

CHART 1   Work Activity Dayshift

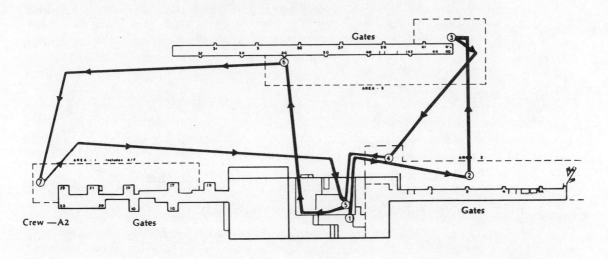

CHART 2   Work Activity Afternoon Shift

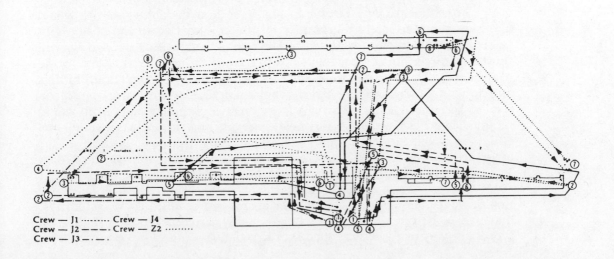

Crew — J1 ....   Crew — J4 ————
Crew — J2 — — —   Crew — Z2 ··········
Crew — J3 —·—·

The result of the old system, when applied to a growing number of crews, was deteriorating operating performance. By Air Canada's standards, this meant an increase in ground elapsed time—the time necessary to service, clean, and prepare the aircraft for takeoff.

QUESTIONS

1. What would be your plan for restructuring the work of the ramp crews?
2. Which of the present problems would this plan reduce or eliminate?
3. Why do you feel that your plan will do this?

CARSTAIRS COMPANY

Doug Stone, project leader for the Carstairs Company, had fifteen computer programmers reporting to him. These programmers were working on the development of three major information systems. Each of the programmers was assigned to one of three teams. Each team was responsible for one of the information systems.

Stone decided that he could best control the development of the projects, and free more time for his administrative responsibilities, by assigning team leaders to each project area. The team leaders, he decided, would be called "lead programmers." Before announcing his decision to all the programmers, Stone decided to discuss it privately with each of the three prospective lead programmers. He wanted to be sure that they understood the project and were willing to accept this new responsibility.

Stone called Dave Fleet into his office and told him that he would like him to be the lead programmer on projects related to the billing and pricing systems. Stone explained to Dave that this position carried the authority to direct the project-related activities of the people assigned to the project area. These people were Bob Strawser, Dave Crumley, Clint Phillips, and Jo Ann Thomas. Stone clearly explained what was meant by project-related activities versus areas of administrative authority, which he would retain. Dave Fleet accepted the new position, and as he was leaving the office, he asked Stone to announce and explain the new position to the other programmers. Stone assured Dave that he would on the next day. The following week Stone began his annual vacation.

One morning, while Stone was still on vacation, Dave Fleet asked Bob Strawser to prepare the computer operator procedure for a system test that had to be run that night. Later that day, Dave asked Bob if the test procedure was ready. Bob replied that it was not.

Dave asked, "Why not, didn't you have enough time?"

"No," Bob replied, "I had enough time, but where I worked before, that task was the responsibility of the project's system analyst."

Dave was getting upset. "Fortunately or unfortunately, it is a programming responsibility here; I've explained that to you earlier. I'm the lead programmer on this project; now why didn't you do as I asked?"

"You're the lead programmer?" Bob seemed surprise. "To my knowledge, we don't have a lead programmer on this project."

Dave pondered what his next step should be. He knew that the test procedure had to be done within three hours, and Bob was the only one who had the knowledge to prepare it.

QUESTIONS

1. What type of organization exists at the Carstairs Company?
2. What changes might be made in the organizational structure?
3. How should the changes be implemented?

KEY WORDS

Organizational design
Division of labor
Functional division of labor
Departmentation
Line activities
Staff activities
Scalar chain of command
Unity of command
Span of control
Suboptimizing

Bureaucratic model
Hierarchy of authority
Centralization
Rules
Procedural specifications
Impersonality
Technical competence
Product form of organization
Matrix organization

REFERENCES

1. Smith, A., *An Inquiry into the Nature and Causes of the Wealth of Nations, 1776* (New York: Modern Library, 1937).

2. Hall D., Some organizational considerations in the professional-organizational relationship, *Administrative Science Quarterly*, 1967, 12, pp. 461–478.

3. Perrow, C., *Complex Organizations:*

A Critical Essay (Glenview, Ill.: Scott, Foresman, 1972); also see Anderson, J. G. Bureaucratic rules: Bearers of organizational authority, *Educational Administration Quarterly*, 1966, 11, pp. 7–34.

4. The battle over bureaucracy, *Time*, March 16, 1978, pp. 16–18.

5. Maniha, J. K., Universalism and par-

ticularism in bureaucratizing organizations, *Administrative Science Quarterly*, 1975, 2, pp. 177–190; Meyer, M. W., and M. C. Brown, The process of bureaucratization, *American Journal of Sociology*, 1977, 83, pp. 364–385.

6.   (Name withheld), The Seven-Eleven organization in relation to the bureaucratic model, unpublished paper, November 1974.

7.   Bacharach, Samuel B., and Michael Aiken, Communication in administrative bureaucracies, *Academy of Management Journal*, 1977, 20, pp. 365–377.

8.   Burns, T., and G. M. Stalker, *The Management of Innovation* (London: Tavistock Publications, 1961); Duncan, R. B., Multiple decision-making structures in adapting to environmental uncertainty: The impact on organizational effectiveness, *Human Relations*, 1973, 26, pp. 273–291; Lawrence, P. R., and J. W. Lorsch, *Organization and Environment* (Boston: Graduate School of Business Administration, Harvard University, 1967).

9.   Hrebiniak, L. G., *Complex Organizations* (St. Paul: West Publishing, 1978); Hummel, Ralph P., *The Bureaucratic Experience* (New York: St. Martin's Press, 1977).

10.   Ford, J. D., and J. W. Slocum, Jr., Size, technology, environment and the structure of organizations, *The Academy of Management Review*, 1977, 2, pp. 561–575; Jackson, J. H., and C. P. Morgan, *Organization Theory: A Macro Perspective for Management* (Englewood Cliffs, N.J.: Prentice-Hall, 1978).

11.   Chandler, A. D., Jr., and S. Salis-bury, *Pierre S. duPont and the Making of the Modern Corporation* (New York: Harper and Row, 1976).

12.   Hellriegel, D., and J. W. Slocum, Jr., *Management: Contingency Approaches* (Reading, Mass.: Addison-Wesley, 1978).

13.   Goggin, W. C., How multidimensional structure works at Dow Corning, *Harvard Business Review*, 1974, 52, pp. 54–66.

14.   Davis, S. M., and P. R. Lawrence, *Matrix* (Reading, Mass.: Addison-Wesley, 1977); Galbraith, J. R., *Organization Design* (Reading, Mass.: Addison-Wesley, 1977).

15.   Dunne, E. J., Jr., M. J. Stohl, and L. J. Melhart, Jr., Influence sources of project and functional managers in matrix organizations, *Academy of Management Journal*, 1978, 21, pp. 135–140.

16.   Burck, C. G., How G.M. turned itself around, *Fortune*, 1978, 97, pp. 86–89+.

17.   Davis, S. M., and P. R. Lawrence, The matrix diamond, *The Wharton Magazine*, 1978, 2, pp. 19–27.

18.   Aldrich, H., and D. Herker, Boundary spanning roles and organization structure, *The Academy of Management Review*, 1977, 2, pp. 217–230; Khandwalla, P. N., *The Design of Organizations* (New York: Harcourt Brace Jovanovich, 1977).

19.   Drucker, P. F., New templates for today's organizations, *Harvard Business Review*, 1974, 52, pp. 45–53; also see Pfeffer, J., and G. R. Salancik, *The External Control of Organizations: A Resource Dependence Perspective* (New York: Harper and Row, 1978).

PART III

INDIVIDUAL DIFFERENCES

5

The Perceptual
Process

5

LEARNING OBJECTIVES

When you have finished reading and studying this chapter, you should be able to:

▲ Describe the basic elements in the perceptual process.

▲ Discuss the factors that affect perceptual selection.

▲ Discuss the factors that affect perceptual organization.

▲ Explain how the perceptual process affects managerial assumptions about people.

THOUGHT STARTERS

▲ What does the perceptual process mean to you?

▲ What factors affect how you perceive the world?

▲ How do certain facts enter your decision process and others get excluded?

▲ How do you ignore threatening information?

▲ What's your philosophy about people?

All of us are aware of our environment. But everything in our environment is not of equal value for the perceptual process. We tune into some perceptual stimuli, while we tune out others. We listen expectantly for our friends' footsteps in the hall, while we ignore the movements of people upstairs. In an office, we ignore the bell announcing the arrival of the elevator, but we jump at the sound of the coffee-cart bell.

We perceive things with which we are in immediate contact, and we perceive other things from afar or through something else. We can turn away from our work and watch someone enter the far side of the room. Or without turning around, we can hear them opening the door and entering. Or they can enter the room silently, but a sudden rush of cold air alerts us to their entry and we turn around.

How we interpret what we perceive varies considerably.[1] You are introduced to someone you have never met before. She smiles at you. Is she indicating pleasure, shyness, nervousness, or perhaps even masking her boredom? How you interpret this smile is affected by how you feel at the moment. Are you yourself pleased, shy, nervous, or bored? Friends of yours who observe this introduction may all form different interpretations as to what the smile means. Responses to any situation differ from person to person. Let's examine one instance:

> *In early 1978, John Fogarty informed his staff that headquarters in New York City had published directions concerning a computerized information and retrieval system that was to be created by each company within the conglomerate. This system was to contain management information on all projects evolved within each company. When the system was finally completed, the general staff in New York could receive up-to-date information from all companies within the organization.*
>
> *Fogarty selected a junior staff member, Morgan Harris, to design and implement the information system within the company. Harris was known for being the first to accept a new project and the last to finish it. Because of a manpower shortage, Fogarty had no choice but to assign the project to Harris and hope that it would be completed on time.*
>
> *Virtually every member of Fogarty's staff was opposed to the computer retrieval system. Comments often made were: "It will be out of date within two months. We work in a fast moving field." "Corporate management is admitting that they cannot do their job and need the electronic brain to do it for them." "It's just plain silly. We already provide New York with monthly and quarterly reports that contain all the needed information if they would just read them."*
>
> *After getting information on each project within the company, Harris discussed the problem with the management systems people and then created the computer files for storing the in-*

*formation. He gave the printout to Fogarty in late November
(it was due in New York in early December) for final review and
approval. Much to the surprise of Fogarty, about 85 percent of
the information proved to be incorrect. It was quite obvious that
either false information had been provided to Harris by members
of top management about the status of their projects or that
Harris had changed the information when entering it into the
computer's files. Time was running out.*[2]

Why did this occur? Did the members of top management provide
incorrect data in order to sabotage the system? Did Harris alter any of the
information provided to him because he wanted to protect individuals or
for his personal ego satisfaction? Had Fogarty made it clear to his staff
and to Harris exactly what New York headquarters wanted? Had New
York made it clear to Fogarty?

Obviously there were differences in the way Fogarty's staff and top
management in New York perceived the project. Fogarty's staff perceived
it as another "make work" project and another means by which control
and decision making could be wrested from them by New York. New York
perceived the project as an important change and something that would
make the company better. The perception by members of Fogarty's staff
may have been false, but what is perceived is most important to the individual and will determine his/her behavior.

Another problem that might have accounted for the staff's attitude
toward the project was the appointment of Harris to head the project. Familiar with Harris' reputation and his low status in the company, they
might not have given much attention to his questions. And Harris might
have delayed pulling the information together until it was too late to verify
it. Whatever the case, it is evident that people often perceive the same
things in different ways. Their responses depend on their perceptions.

THE BASIC ELEMENTS IN THE
PERCEPTUAL PROCESS

Along with learning (discussed in Chapter 6) and motivation (discussed in Chapter 11), perception is a primary psychological process. *The
perceptual process is the selection and organization of environmental
stimuli to provide meaningful experiences for the perceiver.*[3]

As we receive perceptual information, we assemble it and incorporate it into a meaningful experience particular to ourselves. No two people's perceptions are exactly alike. We paint a picture of the world that
expresses our personal view of the "real" world. Fogarty's staff and the general staff in New York had different perceptions of the efficacy of head-

quarter's request. We are all bound by the limits of our own perceptual world.

Our perceptions are affected by the objects perceived, the ways in which we organize these objects, and the meanings we attach to these objects. Individual perceptual awareness varies. Some people who have entered a room only once can describe it in detail, whereas others barely remember anything. How we interpret what we perceive is also affected by our preconceptions. A clenched first raised in the air by a football player can be perceived as an angry threat against the opposition or as an expression of team solidarity. The perceptual environment is constantly changing. Before you can react fully to the dead deer in the road, you realize that it is a pile of brush. And factors affecting perception vary. Drop your books in the library, and everyone will look up; drop them in the machine shop, and no one will notice. The final class bell fills you with joy if you have completed your work and are about to start the weekend; it fills you with dread if you still have three more answers to complete on an important exam. In the first example, an external factor, the amount of noise in the room, affects the impact the dropping of books will have on people in the room. In the second example, an internal factor, your state of mind, affects how you will react to the bell.

Recognition of the difference between the perceptual world and the real world is important to the understanding of organization behavior. With this awareness, we should make decisions with greater care and not make complex and important decisions based on sketchy evidence, as in the following example:

> *The president of a major firm was considering promoting one of the upper-level managers to a top position in the firm. The prospective candidate was invited to the president's home for dinner. At the end of the main course, pie was served. The candidate made the mistake of putting the tines (prongs) of the fork straight into the point of the pie instead of using the side of the fork. The president rejected the candidate because of the individual's lack of sophistication. The president told the Personnel Department that anyone so naive in his approach to such a simple matter as eating pie could not be trusted to make important corporate-wide decisions.*[4]

The president rejected the candidate not because of past experience, but because of what he observed at the dinner party. The president's perception of this minor incident became the basis on which an important career decision was made. To the candidate, how he ate pie was of no consequence; to the president it was crucial. The perceptual world of the president was quite different from the perceptual world of the candidate.

Figure 5–1 summarizes the basic elements in the perceptual process

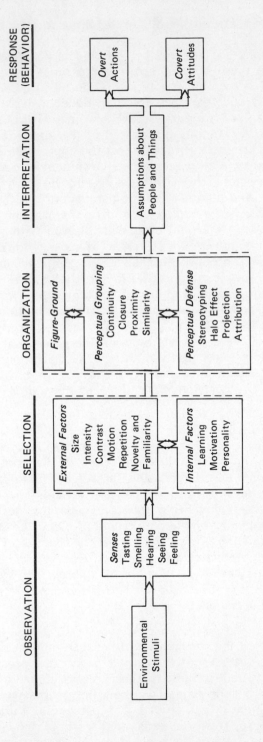

FIGURE 5–1.   The Basic Elements in the Perceptual Process from Observation to Response

Coffey/Athos/Raynolds, *Behavior in Organizations: A Multidimensional View*, 2nd ed., ©
1975, p. 68. Adapted by permission of Prentice-Hall, Inc., Englewood Cliffs, New Jersey.

—from the initial observation to the final response (behavior). Briefly, stimuli in the environment are observed through the five senses—tasting, smelling, hearing, seeing, and feeling. All five senses are important, but in the behavior of individuals in organizations, hearing, seeing, and feeling are the most important. These sensory perceptions are filtered through a selection step that determines what perceptions will receive the most attention. Selection of sensory perceptions is determined by both external factors and internal factors. The sensory perceptions selected to be acted upon are then organized into meaningful patterns. Once a sensory stimuli has been selected and organized, it is open to an interpretation that will lead to a response, either overt (actions) or covert (attitudes) or both. Each person selects and organizes sensory stimuli differently, thus leading to different interpretations and responses.[5]

The basic steps in the perceptual process shown in Figure 5–1 occur, in most cases, almost instantaneously. Rarely can we observe the separate steps between the observation and the response.

PERCEPTUAL SELECTION

The phone is ringing, your roommate is watching television, a dog is barking outside, your kitten is batting at your shoelaces, your electric typewriter is making a strange noise, you smell coffee brewing. Which of these stimuli will you ignore and which will demand your attention? In general, people perceive things that promise to help satisfy their needs and that they have found rewarding in the past. They tend to ignore mildly disturbing things, but will perceive very dangerous ones (e.g. the house is on fire).

Perceptual selection is the process by which we filter out most stimuli so that we may deal with the more important ones. Perceptual selection depends on our preferences and expectations of what is to be perceived and on our previous experience.

External Factors

As indicated in Figure 5–1, both external and internal factors affect perceptual selection. The external factors of perception are outside, or environmental, factors that influence perceptual selection. These external factors include size, intensity, contrast, motion, repetition, and novelty, and familiarity.[6] One, two, or all of these factors may be operating at any one time to affect your perception.

Size. The size principle states that the larger the size of the external factor, the more likely it is to be perceived. Basketball players Wilt Chamberlin, Kareem Abdul-Jabbar, and Bill Walton are likely to "stick out" in a crowd because of their height, just as "Mean" Joe Green, Carl Eller, and Ed "Too Tall" Jones are likely to be noticed in a weight room. In many corporations, the size of your office is preceived as an indication of your power and prestige. The larger your office is, the more likely you are to be paid attention to and respected.

Intensity.   Intensity is closely related to size. The intensity principle states that the more intense the external factor, the more likely it is to be perceived. The ringing of the telephone is more likely to be noticed by you than is your kitten or your typewriter. But if the kitten suddenly digs its claws into your ankle or if your typewriter begins smoking, you might forget all about the ringing telephone. It no longer would be the most intense stimuli. Even the language of a memo from an employer to a staff member can reflect intensity. A memo that reads "Please stop by my office at your convenience" won't fill you with the sense of urgency that you would get from a memo that reads "Report to my office, *immediately!*"

Contrast.   The contrast principle states that external factors that stand out against the background or that are not what people are expecting are the most likely to be perceived. Hunters in Pennsylvania are required to wear a minimum of 250 square inches of fluorescent orange covering. The bright, "unnatural" color stands out against the soft, natural colors of the forest. Someone dressed in cut off jeans and a tee shirt would go unnoticed at a beach but might cause quite a stir in a business setting.

Figure 5–2 demonstrates the contrast principle. Look at the circles in the center. Which is larger? The one on the right appears to be larger, doesn't it? But it isn't. The two circles are the same size. The circle on the right appears larger because its background, its frame of reference, is much smaller circles. The circle on the left appears smaller because it is seen in contrast with larger surrounding circles.

Motion.   The motion principle states that a moving factor is more likely to be perceived than is a stationary factor. Anyone who has ever visited Times Square in New York City will remember the moving signs—the cigarette ad that smokes, the beverage ad that pours a drink, the news flashing around the old Times Building. The lack of motion can also have

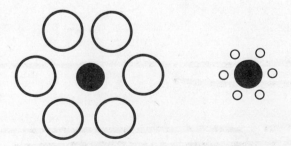

FIGURE 5–2.   Are the Center Circles in Both Figures the Same Size?

its advantages. Geese nesting in the marsh grass are safe from hunters who search the sky for moving flocks.

Repetition. The repetition principle states that a repeated factor is more likely to be perceived than is a single factor. Marketing managers use this principle in trying to get the attention of prospective customers. They create slogans that are used over and over again in ads. Slogans such as "Marlboro Country," "You deserve a break today, so get up and get away to McDonald's," and "Fly the friendly skies of United" are used to alert customers' attention and to affect their buying behavior.

Novelty and Familiarity. The novelty and familiarity principle states that either a novel or a familiar factor in the environment can serve as an attention getter. A large oil company applied both novelty and familiarity to improve perceptual awareness. The company was having teamwork problems with four vice-presidents. For the company to function successfully, it was decided to rotate the executives through each department twice a year. With each shift in job, the executives found themselves in stimulating, novel work situations. As time went on, they became fully familiar with all four departments and thus came to realize how they could help their colleagues in other departments. Results included better teamwork, broadened backgrounds, and a lessening of competition among departments.

Internal Factors

The *internal factors* of perception are aspects of the perceiver that influence perceptual selection. These internal factors include learning, motivation, and personality. Although learning and motivation will be treated in separate chapters, a brief discussion of them here will help you understand the perceptual process. But before examining the internal factors separately, consider the following experiment.

Twenty-three executives were enrolled in a company-sponsored training program. Six were in sales, five in production, four in accounting, and eight in other departments. They were given a ten-thousand word case history dealing with the organization and activities of another company. After examining the case history, they were to indicate what they considered to be the most important problem facing the firm. Five of the six sales persons felt the major company problem was in the sales area. Four of the five production people said the problem was to "clarify relationships within the organization," that is, a production-related problem. Three of the four accounting people had close contact with sales. They stated that sales was the most important problem.

The researchers concluded that although the case history called for looking at the problem from a company-wide perspective rather than a departmental viewpoint, most of the executives perceived the problem in terms of their own background.[7]

Learning.   Learning is an important factor in developing perceptual sets. A *perceptual set* is an expectation of a perception based on past experience with the same or similar stimuli. Here is an experiment you can perform to demonstrate the relationship between learning and the perceptual set principle. As you come into your room carrying some books, say to your roommate, "Is it all right if I bump my books here?" Then ask him/her what you said. Probably your roommate will have heard "bump" as "dump." The other words in your sentence gave your roommate a set that influenced his/her perception. This example shows that learning affects what you perceive. You often perceive what you expect to perceive.

The powerful role that learning and past experience play in perception can be seen in many ways. Stop for a moment and look at Figure 5–3. You know that the young boy cannot be much taller than his mother, yet your eyes tell you that he is. Your eyes are relying on the depth and perspective cues supplied by the apparent shape of the room. What you can't tell from the photograph is that the room is not an ordinary rectangle but an oddly shaped trapezoid. It has been purposefully distorted to fool your eyes. Neither the windows nor the floor tiles have squared corners. The walls, ceiling, and floor slope. The boy is standing higher up and much closer to us than is his mother.

Motivation.   Motivation also plays an important role in determining what you perceive. A hungry person is more sensitive to factors related to food, such as the odors of food cooking, than is a person who is not hungry.

FIGURE 5–3.   Is This Boy a Giant? Or Is His Mother a Midget? (Photo © Baron Wohlman)

In another example, your ability to follow a conversation in a noisy, crowded room depends to a large extent on your motivation. This is known as the cocktail-party effect. If you lose interest in what is being said, you might start picking up another conversation that you think might be more interesting.

A person motivated by a need for power will be attentive to environmental factors that seem to enhance power. Such "empire builders" in business seek to acquire large staffs because they believe that it is a reflection of their power. They also seek to increase their departmental budgets, again perceiving size as an indication of power. It never occurs to them that others might perceive their departments as being overstaffed and over-budgeted.[8]

The following is another example of the effect of motivation on perception in the business world:

> *David Herst, a personnel manager, learned that his boss, the vice-president for corporate personnel would soon retire. Herst and Joseph Wapner were the logical contenders for the job. David felt that his chances of being promoted were slightly less than those of Wapner. In order to eliminate Wapner, David submitted Wapner's name to an executive search firm as a good candidate for a corporate personnel manager. The strategy worked. Wapner took a job in another company and David received the promotion he wanted.*

The motivation to achieve in David's instance made it necessary for him to lessen the competition. He accomplished this by counting on his rival's own achievement motivation. Wapner couldn't resist the better job offered to him by the other firm. When asked sometime later about this strategy, David said that he was helping Wapner out by increasing the probability that another company would seek him out.[9]

Personality. Personality is the total of the emotional and behavioral tendencies that characterize an individual. Your personality is shaped in part by your perceptions. It in turn affects what and how you perceive. Look at Figure 5–4. What do you see? If what you see is an attractive, elegantly dressed woman, your perception concurs with the majority of first-time viewers. But in agreement with a sizeable minority, you may see a poor and ugly old woman. Which woman you see depends on your perceptual set. And this particular perceptual set is based more on personality than on learning.

(You still can't see the two women? To see the old woman, look for her chin buried in her fur collar. See her prominent nose, her small eyes, and her hair falling down over her forehead? To see the younger woman, the old woman's nose becomes her chin; the old woman's fully seen eye,

FIGURE 5–4.   Young Woman or Old Woman?

her ear. The younger woman is turned so you cannot see her mouth. Only the tip of her small nose and a long eyelash show.)

A test has been designed to examine the relationship between personality and perception. What is the man in Figure 5–5 thinking? Write a short story about him.

Depending on your personality, one of three factors may affect your perception of Figure 5–5: achievement, affiliation, power. Each type of individual will come up with a different type of story, even though each person has looked at the same picture.[10]

People who are *highly achievement oriented* tend to see this man as an engineer who wants to win a competition in which the most practical drawing will be awarded the contract to build a bridge. He is thinking now of how happy he will be when he wins. He has been puzzled by how to make a long span strong, but he remembers to specify a new steel alloy of great strength. He submits his entry, but he does not win and he becomes very unhappy.

People who are *highly socially oriented* (seek affiliation) tend to see him as a man who is working late. He is worried that his wife will be annoyed with him for neglecting her. She has been objecting that he cares more about his work than about her and the family. He seems unable to satisfy both his boss and his wife, but he loves his wife very much and will do his best to finish up fast and get home.

People who are *highly motivated by power* tend to see the man as a famous architect who wants to win a competition that will establish who is the best architect in the world. His chief rival has stolen his best ideas, and he is dreadfully afraid of the disgrace of losing. But he comes up with a great new idea that absolutely bowls over the judges, and he wins!

Which type of story did you write? Was it most influenced by achievement, affiliation, or power?

In the preceding pages, we examined the external and internal factors that affect perceptual selection. The external factors include size, in-

FIGURE 5–5.   Look at the Picture Briefly (10–15 Seconds). Then Write the Story It Suggests.

Source: David A. Kolb, Irwin M. Rubin, and James M. McIntyre, *Organizational Psychology: An Experimental Approach*, © 1971, p. 59. Reproduced by permission of Prentice-Hall, Inc., Englewood Cliffs, New Jersey.

tensity, contrast, motion, repetition, novelty, and familiarity. The greater the size, intensity, contrast, and so forth, the greater the chances are that you will perceive the object. These are things that intrude into our perceptual process even when we do not want them to. Bright lights, loud sounds, startling colors, and the telephone ringing are all things that happen externally to influence what we perceive but over which we have little control.

As well as these external factors, there are internal factors that affect perceptual selection. These internal factors include our learning—that is, our past experiences with the same or similar stimuli, our motivation, and our personality. Given the fact that we all have different backgrounds of experience, different aspirations about the future, different feelings toward the environment around us, and different motives and intentions, it is not surprising that individuals do not see the same things.

PERCEPTUAL ORGANIZATION

The pioneer psychologist William James said that "to an infant the world is just a big, blooming, buzzing confusion." All infants are faced with the problem of making sense out of their perceptions. Gradually they learn to organize their perceptions and these perceptual consistencies simplify their world.

Perceptual organization is the process by which we group environmental stimuli into recognizable patterns. Once perceptual selection has occurred, perceptual organization takes over in the perceptual process. The stimuli selected for attention are now seen as a whole. For example, all of us have a mental picture that includes the following properties: wood, four legs, seat, back, armrests, slats. This is our image of a chair. When you see an object that has all these properties, you recognize it as a chair. You organize the incoming information into a meaningful whole, which in this case is a chair.

Three important factors of perceptual selection are figure-ground, perceptual grouping, and perceptual defense.[11]

Figure-Ground

The *figure-ground principle* states that we tend to perceive the factor we are most attentive to as standing out against a background. Look at Figure 5–6 to see what can happen when we are not confronted with a clear figure-ground pattern. These illusions are called reversible figure-ground patterns. In Figure 5–6 (a) do you see a wine glass on a dark background or facing silhouettes on a white background? Figure 5–6 (b) is even harder. How many blocks do you see? Six or seven? Can you see both? (If not, turn the page upside down.) Now try to see both sets of blocks without turning

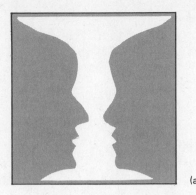
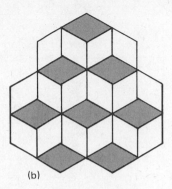

(a)   (b)

FIGURE 5–6.   Reversible Figure-Ground Patterns

the page. This is difficult, because once you are locked into one way of organizing what you see, it is often very hard to change that view. Think how difficult life would be if we were constantly confronted with such figure-ground ambiguity.

Perceptual Grouping

Perceptual grouping is the tendency to form individual stimuli into a meaningful pattern by means of continuity, closure, proximity, or similarity.

Continuity.   Continuity is the tendency to perceive objects as continuous patterns. Look at Figure 5–7 (a). Isn't it easier to visualize a wavy line over a squared-off line than it is to see a complex row of shapes? Continuity has its negative aspects, however. People who are inflexible or noncreative thinkers may be unable to perceive anything unique. Instead, they always seek out continuity. Inflexible managers may insist that employees follow set, step-by-step routines. Random activity, although it may solve problems more imaginatively and proficiently, may not be tolerated because it upsets the manager's unbending need for continuity.

Closure.   Closure is the tendency to complete an object so that it is perceived as a constant overall form. It is the ability to perceive a whole object even though only part of the object is evident. In Figure 5–7 (b) the twenty odd-shaped inkblots are somehow perceived as a dog. Obviously, someone who had never seen a dog would not be able to complete these closures.

Proximity.   The principle of proximity states that a group of objects may be perceived as related because of their nearness to each other. Figure 5–7 (c) illustrates this principle. All four boxes contain pears, but the first

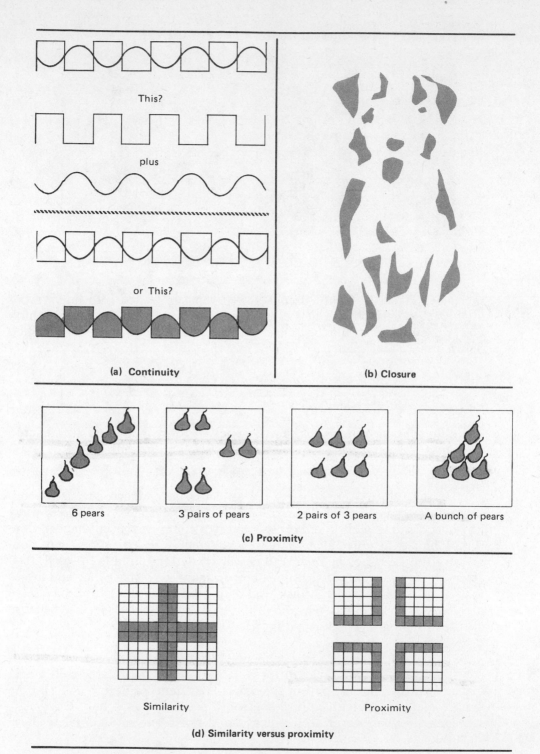

(a) Continuity

This?

plus

or This?

(b) Closure

6 pears   3 pairs of pears   2 pairs of 3 pears   A bunch of pears

(c) Proximity

Similarity   Proximity

(d) Similarity versus proximity

FIGURE 5–7. Perceptual Grouping

has six separate pears; the second has three pairs of pears; the third, two groups of three pears; and the last box, a bunch of (six) pears.

Often people working together in a department are perceived as a unit because of their physical proximity to each other. If four people on the third floor of a large office building quit their jobs for four unrelated reasons, it will still be perceived as a problem on the third floor. Personnel will attempt to determine what is wrong—morale? pay? working conditions?

Similarity. The principle of similarity states that the more alike objects are, the greater is the tendency to perceive them as a common group. In the first part of Figure 5–7 (d), the dark boxes group together as do the light boxes. So in the large square we see a dark cross framed by four light boxes. But move the boxes apart, and proximity takes over. The boxes group by proximity, not by similarity.

Similarity is very important in most team sports. In football, the quarterback must be able to spot teammates without a second's hesitation. The colors of both Penn State and the University of Kentucky are blue and white. When Penn State played Kentucky at home, Penn State players wore white shirts and blue pants; Kentucky, blue shirts and white pants. Otherwise, the uniforms of the two teams would have been too similar. Why is volleyball one team sport in which similarity is not crucial?

Many companies, especially those in buildings with open floor plans, color code the partitions and other accessories of the various departments so that separate functions and responsibilities are visually defined. In another example, a company might require visitors to the plant to wear yellow hard-hats rather than the white hard-hats of the floor supervisors. The workers then recognize that people unfamiliar with everyday precautions and routines are in the work area.

Perceptual Defense

In discussing perceptual selection, it was observed that people perceive things that satisfy their needs and that they tend to ignore disturbing things. Avoiding unpleasant stimuli is more than escapist. Often it is a sensible defensive device. We become psychologically deaf or blind to disturbing parts of our environment. People who live near the railroad tracks don't hear the trains. We don't love someone less because they are physically aging.

Perceptual defense is the tendency to protect oneself against objects or situations that are perceptually threatening. The major categories of perceptual defense that are important for managers to understand are stereotyping, halo effect, projection, and attribution.

Stereotyping. Stereotyping is the tendency to assign attributes to someone solely on the basis of a category to which that person belongs. "Doctor," "president," "minister"—these are categories that usually carry prestige with them. We expect someone so identified to have certain positive attributes, although some doctors, presidents, and ministers have not lived up to these expectations. "Dropout," "ex-con," "alcoholic" are categories that immediately put someone so labeled into a negative perspective. "Black," "elderly," "female" are categories so broad that they should not bring to mind any attributes beyond the obvious physical characteristics. Identifying people by a broad group they belong to can lead to misperceptions. By dwelling on certain expected characteristics, the perceiver may fail to recognize those characteristics that distinguish the person as an individual.

Stereotyping is disturbingly commonplace. In one study of stereotyping in business, a person in a photograph was labeled as either a member of management or as a labor leader. Impressions of the person differed according to how he was labeled and according to who was viewing the photograph. Management and labor formed different impressions, each perceiving the person as less dependable when he was identified as a member of the other group. Managers also felt that other managers were better able to appreciate labor's point of view, while unionists felt that other unionists were better able to appreciate management's point of view.[12]

Halo Effect.   The halo effect is the process in which an impression, either favorable or unfavorable, is used to evaluate a person on other dimensions. The evaluation of one trait, or characteristic, influences the evaluation of all others. The "halo" blinds the perceiver to other attributes that should be evaluated in attaining a complete, accurate impression. The halo effect often plays a major role in the rating of employee performance. A manager may single out one trait and use it as the basis for judgment of all other performance measures. For example, an excellent attendance record may produce judgments of high productivity, quality work, and industriousness.

There is also a tendency to link together certain traits. For example, it may be assumed aggressive people will also have high energy, dominance, and achievement, or that friendly people will also be warm and generous and have a good sense of humor. While the conclusions reached may be correct, how they were reached are examples of the halo effect.

The halo effect can also play a role in forming a general impression of a whole company. In one study, knowledge that the company was in receivership caused employees to devalue the higher pay and otherwise superior working conditions of their company compared with those of financially secure firms.

Projection   Projection is the tendency to see in other persons traits that you yourself possess. That is, you project your own feelings, tendencies, or motives into your judgment of others. This may be especially true for undesirable traits that perceivers possess but fail to recognize in themselves. For example, a manager frightened by rumors of impending organizational changes may not only judge others to be more frightened than they are but may also assess various policy decisions as more frightening than they are. People high in personality traits such as stinginess, obstinacy, and disorderliness tend to rate others higher on these traits than would those who are low in these personality traits.

Attribution. Attribution is the tendency to judge from a person's current behavior whether or not that behavior reflects the "true" person, or what the person is "really like," or what the person "really feels." According to this theory, behavior which is truly reflective of your motives or feelings depends on three things.[13] First, the behavior must be a matter of *free choice.* That is, you must perform the behavior for internal reasons, such as an enjoyment or interest, rather than for external reasons, such as money or social pressure. Second, the *consequences* of that behavior must be important to you. For example, if a stranger tells you that he doesn't like your tie, that behavior might have little consequence to you. However, if your boss tells you that you are a sloppy dresser, you will probably evaluate the consequences of that remark more negatively. Finally, acts of strong *personalism* are more likely to be utilized as bases for inference. Personalism refers to acts which are intentionally directed to you.

Attribution theory suggests, therefore, that when we have confidence that a person's actions are based on free choice, are consequential, and are intentionally directed toward us, we have more confidence in making an attribution or judgment, either negatively or positively, about the person.

The discussion of perceptual organization was concerned with those factors that affect the perceptual process once the information from the situation is perceived and selected by the individual. As indicated in Figure 5-1, it is necessary for the information to be selected by the individual before it can be organized into a meaningful whole. We identified three major factors that can affect the way perceptions are organized: figure-ground, perceptual grouping, and perceptual defense. The figure-ground principle simply means that perceived objects stand out as separable from their general background. The grouping principle states that there is a tendency to group several stimuli together into a recognizable pattern by means of continuity, closure, proximity, or similarity. Perceptual defense occurs because people build up a block against certain objects or situations that they perceive as personally threatening. Stereotyping, halo effect, projection, and attribution were discussed as ways that can prevent people from perceiving threatening information.

MANAGERIAL ASSUMPTIONS ABOUT PEOPLE

Because the people managers interact with during the course of the day are so important to them in determining the effectiveness of the organization, the organization's effectiveness is largely determined by how managers perceive their employees. The kinds of assumptions a manager makes about the nature of people will determine the manager's behavior.[14] If employees are perceived to be indifferent, hostile, motivated only by economic incentives, and hate to work, the managerial strategies used to deal with them are very likely to train them to behave in precisely this manner. In the perceptual process—in the ways we use for organizing perceived information into unique pictures of the world and in the various methods we employ for ruling out much of the data constantly coming in from our environment—lies the origin of our ideas about people.

Our perceptions of others are based on our basic nature and motivations. Douglas McGregor identified two major perceptual sets employed by managers, which he labeled Theory X and Theory Y. The manager who perceives people according to either set will behave in predictable patterns because of personal assumptions, beliefs, and attitudes.

Theory X

The assumptions of Theory X are:

1. People are inherently lazy and must therefore be motivated by outside incentives.
2. People's natural goals run counter to those of the organization; hence, individuals must be controlled by external forces to ensure their working toward organizational goals.
3. Because of irrational feelings, people are basically incapable of self-discipline and self-control.
4. The average person prefers to be directed, wishes to avoid responsibility, and wants security above all.[15]

The manager who accepts Theory X as a good way to manage subordinates will develop perceptual selection and organization techniques that are consistent with these beliefs. The following example of a marketing manager of a large industrial warehouse clearly pinpoints these managerial practices and behaviors:

> We have established sales quotas for each of you this year. For each of you who reaches your quota, the company will pay for a five-day trip for you and your family. This will be in addition to your normal vacation. If you meet your sales quotas for five consecutive years, you are almost guaranteed a permanent position with our firm. Salespersons who are unable to meet their quotas, don't hand in sales reports on time, and who violate company rules, regulations, and channels of command, will probably not be invited to stay on with the company. I will evaluate your work on a regular basis to make sure that it is up to par.[16]

What kind of a picture does this marketing manager create in your mind? Do you see a detailed list of job instructions that each salesperson is to follow: extensive paperwork to check on workers and their performance; close supervision, with the marketing manager hanging over sales personnel and watching for "gold-brickers"; and jobs that discourage creative thinking?

Theory Y

The other perceptual set identified by McGregor is completely different in its assumptions. It stresses:

1. The average human does not inherently dislike work. Depending upon controllable conditions, work may be a source of satisfaction.
2. External control and the threat of punishment are not the only means for bringing forth organizational objectives. Managers will exercise self-direction and control in the service of objectives to which they are committed.
3. The average person learns, under proper conditions, not only to accept but to seek responsibility.
4. The capacity to exercise a relatively high degree of imagination, ingenuity, and creativity in the solution to organizational problems is widely, not narrowly, distributed in the population.[17]

Here again, we can infer how such assumptions can influence perceptions. If you perceive of a person as a responsible individual, you would probably have no second thoughts about giving that person tasks that require trust and commitment. A marketing manager who believed in Theory Y might lead employees in the following manner:

> *You get together on establishing sales quotas for each year. If you achieve your goals, you will receive extra rewards (money, promotion, vacation time, challenging assignments, etc.). High performance as a salesperson is one important factor in being considered for a managerial position. Another important factor besides selling is to keep our product-planning group informed about changes in customers' demand. Many of our new products in the past have stemmed directly from suggestions of salespersons.*

Under which type of manager would you want to work—one motivated by Theory X or by Theory Y?

When Frank Borman, the former astronaut, became Chief Executive Officer and President of Eastern Airlines, he applied Theory Y techniques that he had learned in the space program to turning the company around.[18] In 1973, the year Borman took over, Eastern suffered a loss of $51 million. Its operating costs were 32 percent above the industry average. Yield per passenger mile was a low $0.067; the break-even load factor (59 percent) was one of the worst in the industry. There were 69 vice-presidents distributed between two corporate headquarters (Miami and New York).

Borman introduced a company-wide profit-sharing plan and urged all the employees to become involved in improving the company's performance. Relationships throughout Eastern are now based on mutual trust and confidence. Borman finds out firsthand where there are bottlenecks and seeks out his employees' advice on improving the situation. He has appeared on loading ramps on busy Friday afternoons to assist in passenger loading. And he went directly to the service workers to find out how many planes could be washed each shift. He asked the service workers to set up an evaluation procedure to monitor this task.

In consultation with his top management team, Borman trimmed the number of vice-presidents back to 51. Corporate headquarters were consolidated in New York. Corporate limousines and private jets were done away with. Eastern executives now fly scheduled flights along with their customers. Departments were reorganized not only to cut costs but also to achieve better coordination. Even with increased productivity, the total number of employees was cut back from 34,800 to 33,200.

Has this strategy been successful? Here are some of the results:

1. The loss of $51 million in 1973 was turned around to a profit of $46 million in 1976, despite the fact that 1976 was a poor year for airlines in general.
2. The low yield of $0.067 per passenger mile in 1973 rose to $0.084 in 1977.
3. The break-even load dropped from a high of 59 percent to 53 percent.
4. Customer complaints to the Civil Aeronautics Board dropped by 60 percent and lost bags have dropped by 50 percent.

The key to understanding Borman's managerial actions is to understand his philosophy. His philosophy of what an effective manager should do, learned from previous experience, was then generalized to the situation at Eastern. They became assumptions that provided the framework on how he should manage. These assumptions were then applied to specific actions at Eastern.

SUMMARY

Perception is one of the major psychological processes. Through the perceptual process, we select and organize environmental information into our concept of reality. Selectivity is affected by both external and internal factors. Perceptions may be completely unrealistic, but they constitute our concept of reality; what we see is real for us. External selection is affected by size, intensity, contrast, motion, repetition, novelty and familiarity. Internally, it is influenced by the individual's motivation, learning, and personality.

After the factors in the environment are selected, perceptions are then organized into a meaningful whole for the individual. Figure-ground is the most basic form of organization. Perceptual grouping is the arrangement of selected facts based on continuity, closure, proximity, and similarity. Perceptual defenses are used by individuals to protect themselves from threatening facts. Common factors that increase the tendency for perceptual distortion include stereotyping, halo effect, projection, and attribution.

Managerial practices reflect our perceptions. Theory X assumes that people are inherently lazy, must be forced to work, and are motivated solely by money; this translates into managerial practices such as close supervision, reliance on economic incentives, and use of rules and regulations to control employee behavior. Theory Y assumptions, including that people are not inherently lazy and that they seek challenges in their jobs, lead to a different set of managerial practices. Both sets of assumptions incorporate many aspects of the perceptual process discussed in this chapter.

DISCUSSION QUESTIONS

1. What are the basic elements in the perceptual process?

2. Give examples of how different people might interpret the same incident differently.

3. What are some ways that differences between perceptions might be overcome?

4. How does perception influence an individual's behavior?

5. Why do individuals use perceptual defenses? What kind of defenses are commonly used?

6. Are there any benefits in using stereotypes? What are the dangers?

7. Theories X and Y incorporate many factors of perception as they influence the manager's behavior. Trace through the influences that perceptions have on managerial practices based on Theories X and Y.

8. What perceptual tendencies might create special problems in evaluating the performance of managers?

9. What relevance has perception to an understanding of organizational behavior?

MANAGERIAL PROBLEMS

WHO DID WHAT?

The following is a true account, but it has been altered somewhat for educational purposes.

I was in a supermarket when suddenly a girl, about eight years old, came running around a corner. She looked back and screamed, "Stop! Stop! You're killing him! You're killing my father!" I dropped my things and hurried in the direction from which the girl had come. As I turned the corner I was greeted by a grisly scene. There was a man stretched out on the floor with another on top of him. The guy on top was huge. He must have been 6 feet 6 inches tall and have weighed 300 pounds. He looked only half human. He had his victim by the throat and was beating his head against the floor. There was blood everywhere. I ran for the store manager.

By the time the manager and I returned to the "scene of the crime," the police were just arriving. It took quite a while to straighten things out, but here are the facts that emerged. The man on the floor was a diabetic who had suffered an insulin reaction. As a result, he passed out and hit his head as he went down. This caused the cut (actually quite minor) that accounted for the "blood everywhere." The "guy on top" had seen the first man fall and was trying to prevent him from injuring himself further while unconscious. He was also loosening the man's collar.

If I had never returned, I would have sworn in court that I had seen a murder. This perhaps is understandable. But what I will never quite recover from is the shock I felt when I met the "murderer." This is the man, you will recall, that I had seen a few moments before, in broad daylight, as a huge, vicious, horrible-looking creature. The man was not a stranger. He was a neighbor of mine. I had seen him dozens of times before. I know him by name. He is a rather small man.

QUESTIONS

1. What perceptual factors were involved in the first version of the "murder"?
2. How did the girl affect what was seen?
3. How dependable do you think eyewitness testimony is in a courtroom?
4. Do you think your perceptions of an argument with a friend, parent, or spouse are accurate? What factors might affect your viewpoint?
5. Have you ever had an experience similar to the one described?

SPACE ALLOCATION

Robert Schultz, assistant dean for planning in the College of Business Administration, was chairman of the ad hoc committee for space utilization. The college was soon to move into a new building. Schultz's job was to see that space in the new building was optimally utilized. Before assigning space in the new building, he wanted to be sure that currently available space in the old building was being properly used. Space allocations in the new building were to be based on existing use of space.

Schultz opened his first committee meeting by asking representatives of each department how they saw their space needs. The first to speak was the head of the Accounting Department, who stated:

My department is using every inch of space available to us. We have faculty members sharing offices and graduate assistants without cubicles.

The head of the Management Department was eager to add his input:

We don't have enough space in my department. My secretary doesn't have any room in the office for storing examinations and other supplies. I have repeatedly told the dean that we need more space. After all, our department teaches more students than any other in the college.

Before other department heads could volunteer their versions of space needs, Dean Schultz wisely called the meeting to a close:

Obviously, we have different interpretations of space utilization around here. Before we have any further discussion, I'll call the people in plant and maintenance and ask them to provide us with some objective facts about the space that has been allocated to each department. I'll also check with the director of the undergraduate program to provide us with student trends before our next meeting. Today's meeting is adjourned.

QUESTIONS

1. Why did the different department heads have different interpretations of space utilization?
2. What perceptual principles are evident in this case?
3. What concept was brought out in the management head's comments?
4. Do you think that Schultz's "objective" facts will affect the perceptions of the department heads and faculty members?

KEY WORDS

Perceptual process
Perceptual selection
External factors
Size
Intensity
Contrast
Motion
Repetition
Novelty and familiarity
Internal factors
Perceptual set
Personality
Perceptual organization

Figure-ground
Perceptual grouping
Continuity
Closure
Proximity
Similarity
Perceptual defense
Stereotype
Halo effect
Projection
Attribution
Theory X
Theory Y

REFERENCES

1. Heider, F., On perception, event structure, and psychological environment, *Psychological Issues*, 1959, 1, no. 3.

2. Adapted from Murray, J., and T. Von der Emlose, *Organizational Behavior: Critical Incidents and Analysis* (Columbus, Ohio: Charles E. Merrill, 1973), p. 14.

3. Asch, S., Forming impressions of persons, *Journal of Abnormal and Social Psychology*, 1946, 40, pp. 258–290.

4. Powell, R., *Race, Religion, and the Promotion of the American Executive* (Columbus, Ohio: Faculty of Administrative Studies, 1969), no. AA-3.

5. Anderson, C., and F. Paine, Managerial perceptions and strategic behavior, *Academy of Management Journal*, 1975, 18, pp. 811–823.

6. Coon, D., *Introduction to Psychology: Exploration and Application* (St. Paul, Minn.: West Publishing, 1977), pp. 104–127; Krech, D., R. Crutchfield, and E. Ballachey, *Individual and Society* (New York: McGraw-Hill, 1962), pp. 20–34.

7. Dearborn, D., and H. Simon, Selective perception: A note on the departmental identifications of executives, *Sociometry*, 1958, 21, pp. 140–144.

8. Zaleznik, A., Power and politics in organizational life, *Harvard Business Review*, 1970, 48, no. 3, pp. 47–60.

9. Adapted from Packard, V., *The Pyramid Climbers* (New York: McGraw-Hill, 1962).

10. McClelland, D., J. Atkinson, R. Clark, and E. Lowell, *The Achievement Motive* (New York: Appleton-Century-Crofts, 1953).

11. Gibson, E., *Principles of Perceptual Learning and Development* (New York: Appleton-Century-Crofts, 1969).

12. Haire, M., Perceptions in labor-management relations: An experimental approach, *Industrial and Labor Relations Review*, 1958, 8, pp. 204–216.

13. Staw, B., Attribution of the 'causes' of performance: A general interpretation of cross-sectional research on organizations, *Organizational Behavior and Human Performance*, 1975, 13, pp. 414–432; Kelley, H., *Attribution in Social Interaction* (Morristown, N.J.: General Learning Press, 1971).

14. Child, J., Organization structure, environment, and performance: The role of strategic choice, *Sociology*, 1972, 6, pp. 1–22.

15. McGregor, D., *The Human Side of the Enterprise* (New York: McGraw-Hill, 1960), pp. 33–34.

16. This example and the next was modified from Herbert, T., *Dimensions of Organizational Behavior* (New York: Macmillan Publishing Company, Inc., 1976).

17. Ibid., pp. 47–48.

18. Milks, D., A case study of Eastern Airlines, unpublished paper, Graduate School of Business, Pennsylvania State University, 1977.

Managing Behavior Through Learning and Reinforcement

This Chapter Contributed by

HENRY P. SIMS, JR.

The Pennsylvania State University

6

LEARNING OBJECTIVES

When you have finished reading and studying this chapter, you should be able to:

▲ Describe the unique aspects of the behavioral management approach.

▲ Describe the different types of learning: classical conditioning, operant conditioning, and vicarious learning.

▲ Describe a contingency of reinforcement.

▲ Discuss the positive management of employee behavior.

▲ Discuss the aversive management of employee behavior.

▲ Describe different schedules of reinforcement.

▲ Explain the step-by-step procedures in managing employee behavior.

THOUGHT STARTERS

▲ How would you define learning?

▲ How do employees learn at work?

▲ How does a manager use positive management techniques to improve performance?

▲ How does a manager use aversive management techniques to improve performance?

▲ How does a manager measure employee behavior?

OUTLINE

TYPES OF LEARNING
  Classical Conditioning
  Operant Conditioning
  Vicarious Learning
CONTINGENCIES OF
REINFORCEMENT
  Positive Management of Employee
    Behavior
  Laws of Positive Reinforcement
  Organizational Rewards
  Shaping
  Extinction of Employee Behavior
  Aversive Management of Employee
    Behavior—Punishment
  Aversive Management of Employee
    Behavior—Negative Reinforcement
  Potential Side Effects of Punishment
  The Effective Use of Aversive Management
SCHEDULES OF
REINFORCEMENT
  Fixed Interval
  Variable Interval
  Fixed Ratio
  Variable Ratio
  Stretching the Ratio
PROCEDURES IN MANAGING
EMPLOYEE BEHAVIOR
  Pinpointing Target Behaviors
  Charting Target Behaviors
  Choosing an Intervention Strategy
  First Attempt Doesn't Work?
SELF-CONTROL OF BEHAVIOR
ETHICAL CONSIDERATIONS
SUMMARY
DISCUSSION QUESTIONS
MANAGERIAL PROBLEMS
  Larry Weinstein
  An Exercise in Measuring Managerial Reinforcing Behavior
KEY WORDS
REFERENCES

The management of employee behavior is based on specific principles that have their foundation in an area of psychology called reinforcement theory. Related concepts include operant theory, operant conditioning, and behavior modification. Before discussing these terms, it is useful to consider some of the unique assumptions and features that are part of the behavioral management approach.[1]

First, many of the unique aspects of the management of employee behavior are methodological in nature. For example, the approach stresses the assessment of behavior in objective, measurable (countable) terms. Second, the evaluation of treatments or interventions to change employee behavior is stressed. Third, the focus is on overt or publicly observable employee behavior; unobservable inner cognitive states are deemphasized.

The behavioral management approach is most concerned with the development, maintenance, and change of employee work behaviors. From a managerial viewpoint, the focus is on desirable work behaviors that lead toward organizational goals, or, conversely, on undesirable work behaviors that detract from organizational goals. It is important to recognize, however, that defining behavior as "desirable" or "undesirable" is an entirely subjective decision that depends on the value system of the person making the assessment. For example, an assembly-line worker who returns late from a rest break is exhibiting undesirable behavior from the supervisor's viewpoint, desirable behavior from the viewpoint of friends with whom he chats during the break, undesirable behavior from the viewpoint of his work station replacement, and desirable behavior from his own viewpoint because of his relief from physical fatigue.

Behavior that is viewed as undesirable by management, such as returning late from a break, becomes a potential target for management action (intervention) to bring about change. The emphasis in terms of an intervention is on the control of environmental events, that is, changing something in the environment that will have the effect of changing the frequency of the undesirable behavior. Behavior is not regarded as desirable or undesirable in terms of how it is developed or maintained but in terms of whether the managerial objective is to increase or decrease the frequency of the behavior.

The social environment is important in determining if a behavior is desirable or undesirable. The more a behavior deviates from organizational social norms, the more it might be regarded as undesirable. But norms may be quite different from one organization to another. Behaviors regarded as unacceptable in one organization may be entirely appropriate in another organization. For example, in a research and development laboratory, a scientist may be encouraged to question directives from top management because professional judgment is a critical input to the organization's final output. In a military organization, such questioning might be considered as insubordination and be subject to severe sanctions. Again, labeling a work behavior as "desirable" versus "undesirable" is a subjective process.

The behavioral management approach considers the majority of employee work behaviors to be learned or changed through the processes outlined in this chapter. The focus is directly on the work behaviors that are to be altered. Changing underlying employee personalities or changing fundamental employee inner beliefs are not stressed in this chapter. The manager who uses the behavioral management approach is concerned with the identification of observable employee behaviors and with identifying and managing the environmental conditions that surround the employee's behavior. Environmental conditions include both antecedent events and consequences. The manager looks to the potential of altering these environmental events as a means of managing employee behavior. The manager thus emphasizes external events that can be used to manage employee behavior. This is not to say that events within the individual employee do not influence behavior or are not of interest to the manager. Indeed, although the point remains controversial, many contemporary operant theorists recognize the existence of internal private events and covert behaviors, such as thoughts, feelings, and perceptions, and their influence on overt work behavior. From a behavioral management viewpoint, however, the focus is on external conditions and associated measurable work behaviors.

TYPES OF LEARNING

In behavioral management, *learning is a relatively permanent change in the frequency of the occurrence of a specific employee work behavior.*[2] In organizations, therefore, managers want productive work behaviors to be learned by employees. One of the assumptions of the behavioral management approach is that, to a great extent, learning new work behaviors depends on environmental factors. That is, the degree or intensity of learning is dependent on the way the environment reacts to the performance of a particular behavior. From a managerial viewpoint, the goal of a behavioral management program is to provide learning experiences that promote employee behaviors that are desired by the organization. Generally, learning is considered to take place through one of three procedures or types: classical conditioning; operant conditioning; and vicarious, or observational, learning.[3]

Classical Conditioning

The name most frequently associated with classical conditioning is Ivan Pavlov, the Russian scientist whose experiments with dogs led to the early formulations of classical conditioning. Classical conditioning is concerned with reflexive responses or behaviors. A *reflex* is an involuntary or automatic response that is not under the conscious control of the individual. Examples of reflexive behavior include pupil constriction in response to light, muscle flexes in response to pain, and a startle reaction in response to a loud noise. In classical conditioning, an unconditioned stimulus (environmental event) is said to elicit a reflexive response. Sometimes, a neutral environmental event, called a conditioned stimulus, can be paired with the unconditioned stimulus that elicits the reflex. Eventually the conditioned stimulus alone has the property of eliciting the reflexive behavior. In classical conditioning, environmental events that precede the behavior control a reflexive response. In Pavlov's famous experiment, a bell (the conditioned stimulus) was paired with food (the unconditioned stimulus) so that the experimental dog eventually exhibited a salivation response (the reflex response) to the bell.

Recently, the distinction between reflex and nonreflex behavior has become somewhat blurred. Behaviors that were formerly thought to be exclusively reflex responses have, in some cases, been shown to be under the control of the individual. For example, biofeedback techniques have recently been shown to be effective in changing heart rates, blood pressure, muscle tension, and galvanic skin response. These responses had previously been considered to be exclusively reflexive responses. Biofeedback instruments have permitted individuals to get in touch with very subtle behaviors. Exciting breakthroughs are anticipated in this area of learning.

From a managerial viewpoint, classical conditioning is usually not considered to be of great interest. When managers consider the behavior of employees, they are typically not dealing with reflexive responses that are amenable to change through classical conditioning techniques. Instead, managers are interested in the voluntary behavior of employees. Such voluntary behavior is called *operant behavior*, and the technical term that refers to the management of voluntary behaviors is called *operant conditioning*.

Operant Conditioning

From a behavioral management viewpoint, the objective of operant conditioning is to provoke a change in the voluntary, or operant, work behavior of an employee. Voluntary behaviors are called operants because they operate on, or have some influence on, the environment; they generate some consequence in that environment. Operant behaviors are said to be emitted by the employee. They are controlled, in part, by the consequences that follow the behavior. Virtually all employee work behaviors in an organizational environment are operant behaviors. In fact, most behaviors performed in everyday life are operant behaviors. Operant behaviors include talking, walking, reading, frowning, working, or any behavior that is freely (voluntarily) emitted.[4]

In general, academic treatments of operant behavior in work organizations tend to oversimplify the concept for explanation. In reality, most work behaviors are highly complex combinations of simple operant behaviors. A manager wishing to manage the behavior of an employee frequently will concentrate on a complex combination of behaviors that he might conceptually simplify to one single "target behavior" in order to generate an effective change. The concept of *chaining*, the linking together of simple behaviors into complex sequential combinations, is frequently a useful perspective. For example, the task of typing a letter is actually a chain of many simple operant behaviors.

From the managerial viewpoint, the main point about operant work behaviors is that they are controlled, or managed, by the environmental consequences that are contingent on employee behavior. The frequency of occurrence of an employee behavior can be increased or decreased depending on the consequences that follow the behavior. This is a matter of vital importance to managers, because one of the most important ways managers influence employee behavior is through a change in the environmental circumstances that follow the employee behavior. Therefore, it is critical that managers understand the effects of different kinds of environmental circumstances on the work behaviors of employees. The concept of the contingency of reinforcement is important in this regard and will be covered in some detail in this chapter.

Vicarious Learning

Observational learning, modeling, and imitation are different terms used to indicate vicarious learning. In this type of learning, the employee learns not through direct experience, that is, engaging in the behavior and experiencing the consequence, but through the observation of others performing the behavior and/or experiencing the consequences of the behavior. By observing either live or symbolic models, the observer learns a work behavior without actually having performed the behavior, as the following example illustrates:

When Jim first came to work for the company, he had never actually seen a real computer. He was somewhat frightened when Joe, his supervisor, took him into the computer room with all the complex consoles and machines. Jim had been fairly confident when he applied for the computer operator job, but the first day he doubted that he would be able to learn to operate all that complicated equipment. Joe did two things to help Jim get started. First, he assigned Jim to work with Karen, who had been operating the equipment for over three years. (She would be an excellent live model.) Second, he took Jim down to the personnel training cubicle and showed him how to check out and operate the slide-tape equipment that provided instructions on how to operate the computer. (It would serve as a convenient symbolic model.) The first few days, Jim didn't operate the computer at all, but he observed Karen very closely, and he noted that Karen had certain ways of going about the assignments that were fairly well patterned. In addition, the slide-tape modules presented an opportunity to observe most of the operating tasks in action. As Jim came in for his fifth day of work, he looked forward to actually operating the console, as Karen had promised. Although he had not yet actually performed the task, Jim felt he had learned a lot from observing Karen and the slide-tapes, and he felt confident of being able to undertake most of the operating tasks.

While vicarious learning can be helpful in the development of a new behavior, it does not in itself result in performance, which is the actual accomplishment of the behavior. For sustained maintenance of learned behaviors, performance is a necessary factor. The environmental consequences that follow the performance of a behavior are important in maintaining the frequency of a newly learned task. That is, operant conditioning is important to the subsequent support of vicarious learning.

The effect of vicarious learning on subsequent performance also depends on other factors. Greater imitation usually results when the model is high in prestige, status, or expertise. Note the following example:

For three years, Amy worked for Bob, her supervisor, on the assembly line. Amy knew that Bob was respected by the plant manager because he was demanding of his workers in terms of getting the work out, both in terms of quantity and quality. But Bob was also respected by the workers even though he was demanding; he never failed to recognize a special effort by one of the workers. Bob didn't play favorites. If the worker performed on the job, Bob would provide the recognition that the performance deserved.

When Bob was promoted to general foreman, he recommended that Amy be promoted to line supervisor in his place. Sam Warhourse, the superintendent, agreed. As Amy came into the plant for her first day as line supervisor, she resolved to act toward the workers just as Bob had acted toward her.

Imitation tends to be greater when several models rather than just one are observed. Also, observers tend to imitate models that are similar to them as opposed to models that are different from them.

CONTINGENCIES OF REINFORCEMENT

The concept of contingency of reinforcement is critical to an understanding of operant conditioning. A *contingency of reinforcement* is the relationship between a behavior and the environmental events (both preceding and following) that influence that behavior. A contingency of reinforcement consists of an antecedent, a behavior, and a consequence.[5] Figure 6–1 is a model of a contingency of reinforcement.

An *antecedent* is an environmental stimuli that precedes a behavior and establishes the occasion for the behavior. Antecedents are also called *discriminative stimuli*. They provide the environmental cues that inform individuals about which or what kind of behavior will be reinforced. Behaviors that are influenced by antecedents are said to be under *stimulus control*. The probability of the occurrence of a particular behavior can be increased by presenting or removing a particular antecedent. Goal setting is but one example of the use of stimulus control in organizations. Goal setting can be long term, as in management by objectives, or it can merely be a simple "to do" checklist that a manager uses to organize his everyday work. Instructions on how to carry out a task are another type of stimulus control.

A *consequence* is what results from a behavior. It is contingent upon the behavior. The phrase "contingent upon the behavior" deserves some further explanation. By *contingent*, we mean that a consequence is administered *only* if the employee behavior occurs. That is, the occurrence of the environmental consequence is dependent upon the successful performance of the employee behavior. Figure 6–2 shows a representation of a logic diagram that represents the concept of a contingent consequence in an organizational setting. First, the employee sets a goal that is approved by the supervisor. Next, the employee undertakes the activities to achieve that goal. If the goal is accomplished (i.e., if the behavior occurs), then the employee is provided with a positive consequence (in this case, a verbal compliment) that is contingent upon that accomplishment. If the goal is *not* accomplished, then the positive consequence is *not* provided. This contingency is an example of positive reinforcement where the reinforcer is a verbal compliment from the supervisor. Consider the case of Laura:

Laura approached Harry, her manager, about the possibility of going to Houston in the spring for the annual convention. "I'm very concerned about achieving our fourth quarter quota in your

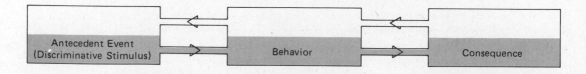

Antecedent event...........what comes before the behavior.

Consequence event.........what comes after the behavior.

FIGURE 6–1.   A Contingency of Reinforcement

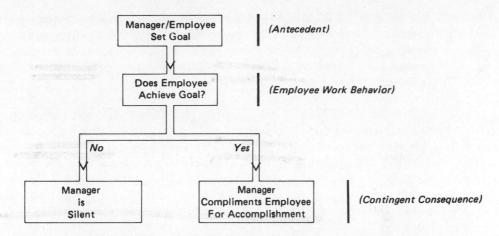

FIGURE 6–2.   The Logic of a "Contingent" Consequence

territory," replied Harry. "I'll tell you what. . . . If you achieve the quota, I'll find the funds somewhere and make sure you get the time to go to Houston."

For Laura, there are at least two possible consequences of her behavior.

> By January 15, Laura knew that the final figures for her territory were at 105 percent of quota. It was now time to bring up the subject of the Houston trip to Harry again.
>
> or
>
> By January 15, Laura knew that the final figures for her territory were at 96 percent of quota. She knew better than to bring up the subject of the Houston trip to Harry again.

To further understand the concept of contingency of reinforcement, it is necessary to identify the type of contingency.[6] First, a contingency can be identified as to whether the environmental event is *presented* (applied) or *withdrawn* (removed). That is, it is possible to present an environmental event contingent upon an employee behavior or it is possible to remove an environmental event contingent upon an employee behavior. It is important to remember that the consequence is presented or removed contingent upon the occurrence of the employee behavior.

Also, it is useful to classify the environmental event as *positive* or *aversive*. Positive events are desired, or pleasing, to the employee, while aversive events are undesired, or displeasing. Naturally, the effect of the contingency on the future behavior of the employee will depend on these factors. The particular combination of whether a positive event is presented or removed, or whether an aversive event is presented or removed, will have

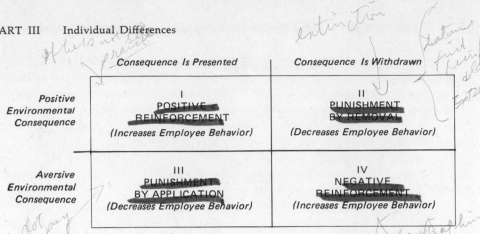

FIGURE 6-3.   Classification of Various Contingencies of Reinforcement

different results in terms of increasing or decreasing the future frequency of the occurrence of the employee behavior. Figure 6-3 shows how these factors can be combined to produce various types of contingencies of reinforcement. In addition, it indicates the effect of the particular type of contingency in terms of whether it increases or decreases the future frequency of the employee behavior. Figure 6-3 is also important because it forms the basis for the following discussion of the various types of contingencies of reinforcement. An important point to note is that reinforcement, whether positive or negative, always has the effect of *increasing* the frequency of the employee behavior, while punishment always has the effect of *decreasing* the employee behavior.

Positive Management of Employee Behavior

Reinforcement refers to a behavioral contingency that has the effect of increasing the frequency of a particular behavior that it follows. *Positive reinforcement* (cell I of Figure 6-3) involves the presentation of a positive environmental consequence contingent upon the occurrence of behavior. In the positive management of employee behavior, the manager uses positive reinforcement behavioral contingencies to increase or maintain the frequency of desired employee behavior. That is, a manager provides some positive reward contingent upon the occurrence of an employee's behavior that the manager views as desired or leading toward the organization's goals.

Reinforcement versus Reward.   The terms *reinforcement* and *reward* are frequently confused in everyday usage.[7] A reward is an environmental event (consequence) that at least one individual would define as desirable or pleasing. What is defined as a reward is thus a subjective choice. A reward is not necessarily a reinforcer. In order to qualify as a reinforcer, a reward must influence the frequency of behavior. If a reward does not increase (or maintain) the frequency of the behavior that it follows, it is not a reinforcer. Note in the following example a reinforcer that is not a reward.

Joyce was concerned because her subordinate Mike frequently did not return from lunch on time. In her evening class, she discussed the problem with Professor Snow, who suggested that she try to reinforce Mike positively by giving him verbal approval when he did return on time. Joyce decided to give it a try.

By the end of the semester, Joyce came to see Professor Snow again. "I've tried what you suggested," said Joyce. "I've told him several times that I appreciate it when he gets back on time. It just hasn't had any effect. He's late just as often now as he was before. My verbal reinforcement hasn't worked."

"It's apparent," said Professor Snow, "that your verbal approval is really not a reinforcer. You and I might consider it to be a reward because we define it so, but is not really a reinforcer because it hasn't had any effect on Mike's behavior." Professor Snow and Joyce then explored some of the reasons why Joyce's approach had not worked and discussed several alternative management strategies.

Technically, a reinforcer might not even be a reward, although this situation is unusual. This might occur when a consequence which a supervisor assumes to be punishing has the unintended effect of *increasing* employee behavior. For example, a manager might think he is "bawling out" a subordinate, but the real effect might be reinforcing because the employee desires the personal attention that is part of the reprimand. This situation is most likely when an employee has been previously deprived of attention.

Jerry couldn't understand why every time he walked past Hank's work station the machine seemed to break down. The thing that was puzzling to Jerry was the fact that he made it a practice to "ream Hank out" every time a breakdown occurred. What Jerry didn't know was that Tom and Harv, who had the machine next to Hank, made a practice of smirking and laughing behind Jerry's back while he was reprimanding Hank. Hank, of course, could see Tom and Harv, and they laughed together when Jerry had gone. Jerry couldn't understand why his "punishment" of Hank seemed to make the problem more severe.

In this example, Jerry is not really "punishing" Hank because Hank's undesirable behavior has a tendency to increase as a result of Jerry's attention (and also as a result of Tom and Harv's reinforcing behavior). Jerry may be inadvertently reinforcing Hank's undesirable behavior. In this case, the reprimand is serving as a positive reinforcer, but most people would not refer to the reprimand as a reward. Once again, the term reward is not necessarily synonymous with reinforcer.

Whether a reward is a positive reinforcer or not is an empirical question. Only if the frequency of a desired behavior increases as a result of the contingent administration of the reward can the reward be said to be a reinforcer. Another way of viewing this phenomenon is to see a reinforcer as "functionally determined." That is, if any contingent environmental consequence has the effect of increasing the frequency of the target employee behavior, then that contingent environmental consequence is said to be a reinforcer.

Primary and Secondary Reinforcers.   A primary reinforcer is a consequence where the employee does not have to learn the reinforcing value. Food and drink are primary reinforcers for hungry and thirsty people. This is not to say that primary reinforcers are reinforcing all the time. If an individual is *satiated* with the consequence, then the consequence may not be reinforcing. For example, food may not be a reinforcer to someone who has just completed a twelve-course meal. The opposite of satiation is *deprivation.* An environmental event is more likely to be reinforcing if the individual is deprived of the event.

Most behavior in organizations is influenced not by primary reinforcers but by secondary reinforcers, which are events that once had neutral value but that have taken on some value (positive or negative) for the individual because of past experience. Money is the most evident example of a secondary reinforcer. It has no inherent value in itself, but assumes value to the individual employee.

The Premack Principle.   Managers in organizations frequently apply the Premack principle, even though they may be unaware of it. According to the Premack principle,[8] if two behaviors are paired together, the more probable behavior will tend to reinforce the less probable behavior. Often, a supervisor will assign an undesirable task to a subordinate and pair it with the assignment of a desirable task. The opportunity to undertake the desirable task is sometimes made contingent upon the accomplishment of the undesirable task, as in this example:

> *Mary Orcutt, a flight attendant for Overmountain Airlines, walked into the scheduling office to talk to Tricia Peterson, the scheduling supervisor. "Well," said Tricia, "here's your schedule for next month. The majority of your runs are to the coast. I'm sorry I had to schedule you on several short runs to Podunk, but, at the end of the month, I've scheduled you on the special charter to London, and you'll have a one-week layover there."*

Laws of Positive Reinforcement

Several factors have the potential of influencing the effectiveness of the intensity of a positive reinforcement contingency.[9] These factors can loosely be thought of as "laws," because they help to explain conditions of optimum reinforcement.

Law of Contingent Reinforcement. According to the law of contingent reinforcement, for a reinforcer to have maximum effectiveness, the reinforcer must be administered *only* if the desired target behavior is performed.[10] This is another way of stating that the reinforcer must be contingent upon the behavior of the employee. According to this law, therefore, a reinforcer loses effectiveness if it is administered when the desired behavior has *not* been performed. To determine if the law was followed, ask the question: Was the reinforcer given only when the target behavior occurred?

Law of Immediate Reinforcement. Next, the law of immediate reinforcement states that the more immediate the administration of a reinforcer after the target behavior has occurred, the more effect the reinforcer will have on the future occurrence of that behavior.[11] In general, delivery of the reinforcer should coincide as much as is practical with the completion of the target behavior. The following illustrates what can result if the law of immediate reinforcement is not applied:

> Chuck brought the "hot" report into Dan's office half a day early. Dan was distracted and merely said, "Leave it on the desk." A week later, Dan told Chuck that he appreciated receiving the report before the deadline. Chuck thought to himself "If it was so important, why didn't he say something when I delivered the report?"

Do you think that in the future Chuck will make a special effort to get his reports in before the deadline?

Law of Reinforcement Size. The amount or size of the reinforcer can also have an effect. The law of reinforcement size states that the larger the amount of reinforcer that is delivered after the occurrence of a target behavior, the more effect the reinforcer will have on the rate of the response.[12] The amount, or size, of a reinforcer is relative. It is important to determine if the amount of the reinforcement is *worthwhile*. What might be a large reinforcer to one person may be small to another person:

> In March, the president of the small company that Dave worked for gave the dock crew a bonus of $50 each because they had

done so well in shipping out the special order. Dave was pleased, and he intended to be able to provide the same kind of special service to future special orders.

The president also provided a bonus of $50 to Connie, his marketing vice-president, for meeting the March sales quota. In the privacy of her home, Connie remarked to her husband, "The president really is cheap. He only gave me 50 bucks for meeting that impossible March quota."

Law of Reinforcement Deprivation.   Last, the law of reinforcement deprivation states that the more deprived a person is of the reinforcer, the more effect it will have on the future occurrence of the target behavior.[13] But if, as in the following example, an employee has recently had his fill of a reinforcer, that is, if he is satiated, the reinforcer will have less effect:

When the staff psychologist implemented the lottery system to reinforce perfect attendance, Bob, the foreman, saw a substantial drop in the absenteeism rate of most of his staff. The way the lottery system worked, a color television was raffled off each month. An employee had to have a perfect attendance record to be eligible for the drawing.

Bob observed that Jim was an exception to the majority of his staff. Jim had been missing about two days a month before the lottery began, and he was still missing about two days a month. Bob knew that Jim had not been eligible to participate in any of the drawings to date. He asked Jim why he wasn't interested in the lottery. Jim replied, "My wife just won a new color TV in the church drawing four months ago. I really don't need another TV."

Organizational Rewards

What types of rewards are used in organization settings? The answer that comes to mind most immediately is material rewards—money, salary, fringe benefits, and so forth. However, organizations offer a wide range of rewards, many of which are not immediately apparent. Included among these other rewards are such things as verbal approval, assignment to desired tasks, improved working conditions, and extra time off. In addition, an important class of rewards—sometimes called covert, or private, events—are self-administered. Indeed, a reward such as self-congratulations for accomplishing a particularly difficult assignment can be a potent reinforcer. Table 6–1 gives an extensive list of organizational rewards.[14]

TABLE 6-1. Typical Rewards from Organizational Environments

Material	Fringe Benefits	Status Symbols	Social/Interpersonal	From the Task	Self-Administered
Pay	Medical plan	Corner office	Informal recognition	Sense of achievement	Self-recognition
Pay raise	Company automobile	Office with window	Praise	Job with more	Self-praise
Stock options	Insurance	Carpeting	Smile	responsibility	Self-congratulations
Profit sharing	Pension contributions	Drapes	Evaluative feedback	Job rotation	
Bonus plans	Product discount plans	Paintings	Compliments	Output feedback	
Incentive plans	Vacation trips	Watches	Nonverbal signals		
Christmas bonus	Recreation facilities	Rings	Pat on the back		
	Work breaks		Ask for suggestion		
	Club privileges		Invitations to coffee/		
	Expense account		lunch		
			Newspaper article		
			Formal awards/		
			recognition		
			Wall plaque		

Shaping

Sometimes it is impossible to reinforce a desired target behavior because the behavior may be so complex as to be beyond the present capability of the employee. In this case, the reinforcement of successive approximations of the final target behavior might be used. This procedure —the reinforcing of small steps or approximations toward a final target behavior rather than reinforcing the target behavior itself—is called *shaping.* By reinforcing successively closer and closer approximations of the final behavior, the desired final employee target behavior is gradually achieved.

Shaping requires the reinforcement of acts that resemble or approximate the final behavioral goal. As the initial act is performed more and more consistently, the reinforcement is altered slightly so as to reinforce elements that are closer to the final behavior. The earlier act that was first reinforced is no longer reinforced. This procedure of differential reinforcement of successive approximations is continued until the final behavior is achieved. Note the following example of successful shaping:

When John Friday first joined the skilled craft apprenticeship program, he was assigned to work with Joe Hooks, an experienced hydraulic repair journeyman. At first, John was completely confused by the complex work that Joe carried out, and about the only thing that John was able to do was to carry the tools and to get the parts. He was particularly apprehensive about changing the main cylinder on the 15-ton hydraulic press. He knew from Joe's seriousness about that job that it was important to do the job right. The first time, John merely handed Joe the tools, and Joe did all the work. John was surprised when Joe thanked him for helping when the job was completed. The next time, Joe had John disconnect all the external hydraulic lines before Joe did the main work. From then on, whenever they changed the cylinder, Joe had John do a little more of the work. After a year had passed, John did the entire job when Joe was on vacation, and the foreman complimented John for doing the job so well.

In the true literal sense, shaping is not common in organizations. In true shaping, the employee must perform a behavior before it can be reinforced. In organizations, the successive approximations are typically combined with verbal instructions, which form a type of discriminative stimuli interspersed with reinforcement of the successive approximations. Nevertheless, the general idea of shaping has value because it provides a systematic model by which new employees can acquire the complex skills that are required.

Extinction of Employee Behavior

While reinforcement is a technique to increase the frequency of a work behavior, *extinction* is a procedure to decrease the frequency of a behavior and eventually to extinguish it. From a managerial viewpoint, extinction is used to diminish undesirable employee behaviors. That is, extinction is a behavioral management procedure where employee behaviors that do not lead toward organizational goals are reduced.

There are three steps in the extinction procedure:

1. Identifying the target behavior the manager wants to reduce or eliminate.
2. Identifying the reinforcer that maintains the target behavior.
3. Stopping the reinforcer.

Once the reinforcer is no longer administered contingent upon the target behavior and the behavior starts to decrease in frequency, then extinction is taking place.

Extinction applies to stopping consequence events that are reinforcers. This means that the reinforcing event that is stopped has previously occurred after the target behavior. For extinction to occur, the event that is stopped must previously have followed the target behavior, and the frequency of the target behavior must decrease. Extinction can also be regarded as a failure to positively reinforce a behavior.

Extinction is a useful behavioral management technique for reducing behaviors that are undesirable or disruptive to the normal work flow. For example, a group might reinforce the disruptive behavior of a member by laughing at the behavior. By stopping the laughing (the reinforcer), the disruptive behavior will diminish and eventually stop.[15]

Extinction is a powerful tool to change employee work behavior. Like reinforcement, it can be used wisely or unwisely. The extinction of desirable behavior can unintentionally occur. If a desirable behavior is never reinforced, a manager may, without recognizing it, be using a process of extinction. The desired behavior may inadvertently decrease in frequency.

Extinction is enhanced when combined with positive reinforcement of behavior that is incompatible with the extinguished behavior. If other reinforcers are developed to support desirable behavior, then step 2, the precise identification of the reinforcer that supports the undesirable behavior to be extinguished, is not so critical. Potential side effects of extinction (e.g., emotional behavior) are diminished if reinforcements are provided for alternative behaviors.

Although extinction may effectively decrease undesirable employee behavior, it does not guarantee that a desirable target behavior will replace the undesired behavior. When extinction is terminated, the undesired behavior is likely to return if alternate desirable behaviors have not been developed to replace the extinguished behavior. Therefore, when extinction is used, a combination strategy of reinforcement should be used to develop desirable behavior to replace the behavior to be extinguished.

Aversive Management of Employee Behavior—Punishment

Aversive control is an important aspect of the management of employee behavior. *Aversive* means unpleasant, and aversive control is the use of unpleasant or displeasing events to manage behavior. The common assumption that aversive control techniques should generally be avoided by managers is an oversimplification. While aversive control can have undesired side effects, it can, given the right conditions, be a useful part of the management of employee behavior. Generally, two types of aversive control are recognized: *punishment* and *negative* reinforcement. These two concepts are frequently confused with each other, and it is important to understand the differences.

Perhaps the easier of the concepts to understand is punishment. The common definition of punishment is doing something unpleasant to someone. In behavioral terms, punishment is a complex technical term. First, a punisher is an aversive event that *follows* a behavior and *decreases* the frequency of that behavior. As in positive reinforcement, a punishment contingency may include a specific discriminative stimulus that cues the employee that a punisher will be the consequence of a specific behavior. While a positive reinforcement contingency encourages the frequency of a target behavior, a punishment contingency suppresses the frequency of a target behavior.

In order for a consequence to qualify as a punisher, the target behavior must decrease. In other words, just because an event is thought of as displeasing (aversive), it is not necessarily a punisher. The event must have the effect of suppressing behavior before it can be defined as a punisher. The important point is that punishment is an aversive consequence that follows behavior and has the effect of decreasing the frequency of the behavior.

In organizations, several types of aversive events are typically used as punishers. Material consequences, for example, include such events as a cut in pay, disciplinary layoff without pay, a disciplinary demotion in salary grade or job classification, or a job transfer because of failure to adequately perform in the past. The ultimate punishment in organizations is dismissal, getting fired for failure to perform duties (some would refer to this as organizational "capital punishment"). In general, material aversive consequences are not widely used in organizations except for very serious behavior problems.

Interpersonal aversive consequences tend to be much more widely used on a day-to-day basis. An example of an interpersonal punisher would be the oral reprimand from a manager to an employee because of unacceptable behavior. In addition, nonverbal aversive events such as frowns, grunts, and aggressive body language can also qualify as punishers. Sometimes the task itself can provide aversive consequences. The fatigue that follows hard physical labor can be considered as a type of punishment. Harsh or dirty working conditions might also be considered aversive events that are contingent on job incumbency.

The laws previously discussed with reinforcement have their equivalents with punishment. For maximum effectiveness, a punisher should be directly linked to the target behavior (law of contingent punishment), it should be administered as immediately as possible (law of immediate punishment), and the greater the size of the punisher, generally, the stronger the effect will be on the target behavior (law of punishment size).

In addition to punishment through the application of an aversive consequence (Figure 6–3, cell III), another type of punishment contingency is possible: punishment by contingent removal of a pleasant event (Figure 6–3, cell II). This type of contingency entails the withdrawal of a pleasant event, subsequent to an undesired behavior, that has the effect of decreasing the frequency of that behavior. Note that the withdrawal takes place *after* the specific behavior, and in order to qualify as punishment, the behavior must *decrease* in frequency.

Thus there are two types of punishment. The first features the presentation of an aversive event after an undesired behavior has occurred. The second features the withdrawal of a pleasing event after an undesirable behavior has occurred. Both types of punishment have the effect of decreasing the frequency of the target behavior.

Punishment by withdrawal can take several forms. One type is a fine, where money is withdrawn from a person because of an undesirable behavior. Another type is the temporary loss of a privilege because of the occurrence of an undesired behavior.

Punishment by withdrawal should not be confused with extinction. In punishment by withdrawal, the event that is withdrawn is normally present unless the undesirable behavior occurs. In extinction, a pleasant event that was previously contingent upon a specific behavior is no longer administered contingent upon that behavior. A useful question can distinguish between the two types of contingencies: Is the event usually in the employee's environment *before* the behavior, or does the event occur *after* and contingent upon the behavior? If the event is normally in the person's environment and is withdrawn contingent upon the occurrence of the undesirable behavior, the contingency can be regarded as punishment by contingent withdrawal. If the event has been previously dependent upon the employee's behavior and is then no longer administered contingent upon the behavior, then the procedure can be regarded as extinction.

In summary, punishment is an aversive control technique that manages the behavior of employees by administration of events subsequent to an undesired behavior. Punishment has the effect of decreasing the frequency of the behavior in question.

Aversive Management of Employee Behavior—Negative Reinforcement

In *negative reinforcement,* an aversive event is presented *before* the employee behavior and is then terminated when the behavior occurs. This procedure has the effect of increasing the frequency of the specific behavior. In common usage, negative reinforcement is sometimes incorrectly confused with punishment because both use aversive events to control behavior. For example, the use of an oral reprimand that is contingent upon poor employee performance is sometimes mistakenly called negative reinforcement when, in actuality, the procedure is one of punishment. Negative reinforcement is used to *increase* the frequency of a desired target behavior; punishment is used to *decrease* the frequency of an undesired target behavior.

Negative reinforcement is frequently used when an employee has *not* done something that is desired. For example, when a supervisor "bawls out" a worker for not cleaning up a machine, the procedure is negative reinforcement because the oral reprimand terminates when the worker begins to clean up the machine, and the probability of cleaning up the machine *increases* in the future. This type of procedure is also called *escape* because the employee begins cleaning up the machine to "escape" from the oral reprimand of the supervisor. Escape is the procedure where an aversive event is present until an employee performs a behavior to terminate the aversive event. The behavior is called an *escape response.*

Avoidance is a procedure closely connected with escape. With avoidance, an aversive event is *prevented* from occurring because the person completes the target behavior before the aversive event is presented. After some encounters with an angry supervisor over a dirty machine, for example, the employee may clean the machine in order to *avoid* an oral reprimand from the supervisor. Like escape, avoidance has the effect of *increasing* the target behavior.

With an escape procedure, the aversive event is present in the employee's environment. With avoidance, however, the aversive event is likely to take place, but does not actually take place because the employee undertakes the appropriate behavior. In order to distinguish whether the procedure is escape or avoidance, ask yourself: Is the aversive event present or absent when the target behavior takes place? If the aversive event is present, the procedure is escape.

In summary, escape and avoidance are both types of negative reinforcement that result in an increase in the target behavior and make use of aversive events.[16]

Potential Side Effects of Punishment

An argument against the use of punishment is the possibility of undesirable side effects, especially over long periods of time or through sustained periods of punishment incidents.[17] Even though an undesirable employee target behavior may be eliminated, the secondary consequences that could result from punishment might be more of a problem than the original undesirable behavior or at least be a problem in their own right. Figure 6–4 is a diagrammatic representation of the potential side effects of punishment.

Undesirable emotional reactions may result from punishment. For example, a worker who has been reprimanded for staying at a break too long may react with anger toward his manager and toward the organization. This anger may lead to aggressive behavior that is detrimental to the organization. Sabotage behavior, for example, is typically a result of a punishment-oriented behavioral management system. At the very least, the anger of one employee tends to be disruptive to other employees.

Punishment frequently leads only to short-term suppression of the undesirable employee behavior rather than to sustained elimination of the behavior. This means that continued punishment is likely to be required over a long period of time if the undesirable behavior is to be continually suppressed. Another problem is that the absence of the undesired behavior becomes contingent upon the presence of the punishing agent. When the punishing agent is not present, the undesirable employee behavior is likely to reoccur.

In addition, punishment may lead to future attempts to avoid or to escape the punishment situation. From an organizational viewpoint, this reaction may sometimes be undesirable because an employee may avoid a particular job situation that is necessary for normal job performance. The ultimate form of escape, of course, is voluntary termination. Most management scholars would agree that organizations that depend on punishment as the dominant mode to manage employee behavior are likely to have higher rates of employee turnover. While some turnover is desirable from an organizational viewpoint, excessive rates are generally considered to be costly and unhealthy because useful and adequate performing employees are more likely to leave. Absenteeism is another form of avoidance that is likely to occur in situations where punishment is used frequently.

Another problem with punishment is its potential to suppress employee initiative and flexibility. At one time or another, most of us have heard an employee say that "I'm going to do just what I'm told, and nothing more." This type of reaction to punishment is undesirable because organizations depend on the personal initiative and creativity that individual employees bring to their jobs. An overuse of punishment tends to produce apathetic employees who are generally not an asset to the organization. Sustained punishment can also lead to a generalized negative self-evaluation on the part of the employee, which, in turn, is detrimental to the confidence that is necessary for most organizational jobs.

Punishment also tends to produce a conditioned fear of the punishing agent. That is, the employee tends to develop a general fear of whoever administers the punishment, usually the manager, even though many day-to-day situations might require a normal and positive interaction between

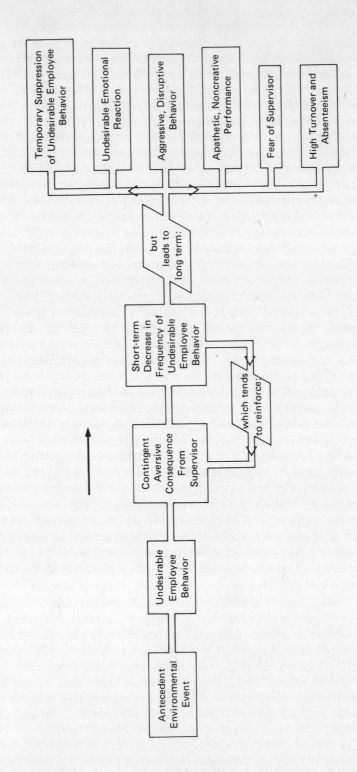

FIGURE 6–4. Potential Side Effects of Punishment

employee and manager. Behavior such as "hiding" to avoid a manager or reluctance to communicate with a manager may well hinder the normal performance of the employee. This type of reaction occurs because the manager becomes an environmental cue that indicates the probability of the occurrence of an aversive event to the employee.

One reason why many managers tend to rely on punishment as a behavioral management technique is that punishing behavior often produces fast results in the short run. In essence, the manager is reinforced for using punishment because the approach does produce an immediate change in an undesirable employee target behavior. However, this manager overlooks the long-term detrimental side effects of punishment, which can have a cumulative effect. That is, while a few incidents of punishment may not produce these undesirable side effects, the long-term sustained use of punishment as a dominant mode of managing employee behavior will invariably result in unproductive organizational outcomes, as in the following example:

When the new department was formed, Chris was appointed manager. This was Chris's first managerial assignment, although she had considerable experience in the technical aspect of the work and she had been considered a top performer by her previous bosses. Chris was resolved that the department was going to be "run right." She had had experience with weak managers before, and she was determined that the performance of her department was going to be outstanding. Above all, she was not going to be tolerant of any subordinates who were not willing to do the work in the way Chris thought it should be done.

Within a month, Chris's subordinates knew she "meant business." The first week, she had given Mary a public "dressing down" because Mary arrived five minutes late for work. Chris also became quite distressed and expressed her displeasure when one of her staff made an error in the work. When Skip made a special effort to complete the report that Chris wanted, Chris said nothing about his extra effort. In addition, within the first month, Chris had Skip transferred to a lower paying job because "he couldn't do the work."

When a year had gone by, Dale Slobin, the assistant personnel manager, was called into the office of Chris's boss, the district vice-president. "I'd like to take some special time to look at Chris's department," said the vice-president. "We thought that Chris had the potential to do an excellent job, and the first few months, the performance of her department got off to a good start. Lately, however, things seem to keep going wrong. First, the turnover and absenteeism in her department is terrible. Over 50 percent of her employees have quit or requested a transfer in the first year. In addition, we seem to have a great deal of trouble when something unusual comes up. Chris's department seems to be able to handle the routine things okay, but when we get special requests, or when we have to develop a new procedure, we seem to have a lot of trouble. Her people don't seem to have the creativity and the 'get up and go' that I thought she'd be able to inspire. In addition, I just haven't seen any signs of loyalty and cohesiveness within her department."

"Most of all," he continued, "I'd like you to make an assessment of Chris's health and emotional stability. The launching of this new department has been stressful, and I'm beginning to worry about Chris herself, and her capabilities to take care of herself under difficult conditions. The bottom line of what I'm asking you to do is to help me in my decision of whether I should replace Chris as manager or not."

Pretend that you are Dale Slobin. Employing what you have just learned about the potential side effects of punishment, analyze Chris's problem.

The Effective Use of Aversive Management

Most contemporary behavioral management scholars recommend an emphasis on positive management techniques. That is, research has generally shown that the use of positive reinforcement as a dominant practice is generally regarded as more effective in managing employee behavior in the long term than the use of aversive control. Yet aversive control has an appropriate place in the management of employee behavior, and it is useful to examine some of the factors that influence the effective use of aversive management.

In organizations, the most common form of aversive management is an oral reprimand, which is intended to diminish or stop an undesirable employee target behavior. An old rule of thumb says, "praise in public, punish in private." Private punishment does indeed establish a different type of contingency than public punishment. In general, a private reprimand can be constructive and instructive in nature, while a public punishment is likely to bring forth undesirable emotional side effects.

Punishment should be as immediate to the occurrence of the undesired target behavior as possible. By waiting an unnecessary length of time, the punishment has a greater possibility of losing effectiveness, as in the following example:

Ms. Frisch wondered why she was being called into the assistant manager's office. When she arrived, she knew from the serious look on Mr. Jenkins' face that the visit wasn't going to be pleas-

ant. Mr. Jenkins began, "I just wanted you to know that I noticed it when you were discourteous to that customer last month, and I plan to remember it when your performance evaluation comes up." Ms. Frisch was shocked. "Which customer are you talking about?" she calmly asked, even though she was trembling inside. After several minutes of discussion, Ms. Frisch still wasn't sure of the incident that Mr. Jenkins was referring to. As she left his office, she thought about whether she should begin to look for a new job.

Aversive control should be tied as directly and obviously as possible to the particular undesirable target behavior. Verbal reprimands should never be delivered about behavior in general, and especially should never be delivered about a so-called bad attitude. In order to be effective, the reprimand must pinpoint and specifically describe the undesirable behavior that is to be avoided in the future. It is important to focus on the specific undesirable target behavior and to avoid threatening the intrinsic worth of the employee. In essence, punish *specific* undesirable behavior, not the person. See how the last example could have been handled more effectively:

After the customer left, Mr. Jenkins came up to Ms. Frisch and quietly said, "Let's talk about that last customer. First, your decision was correct; his requests were out of line and it was not appropriate to provide a service that was against company policy. However, the way you handled him was not up to the standards that we expect. First, it's important to keep your voice at a normal tone. Even if he is annoying you, it's never acceptable to raise your voice. Next, it's very important to smile rather than frown, especially at the end of the conversation. This way, you let him know that your decision is based on company policy and that you are still friends with him and value him as a customer. Last, if he is insistent, it is important for you to refer him to me so that I can take the time to explain the reasons for the policy, or to see if I can find some special way to help him solve his problem. This is the kind of friendliness and courtesy that our company expects when our employees deal with our customers. Do you have any questions, or do you need any help in your work?"

"No," Ms. Frisch replied. "I appreciate your suggestions and I'm sure I'll do better the next time I have that problem." At lunch that day, she commented to a coworker about how lucky they were to have Mr. Jenkins as assistant manager.

An unfortunate characteristic of aversive control is that it trains a person in what *not* to do but not in *what* to do. If a punishment focuses on what an employee *should not* be doing, it is also important to be specific about the behavior than an employee *should* be doing. An alternate, incompatible behavior should be made clear to the employee. When the employee performs the desired alternate behavior, it is most important to positively reinforce that desired target behavior. In summary, if an undesired behavior is to be punished, then an incompatible desired behavior should be identified and reinforced.

Last, but not least, there should be an appropriate balance between the use of positive management incidents and aversive management incidents. It is not the absolute number of aversive management incidents that is really important, but the ratio of positive incidents to aversive incidents. When a manager has a practice of using positive reinforcement frequently, the use of an occasional deserved punishment incident can be quite effective. However, if a manager *never* uses positive reinforcement, but relies entirely on aversive management procedures, then the long-run side effects are likely to counteract any short-term benefits from the use of punishment. It is important to remember that most behaviorists recommend relying on positive management procedures as the dominant theme in any complete behavioral management program.

Before going on to the next section on schedules of reinforcement, read the two real-life examples of the application of positive management given in Figures 6–5 and 6–6.

FIGURE 6–5.   Fran Tarkenton on Positive Feedback/Positive Reinforcement

Francis Asbury Tarkenton is a professional quarterback. Francis Asbury Tarkenton is also a professional trainer—chief executive officer of Behavioral Systems Inc., one of the largest and most successful promotors of performance feedback and positive reinforcement systems. In his role as a trainer, the problems Tarkenton encounters are performance problems. "If, the marketing vice president is interested in improving performance, he has got to get involved and accept and acknowledge his responsibility for the performance he wants," Tarkenton emphasizes. "He has to learn to do things differently to fulfill that responsibility. He is going to have to learn about behavior—to control consequences, to use positive reinforcement, to give feedback, to manage people for long-range payoff, rather than to let them skate from sales campaign gimmick to sales campaign gimmick. And that means making a systematic change in how that marketing vice president manages. It means arranging the management system so people know how they are doing and get rewarded when they are doing things correctly."

In discussing whether behavior management has a place on the gridiron, Tarkenton says: "Yes, we do have a performance feedback system." It turns out that managing behavior through consequences is an important part of managing the Viking's offense. Extensive data is collected on 20 variables which history and a good computer have proven to bear directly on the offensive team effort. During the Wednesday showing of Sunday's game films, the offensive unit is evaluated on those 20 variables. Perfect performance on 11 or 12 of these critical variables usually leads to a winning effort. "We get feedback on the variables, we get reinforced on the variables, and it gets our people to concentrate on the things that are important to us winning. We find the most effective reinforcement is social reinforcement, peer reinforcement of each other."

Tarkenton also comments on former Green Bay Packer coach, Vince Lombardi. "Everyone thinks of him as very punitive, very negative, but he was no ranting, raving lunatic," Tarkenton emphasizes. "He was a very organized, systematic person. He pinpointed exactly what he wanted, and he gave feedback, sometimes loudly, but feedback. As a reinforcing agent, he was unbelievable. A nod from Lombardi could be a more powerful reinforcer than 20 minutes of gushing from anyone else."

He also talked about Ohio State Coach Woody Hayes slapping Buckeye decals on his player's helmets when they perform well. "Some people think that's all Mickey Mouse, stars on the helmet," answers Tarkenton. "It isn't. Recognition for doing a good job, especially from those who know good performance from bad performance, means a lot. Recognition means a lot to the 50-year-old guy working on the plant floor, and to the guy sitting in the chairman-of-the-board chair, and to the college football player. It means a lot to know you did something well, and somebody saw it, and somebody acknowledged it. People don't just work from paycheck to paycheck, at least not any more. Those stars on the helmets—be they real stars or metaphorical stars— mean a lot."

Tarkenton comments further: "We're all reinforcing agents and feedback agents for each other, each and every one of us. I'm a great believer in feedback, positive and negative. When something isn't right, tell the performer what and why and how to correct it. And when it's right, deliver the positive reinforcement and positive feedback."

FIGURE 6–6.   Application of Positive Reinforcement:
Emery Air Freight Corporation

Adapted from Feeney, E. J., At Emery Air Freight: Positive reinforcement boosts performance, *Organizational Dynamics*, 1973, 1, pp. 41–50.

E. J. Feeney, vice-president for Emery Air Freight Corporation, designed a positive reinforcement program at Emery. First, he introduced a performance audit that indicated which were the biggest potential profit payoffs for the company and areas that needed substantial improvement. For example, managers at Emery were certain that containers were used for shipping about 90 percent of the time. The performance audit indicated that containers were used only 45 percent of the time. Thus, the performance audit provided a specific objective baseline against which to measure future performance.

Second, Feeney established performance standards and goals for each worker. The goals were defined in measurable terms. It is important that the goal-setting activity follow the performance audit and that the goals be tied directly to the job. The involvement of employees in setting standards was encouraged.

Third, each employee was given the basic data so that he or she could keep track of the work. This gives the worker immediate knowledge about the results of his work and whether or not the goals are being met. Prompt, direct feedback, of course leads to knowledge of results, which is one of the most important principles of learning.

The fourth step involves the use of supervisor performance reports to the worker. The behavior should be reinforced as soon as possible and be expressed in specific rather than nonspecific phrases. For example, "Keep up the good work, Harry" is an example of what Feeney calls "gumdrops," generalized praise. Specific phrases such as "Marie, I liked the imagination you used in scheduling production," or "Ildiko, you are running fairly consistent at 98 percent of standard" are specific positive reinforcers. Emery Air Freight encourages a variable-ratio reinforcement, with supervisors giving praise and recognition to each employee. The use of aversive management is discouraged.

The results at Emery have been exceptionally good. In the three divisions that are using the positive reinforcement approach, management has reported a saving of over $3 million in the past three years. What does this prove? In those instances in which Emery has used positive reinforcement, behavior modification has been dramatic, sustained, and uniformly in the desired direction. Positive reinforcement has been used selectively at Emery in areas where work could be measured and quantifiable standards set if they did not already exist, and areas where observation showed *that existing level of performance was far below standard. On the basis of Emery's success, other corporations, such as United Airlines, IBM, IT&T, Procter and Gamble, and Ford Motor Company, have used positive reinforcement approaches with tentative but similar results.*

SCHEDULES OF REINFORCEMENT

The rules that describe the manner in which consequences are made contingent on employee behavior are known as *schedules of reinforcement*.[18] Whether deliberate or not, reinforcement is always delivered according to some schedule. The simplest schedule of all is known as *continuous reinforcement*, where the behavior is reinforced each time it occurs.

When Harv began work in the machine shop, Mike, the foreman, showed him how to run the valve-turning machine. Mike showed Harv how to adjust the machine, and told Harv that the machine would need to be adjusted several times each shift because of tool wear. Harv was concerned about how to adjust the machine until Mike showed him the "go/no-go" gauge. When each valve completed the machining cycle, it automatically entered the "go/no-go" gauge, and the dial showed the diameter of the valve. In addition, the dial was marked into a "green" area, and into two "red" areas. If the needle on the dial was in the green area, Harv knew that the valve was okay. If the needle went into the red area, Harv knew that the machine needed adjustment. Thus, after each valve that he machined, Harv was provided with the information he needed so that he knew whether the valve had been machined properly.

In this example, the visual event of the needle on the "go/no-go" gauge provided an environmental consequence to Harv that reinforced his correct machining behavior. It was a case of continuous reinforcement because the consequence was provided after each incidence of the correct behavior.

The alternate to continuous reinforcement is *intermittent reinforcement*, where a reinforcer is delivered after some, but not every, instance of the behavior. Intermittent reinforcement can be subdivided. First, reinforcers can be delivered after the passage of a certain amount of time separates the reinforcers. This is known as an *interval* schedule. The other type of schedule is known as a *ratio* schedule, because the reinforcer is delivered after a certain number of behaviors have been performed.

A second type of distinction of intermittent schedules is *fixed* (not changing) versus *variable* (constantly changing) schedules. Thus, four types of reinforcement schedules can be identified: fixed interval, variable interval, fixed ratio, and variable ratio.

Fixed Interval

A *fixed interval* schedule means that a constant amount of time must pass before a reinforcer can be provided. The first behavior to occur after the interval had elapsed would be reinforced. For example, a FI:1hr. (fixed interval, one hour) schedule would mean that the first target behavior that occurs after one hour had elapsed would be reinforced.

Pete asked Dr. Benoit, the management behavioral consultant, "Aren't fixed interval schedules rare in organizations? I can't think of one case where we reinforce performance by a fixed interval schedule." Dr. Benoit replied, "You're right about fixed interval schedules being rare in work organizations. However, I think one of the most visible rewards in the organization is provided on a fixed interval schedule. How often is your pay provided to you?" "Well," said Pete, "I get my paycheck once a month. But, in the short term at least, my pay is not dependent on my performance. Over the long term I suppose it is dependent on performance, but in our organization that connection is not always very obvious." "What you're telling me," replied Dr. Benoit, "is that your pay is not contingent on performance, but is contingent on organizational membership behavior. The behavior that is reinforced is organizational membership, and the pay reinforcing schedule is a fixed interval schedule."

Variable Interval

In a *variable interval* schedule, the reinforcer is also dependent upon the passage of a certain amount of time, but that amount of time tends to vary around some average. That is, the length of the interval is not always exactly the same but varies around an average length of time. For example, the manufacturing vice-president at Standard Steel Corporation makes it a point to walk through the melting shop on the average of once a day but at varied times, i.e., twice on Monday, once on Tuesday, not on Wednesday, not on Thursday, and twice on Friday. The first behavior that occurs after the selected variable has elapsed is reinforced.

Fixed Ratio

In a *fixed ratio* schedule, a certain number of the target behaviors must occur before the behavior is reinforced.

> *When Roseann first started work in the shirt factory, she knew that she would be paid at least the minimum federal wage. But the foreperson explained to Roseann that she could also make more than the minimum wage according to how many sleeves she sewed on. Her job was to sew the right sleeves on the men's shirts that were produced at the factory. According to the foreperson, Roseann would be paid the incentive rate for each dozen sleeves that she completed and that passed inspection. Roseann was very tired after the first day, and she had not made enough to exceed the minimum wage. By her second week, however, she was able to make more than the minimum wage, and she wasn't as physically tired as she had been. The woman who worked next to Roseann was able to make double the minimum wage. Her wage incentive was the same as Roseann's; she was paid the same incentive for each dozen left sleeves she sewed on.*

Roseann and her coworker work under a fixed ratio schedule, FR : 12, where every 12 sleeves that are sewn on are reinforced with a wage incentive.

Variable Ratio

The last type of reinforcement schedule is the *variable ratio* schedule, where a certain number of the target behaviors must occur before the reinforcer is delivered, but the number of behaviors varies around some mean. Variable ratio schedules are frequently used in organizations for nonmaterial reinforcers. Verbal praise and recognition, for example, are typically given on some type of variable ratio schedule. Not every behavior is reinforced, and the number of behaviors that occur before verbal approval is given varies from one time to the next, as in the following example:

> *Tony owns a small neighborhood bakery that sells retail baked goods and also furnishes rolls to the neighborhood restaurants. After school, Tony's son, Carlo, helps Tony by delivering the rolls to the restaurants. Tony doesn't pay Carlo through a normal payroll because Carlo is too young to be legally working for the bakery. However, Tony tries to remember to give Carlo five dollars for every 100 dozen that Carlo delivers. Sometimes Tony remem-*

bers early and Carlo gets five dollars for delivering less than 100 dozen. However, sometimes Tony forgets and Carlo delivers more than 100 dozen before he gets the five dollars.

Without knowing it, Tony is applying a variable ratio schedule.

Based on laboratory experimentation, the highest rates of behavioral frequency are usually achieved with ratio rather than with interval schedules or with continuous schedules.[19] In addition, intermittent schedules are important for developing a resistance to extinction. Unfortunately, these generalizations have not yet been well validated with people in ordinary work settings.

Table 6–2 presents a summary of reinforcement theory.

TABLE 6–2.   Summary of Reinforcement Theory

Type of Reinforcement	Schedule of Reinforcement	Effect on Behavior When Applied to the Individual	Effect on Behavior When Removed from the Individual
	Continuous Reinforcement	Fastest method to establish a new behavior.	Fastest method to extinguish a new behavior.
	Intermittent Reinforcement	Slowest method to establish a new behavior.	Slowest method to extinguish a new behavior.
	Variable Reinforcement Schedules	More consistent response frequencies.	Slower extinction rate.
	Fixed Reinforcement Schedules	Less consistent response frequencies.	Faster extinction rate.
Positive Reinforcement		Increased frequency over preconditioning level.	Return to pre-conditioning level.
Negative Reinforcement			
Punishment		Decreased frequency over preconditioning level.	Return to pre-conditioning level.

Adapted from Behling, O., C. Schriesheim, and J. Tolliver, Present theories and new directions in theories of work effort, *Journal Supplement and Abstract Service of the American Psychological Corporation,* 1974, no. 385, p. 57. Reprinted by permission.

Stretching the Ratio

Closely associated with schedules of reinforcement is the procedure called *stretching the ratio*. In stretching, the number of occurrences of the behavior between reinforcers is gradually increased as time goes by. For example, the schedule may start out to be a VR:2 schedule (variable ratio, approximately every second behavior gets reinforced). Over time, the schedule is "stretched" to a VR:8 schedule (variable ratio, approximately every eighth behavior gets reinforced). From an organizational viewpoint, stretching has the advantage of maintaining a certain level of behavior with a lesser expenditure of resources. Stretching is not frequently used deliberately in organizations, but is sometimes used without conscious knowledge, especially in giving verbal approval. The inherent danger in stretching, of course, is the possibility of overstretching, where the behavior is not reinforced with sufficient frequency to maintain the behavior. In the case of overstretching, extinction would occur.

PROCEDURES IN MANAGING EMPLOYEE BEHAVIOR

In order to manage employee behavior, certain procedures, or steps, are typically recommended. Figure 6–7 diagrams these steps in the appropriate logical sequence. The diagram reflects the managerial viewpoint that it is the appropriate responsibility of the manager to manage the behavior of subordinate employees. The diagram identifies the most useful sequence of steps to accomplish this objective. The following is a discussion of the steps in the diagram.

Pinpointing Target Behaviors (Box 1)

The first and most critical step in the behavioral management process is the identification of performance-related target behaviors. By *target* behavior, we mean an important employee behavior that the manager chooses to focus upon—a work behavior that has an important impact on the overall performance of the employee. From a managerial viewpoint, a target behavior is considered to be a desirable behavior if it *contributes toward* the goals of the organization. A target behavior is considered to be undesirable if it detracts from the goals of the organization. Obviously, a manager wishes to increase or maintain the frequency of the desirable target behaviors and to decrease or eliminate the frequency of undesirable target behaviors. Not all employee behaviors are necessarily "desirable" or "undesirable" from a managerial viewpoint. Many behaviors are neutral in that they neither contribute to nor detract from the goals of the organization.

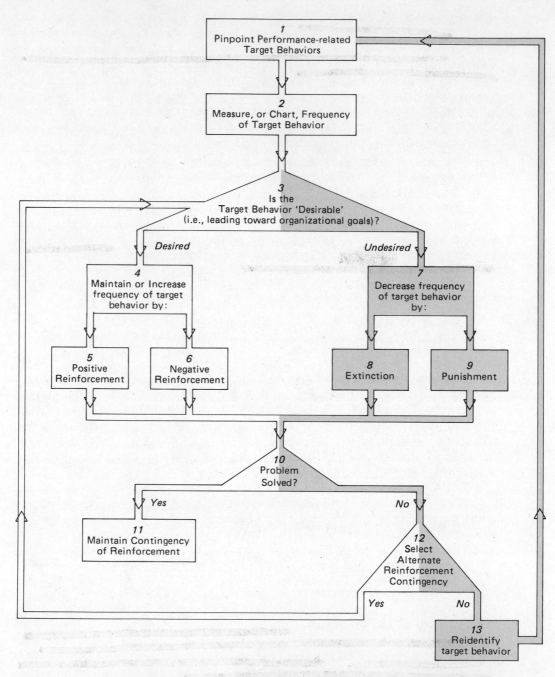

FIGURE 6–7.   Procedures in Managing Employee Behavior

In addition, even though a behavior may be desirable or undesirable, it may not become a target behavior because it makes only a relatively unimportant contribution to overall employee performance. Target behaviors are only those most important employee behaviors that a manager identifies as having a major impact and that the manager chooses to concentrate on.

The procedure for identifying the target behavior is called *pinpointing* because an employee's behavior is pinpointed as being particularly important in regard to overall employee performance. In pinpointing, it is important to be able to do three things:

1. *See* the behavior.
2. *Count* or measure the behavior.
3. *Describe* the situation in which the behavior occurs.

Pinpointing is not as easy as it might originally seem. Training or orientation is needed to be able to pinpoint behaviors adequately. Frequently, managers confuse attitudes, feelings, and temperament with behaviors. For example, manager Phil Oaks might describe his subordinate employee Joe Scotto as follows:

> *Well, Joe is just not easy to get along with. He's so disagreeable and negative all the time. He's very aggressive and disruptive. When he's unhappy he just sulks a lot and he daydreams. He's also insubordinate and doesn't follow the rules. I don't know if he's immature, not intelligent, or whether he just doesn't think rationally. Overall, his motivation is very low. He lacks drive and is generally hostile. I suspect that there may be a home problem also.*

Phil obviously has had no training in pinpointing target behaviors. Many of the labels that he attaches to Joe deal with Joe's inner state. While they may in actuality be true, they do not provide a useful basis for Phil to begin to manage Joe's behavior. Most of all, Phil cannot count or measure such attributes as "disagreeable," "aggressive," "daydreams," "hostile," and "low motivation." (Usually when managers use the term "low motivation," they mean that employee behavior is not contributing toward the goals of the organization.) There is another problem with Phil's approach. If Joe were able to hear Phil's comments, he would not know *specifically* how to improve his performance. In contrast, if Phil had training in pinpointing behaviors, he might describe Joe as follows:

> *Well, whenever Joe is given some direction, he responds by immediately telling you why it can't be done. He frequently threatens other employees and has even been in one or two fights. He leaves his own work area to tell jokes to other workers. Sometimes he just sits in a corner, or stares out the window for several minutes.*

He has violated several company rules such as smoking in
a nonsmoking zone, working without safety goggles, and parking
in a fire lane. Also, he has arrived late for work 10 times in the
last month and has returned from his break late on 12 occasions.

Phil now is quite adept at pinpointing employee behaviors. Most of all, he is now able to describe Joe's behavior in specific terms that can be counted. Once he's able to do this, Phil has a useful base to begin his attempts to manage Joe's behavior. Note that several of the behaviors could be considered undesirable.

1. Telling you it can't be done
2. Threatening other employees
3. Fighting
4. Leaving own work area
5. Parking in fire lanes
6. Working without safety goggles
7. Arriving late for work

Most of these undesirable behaviors can be redefined as desirable behaviors by stating the converse. For example:

1. Agreeing that it can be done
2. Staying in own work area
3. Parking in assigned parking area
4. Working with safety goggles
5. Arriving for work on time

Stating these behaviors as desirable behaviors has a substantial advantage. It is much easier to utilize positive behavioral management techniques that emphasize increasing the frequency of desirable behavior than to focus on undesirable behaviors that may require aversive behavior management techniques. Phil's next step will be to select which of Joe's behaviors he identifies as target behaviors—those behaviors on which he wants to concentrate his managerial attention.

Charting Target Behaviors (Box 2)

One of the best ways to keep track of employee target behaviors is through the technique known as charting. *Charting* measures the frequency of an employee's behavior over some time dimension. Charting provides an opportunity for an overall visual impression of when and how frequently a behavior occurs. Figure 6–8 shows an example of a chart. The time dimension is shown on the x axis (the abscissa), and the count of the employee behavior is shown on the y axis (the ordinate). Each entry on the chart is therefore a measure of the frequency (the count) of an em-

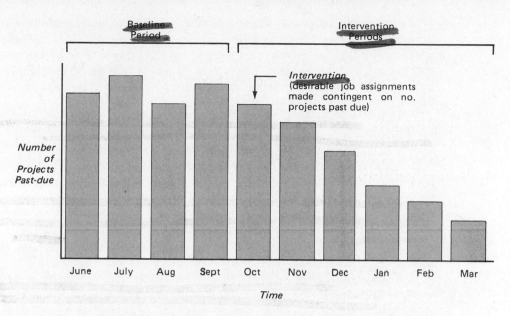

FIGURE 6–8.   Example of Employee Behavior Chart

ployee's behavior during one unit of time. Frequency simply means "how often" the target behavior occurs during a given unit of time.

In charting a target behavior, the chart is divided into at least two parts. The first part is known as the *baseline* period because it measures the existing behavior of the employee before any attempt is made to change the behavior. In Figure 6–8, these are the months of June through September. The term baseline is used because this time period provides a base to which future behavior frequency can be compared. Usually, observations during the baseline period are done unobtrusively, without the employee's knowledge. If the employee should be aware of the observation during the baseline period, then this awareness might constitute a treatment in itself and destroy any true baseline measure.

The second part of the chart is known as the *intervention* period because it measures the employee target behavior after some type of intervention strategy (e.g., positive reinforcement or punishment) has been implemented. During the intervention period (see Figure 6–8, October through March), the employee might be made aware of the chart, which forms a type of feedback or knowledge of results. Sometimes this feedback has sufficient power all in itself to cause a change in employee behavior. However, the feedback frequently is accompanied by the contingent administration of a reward or penalty.

If the intervention is discontinued, and the conditions revert to the same as the baseline period, then this phase is known as a reversal. This technique is especially useful for research into employee behavior because it helps to verify with some assurance if the intervention was truly the cause of a change in behavior. Reversals are used with less frequency in work organizations, however, because a manager seldom wants to reverse a successful attempt to manage an employee's behavior. From the manager's viewpoint, it may be less important to know the precise reason that a behavior has changed than to know that the behavior has actually changed in the direction desired by the manager.

Charting has two overall objectives. First, the baseline period provides an accurate picture of the actual frequency of a target behavior. Sometimes, charting a behavior will reveal that the behavior was not truly as much of a problem as was originally thought. Reliance on human judgment alone may distort the extent to which the behavior is actually being performed. Second, by charting through an intervention period, the manager is able to get a useful visual scan of whether or not the intervention strategy is actually working. Charting then becomes a means of evaluation. Sometimes, a chart will reveal no change in behavior, which means that the attempted intervention to manage behavior was not successful.

There are three basic ways of counting or measuring a target behavior: event counting, time sampling, or output counting.[20] *Event counting* is simply a direct count of the number of times an employee's behavior occurs within the given time period, as in this example:

> *As manager of the typing pool, Jessica was having trouble with Lorraine coming late to work. In order to be sure that she wasn't overemphasizing the problem, Jessica identified a desirable target behavior of "coming to work on time," and began recording the number of times that Lorraine was at work on time during the week. Jessica selected a "baseline" period of four weeks to be sure. At the end of four weeks, Jessica's chart showed that Lorraine had been on time 4, 3, 3, and 4 times. She was averaging 1.5 times late per week. Jessica's next step was to consider how she was going to "manage" Lorraine's behavior so that late behavior would be less than 1 day per month.*

Time sampling involves taking a series of checks throughout the time period to check on a target behavior. Typically, this procedure involves the observation of whether a behavior was or was not occurring when the observation was made.

> *Jack was concerned about Fred spending too much time away from his desk talking to other engineers in the office. In addition to losing time on his own engineering projects, Jack felt that Fred was disruptive to the work of the other engineers. In order to be sure, Jack decided to chart Fred's frequency of "at-desk" behavior versus "away-from-desk" behavior. He decided to unobtrusively observe Fred and two other engineers about once an hour each day for three weeks. At the end of the three weeks, the chart*

showed that Fred had averaged 28 percent time "away-from-desk," while the other two engineers had averaged 13 percent and 15 percent. Jack was then sure of his problem with Fred. Somehow, he had to increase the percent of Fred's "at-desk" behavior.

Output counting involves counting the results of a target behavior (or a chain of target behaviors) rather than the target behavior itself. Examples are the number of typing errors in a letter, the number of sales calls made, the number of orders received, rejects on a production line, and achievement of a budgeted profit goal. The practice of counting output behavior is widely used in organizations. Management by objectives, for example, focuses on setting goals for output behaviors and in evaluating overall employee performance on the basis of output behaviors. The management of behavior through the use of output target behavior is especially appropriate for managerial and professional personnel. Here is Jack's problem with Fred handled from an output counting approach:

One of Fred's main problems was his practice of completing his engineering projects past the due date. In order to check on Fred's performance in this key target behavior, Jack began to keep a chart of Fred's on-time project completion performance. Over a period of three months, Jack found that only 32 percent of Fred's projects were completed on time.

Choosing an Intervention Strategy (Boxes 3 to 9)

Once a target behavior has been identified and a baseline period has been charted, the manager must decide what kind of behavioral management strategies should be implemented in order to change the frequency of the target behavior. Different strategies would be appropriate depending on whether the behavior is seen to be desirable or undesirable by the manager. For desirable employee behaviors, the manager will use a behavioral management technique that has the effect of increasing or maintaining the desirable target behavior. The first alternative to consider would be positive reinforcement (the administration of a positive reward that is made contingent upon the performance of the target behavior). The manager must make an "educated guess" as to which reward will have the desired effect of increasing the target behavior. Another alternative to consider would be negative reinforcement (the administration of an aversive event that is terminated when the target behavior is performed). The purpose of either positive reinforcement or negative reinforcement would be to increase the frequency of the desired target behavior.

If the target behavior is seen as undesired by the manager, then a different intervention strategy would be appropriate. Since the purpose would be to decrease or eliminate the target behavior, then either extinction (the removal of a contingent positive event) or punishment (the administration of a contingent aversive event) would be appropriate. In addition, the manager might choose to use a combination intervention strategy to punish or extinguish undesired behaviors while reinforcing (increasing) desired behaviors.

Since the manager would be using a chart to monitor the progress of the intervention, the effect of the chosen behavioral management technique will become apparent after a certain length of time. If the intervention strategy is successful, then the contingency of reinforcement should be continued in order to maintain the desired level of the target employee behavior.

First Attempt Doesn't Work? (Boxes 10 to 13)

There is no guarantee that a chosen intervention technique will be effective. Indeed, part of the "art" of being a manager is the ability to evaluate ahead of time just which behavioral management techniques are likely to be successful and which are not likely to be successful. Part of the behavioral management "art" comes from experience; the ability of the manager to generalize from similar situations in the past or from similar incidents with the same employee. Nevertheless, every manager encounters situations when the first intervention strategy fails. What does the manager do?

The simple, straightforward answer is that the manager tries again. He begins the process over again. However, several questions can serve to simplify the procedure. First, does the manager wish to attempt to structure a new reinforcement contingency? If the answer is yes, several alternative changes might be attempted. For example, the contingent environmental event (e.g., reward) might be changed. The manager might select a new contingent consequence in an attempt to increase the frequency of the target behavior. As another alternative, the manager might try an alternative type of reinforcement contingency. He might, for instance, change from a negative reinforcement contingency to a positive reinforcement contingency. He might also choose to attempt a combination intervention strategy.

SELF-CONTROL OF BEHAVIOR

For the most part, reinforcement theory has tended to focus on the management of behavior through the control of environmental events that are exclusively external to the individual. However, more recently, contemporary behaviorists have shown strong interest in using reinforcement principles to describe and to investigate covert, or private, events that occur within the individual.[21] This approach clearly represents a thrust into what previously might have been exclusively termed "cognitive" areas of psychology, and the difference between cognitive and operant approaches to behavior are becoming considerably less distinct.[22] While overlap between cognitive and operant approaches remains controversial, the issues become important when one considers the question of self-control. Self-control of behavior is especially salient in organizational environments because most managers expect employees to be able to perform at some minimum level without the support of sustained external reinforcers. Frequently, managers use the term "self-motivated" to describe employees who are capable of invoking self-control procedures to manage their own behavior.

The management of employee behavior approach described in this chapter concentrates on describing relations between an individual employee's behavior and the environment that surrounds that behavior. Most of the principles and techniques described in his chapter focus on instances where an agent (usually the manager) structures environmental contingencies to manage the behavior of another (usually a subordinate employee).[23] Nevertheless, the techniques and principles can be used by individual employees to manage their own behavior. This section focuses on the use of self-control to manage one's own work behavior in an organization.

There are several reasons why individuals who structure their own contingencies of reinforcement have advantages in an organization. First, managers may miss a great deal of employee behavior when applying reinforcements or punishments. Second, managers who administer reinforcements or punishments frequently become a cue (discriminative stimulus) for the target behavior, and the target behavior is not performed when the manager is not present. Behavior may be performed only in the presence of the agent who administers reinforcements. Third, it appears that employees may perform better when they are allowed to contribute to the planning of the contingencies of reinforcement rather than having the contingencies imposed upon them. Thus, performance may be enhanced by allowing individuals some self-control over their behavior.

The concept of self-control entails the use of private events, by which individual employees structure their own contingencies of reinforcement. Individuals manage their own behavior using techniques that resemble those a manager would use for behavior management—by altering (managing) the antecedent and consequent events that control their own behavior. Self-control refers to those behaviors that an individual deliberately undertakes to achieve self-selected outcomes. The individual employee selects the goals and implements the procedures to achieve these goals. For example, some individuals are much more experienced than others when it comes to the process of internal standard setting and providing internal consequences for the achievement of goals. Individuals can achieve this self-management of behavior through stimulus control (e.g., internal goal setting), self-observation and measurement of one's own behavior, self-reinforcement (e.g., self-congratulations, self-satisfaction), and self-punishment (e.g., self-reprimand).

One reason for self-control being such a powerful factor in the management of behavior is the influence of immediacy—the reinforcer is available for delivery immediately after the behavior occurs. Delivery of a reinforcer from an external agent might not occur until a period of time had elapsed. In addition, the immediacy and acceptance of self-defined goals (antecedents) may be critical to the performance of a specific target behavior.

The traditional management literature has emphasized the value and need for participatory management techniques. The concept of self-control may be an important reason underlying the success of participatory management techniques. In essence, participatory management provides a shift in the contingencies of reinforcement from the external agent to the individual employees themselves. With no participation, the behavioral contingency is defined externally. With participation, a behavioral contingency is defined externally, but the individual employee also structures a contingency of reinforcement by accepting goals and providing self-recognition for achievement. This covert contingency of reinforcement, stimulated by the participation, may indeed have a more powerful effect on the employee behavior.

From a long-term managerial viewpoint, it is desirable to select individuals who are capable of self-control and to develop self-control techniques among current employees. Indeed, the ability to utilize self-control may be the best sign of the so-called "mature" employee. Above all, it is important to recognize that identical external contingencies of reinforcement may have different effects on different individuals, and one dominant reason that this may occur is the variable degree of self-control capability between individual employees. Observe the following example:

Robert and Ben came to work for Harry during the same week, after they had both graduated from the College of Engineering at the State University. Within three months, Harry was able to observe substantial differences in the way Robert and Ben handled their jobs. Robert had developed his own project control system. He used a "current status" book that listed all the important target dates for his projects, along with his coded notations of the work that had been completed on each project. In addition, Robert kept a weekly "tasks-to-do" list that planned most of his work for a week in advance. Whenever Harry asked Robert about a specific project, Robert usually had the answer within a minute or so after looking at his current status book, or his tasks-to-do list.

Ben was just the opposite. While his engineering capability was just as good as Robert's, Harry had a difficult time keeping track of Ben's progress on his projects, mainly because Ben himself was sloppy about target dates and work accomplished to date. In his annual review of his subordinates with his boss, Harry re-

marked: "Robert is excellent at controlling his own activities. He sets his own goals and he is aware of his progress. Ben is just the opposite. He has very little self-control, and I have to keep on top of him. I'm just not sure that Ben is going to work out in the department."

To require continuous external control over employee behavior is certainly not a managerial end in itself. Most good managers desire individual employees to be able to control their own behavior and to be able to achieve self-specified goals. External control should, wherever possible, be used to promote self-control, and good managers recognize that employee behavior is the function of some combination of the external contingencies of reinforcement and those contingencies that are derived from self-control.

ETHICAL CONSIDERATIONS

The most frequent criticisms of the behavioral management approach revolve around the question of whether a manager has an ethical right to manage the behavior of a subordinate employee. Typically, these concerns about ethics focus on value-laden terms such as *manipulate* and *control*. Our culture places substantial value on the concepts of freedom and free will, and the words manipulate and control imply some threat to free will.

In fact, behavioral management principles and technology are neither ethical nor unethical in themselves. A manager has not only the right but also the responsibility to guide employee behaviors toward organizational objectives. This basic management responsibility has been accepted and recognized for many years. Research has shown that most individuals in organizations desire some clarification of expected behaviors, and there is no doubt that most individuals do desire rewards when they are deserved.

In order to reduce fears and reservations about the ethics of behavioral management, several recommendations are in order. First, knowledge about organizational reinforcement systems should be as open as possible. Employee knowledge about what is required to get reinforced can significantly reduce doubts about manipulation and secrecy. Second, managers should emphasize the development of self-control. Third, organizations should rely predominately on reinforcement systems where positive control dominates over aversive control. Last, contingencies of reinforcement should be structured to reinforce ethical goals, rather than structured to reinforce unethical goals.

Interestingly, these recommendations are generally consistent with prescriptions normally provided to achieve productivity and efficiency in the management of employee behavior. Above all, behavioral management techniques are not inherently ethical or unethical. They can, however, be instrumental for managers to achieve organizational goals, and can be applied in a manner acceptable and desired by employees.

SUMMARY

This chapter has concentrated on the behavioral approach to the management of employee behaviors that contribute toward organizational objectives. The unique aspects that characterize the management of behavior approach, with special focus on the idea of managing measurable and observable employee behaviors, were discussed. Three types of learning—classical conditioning, operant conditioning, and vicarious learning—were described. Next, the different contingencies of reinforcement—positive reinforcement, negative reinforcement, and punishment—were introduced and defined. The most useful means of utilizing these contingencies—through positive or aversive management—were identified. The four types of schedules of reinforcement—fixed interval, variable interval, fixed ratio, and variable ratio—were defined and illustrated. Most important, a step-by-step set of procedures was identified that provided a systematic approach to managing employee behavior. The major steps are pinpointing target behaviors, charting target behaviors, and choosing an intervention strategy. The application of reinforcement theory to the self-control of employee behavior was discussed. Finally, the ethical considerations of the management of employee behavior were reviewed. Above all, this chapter has been based on the notion that the best way to manage employee behaviors is through the systematic control of the environmental events, both antecedents and consequences, that surround the employee.

DISCUSSION QUESTIONS

1. How is the management of behavior approach different from other approaches to questions of employee performance?

2. Which type of learning is most important for organizational environments?

3. How does a manager use positive management of employee behavior?

4. How does a manager use aversive management of employee behavior?

5. How can the effectiveness of aversive management be maximized?

6. What are some examples of the use of various schedules of reinforcement in organizations?

7. How does a manager go about pinpointing an employee target behavior?

8. How can charting be used to manage employee behavior?

9. What should a manager do when the first attempt at managing employee behavior fails?

10. How are reinforcement theory and the self-control of behavior related?

11. What ethical considerations must be taken into account before applying the management of employee behavior?

MANAGERIAL PROBLEMS

LARRY WEINSTEIN

Larry Weinstein had been assistant manager of the big north-side store for five years when he was promoted to manager of the smaller south-side store. When Larry started on Monday, he decided that the first week he would mainly spend his time observing what went on in the store so he could make an assessment of the important decisions and directions that the store needed.

Larry found that he had problems with Frank and Lester, the stock clerks. Larry knew that a well-run store tried to keep the shelves stocked at an 80 percent level at the end of each day. In the first week, Larry noted that the stock rate averaged 60 percent and that one day it was less than 50 percent. Larry observed that Frank and Lester spent a substantial part of their day in the back room, smoking and talking. In addition, Frank and Lester were frequently slow to answer the call for carry-out services. Sometimes, a customer had to wait more than five minutes and three calls before Frank or Lester would show up at the checkout counter. Finally, on Saturday, Frank came to Larry and requested to leave work two hours early because of his Saturday evening activities.

Larry knew from his previous experience that the store was not understaffed in relation to its size and sales volume. Frank and Lester should be able to carry the load. As Larry came into the store on Monday of his second week, he thought about his plan to get the stock clerks' performance up to par.

EXERCISE

Outline what you think would be a good plan for Larry to use. Then indicate what reinforcement principles are applied in this plan.

AN EXERCISE IN MEASURING MANAGERIAL
REINFORCING BEHAVIOR

Managerial Behavior Questionnaire

The questionnaire is part of an exercise designed to teach about managerial behavior. It is not a "test": there are no "right" or "wrong" answers.

Please think about managers you have known or know now. Then, think about the *most effective* manager, and the *least effective* manager. (Effective is defined as being able to substantially influence the effort and performance of subordinates.)

Read each of the following statements carefully. For the *most effective* manager, place an X over the number indicating *how true* or *how untrue* you believe the statement to be. For the *least effective* manager, place a circle around the number indicating how true you believe the statement to be.

Most effective: X Least effective: O	Definitely Not True	Not True	Slightly Not True	Uncertain	Slightly True	True	Definitely True
1. My manager would pay me a compliment if I did outstanding work.	1	2	3	4	5	6	7
2. My manager maintains definite standards of performance.	1	2	3	4	5	6	7
3. My manager would give me a reprimand if my work was consistently below standards.	1	2	3	4	5	6	7
4. My manager defines clear goals and objectives for my job.	1	2	3	4	5	6	7
5. My manager would give me special recognition if my work performance was especially good.	1	2	3	4	5	6	7
6. My manager would "get on me" if my work were not as good as he or she thinks it should be.	1	2	3	4	5	6	7
7. My manager would tell me if my work were outstanding.	1	2	3	4	5	6	7
8. My manager establishes clear performance guidelines.	1	2	3	4	5	6	7
9. My manager would reprimand me if I'm not making progress in my work.	1	2	3	4	5	6	7

Scoring Instructions

For each of the three "scales" (A, B, and C), compute a total score by summing the answers to the appropriate questions, and then subtracting the number 12. Compute a score for *both* the "most effective" and the "least effective" managers.

Question Number	Most Effective	Least Effective	Question Number	Most Effective	Least Effective	Question Number	Most Effective	Least Effective
2.	+ ( )	+ ( )	1.	+ ( )	+ ( )	3.	+ ( )	+ ( )
4.	+ ( )	+ ( )	5.	+ ( )	+ ( )	6.	+ ( )	+ ( )
8.	+ ( )	+ ( )	7.	+ ( )	+ ( )	9.	+ ( )	+ ( )
Sub total	( )	( )	Sub total	( )	( )	Sub total	( )	( )
	− 12	− 12		− 12	− 12		− 12	− 12
Total Score	A	A	Total Score	B	B	Total Score	C	C

Next, on the following graph, write in a large X to indicate the total score for scales A, B, and C, for the most effective manager. Use a large O to indicate the scores for the least effective manager.

A. Setting goals and expectations

B. Positive reward behavior

C. Punitive reward behavior

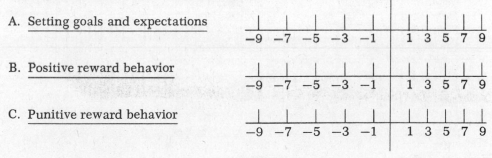

KEY WORDS

Behavioral management approach	*Shaping*
Learning	*Extinction*
Classical conditioning	*Aversive control*
Reflex	*Punishment*
Operant behavior	*Punisher*
Operant conditioning	*Law of contingent punishment*
Chaining	*Law of immediate punishment*
Vicarious learning	*Law of punishment size*
Modeling	*Negative reinforcement*
Imitation	*Escape*
Contingency of reinforcement	*Avoidance*
Antecedent	*Schedule of reinforcement*
Consequence	*Continuous reinforcement*
Discriminative stimulus	*Intermittent reinforcement*
Stimulus control	*Fixed interval reinforcement*
Reinforcement	*Variable reinforcement schedule*
Positive reinforcement	*Fixed ratio reinforcement*
Reward	*Variable ratio reinforcement*
Primary reinforcer	*Stretching the ratio*
Secondary reinforcer	*Target behavior*
Deprivation	*Charting*
Satiation	*Baseline*
Premark principle	*Intervention*
Law of contingent reinforcement	*Reversal*
Law of immediate reinforcement	*Event recording*
Law of reinforcement size	*Time sampling*
Law of reinforcement deprivation	*Output counting*
	Self-control

REFERENCES

1. Tarpy, R. M., *Basic Principles of Learning* (Glenview, Ill.: Scott, Foresman, 1974), p. 4.

2. Kazdin, A. E., *Behavior Modification in Applied Settings* (Homewood, Ill.: Dorsey Press, 1975), 21–24.

3. Ibid., pp. 13–24.

4. Craighead, W. E., A. E. Kazdin, and M. J. Mahoney, *Behavior Modification: Principles, Issues, and Applications* (Boston: Houghton Mifflin, 1976), pp. 111–133.

5. Luthans, F., and R. Kreitner, *Organizational Behavior Modification* (Glenview, Ill.: Scott, Foresman, 1975), p. 44.

6. Craighead, Kazdin, and Mahoney, *Behavior Modification*, pp. 111–133.

7. Mawhinney, T. C., Operant terms and concepts in the description of individual work behavior: Some problems of interpretation, application, and evaluation, *Journal of Applied Psychology*, 1975, 60, pp. 704–712.

8. Craighead, Kazdin, and Mahoney, *Behavior Modification*, p. 115.

9. These are not "laws" in any scientific sense, but are probability statements loosely based on Thorndike's law of effect. (Thorndike, E. L., *Educational Psychology: The Psychology of Learning, Vol. II* (New York: Columbia University Teachers College, 1913.) In addition, the practice of generalization of research results based on animal subjects to human subjects, which has been done in this chapter, is a controversial issue. Some theorists believe such generalization is acceptable, others believe it to be misleading.

10. Miller, L. K., *Principles of Everyday Behavior Analysis* (Monterey, Calif.: Brooks/Cole, 1975), p. 155.

11. Ibid.

12. Ibid.

13. Ibid.

14. Luthans, and Kreitner, *Organizational Behavior Modification*, p. 101.

15. Ibid., p. 125.

16. Miller, *Everyday Behavior Analyses*, pp. 276–277.

17. Kazdin, *Behavior Modification*, pp. 160–164.

18. Hamner, W. C., Reinforcement theory and contingency management in organization settings, in H. L. Tosi and W. C. Hamner, *Organizational Behavior and Management: A Contingency Approach*, rev. ed. (Chicago: St. Clair Press, 1977), pp. 93–112.

19. Behling, O., C. Schriesheim, and J. Tolliver, Present theories and new directions of work effort, *Journal of Supplement and Abstract Service of the American Psychological Corporation*, 1974, ms. no. 385, p. 57.

20. Miller, *Everyday Behavior Analyses*, p. 15.

21. Kazdin, *Behavior Modification*, pp. 189–211.

22. Mahoney, M. J., *Cognition and Behavior Modification* (Cambridge, Mass.: Ballinger Publishing, 1974).

23. Sims, H. P., The leader as a manager of reinforcement contingencies: An empirical example and a model, in J. C. Hunt and L. L. Larson (eds.), *Leadership: The Cutting Edge* (Carbondale, Ill.: Southern Illinois University Press, 1977), pp. 121–137.

7

Personality and Problem Solving

7

LEARNING OBJECTIVES

When you have finished reading and studying this chapter, you should be able to:

▲ Describe what is meant by the concept of personality.

▲ Understand the basic factors that influence the development of personality.

▲ Discuss a model that explains personality differences in terms of four basic problem-solving styles.

▲ Have an understanding of some contingencies under which certain problem-solving styles are likely to be more effective than others for individual and organizational performance.

▲ Further develop the ability to diagnose and recognize differences in personality, especially as they affect problem-solving styles.

▲ Increase personal insight and understanding of individual differences.

THOUGHT STARTERS

▲ How would you describe your personality?

▲ How do you solve problems?

▲ How might your personality affect the way you solve problems?

OUTLINE

PERSONALITY
  Nature of Personality
  Influences on Personality
      Development
    Heredity
    Group Membership
    Role
    Situation
    Interdependence of Influences
PERSONALITY AND PROBLEM SOLVING
  Jung's Personality Theory
  Emotional Orientations
PSYCHOLOGICAL FUNCTIONS IN PROBLEM SOLVING
  Sensation versus Intuition in
      Gathering Information
    Sensation Type Individuals
    Intuitive Type Individuals
  Feeling versus Thinking in
      Evaluating Information
    Feeling Type Individuals
    Thinking Type Individuals
MODEL OF PROBLEM-SOLVING STYLES
  Sensation-Feeling Style
    Stewart Mott
  Intuition-Feeling Style
    Steve Carmichael
  Sensation-Thinking Style
    John de Butts
  Intuition-Thinking Style
    Irving Shapiro
  Overview of Problem-Solving Styles
SUMMARY
DISCUSSION QUESTIONS
MANAGERIAL PROBLEMS
  Sue Klein
  Diagnosing Your Problem-Solving
      Style
KEY WORDS
REFERENCES

Donald C. Burnham is a shy executive who shuns the spotlight, keeps his distance from the press, and nurses a long glass of tomato juice at cocktail parties. . . . Robert E. Kirby . . . not only will take a hard drink, he'll also take your picture, join a jazz band for a few riffs, and maybe even do a few magic tricks. The two men do, however, have one thing in common: both have held the chief executiveship of Westinghouse Electric Corporation. . . . Whereas Burnham (1963 through 1974) kept in touch with Westinghouse's multifarious activities through a staff of specialists . . . Kirby has formed an operations committee of seven members, all of whom are encouraged to render advice on any of all segments of the company. Then, too, Burnham used his staff as a screen between himself and his line managers. Kirby prefers face-to-face contact.[1]

The differences between Burnham and Kirby represent the heart of this chapter—differences in personality, especially in terms of problem-solving styles, that can influence individual behavior and effectiveness within organizations. The types of personality differences discussed in this chapter are not likely to have a significant impact on highly structured, stable organizational situations. For example, differences in problem-solving styles among assembly-line workers are not likely to influence the types of tasks they perform or how they go about performing them. These tasks have already been spelled out in detail by the organization. However, when individuals are dealing with changing, nonroutine, and complex organizational problems, differences in personality can influence what problems are perceived and how they are evaluated.

This chapter selectively draws upon a limited body of personality theory. It makes no attempt to discuss the numerous approaches or conflicting positions existing within the field of personality theory. The selective application of personality theory is based on the conclusion that "no substantive definition of personality can be applied with any generality" and the recommendation that personality should be "defined by the particular empirical concepts which are a part of the theory of personality employed by the observer."[2] It is recognized that there are personality concepts and theories different from the ones discussed here that could also be used to examine some of the issues and questions of concern in this chapter.

The major thrust of this chapter is to explore individual differences in terms of several basic problem-solving styles. No assumption is made that there is only one ideal problem-solving style nor that a single individual can utilize only one problem-solving style. Either consciously or subconsciously, individuals may be capable of using different problem-solving styles to deal with different situational requirements and personal needs. However, individuals have a tendency to use one problem-solving style more often than the others.

PERSONALITY

The preceding two chapters discussed two of the important basic concepts for understanding individual behavior in organizations—perception and learning. These two concepts are brought together in this chapter. Managers need more facts than those provided by perception and learning alone in order to understand individual behavior. Because each individual operates as a "whole" person, behavior cannot be understood as distinct parts. The process of tying together these parts is accomplished through the study of personality. *Personality* is defined as "how a person affects others, how he understands and views himself, and his pattern of inner and outer measurable traits."[3] There are three important assumptions in this definition. First, how a person affects others depends primarily on external appearance (height, weight, and so forth) and behavior. Second, each person is unique. Each individual forms a self-concept that is based upon continuous interaction with the environment. Third, each individual possesses traits, or characteristics, and it is how these traits interact that shape the total pattern of the individual's personality.

An individual's personality can change. Situational factors influence personality. People learn new ways and vary their behavior in many of their more accustomed roles. A new employee will be significantly influenced by the demands of the organization's environment. Personality may change somewhat as a result of the socializing influence of the organization. Personality development may occur as a result of everyday experience within an organization. Different situations bring different responses, which may be either strengthened or weakened as a result of reinforcement.

This concept of personality goes beyond the assertion that the individual's "basic" personality is formed by the age of five. We agree with this statement as long as it is not interpreted to mean that an individual's personality is absolutely fixed or rigid.

Nature of Personality

The concept of personality as a potentially changing and developing system can be more easily understood through several propositions. Each of these propositions is explained here along with some indication of its relevance to managers.[4]

1. *Human behavior consists of acts.* In any complex behavior, a person responds as a whole. Learning and perception are only part of the total behavioral pattern of the individual. A view of personality must focus on the pattern of the total act rather than on specific aspects of it. For example, in responding to a managerial request to increase productivity, workers may respond in various ways. The consequences of the managerial request may be the desired increased productivity or it may be the formation of a union.

2. *Personality conceived of as a whole actualizes itself in a specific*

environment. This proposition indicates that people cannot be understood apart from the environment in which they are operating. Employees are part of a work unit, and this affiliation interacts with the total organizational atmosphere to influence their personalities. Other people are important sources of an individual's identity and self-concept. Various aspects of one's personality can be drawn out by aspects of others' personalities. Thus individuals can change as a result of the characteristics of those around them. The interrelationship between the individual, the small group, and the formal organization is a theme throughout this book.

3. *Personality is characterized by self-consistency.* A healthy personality is in a state of dynamic equilibrium. This means it is flexible but that it tries to maintain consistency. For example, people who are internally oriented (who see themselves as able to control their environment) show higher motivation toward achievement than do people who are externally oriented (who believe that others control their fate).[5] This does not mean that in every instance internally oriented people demonstrate achievement. However, over the long run, they tend to demonstrate this type of behavior. Attempts to maintain self-consistency do not always lead to improved organizational effectiveness. People may learn to avoid discussing various topics and avoid noticing disturbing events in their environment as means of protecting their self-concepts.

4. *Personality is concerned with goal directed behavior.* The choice among goals or motives is a distinguishing feature of individuals. People strive for more than self-consistency; they try to obtain goals and satisfy needs. For example, most people have a need to be accepted by their co-workers. Workers who attain this goal are more satisfied with their jobs than those who do not.

5. *Personality is a time-integrating structure.* Personality takes in the past, the present, and the future. People are partly a product of conditioned responses and habits learned from past reinforcement. However, people are also future oriented. The planning function in an organization is an example of the organization's future orientation, just as a person planning a career is an example of individual future orientation.

6. *Personality is a process of growth.* Each individual personality is striving to grow—to become all that one is capable of becoming. As indicated in Chapter 3, the quality-of-work-life managerial value system attempts to create an environment that allows employees to participate in determining their own work goals to help achieve personality growth. The concept of growth is important in most discussions of motivations and employee job involvement.[6]

Influences on Personality Development

What determines personality? There is no single answer to this question because there are too many variables that contribute to personality. However, several researchers suggest that clear and orderly thinking about personality formation will be increased if four basic influences and their interaction are examined: heredity, group membership, role, and situation.[7]

Heredity.   Factors such as body type, sex, muscular and nervous systems, and some glandular processes are determined by heredity. As a result of heredity, people appear to have varying potentials for learning and different biological rhythms, reaction times, and tolerances of frustration. Such characteristics influence our needs and expectations. The way others react to our appearance and physical capacities can affect our personality formation. Occasionally, a physically weak youth, such as Theodore Roosevelt, may be driven to achieve feats of physical strength as a form of overcompensation. But most people instead learn to avoid situations that they perceive as threatening to their self-concept.

Group Membership.   Anthropologists working in different cultures have clearly demonstrated the important role that culture plays in the formation of personalities. Individuals within any given culture are exposed to existing values. For example, our culture rewards people for being independent and competitive. However, there are extreme differences among individuals within any single culture. The Protestant work ethic is usually associated with Western culture, but it is wrong to assume that all individuals within this culture hold this value to the same degree. It is important for the manager to recognize that culture does have an impact on the development of workers' personalities. But it is wrong to assume that all individuals are equally influenced by their culture or that all cultures are homogeneous.[8]

Membership in a group also carries with it exposure to a social environment. The individual adjusts in the presence of others. Our personality is molded by the members of the group with whom we have personal contact and by our perceptions of the group as a whole. Groups influence the roles played by individuals along with their social standing in the group.

Role.   Culture defines how the different roles necessary to group life are to be performed. In this sense, the role influences are a special class of group membership influences. People are called upon to play a number of different roles at various times. This is because everyone participates in several groups and the roles of individuals are influenced by the groups within which they participate. For example, the roles of a husband and father are partially determined by the cultural environment of the family, while the roles of a shop supervisor or secretary are largely influenced by their immediate work groups. The medical doctor who demonstrates little emotional distress in emergency situations has been trained in medical school to adopt that role.

Situation.   Situational influences are unique factors that influence individual personalities. For example, a student who is undecided as to her professional career, or who is equally drawn to several different vocations, happens to sit down in an airplane next to a lawyer who is an engaging and persuasive advocate of the legal profession. This may set off a chain of events that puts the student into situations that are decisive in further shaping her personality and/or changing her academic program.

Situational determinants also include things that happen in the immediate family. A divorce, a father whose occupation keeps him away from home much of the time, being the only child or the youngest or eldest in a series may all affect individual personality development. One research study of twenty executives who had risen from a lower-class neighborhood to hold top-ranking positions with business firms clearly indicated that parents who reinforce values supportive of achievement have a great deal of influence on the personalities of their offspring.[9]

Interdependence of Influences. An individual's personality is the product of inherited traits, or tendencies, and experiences. These experiences occur within the framework of one's biological, physical, and social environment—all of which are modified by the culture and immediate group ties. A balanced consideration of all these influences is needed. For example, it is common in all cultures, to varying degrees, to socialize children differently according to sex. Also, in every society different behavior is expected of people in different age groups. But each culture makes its own unique prescriptions as to what behavioral responses are to be reinforced. The personalities of men and women, of the young and old, are differentiated, in part, by the experience of playing these various roles in conformity to cultural norms. Since sex and age are also biological facts, they also operate as heredity influences on personality.

PERSONALITY AND PROBLEM SOLVING

The theoretical and empirical work that serves as the primary basis for this discussion of problem-solving styles was originally undertaken by Carl Jung.[10] We draw primarily upon his framework of the emotional orientations of personality, including extroversion and introversion, and the four basic psychological functions: sensing, intuiting, thinking, and feeling. Before reading further, we would like you to take a few minutes to complete the questionnaire shown in Table 7–1.

Jung's Personality Theory

There are three basic assumptions in Jung's personality theory. First, our behavior and personality are influenced by our history as well as by our goals and aspirations for the future. We are not simply "slaves" to the past. Rather, we can be proactive in selecting goals and influencing our

TABLE 7–1.   Diagnostic Questionnaire

Please respond to the following questionnaire. You may want to indicate your responses on a separate sheet of paper. The key for diagnosing your responses is presented in the "Managerial Problems" section toward the end of the chapter. There are no "right" or "wrong" responses to any of these items.

PART I.   Circle the response that comes closest to how you usually feel or act.

1. Are you more careful about:
    A. people's feelings
    B. their rights
2. When you have to meet strangers: do you find it:
    A. something that takes a good deal of effort
    B. pleasant, or at least easy
3. Do you usually get on better with:
    A. imaginative people
    B. realistic people
4. Are you naturally:
    A. rather quiet and reserved in company
    B. a good "mixer"
5. Which of these two is the higher compliment:
    A. he is a person of real feeling
    B. he is consistently reasonable
6. Would you judge yourself to be:
    A. more enthusiastic than the average person
    B. less excitable than the average person
7. In doing something with many other people, does it appeal more to you:
    A. to do it in the accepted way
    B. to invent a way of your own
8. Do you get more annoyed at:
    A. fancy theories
    B. people who don't like theories

9. It is higher praise to call someone:
    A. a person of vision
    B. a person of common sense
10. Do you more often let:
    A. your heart rule your head
    B. your head rule your heart
11. Can you:
    A. talk easily to almost anyone for as long as you have to
    B. find a lot to say only to certain people or under certain conditions
12. Do you think it is a worse fault:
    A. to show too much warmth
    B. to be unsympathetic
13. If you were a teacher, would you rather teach:
    A. courses involving theory
    B. fact courses
14. Can the new people you meet tell what you are interested in:
    A. right away
    B. only after they really get to know you.
15. In a large group, do you more often:
    A. introduce others
    B. get introduced

PART II.   Which word in the following pair appeals to you more? Circle A or B.

16. A. Compassion   B. foresight
17. A. justice   B. mercy
18. A. production   B. design
19. A. gentle   B. firm
20. A. uncritical   B. critical
21. A. calm   B. lively
22. A. literal   B. figurative
23. A. imaginative   B. matter-of-fact

own destiny. Second, the possibility exists for constant and creative development of individuals. Jung's personality theory assumes an optimistic view of individuals and their potential for growth and change. Third, Jung suggests an open systems view of personality. Personality is said to consist of a number of different but interacting subsystems.

The open systems view of personality leads to two important considerations. First, the subsystems within the personality can be receptive to inputs and exchanges with each other. Second, the personality as a whole, or one of its subsystems, can change as a result of inputs and interactions with the external environment, particularly influences from other individuals. The subsystems within Jung's personality theory that will be considered here are the ego, personal unconscious, emotional orientations (extroversion and introversion), and the psychological functions (sensing, intuiting, thinking, and feeling).

The *ego* is the conscious mind. It consists of feelings, thoughts, perceptions, and memories of which we are aware and which we can articulate to ourselves and others. The *personal unconscious* includes experiences and wishes that have been repressed (that is, pushed below the level of consciousness); feelings and thoughts that lie below conscious awareness; and thoughts that have not yet reached consciousness but that provide the basis for certain forms of future consciousness, such as creativity. The personal unconsciousness is often first expressed in the form of dreams. It can change its "contents" in coordination with the conscious mind.[11]

The personal unconscious and conscious are often in a compensatory relationship to one another. A key element in Jung's personality theory is the *principle of compensation* which states that, for the normal personality, one subsystem may compensate for the weakness of another subsystem. A period of intense extroverted behavior may be followed by a period of introverted behavior. A person characterized by the psychological functions of thinking and feeling in the conscious mind may emphasize the intuitive and sensation psychological functions in the unconscious mind. The principle of compensation serves as a means of balancing contrasting types, thus preventing the personality from becoming neurotically unbalanced.[12]

Emotional Orientations

The two emotional orientations of the personality are extroversion and introversion. While these are opposing orientations, both are present in one's personality. One of them is usually dominant and exists in the conscious mind, while the other is subordinate and exists in the unconscious. Jung contends that the balance between extroversion and introversion is potentially variable within an individual, that is, it can change over one's lifetime. The extreme introvert is "normally characterized by a hesitant, reflective, retiring nature that keeps to itself, shrinks from objects, is always slightly on the defensive, and prefers to hide behind mistrustful scrutiny." On the other hand, the extreme extrovert is "normally characterized by an outgoing, candid, and accommodating nature that adapts itself easily to a given situation, quickly forms attachments, and setting aside any possible misgivings, will often venture forth with careless confidence into unknown situations."[13] In relation to problem-solving styles, an introvert often likes "quiet for concentration, uninterrupted work on one subject, has some problems communicating (with others) and works contentedly alone." On the other hand, extroverts "like variety and action, are impatient with long, slow jobs, usually communicate well, like to have people around, and are good at greeting people."[14]

Most of us can probably think of individuals who tend to characterize the extremes of introversion and extroversion. But, as suggested by Figure 7–1, individuals vary in the degree to which they are extroverted, introverted, or relatively balanced between the extremes. You might want to take a moment to reread the descriptions of the extrovert and introvert types and think about where you might fit on the continuum in Figure 7–1 with respect to your conscious mind. There are obvious problems of distortion in any assessment process that relies on perception, especially self-perception. Thus, it might be useful to also ask people who know you well how they perceive you in terms of the continuum in Figure 7–1. In sum, the extreme extrovert and introvert types are so contrasting that their differences become obvious to almost everyone once they are pointed out.[15]

Extrovert and introvert types are widely distributed among the population within such categories as educational level, sex, and occupational classification. As might be expected, extroverts seem to be disproportionately represented in the managerial occupation. Some research even suggests that extroversion is important to managerial success.[16] Since the manager's role often involves identifying and solving problems with and through other individuals, a certain degree of extroversion is likely to be essential. But an extremely extroverted orientation can result in individuals literally sacrificing themselves to external conditions and demands. A manager who becomes totally immersed in his or her job at the cost of all other concerns is one example of this.

Introverts, on the other hand, tend to interject a personal view between their perception of external demands and factors and their decisions. As a result, introverts may choose courses of action that do not as readily fit external situations. There tends to be more concern with personal factors in relation to external factors. As Jung emphasized, when external understanding is overvalued, we are actually repressing the importance of

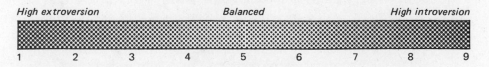

FIGURE 7–1.   Continuum of Emotional Orientations

the subjective, or personal, factor. This simply means we are denying ourselves. Perception and knowledge are not simply externally determined; they are also personally determined and conditioned. The world exists not merely in itself, but also as it appears to us.[17]

At this point we want to reemphasize that there are no "right" or "wrong" problem-solving styles for individual effectiveness in organizations. Rather, it is more useful to gain an insight into the nature of each style, the unique advantages and potential limitations of each, and the conditions under which each could be relatively more effective.

PSYCHOLOGICAL FUNCTIONS IN PROBLEM SOLVING

As mentioned previously, Jung identified four psychological functions that go into making up the different problem-solving styles: sensation, intuition, thinking, and feeling.[18] The sensation and intuition functions represent the extreme orientations preferred by individuals for gathering or perceiving information. Information-gathering orientations are concerned with the approaches by which we can become aware of people, things, situations, or ideas. As shown in Figure 7–2, sensation and intuition are opposite ways of gathering information and may be thought of as the extremes of a continuum.

In contrast, the thinking and feeling functions represent the extreme orientations preferred by individuals for evaluating information (making judgments) about external "facts." As shown in Figure 7–3, thinking and feeling are also viewed as opposites that can vary along a continuum.

According to Jung, only one of the four functions is dominant in each individual. However, the dominant function is normally backed up by only one of the functions from the other set of paired opposites. For example, the thinking function may be supported by the sensation function, or sensation may be supported by thinking. The sensation-thinking combinations are regarded as most characteristic of modern humanity in Western industrialized societies. As a result, feeling and intuition are the functions most likely to be disregarded, undeveloped, or repressed. We will first consider each of the four psychological functions as a dominant type, and then consider the two information-gathering orientations (sensation and intuition) in combination with the two information-evaluation orientations (thinking and feeling).

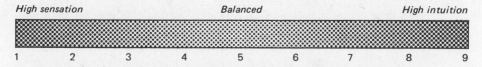

FIGURE 7–2.   Continuum of Information-gathering Orientations

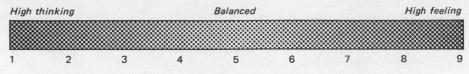

FIGURE 7–3.   Continuum of Information-evaluation Orientations

Sensation versus Intuition in Gathering Information

Sensation versus intuition refers to basic differences in the ways individuals perceive or gather information. For example, some individuals tend to integrate information into dynamic wholes (systems minded) whereas others tend to make collections of unrelated data. In everyday terms, some people emphasize well-defined details, whereas others tend to perceive the big picture.[19]

Sensation Type Individuals.   Sensation type individuals "dislike new problems unless there are standard ways to solve them, like an established routine, must usually work all the way through to reach a conclusion, show patience with routine details, and tend to be good at precise work."[20] Sensation types are likely to be satisfied and good performers as "detail" persons. A detail person is someone whose organizational life primarily revolves around the implementation and use of rules, regulations, and standard operating procedures. Many lower level organization jobs are designed like this. Of course, this is not to suggest that most individuals occupying such jobs are sensation types. Sensation types may adequately fill such jobs because they require a minimal need to exercise discretion. *Discretion* is the amount of authority and the level of responsibility in a job.[21] In terms of a problem style, the sensation type tends to:

1. Dislike new problems unless there are standard ways to solve them.
2. Enjoy using skills already learned more than learning new ones.
3. Work more steadily, with realistic idea of how long it will take.
4. Usually work all the way through to reach a conclusion.
5. Be impatient when the details get complicated.
6. Distrust creative inspirations, and don't usually get inspired.

The sensation type dislikes dealing with unstructured problems because they contain considerable uncertainty. In most cases, unstructured problems require the individual to exercise some degree of judgment in deciding upon a course of action and how to implement it. A sensation type may experience considerable anxiety because of the uncertainties that are a part of making decisions in "hazy" areas. The mental set of the sensation type is oriented to realism, external facts, and concrete experiences. Along with the love of concrete or physical reality, this type is not inclined toward personal reflection and introspection into their experiences or selves.

Intuitive Type Individuals.   The type of job (routine and structured) enjoyed and performed well by a sensation type is likely to be disliked and poorly performed by an intuitive type. An intuitive type individual is one who "likes solving new problems, dislikes doing the same things over and over again, jumps to conclusions, is impatient with routine details, and dislikes taking time for precision."[22] Where the sensation type tends to perceive the external environment in terms of details and parts, the intuitive type tends to perceive the whole or totality of the external environment —as it is and as it might change. In terms of a problem-solving style, intuitives tend to:

1. Keep the "total" or overall problem continually in mind as the problem solving process develops.
2. As the process unfolds, show a tendency, willingness, and openness to continuously redefine the problem.
3. Rely on hunches and unverbalized cues.
4. Almost simultaneously consider a variety of alternatives and options.
5. Jump around or back and forth in the elements or steps in the problem-solving process. (After presumably defining a problem, identifying alternatives to the problem, and evaluating consequences of each alternative, the intuitive individual may suddenly jump back to a reassessment as to whether the "true" problem has even been identified!)
6. Quickly consider and discard alternatives.[23]

Unlike the sensation type, the intuitive type is suffocated by stable conditions and seeks out and creates new possibilities. Intuitives may often be found among business tycoons, politicians, speculators, entrepreneurs, stockbrokers, and the like. This type can be extremely valuable to the economy and society by providing a service as initiators and promoters of new enterprises, services, concepts, and other innovations in both the public and private sectors. If the intuitive is oriented more to people than to tangible things, he or she may be exceptionally good at diagnosing the abilities and potential of other individuals. This diagnostic capacity may be combined with a talent for anything new.[24]

Feeling versus Thinking in Evaluating Information

Feeling versus thinking refers to basic differences in the ways individuals evaluate information.

Feeling Type Individuals.   Feeling type individuals are "aware of other people and their feelings, like harmony, need occasional praise, dislike telling people unpleasant things, tend to be sympathetic, and relate well to most people."[25] Feeling types are likely to engage in a high degree of conformity and to accommodate themselves to other people. They tend to make decisions that result in approval from others (peers, subordinates, and superiors). In terms of a problem solving style, feeling types tend to:

1. Like solving problems that will please other people, even in unimportant things.
2. Dislike dealing with problems that require them to tell people unpleasant things.
3. Be responsive and sympathetic to other people's problems.
4. Heavily emphasize the human aspects in dealing with organizational problems.
5. See problems of inefficiency and ineffectiveness, as caused by interpersonal and other human difficulties.

Feeling types have a strong tendency to avoid problems that are likely to result in disagreements. When avoidance or smoothing of differences is not possible, they are likely to change their positions to ones more acceptable to others. The establishment and maintenance of friendly relations may be more important to them than a concern for achievement, effectiveness, and decision making.[26] Feeling type managers may have a difficult time suspending or discharging subordinates for inadequate performance even when it is widely recognized by others, including the poor performer's own peers. In sum, feeling types are likely to emphasize emotional and personal factors in decision making.

Thinking Type Individuals. At the other extreme, thinking type individuals are "unemotional and uninterested in people's feelings, like analysis and putting things into logical order, are able to reprimand people or fire them when necessary, may seem hard hearted, and tend to relate well only to other thinking types."[27] The activities and decisions of these individuals are usually controlled by intellectual processes based upon external data and/or generally acceptable ideas and values. There tends to be a desire to fit problems and their solutions into standardized formulas. The application of external data and impersonal formulas to decision situations may result in the loss of all personal considerations even when they affect these decision makers' own welfare. For the sake of some goal, thinking types may neglect health, finances, family, or other interests that others would normally regard as important.

The thinking function, when dominant, is often positive and productive because it results in the discovery of new facts, new concepts, or new models, which are based upon seemingly unrelated empirical data. In terms of a problem-solving style, thinking types are likely to:

1. Make a plan and look for a method to solve the problem.
2. Be extremely conscious and concerned with the approach they take to a problem.
3. Carefully define the specific constraints in the problem.
4. Proceed by increasingly refining their analysis.
5. Obtain and search for additional information in a very orderly manner.[28]

There is considerable similarity between the thinking type, the major elements in the scientific method, and what our society characterizes as rational problem solving. Our educational institutions have also been most concerned with developing the thinking type of function. The characteristics of this type are obviously important to an advanced industrialized society. But there has been overemphasis on the assumed functional nature of thinking versus feeling.

A useful summary of the difference between the thinking and feeling types has been expressed this way:

> A thinking individual is the type who relies on the cognitive process. His evaluations tend to run along the lines of abstract true-false judgments and are based on formal systems of reasoning. A preference for feeling, on the other hand, implies the type of individual who relies primarily on affective processes. His evaluations tend to run along personalistic lines of good/bad, pleasant/unpleasant, and like/dislike. Thinking types systematize; feeling types take moral stands and are interested and concerned with moral judgments.[29]

The discussion to this point has focused on each of four pure and dominant psychological functions for considering individual differences in problem solving. As suggested earlier, each dominant type is likely to be supplemented and backed up by one of the other paired opposite types. Thus, the discussion of individual problem-solving styles needs to be carried one step further. This will be accomplished by considering the four major styles that can exist when combining the two information-evaluation orientations with the two information-gathering orientations.

MODEL OF PROBLEM-SOLVING STYLES

Figure 7–4 is a simplified model of individual problem-solving styles. It is based on the information-evaluation orientations of thinking and feeling and the information-gathering orientations of sensation and intuition.

The nature of the four psychological functions when each is dominant in an extroverted individual has already been presented. This section examines the four "pure" combined types shown in Figure 7–4.[30] Following the explanation of each combined type, a profile of a specific individual who seems to fit the characteristics of the combined type is presented. However, we want to reemphasize that according to Jung only one of the four functions is dominant in each individual. The individual's dominant function is backed up by one of the functions from the other set of paired opposites. The classification of these individuals into different problem solving styles is based on secondary data. Accordingly, you should be more concerned with the behaviors described than with whether the specific individuals are truly of a particular combined type.

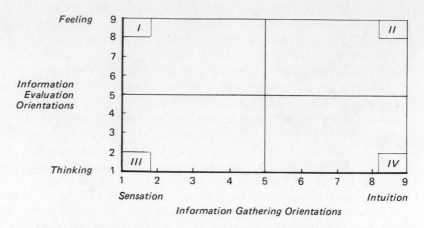

FIGURE 7–4.   Model of Problem-Solving Styles

Sensation-Feeling Style

Individuals in cell I of Figure 7–4 rely primarily on sensing for purposes of gathering information and on feeling for purposes of evaluating information. These individuals are mainly interested in detailed facts that can be collected and verified directly by the senses. They approach these facts with personal and human concern because they are more interested in facts about people than about things. Sensation-feeling types are friendly, tactful, sympathetic, and highly receptive to approval by others. When asked to write a paragraph or two on what they perceive as the ideal organization, these individuals often describe an organization with a well-defined hierarchy and a set of rules that exist to maximize member motivation. The organization should, they feel, also satisfy member needs and enable them to openly communicate with one another.

Occupations.   Sensation-feeling types are likely to be interested in jobs that require many human contacts. They may do well in occupations such as selling, some types of direct supervision, counseling, teaching, preaching, face-to-face cooperative work, and many other kinds of "helping" occupations. Sensation-feeling types enjoy talking with other people. For them, organizational effectiveness is likely to focus on such variables as employee loyalty, quality of interpersonal relationships, number of grievances, employee attitudes, absenteeism, and turnover.[31]

Stewart Mott.   Stewart Rawlings Mott, a multimillionaire philanthropist, seems to have a number of the characteristics of the sensation-feeling type.[32] Mott's fortune was inherited from his father, who was a major stockholder of General Motors. Mott's annual income has ranged between $950,000 and $1.5 million. He greets people with a friendly and open smile and is quite willing to discuss any aspect of his life in an open and candid manner. His sixteenth story penthouse on New York's Park Avenue serves as his office and home. Mott's main office, his bedroom, is filled with piles of papers scattered around the room in an organized manner. He says "I don't know how to throw things out—people, old newspapers, or cigarette boxes." He is fascinated by details. The long hours he works are a result of his insistence on being informed on all the major and many of the minor activities of the organizations he helps support. Thus, he constantly reviews numerous reports and memoranda.

Mott feels that the two major problems facing the world are population control and arms control. Thus, most of the money (over $6 million) he has donated has gone to charitable and political groups concerned with these two causes. Insight into his "feeling" self was developed around 1960, when, through psychoanalysis, he came to realize how supersensitive he was to possible rejection by his parents and girl friends.

While Mott is an activist for people causes, he is not interested in taking the time for abstract reflection or for considering global philosophies. Mott says: "I'm no ideologue. I feel uncomfortable when asked to explain in some cogent, complete, lucid way a blueprint of my political perceptions. I believe in chipping away at the defects in the present system without attempting to change the way it fundamentally works."

Intuition-Feeling Style

Individuals in cell II of Figure 7–4 rely primarily on intuition for purposes of gathering information and feeling for purposes of evaluating information. They tend to focus on changing possibilities such as new projects, new approaches, new "truths"—on events that might happen. They approach these possibilities in terms of meeting or serving the personal and social needs of people in general. Intuitive-feeling types tend to avoid specifics and focus on broad themes that revolve around the human purposes of organizations, such as serving humanity or the organization's clientele.

The ideal organizations for these individuals tend to be decentralized, with flexible and loosely defined lines of authority, no strong or central leaders, and few required rules and standard operating procedures. Intuitive-feeling types prefer organizations that are adaptive and run in a relatively democratic manner.

Occupations.   Intuitive-feeling types, as with sensation-feeling types, are likely to be interested in occupations that deal with the human side of the organization. However, the jobs need not have as many personal and detailed contacts with others. These individuals may be comfortable in dealing with groups of people either directly or indirectly. Intuitive-feeling types may do well in occupations such as public relations, politics, advertising, personnel, some types of sales, art, and teaching. For them, organizational effectiveness is likely to focus on such variables as consumer satisfaction, social responsibility, ability to identify problems or new opportunities, quality of life, and community satisfaction with the organization.

Steve Carmichael.   Our profile of the intuitive-feeling type is Steve Carmichael, a fictitious name for a project manager with nine subordinates. He worked for a city Neighborhood Youth Corps that was federally funded by the Office of Economic Opportunity. The following description is from Studs Terkel's book *Working*.[33] At the time of the interview, Carmichael was twenty-five years old, married, and had one child. The following excerpts are in Carmichael's own words:

> They say I'm unrealistic. One of the fellas that works with me said, "It's a dream to believe this program will take seventeen-year-old dropouts and make something of their lives." This may well be true, but if I'm going to think that I can't believe my job has any worth. . . . We've got five or six young people who are burning to get into an automotive training program. Everybody says, "It takes signatures, it takes time." I follow up on these things because everybody else seems to forget there are people waiting. So I'll get that phone call, do some digging, find out nothing's happened, report that to my boss, and call back and make my apologies. . . . The most frustrating thing for me is to know that what I'm doing does not have a positive impact on others. I don't see this work as meaning anything. I now treat my job disdainfully.

Sensation-Thinking Style

The sensation-thinking problem-solving style is shown in cell III of Figure 7–4. These individuals emphasize external factual details, specifics of a problem, analysis, logic, and decisiveness. The facts of a problem are often analyzed through a step-by-step logical process of reasoning from cause to effect. The problem-solving style of sensation-thinkers tends to be practical and matter-of-fact.

Sensation-thinking types are likely to be more comfortable in working with things or numbers than with people. They often accept the organization as it exists. Sensation-thinking types prefer to deal with relatively structured problems and may feel restless or anxious until a decision is reached on a thing, situation, or person. Whereas sensation-feeling and intuitive-feeling types may overemphasize the human side of the organization, sensation-thinkers may underemphasize it. Sensation-thinkers may lack sensitivity in dealing with interpersonal conflict and may be quick to use punishments on others.

When asked to describe their ideal organization, these individuals often write about an extreme form of bureaucracy. This organization emphasizes extensive use of rules and regulations; well-defined positions (the do's and don't's of each position are specific and written down); technical ability as the primary if not the only basis for judging individuals; a specific organizational hierarchy; high control, specificity, and certainty; and existing, limited, and short-term goals.

Occupations.   Sensation-thinking types are likely to be interested in occupations that deal with the details of the physical and impersonal side of the organization. These individuals may be attracted to occupations such as accounting, production, market research, computer programming, clerical, scheduling, copy-editing, drafting, engineering, statistics, staff analysis, librarianship, assembling, and applied science. For them, organizational effectiveness is likely to focus on such variables as sales per full-time salesperson, inventory cost per dollar of sales, scrap loss per unit produced, rate of return on invested capital, short-term profits, value of production per work hour, and costs of goods sold. As mentioned earlier, most organizations and advanced industrialized societies place considerable emphasis (especially through the educational system) on developing and using the problem-solving style characteristic of sensation-thinkers.

John de Butts.   While apparently not an extreme sensation-thinking type, John de Butts, the past chairman of the board of the American Telephone and Telegraph Company, seemed to reveal characteristics of this type in an interview published in the *Harvard Business Review*.[34] To judge by this interview, he appears to focus on short-term problems using standard operating procedures to solve problems and on keeping the system in control. To paraphrase de Butts:

> The quality of your decisions depends on the quality of your input, on how unvarnished your information is after it has passed up the chain of command. And I do get information of that quality—the constant contact I have with the key people at AT&T and the top people of our subsidiaries give me that quality. The organizational structure we have here helps provide quality information too. . . . Every other week, I meet with all the officers of AT&T; and practically every month I meet with all the presidents of our subsidiaries. In between, I have many conversations with individuals in these groups. These contacts give me a lot of my input.

In response to the question of whether he ever finds himself unprepared or surprised by something, de Butts stated:

> Seldom is there a significant surprise. Naturally, details come up with which I am not familiar. That's why we have discussions. . . . The key, for me, has been to set up my broad objectives and then deal with the tasks within that framework.

In response to the question of how he spends his day, de Butts replied:

> Usually, before I arrive at the office, I try to get into my mind the things I want to accomplish that day. I also jot down notes to myself. Today, for

example, I've got several things I need to talk to people about. Then I'll try to take care of the mail. Incidentally, I read every letter that's addressed to me, either by name or by title. . . . Nobody signs my name but me. I personally sign the reply on every letter that's addressed to me. Many answers are prepared for me, of course. I usually check the reply, and I frequently change it.

Intuition-Thinking Style

The last "pure" problem-solving style is shown in cell IV of Figure 7–4. Intuitive-thinking types tend to focus on changes and new possibilities, but they approach them through impersonal analysis. Rather than emphasizing the human element, they consider possibilities that are more often theoretical or technical. They are likely to enjoy positions that are unstructured and require abstract thinking skills, such as long-range planning and searching for new goals.

Intuitive-thinking types often consider problems that are complex, novel, and changing as positive challenges and opportunities rather than as burdens or sources of threat. They enjoy being the "architects" of ideas. They enjoy the creative process (such as developing new goals or solutions to problems). But, once the "castle" is designed or changed, they are often willing to let others take over to keep things running. Thus, they may be more interested in solving problems than in putting the solutions into practice. Intuitive-thinking types often feel restless and unfulfilled under stable conditions. As a result, they tend to escalate standards for themselves and others as well as fall into the trap of encouraging change for the sake of change.

They are interested in the "whys" of events and situations, in contrast with sensation-thinkers who limit their concerns to the "whats" and "hows." Intuitive-thinkers see relationships among the parts of the organizational system in which they work and between their organization and the external environment. They are likely, from an impersonal point of view, to immediately recognize and analyze the power structure of an organization.

The ideal organization for these individuals is one that is impersonal and conceptual. The goals of the organization should be consistent with environmental needs (such as pure air, clear water, and equal opportunity) and the needs of organizational members. However, these issues are considered in an abstract and impersonal frame of reference.

•*Occupations*.   Intuitive-thinkers are likely to be interested in occupations that deal with the "big picture" and the impersonal side of the organization. They are attracted to occupations such as middle to higher level managers; systems designers and analysts; architectural designers; pure scientists; scholar-teachers in such fields as economics, business, philosophy (they may care more for their subject than their students); lawyers; mathematicians; and creative engineers. For them, organizational effectiveness is likely to focus on such variables as rate of new product development, market share, cost of capital, growth in earnings and long-run profits, new market development, and acting on and responding to environmental changes.

Irving Shapiro.   Our profile of the intuitive-thinking type is Irving Shapiro, who in 1974, at the age of fifty-seven, became the chairman of the board and chief executive officer of E. I. duPont de Nemours and Company. The description of Shapiro is based upon an article in *Fortune* magazine.[35] Shapiro is regarded by others in duPont as well suited to dealing with the wide-ranging changes affecting duPont and all other multinational corporations. It is said that no one else in duPont's top management has his ability to analyze risks, comprehend complex issues of law and politics, negotiate and devise solutions that the company—and those watching it—can accept. He holds strong opinions but listens carefully to others. He is cautious but willing, if the odds are right, to take big risks. Bill McCoy, who chose Shapiro as his successor, says that he quickly learned how to make decisions.

Prior to joining duPont, Shapiro had worked at the Office of Price Administration (OPA) at the start of World War II. While there, he helped set up rationing systems for sugar, automobiles, and bicycles. After a while, he became bored with OPA and took a job in the Criminal Division of the Justice Department. Shapiro soon had a reputation as an outstanding writer of briefs, with an ability to grasp the critical issues in a case, clarify them, and argue in support of the government's position. The Justice Department at that time was divided into two factions, and both considered him a member; he was smart enough to debate the intellectuals and practical enough to satisfy the activists. Thus he showed a keen awareness of power structures and how to work within them early in his career.

After joining duPont in 1951, Shapiro soon became known as the "can-do" lawyer. Instead of putting up legal roadblocks, he suggested how duPont management could accomplish their objectives legally. Shapiro's associates say that one of his greatest gifts is his ability to put complex and often emotional issues into simple, practical terms. One executive tells about a personal problem he was unable to resolve. He phoned Shapiro at home one afternoon and was immediately invited over for a drink. The executive said he laid out three alternatives. After talking them over with Shapiro for only fifteen minutes, the best alternative became obvious.

Overview of Problem-Solving Styles

The four problem-solving styles discussed here comprise only one of a number of useful models and sets of concepts that have been developed in this area. The validity and long-term utility of this model for considering differences in individual problem-solving styles within organizations is still being developed. The research cited in this chapter and our own applied research with more than 1,000 college students and about 300 managers suggest it is worthy of recognition, discussion, and further research. In addition, the model presented is consistent with a number of key assumptions and findings of other models concerned with individual problem solving. Among these assumptions and findings are:

1. Individual differences in judgments (decisions) reflect the characteristic styles by which individuals perceive and organize their environment.
2. Individuals differ in how they perceive or gather information from the environment and in how they evaluate it.
3. Differences in individual problem solving can also be influenced by a wide variety of other individual characteristics (which were not discussed in this model of problem-solving styles), such as intelligence and values.
4. The environment in which individuals function can be as important or more important than the problem-solving styles of individuals.[36]

SUMMARY

The discussion of personality, especially in terms of problem-solving styles, focused on why and how individuals differ in organizations. As a further development of the preceding two chapters on perception and learning, this chapter suggested additional ways for understanding how individuals can affect others, how we can view ourselves and others, and how we can learn to appreciate and build upon differences in others.

Four pure problem-solving styles were discussed, but there was no intent to suggest that every individual can be characterized as one of the four pure types. According to Jung, the developing individual tends to move toward a balance and integration of the four psychological functions. (This balance would exist in the center of Figure 7–4). Since each individual is rich in variety and complex in nature, we need to be especially cautious in pigeon-holing individuals and inferring that they cannot adapt to or learn from situations that do not "fit" their style.

The intent of this chapter has been to (1) foster empathy for and understanding of the potential impact of personalities in organizations; (2) increase self-insight as to your characteristic problem-solving style and how it might influence your actions and reactions to certain problems, particularly in group problem-solving situations; and (3) provide a framework for possible forms of desired individual growth and development. There is no assumption that one pure style is necessarily better than another. However, the requirements of certain positions or roles in organizations may be more natural to one style than to others.

DISCUSSION QUESTIONS

1. How would you rank the importance of the major influences that were identified as affecting personality development?

2. When should managers be concerned with the personalities of employees?

3. How would you characterize yourself in terms of the various problem-solving styles presented? What is the basis for your conclusions?

4. How would you characterize the problem-solving style of someone who has served as your supervisor, manager, or academic advisor? What is the basis for your conclusion?

5. Is it important for a manager to be extroverted? Are some management positions more likely to require extroversion than others?

6. Do you think someone with a high feeling orientation can be effective and successful in an organization? Explain.

7. Should there be an attempt to select people for positions on the basis of their problem-solving styles? What virtues and problems might there be in such an attempt?

MANAGERIAL PROBLEMS

SUE KLEIN

Sue Klein had recently been made supervisor of a production line at Hermes Manufacturing, Inc. She is responsible for keeping the product line operating effectively and efficiently. Klein supervises five floor managers who, in turn, have fifty assembly-line workers reporting to them. She feels that her job is to maintain the assembly line at 80 units of output per hour.

Prior to Klein's being appointed supervisor, the production line was losing 10 minutes of production per day. A variety of causes seemed to be contributing to this production loss—which amounted to more than 20 percent of the daily production schedule. Klein tried to correct this problem through a number of steps, such as discharging several workers and keeping the main production line going even when some feeder lines broke down.

The production-line workers became increasingly disgruntled over these and other steps that had been taken. The workers claimed that Klein was using "speed up" tactics. Last week, four of the workers filed a formal grievance against Klein. Many workers are also increasingly making verbal protests to their floor managers. The plant manager, Ed Mitras, became aware of the situation when the grievance was filed. After some checking, Mitras is convinced that the situation is potentially explosive.

QUESTIONS

1. How would Mitras proceed if he had a strong sensation-thinking problem-solving style?
2. How would Mitras proceed if he had a strong intuitive-feeling problem-solving style?
3. How would Mitras proceed if he had a strong sensation-feeling problem-solving style?
4. How would you characterize Klein's problem-solving style?

DIAGNOSING YOUR PROBLEM-SOLVING STYLE

This key is to be used to diagnose your responses to the questionnaire in Table 7–1. Count one point for each response on the following six scales. Then, total the number of points recorded in each column. Instructions for classifying your scores are indicated below.

Extroversion	Introversion	Sensation	Intuition	Thinking	Feeling
2B ____	2A ____	3B ____	3A ____	1B ____	
4B ____	4A ____	7A ____	7B ____	5B ____	5A ____
6A ____	6B ____	8A ____	8B ____	10B ____	10A ____
11A ____	11B ____	9B ____	9A ____	12A ____	12B ____
14A ____	14B ____	13B ____	13A ____	16B ____	16A ____
15A ____	15B ____	18A ____	18B ____	17A ____	17B ____
21B ____	21A ____	22A ____	22B ____	19B ____	19A ____
		23B ____	23A ____		20A ____
Totals					

CLASSIFYING TOTAL SCORES

Write introversion if introversion is greater than extroversion
Write extroversion if extroversion is equal to or greater than introversion _____

Write intuitive if intuitive is equal to or greater than sensation
Write sensation if sensation is greater than intuitive   _____

Write feeling if feeling is greater than thinking
Write thinking if thinking is greater than feeling   _____

When thinking equals feeling, you should write feeling if a male and thinking if a female.

KEY WORDS

Personality
Ego
Personal unconscious
Principle of compensation
Extroversion
Introversion
Sensation type individual

Intuitive type individual
Feeling type individual
Thinking type individual
Sensation-feeling style
Intuition-feeling style
Sensation-thinking style
Intuition-thinking style

REFERENCES

1. Hoffman, G., The Baker Scholar at Westinghouse, *MBA*, 1975, 9, pp. 34–40.

2. Hall, C. S., and G. Lindzey, *Theories of Personality*, 2nd ed. (New York: John Wiley & Sons, 1970), pp. 78–116.

3. Ruch, F., *Psychology and Life*, 6th ed. (Chicago: Scott, Foresman, 1963), p. 354.

4. Bonner, H., *Psychology of Personality* (New York: Ronald Press, 1961), pp. 38–40.

5. Lefcourt, H. M., *Locus of Control: Current Trends in Theory and Research* (New York: John Wiley and Sons, 1976).

6. Rabinowitz, S., D. T. Hall, and J. G. Goodale, Job scope and individual differences as predictors of job involvement: independent or interactive? *Academy of Management Journal*, 1977, 20, pp. 273–281.

7. Sarason, I., R. Smith, and E. Diener, Personality research: Components of variance attributed to the person and the situation, *Journal of Personality and Social Psychology*, 1975, 32, pp. 199–204.

8. Donleavy, M. R., and C. A. Pugh, Multi-ethnic collaboration to combat racism in educational settings, *Journal of Applied Behavioral Science*, 1977, 13, pp. 360–372.

9. Abegglen, J., Personality factors in social mobility: A study of occupationally mobile businessmen, *Genetic Psychology Monographs*, 1958, 58, pp. 101–159.

10. Jung, C. G., *Collected Works* (esp. Vols. 7, 8, 9, Part I), H. Read, M. Fordham, and G. Adler (eds.) (Princeton: Princeton University Press, 1953).

11. Campbell, J. (ed.), *The Portable Jung* (New York: Viking Press, 1971), pp. 70–74.

12. Hall, and Lindzey, *Personality*, pp. 90–91.

13. Wehr, G., *Portrait of Jung: An Illustrated Biography* (New York: Herder & Herder, 1971), pp. 64–65.

14. Myers, I. B., and K. C. Briggs, *Myers-Briggs Type Indicator* (Princeton: Educational Testing Service, 1962).

15. Campbell, *Jung*, p. 179.

16. Harrel, T. W., *Managers' Performance and Personality* (Cincinnati: South-Western, 1961).

17. Campbell, *Jung*, p. 130.

18. Ewing, D. W., Discovering your problem-solving style, *Psychology Today*, 1977, 11, pp. 68–73+.

19. Maccoby, M., *The Gamesman* (New York: Simon and Schuster, 1976).

20. Myers, and Briggs, *Myers-Briggs Type Indicator*.

21. Jacques, E., *Equitable Payment* (London: Heineman Educational Books, 1961).

22. Myers, and Briggs, *Myers-Briggs Indicator*.

23. McKinney, J. C., and G. W. Keen, How managers' minds work, *Harvard Business Review*, 1974, 51, pp. 79–90.

24. Campbell, *Jung*, p. 224.

25. Myers, and Briggs, *Myers-Briggs Type Indicator*.

26. Boyatzis, R. E., The need for close relationships and the manager's job, in *Organizational Psychology: A Book of Readings*, 2nd ed. Kolb, D. A., I. M. Rubin, and J. C. McIntyre (eds.) (Englewood Cliffs, N.J.: Prentice-Hall, 1974), pp. 183–187.

27. Myers, and Briggs, *Myers-Briggs Type Indicator*.

28. McKinney, and Keen, Managers' Minds.

29. Mason, R. O., and I. I. Mitroff, A program of research on management information systems, *Management Science*, 1973, 19, pp. 475–487.

30. Bates, M., and D. W. Keirsey, Managerial styles, unpublished manuscript, 1974; Kilmann, R. H., I. I. Mitroff, *Defining Real World Problems: A Social Science Approach* (New York: North Holland, in press).

31. Kilmann, R. H., and R. P. Herden, Towards a systemic methodology for evaluating the impact of interventions on organizational effectiveness, *The Academy of Management Review*, 1976, 1, pp. 87–98.

32. Ross, I., The view from Stewart Mott's penthouse, *Fortune*, 1974, 89, pp. 133–134.

33. Terkel, S., *Working* (New York: Pantheon Books, 1974), pp. 341–343.

34. An interview: The management style of John deButts, *Harvard Business Review*, 1974, 52, pp. 34–42+.

35. Vanderwicken, P., Irving Shapiro takes charge at duPont, *Fortune* 1974, 89, pp. 79–81+.

36. Wiggins, N., Individual differences in human judgments: A multivariate approach, in *Human Judgment and Social Interaction*, Rapport, L. and D. A. Summer (New York: Holt, Rinehart and Winston, 1973).

Interpersonal
Communication

8

LEARNING OBJECTIVES

When you have finished reading and studying this chapter, you should be able to:

▲ Explain the basic process that must exist for communication to take place between two individuals.

▲ Identify several forms of verbal and nonverbal communication and understand how they are likely to influence the relative effectiveness of interpersonal communication.

▲ Describe five basic communication networks that can be used by a manager.

▲ Diagnose your own and other individual's style of interpersonal communication.

▲ Improve your own effectiveness in several key areas of interpersonal communication.

THOUGHT STARTERS

▲ How important do you think interpersonal communication is in organizations?

▲ How many means of communication can you think of?

▲ In what areas would you like to improve your own communication ability?

OUTLINE

BASIC COMMUNICATION PROCESS
  Sender and Receiver
  Transmitters and Receptors
  Messages, Channels, and Noise
  Decoding, Meaning, and Encoding
  Feedback
FORMS OF INTERPERSONAL COMMUNICATION
  Verbal Communication
  Nonverbal Communication
INTERPERSONAL COMMUNICATION NETWORKS
  Types of Networks
  Effects of Different Networks
  Guidelines for Application
MODEL OF INTERPERSONAL COMMUNICATION STYLES
  Framework
  Five Styles
    Self-denying
    Self-protecting
    Self-exposing
    Self-bargaining
    Self-actualizing
  Effective Feedback
  Diagnosing Feedback Practices
PERSONAL CONTINGENCIES
INFLUENCING INTERPERSONAL COMMUNICATION
  Self-concept
  Self-disclosure
  Listening Ability
  Expression Ability
SUMMARY
DISCUSSION QUESTIONS
MANAGERIAL PROBLEMS
  Manager-Subordinate Meeting
  Mr. Hart and Bing
KEY WORDS
REFERENCES

In the middle of a conversation with a personnel manager, a twenty-three-year-old college graduate states:

A person can't spend a lifetime working for a boss like that. I'm going to get away from him as fast as possible—even if I have to leave the company. The other day he came down and really read the riot act to us. I won't take that kind of stuff. He wanted me to do the whole thing over—after hours! He wouldn't give it to the staffers—he knew they wouldn't come through for him. Well! Isn't he going to be surprised at the end of the week when he discovers I haven't even started his dirty work—and I'm not going to do it either!

Assuming you were the personnel manager, which of the following responses would you make to this person?

_____1. "All of us feel like that at one time or another. You must not let your feelings get the best of you."

_____2. "The job has been made unbearable by your boss, and the way he treats people makes it impossible for you to work under him."

_____3. "You feel that the best solution is not to give an inch on this extra work."

_____4. "You want a transfer to get away from him as soon as possible."

A young employee whose work showed a sudden drop in quality was sent to the employment manager for a counseling interview. The first thing the employee said upon arriving was: "I don't know why I should be asked to talk to you about my work. I haven't complained and I haven't time for this kind of chit-chat. So give me what help you have in mind and I'll be on my way."

Assuming you were the employment manager, which of the following responses would you make to this employee?

_____1. "You came to see me because you were sent and not because you feel any need for help."

_____2. "Don't you feel that with my experience in the company I might be of some help?"

_____3. "You feel irritated for coming here because you don't think I can help you."

_____4. "You mustn't jump to conclusions. Often people need help when they are unaware of the need."

This chapter is designed to develop your knowledge and skills for effective interpersonal communications. After reading this chapter, refer back to the two examples just presented. You may conclude that the answers you initially chose were not the most effective. Even if your answers don't change, you may have a better understanding as to why they were probably the best choices.

This chapter discusses the process, patterns, and characteristics of communication by and between people rather than considering the content of what people communicate. Moreover, its primary interest is limited to interpersonal communications between two to about ten people. A number of studies clearly demonstrate that most of a manager's work day is spent in dealing with tasks that rely upon verbal (and nonverbal) interpersonal communications. One study at DuPont showed the distribution of time spent in communicating by supervisors as follows: meetings (administrative and technical), 53 percent; writing, 15.5 percent; reading, 14.9 percent; telephoning, 8.0 percent; and other, 7.7 percent.[1] Other studies show that managers and executives may spend up to 80 percent of their time in verbal (interpersonal) communications. From the standpoint of the individual, there appears to be much potential for personal gain through improved interpersonal communication. For example, one study found that interpersonal (including group) communication effectiveness was of very high importance in promoting organizational success.

Applying the adage, "There's more than one way to skin a cat," the area of communications is discussed from a number of approaches. As a result, no single definition of communication adequately takes into account all these approaches. One book, which attempts to capture the diversity in this area, identifies twenty-four approaches to human communication, including such points of reference as art, general semantics, mass media, nonverbal behavior, linguistics, and symbolic interaction.[2] While recognizing the inadequacy of any one definition, *interpersonal communication* is defined as the "transmission and reception of ideas, feelings, and attitudes—verbally and/or nonverbally—which produce a response."[3]

BASIC COMMUNICATION PROCESS

What is involved in interpersonal communication? On the surface, this probably appears to be a trivial question. But in fact, a number of elements (variables) and relationships between these elements are involved in interpersonal communication. Communication occurs "when individuals send and receive messages in an effort to create meaning in their own minds . . . or in the minds of others."[4] Figure 8–1 shows the elements (variables) and processes that are necessary for communication to occur. This figure presents a basic model of the interpersonal communication process. It shows that accurate interpersonal communications between two (or more) people only takes place if there is a sharing of experiences, perceptions, ideas, facts, or feelings. As discussed in Chapter 5, factors within and external to individuals often lead to inaccurate perceptions and poor interpersonal communications. It should be stressed that agreement does not need to exist between individuals for accurate interpersonal communication. Management and labor representatives may well disagree with each other while negotiating a new contract. But so long as

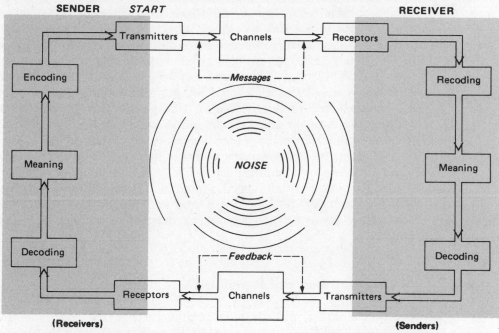

FIGURE 8–1.   Basic Model of Interpersonal Communication Process

these opposing viewpoints are being transmitted, received, and understood with the intended meaning, accurate interpersonal communication is taking place. Let's now consider the elements and relationships in the model of interpersonal communication.

Sender and Receiver

Interpersonal communication obviously requires two or more people. Figure 8–1 presents the communication process when only two people are involved. Since interpersonal communication often includes a number of exchanges between people, the labeling of one person as the sender and the other as the receiver is a relative matter. These roles shift back and forth, depending on where we are in the process shown in Figure 8–1.

The characteristics of the senders and receivers have a substantial influence on the communication process. For example, the sender may have certain goals for engaging in communications, such as changing the opinion, perception, behavior, or relationship with the receiver.[5] If the receiver is antagonistic toward these goals, the probability of distortion and misunderstanding will be quite high. The less the goals for communication are concerned with differences in attitudes and values, the greater the probability of accurate interpersonal communication.

Another way of considering the characteristics of senders and receivers as influences on interpersonal communication is in terms of differences in problem-solving styles. Chapter 7 described people who are strongly characterized as intuition, thinking, feeling, or sensation types. Interpersonal communications are more difficult between people who are different types rather than like types. *Intuition types* are often wordy, aloof, and impersonal. They may converse in intellectual and abstract terms. In contrast, *sensation types* are often abrupt and to the point. They may communicate in the briefest of terms and with a sense of urgency. *Feeling types* tend to converse in warm, friendly and humorous terms. They enjoy abundant interpersonal communication that is highly personalized. In contrast, *thinking types* tend to be very business-like and orderly in their interpersonal communication. They often speak or write in a well-organized, structured, and specific manner.[6] These characteristics and several others that will be considered later in this chapter can influence the probability of accurate interpersonal communications between two or more people.

Transmitters and Receptors

Transmitters and *receptors* simply refer to the means available for sending and receiving messages. In interpersonal communication, this usually focuses on the senses—the ability to see, hear, touch, smell, and taste. Transmission takes place through verbal and/or nonverbal communications. Once the transmitters are in operation, the communication process has moved outside of and beyond the control of the sender. A message that has been transmitted cannot be brought back. How many times have you thought to yourself "I wish I hadn't said that"?

Messages, Channels, and Noise

In interpersonal communications, *messages* are transmitted. A feature that distinguishes human beings from other creatures is the ability to transmit messages through the use of language. The messages that are transmitted are not our original meaning but a coded symbol of that meaning. We hope that these messages are as close as possible to the meanings that we had in our minds. The difference between our meaning and messages is easily grasped if you think about an occasion when you tried to convey your inner thoughts and feelings of love, rage, or fear to another. Did you find it difficult or impossible to transmit truly your "inner meaning"? The greater the difference between our meanings and the messages transmitted, the poorer the interpersonal communications. For communication to occur at all, there must be some level of shared meanings between two or more people. Words or nonverbal symbols have no meanings in themselves; their meanings are created by the sender *and* the receiver.

Channels are the means by which messages travel from a sender to a receiver. For example, a conversation may be carried by the air in a face-to-face conversation or by a telephone line. *Noise* is any interference in the channel other than the intended message. A radio playing loud music while someone is trying to talk to someone else is an example of noise. Noise can be overcome by repetition of the message or by increasing the intensity (e.g., volume) of the message.

Decoding, Meaning, and Encoding

As indicated in Figure 8–1, messages arrive at receiver's receptors. The receptors are nothing more than the receiver's senses—sight, hearing, touch, smell, and taste. These are the only means available to us for receiving incoming signals. Through our senses, we take in messages and change them from their symbolic form (such as spoken words) so that they have some meaning. *Decoding* is the translation of received messages (signals) into interpreted meanings. Through a shared language, we are able to decode many messages so that the meanings transmitted are reasonably close to the meanings received. The importance of this point can be easily appreciated if you have ever tried to communicate with someone who spoke a different language.

Meanings are the ideas, thoughts, images, feelings, or facts that exist within us. The accuracy of interpersonal communications increases in relation to the "ideal" state where the sender's "meanings" are the same as the receiver's "meanings." This "ideal" state is most closely approximated when factual information of a nonthreatening nature is being transmitted. For example, communicating the recipe for making a cake will generally result in easier and more accurate interpersonal communication than the communication that takes place between a manager and a subordinate in a performance evaluation session.

Encoding is the sender's translation of "meanings" into messages that can be transmitted. The vocabulary and knowledge we possess play an important role in our ability to encode our thoughts, images, feelings, and ideas. Professionals often have difficulty in communicating with laypersons because they tend to encode "meanings" in a form that can only be understood by other professionals in the same field. The current pressure to have contracts written in a form that can be understood by consumers is an example of a reaction to self-serving encoding. Most contracts that directly affect consumers have been written on the assumption that the encoding and decoding will take place only between lawyers.

Feedback

The last element in the model of interpersonal communications is feedback. *Feedback* is the response by the receiver to the sender's message. Feedback makes communication a process rather than just an event.

Through feedback, interpersonal communication becomes a dynamic (on-going), two-way process. Feedback may be of two kinds—positive or negative. Positive feedback informs the sender that the intended meaning of a message was achieved. *Negative feedback,* on the other hand, informs the sender that the intended meaning of a message was not achieved. Since negative feedback is often disruptive to the relationship between the sender and receiver, it can create tension or hostility between them. Because it causes disruptions, it is likely to be unrewarded or even punished. Later in this chapter, guidelines will be presented for improving your skills in giving feedback.

Failures in interpersonal communication can occur at any point in the basic communication process. To a considerable extent, this discussion has provided the skeleton or framework of interpersonal communication. The remainder of the chapter will focus on adding "flesh and meat" to the presentation.

FORMS OF INTERPERSONAL COMMUNICATION

The two primary forms of interpersonal communication are verbal and nonverbal. The discussion of verbal communication is limited here to a presentation of some "bad habits" that are often revealed in communicating with others. The discussion of nonverbal communication focuses on raising your consciousness as to its wide-ranging impact and how it can influence the directions and outcome of verbal communication.

Verbal Communication

Interpersonal verbal communications are often negatively affected by the use of pseudoquestions and clichés.[7]

Pseudoquestions.   Pseudoquestions are questions that are not really designed to obtain information or answers. Instead, questions are used to present opinions or make statements. This reduces the risk of having one's ideas rejected and possibly increases the ability to force the other person(s) to agree with the sender. Some types and examples of pseudoquestions commonly used are:

1. *Co-optive questions* attempt to get the sender's desired answer by working in restrictions and limitations to the possible responses of the receiver(s). These questions are likely to begin with phrases such as "Don't you think that . . . ?" "Wouldn't you rather . . . ?" and "Isn't it true that . . . ?"

2. *Imperative questions* attempt to make a demand or request of the receiver(s). These questions often start with phrases such as "Have you done anything about . . . ?" or "When are you going to . . . ?"

3. *Screened questions* occur when the sender asks the receiver(s) what they like or want to do, while really hoping the responses will be what the sender secretly desires. These questions may be employed when the sender is fearful of simply stating his or her own preference. An example of a screened question is a manager asking a subordinate "Would you like to work overtime tonight on the Jones order?" when the real statement should be "I need you to work overtime tonight to get the Jones order out first thing in the morning. Will you?" Even in the rephrased question, there could be the possibility of its being intended or perceived as an imperative question.

4. *"Got-cha"* or *set-up questions* are used by the sender to trap, intimidate, or embarrass the receiver(s) rather than to obtain a meaningful response.[8] "Got-cha" questions might start with phrases such as "Weren't you the one who . . . ?" "Didn't I see you . . . ?"

Clichés.   A cliché is a standard, routine, habitual way of responding. People use clichés when they don't really want to spend much effort in communicating anything of significance. We all use clichés occasionally. It is the overuse of phrases such as the following that diminish communication effectiveness. "If you've seen one, you've seen them all." "You hit the nail on the head." "It's an open-and-shut case." "Better late than never." "Better safe than sorry." "Let's get it over and done with."

The next time you are in a conversation, try to check yourself or listen to others for their use of pseudoquestions and clichés. Try to analyze the effect these habits may have on the communication process.

Nonverbal Communication

Since the late 1960s, interest in nonverbal communication has increased considerably. *Nonverbal communication* is defined as all behavior expressed consciously or unconsciously, done in the presence of another (or others) and perceived either consciously or unconsciously. Within this definition, "it follows that no matter how one may try, one cannot *not* communicate. Activity or inactivity, words or silence all have message value; they influence others and these others, in turn, cannot *not* respond to these communications and are thus themselves communicating."[9] Even if you are silent or inactive in the presence of others, you may send a message, which may or may not be your intended message. You may appear to be signaling that you are bored, fearful, angry, or depressed.

Let's consider a hypothetical incident of this process:

Susan Rollich, a departmental manager, calls the usual monthly review and planning meeting with her five subordinates. These meetings typically last four hours and are concerned with re-

viewing the previous month's accomplishments and problems and developing working plans for the coming month.

Unknown to her subordinates, Susan attended a two-day communication-skills seminar three days before their meeting. At the meeting she learned about such things as the tendency of superiors to dominate communication flow when interacting with subordinates; the need for greater active listening by superiors; the impact of nonverbal communications, such as frowns or smiles as indicators of disapproval or approval. Based on exercises in the seminar and personal introspection, Susan has concluded that there is a need for major changes in how she communicates. So for this staff meeting, Susan decided to vary past practice by being almost exclusively a listener and by controlling her nonverbal responses by retaining a "poker face."

What happens? The meeting is likely to be a complete disaster. One subordinate perceives Susan's "new" behavior as an obvious sign that she is terribly upset about "something," and thus becomes quite anxious. Another subordinate interprets Susan's behavior as a sure indicator of complete boredom and becomes quite frustrated because of the inability to draw her out. A third subordinate suspects that Susan is fearful of something, such as getting fired or demoted because the unit has been having more than its share of problems over the past three months.

While the specifics of this incident are hypothetical, the issues and concepts within the incident are real. The overriding implication of this incident is the failure of Susan to communicate about how she would like to communicate in this meeting and how it might be different from past approaches. Any radical change from behavior that others have learned to anticipate and to interpret with reasonable accuracy may result in messages being misinterpreted by the different receivers. The sender's intended message is never received by anyone. Over the long run, relearning would take place so that the intended verbal and nonverbal messages would more closely match the received or interpreted messages.

Types of Nonverbal Communication.   To develop a more specific understanding of the rich scope and depth or nonverbal communication, Table 8–1 provides a classification system and explanation of four major sets of nonverbal codes: performance codes, artifactual codes, mediational codes, and contextual codes. The classification scheme in Table 8–1 serves to illustrate dramatically the numerous ways in which we can and do communicate without saying a word. This figure also suggests the subtle, unrecognized, and often unconscious role of nonverbal communications.

TABLE 8–1. Classification System of Nonverbal Communication Codes

Major Codes	Explanation and Examples
Performance Codes	Nonverbal signs originating through differences and changes in bodily action, such as facial expression, eye movement, gestures, body posture, tactile (touch) contact
Artifactual Codes	Nonverbal signs originating through differences and changes in cosmetics, dress, furnishings, art objects, status symbols (such as make of car), architecture, and the like.
Mediational Codes	Nonverbal signs originating through differences and changes in an intervening or intermediary communication medium such as television, radio, magazines, and newspapers. Through decisions by the intervening media, the sent nonverbal or verbal message can be influenced. For example, the message from nonverbal behavior can be influenced somewhat by use of color or black-and-white, photography or cartoon, and close-up or long-shot.
Contextual Codes	Nonverbal signs originating through differences and changes in the use of time and space. Time might be divided up very precisely and used efficiently, such as within work organizations or viewed and used casually in between. Space between individuals might vary for different types of interaction, such as a small zone for intimate interaction and a large zone for interaction with strangers.

Adapted from Harrison, R. P., Nonverbal behavior: An approach to human communication, in Budd, R. W., and B. D. Ruben (eds.), *Approaches to Human Communication* (Rochelle Park: Spartan Books, 1972), pp. 253–268.

Impact of Nonverbal Communication. Nonverbal communication appears to have preceded verbal communication in the development of individual human beings. It may also strongly influence the content of verbal communication and the likelihood of its even taking place. The three major functions of nonverbal communications and examples of each have been aptly summarized by R. P. Harrison as follows (italics added):

First, they *define, condition,* and *constrain* the communication system between individuals. For instance, the time of day, or allotted time, the setting, and the arrangement of props may cue the participants on who is in the system, what the pattern of interaction will be, and what is appropriate or inappropriate conversational fare.

Secondly, nonverbal cues help to *regulate* the communication system. They signal status hierarchies, indicate who is to speak next, provide feedback about evaluations and intentions.

Finally, nonverbal signs (cues) communicate *content*. Sometimes, the nonverbal code is more efficient; for example, relationships are more easily preserved in an analogic code, such as a map, a blueprint, a picture, a model. Sometimes, the nonverbal code is more effective, perhaps because it uses an additional modality such as touch, or odor, or even taste. And sometimes, the nonverbal code increases the efficiency and effectiveness because it provides redundancy, another way of saying the same thing.[10]

In sum, nonverbal communications are a crucial component of all interpersonal communications. Later sections of this chapter consider some of the personal contingencies that might explain why the nature and quality of verbal and nonverbal communications are "what they are." But first developed are the ideas that (1) much interpersonal communication in organizations takes place in networks and (2) individuals often play different communication roles in organizations.

INTERPERSONAL COMMUNICATION NETWORKS

An *interpersonal communication network* is defined as "those interconnected individuals who are linked by patterned flows to any given individual."[11] The focus is on communication *relationships* between individuals rather than on the individuals themselves. What is of interest is the flow of verbal, nonverbal, written, or other forms of signals (data) between two or more group members. Since the concern is on relationships, the emphasis is on the pattern of signal flow, such as between member A and member B, or member A and all other members simultaneously, rather than on whether the signal sent was received as intended by the sender. Of course, communication networks can influence the likelihood of a match between the intended sent messages and the messages received.

The basic model of the communication process (Figure 8–1) assumed only two people were involved. But, of course, interpersonal communication often takes place in larger groups. In studying the possible direct effects of different communication networks, a single group of five members will be considered. This will minimize the complicating effects of different numbers of members in a group.

Group size places limits on the possible communication networks within a group. In principle, as the size of a group increases arithmetically, the number of possible interrelationships increases geometrically. Accordingly, there is, for example, a potential for disproportionately more variety and complexity in communication networks in a twelve-person group than in a five-person group.

While every member may theoretically be able to communicate with all other members in real-life groups, the direction and number of communication channels is often somewhat limited.[12] For example, in committee meetings, varying levels of formality in the rules and procedures influence who may speak, what may be discussed, and in what order. The relative status or ranking of group members also may differ, with the likely result of higher status members dominating the communications network. Finally, even where an open network is encouraged, the members may actually use a more constrained or limited network arrangement.

Types of Networks

Although there are about sixty possible communication networks for a five-person group, this section will concentrate on five basic communication networks of a five-person group. As a practical matter, the five networks presented in Figure 8–2 illustrate the major differences that may be found in a five-person group. These five basic communication networks are the *star* (sometimes called the *wheel*), the Y, the *chain*, the *circle*, and the *all-channel* network.

Each line between every pair of names represents a two-way communication channel. The networks are presented in terms of the degree of restriction on members in the use of communication channels. An inspection of the networks reveals that the star configuration is the most restricted since all communications must flow between Jane and each of the other members. At the other extreme, the all-channel network is the least restricted and most open, since each member may communicate with all other members simultaneously.

Effects of Different Networks

The importance of communication networks lies in the potential effects of different networks on such things as predicting group leaders, effectiveness, efficiency, and member satisfaction.[13] Table 8–2 provides a rough synthesis and comparison of the communication networks in terms of five assessment criteria. The first criterion, *degree of centralization,* is the extent to which some group members have access to more communication channels than other members. The star network is regarded as the most centralized, because all communications flow from and to only one member. The all-channel network is the least centralized because any member can communicate with any other member or all other members at the same time. The second criterion, *number of possible communication channels*, is closely related (but in the opposite direction) to the degree-of-centralization criterion. The number of possible communication channels is the extent to which an increased number of members have access to channels of communication. The number of possible communication

TABLE 8–2.   Some Comparisons of Five Communication Networks for Five-person Groups

	Types of Communication Networks				
	Star	"Y"	Chain	Circle	All-channel
Assessment Criteria					
Degree of centralization	Very high	High	Moderate	Low	Very low
Number of possible communication channels	Very low	Low	Moderate	Moderate	Very high
Leadership predictability	Very high	High	Moderate	Low	Very low
Average group satisfaction	Low	Low	Moderate	Moderate	High
Range in individual member satisfaction	High	High	Moderate	Low	Very low

channels for the members as a whole is at a minimum in the star network and at a maximum in the all-channel network. The criterion of *leadership predictability* measures the ability to anticipate which group member is likely to emerge as the group leader. In Figure 8–2, the following individuals are likely to emerge as leaders: Jane in the star network; Sam in the Y network; and possibly Sam in the chain network. In each of these three networks, the anticipated leader should have greater amounts of information and greater control over the dissemination of information, suggestions, and the like, than the other group members.

The fourth and fifth assessment criteria in Table 8–2 measure the *average satisfaction* of the group members as a whole within each network and the *range in satisfaction* between group members. There are a number of interesting relationships between these two criteria. In the star network, the *average* member satisfaction in the group is likely to be the lowest compared with the other networks. But the *range* in individual member satisfaction is likely to be high relative to the other networks. Why might this be the case? First, Jane would find the star network highly satisfying because she is the center of attention and has considerable influence over the group. But the other members are highly dependent on Jane and may well play a marginal role to her in the decision process. Accordingly, the average satisfaction of the group as a whole is likely to be relatively low. In contrast, the all-channel network creates the potential for greater participation by all members in terms of their interest and

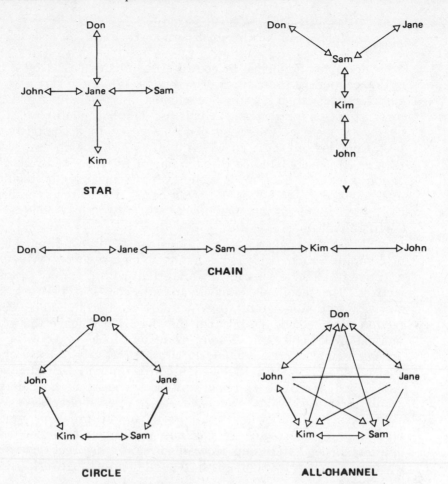

FIGURE 8–2.   Five Basic Communication Networks for Five-person Groups

ability to contribute to the group. Thus, while the average group satis-faction may be relatively high, there is likely to be a lower range between the satisfaction scores of individual members.

Guidelines for Application

As usual, the guidelines for using these and other findings regard-ing communication networks cannot be presented as a simple cookbook recipe to be applied under all conditions. At a basic level, communication problems can be differentiated as being simple or complex. Simple prob-lems make few demands on the members in terms of:

1. Collecting, categorizing, and evaluating information.
2. Generating goals or objectives to be achieved.

3. Developing and evaluating alternatives.
4. Coping with human problems associated with the task at hand.

Complex problems, in contrast, are characterized by a high degree of one or more of these types of demands. While the star network may be sufficiently effective for simple problems, the all-channel network is often most effective for complex problems. Another qualifying factor is the degree of member interdependence required to accomplish the group's task. Complex problems, in which there is little member interdependence, may be effectively handled through one of the more centralized communication networks. But since complex problems usually require member interdependence, this does not often occur. For complex problems requiring a high degree of member interdependence, the all-channel network is the most likely to be effective.

Several managerial implications can be drawn from this discussion of communication networks. First, no single network is likely to prove effective in all situations for a work group with a variety of tasks and objectives. The seemingly efficient and low-cost star network, if used exclusively by a work group, may actually be dysfunctional. Member satisfaction may become so low that individuals will leave the group or lose motivation to contribute. Second, complex problems requiring high member interdependence may be dealt with ineffectively because of inadequate sharing of information, inadequate consideration of alternatives, and the like. Third, trade-offs or opportunity costs must be considered. A work group committed to the exclusive use of the all-channel network could experience inefficiency in dealing with simple problems requiring little member interdependence. In such cases, members may also become bored and dissatisfied with group processes because they feel their time is being wasted. Another trade-off with the all-channel network is its implied labor costs.

In sum, whatever network most appropriately serves the group tasks or problems at hand should be used, with the simultaneous recognition of the impact on member satisfaction.

MODEL OF INTERPERSONAL COMMUNICATION STYLES

The styles by which people communicate in their communication networks can vary substantially. We mentioned earlier how people with different personality traits (sensation, intuition, thinking, and feeling types) would tend to send messages. This section describes five basic styles of interpersonal communication, the possible effects of each, and how each of us can improve our skills in giving feedback.[14]

The model of communication styles, as shown in Figure 8–2, is built upon a number of concepts and perspectives already presented. This model also serves to develop explicitly the concept and role of feedback in interpersonal communication styles.

Framework

Figure 8–3 is based upon two dimensions of interpersonal communications. One dimension, which is shown on the vertical axis as varying from low to high, is labeled as *openness to and from others*. This dimension attempts to capture both the idea of self-disclosure (opening or revealing oneself to others) and being receptive to feedback from others, particularly about how others perceive you and your actions. The second dimension, which is shown on the horizontal axis as varying from low to high, is labeled as *giving feedback*. This dimension is the degree to which individuals communicate their thoughts and feelings toward one or more individuals. The giving-feedback dimension can focus on very personal aspects of others or on more abstract aspects such as feeding back reactions to the ideas or proposals of others. Thus, the emotional impact of feedback is likely to vary as to how "personal" is its focus.

Five Styles

The five interpersonal communication styles identified in Figure 8–3 are: self-denying, self-protecting, self-exposing, self-bargaining, and self-actualizing.

Self-denying. The self-denying style refers to individuals who are isolated from others and very withdrawn. Introverted individuals are

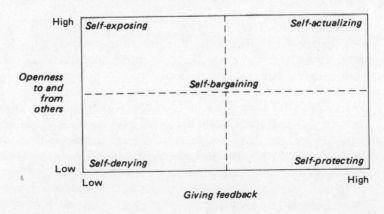

FIGURE 8–3.   Model of Interpersonal Communication Styles

Adapted from Polsky, H. W., "Notes on Personal Feedback in Sensitivity Training," Sociological Inquiry, 1971, 41, p. 179. Used with permission.

likely to be more prone to this communication style than are extroverted individuals. Self-denying individuals are low on openness to and from others and low on giving feedback.

Self-protecting.   The self-protecting style refers to individuals who probe others or make comments to others. However, the motivation in giving feedback may be a defensive measure to prevent the possibility of self-exposure and comments from others about themselves. The self-protecting style is high on giving feedback to others, but low on openness to and from others.

Self-exposing.   With the self-exposing style, individuals attempt to get others to focus on them by constantly asking for reactions to their behavior. Moreover, there is likely to be little internalization of the feedback by self-exposing individuals. It's like "water off a duck's back." The self-exposing style is low on giving feedback, but high on openness to and from others.

Self-bargaining.   The self-bargaining style refers to individuals who are willing to give feedback and open up in direct relation to the same process taking place with the others in the interaction. These individuals use themselves as a point of bargaining or negotiation. The self-bargaining style is moderate on giving feedback as well as moderate on openness to and from others.

Self-actualizing.   The self-actualizing style refers to individuals who spontaneously provide the appropriate amount of information about themselves, ask for feedback, and provide feedback in a constructive and non-defensive manner. The self-actualizing style is high on giving feedback as well as high on openness to and from others. Under ideal conditions, the self-actualizing communication style might be one we would like to experience. But even if we desire to produce the self-actualizing style, we may experience situational factors that motivate us to use some other style. One key situational factor is the approach that others take in communicating with us. If a superior is not receptive to receiving feedback, we may be reluctant to give feedback. Although it would be simplistic and unrealistic to suggest that there should be only one communication style for all situations, our biases, which are based on some research and personal values, lead us to conclude that the self-actualizing style is a desirable one to develop and use when possible.

Effective Feedback

Giving feedback is a crucial dimension in the model of interpersonal communication styles shown in Figure 8–2. Thus it is useful to consider some concepts and techniques for giving effective interpersonal feedback. These concepts and techniques are used by Proctor and Gamble and many other organizations as part of their development programs to build more effective working relationships on the job.[15] Of course, researchers in other settings have also found them helpful.[16] To be maximally useful to the receiver, feedback should be offered with the following concepts and techniques in mind:

1. Feedback should be *intended to help* the receiver. One question for testing this is to ask yourself: "Do I really feel that what I am about to say is likely to be helpful to the receiver?" While there may be circumstances in an organization where this is not possible, you are at least more likely to be aware of potential negative reactions by the receiver and possibly be prepared to cope with these reactions constructively rather than defensively.
2. Feedback should ideally be based upon a *foundation of trust* between the senders and receivers. If the organizational environment is characterized by extreme personal competitiveness, emphasis on the use of power to punish and control, rigid boss-subordinate relationships, and the like, the level of trust necessary for effective helping feedback will be lacking.
3. Feedback should be primarily *descriptive rather than evaluative*. If you describe a specific situation (in time and place) and tell the receiver(s) of the effect it had on you, the feedback is more likely to lead to further dialogue. This is in contrast to evaluating a situation or, more seriously, the receivers in terms of good or bad and right or wrong.
4. Feedback should be *specific rather than general*, with clear and preferably recent examples. To be told one is "dominating" will not be as useful as to be told "just now when we were deciding the issue you did not listen to what others said and I felt I had to accept your argument or face attack from you."
5. Feedback should be given at a time when the receiver appears to be in a condition of readiness to accept it. Thus, if a person is angry, upset, or defensive, it is probably not the time to bring up other and new issues.
6. Feedback should be checked with the receiver(s) to determine if it seems *valid to the receiver(s)*. One way of doing this is to have the receiver(s) rephrase and restate the feedback to see if it matches what the sender intended.
7. Feedback should include only those things that the receiver *might be capable of doing something about*.
8. Feedback should *not include more than the receiver can accommodate* at any particular time. For example, the receiver may become threatened and defensive if you unload "everything that bothers you" about the receiver.

In a study based on data collected from approximately 1,000 managers, which focused on the managers' perceptions of their use of self-disclosure and feedback with other employees—such as subordinates, peers, and colleagues, J. Hall reached the following conclusions, among others:

1. Power differences among organizational members appear to influence their willingness to communicate openly. More specifically, there seems to be an implicit mistrust in relationships with peers and qausi-sub-servient withdrawal tendencies in relationships with superiors.
2. Strong correlations between personality traits and communication styles (in a subsample of MBA students) served to emphasize the importance of individual characteristics in effective or ineffective commnunciation. Thus, a portion of communication problems in organizations is traceable to factors within individual members.[17]

The model of communication styles in Figure 8–3 should not be interpreted narrowly and mechanistically. It should serve as a diagnostic tool for considering your own and other styles. It is also a broad framework for considering paths for improving interpersonal communications by indicating the alternative styles that might be necessary and appropriate for individual "survival" under varying situations.

Personal feedback helps people to consider changing behavior by revealing to them the feelings aroused in others or by enabling them to see themselves as others do. It does not mean that if someone is given accurate feedback, which is accepted, that one has to change in the direction implied by the observation or impression.

Diagnosing Feedback Practices

Within organizations, various types of feedback take place. For a more personalized feel for feedback practices in organizations, turn to Figure 8–4. This figure provides a questionnaire that can be used to diagnose some of these feedback practices. Read each of the items presented in the diagnostic questionnaire and record your responses on a separate sheet of paper as to how you experienced the feedback practices in an organization that has employed you.

The first seven items are concerned with various aspects of negative feedback. Remember that negative feedback is not necessarily bad for the person who is receiving it. One of the keys in determining whether negative feedback will be effective is in terms of *how* it is done. A number

FIGURE 8–4.   Diagnosis of Feedback Practices*

Directions. Read each of the following statements and record your perceptions as to the feedback practices you have experienced in a previous or present job. Respond on the seven point continuum that ranges from "never" to "extremely often." Notice that the midpoint is "occasionally."

FACTORS AND ITEMS   *Scale*

Negative Feedback

	Never	*Occasionally*	*Extremely Often*
1. Your supervisor tells you that you are doing a poor job.	____	_____	_____
2. You receive a formal report of poor performance.	____	_____	_____
3. The supervisor really lets you have it.	____	_____	_____
4. The supervisor makes backhanded comments (like "Have a hard night?").	____	_____	_____
5. Your coworkers kid you about doing too little.	____	_____	_____
6. Coworkers tell you you've done something wrong.	____	_____	_____
7. You are told you should be doing something else.	____	_____	_____

Positive Feedback from Above

	Never	*Occasionally*	*Extremely Often*
8. You receive comments about completed jobs.	____	_____	_____
9. You receive a formal report of good performance.	____	_____	_____
10. Your supervisor tells you that you are doing a good job.	____	_____	_____
11. You have a regular performance review with your supervisor.	____	_____	_____
12. The supervisor treats you as an equal.	____	_____	_____

Positive Feedback from Nonhierarchical Others

	Never	*Occasionally*	*Extremely Often*
13. Coworkers kid you about doing too much.	____	_____	_____
14. Coworkers kid you about doing too well.	____	_____	_____
15. You know more people are using the company's product or service.	____	_____	_____
16. Coworkers like you a great deal.	____	_____	_____

Internal Feedback

	Never	*Occasionally*	*Extremely Often*
17. You meet your own goals.	____	_____	_____
18. You find better ways of doing the job.	____	_____	_____
19. You know how much you can do without making a mistake.	____	_____	_____

Adapted and modified from Herold, D. M., and M. M. Greller, "Feedback: The definition of a construct," *Academy of Management Journal,* 1977, 20, pp. 144–145. Used with permission.

of guidelines were presented in the previous section for giving constructive negative feedback.

The second factor has the common theme of positive feedback from individuals at higher organizational levels (items 8–12). Positive feedback attempts to reinforce and reward certain behaviors so that they are repeated in the future. The third factor (items 13–16) is also concerned with positive feedback, but it comes from individuals who are *not* in a hierarchical authority relationship. These first three factors are all concerned with feedback that comes from sources external to the individual.

By contrast, the fourth factor—internal feedback (items 17–19)—focuses on feedback that is created by your own observations and assessment of yourself. It is concerned with comparing your own observations of yourself with the criteria you hold within yourself. Someone who thought "I did a good job on this paper regardless of what the prof thinks" would be an example of this.

The diagnostic questionnaire in Figure 8–4 clearly shows that there are several forms of feedback available to individuals in organizations. The greater the compatibility between these forms of feedback, the less conflict can be expected within an individual or between individuals. Lack of compatibility between these forms of feedback may indicate that there are serious problems in interpersonal communication processes that need to be corrected.

PERSONAL CONTINGENCIES INFLUENCING INTERPERSONAL COMMUNICATION

The objective of this section is to consider several personal contingencies that influence the styles of interpersonal communication individuals are likely to use. The personal contingencies discussed are self-concept, self-disclosure, listening ability, and clarity of expression ability.[18]

Self-concept

Self-concept refers to how individuals see themselves and how they feel about what they see. It is a personal judgment of the degree of worthiness individuals hold toward themselves.[19] Ones self-concept is multidimensional, with some dimensions contributing more than others to the overall self-concept.[20] Self-concept may include such wide-ranging dimensions as height, weight, physical attractiveness, honesty, intelligence, and athletic ability. Evaluations of each dimension are determined by how you judge your own worth on that dimension and the degree of importance you assign to it. If you evaluate your athletic ability as very low but do not regard it as an important issue, it is not likely to affect your overall self-concept greatly.

Several crucial relationships exist between self-concept and communication styles. *First,* individuals whose self-concept involves inferiority, weakness, or inadequacy may have difficulty in conversing with others, expressing personal feelings, admitting when they have been wrong or in error, accepting constructive criticism from other persons, or taking a position contrary to others. Individuals with a weak self-concept are likely to be guarded and seclusive in interpersonal communication. They are most likely to use the self-denying or self-protecting styles of interpersonal communication.

Second, the relationship between self-concept and communication style seems to be circular. An important influence on the formation of and changes in one's self-concept is the verbal and nonverbal communications you receive from people who are significant to you. Communications from others influence learning about yourself as to whether you are liked or disliked, loved or hated, acceptable or unacceptable, and the like.

Third, individuals with strong self-concepts have usually had their needs for security, love, respect, and acceptance met from others who were significant, particularly in the childhood years.[21] As a result, their communication may be less inhibited and evaluative. They have an easier time using the self-actualizing style of interpersonal communication.

Self-disclosure

Self-disclosure is any information individuals consciously communicate verbally or nonverbally about themselves to one or more other individuals. You often unconsciously disclose much about yourself through what you do, how you act and react, your mannerisms, and how you say what you say.[22] However, this discussion of self-disclosure is limited to verbal and nonverbal communication about oneself that is consciously chosen for transmission.

While self-concept may influence self-disclosure, the two contingencies are not the same and do not necessarily vary with one another. Individuals with positive self-concepts may vary from high to very little disclosure about themselves. A crucial intervening variable between self-concept and self-disclosure in interpersonal communications is the *social norms* (standards as to acceptable and unacceptable actions) that have been formed in the particular group. Norms are important in determining what, when, where, and with whom it is regarded as appropriate to be relatively open or closed about oneself in interpersonal communications. Work groups often have social norms that make it inappropriate to give negative feedback to the boss about actions that may be interfering with productivity.

The ability to expose or express one's real self to one or a few significant other individuals is often a prerequisite for the development and maintenance of a healthy personality. The specific relationship between self-disclosure and mental health appears to be curvilinear. Nondisclosing individuals may be repressing their "selves" because to reveal themselves is seen as threatening. This could be represented by the self-protecting or self-denying communication style. Total-disclosure individuals, who continuously expose a great deal about themselves to anyone they meet, may be unable to relate and communicate with others because of a preoccupation with their own selves. This could be characteristic of the self-exposing style. A medium level of disclosure may be found in individuals who are quite open with a select number of very close individuals and moderately open with others consistent with the specific requirements of their social relationships. These individuals may tend to make relatively great use of the self-bargaining and self-actualizing styles. A healthy openness in a work setting might facilitate discussion and sharing of work-related problems individuals are having with their superiors. Of course, we are assuming that the superiors are approachable and receptive. A form of self-disclosure in the work setting that may not be consistent with a healthy personality would be a constant preoccupation with describing to superiors and peers sexual experiences in great detail.

The possible ties between personality, self-disclosure, and communication style have been dramatically expressed by S. M. Jourard:

> Healthy personality is manifested by a mode of what we call *authenticity*, or more simply, honesty. Less healthy personalities, people who function less than full, who suffer recurrent breakdowns or chronic impasses, may usually be found to be *liars*. They say things they do not mean. Their disclosures have been chosen more for cosmetic value than for truth. The consequence of a lifetime of lying about oneself to others, of saying and doing things for their sound and appearance, is that ultimately the person loses contact with his real self.
>
> The authentic being manifested by healthier personalities takes the form of unself-conscious disclosure of self in words, decisions, and actions.[23]

Self-disclosure between Hierarchical Levels.   The issue of authenticity and self-disclosure in interpersonal communications within organizations is often compounded between hierarchical levels. Individuals at one level have formal power (i.e., the ability to influence the allocation of rewards such as pay raises and promotions and punishments such as demotion or dismissal) relative to individuals at another level. Even if individuals are able and willing to engage in "appropriate" forms of self-disclosure at work, the degree to which superiors are perceived as trustworthy in not using the revealed information to punish, intimidate, or suppress is likely to influence the amount and form of self-disclosure. While this discussion has focused on self-disclosure as a function of the individual, the organizational climate and the leadership style of superiors can also influence levels of self-disclosure.

In recognition of hierarchical power relationships, the New England

Telephone Company introduced an upward communications program that had the goal of increasing self-disclosure. To have a system that could be trusted rather than feared, the communication program started with "private lines." This technique enabled all employees to discuss or question any issue of concern anonymously by mailing in a form or calling the full-time coordinating staff that administered the upward communications program. This staff then transmitted the issue, without identifying the employee, to the individuals who were responsible and/or had the necessary expertise to answer the problem. The coordinators received the reply, which was, in turn, fed back to the employee. Questions and answers of general interest were often published in the company newspaper.

In one two-year period, 2,500 questions or comments were processed, principally within the following categories: working conditions, benefits, promotions, transfers, assignments and compensation. A survey of employees (75 percent nonmanagement and 25 percent management) using the private-line program indicated that 79 percent were satisfied with the response to their questions and 93 percent indicated that they would use the private-line again.[24] While it may be unfortunate that a program such as this should even be necessary to get issues expressed, it does represent a constructive attempt to increase self-disclosure and, thus, communications within the context and realities of organizational power.

Listening Ability

Listening is defined as "an intellectual and emotional process that integrates physical, emotional, and intellectual inputs in a search for meaning and understanding."[25] Listening is effective when the sender's intended message is received and understood by the listener.

It has been estimated that as much as 40 percent of the work day of many white-collar workers is devoted to listening. However, tests of listening comprehension suggest that these employees listen at 25 percent efficiency.[26] While these figures might be quibbled over, the key point is that listening requires a meaningful portion of most employees' work day, particularly those in white-collar and managerial jobs. The quality and effectiveness of peer and superior-subordinate relationships is likely to be influenced somewhat by their listening ability when engaged in interpersonal communications.

A potential basic barrier to listening ability may exist in the fundamental nature of the listeners in terms of such previously discussed dimensions as self-concept, attitudes and values, level of knowledge, and problem-solving styles. If employees have developed an attitude of dislike for their superior, it may be extremely difficult to listen truly to the comments being made by the superior during performance review sessions. If a trainer is trying to explain something that so exceeds the trainee's basic level of knowledge, frustration may develop to such a high level that the individual simply "turns off" the trainer.

Improving Listening Ability.   The following concepts and guidelines can aid in increasing listening ability:[27]

1. Listeners should have a *reason or purpose* for listening. Good listeners tend to search for value and meaning in what is being said, even if they are not predisposed to be interested in the particular issue or topic. Poor listeners tend to rationalize any or all inattention on the basis of initial interest or noninterest.
2. Listeners should *suspend judgment*, at least initially. Good listening requires concentrating on the whole message of the sender, rather than forming evaluations of good or bad on the basis of the first few ideas presented.
3. Listeners should *resist distraction*, such as noises, views, and other people, and focus on the sender.
4. Listeners should wait *before responding* to the sender.
5. When the message is heavily emotion-laden or there is doubt as to what was intended, listeners should *rephrase* in their own words the content and feeling of what the sender appeared to be saying.
6. Listeners should *seek the important themes* of the sender by listening for the overall content-and-feeling message.
7. Listeners should use the time differential between rate of thought (400–500 words per minute) and rate of speech (100–150 words per minute) to *reflect upon content* and to *search for meaning*.

Most of these guidelines and concepts for improving listening ability are interrelated—you can't practice one without improving the others. As with the guidelines presented for improving feedback, it is much easier to understand or even be able to recall these guidelines and concepts than to develop them as a skill to be used in day-to-day interpersonal communications. Moreover, the guidelines for improving listening and feedback skills need to be linked up in the overall process of enhancing interpersonal communication. A variety of experiential exercises are available for assisting individuals in diagnosing and improving their listening ability.[28]

Example of Poor Listening.   This section is capstoned with a short, hypothetical incident between a college president and a student activist, which serves to capture the essence of the discussion of listening abilities. The incident is drawn from James and Jongeward.[29]

President:	What can I do for you, son?
Student:	Don't call me son! I'm not your son! I've talked to you before and you obviously didn't listen to a word I said. The demands I have represent a majority of the students here. You can't ignore them.
President:	I know those demands: I've read them before.
Student:	Do you understand them?
President:	Yes, I understand them, and for your own good, I can't accept any of these demands.

Student: You and your pompous friends had better start listening to us, because we're going to sit in your office forever!

President: O.K., I will listen to you, but I'll tell you right now, before you begin, that for your own good these demands are not being met.

One interpretation of the president's behavior is that he or she assumed that students must be controlled by authority, direction, and responsibility. The president was unwilling to discuss a new approach or listen to new ideas. Even when the president asserted, "O.K., I will listen to you . . . ," there was no active listening. For the most part, the president's "listening" was used to form challenging questions, create diversions, and plan counterattacks. Given this analysis of the president's listening and communication approach, how would you characterize and assess the student's listening skill? How would this script be rewritten if either party was trying to practice the guidelines for listening and giving feedback previously outlined?

Expression Ability

The fourth and last contingency to be considered in this section is facility of expression. *Expression ability* is the skill to say what we mean or to express what we feel. Lack of expression ability is due to such things as carelessness in speech, assuming other individuals understand what we mean, placing the burden of communication on the listener (i.e., "If it is clear to me, it must be clear to you"), and lack of knowledge or vocabulary in communicating thoughts so that they are interpretable by the listener. Feedback is one means for improving expression ability.

SUMMARY

The lifeblood of organizations is communication. This chapter has dealt with one part of the total system of communication that takes place in organizations—interpersonal communication. First, the chapter outlined the basic elements in the communication process: sender and receiver; transmitters and receptors; messages, channels, and noise; decoding, meaning, and encoding; and feedback. It then differentiated between and gave examples of verbal and nonverbal communication. Two types of verbal communication to minimize—pseudoquestions and clichés—were presented. Five basic communication networks were illustrated, and their advantages and disadvantages were detailed. A model of interpersonal communication styles was drawn with five basic styles: self-denying, self-protecting, self-exposing, self-bargaining, and self-actualizing. Finally, four personal contingencies—self-concept, self-disclosure, listening ability, and expression ability—that influence interpersonal communication were analyzed.

Our ability to engage in effective interpersonal communications plays an important part in determining our own sense of well-being as well as the probability of being viewed by others as a good employee. It is hoped that this chapter has provided some insight into developing your conceptual understanding of interpersonal communications as well as your human skills for communicating effectively.

This chapter has built upon earlier discussions, particularly Chapter 5 on the perceptual process and Chapter 8 on individual personality and problem solving. It should be apparent that our perceptions and tendencies to deal with problems in particular ways can influence the process of interpersonal communication. By introspecting into yourself in terms of these dimensions, you should be able to improve your own communication effectiveness as well as have greater empathy for and understanding of the strengths and limitations of others.

Refer back now to the two brief incidents presented at the beginning of this chapter and check your responses. The "best" answers in terms of applying the listening and feedback guidelines are number 3 for the first incident and number 1 for the second incident.

DISCUSSION QUESTIONS

1. What is the difference between encoding and decoding?

2. Describe the various nonverbal forms of communication utilized by someone you have worked for (or studied under). Were the nonverbal communications consistent or inconsistent with his or her verbal communications? Explain.

3. Is there one best communication network for a five-person group? Explain.

4. How would you compare the self-actualizing communication style with the self-exposing communication style?

5. Describe a situation in which you have used one or more of the communication styles presented. Do you think the style was effective or ineffective? Why do you feel as you do?

6. What problems and limitations do you see in obtaining meaningful self-disclosure between superiors and subordinates?

7. What similarities and differences are there in the recommendations for improving feedback and listening skills?

MANAGERIAL PROBLEMS

MANAGER-SUBORDINATE MEETING

The following meeting took place between a manager and subordinate.

Manager:	"Jim, I'd like to talk to you about your work. Will you join me in my office?"
Jim:	"Oh, okay, I'll be right with you."
Manager:	"I'll come right to the point. Your work has been deteriorating recently. Your productivity has fallen off and you've failed to meet three deadlines."
Jim:	"My work is as good as ever."
Manager:	"I'm not talking about how well you do things. I'm referring to how much you do and how quickly you do them."
Jim:	"Well, ever since we had to start using the new set-up procedure, nobody has been doing as much as before."
Manager:	"Jim, everyone in the section was consulted for their opinions before we installed it—including you. Nobody expressed any objections. If you want to talk about the production of the others, take a look at this production chart first."
Jim:	"Well, okay—so they're doing fine, but this new set-up throws me off."
Manager:	"Jim, your production started dropping before we began the new procedure."
Jim:	"Well, okay—so they're doing fine, but this new set-up Anyway, as they say, you can't teach an old dog new tricks."
Manager:	"Didn't your team leader explain it all to you?"
Jim:	"Yes, he did—but I guess I just didn't get it."
Manager:	"He told me he spent several hours with you."
Jim:	"I suppose he did—maybe I'm just thick."
Manager:	"We'll give you whatever assistance you need to understand it. If necessary, I'll arrange to streamline the production procedure on your line. Now, what about the deadlines, Jim —that's another matter."
Jim:	"Yes, but I can't possibly meet them with all these changes taking place."
Manager:	"Jim, you can take measures to make yourself more effective. I will do what I can to remove barriers to your performance. I'm setting up another meeting with you to go over positive measures that you can take to meet production standards. I expect you to . . ."

QUESTIONS

1. What interpersonal communication styles are apparently being used by the manager and Jim?
2. Do you feel that the guidelines for listening and giving feedback are being applied? Explain.
3. Did the manager do a good job in handling this meeting? Explain.

MR. HART AND BING*

The case is presented in two versions, A and B. Version A presents Mr. Hart's point of view, and version B presents Bing's point of view.

The shop situation reported in this case occurred in a work group of four men and three women who were engaged in testing and inspecting panels for electronic equipment. The employees were paid on a piecework incentive basis. The personnel organization of the company included a counselor whose duty it was to become acquainted with the workers and talk over any problems they wished to discuss with him. The following statements of the views of two men consist of excerpts from five interviews that the counselor had with each of them within a period of about two weeks.

Version A (Mr. Hart)

Say, I think you should be in on this. My dear little friend Bing is heading himself into a showdown with me. Recently it was brought to my attention by the Quality Control checker that Bing has been taking double and triple set-up time for panels which he is actually inspecting at one time. In effect, that's cheatin', and I've called him down on it several times before. A few days ago it was brought to my attention again, and so this time I really let him have it in no uncertain terms. He's been getting away with this for too long and I'm gonna put an end to it once and for all. I know he didn't like my calling him on it because a few hours later he had the union representative breathin' down my back. But you know what talkin' to those people is like; they'll sometimes defend an employee, even though they think he's takin' advantage of the company. Well, anyway, I let them both know I'll not tolerate the practice any longer, and I let Bing know that if he continues to do this kind of thing, I'm gonna take official action with my boss to have the guy fired or penalized somehow. This kind of thing has to be curbed. Actually, I'm inclined to think the guy's mentally deficient, because talking to him has actually no meaning to him what-

* This case, Mr. Hart and Bing, was prepared by Harriet Ronkin under the direction of Professor George F. F. Lombard as the basis for classroom discussion and not to illustrate either effective or ineffective handling of an administrative situation. Copyright 1949 by the President and Fellows of Harvard College. Reproduced by permission.

soever. I've tried just about every approach to jar some sense into that guy's head, and I've just about given it up as a bad deal. I just can't seem to make any kind of an impression upon him. It's an unpleasant situation for everyone concerned, but I'm at a loss to know what more I can do about it.

I don't know what it is about the guy, but I think he's harboring some deep feelings against me. For what, I don't know, 'cause I've tried to handle that bird with kid gloves. But his whole attitude around here on the job is one of indifference, and he certainly isn't a good influence on the rest of my group. Frankly, I think he purposely tries to agitate them against me at times, too. It seems to me he may be suffering from illusions of grandeur, 'cause all he does all day long is sit over there and croon his fool head off. Thinks he's a Frank Sinatra! No kidding! I understand he takes singin' lessons and he's working with some of the local bands in the city. All of which is OK by me; but when his outside interests start interfering with his efficiency on the job, then I've gotta start paying closer attention to the situation. For this reason I've been keepin' my eye on that bird and if he steps out of line any more, he and I are gonna part ways.

I feel quite safe in saying that I've done all I can rightfully be expected to do by way of trying to show him what's expected of him. You know there's an old saying, "You can't make a purse out of a sow's ear." The guy is simply unscrupulous. He feels no obligation to do a real day's work. Yet I know the guy can do a good job, because for a long time he did. But in recent months, he's slipped for some reason and his whole attitude on the job has changed. Why, it's even getting to the point now where I think he's inducing other employees to "goof off" a few minutes before the lunch whistle and go down to the washrooms and clean up on company time. I've called him on it several times, but words just don't seem to make any lasting impression on him. Well, if he keeps it up much longer, he's gonna find himself on the way out. He's asked me for a transfer, so I know he wants to go. But I didn't give him an answer when he asked me, 'cause I was steamin' mad at the time, and I may have told him to go somewhere else.

I think it would be good for you to talk with him frequently. It'll give him a chance to think the matter through a little more carefully. There may be something that's troubling him in his personal life, although I've made every effort to find out if there was such a thing, and I've been unsuccessful. Maybe you'll have better luck.

Version B (Bing)

According to the system 'round here, as I understand it, I am allowed so much "set-up" time to get these panels from the racks, carry them over here to the bench and place them in this jig here, which holds them in position while I inspect them. For convenience's sake and also to save time, I sometimes manage to carry two or three over at the same time and inspect them all at the same time. This is a perfectly legal thing to do. We've always been doing it. Mr. Hart, the supervisor, has other ideas about it, though; he claims it's cheating the company. He came over to the bench a day or two ago and let me know just how he felt about the matter. Boy, did we go at it! It wasn't so much the fact that he called me down on it, but more the way in which he did it. He's a sarcastic bastard. I've never seen anyone like him. He's not content just to say in a manlike way what's on his mind, but he prefers to do it in a way that makes you want to crawl inside a crack in the floor. What a guy! I don't mind being called down by a supervisor, but I like to be treated like a man, and not humiliated like a school teacher does a naughty kid. He's been pullin' this stuff ever since he's been a supervisor. I knew him when he was just one of us, but since he's been promoted he's lost his friendly way and seems to be havin' some difficulty in knowin' how to manage us employees. In fact, I've noticed that he's been more this way with us fellows since he's gotten married. I dunno whether there's any connection there, but I do know he's a changed man over what he used to be like when he was a worker on the bench with us several years ago.

When he pulled this kind of stuff on me the other day, I got so damn mad I called in the union representative. I knew that the thing I was doing was permitted by the contract, but I was just intent on making some trouble for Mr. Hart, just because he persists in this sarcastic way of handling me. I'm about fed up with the whole damn situation. I'm tryin' every means I can to get myself transferred out of his group. If I don't succeed and I'm forced to stay on here, I'm going to screw him every way I can. He's not gonna pull this kind of kid stuff any longer on me. When the union representative questioned him on the case, he finally had to back down, 'cause according to the contract an employee can use any timesaving method or device in order to speed up the process as long as the quality standards of the job are met. During the discussion with me and the union representative, Mr. Hart charged that it was a dishonest practice and threatened to "take it up the line" unless the union would curb me on this practice. But this was just an idle threat, 'cause the most he can do is get me transferred out of here, which is actually what I want anyway.

You see, he knows that I do professional singing on the outside. He hears me singin' here on the job, and he hears the people talkin' about my career in music. I guess he figures I can be so cocky because I have another means of earning some money. Actually, the employees here enjoy havin' me sing while we work, but he thinks I'm disturbing them and causing them to "goof off" from their work. It's funny, but for some reason I think he's partial to the three female employees in our group. He's the same with all us guys as he is to me, but with the girls he acts more decent. I don't know what his object is. Occasionally, I leave the job a few minutes early and go down to the washroom to wash up before lunch. Sometimes several others in the group will accompany me, and so Mr. Hart automatically thinks I'm the leader and usually bawls me out for the whole thing.

So, you can see, I'm a marked man around here. He keeps watchin' me like a hawk. Naturally, this makes me very uncomfortable. That's why I'm sure a transfer would be the best thing. I've asked him for it, but he didn't give me any satisfaction at the time. While I remain here I'm gonna keep my nose clean, but whenever I get the chance I'm gonna slip it to him, but good.

QUESTIONS

1. How would you characterize the styles of interpersonal communication of Mr. Hart and Bing?
2. What personal contingencies in interpersonal communications seem to be operating in this case?
3. What problems and failures in interpersonal communication have taken place in this case?
4. What can be done to improve the interpersonal communications?

KEY WORDS

Interpersonal communication
Channels
Noise
Decoding
Meaning
Encoding
Feedback
Positive feedback
Negative feedback
Pseudoquestion
Cliché
Nonverbal communication
Interpersonal communication
   network

Self-denying communication
   style
Self-protecting communication
   style
Self-exposing communication
   style
Self-bargaining communication
   style
Self-actualizing communication
   style
Self-concept
Self-disclosure
Listening
Expression ability

REFERENCES

1. Roth, R. A., Control of the technical function, *Advanced Management-Office Executive*, 1963, pp. 20–24.

2. Budd, R. W., and B. D. Rubin (eds.), *Approaches to Human Communication* (Rochelle Park, N.J.: Spartan Books, 1972).

3. Sigband, H., *Communication for Management.* Glenview, Ill.: Scott, Foresman, 1969), p. 10.

4. Baird, J. E., Jr., *The Dynamics of Organizational Communication* (New York: Harper and Row, 1977), p. 6.

5. Herbert, T. T., Toward an administrative model of the communication process, *Journal of Business Communications*, 1977, 14, pp. 25–35.

6. Lynch, D., In style with the other guy, *TWA Ambassador*, 1977, 10, pp. 28–31.

7. Adapted from Pfeffer, J. W., and J. E. Jones, Don't you think that . . . ? An experimental lecture on indirect and direct communication, in Pfeffer, J. W., and J. E. Jones, *1974 Annual Handbook for Group Facilitators* (La Jolla, Calif.: University Associates, 1974), pp. 203–208.

8. Berne, E., *Games People Play* (New York: Grove Press), 1964.

9. Watzlawick, D., J. H. Beavin, and D. D. Jackson, *Pragmatics of Human Communication: A Study of Interactional Patterns, Pathologies, and Paradoxes* (New York: W. W. Norton, 1967), p. 9.

10. Harrison, R. P., Nonverbal behavior: An approach to human communication, in *Approaches to Human Communication*, Budd, R. W., and B. A. Ruben (eds.) (Rochelle Park, N.J.: Spartan Books), 1972, p. 258.

11. Laumann, E. O., *Bonds of Pluralism: The Form and Substance of Urban Social Networks* (New York: Wiley-Interscience, 1973), p. 7.

12. Glazer, M., and R. Glazer, *Techniques for the Study of Team Structure and Behavior*, Part II: Empirical studies of the effects structure (Pittsburgh: American Institute for Research, 1957).

13. Guetzkow, H., and H. Simon, The impact of certain communication nets upon organization and performance in task-oriented groups, *Management Science*, 1, 1955, pp. 233–250.

14. This section is adapted from Polsky, H., Notes on personal feedback in sensitivity training, *Sociological Inquiry*, 1971, 41, pp. 175–182.

15. Anderson, J., Giving and receiving feedback, in *Managers and Their Careers: Cases and Readings*, Lorsch, J. W., and L. B. Barnes (eds.) (Homewood, Ill.: Richard D. Irwin, 1972), pp. 260–267.

16. Mead, W. R., Feedback: A how to primer for T-group participants, in *Sensitivity Training and the Laboratory Approach: Readings, Concepts and Applications*, Golembiewski, R. T., and A. Blumberg (eds.) (Itasca, Ill.: F. E. Peacock Publishers, 1977), pp. 66–69.

17. Hall, J., Interpersonal style and the communication dilemma: Managerial implications of the Johari awareness model, *Human Relations*, 1974, 27, pp. 381–399.

18. Adapted from Bienvenu, M. J., Jr., An interpersonal communication inventory, *The Journal of Communication*, 1971, 21, pp. 381–388; Chartier, M. R., Five components contributing to effective interpersonal communications, in Pfeffer and Jones *Annual Handbook*, pp. 125–128.

19. Coppersmith, S., *The Antecedents of Self-Esteem* (San Francisco: W. H. Freeman, 1967), p. 95.

20. Sherwood, J. J., Self-identity and referent others, *Sociometry*, 1965, 28, pp. 66–81.

21. Arieti, S., *The Intrapsychic Self: Feeling, Cognition, and Creativity* (New York: Basic Books), 1967.

22. Cozby, P. C., Self-disclosure: A literature review, *Psychological Bulletin*, 1973, 79, no. 2, pp. 73–91.

23. Jourard, S. M., *Disclosing Man to Himself* (New York: Van Nostrand Reinhold, 1968), pp. 46–47.

24. Harriman, B., Up and down the communication ladder, *Harvard Business Review*, 1974, 52, pp. 143–151; also see Bacharach, S. B., and M. Aiken, Communication in administrative bureaucracies, *Academy of Management Journal*, 1977, 20, pp. 365–377; Muchinsky, P. M., Organizational communication: Relationships to organizational climate and job satisfaction, *Academy of Management Journal*, 1977, 20, pp. 592–607.

25. Chartier, Interpersonal communications, p. 126.

26. Listening is a 10-part skill, in Nicholas, R. G., *Successful Management* (New York: Doubleday, 1957).

27. Reik, T., *Listening with the Third Ear* (New York: Pyramid Publications, 1972).

28. Ruben, B. A., and R. W. Budd, *Human Communication Handbook: Simulations and Exercises* (Rochelle Park, N.J.: Hayden Book, 1975).

29. James, J., and A. Jongeward, *Born to Win: Transactional Analysis with Gestalt Experiments* (Reading, Mass.: Addison-Wesley, 1971), pp. 227–230.

PART IV

GROUP
PROCESS

9

Dynamics Within Groups

9

LEARNING OBJECTIVES

When you have finished reading and studying this chapter, you should be able to:

▲ Understand why people do what they do in work groups.

▲ Perceive trouble spots and possible reasons why work groups may be operating at a less than optimal level.

▲ Consider alternative ways of behaving to increase the personal rewards available to people in work groups.

▲ Appreciate the contingencies that influence groups, and thereby understand how group members can play a positive role in determining their ultimate achievement level.

▲ Recognize that the managerial role requires dealing with both individuals and groups.

▲ Present some ways for diagnosing and assessing work groups.

THOUGHT STARTERS

▲ Why are some groups more successful than others?

▲ What makes a good group leader? A good group member?

▲ Why do people join groups?

Recently Alice, a first-line supervisor, sat at her desk wondering about a problem that faced her. Maria was a newly hired clerk in Alice's unit whose acceptance into the group was not going well. Although Alice was a relatively new supervisor, she had been a senior clerk in this unit and had seen many new employees come into the group. All these people, as far as Alice could remember, had easily fitted into the scheme of things. Alice was perplexed by Maria's case because she was unable to pinpoint what was going wrong and felt that she did not have the tools for deciding how to help make Maria's transition into the group successful.

Maria was a young Hispanic who had been with the company for two months. She had come directly from a training program in the inner city. Maria's level of office skills was below standard when she was hired and, although she had been working hard, she was progressing at a slow pace. A number of events complicated Maria's situation. For example, the members of the unit did not accept Maria. Alice was especially concerned when she overheard some of the employees complain that it was difficult to understand Maria's "broken English" and that they thought Maria was "strange." The group's rejection of Maria, Alice was convinced, caused her on-the-job training to suffer significantly. In addition, her indoctrination to the department was less thorough than for others who had entered the group, and she appeared to be isolated from the emotional support of the group members—support that had been important to new employees in the past.

No easy prescriptions are available to Alice that will guarantee sure-fire solutions in handling the situation between Maria and her coworkers.[1] However, this chapter should go a long way in helping Alice diagnose and understand the types of group problems in this situation and some of the ways by which she might solve or reduce them.

The preceding four chapters focused on the individual, particularly in terms of perceptions, learning, personality and problem solving, and interpersonal communications. The insights provided in these chapters could certainly be of help to Alice. However, they are not likely to provide Alice with the whole picture in dealing with this case. She needs knowledge and skills for dealing with groups as well as with individuals. The next two chapters focus on groups and relations between groups within formal organizations.

These two chapters discuss only concepts and findings that are potentially useful in assisting individuals within organizations to better understand, diagnose, and possibly improve the groups within which they function. The specific "technologies" for improving the effectiveness of groups and intragroup relations will be considered more directly in the last part of the book, which is concerned with organizational change and intervention.

The strategy of this chapter is to discuss five major components for considering groups, while explicitly recognizing the interdependencies between them. The major components discussed in this chapter are: (1) the relation between individuals and groups; (2) the sources of attraction to groups for individuals; (3) some major contingencies that have been identified as affecting group members and the ways groups operate; (4) decision processes within groups; and (5) methods for diagnosing work groups. The issue of group effectiveness is also considered throughout the chapter. For the purposes of this chapter, a *group* is defined as "a number of persons who communicate with one another often over a span of time, and who are few enough so that each person is able to communicate with all the others, not at secondhand, through other people, but face to face."[2] The focus is on the interactions of group members and/or the outputs of the group as a whole, rather than on several individuals who just happen to be close to each other over some period of time. Groups differ from larger systems, such as a division of an organization or an entire organization, in several fundamental ways. *First,* for a group to exist, the members must be able to see and hear each other. *Second,* each group member must engage in two-way personal communication with every other member. *Third,* there must be minimal hierarchical distinctions in the sense of a chain of command such as one might find in the military or other formal organizations. However, this is not to suggest that there are no status distinctions or differences between members in their relative influence in the group.

INDIVIDUAL-GROUP RELATIONS

Within the United States, there is strong belief in the importance and centrality of the individual. Our educational, governmental, religious, and business institutions frequently proclaim that their reason for existence is intimately related to enhancing the welfare of the individual. We are in substantial agreement with the assertion that "individuals are the foci of human value, dignity, and worth; individuals are the source of new ideas; the growth of society depends on the creativity of individuals; and new values originate in the minds of individuals."[3] But our concern is that this view of the individual leads to a narrow restriction in the understanding of organizational behavior. Viewing the individual as the major and/or only unit of analysis worthy of consideration limits the potential understanding of organizational behavior.

Social Component of Individuals

Nineteenth-century individualism, which idealized self-reliance, self-determination, and self-made men, ignored the social component of the individual. But with the disappearance of the land frontier of the United

States in the early 1900s, the social component began to be acknowledged. The abstractions of pure rugged individualism and self-sufficiency began to lose their validity. Since then, the complexity of relations between individuals has become increasingly apparent. While individuals play a substantial role in choosing the kind of persons they want to become, many skills, values, and modes of behavior must be acquired through group relations. The importance of groups and their relation to the social component of individuals, who are often lauded as being "self-made," was expressed by Marian Anderson (the contralto who became the first black to sing a leading role at the Metropolitan Opera). Anderson was asked why she used "one does" and "we do" instead of using "I."

> Possibly because the longer one lives, one realizes that there is no particular thing that you can do alone. With the execution of the work that we do there are many people—those who write the music, those who made the piano on which the accompanist is playing, the accompanist who actually lends support to the performance. To go out without any of these things, to stand on your own, even the voice, even the breath, the notion that you have, to go to the platform, is not your own doing. So the "I" in it is very small after all.[4]

While neither society nor organizations can be adequately envisioned as a set of isolated individuals, the 1950s ushered in a new series of worries. Some social critics began to suggest that the pendulum had swung to excessive subordination of the individual to groups.[5] Similarly, in the late 1960s, more and more young people began to worry that organizational life required conformity and "groupthink" for success. Such conformity and suppression of individual qualities were increasingly perceived as being antagonistic to one's personal self and immediate role as a unique being.

Importance of the Group to the Individual

Although there is certainly the potential for individuals and groups to have incompatible interests, it is just as important to recognize that these interests and relations need not be conflicting and are often compatible. This position is summed up in five assertions presented by Cartwright and Lippitt about individuals and groups:

1. Groups do exist; they must be dealt with by any man of practical affairs, or indeed by any child, and they must enter into any adequate account of human behavior. . . .
2. Groups are inevitable and always present. . . .
3. Groups mobilize powerful forces that produce effects of the utmost importance to individuals. . . .
4. Groups may produce both good and bad consequences. . . .
5. A correct understanding of group dynamics permits the possibility that desirable consequences from groups can be deliberately enhanced.[6]

Accordingly, our position is a highly contingent one. Some processes and problems may appropriately be solved by the individual; others, by the group; and still others, by consideration of both.

Types of Groups

Individuals may become members of many types of groups. There is no right or wrong way of classifying groups. If you are concerned with the degree of difficulty in gaining membership or becoming accepted as a group member, you might develop a classification scheme that differentiates groups according to whether they are open or closed to new members. If you are evaluating groups in an organizational setting according to the primary purpose they seem to be serving, the classifications of friendship groups and task (work) groups might be useful. *Friendship groups* serve the primary purpose of meeting the members' personal needs of security, esteem, and the like. *Task groups* interact for the primary purpose of accomplishing organizationally defined goals. Of course, a single group in an organization can serve both friendship and task purposes.

Task groups can be further classified on the basis of the nature of the interdependencies between group members in accomplishing some task or objective. For example, three types of task groups have been identified in terms of the nature of member interdependency: interacting, coacting, and counteracting.[7]

An *interacting group* exists when a group cannot perform a task until all members have completed their share of the task. This is illustrated by a production group, such as the assembly teams utilized at Samsonite Luggage. Each team consists of about ten people who perform the separate tasks required to assemble a complete piece of luggage. If one task is not undertaken, the complete task—the finished suitcase—is not realized.

A *coacting group* exists when the group members perform their jobs relatively independently, in the short run, of each other. The qualifiers "relatively" and "in the short run" are added because if there was no interdependency over time, there would not be a work group. For example, faculty members may be independent in the day-to-day teaching of their courses but highly interdependent in considering changes in courses or new course offerings.

A *counteracting group* exists when members interact to resolve some type of conflict, usually through negotiation and compromise. Labor-management negotiating teams illustrate counteracting groups. The discussion in this chapter emphasizes interacting groups.

SOURCES OF ATTRACTION TO GROUPS

In the opening pages of this chapter, several desirable and undesirable impacts of groups on individuals were suggested. Now considered are the sources of attraction of groups for individuals. Depending upon how the individual perceives them, each of the sources of attraction could also represent sources of rejection. This presentation draws heavily from the scheme presented by Shaw.[8] The types of personal needs satisfied from membership within a group include interpersonal factors, group activities, and group goals. In addition, some personal needs could be satisfied outside the group, but only through group membership. In this instance, the group becomes a means and the ultimate attraction may be to others or goals outside the group. These sources of attraction to a group are depicted in Figure 9–1.

Although all these sources of attraction are discussed as if they were independent of each other, there are several complicating factors worth noting. *First*, each factor can vary in intensity, or strength, of attraction. For example, interpersonal factors could weigh heavily in the attraction a group holds for an individual, but group activities may have little significance. *Second*, the presence and intensity of all four factors simultaneously are likely to increase the strength of attraction relative to fewer factors and/or lower intensities. *Third*, these four factors are also potential sources of rejection of the group, depending upon the individual's perception of them (as suggested by the minus signs in Figure 9–1). *Fourth*, some factors may be sources of attraction and others sources of rejection, raising the possibility of internal conflict for the individual.

Interpersonal Factors

An individual may obtain personal satisfaction in a group because of the perceived attractiveness in the physical appearance, attitudes and values, or abilities of other members or because of the psychological comforts the group offers. In some cases, such as a work group where the members have little or no influence in the choice of individuals who join them, interpersonal factors are not likely to have a major influence on the decision to join the work group. Interpersonal factors, however, often influence the job applicant and prospective superior and/or peers when they participate in the selection process.

Physical attractiveness is one of the more obvious sources of attraction of an individual to a group. The importance of this dimension can vary widely within work groups. The difficulties extensively reported by some women and minority members in gaining full acceptance into work groups composed of white males is a notable case. Apparently, sex and race are unfortunately sometimes perceived as undesirable physical characteristics in the work group.

The similarity of an individual to the group, particularly in terms of attitudes and values, may play a significant role in organizational settings. You can well imagine the potential for mutual rejection between an individual and group who do not share compatible values. In a CBS television

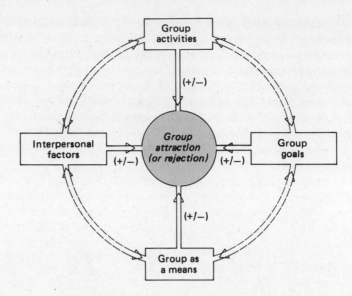

FIGURE 9–1.   Possible Sources of Attraction to or Rejection by a Group

special on Phillips Petroleum Co., several Phillips' executives indicated that they investigate and evaluate the attitudes and values of college recruits to determine whether they are compatible with the company. Even where the issue of attitude similarity is not explicit, it plays some role, possibly at a subconscious level, in many work-group situations. The excessive demand and pressure for maintaining and creating attitude similarity raises the oftentimes expressed concerns about conformity, groupthink, "sheeplike" behavior, and lack of individual freedom. While there is often considerable diversity evidenced in organizations and society, it should be noted that much of this apparent diversity is *between* groups or organizations. Diversity *within* small groups is likely to be considerably less. This point will be developed later in the chapter.

The perceived ability or similarity in the ability of others may be a particularly strong form of attraction. If an individual needs to accomplish certain tasks that are interdependent with the tasks being performed by others (such as in interacting or coacting groups), it is apparent that there might be a motivation to avoid affiliating with an incompetent and ineffective group.

Finally, an individual may be attracted to a group because it provides a setting in which the need for affiliation, survival, and security is met. Membership in a group may reduce a real or imagined threat, such as a new superior that threatens members of the work group with dismissal if they don't shape up. This is also true for large-scale organizations such as labor unions or trade organizations. Regardless of group size, the underlying rationale is the same: In unity there is strength. Even if no real threat exists, group membership may reduce the debilitating condition of excessive anxiety by meeting the individual's need for affiliation.

Group Activities

Attraction to a group may occur simply because the individual likes the activities or things done by the group. This has probably increased in relevance as individuals with higher educational levels and more specific skills seek out opportunities to apply their skills and talents within organizations. These individuals seek out work groups in which the other members have complementary and supporting skills. For example, a student who has developed accounting skills and enjoys these activities will seek out those work groups that need the application of these skills.

Group Goals

The goals of a group and its activities may be, but are not inherently, interrelated. Similar activities may be used to accomplish different goals. Moreover, individual goals and values may be compatible, neutral, or incompatible with group goals. An engineering graduate might be highly attracted to the general types of activities performed by a work group in a chemical firm, until he or she learns that the ultimate purpose of this group is to provide fundamental knowledge that can be used to increase the kill power of a chemical manufactured by the firm. If the individual is a pacifist, the group goals and personal goals are likely to be in sharp conflict with each other. Or a new employee might be attracted to the types of activities of a work group, but decide to leave when it is determined that their real purpose is to fight management, "goof off," and minimize output. The assumption here is that the individual's goals include high achievement and performance.

Group as a Means

A group is a means when the individual is attracted to it in order to attain one or more goals external to the group. This can occur in small groups or in large groups such as fraternities, sororities, country clubs, and political groups. For example, one study found that belonging to certain business firms increased the recognition and status of the members in the community.[9] Some work groups receive recognition and status from others outside the group because of such things as having more autonomy or more interesting work. Thus the attraction to the group may be based on several factors, including the nature of the group activities and the ability of the group to serve as a means for obtaining external recognition and status.

In sum, a group can have a powerful attraction to an individual for a variety of reasons. At the same time, groups often hold an inherent dilemma for the individual. One author suggests that the individual "wishes to be part of the group and at the same time to remain a separate, unique individual. He wants to participate, yet observe; to relate to, yet not become the other, to join, but to preserve his skills as an individual."[10]

SOME CONTINGENCIES
AFFECTING GROUPS

This section presents some of the major contingencies that can affect groups, particularly work groups, in terms of their behavior and outputs. By behavior is meant the activities and interactions within the group. *Activities* of a group are the "things that people do: work on the physical environment, with implements, and with other persons."[11] Activities is a broad concept that can include a variety of behaviors, such as writing, walking, drinking, typing, sawing, giving instructions. *Interactions* in a group refer to the "fact that some unit of activity of one man follows, or, if we like the word better, is stimulated by some unit of activity of another, aside from any question of what the units (of activity) may be."[12] Again, interaction is a broad concept and most often takes place through verbal and nonverbal communications. The *outputs* of a group are such things as member sentiments and the achievement of certain tasks and goals. *Sentiments* are "internal states of the human body . . . and range . . . all the way from fear, hunger, and thirst, to such probably far more complicated psychological states as liking or disliking for individuals, approval or disapproval of their actions."[13] The achievement of tasks and goals can vary from the making of decisions to the creation of physical objects. Typically, a staff or managerial group primarily has decisions as their outputs, whereas a work group in a manufacturing plant primarily has physical objects as their outputs, such as assembled luggage.

Figure 9–2 identifies a number of contingencies that can influence the behavior and outputs of a group, from the standpoint both of the group as a whole and of the individual members. Of course, these contingencies are interrelated, as suggested by the line between each of them in Figure 9–2. For example, the size of a group is likely to have an impact on member composition, which in turn, is likely to influence the norms in the group. To keep the discussion from becoming excessively complex, only some of the more important interrelationships between these variables are mentioned.

Keep in mind three fundamental points in reading this section. *First*, the nature of each of these contingencies can vary between groups and within a group over time. *Second*, these variables can be consciously influenced by the members, unconsciously influenced by the members, and/or influenced by factors external to the group. Thus the variables affecting groups, particularly work groups, can be dynamic and changing over time. *Third*, the behavior and outputs of groups can also be variables that ultimately influence a group. This is suggested by the lines with double arrow-

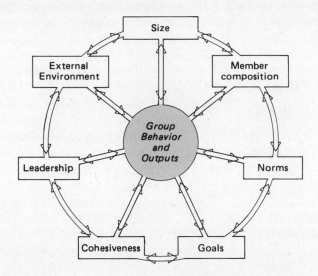

FIGURE 9–2.   Some Contingencies Affecting Groups

heads between a contingency and the box labeled "Group Behavior and Outputs."

Size

The size of a group can range from two members to a normal upper limit of twelve members and rarely more than sixteen members. In the way a group is defined in this chapter, twelve members is probably the upper limit for each member to react and interact with every other member simultaneously.[14] Table 9–1 lists some of the possible effects of size on groups. The table shows nine dimensions of groups within the three categories of leadership, members, and group process. The likely effects of group size for each of these dimensions is shown as varying from low, to moderate, to high. The tendencies identified indicate changes that are likely to occur with increases in the number of group members. As suggested in Table 9–1, groups of eight or more members are often quite different from groups with two to seven members. A sixteen-member board of directors is likely to operate quite differently from a board of seven members. Of course, boards of directors often form subgroups of five to seven members to consider specific decisions in greater depth than is possible with the whole board meeting at the same time.

As with all the contingencies that can affect groups, a number of qualifications can be introduced to the tendencies identified in Table 9–1.[15] For example, if there is considerable time available to the group and the members are sufficiently committed to the group activities and goals, the tendencies identified might not become nearly so pronounced beyond seven

TABLE 9–1.   Some Possible Effects of Size on Groups

Dimensions	Group Size		
	2–7 Members	8–12 Members	13–16 Members
LEADERSHIP			
1. Demands on leader	Low	Moderate	High
2. Differences between leaders and members	Low	Low to moderate	Moderate to high
3. Direction by leader	Low	Low to moderate	Moderate to high
MEMBERS			
4. Tolerance of direction from leader	Low to high	Moderate to high	High
5. Domination of group interaction by a few members	Low	Moderate to high	High
6. Inhibition in participation by ordinary members	Low	Moderate	High
GROUP PROCESS			
7. Formalization of rules and procedures	Low	Low to moderate	Moderate to high
8. Time required for reaching judgmental decisions	Low to moderate	Moderate	Moderate to high
9. Tendency for subgroups to form within group	Low	Moderate to high	High

members. If the group's primary activity and goal is to bring together the expertise of each respective member to arrive at decisions primarily based on expertise rather than judgment, a larger group would not necessarily experience the tendencies identified.

Member Composition

Similarities or differences among individual members and the roles they prefer to assume in the group can also influence the processes and outcomes of a group.[16] Recall the discussion in Chapter 7 about differences in individual problem-solving styles. Individuals were differentiated by their preference for taking in information from the outside world—either by sensation or by intuition—and by the two basic ways of reaching a decision

—either by thinking or by feeling. Combining the two information-input approaches and the two decision-making approaches results in a model of problem-solving styles with four basic types: sensation-thinking, sensation-feeling, intuition-thinking, and intuition-feeling. Problem-solving groups can have their processes and decisions affected by the particular combination of member personalities in the group. For example, a group with three strong sensation-thinking types and three intuition-feeling types is likely to generate more conflict and divergence of opinion than if the group consisted of members of one type. Of course, this divergence of viewpoint may be highly desirable. On the other hand, differences in group members can lead to conflict that escalates to the point that no agreement can be reached. Since a manager can rarely alter the personalities of members of a task group, it may be more useful to focus on influencing the behavioral roles in the group.

In general, roles in groups can be classified as to whether they are task-oriented, relations-oriented, or self-oriented.[17] The *task-oriented role of members facilitates and coordinates problem-solving activities*. It may be broken down into the following subroles:

1. *Initiator:* Offers new ideas or modified ways of regarding group problems or goals; suggests solutions to group difficulties, new group procedures, and new group organization.
2. *Information seeker:* Seeks clarification of suggestions in terms of factual adequacy and/or authoritative information and pertinent facts.
3. *Information giver:* Offers facts or generalizations that are "authoritative" or relates own experience pertinent to group problem.
4. *Coordinator:* Clarifies relationships among ideas and suggestions, pulls ideas and suggestions together, or tries to coordinate activities of members of subgroups.
5. *Evaluator:* Assesses "standards" of group functioning; may evaluate or question "practicality," "logic," "facts," or "procedure" of suggestions or of some unit of group discussion.

The *relations-oriented role of members builds group-centered activities and viewpoints*. It may be broken down into the following subroles:

1. *Encourager:* Praises, agrees with, and accepts others' ideas; indicates warmth and solidarity in attitude toward other members.
2. *Harmonizer:* Mediates intragroup scraps; relieves tension.
3. *Gatekeeper:* Encourages and facilitates participation of others by using such expressions as, "Let's hear . . ." "why not limit length of contributions so all can react to problem?"
4. *Standard setter:* Expresses standards for group to attempt to achieve in its functioning or applies standards in evaluating the quality of group processes; raises questions of group goals and purpose and assesses group movement in light of these objectives.
5. *Follower:* Goes along passively; provides friendly audience.
6. *Group observer:* Stays out of group's proceedings; functions by giving feedback as to what goes on during various phases of the meeting.

Finally, the *self-oriented role focuses only on the members individual needs, often at the expense of the group*. It may be broken into the following subroles.

1. *Blocker:* Negativistic; stubbornly and unreasoningly resistant; tries to bring back an issue the group intentionally rejected or bypassed.
2. *Recognition-seeker:* Tries to call attention to self; may boast, report on personal achievements, and, in unusual ways, struggles to prevent being placed in "inferior" position.
3. *Dominator:* Tries to assert authority in manipulating group or some individuals in group; may use flattery or assertion of superior status or right to attention; interrupts contributions of others.
4. *Avoider:* Maintains distance from others; passive resister; tries to remain insulated from interaction.

Effective problem-solving groups are often composed of group members who serve both the task- and relations-oriented subroles. Obviously, one individual may act out two or more of these subroles. An individual who is adept at acting out several of the task- and relations-oriented subroles is likely to have relatively high status in the group. Status simply refers to the relative ranking of an individual in comparison with others in the group. A group that is dominated by individuals who are primarily acting out the self-oriented subroles is likely to be ineffective.

Table 9–2 provides a concise summary of the task-oriented, relations-oriented, and self-oriented role behaviors. Moreover, it provides a scale for ranking how often these role behaviors occur in a task group.

In sum, a key contingency in influencing group behavior and outputs is the composition of group members and the role behaviors they act out. In attempting to draw conclusions about the effects of member composition on group effectiveness or performance, it should be recognized that either too much or too little of certain attributes of members could adversely influence group effectiveness.[18]

Norms

In the most limited sense, *norms* are generally agreed upon standards of member and group behavior that have emerged as a result of member interaction over time. In the broader sense, a norm is the "behavior that is anticipated and expected by the group of its members."[19] Thus individuals may join or form groups in which many of the norms actually exist prior to group interaction. For example, bricklayers who have never worked together before may begin work at a construction site with a common norm as to about how many bricks should be laid on an average workday.

Norms differ from organizational rules in that they are unwritten and must have some degree of acceptance and implementation by members before they can be said to exist. Rules may be written and distributed to all

TABLE 9–2.   Role Behaviors of Members in Task Groups

	Never	Seldom	Often	Frequently
Task-oriented Behavior				
1. Initiates ideas or actions	1	2	3	4
2. Facilitates introduction of facts and information	1	2	3	4
3. Clarifies issues	1	2	3	4
4. Evaluates	1	2	3	4
5. Summarizes and pulls together various ideas	1	2	3	4
6. Keeps the group working on the task	1	2	3	4
7. Consensus taker—asks to see if group is near decision	1	2	3	4
8. Requests further information	1	2	3	4
Relations-oriented Behaviors				
1. Supports, encourages others	1	2	3	4
2. Reduces tension	1	2	3	4
3. Harmonizer—keeps peace	1	2	3	4
4. Compromiser—finds common ground	1	2	3	4
5. Encourages participation	1	2	3	4
Self-oriented Behaviors				
1. Expresses hostility	1	2	3	4
2. Seeks recognition	1	2	3	4
3. Avoids involvement	1	2	3	4
4. Dominates group	1	2	3	4
5. Nitpicks	1	2	3	4

members in the form of manuals and memorandums, but they may be widely ignored and not accepted. But a norm must also be backed up by some type of power or influence system. If a member consistently and excessively violates the group's norm(s), the other members use some type of negative and/or positive sanction against the individual. Sanctions can range from physical abuse or threats to the withdrawal of rewards such as praise, recognition, and acceptance. Specific norms are often interdependent and mutually reinforcing to one another. That is, they form part of the group's total normative system.

Even though norms may be a powerful influence on group and member behavior, group members often have only a vague conscious awareness of the norms by which they live. For two reasons it is imperative that these subconscious group forces be brought to the level of conscious awareness: *First,* awareness increases the potential for individual and group freedom.

This is based on the assumption that self-awareness and awareness of one's environment is a necessary (even though insufficient) condition for freedom. *Second,* norms and normative systems can have positive and/or negative influences on the effectiveness of individuals, groups, and organizations.

Categories of Norms.   Table 9–3 identifies nine categories of norms that are obviously somewhat interrelated and can influence the effectiveness of work groups, departments, or even entire organizations. For each category, an illustration of a possible positive and negative norm is given.

Many popular articles criticize large-scale organizations for maintaining and encouraging norms such as "It is best to keep opinions to yourself and play it safe" and "The most important thing is to appear to work hard, regardless of the results." Unfortunately, there is little data to demonstrate the extent to which such norms actually exist in organizations.

Conformity.   An important issue for work groups is that norms and the pressures to adhere to them may result in conformity. There are actually two types of conformity: compliance and personal acceptance.[20] *Compliance* is the behavior of an individual that becomes or remains similar to the group's wishes because of real or imagined group pressure. A considerable amount of the conformity found in organizations and work groups is most likely of this type. Compliance does not mean that the individual personally believes in the desirability or appropriateness of the actions. A variety of reasons result in compliance without personal acceptance. Group members might feel that the appearance of a "united front" is necessary for them to succeed in accomplishing their goals. The president of General Motors would not announce "After considerable argument and debate, the majority of my executive committee finally agreed to increase car prices by an average of 6 percent this year." Rather, the GM president might say: "After considerable study, the Executive Committee of GM unanimously agrees that it is essential to raise the price of our cars by an average of 6 percent even though the costs of producing a car exceed this percentage." On a more personal level, individuals may conform because it is important in meeting their needs to be liked and accepted by others. This may be especially true for lower status members in relation to higher status members, such as a subordinate and a superior. Finally, individuals often comply because the costs of conformity are much less than the costs of nonconformity, which could serve to threaten the maintenance of the existing relationship in the group. Another way of stating this is that the individual makes some trade-offs and attempts to maximize rewards and minimize costs.

The second type of conformity is based on the personal acceptance of the group's wishes by the individual. In *personal acceptance conformity,* the person's behavior and attitudes or beliefs are consistent with the group's norms and wishes. The strength of this type of conformity is, by definition, much stronger than the compliance type of conformity.

TABLE 9–3. Categories of Organizational Norms with Positive and Negative Examples.

| | Examples | |
Categories	Positive Norms	Negative Norms
Organizational and personal pride	Members speak up for the company when it is criticized unfairly	Members don't care about company problems
Performance/ Excellence	Members try to improve, even if they are doing well	Members are satisfied with the minimum level of performance necessary
Teamwork/ Communication	Members listen and are receptive to the ideas and opinions of others	Members gossip behind the backs of others rather than deal with issues openly and constructively
Leadership/ Supervision	Members ask for help when they need it	Members hide their problems and avoid their superiors
Colleague/Associate relations	Members refuse to take advantage of fellow workers	Members don't care about the well-being of fellow workers
Customer/Consumer relations	Members show concern about serving the customers	Members are indifferent and, when possible, hostile to customers
Honesty and security	Members are concerned about dishonesty and pilferage	Members are expected to steal a little and be honest only when necessary
Training and development	Members really show they care about training and development	There is much talk about training and development but no one takes it seriously
Innovation and change	Members are usually looking for better ways of doing their job	Members stick to the old ways of doing their jobs

Adapted by permission of the publisher from *Organizational Dynamics*, Spring 1973. Copyright © 1973 by Amacom, a division of American Management Association.

Let's consider a hypothetical example of these two types of conformity for two employees in a battery assembly plant.

The work group has norms as to the appropriate output for a day's work—between 90 and 100 batteries assembled. High conformity exists within this allowable range of output. Management feels that the workers could produce substantially more units without sacrificing quality. After much study, management decides to implement an incentive system, on an experimental basis, subject to modification or elimination by either party (workers or managers) after a six-month trial period. To minimize problems of possible distrust and meet the security needs of workers, the incentive plan is designed as a supplement to the present hourly pay system. What happens? Bob, who has been conforming to the output norms on the basis of compliance, is quite enthusiastic toward management's proposal. However, Sam, who has been conforming to the output norms on the basis of personal acceptance, receives management's proposal with considerable distrust, anxiety, and opposition.

These two types of conformity provide major insight into why some members of highly conforming groups may easily change behavior while others may oppose and/or find the process of change stressful.

There is no simple answer to the issue of conformity in work groups.[21] Without norms and some conformity to them, work groups would be chaotic and random environments in which few tasks could be accomplished. At the other extreme, excessive and mechanistic conformity threatens the important place claimed for the individual in our society, as well as the ability of groups to deal with change, uncertainty, and complex problems. One possible recommendation in coping with the dilemmas of conformity is that work groups can learn to become more aware of the conformity and its possible positive and negative consequences. They can then reassess or change the norms and the sanction system that serves as the underlying base of conformity. From the standpoint of group members, it appears that the functional or dysfunctional nature of conformity may depend on the norms of the group itself.

Effects on Productivity.   Work groups do not always have well-defined norms regarding standards of productivity. This conclusion is brought into clear focus in an interview and questionnaire study of workers in the engineering divisions and power plants of the Tennessee Valley Authority. The subjects were asked, "If a person on your job were known as a fast, energetic worker, how would this affect his chances of being close friends with people on his own level on the job?"[22] The findings were somewhat surprising: 56 percent indicated it wouldn't matter one way or the other in terms of acceptance; 27 percent thought hard work would make it easier to gain acceptance in the work group; and 16 percent thought an energetic worker would find it harder to make friends.

Goals

Generally, there is a natural correspondence between group goals and group norms. It is logical, but not always true, that groups adopt norms to facilitate the attainment of their goals. One purpose of some organizational development efforts is to assist group members in assessing whether the norms they follow are consistent, neutral, or actually conflicting with the group and/or organizational goals. For example, a work group may claim and believe that one of its goals is to improve its efficiency, which is likely to be compatible with the productivity goals "assigned" to the work group by higher management. Close inspection of the members' behavior might actually reveal norms counterproductive to this expressed goal. There may be norms of "Don't produce too much" and "Don't make too many changes." Norms such as these, even if the members are consciously aware of them, could be rationalized as being instrumental to their efficiency goal. Members could claim that producing more than the norm will "burn them out," resulting in lower long-term efficiency. On the other hand, always looking for and introducing changes takes members away from their primary tasks and is too disruptive to their operation. However, if the work group goals are concerned with such things as minimizing managerial influence and increasing the opportunity for social interaction among members, norms placing some restrictions on worker output could be perceived by the members as functional.

Relation to Individuals.   Group goals do not exist outside the minds of the members. Group goals, however, cannot be directly determined from the goals of individual members, nor can they be summed up by simply adding together the individual member goals. *Group goals are the objectives or states desired for the group as a whole, not just the objectives desired by each individual member.* This definition is based on the idea that the whole is greater than and different from the simple sum of the individual parts. For example, the positive and negative norms illustrated in Table 9–3 have primary meaning in relation to group goals and groups as a whole (where the focus is on structure, size, norms, and the like). In sum, group goals refer to the group as a unit or system, that is, they refer to desired states of the unit, not just individual members.[23]

Pervasiveness of Goals.   Throughout this book, we keep returning to the concept of goals as important to understanding, predicting, and changing individuals, groups, and organizations. Each of these systems is partially defined as possessing the characteristic of being a goal-oriented system. Accordingly, because of our concern with variables affecting group behavior and sentiments, we must always try to make some assessment of group goals. Of course, individual goals and the organizational goals within which the group functions are likely to influence both the types of group goals and the actual behavior and outputs of the group. A number of possibilities exists for compatible and conflicting goals within each system (individual, group, and organization) as well as between systems. For example, work groups typically have both relations-oriented goals and task goals. In effective work groups, there appears to be concern with both these goals, with about two-thirds of the time spent on task issues and one-third on relations-oriented issues.[24] The sole pursuit of only one or the other of these goals over the long run would reduce effectiveness, increase conflicts, and possibly result in dissolution of the group. The role of goals in influencing work-group behavior and outputs becomes even more complex when the possible compatibilities and conflicts between group goals, individual member goals, and organizational goals are considered.

Cohesiveness

One contingency affecting groups, cohesiveness, is substantially influenced by the degree of compatibility between group goals and individual member goals. *Cohesiveness* is the strength of the members' desires to remain in the group and their commitment to the group. A group whose members have a strong desire to remain in the group and personally accept its goals would be considered as a highly cohesive group relative to a group where the opposite was found.

Relation to Conformity.   No one-to-one relationship exists between cohesiveness and conformity. Although low cohesiveness is usually associated with low conformity, there is no inherent requirement that high cohesiveness exists only in the presence of high conformity. Mature groups may have high member commitment and stick-togetherness while simultaneously respecting individual differences in terms of behavior and thought. This might occur more frequently when the cohesion is substantially based on a common commitment to group task goals. Moreover, if the group confronts complex problems, low or moderate conformity may not only be tolerated but may actually be encouraged and supported by members.

Relation to Groupthink.   When decision-making groups are both conforming and cohesive, a phenomenon called *groupthink* may take place. Irving Janis, who coined the term "groupthink," focused his research on high level policy groups in the government faced with difficult problems in a complex/dynamic environment.[25]

Figure 9–3 summarizes the initial conditions that are likely to lead to groupthink, the characteristics of groupthink, and the types of defective decision making that will result from groupthink. The initial conditions and the types of defective decision processes are self-explanatory. We will concentrate on the eight characteristics of groupthink:[26]

1. An *illusion of invulnerability,* shared by most of or all the members, which creates excessive optimism and encourages taking extreme risks.

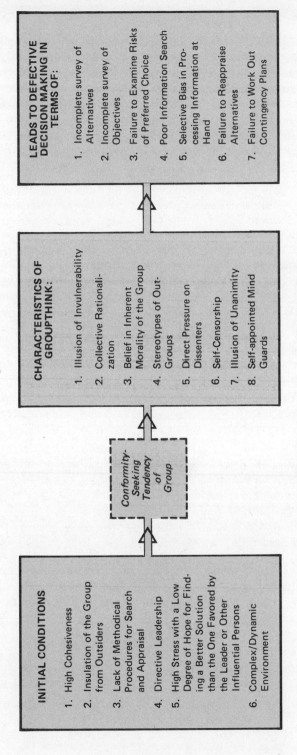

INITIAL CONDITIONS

1. High Cohesiveness
2. Insulation of the Group from Outsiders
3. Lack of Methodical Procedures for Search and Appraisal
4. Directive Leadership
5. High Stress with a Low Degree of Hope for Finding a Better Solution than the One Favored by the Leader or Other Influential Persons
6. Complex/Dynamic Environment

Conformity-Seeking Tendency of Group

CHARACTERISTICS OF GROUPTHINK:

1. Illusion of Invulnerability
2. Collective Rationalization
3. Belief in Inherent Morality of the Group
4. Stereotypes of Out-Groups
5. Direct Pressure on Dissenters
6. Self-Censorship
7. Illusion of Unanimity
8. Self-appointed Mind Guards

LEADS TO DEFECTIVE DECISION MAKING IN TERMS OF:

1. Incomplete survey of Alternatives
2. Incomplete survey of Objectives
3. Failure to Examine Risks of Preferred Choice
4. Poor Information Search
5. Selective Bias in Processing Information at Hand
6. Failure to Reappraise Alternatives
7. Failure to Work Out Contingency Plans

FIGURE 9–3.   Model of Groupthink*

Modified with permission of Macmillan Publishing Co., Inc., from *Decision Making: A Psychological Analysis of Conflict, Choice, and Commitment*, by Irving L. Janis and Leon Mann. Copyright © 1977 by The Free Press, a division of Macmillan Publishing Co., Inc.

2. *Collective rationalization* in order to discount warnings that might lead the members to reconsider their assumptions before they commit themselves to their policy decisions.
3. An unquestioned belief in the group's *inherent morality*, inclining the the members to ignore the ethical or moral consequences of their decisions.
4. *Stereotyped views* of rivals and enemies (outgroups) as being too evil to warrant genuine attempts to negotiate or too weak or stupid to counter whatever attempts are made to defeat their purposes.
5. *Direct pressure* on any member who expresses strong arguments against any of the group's illusions, stereotypes, or commitments, making clear that such dissent is contrary to what is expected of all loyal members.
6. *Self-censorship* of deviations from the apparent group consensus, reflecting the inclination of members to minimize to themselves the importance of their doubts and counterarguments.
7. A shared *illusion of unanimity*, partly resulting from self-censorship and reinforced by the false assumption that silence implies consent.
8. The emergence of *self-appointed "mindguards"*—members who protect the group from adverse information that might shatter their shared complacency about the effectiveness and morality of their decisions.

Janis reports that these characteristics of groupthink existed in the group decision making that was undertaken by President Kennedy and his top policy advisors in the decision to invade Cuba. The invasion of Cuba, commonly known as the Bay of Pigs fiasco, took place in April 1961 and was a complete failure. The group members had felt that they were invulnerable. For example, Robert Kennedy reported on the eve of the invasion that he felt that with such talent, "bold new ideas," and "common sense and hard work," they would overcome whatever challenged them. The reports from inside the Executive Committee were that everyone was unanimously in support of the President's decisions. It was only later that doubts were mentioned. For example, Arthur Schlesinger, Jr., reported that he had doubts about the decision being made. He felt, however, that everyone else was in agreement and that he was the only one with divergent views. Rather than appear "soft" or "compromising," he kept his feelings to himself. He later regretted his self-censorship and part in the illusion of unanimity.

When discussions were held, President Kennedy would occasionally call in an "expert" and have him respond to any critical questions that came up. Instead of actively inquiring about the extent of dissent or seeking divergent views, the President would simply let the expert silence the critic. Informal pressure was also placed on members of the Executive Committee. Schlesinger reports for example, that Robert Kennedy took him aside and mentioned that while he could see there might be some problems with the President's decision, the President needed unanimous support on this issue. This was an appeal for group solidarity.

Finally, because of the similarity of attitudes of the group members, their liking for one another, and the pressure for conformity, outside criticism was dismissed prematurely. Considerable evidence existed suggesting that the Bay of Pigs invasion would fail. However, due to groupthink, this evidence was never given proper consideration.

This discussion of groupthink points out how, under certain conditions, high group cohesiveness and conformity can hinder the effectiveness of decision-making groups. However, Janis points out that groupthink is not inevitable. Several steps can be taken to decrease groupthink. For example, a leader should try to stay neutral and should encourage criticism and new ideas. Small subgroups or outside consultants may come up with a different viewpoint. People sympathetic to an alternative view should be encouraged to present their views. More will be said about increasing the effectiveness of decision-making groups as the chapter unfolds.

Impact on Productivity.   The degree of group cohesion is especially important because of its potential impact on group productivity. Actually, it might be more appropriate to think of cohesion and productivity as potentially interdependent. This is particularly true for groups who have highly task-related goals. If the group is successful in reaching its goals, the positive feedback of its attainments may serve to increase member commitment.[27] A winning football team, everything else equal, is more likely to be cohesive than one with a mediocre record. Of course, the cause-and-effect relation can work in both directions. Thus, a cohesive football team may also be more likely to win games.

On the other hand, low cohesiveness may interfere with the ability to obtain task goals because group resources are not as likely to be shared and interactions are not as likely to take place as frequently as is necessary. High cohesiveness in work groups may actually be associated with low productivity *if* the group goals are contrary to organizational or managerial goals. Thus the relation between cohesion and productivity cannot be anticipated or understood unless the group's goals and norms are also known.

The potentially complex relationship between cohesion, productivity, and other variables was suggested in a study of 228 small work groups in a plant manufacturing heavy machinery.[28] Cohesiveness was evaluated in terms of the degree to which members perceived themselves to be part of the group; members preferred to remain in the group rather than leave; and members perceived their group to be superior to other groups with respect to the way the members stuck together, helped each other out, and got along together. The productivity measure was obtained from a single productivity average for each respondent for a three-month period prior to completing the questionnaires. The major findings obtained were:

1. Productivity between workers was more uniform in high-cohesiveness groups than in low-cohesiveness groups, suggesting that cohesiveness had a conformity effect.
2. Productivity differences between work groups were greater in high-cohesiveness groups than in low-cohesiveness groups.

302 PART IV Group Process

3. High cohesiveness was associated with high or low productivity, depending upon the degree to which members felt management was supportive or threatening to them.

Leadership

Studies of small groups within organizations have emphasized the importance of emergent or informal leadership, especially as related to the accomplishment of task goals. An *informal leader* is an individual who emerges over time with relatively high influence in the group.

Multiple Leaders. Leadership in a group has popularly been regarded as the province of a single individual. As mentioned earlier, work groups often have at least two major classes of goals—relation-oriented goals and task goals. It is quite possible for a group to have two leaders—one who provides leadership with respect to relation-oriented goals and the other who provides leadership with respect to task goals. These two goals may require different personal skills for attainment and they may be conflicting at times—a combination of demands difficult to fulfill in one person.[29]

Some research indicates that informal task leaders do emerge in groups with formal (designated) leaders. For example, in a study of seventy-two decision-making groups with between five and seventeen members, the informal emergent task leaders were generally characterized as follows:

1. Very high on total participation.
2. Members of conference groups in which the formal leaders did not engage in behavior that would have facilitated discussion and problem solving.
3. Exhibiting much more facilitating discussion and problem-solving behavior than did the formal leader or other high participators who were not identified as informal leaders.
4. Called "more needed" significantly often by the chairperson and other members.[30]

This and other studies suggest that informal task leaders of work groups, where a formal leader already exists, are unlikely to emerge unless the formal leader abdicates the task-related responsibilities or lacks the necessary abilities to carry them out. In contrast, relations-oriented leaders of work groups are more likely to emerge informally.

Effective Group Leaders. Effective leaders of work groups generally exhibit more of the following types of behavior than other members:

1. Creating and maintaining a clear conception of the primary group task or goal.

2. Maintaining a unique position in the group by both participating in it and yet remaining sufficiently detached so as to observe the group as a whole.
3. Assuming primary responsibility for the regulation or control of inter-actions (i.e., exchanges and interrelationships) between the group and other groups or individuals.
4. Permitting and encouraging some shifting of leadership tasks among members who are more qualified to meet the changing demands of the group.

These behaviors provide only an outline of basic qualities needed for effective work-group leaders. The extent to which activities and processes are accommodated by formal or informal leaders can have substantial im-pact on group behavior and outcomes, including productivity and member satisfaction.

The importance of group leadership may be especially profound in its indirect and subtle effects. Virtually all the variables affecting groups (size, member composition, norms, and goals) will be disproportionately influenced by the person or persons in the group leadership position(s). For example, the effective group leader often assumes a key role in the relations between the group and its external environment. This person is likely to have substantial influence over the selection of new group members, a process that is virtually universal in work groups. Even when the work-group members participate in the selection of new members, it is common for the group leader to provide some screening of potential members, thereby limiting the alternative choices available to the members.

External Environment

The last contingency affecting groups considered in this part of the chapter is the external environment of the group. The *external environment* is the conditions and factors that are not substantially controlled by the work group and represent "givens" for the members. Some dimensions that might be considered as part of the external environment for a work group are the technology, physical conditions, management practices, rules, lead-ership of the designated supervisors and managers, and rewards and pun-ishments from the organization.[31] Since these external environmental fac-tors often play such a crucial role in the day-to-day behavior and output of a work group, it is likely that they will become blurred with the variables within the group, which can also influence group behavior and output.

Up to this point, the discussion of contingencies affecting groups focused on the internal character and dynamics of the group. The external environment can affect each of the variables presented, such as member composition and leadership, as well as directly affect the behavior and out-puts of a group. For example, management may want to introduce a tech-nological change, such as automatically controlled machines, to a work group. From the perspective of the work group, this might be considered as an external force. But by acting in a united manner, the work group might be able to influence the conditions under which the machines are introduced. Thus, the influences between the external environment and work group can be two-way, rather than just from the external environment to the group.

Much of the discussion in Chapter 3 on environmental influences and in the next chapter on intergroup relations addresses issues and concepts related to the external environment of work groups. Thus, the "external environment" contingency will not be explored any further here. But one point should be made explicit: Work groups can be and often are dramatically changed in response to higher management-initiated changes in the areas of technology, job design, structure, rules, and formal supervision.

This part of the chapter emphasized some contingencies that can influence the behavior and outputs of work groups. These contingencies are group size, member composition, norms, goals, cohesiveness, leadership, and the external environment of the group. Obviously, groups are not easy to understand or manage. However, it is hoped that this part of the chapter will increase your "batting average" in being an effective member or leader of groups. This part should also provide a good foundation for your consideration of decision processes within groups, which is the focus of the next part.

GROUP DECISION PROCESSES

Six areas of group decision making will be covered in this part of the chapter (1) individual versus group decision making; (2) degrees of participation in group decision making; (3) content of group decisions; (4) potential benefits and limitations to group participation in decision making; (5) phases of integrated group problem solving; and (6) interacting versus nominal decision groups.[32]

Individual versus Group

Which is better—individual decision making or group decision making? While this is the way the issue of individual versus group decision making is popularly formulated, it is probably an inappropriate and meaningless question. It accomplishes little more than locking people into "either-or" positions. It would be much more useful to ask: Under what conditions does individual or group decision making, or some combination of the two, appear to be relatively more effective? Some research suggests that a key situational factor that indicates a superiority of one approach over the other is the nature of the problem. In making decisions, groups often appear to be superior to an individual (or the same number of individuals working independently) when the tasks involve generating many ideas or very unique ideas, recalling information accurately, and estimating and evaluating ambiguous or uncertain situations. Individuals seem to have the edge for "thinking out" problems that require long chains of decisions to be made for solution.[33] The latter type of task is concerned with the implementation of predesigned plans, rules, or instructions. If group members can perform their jobs relatively independent of others, individual decision making is likely to be the more appropriate mode. However, if group members are interdependent and must cooperate with one another, greater group decision making is probably needed for effective performance.[34]

As suggested earlier in this chapter, work groups over time often confront different types of tasks and experience varying degrees of member interdependency for different problems. Thus we would fully expect both individual and group decision making in effective groups. The intent here has been to suggest several underlying criteria that a work group or its leadership should consider in deciding when to use individual decision making and when to use group decision making. There are costs associated with inappropriate use of either individual or group decision modes. The inappropriate use of group decision making may have dual costs: organizational resources are wasted because members' time could have been used in other pursuits; and member motivation is reduced because of boredom and a feeling that their time has been wasted. The inappropriate use of individual decision making can result in poor coordination, lower quality and creativity in decision making, greater errors, and the like.

Degrees of Participation

Vroom and Yetton have developed a model that helps managers determine the types of decision problems facing them and how much participation in decision making they should encourage.[35] As shown in Figure 9–4, there are five degrees or amounts of participation in group decision making. The situations range from no participation, to consultation with group members, to a group as a whole making the decision.

Vroom and Yetton contend that the proper degree of group participation in decision making should be contingent upon the type of decision problem. They identify seven diagnostic questions that managers should ask themselves in determining the type of decision problem. From this, they prescribe the amount of participation that would be appropriate by indicating yes or no to a list of questions. The diagnostic questions are:

1. Is there a criterion that will show that one solution is better than another?
2. Do I have enough information?
3. Is the problem structured?
4. Do I need subordinate acceptance?
5. Will I get acceptance if I decide alone?
6. Do subordinates share the organizational goals?
7. Is conflict among subordinates likely?

FIGURE 9–4.   Degrees of Group Participation in Decision Making

Degrees of Participation	Key	Explanation
None		
Alone	A I	Manager makes the decision alone.
	A II	Manager asks for information from subordinates but makes the decision alone. Subordinates may or may not be informed about what the problem is.
Consultation	C I	Manager shares the problem with and asks for information and evaluations from them. Meetings take place as dyads, not as a group, and the manager then goes off and makes the decision.
	C II	Manager and subordinates meet as a group to discuss the problem, but the manager makes the decision.
Group	G	Manager and subordinates meet as a group to discuss the problem, and the group as a whole makes the decision.
High		

The various combinations of answers to these questions determine the types of problems facing managers. Table 9–4 summarizes the basic types of decision problems that are arrived at from the responses to the seven diagnostic questions. The fourteen basic types of problems are shown in the left-hand column of the figure. The right-hand side of the figure shows the degree of participation that is prescribed when dealing with each problem type.

The Vroom and Yetton model is useful in helping individuals diagnose their decision problems and in guiding them in the choice of the degree of group participation to employ. This model pulls together a variety of our previous comments on groups in terms of the degree of participation that should be encouraged. Of course, it needs to be emphasized that this model should not be used as a simple cookbook for group participation. The world of management is much too complicated to assume that this model provides all the answers.

Application of Vroom and Yetton Model.   To sharpen your skills in applying this model, we would like you to read and diagnose the following case incident.

John Stevens, plant manager of the Fairlee Plant of Lockstead Corporation, attended the advanced management seminar conducted at a large midwestern university. The seminar, of four

TABLE 9–4. Summary of Vroom and Yetton Contingency Model of Group Decision Making

TYPES OF PROBLEMS	DIAGNOSTIC QUESTIONS							DEGREE OF GROUP PARTICIPATION
	1 Is there a criterion which will show that one solution is better than another?	2 Do I have enough information?	3 Is the problem structured?	4 Do I need subordinate acceptance?	5 Will I get acceptance if I decide alone?	6 Do subordinates share the organizational goals?	7 Is conflict among subordinates likely?	
1	No			No				A I
2	No			Yes	Yes			A I
3	No			Yes	No			G
4	Yes	Yes		No				A I
5	Yes	Yes		Yes	Yes			A I
6	Yes	Yes		Yes	No	Yes		G
7	Yes	Yes		Yes	No	No	Yes	C II
8	Yes	Yes		Yes	No	No	No	C I
9	Yes	No	Yes	Yes	Yes			A II
10	Yes	No	Yes	No				A II
11	Yes	No	No	Yes	Yes			C II
12	Yes	No	No	Yes	No	Yes		G
13	Yes	No	No	Yes	No	No		C II
14	Yes	No	No	No				C II

Blanks simply mean that the information is not relevant due to the response to some other question.

weeks in duration, was largely devoted to the topic of executive decision making.

Professor Mennon, of the university staff, particularly impressed John Stevens with his lectures on group discussion and group decision making. On the basis of research and experience, Professor Mennon was convinced that employees, if given the opportunity, could meet together, intelligently consider, and then formulate quality decisions that would be enthusiastically accepted.

Returning to his plant at the conclusion of the seminar, Mr. Stevens decided to practice some of the principles which he had learned. He called together the twenty-five employees of Department B and told them that production standards established several years previously were now too low in view of the recent installation of automated equipment. He gave the men the opportunity to discuss the mitigating circumstances and to decide among themselves, as a group, what their standards should be. Mr. Stevens, on leaving the room, believed that the men would doubtlessly establish much higher standards than he himself would have dared propose.

After an hour of discussion the group summoned Mr. Stevens and notified him that, contrary to his opinion, their group decision was that the standards were already too high, and since they had been given the authority to establish their own standards, they were making a reduction of 10 percent. These standards Mr. Stevens knew, were far too low to provide a fair profit on the owner's investment. Yet it was clear that his refusal to accept the group decision would be disastrous. Before taking a course of action, Mr. Stevens called Professor Mennon at the university for his opinion.

You should now try to diagnose the errors made by John Stevens by responding to as many of the questions as possible that are shown in Table 9–4. From this diagnosis, how do you think that John Stevens should have approached this situation. It will be necessary for you to make some assumptions and inferences.

Content of Group Decisions

While the previous section was concerned with the degree of group participation in decision making, this section focuses on the content of decision problems that may be made by a work group. As work groups deal with decision problems that are of increasing importance to them, we would conclude that they have increasing autonomy.

Some of the content areas for group decision making and the corre-

FIGURE 9–5.   Continuum of Work Group Autonomy

Content of Decision Areas

Level of
Group Autonomy

High

Group has influence on its qualitative goals.   ____
Group has influence on its quantitative goals.   ____
Group decides on questions of external leadership.   ____
Group decides on what additional tasks to take on.   ____
Group decides when it will work.   ____
Group decides on questions of production.   ____
Group determines internal distribution of tasks.   ____
Group decides on questions of recruitment.   ____
Group decides on questions of internal leadership.   ____
Group members determine their individual production methods. ____

Low

Adapted from Gulowsen, J., A measure of work-group autonomy, in Davis, L. and J. Taylor (eds.), *Design of Jobs* (Middlesex: Penguin Books, 1972), pp. 374–390.

sponding levels of group autonomy are shown in Figure 9–5. The autonomy of a work group increases as you read *up* the list of decisions in Figure 9–5. Moreover, it is generally assumed that these types of decisions are cumulative. A group that can decide on questions of recruitment will also have an influence on questions of internal leadership and production methods.

The relationships between degrees of group participation (as shown in Table 9–4) and degrees of work-group autonomy (as shown in Figure 9–5) might be summed up this way: *First*, Table 9–4 is primarily concerned with the amount of participation in group decision making, whereas Figure 9–5 is concerned with the content or substance of decisions made by and within the group. *Second*, a group may make extensive use of a high level of group participation in decision making without necessarily being highly autonomous. However, a highly autonomous group must use a high level of group participation. For example, a group may have a high level of group participation with respect to determining its internal distribution of tasks, but have little or no influence over the qualitative and quantitative goals "assigned" to it by higher management.

Benefits and Limitations to Group Participation

Work group participation is often closely linked to the distribution of power[36] and the control structure[37] in organizations. These issues will be taken up in the next chapter. For now, we will describe one organizational study indicating the possible benefits of group participation in decision making. This will be balanced by a presentation of several limitations to participation.

  Possible Benefits.   This section reviews a field and experimental study conducted by J. Bragg and I. Andrews.[38] *Participative decision making* (hereafter PDM) is a form of involvement in which decisions as to the work group's activities are heavily influenced, if not arrived at, by the work group that has to implement the decisions.[39] PDM was introduced into the laundry department of one hospital. Two other hospital laundries were used as comparison groups, that is, no formal changes were made in their level of PDM. Before PDM was implemented, the laundry supervisor accepted the idea and fundamental changes involved in the experiment. When PDM was introduced to the 32 laundry workers, the supervisor honestly stated that the basic purpose of this change was to create more interesting jobs. Higher level management was already quite happy with the productivity of the laundry. The laundry workers were assured that they (the laundry workers) could discontinue PDM if they did not like it. The union leadership gave their approval, but not active support, to the program. The major transfer in decision-making power was from the laundry supervisor to the work group, consisting of all the laundry employees. The work group could consider any and all aspects of managing the laundry. It was agreed that the meetings of the work group would be limited in length to 30 or 40 minutes and would only be called if there were specific problems or proposals to discuss. Much PDM was also achieved outside of formal meetings. Typically, the work group's decisions could be implemented within one or two weeks, since prior approval from higher management was usually not necessary before taking action.

  Measurements were taken in the areas of employee attitudes, absenteeism, and productivity. At the end of fourteen months, 90 percent of the employees had positive attitudes toward PDM. This is an increase from 62 percent with positive attitudes at the end of the first two months of the program. The absenteeism record (compared to the rest of the hospital) became significantly better after the introduction of PDM. The laundry group had an overall absence rate of 2.95 percent before PDM and only 1.77 percent after the introduction of PDM. Productivity averaged 50 pounds of laundry processed per paid employee hour in the year prior to the introduction of PDM. During the third six-month period after PDM, productivity had increased to 73 pounds per paid employee hour. The productivity in the two comparison hospitals had declined slightly over the eighteen-month study period.

  Possible Limitations.   While this study seems to be building the case for PDM, some of the possible limitations with participatory groups need to be kept in mind. Participatory groups are generally faced with the potential limitations of *time*, *personalization*, and *inequality*.[40] *First,* a greater length of time is usually required with group decision making. This could have the further consequences of making quick decisions in emergencies almost impossible, causing frustration and boredom among members and creating conflicts among members who see their time as more or less valuable in relation to the group. *Second,* group decision making may increase the possibility of issues becoming personalized. Members' ideas can become interrelated with their own emotional psychological selves. Members who present ideas may take criticism of these ideas as criticism of themselves. Members who are not subtle and who possess little interpersonal skill may have their ideas ignored or rejected, even though they are of high quality. *Third,* group decision making may not adequately consider inequalities of abilities between members in making decisions. Problems of time, personalization, and inequality are not always inevitable, and they may be more than offset by other benefits. Yet they need to be recognized.

Integrated Group Problem Solving

Once the decision has been made that a high degree of group participation is appropriate and that important content areas should be considered by the group, how should the manager implement group problem solving? W. C. Morris and M. Sashkin have developed a useful model of the phases of integrated group problem solving that can be used and followed by managers and group members. Table 9–5 summarizes the six phases of their integrated group problem-solving model.

Morris and Sashkin indicate that each of the six phases should be characterized by the following problem-solving format:[41]

Phase I: *Problem Definition.* Often we assume that we know what the problem is, but just as often we are wrong and are looking only at a symptom or, at best, only part of the problem. Phase I is intended to encourage the group to fully explore, clarify, and define the problem.

Phase II: *Problem Solution Generation.* People tend to be solution minded, rather than problem oriented. Phase II is designed to prolong the idea-generating process and prevent premature decisions. Although the solution we choose is often the first or one of the first suggested, research has clearly shown that solutions can be greatly improved by looking at as many alternatives as possible. The more ideas we consider, the more likely we are to come up with a greater number of good ideas.

Phase III: *Ideas to Actions.* Now the group is ready to evaluate the ideas and come up with a solution. Even though an idea may not work alone, it may provide a good "part." Time can be taken to combine the good parts of various ideas. Each alternative can then be carefully evaluated. People will be more able to help and participate if they do not feel attacked or threatened. Rather than weeding out poor alternatives (and making those who suggested them feel defensive), it is better to select the best ones and concentrate on those until everyone can agree on one or two solutions.

TABLE 9–5.   Summary of Morris and Sashkin's Integrated Group Problem-Solving Model

Phases	Activities
I Problem Definition	Explaining the problem situation, generating information, clarifying and defining the problem.
II Problem Solution Generation	Brainstorming solution alternatives; reviewing, revising, elaborating, and recombining solution ideas.
III Ideas to Actions	Evaluating alternatives, examining probable effects and comparing them with desired outcomes; revising ideas; developing a list of final action alternatives and selecting one for trial.
IV Solution Action Planning	Preparing a list of action steps, with the names of persons who will be responsible for each step; developing a coordination plan.
V Solution Evaluation Planning	Reviewing desired outcomes and development of measures of effectiveness; creating a monitoring plan for gathering evaluation data as the solution is put into action; developing contingency plans; assigning responsibilities.
VI Evaluation of the Product and the Process	Assembling evaluation data to determine the effects of actions and the effectiveness of the group's problem-solving process.

Phase IV: *Solution Action Planning.* Now that there is a solution to try out, chances are that it will work more smoothly if the actions needed to put it into operation are carefully planned. This means looking for problems in advance, planning to involve those persons whose support will be needed, and assigning and accepting action responsibilities. Only if the group determines *who* is to do *what* and *when* can the solution have a fair test.

Phase V: *Solution Evaluation Planning.* Unfortunately, most groups stop at Phase IV, losing the chance to learn from experience. Even if a solution is a tremendous success, it is useful to know exactly what it was about the actions taken that made the solution work so well. It can then be repeated more easily. If a solution is a total disaster, we may feel like hiding the fact that we had anything to do with it, but it is necessary to know exactly what went wrong so that the same things can be avoided in the future. Of course, in real life, solutions generally work moderately well—they are neither great successes nor great failures. Keeping track of exactly what is happening allows minor improvements or adjustments that will help significantly in solving the problem.

This is best done not by guesswork or trial and error, but on the basis of hard, accurate information about the effects of actions. This phase offers the greatest potential for learning to solve problems. Again, *what* kind of evaluation information is needed, *who* will obtain it, and *when* must it be specified?

Phase VI: *Evaluation of the Product and the Process.* When there is enough information to evaluate how well and to what degree the solution worked, it is time for another group evaluation meeting. At this point, it is possible to see what the outcomes were and whether the problem was solved. If the problem or some part of it remains, the group can "recycle" it by looking at the information, perhaps even redefining the problem, and coming up with new ideas or trying out a previously rejected alternative. This is also the time to review and evaluate how well the group worked together.

Obviously, group problem-solving processes rarely proceed so neatly. Real-life problem-solving groups often jump around or skip phases. But, Morris and Sashkin's model, if followed, should go a long way in improving the effectiveness of problem solving in your group. A diagnostic questionnaire that can be used to help implement this model is presented after the following discussion of interacting and nominal groups.

Interacting versus Nominal Decision Groups

Much of the discussion in this section on group decision making has assumed the presence of an interacting work group. Here the definition of an interacting decision group is further narrowed to: "(1) an unstructured group discussion for obtaining and pooling ideas of participants; and (2) majority voting on priorities by hand count."[42] Interacting groups may be most effective for the evaluative phase of a group decision process that involves synthesis of information and development of alternative solutions; evaluation of information and assessment of alternative solutions; and development of group consensus and agreement on a particular solution.[43] While this and previous chapters have provided many suggestions for improving the effectiveness of interacting groups, the creative or fact-finding phase of group decision making could benefit by a different group process.

One such process involves the use of the *nominal group technique* in the creative and fact-finding phase of group decision making. As outlined by A. L. Delbecq, A. H. Van de Ven, and D. H. Gustafson, the process of group decision making with the nominal group technique is as follows:[44]

1. A group size of about seven to ten individuals.
2. Members silently express their ideas in writing as to the nature of the problem or alternative solutions to the problem, if it has already been identified. The members may work alone in separate rooms or around a table in full view of each other.

3. At the end of some time period (10 to 15 minutes), the members share their ideas with each other. This sharing is very structured in that each member presents, in round-robin fashion, only one idea in each round from her or his list.
4. In full view of all members, a recorder writes a short, paraphrased version of each idea on a flip chart or board. This continues until all ideas, possibly eighteen to twenty-five, have been expressed. There is no recorded identification of ideas with members.
5. Each idea is then openly discussed by asking for clarification or stating support or nonsupport of it.
6. Each member privately and in writing rank-orders the ideas in order of preference. The group decision or recommendation would be the mathematically polled outcomes of the member rankings of each idea.

The potential advantages of the nominal group technique over the usual interacting group are greater emphasis and attention to idea generation, increased attention to each idea, and a greater likelihood of balanced participation and representation of each member in the group. However, some research suggests that nominal groups may not be superior to interacting groups "when the task of problem identification is performed by persons who are both (a) pervasively aware of the existing problems and (b) willing to communicate them."[45] It appears that the nominal group technique may be most effective when there are certain blocks or problems in a group, such as a few dominating members.

Review of Group Decision Processes

Several themes have run through this entire discussion of group decision processes. These themes might be summed up in the form of the questions we have addressed. How can we differentiate the degree of participation in group decision making? What is the relation between group decision processes and the relative autonomy of groups? What role does the process of group decision making and the content of decisions made by a work group have in evaluating the concept of participation? What are the possible effects, both positive and negative, of group decision making? What are some of the contingency factors to be considered in group decision processes? How should one go about using group problem solving? What is the nominal group technique and when should it be used?

DIAGNOSING YOUR WORK GROUP

The last part of this chapter presents two illustrative diagnostic and assessment approaches for evaluating work groups and serves two objectives. *First*, it provides you with some knowledge and awareness of the limitations we face in learning about, diagnosing, and assessing groups.

Second, it explains two of the available means for better understanding and improvement of the groups in which we participate here and now and in the future. Two of the ways for diagnosing and assessing intragroup relations are through Morris and Sashkin's Integrated Group Problem-Solving Diagnostic Questionnaire and Bales' Interaction Process Analysis.

Morris and Sashkin's Integrated Group Problem-Solving Diagnostic Questionnaire

One of the best diagnostic questionnaires for assessing and guiding the problem-solving process of a work group is that developed by Morris and Sashkin.[46] Their instrument draws out the observations and perceptions of the group members and outside observers on a systematic basis. Their questionnaire directly follows each of the phases of their integrated group problem-solving model (given in Table 9–5). As shown in Figure 9–6, the questionnaire requires members to respond to a series of questions for each of the six phases of group problem solving. Moreover, separate questions are asked in terms of both the *tasks* and the *processes* of group problem solving. This forces the group members to consider *what* they are doing in each phase and *how* they are going about doing it. The diagnostic questions concerned with the content (i.e., the tasks the group is working on) are shown on the left-hand side of Figure 9–6 for each of the six phases of group problem solving. Likewise, the processes (i.e., how the group is engaging in its problem solving) are diagnosed through the questions shown on the right-hand side of Figure 9–6. For each of the questions presented, the group member or observer is asked to respond on a five-point scale that ranges from "not at all" to "fully." This questionnaire serves to identify perceived trouble spots in the group's functioning as well as to identify possible ways for improving the effectiveness of the group.

We would like you to take a few minutes to work through the questionnaire shown in Figure 9–6 by applying it to a problem-solving group in which you have been a member. You may want to use a separate sheet of paper to record your responses. From this exercise, you may be able to single out some problem areas or better understand why your group operated so effectively.

Bales' Interaction Process Analysis

Bales' Interaction Process Analysis is a well-developed technique designed to record or collect information on the behavior of the group as a whole and the behavior of the group members. Observations are typically made by someone or some mechanical device (television or tape recorder) "external" to the group. By external, we mean the observing individual or machine is not intended to be an active participant or influence on the

FIGURE 9–6.   Morris and Sashkin's Integrated Group Problem-Solving
               Diagnostic Questionnaire

Phase I. Problem Definition: Exploring, Clarifying, Defining

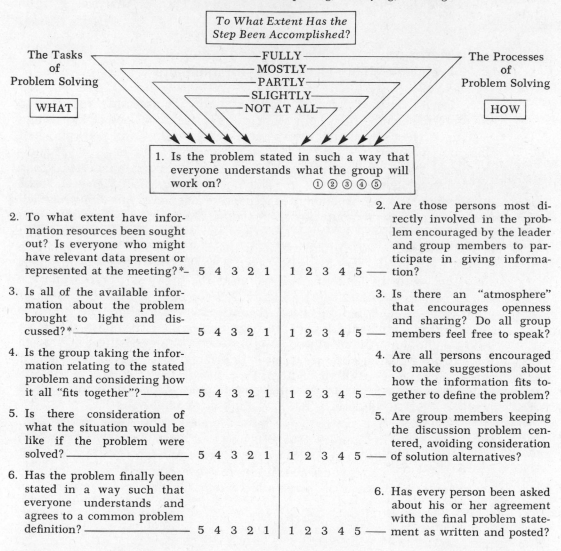

1. Is the problem stated in such a way that everyone understands what the group will work on?   ① ② ③ ④ ⑤

The Tasks of Problem Solving (WHAT)		The Processes of Problem Solving (HOW)
2. To what extent have information resources been sought out? Is everyone who might have relevant data present or represented at the meeting?*– 5 4 3 2 1	1 2 3 4 5 ——	2. Are those persons most directly involved in the problem encouraged by the leader and group members to participate in giving information?
3. Is all of the available information about the problem brought to light and discussed?*——————— 5 4 3 2 1	1 2 3 4 5 ——	3. Is there an "atmosphere" that encourages openness and sharing? Do all group members feel free to speak?
4. Is the group taking the information relating to the stated problem and considering how it all "fits together"?——— 5 4 3 2 1	1 2 3 4 5 ——	4. Are all persons encouraged to make suggestions about how the information fits together to define the problem?
5. Is there consideration of what the situation would be like if the problem were solved? ———————— 5 4 3 2 1	1 2 3 4 5 ——	5. Are group members keeping the discussion problem centered, avoiding consideration of solution alternatives?
6. Has the problem finally been stated in a way such that everyone understands and agrees to a common problem definition? —————— 5 4 3 2 1	1 2 3 4 5 ——	6. Has every person been asked about his or her agreement with the final problem statement as written and posted?

Phase II. Problem-Solution Generation: Brainstorming, Elaborating, Creating

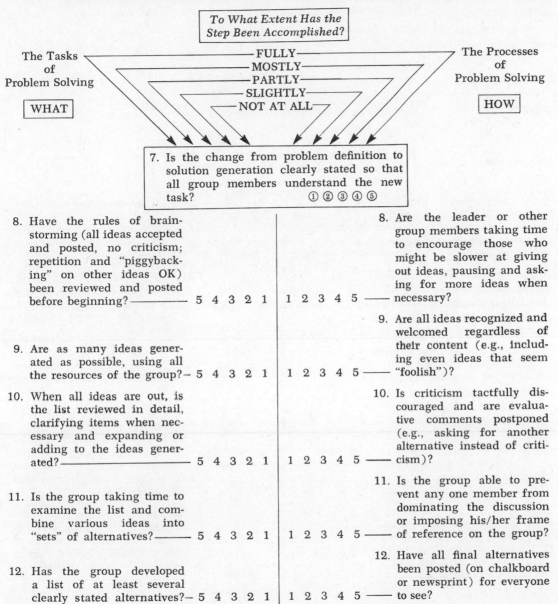

To What Extent Has the Step Been Accomplished?

The Tasks of Problem Solving

WHAT

—FULLY—
—MOSTLY—
—PARTLY—
—SLIGHTLY—
—NOT AT ALL—

The Processes of Problem Solving

HOW

7. Is the change from problem definition to solution generation clearly stated so that all group members understand the new task?   ① ② ③ ④ ⑤

8. Have the rules of brainstorming (all ideas accepted and posted, no criticism; repetition and "piggybacking" on other ideas OK) been reviewed and posted before beginning?————— 5 4 3 2 1 | 1 2 3 4 5

8. Are the leader or other group members taking time to encourage those who might be slower at giving out ideas, pausing and asking for more ideas when necessary?

9. Are as many ideas generated as possible, using all the resources of the group?— 5 4 3 2 1 | 1 2 3 4 5

9. Are all ideas recognized and welcomed regardless of their content (e.g., including even ideas that seem "foolish")?

10. When all ideas are out, is the list reviewed in detail, clarifying items when necessary and expanding or adding to the ideas generated?————— 5 4 3 2 1 | 1 2 3 4 5

10. Is criticism tactfully discouraged and are evaluative comments postponed (e.g., asking for another alternative instead of criticism)?

11. Is the group taking time to examine the list and combine various ideas into "sets" of alternatives?————— 5 4 3 2 1 | 1 2 3 4 5

11. Is the group able to prevent any one member from dominating the discussion or imposing his/her frame of reference on the group?

12. Has the group developed a list of at least several clearly stated alternatives?— 5 4 3 2 1 | 1 2 3 4 5

12. Have all final alternatives been posted (on chalkboard or newsprint) for everyone to see?

Phase III. Ideas to Actions: Evaluating, Combining, Selecting

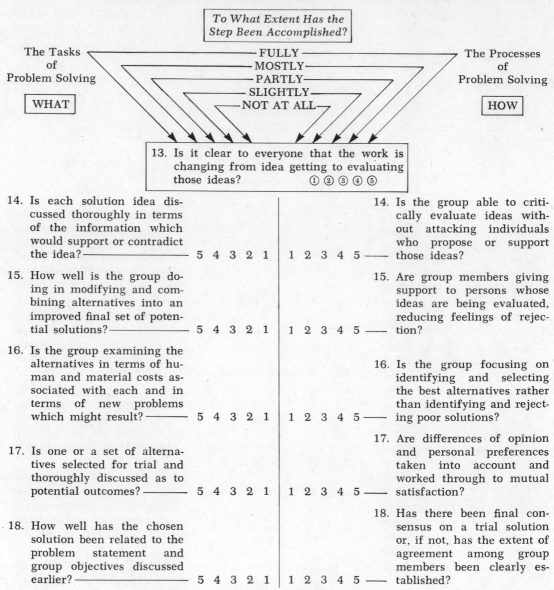

To What Extent Has the
Step Been Accomplished?

The Tasks
of
Problem Solving

WHAT

FULLY
MOSTLY
PARTLY
SLIGHTLY
NOT AT ALL

The Processes
of
Problem Solving

HOW

13. Is it clear to everyone that the work is changing from idea getting to evaluating those ideas?   ① ② ③ ④ ⑤

14. Is each solution idea discussed thoroughly in terms of the information which would support or contradict the idea?——— 5 4 3 2 1

14. Is the group able to critically evaluate ideas without attacking individuals who propose or support those ideas?

15. How well is the group doing in modifying and combining alternatives into an improved final set of potential solutions?——— 5 4 3 2 1

1 2 3 4 5 ——

15. Are group members giving support to persons whose ideas are being evaluated, reducing feelings of rejection?

16. Is the group examining the alternatives in terms of human and material costs associated with each and in terms of new problems which might result?——— 5 4 3 2 1

1 2 3 4 5 ——

16. Is the group focusing on identifying and selecting the best alternatives rather than identifying and rejecting poor solutions?

17. Is one or a set of alternatives selected for trial and thoroughly discussed as to potential outcomes?——— 5 4 3 2 1

1 2 3 4 5 ——

17. Are differences of opinion and personal preferences taken into account and worked through to mutual satisfaction?

18. How well has the chosen solution been related to the problem statement and group objectives discussed earlier?——— 5 4 3 2 1

1 2 3 4 5 ——

18. Has there been final consensus on a trial solution or, if not, has the extent of agreement among group members been clearly established?

Phase IV. Solution-Action: Planning, Assigning, Coordinating

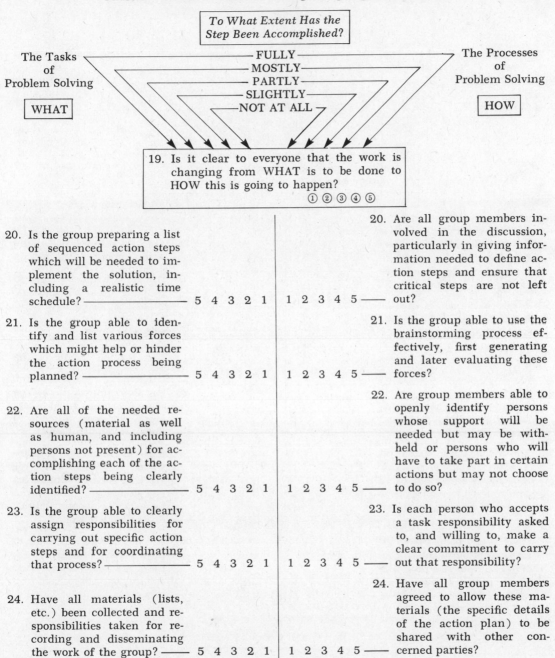

To What Extent Has the Step Been Accomplished?

The Tasks of Problem Solving

WHAT

FULLY
MOSTLY
PARTLY
SLIGHTLY
NOT AT ALL

The Processes of Problem Solving

HOW

19. Is it clear to everyone that the work is changing from WHAT is to be done to HOW this is going to happen?
① ② ③ ④ ⑤

20. Is the group preparing a list of sequenced action steps which will be needed to implement the solution, including a realistic time schedule? —— 5 4 3 2 1 | 1 2 3 4 5 ——

21. Is the group able to identify and list various forces which might help or hinder the action process being planned? —— 5 4 3 2 1 | 1 2 3 4 5 ——

22. Are all of the needed resources (material as well as human, and including persons not present) for accomplishing each of the action steps being clearly identified? —— 5 4 3 2 1 | 1 2 3 4 5 ——

23. Is the group able to clearly assign responsibilities for carrying out specific action steps and for coordinating that process? —— 5 4 3 2 1 | 1 2 3 4 5 ——

24. Have all materials (lists, etc.) been collected and responsibilities taken for recording and disseminating the work of the group? —— 5 4 3 2 1 | 1 2 3 4 5 ——

20. Are all group members involved in the discussion, particularly in giving information needed to define action steps and ensure that critical steps are not left out?

21. Is the group able to use the brainstorming process effectively, first generating and later evaluating these forces?

22. Are group members able to openly identify persons whose support will be needed but may be withheld or persons who will have to take part in certain actions but may not choose to do so?

23. Is each person who accepts a task responsibility asked to, and willing to, make a clear commitment to carry out that responsibility?

24. Have all group members agreed to allow these materials (the specific details of the action plan) to be shared with other concerned parties?

Phase V. Solution-Evaluation Planning: Describing, Monitoring, Contingency Planning

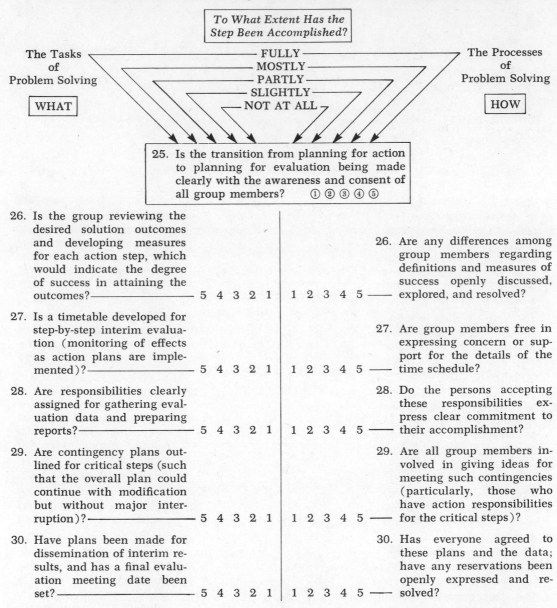

To What Extent Has the Step Been Accomplished?

The Tasks of Problem Solving

WHAT

FULLY
MOSTLY
PARTLY
SLIGHTLY
NOT AT ALL

The Processes of Problem Solving

HOW

25. Is the transition from planning for action to planning for evaluation being made clearly with the awareness and consent of all group members?   ① ② ③ ④ ⑤

26. Is the group reviewing the desired solution outcomes and developing measures for each action step, which would indicate the degree of success in attaining the outcomes?————— 5 4 3 2 1 | 1 2 3 4 5 ——— 26. Are any differences among group members regarding definitions and measures of success openly discussed, explored, and resolved?

27. Is a timetable developed for step-by-step interim evaluation (monitoring of effects as action plans are implemented)?————— 5 4 3 2 1 | 1 2 3 4 5 ——— 27. Are group members free in expressing concern or support for the details of the time schedule?

28. Are responsibilities clearly assigned for gathering evaluation data and preparing reports?————— 5 4 3 2 1 | 1 2 3 4 5 ——— 28. Do the persons accepting these responsibilities express clear commitment to their accomplishment?

29. Are contingency plans outlined for critical steps (such that the overall plan could continue with modification but without major interruption)?————— 5 4 3 2 1 | 1 2 3 4 5 ——— 29. Are all group members involved in giving ideas for meeting such contingencies (particularly, those who have action responsibilities for the critical steps)?

30. Have plans been made for dissemination of interim results, and has a final evaluation meeting date been set?————— 5 4 3 2 1 | 1 2 3 4 5 ——— 30. Has everyone agreed to these plans and the data; have any reservations been openly expressed and resolved?

Phase VI. Evaluation of the Product and the Process

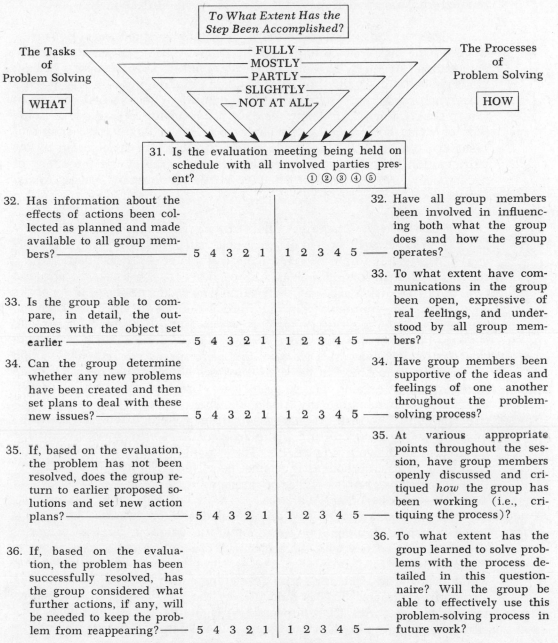

To What Extent Has the
Step Been Accomplished?

The Tasks
of
Problem Solving

FULLY
MOSTLY
PARTLY
SLIGHTLY
NOT AT ALL

The Processes
of
Problem Solving

WHAT

HOW

31. Is the evaluation meeting being held on schedule with all involved parties present?   ① ② ③ ④ ⑤

32. Has information about the effects of actions been collected as planned and made available to all group members? ——— 5 4 3 2 1

32. Have all group members been involved in influencing both what the group does and how the group operates?

33. Is the group able to compare, in detail, the outcomes with the object set earlier ——— 5 4 3 2 1

33. To what extent have communications in the group been open, expressive of real feelings, and understood by all group members?

34. Can the group determine whether any new problems have been created and then set plans to deal with these new issues? ——— 5 4 3 2 1

34. Have group members been supportive of the ideas and feelings of one another throughout the problem-solving process?

35. If, based on the evaluation, the problem has not been resolved, does the group return to earlier proposed solutions and set new action plans? ——— 5 4 3 2 1

35. At various appropriate points throughout the session, have group members openly discussed and critiqued *how* the group has been working (i.e., critiquing the process)?

36. If, based on the evaluation, the problem has been successfully resolved, has the group considered what further actions, if any, will be needed to keep the problem from reappearing? —— 5 4 3 2 1

1 2 3 4 5 ——— operates?

1 2 3 4 5 ——— bers?

1 2 3 4 5 ——— solving process?

1 2 3 4 5 ——— tiquing the process)?

36. To what extent has the group learned to solve problems with the process detailed in this questionnaire? Will the group be able to effectively use this problem-solving process in future work?

1 2 3 4 5 ——— future work?

37. Overall, how satisfied are you with the way your group solves problems?

processes and behavior of the group. However, it must be acknowledged that external observation may well influence the group's behavior.

Observer Role.   The observer(s) is usually assigned one of two tasks, or both. One task may be to assign the behavior being observed into predetermined categories. This often involves counting how frequently certain kinds of behavior occur. For example, the observer may record the frequency of laughter or disagreement in the group. A second task may be to assign some numerical index to the observed behavior by rating it on some type of scale. For example, the observer might evaluate the amount of member participation on the scale ranging from high participation to low participation. A technique emphasizing the recording of the frequency of occurrence of specific kinds of behavior is Bales' Interaction Process Analysis.

Observational Categories.   Bales' Interaction Process Analysis (hereafter IPA) consists of twelve observational categories. It is called IPA because "it attempts to abstract from the raw material of observation . . . the . . . problem-solving relevance of each act for the total on-going process."[47] IPA is particularly useful for gaining a specific understanding of the decision-making process within one's group and identifying areas for improvement. Bales suggests that group processes may be broken down into the broad areas of *socioemotional* (relations) *orientation* and *task orientation*. These basic categories are quite similar to our discussion in the section on member composition in terms of the types of role behaviors that group members might exhibit. The socioemotional orientation is further broken down into the two major categories of showing positive reactions and negative reactions. The task orientation is further broken down into the categories of asking questions and giving answers. These categories are further subdivided as shown in Figure 9–7. The various categories of behavior are related to six basic problems that must be solved if the group is to accomplish its objectives or task. Three of these problems are in the task area and three are in the socioemotional area.

In the task area, the first problem is one of orientation. *Orientation* involves arriving at a common definition of the situation. The subcategories of behavior concerned with the problem of orientation are giving information and asking for information. The second problem is one of *evaluation*, which is primarily concerned with developing a common way of evaluating alternative solutions. This is indicated by the giving-opinion and asking-for-opinion categories. The third problem is one of *control*, and deals with efforts by the group members to influence one another. This is indicated by the behavior of giving suggestions and asking for suggestions.

In the socioemotional area, the three major problems are those of decision, tension management, and integration. The problem of *decision* is concerned with the resolution of the problem or problems before the group, and is indicated by the behavioral categories of showing agreement and showing disagreement. The problem of *tension management* concerns the

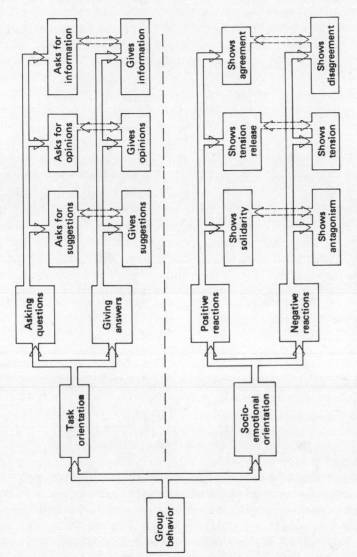

FIGURE 9–7. Simplified Bales' IPA Scheme

expression and reduction of tension. This is recorded in the categories of showing tension and tension release. Lastly, the problem of *integration* concerns the binding together and breakdown in the group. Integration is primarily evaluated through the behavioral categories of solidarity and antagonism.

Choosing a Diagnostic Approach

The choice involved in deciding to use some sort of self-report or an observational approach is certainly not a simple one. The self-report approach has the advantage of drawing from the members what they see happening in their group and how they feel about it. Measurement of the members' attitudes is at times a relatively accurate and at other times a relatively inaccurate indicator of the group's behavior.[48] The observational approach may be somewhat more accurate in reporting actual group behavior. But this is true only if the process of observing does not radically change the way the group would have behaved if it had not been under observation. The observation approach may not tell you as much about the significance and meaning of the group to the members as would the self-report approach. Many other approaches for diagnosing a group could be considered; these are described in the literature.[49]

SUMMARY

A considerable body of knowledge has been developed during the past thirty years about the functioning of groups and how they can be improved. This chapter has attempted to pull together those streams of knowledge and techniques that will help you to understand, diagnose, and improve work groups that you will be a member of and possibly lead in the future.

We wish it were possible to present you with simple and straightforward prescriptions that would guarantee you success as a member or leader of work groups. Unfortunately, the real world of organizations and work groups does not fit such neat formulas. Instead, we have opted to throw our net out to provide you with a fairly broad foundation of what is known about groups in terms of the key factors that can influence their functioning and effectiveness. First discussed were the interrelations between individuals and groups. Then types of groups were listed. Task (or work) groups were subdivided into interacting, coacting, and counteracting groups.

Next analyzed was why individuals are attracted to groups. The attractions come under the categories of interpersonal factors, group activities, group goals, and the group as a means. Major contingencies affecting groups were discussed: size, member composition, norms, goals, cohesiveness, leadership, and the external environment. Group members were distinguished as to whether they were task-oriented, relations-oriented, or self-oriented. Norms, which can be positive or negative in relation to organizational goals and productivity were distinguished from rules. Under norms, two types of conformity—compliance and personal acceptance—were compared and contrasted. Cohesiveness was related to conformity, groupthink, and productivity. Under leadership it was shown that a group can have both formal and informal leaders.

The next major section of the chapter provided concepts and techniques about how groups make decisions as well as how group decision making should be implemented and when it should be used. The six areas covered were individual versus group decision making, degrees of participation in decision making, content of group decisions, benefits and limitations of group participation, phases of integrated group problem solving, and interacting versus nominal decision groups.

Finally, two basic approaches for diagnosing work groups were presented. Without proper diagnosis, it is likely that the wrong problems will be identified and the wrong prescriptions implemented for improving the groups' functioning.

Although the next chapter focuses on relations between groups, much of it naturally has implications for relations within groups. Thus, this chapter has certainly not presented all issues or suggestions associated with dynamics within groups, particularly work groups.

DISCUSSION QUESTIONS

1. Identify a group in which you are presently a member. By utilizing the framework presented in Figure 9–1, analyze the specific sources of attraction and/or rejection of this group for *you* in terms of interpersonal factors, group activities, group goals, the group as a means.

2. How would you assess the effects of group size on the group you identified in question 1? Is your group characterized by effects of group size as presented in Table 9–1?

3. Identify three prevalent norms of a work group in which you have been a member. Table 9–3 might be helpful in stimulating your thinking. Do you think that you or other group members conformed to these norms on the basis of compliance or personal acceptance? Explain.

4. Describe the leadership process of a work group in which you have been a member. Did there seem to be a task leader and a socioemotional leader, or did one person perform both these tasks? Evaluate the group leader or leaders in terms of the types of behavior identified for effective group leaders in the chapter.

5. Describe and evaluate the content of group decisions that were (or are) made by your work group. Table 9–4 should be helpful in performing this task. Should the group decisions be changed for improved effectiveness? Explain.

6. What is meant by group cohesiveness? How is it related to group conformity?

7. What is meant by groupthink? Why is it likely to be a problem?

8. Is group decision making superior to individual decision-making? Explain.

MANAGERIAL PROBLEMS

GROUP DECISION MAKING

The following conversation took place between a team of postal supervisors, carrier examiners, finance personnel, and a trainer-consultant (Mr. Saxbe). This team was attempting to learn to be a more effectively functioning group.*

*Excerpted from Joyce, R. D., *Encounters in Organizational Behavior* (New York: Pergamon Press, 1972), pp. 54–57. Used with permission.

Wrigley:	Well, so far we've agreed to eliminate numbers 1, 2, and 4 as problems this group would like to work to improve. Now then, let's take a straw vote on the remaining problems. How many would like to work on number 3, *How to prevent mis-sent mail to direct firm holdouts?* (*counts raised hands*) One . . . two . . . three . . and I make four. How about *Better internal communication?* (*counts hands*) One . . . two. Okay, reducing absenteeism? One . . . two.
Hernandez:	Hey, who didn't vote?
Evans:	Saxbe and Cline.
Saxbe:	The facilitator has no vote.
McCleary:	(*smiling*) Stand up and be counted, Mrs. Cline.
Cline:	I hesitated because I think they are all very interesting problems and I'll go along with the majority.
Hernandez:	Well, that settles it . . . we'll work on mis-sent mail. . . .
Evans:	(*upset*) Now wait a second! If we've been assembled to meet here four hours each week for eight weeks, I think we should tackle a really big problem like communication. Lord knows we need better communication!
Lowell:	I agree with Mr. Evans. Communication is a terribly important problem.
Wrigley:	But, as stated, it's so vague. How do we begin to go about attacking the problem?
Hernandez:	It's like the weather. You can talk about it all you want but nobody's going to be able to do much about it.
Smith:	That's for sure!
Fisher:	(*irritated*) Let's get on with it! We're not getting anywhere.
Hernandez:	Majority rules. We'll work on mis-sent mail.

Saxbe: (*breaking in on group discussion*) Since our purpose here is to better understand the nature of leadership and group process methods as well as solving particular Postal Service problems, I feel I am justified in intervening at this point. Behavioral scientists agree that the majority vote, or so-called democratic process, is generally better for obtaining personal decision commitment than, say, autocratic choice of the leader. . . .

Hernandez: That's what I just said . . . majority rules . . . we'll work on mis-sent. . . .

Saxbe: (*interrupting Hernandez*) But majority rule, although a reasonable expedient for the sake of time, is not always the best way. . . .

Blackman: What other way is there?

Saxbe: Consensus. Although procedurally slower at first, it can often prove to be better than majority rule.

Blackman: I don't see the difference.

Saxbe: Consensus is a working through of differences to ultimately arrive at a decision, whereas the democratic vote has a tendency to arbitrarily cut off all objections, reasonable or not, at a fixed point in time. This can often suppress further involvement or commitment by someone whose views have been overruled or denied expression.

Smith: Good grief! You mean we have to get *everyone* to agree before we move on? We'll be as deadlocked as a hung jury!

Blackman: Exactly what are the implications of consensus to group progress, Mr. Saxbe

Saxbe: Not nearly as bad as I have apparently made it appear. Your straw vote was procedurally sound. It showed where the majority stands on the issue. My only concern is that the minority should not now be arbitrarily shut off.

Fisher: You mean we keep talking until Evans wins us over to *his* point of view?

Saxbe: Not necessarily, although that could happen. We're not severely time limited. I prefer to see consensus within the group before moving on than to have us work on a democratically chosen problem and not have the full and active support of several persons.

Wrigley: I'm a little confused. What should we do next? What is my role as the leader?

Saxbe: I'd ask the group what they think.

Wrigley: Okay. (*to group*) Where do we go from here?

Lowell: I still stand with Mr. Smith, but I do see that we will have some difficulty addressing ourselves to a problem as complex and vague as communication unless we break it down in some way. I suggest we ask our two members who voted for *reducing absenteeism* for their comments.

Wrigley: Good idea. Who voted for working on the absenteeism problem? (*McClearly and Blackman raise hands*)

McCleary: Let's not fight, team. (*smiling*) I voted for absenteeism because I see it as a big problem. However, at the large mail processing and distribution center, absenteeism could be job related . . . that is, somehow tied in with carelessness and poor motivation. If I have to make a choice between the two, I lean toward working on the problem of mis-sent mail. (*pause*) Even in discussing that problem I'll still get in some shots at the absenteeism problem. (*general laughter*)

Wrigley: I think you're right, McCleary. I have a feeling that excessive absenteeism may well be a symptom of low job motivation. (*momentary silence*)

Blackman: Well, I voted for absenteeism as well. I lean toward taking communication as our problem but it really is too vague as we've stated it up to this point. We'd really have to break it down.

Hernandez: Hey! If we're going to take one aspect of improving communication, why not tie it in with the mis-sent mail problem? Maybe the clerks don't fully understand the implications when they don't "stick" mail correctly? Maybe we have to communicate better or give them better instruction or training. Maybe mis-sent mail involves communication.

Cline: That's a good idea Mr. Hernandez. I'll go along with that and support the mis-sent mail problem.

Blackman: (*smiling*) I wouldn't want it to get around that I actually agreed on something with Hernandez (*a few chuckles*) but he does have a point. I'll go along with mis-sent mail.

Wrigley: All right, that makes seven who support the idea of working on the problem of mis-sent mail.

Lowell: I really have no objections either, except that as a customer service representative I have no knowledge of operations at the mail processing and distribution centers. I don't feel I will be able to contribute very much.

Wrigley: That's not really true, Mrs. Lowell. Some of us are too close to the problem and may not be able to see the forest for the trees. You can check our thinking by asking questions and by offering fresh and unbiased ideas.

Lowell: You make my role sound very important, Mr. Wrigley. I'm glad we made you the leader. (*general laughter*) I hope I don't ask too many dumb questions.

Hernandez: (*emphatically*) There is no such thing as a dumb question. Right, Mr. Saxbe?

Saxbe: Right.

(*momentary silence*)

Fisher: Well, what do you say, Mr. Evans? You going to join us?

Evans: The ground has my support. I'm sorry if I was divisive and held up progress. It's just that I feel so strongly about the communications problem. . . .

Wrigley: Not at all, Evans. All of us share your general sentiments.

McCleary: Hey, Evans, you can still get your shots in . . . like I'm going to.

Wrigley: (*summarizing*) It appears then that we have indeed reached a consensus that this group will work on the problem of mis-sent mail to direct firm holdouts.

Lowell: Mr. Saxbe, is this what you meant by working through differences in arriving at a decision?

Saxbe: Essentially. It took a few minutes longer but the group is now more likely to make better progress from this point forward . . . and with everyone's active support.

Cline: I think we really work well together.

Saxbe: You do. (*winking*) For all practical purposes I might as well go home.

Fisher: I'll buy that! I'd like to go home too.

QUESTIONS

1. What ideas and concepts about group participative decision making does this illustrate?
2. What is your diagnosis of the effectiveness of this group? You should use Morris and Sashkin's Integrated Group Problem Solving Diagnostic Questionnaire to undertake this task.
3. What might have been done to make this group more effective?

PARMA PLANT

Alvin Brown, a plant manager of the Parma Plant of Wiley Corporation attended a management seminar conducted at a large university. The two-week seminar primarily emphasized managerial decision making.

Professor Scholar of the university staff especially impressed Alvin Brown with the lectures on group processes and decision making. On the basis of research and experience, Professor Scholar told the managers that employees, if given the opportunity, could diagnose and evaluate many problems and arrive at quality decisions that would be enthusiastically accepted.

Upon returning to his plant, Mr. Brown decided to practice some of the principles presented. He called together the fifteen employees of Department A and told them that production standards established several years previously were now too low in view of the recent installation of automated equipment. He was giving them the opportunity to discuss these circumstances and to decide among themselves as a group, what their production standards should be. On leaving the room, Mr. Brown believed the workers would establish much higher standards than he would ever dare propose.

After three hours of discussion over a three-day period, the workers summoned Mr. Brown and notified him that, contrary to his opinion, their group decision was that the standards were already too high, and since they had been given the authority to establish their own standards, they were making a reduction of 5 percent. Mr. Brown knew these standards were far too low to provide an adequate profit on the owners' investment. Yet, as Professor Scholar emphasized in the seminar, the refusal to accept a work group's decision could be disastrous. Before doing anything, Mr. Brown called Professor Scholar at the university for his opinion.

QUESTIONS

1. Assuming you are Professor Scholar, what "errors" do you think were made by Mr. Brown?
2. What advice might you give to Mr. Brown?

KEY WORDS

Group	*Conformity*
Friendship group	*Compliance*
Task group	*Personal acceptance conformity*
Interacting group	*Group goals*
Coacting group	*Cohesiveness*
Counteracting group	*Groupthink*
Activities	*Informal leader*
Interactions	*External environment*
Outputs	*Participative decision making*
Sentiments	*Integrated group problem solving*
Task-oriented role	*Nominal group technique*
Relations-oriented role	*Semantic differential technique*
Norms	*Interaction process analysis*

REFERENCES

1. Summers, D. B., Understanding the process by which new employees enter work groups, *Personnel Journal*, 1977, 56, pp. 394–397+; Wanous, T. P., Organizational entry: Newcomers moving from outside to inside, *Psychological Bulletin*, 1977, 84, pp. 601–618.

2. Homans, G. C., *The Human Group* (New York: Harcourt, Brace and World, 1950), p. 2; also see Miller, J., Living systems: The group, *Behavioral Science*, 1971, 16, pp. 302–398.

3. Miller, D., *Individualism: Personal Achievement and the Open Society* (Austin: University of Texas Press, 1967), p. 85.

4. An account by Edward R. Murrow, in *S. Hurok Presents Marian Anderson*, quoted from Miller, Living systems.

5. Riesman, D., *Individualism Reconsidered* (New York: Free Press, 1954); Fildman, D. C., A contingency theory of socialization, *Administrative Science Quarterly*, 1976, 21, pp. 433–452.

6. Cartwright, D., and R. Lippitt, Group dynamics and the individual, *International Journal of Group Psychotherapy*, 1957, 7, pp. 86–102.

7. Fiedler, F., *A Theory of Leadership Effectiveness* (New York: McGraw-Hill, 1967).

8. Shaw, M., *Group Dynamics: The Psychology of Small Group Behavior* (New York: McGraw-Hill, 1971); also see Hill, R. A., Interpersonal compatibility and workgroup performance, *Journal of Applied Behavioral Science*, 1975, 11, pp. 210–240.

9. Ross, I., and A. Zantler, Need satisfaction and employee turnover, *Personnel Psychology*, 1957, 10, pp. 327–338.

10. Turquet, P., Leadership: The individual and the group, in Gibbard, G., J. Hartman, and R. Mann (eds.), *Analysis of Groups* (San Francisco: Jossey-Bass, 1974), pp. 349–386.

11. Homans, *Human Group*, p. 368.

12. Ibid., p. 36.

13. Ibid., p. 38.

14. Turquet, *Leadership*, p. 350.

15. Berelson, B., and G. Steiner, *Human Behavior: An Inventory of Scientific Findings* (New York: Harcourt, Brace and World, 1964), esp. pp. 356–360.

16. Melnick, J., and M. Wood, Analysis of group composition research and theory

for psychotherapeutic and growth-oriented groups, *The Journal of Applied Behavioral Science,* 1976, 12, pp. 493–512; Mieker, B. F., and P. A. Weitzel-O'Neill, Sex roles and interpersonal behavior in task-oriented groups, *American Sociological Review,* 1977, 42, pp. 91–105; White, J. K., generalizability of individual difference moderators of the participation in decision-making employee response relationship, *Academy of Management Journal,* 1978, 21, pp.36–43.

17.   Bales, R. R., *Interaction Process Analysis a Method for the Study of Groups* (Reading, Mass.: Addison-Wesley, 1950).

18.   McGrath, J. E., and J. E. Altman, *Small Group Research* (New York: Holt, Rinehart and Winston, 1966), p. 65.

19.   Allen, P. F., and S. Pilnick, Confronting the shadow organizations: How to detect and defeat negative norms, *Organizational Dynamics,* 1973, 1, pp. 3–18.

20.   Kiesler, C., and S. Kiesler, *Conformity* (Reading, Mass.: Addison-Wesley, 1969).

21.   Rothlisberger, F. J., and W. J. Dickson, *Management and the Worker: Technical Versus Social Organization in an Industrial Plant* (Cambridge: Harvard University Press, 1939).

22.   Patchen, M., *Participation, Achievement, and Involvement on the Job* (Englewood Cliffs, N.J.: Prentice-Hall, 1970).

23.   Mills, T. M., *The Sociology of Small Groups* (Englewood Cliffs, N.J.: Prentice-Hall, 1967).

24.   Philip, H., and D. Dunphy, Development trends in small groups, *Sociometry,* 1954, 22, pp. 162–174.

25.   Janis, I. L., *Victims of Groupthink: A Psychological Study of Foreign Policy Decisions and Fiascos* (Boston: Houghton Mifflin, 1972).

26.   Janis, I. L., and L. Mann, *Decision Making: A Psychological Analysis of Conflict, Choice, and Commitment.* New York: The Free Press, 1977.

27.   Sherif, M., and C. Sherif, *Groups in Harmony and Tension.* New York: Harper & Row, 1953; Shirom, A., On some correlates of combat performance, *Administra-*

tive Science Quarterly, 1976, 21, pp. 419–432.

28.   Seashore, S., *Group Cohesiveness in the Industrial Work Group* (Ann Arbor: Survey Research Center, University of Michigan, 1954.

29.   Bales, R., *Interaction Process Analysis* (Reading, Mass.: Addison-Wesley, 1950).

30.   Crockett, W., Emergent leadership in small, decision-making groups, *Journal of Abnormal and Social Psychology,* 1955, 51, pp. 378–383.

31.   Nemiroff, P. M., and A. L. Ford Jr., The "fit" between work group structure and tasks: Its influence on task effectiveness and human fullfillment, *Organization and Administrative Sciences,* 1977/1978, 8, pp. 15–34.

32.   Zander, A., *Groups at Work* (San Francisco: Jossey-Bass, 1977).

33.   Geer, J., *A Psychological Study of Problem-Solving* (Holland: de Toarts, 1957); Schoner, B., and G. Rose, Quality of decisions: Individual versus real and synthetic groups, *Journal of Applied Psychology,* 1974, 59, pp. 424–432.

34.   Sashkin, M., Changing toward participative management approaches: A model and methods, *Academy of Management Review,* 1976, 1, pp. 75–86.

35.   Vroom, V. H., and P. W. Yetton, *Leadership and Decision Making* (Pittsburgh: University of Pittsburgh Press, 1973).

36.   Wood, M., Power relationships and group decision-making in organizations, *Psychological Bulletin,* 1973, 74, pp. 280–293.

37.   Levine, E., Problems of organizational control in microcosm: Group performance and group member satisfaction as a function of differences in control structure, *Journal of Applied Psychology,* 1973, 58, pp. 186–196.

38.   Bragg, J., and I. Andrews, Participative decision-making: An experimental study in a hospital, *Journal of Applied Behavioral Science,* 1973, 9, pp. 727–735.

39.   Lowin, A., Participative decision-making: A model, literature critique, and

prescriptions for research, *Organizational Behavior and Human Performance*, 1968, 3, pp. 68–106.

40.   Mansbridge, J., Time, emotion, and inequality: Three problems of participatory groups, *Journal of Applied Behavioral Science*, 1973, 9, pp. 351–368.

41.   Morris, W. C., and M. Sashkin, *Organization Behavior in Action: Skill Building Experiences* (St. Paul, Minn.: West Publishing, 1976).

42.   Van de Ven, A. H., Group decision-making and effectiveness: An experimental study, *Organization and Administrative Sciences*, 1974, 5, pp. 1–110.

43.   Van de Ven, A. H., Nominal versus interacting group processes for committee decision-making effectiveness, *Academy of Management Journal*, 1971, 14, pp. 203–212.

44.   Delbecq, A. L., A. H. Van de Ven, and D. H. Gustafson, *Group Techniques for Program Planning: A Guide to Nominal and Delphi Processes* (Glenview, Ill.: Scott, Foresman, 1975), pp. 7–10, 17–18.

45.   Green, T. B., An empirical analysis of nominal and interacting groups, *Academy of Management Journal*, 1975, 18, pp. 63–73.

46.   Morris, and Sashkin, *Skill Building Experiences*.

47.   Bales, R., A set of categories for the analysis of small group interaction, *American Sociological Review*, 1950, 15, pp. 257–263.

48.   Liska, A., Emergent issues in the attitude-behavior consistency controversy, *American Sociological Review*, 1974, 39, pp. 261–272.

49.   Madron, T., *Small-Group Methods and the Study of Politics* (Evanston, Ill.: Northwestern University Press, 1969).

10

Dynamics Between Groups

10

LEARNING OBJECTIVES

When you have finished reading and studying this chapter, you should be able to:

▲ Explain how the following contingencies can influence the dynamics between groups: goals, uncertainty absorption, substitutability, task relations, resource sharing, and attitudinal sets.

▲ Diagnose the possible causes of problems between groups.

▲ Know how and when to use the six formal mechanisms for managing the dynamics between groups: hierarchy, plans, linking roles, task forces, integrating roles, and matrix organization.

▲ Describe the four formal mechanisms that are used to deal with the relations between workers and management as distinct groups: hierarchy, joint consultation, collective bargaining, workers' control.

THOUGHT STARTERS

▲ How do you think dynamics between groups differ from dynamics between individuals?

▲ What factors do you think can effect dynamics between groups?

▲ How can a manager improve the effectiveness of dynamics between groups?

OUTLINE

MAJOR CONTINGENCIES
INFLUENCING DYNAMICS
BETWEEN GROUPS
  Goals
  Uncertainty Absorption
  Substitutability
  Task Relations
  Resource Sharing
  Attitudinal Sets
FORMAL MECHANISMS FOR
MANAGING THE DYNAMICS
BETWEEN LATERAL GROUPS
  Factors Influencing Lateral Relations
  Overview of Formal Mechanisms
  Hierarchy
  Plans
  Linking Roles
  Task Forces
  Integrating Roles
  Matrix Organization
FORMAL APPROACHES FOR
MANAGING THE DYNAMICS
BETWEEN WORKERS AND
MANAGEMENT
  Joint Consultation
  Collective Bargaining
  Workers' Control
SUMMARY
DISCUSSION QUESTIONS
MANAGERIAL PROBLEMS
  Inland Division: Group and Intergroup Relations
  Lindell-Billings Corporation
KEY WORDS
REFERENCES

There was a time when conversation in the judges' lunchroom atop the State Supreme Court Building in Manhattan centered on fine legal points—the handling of a motion, say, or the implications of a decision.

Now, discouraged by cuts in their budgets, distracted by charges of corruption in the courts, and vexed by an administrative struggle that they contend threatens their independence and dignity, judges are exchanging notes on the lack of morale. "I love the work," one judge commented recently over lunch, "but I hate the job."

After frequent informal discussions of the problem, the 120 State Supreme Court justices in New York City were invited to join a committee last week to "act as one voice in a time of crisis."

The committee's acting president, Justice Edward J. Greenfield, said that the justices' first worry was how they would be able to function without their confidential aides, who were scheduled to lose their jobs today for budgetary reasons. The aides type decisions, answer phones, and perform other clerical functions for the justices.

More generally, Justice Greenfield said his colleagues were concerned about their reputations and credibility, which they maintained have been damaged by the charges being made by Maurice H. Nadjari, the special state prosecutor investigating corruption in the criminal-justice system.

But the issue that has preoccupied the judges, according to Justice Greenfield, is how to fight domination by the state's Office of Court Administration under the direction of Justice Richard J. Bartlett. "We want the right to give the orders," said Justice Moses M. Weinstein, deputy administrative judge in charge of Queens, who is also a member of the committee. "Who knows the courts better than a judge right on the scene?"

At issue is who should oversee the nonjudicial matters of State Supreme Court: the Office of Court Administration or deputy borough administrators under the direction of Justice David Ross.

Up until last November Justice Ross and his deputies were responsible for the management of nonjudicial personnel: court officers, secretaries, stenographers, and so on. In November this authority was signed over to Justice Bartlett's office. The justices' fight is to regain this responsibility. They view the matter as crucial to maintaining the judiciary's independence.

Justice Bartlett, a Glens Falls judge who was appointed state administrator in January 1974 by Chief Judge Charles D. Breitel of the State Court of Appeals in a move to spur statewide improvements in the judicial system, said he viewed the matter in terms of efficiency. "There are many advantages," said Justice

Bartlett, commenting on centrally managed personnel. "Non-judicial needs could be viewed from a citywide perspective, the city court system could be viewed as a single budgetary entity and costs could be handled on a uniform basis."

The justices contend that they are not opposed to central-ization as such but rather are concerned about taking directions from a central administrator who is not a judge. Peter Preiser, Justice Bartlett's deputy administrator in charge of the city's courts, is not a judge. The judges maintain that Mr. Preiser's appointment is a first step to taking judicial power away from the judiciary.[1]

This incident addresses a number of issues and aspects of the dynamics between two key groups within the New York state court system—the judges and the Office of Court Administration. It directly or indirectly touches on a number of issues that are of direct concern in this chapter —goal incompatibility, power relations, task relations, resource sharing, hierarchy, bargaining, and others. Although the problems and issues of managing intergroup relations are not always so dramatic or so intense as in this case incident, the need for managing the dynamics between groups is ongoing in all types of organizations. This incident sharply illustrates that an understanding of intergroup relations is important to all of us because: (1) we often have to work with and through other groups to accomplish our objectives; and (2) other groups within the organization often create problems and demands on our own work groups. Thus other groups within the organization may be an important component to the "external" environment of your work group.

The previous chapter focused on the dynamics within an interact-ing group of twelve or fewer individuals. In this chapter, the primary focus is on the dynamics between groups of various sizes. Most of this chapter could be relevant for: (1) two groups within a single functional area, such as marketing research and sales; (2) two different functional departments, such as personnel and production; (3) a product unit, such as a car division and corporate headquarters; (4) a staff unit, such as a planning group and top management; and (5) other formal or informal groupings that can be identified as being interdependent. The use of the word *group* in this chapter goes beyond the definition of group—face-to-face relations—used in the previous chapter. In this chapter, group is used synonymously with *department* and *unit*. Although this chapter con-siders some aspects of intergroup conflict, a more extensive presentation of this topic is made in Chapter 14 on conflict processes.

MAJOR CONTINGENCIES INFLUENCING DYNAMICS BETWEEN GROUPS

Consistent with the discussion of dynamics within groups, no single contingency or factor can serve as a simple explanation of dynamics between groups. The primary strategy in this section is to explain how and why each contingency can influence the dynamics between groups. The secondary strategy is selectively to explain how two or more of these contingencies can interact to influence intergroup dynamics. Figure 10–1 identifies six major contingencies that may have an impact on the dynamics between two or more groups: goals, uncertainty absorption, substitutability, task relations, resource sharing, and attitudinal sets. The dashed lines between the contingencies are intended to reflect their potential interconnectedness.

Goals

The goals of two groups can have a powerful impact on their relationships with one another. *Goals* are desired end states. Decision makers often use goals to indicate their relative preferences:

> *The corporate directors of the Nu-made Plastics Company determined that the short-run goal of their firm should be a 10 percent increase in profits. To reach this goal, Nu-made's production department might have a goal of a 5 percent increase in*

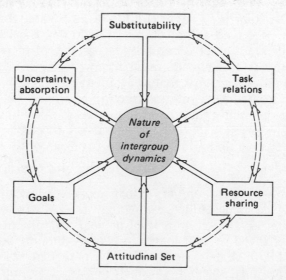

FIGURE 10–1.   Some Contingencies Influencing Dynamics Between Groups

*efficiency; the marketing department might have a goal to intro-
duce three new products or services; the research department
might have a goal to develop less expensive materials of equal
quality for one of Nu-made's product lines; the personnel department might have a goal to reduce turnover of blue-collar workers
by 10 percent; and the finance department might have a goal to
reduce the average time period for accounts receivable from 40
to 37 days.*

Three ideas are important in these goals (1) Each goal represents
an example of only one of the several goals each of these departments is
likely to have. (2) The goals for each of the groups (production, personnel, marketing, etc.) are intended as subgoals to help the organization obtain the stated broader goal of a 10 percent increase in profits. (3)
The accomplishment of the stated goal of each group may require interaction with one or more of the other groups. For example, the personnel
department might need the cooperation of production supervisors in reducing turnover or the finance department might need more information
from the marketing department regarding the financial status of customers.

The ideal state might exist when each group perceives its goals,
the goals of the organization as a whole, and the goals of other groups as
compatible with one another and mutually reinforcing. This would be a
win-win situation. Each group can gain or attain its goal if the other groups
attain their goals. In such a case, we are likely to find open and free-
flowing communications between groups, cooperation, mutual concern,
and respect for each other's problems, and rapid problem solving. However, goals are not always perceived or designed to be quite so compatible
and mutually reinforcing.

Goal Conflict.   Goal conflict occurs when goal achievement by one
group is perceived as preventing or reducing the level of goal attainment
by one or more other groups. Widespread goal incompatibility of the win-
lose variety is unlikely within an organization. But a win-lose situation does
exist when one group's goal attainment is at the direct expense or cost of
another group. This might occur at Nu-made when the production department perceives that the introduction of three new products by the marketing group might decrease the former's reported efficiency by 5 percent
rather than enabling it to realize its goal of a 5 percent increase in
efficiency.

Mixed Goal Conflict.   Goal conflict between departments is more
often mixed goal conflict, rather than a total win-lose situation. This may
mean that up to a certain level of goal attainment for each group, there
is no perceived or real conflict. The production department at Nu-made
might believe that it can attain its 5 percent efficiency goal if marketing
introduces only one new product, a 2 percent improvement in efficiency
with the introduction of two products, and a 5 percent drop in efficiency

with the introduction of three products. This example assumes that three new products are likely to have an impact on the production department's efficiency because of the new learning and start-up costs experienced by production personnel. It also assumes that certain thresholds exist for the production department: one new product can be accommodated and still allow the department to meet its goals, some impact occurs with two new products, and chaos starts to set in for the production unit with the introduction of three new products.

These assumptions clarify why the production department might perceive its goals, at some point, as being potentially incompatible with those of marketing. Production may claim that the lost efficiencies are not offset by the possible gains of introducing three new products within a one-year time period. But the introduction of these products over three years, rather than one year, could enable production to meet its efficiency goal and marketing to meet its long-term goal of being responsive to changing customer needs. Can you think of some counterarguments marketing might present?

One way for reducing this goal conflict is for higher management simply to relax the requirement of a 5 percent improvement in efficiency for the production department. However, if the members of the production department had personally accepted (internalized) the efficiency goal, the willingness of higher management to relax or modify it may not reduce resistance to or questioning of the desirability of introducing three new products. In the first place, it is extremely difficult to establish meaningful production goals for the new products when they are first manufactured because each production worker has to be trained to perform the new tasks and new machine standards have to be set. Thus the production members could experience some short-run losses in the reduced sense of accomplishment or achievement unless new standards and goals are reached. New products may also require changing comfortable habits and work patterns and demand new skills. If the production unit had not been accustomed to change, these new requirements could create considerable frustration and anxieties for workers.

Intergroup Competition: An Application of Goal Conflict.   Structured competition *between* groups often represents an application of goal conflict. Of course, intergroup competition is likely to relate most dramatically to goal conflict when the groups must interact interdependently. When Penn State and Pittsburgh or Texas A&M and the University of Texas meet on the football field each year, each wants to win over the other. As fans at Texas A&M are so fond of saying, "beat the h--- out of Texas." They are supposed to compete, not collaborate.

Research has shown that there are some very predictable outcomes between competing groups that must interact with each other. You may want to think about the dynamics between competing groups that you are familiar with in terms of the following questions.[2] We will have more to say about this in Chapter 14 on conflict processes.

What happens within each competing group?   Each group becomes more cohesive and obtains greater loyalty from its members; members close ranks and bury some of their differences. The group increases its task orientation relative to socioemotional concerns. Leadership becomes more structured and authoritarian, and the group members become more accepting of this type of leadership. Finally, the group demands more loyalty and conformity so that it can present a solid front.

What happens between the competing groups?   Each group may begin to see the other as the enemy. Distortion of perceptions sets in, such as perceiving your own group in positive terms and the other group in negative terms. Thus, stereotypes are soon formed ("They are dirty players"), with increasing hostilities toward each other. Interaction and communication decline. When the groups do interact, there is a tendency to emphasize and listen only to their own self-concerns and to discount the statements of the other group.

What happens to the winner?   The winning group often becomes more cohesive and tends to release its tension in the victory celebration. Over time, the winner may become complacent ("fat and happy") and feel there is little need to reexamine its own internal functioning.

What happens to the loser?   When possible, the loser may deny or distort the reality of losing: "The referees were biased," "It was an unlucky day," and so forth. When the loss is accepted, conflicts may come to the surface, fights may break out or blame-placing may be emphasized. As a result, there is more tension and less intragroup cooperation. Over time, the group may reevaluate its self-perceptions and stereotypes, which could lead to a reorganization and other changes.

Significance to Management.   The degree to which two interacting groups perceive their goals as compatible or in conflict with each other may have considerable impact on the nature of their relations. Complete compatibility in goals between units is neither possible nor necessarily even desirable. The specialization of labor that is inherent in organizations creates the inevitable condition of some degree of tunnel vision, or narrowness in goal orientation by the members comprising a group. The question of goal conflict is not whether or not it occurs, but to what degree goal conflict occurs, what its effects are, and what mechanisms are available to manage it creatively.

Uncertainty Absorption

Uncertainty is the complement of knowledge. "It is the gap between what is known and what needs to be known to make correct decisions."[3] One way of managing uncertainty is to create particular groups or assign particular people to deal with it. Here the focus is on uncertainty absorption by a group rather than an individual. Some groups absorb particular types of uncertainty for other groups in the organization.[4] *Uncertainty absorption* occurs when one group makes particular decisions for another group or sets the decision premises for another group. For example, the accounting department might develop uniform procedures and guidelines for handling expense accounts. Thus a sales manager would have many ready-made answers provided by accounting regarding how to process expense accounts and how to determine what is allowable. Accounting has absorbed the uncertainty the sales manager might have experienced in handling expense-account matters with sales representatives.

Effects on Relative Power. An important effect of uncertainty absorption is the impact it can have on the relative power of groups. The power of one group may serve as the basis for influencing the behavior of another group. Power has three major dimensions: weight, domain, and scope.[5] The *weight* of power is the degree to which one group can affect the behavior of another group. The *domain* of power for a group is the number of other groups it affects. The *scope* of power is the range of behaviors or decision issues that are determined by one group for another group. In relation to our earlier example, accounting carries a heavy *weight* with respect to expense-account procedures; the *domain* of accounting in expense-account matters is relatively encompassing, affecting virtually all members in marketing as well as in other groups; and the *scope* of behaviors affected in marketing by these procedures is probably small relative to marketing's important behaviors and goals.

The actual power of accounting relative to marketing in expense-account procedures (or any two groups on any issues) cannot be assumed. For example, marketing could require accounting to change its expense-account procedures because they are too cumbersome or time-consuming. Or, accounting might have to discuss and obtain approval from the top management in marketing before making any changes in expense-account matters. In this situation, it would be very deceiving to see the statement of procedures and rules from accounting regarding expense-account matters and to conclude that they have high power even in this single area. The real power of accounting relative to expense accounts may be more to enforce the procedures and rules. Of course, this could become a major source of power.

Case Study of Uncertainty Absorption. Since uncertainty absorption is an important contingency for understanding intergroup dynamics, an abridged version of an actual case study that dramatically demonstrates this concept is provided here. This case study, by Fred Goldner, focuses on the relationship between the industrial relations department and the production department of one of the companies of a multicompany corporation.[6] Most of the data were obtained from the main plant of the company, which used a continuous-process technology that converted a raw material into a product used in construction.

Role of Unions: *The most important tasks of the industrial relations department were those related to the unions, including negotiating union-management agreements, processing working grievances, and interpreting issues covered in the agreement. The mechanisms and practices by which the industrial relations department absorbed uncertainty for the production department stemmed heavily from the union's existence. A significant source of the industrial relations power relative to other departments within the scope of plant-level issues stemmed from their (I.R.'s) use of the union as an "outside" threat that could adversely affect the whole organization.*

One industrial relations manager recognized that their supposed antagonists, the unions, were a major source of their internal power in these words: "As I told one of the (other I.R.) guys who was damning the unions, 'Don't bite the hand that feeds you.' "[7] The union increased the need to maintain uniformity and coordination in industrial relations policies, practices, procedures, and rules. Without coordination, one plant might yield on union demands unimportant to them but of relevance to other companies or plants.

Appeal to Superior Knowledge: *To maintain and increase its autonomy and power, the industrial relations department always claimed to possess the "bigger picture," which must be considered for decision making related to the organization's human resources. The inconsistent pressures of maintaining uniform labor relations policies, rules, procedures, and the like, while also trying to give a reasonable amount of autonomy to managers within the companies and plants, created considerable uncertainty and some conflict. Because of these conflicting pressures both within management and between management and the union, the industrial relations department played a key role in absorbing many of the uncertainties created.*

The industrial relations department had superior knowledge of the bargaining agreements. They also had considerable ability to apply the knowledge. Industrial relations people often asserted: "You never go by the wording in contracts. You go by the interpretation."[8] Thus uncertainties in the meaning and interpretation of agreements were primarily absorbed by the industrial relations department. Since the industrial relations department was not part of the production department's chain of authority, it could obtain information unavailable to others and bypass the plant's hierarchy. For example, industrial-relations personnel regularly obtained information in their tours of all plant facilities. Employees also came to industrial relations personnel when they were fearful of going to their supervisors. Through such means, industrial relations could legitimately pick up bits and pieces of information and feelings about the true state of the organization that didn't get into the production unit's communication channels. As a result, the industrial relations department absorbed considerable uncertainty as to emerging human problems.

Significance to Management.   There are three reasons why uncertainty absorption is an important concept for management. *First,* uncertainty absorption forces higher management to think through which groups or individuals are to have the discretion to make decisions that affect other groups or individuals. *Second,* uncertainty absorption influences the relative power of various groups in organizations. These power differences can be an important factor in understanding conflicts and other problems between groups. *Third,* uncertainty absorption requires us to make sure that the uncertainties being absorbed by groups or individuals are consistent with their knowledge and expertise.

Substitutability

Substitutability is the degree to which a group (or individual) can obtain the services, inputs, or activities provided by another group (or individual) from alternative sources. While the concept of substitutability applies between individuals, our focus will be on groups. If alternative services, inputs, or activities are readily available, the power of the "service" group is likely to be weaker than if no alternatives existed.[9] For example, in the case just presented, no ready substitute for the industrial relations department existed. However, if the organization had been willing to spend the additional resources, they could have hired external industrial relations consultants. The consultants could have evaluated the same issues as the industrial relations department and provided independent diagnoses and recommendations to management. While the consultants would also be absorbing uncertainty, it might enable top management to question and evaluate the activities of the industrial relations department more effectively.

Limits on Substitutability.   To increase the probability of full utilization of resources, top management frequently issues rules requiring that departments use the services provided by other units within the organization. For example, a marketing department that wants a new sales brochure run off might have to go through the printing department rather than contracting with an outside printing firm. This rule might be enforced even if the marketing department could get the job done faster and at a lower price from the outside firm. From an organizational standpoint, the increased costs to marketing might be less significant than the lower utilization of manpower and equipment in the printing department.

The impact of limitations on substitutability was experienced by one individual when he served as coordinator of a committee that was re-sponsible for the development and planning of a Behavioral Learning Center in the College of Business at Penn State. The University had a rule that all electronic design work had to be done by a special internal depart-ment rather than by an external consultant. Once the design work was completed, it was given to the purchasing department, which sought the approval of the facility from a government agency in the state capital. Since the internal design department had so many demands for its ser-vices, it took approximately nine months to obtain the specifications state-ment from the time the desired capabiliies were indicated for the Be-havioral Learning Center. Because the rules prevented the use of any substitute for this department, the full use of the Behavioral Learning Center was delayed by over one year.

Significance to Management.   Everything else being equal, the lower the substitutability of the services or activities of a group, the greater its power within the organization.[10] Groups that provide vital, but non-substitutable, services often find the groups to which they provide services trying one of two extreme strategies—to win them over through the pro-vision of extra rewards or to eliminate the group or its management by complaints to higher management. Many managers of electronic data processing departments, for example, are dismissed because they become threats to higher management and other line groups. Although such de-partments provide vital and nonsubstitutable services, the apparent at-tempt to exercise too much power and control can lead to a backlash for managers of data processing departments.

Task Relations

Task relations are related to the concept of substitutability. The quesion of substitutability would not exist if there were no task relations between groups. The three basic types of possible task relations between any two groups within an organization are independent, interdependent, and dependent. It is useful to think of relations between groups as varying along a continuum from relative independence, through varying degrees of interdependence, to relative dependence.

Independent Task Relations.   Task relations are independent when interactions and mutual decision making between two groups occurs only at the discretion of both groups. An independent task relation between two groups is almost a contradiction in terms. If the groups are inde-pendent of each other, how can it be said that they have task relations? So the term is used to denote infrequent task relations between two groups that occur at the discretion of both groups.[11] For example, some large or-ganizations maintain internal consulting groups that contract, on mutually agreeable terms, to work with other units. Corning Glass Company has an

Organizational Development Group that operates principally along these lines. If a unit at Corning wants to improve its problem-solving effectiveness in committee meetings, it might call in a representative from the Organizational Development Group to diagnose the problems and assist in changing the processes. Once the groups start working together, it is probably more reasonable to identify their relations as interdependent for the duration of the project. However, if both groups have the discretion to withdraw from the relationship at will, they are likely to perceive a relatively independent task relationship.

Interdependent Task Relations.   Interdependent task relations occur when collaboration, coordination, and mutual decision making between two groups is necessary and desirable for each group to achieve its own goals. *Collaboration* occurs when the two groups share joint responsibility for certain tasks. *Coordination* occurs when the subtasks allocated to different units need to be sequenced and agreed upon by the two groups. For instance, coordination and collaboration are often needed between production and marketing. Marketing must not promise customers orders that would create chaos for the production unit. Production must also be responsive to customer wants. For an effective interdependent task relation to exist, neither group can have the power to dictate or unilaterally determine the outcome of the interaction.[12] As illustrated in this and other chapters, numerous issues and problems in organizations create interdependent task relations between groups.

Dependent Task Relations.   Dependent task relations occur when one group has the ability and power to dictate or unilaterally determine the outcomes from the interactions between the two groups. Dependent task relations between two groups often occur when one group absorbs uncertainty for the other group, the activities of the latter group are readily substitutable, or the latter group is dependent upon the former for resources. A dramatic example of a dependent task relation may occur between the top-management planning or budget committee and lower level organizational units. The budget levels and possibly the survival of the lower level units may be dependent upon the stroke of a pen by the top-management planning committees.

Case Study of Task Relations.   This study by George Strauss concerns the tactics used by purchasing departments in their interactions with other units, such as engineering, manufacturing, sales, and production scheduling.[13] It also brings out several of the previously mentioned contingencies affecting intergroup relations, such as uncertainty absorption and substitutability. Here the focus is on the tactics used by purchasing in dealing with task interdependencies with other units and the conflicts that frequently result. The majority of contacts between purchasing and other units were handled routinely, according to standard operating procedures, and without conflict. But there were still many difficult task interdependencies that could not be handled in a standardized or routine way.

> *On the surface, in the firms studied, purchasing had two major functions: (1) to negotiate and place orders at the best terms possible, according to specifications laid down by other units; and (2) to expedite orders by making sure deliveries were made according to schedule. However, the purchasing unit and/or many of its member agents often viewed their responsibilities more broadly. While purchasing recognized that its job was to serve the needs of departments, it also considered its job to be proactive with other departments. Purchasing often was proactive in making suggestions to other units regarding such issues as: (1) the use of alternative parts or raw materials; (2) modifications in specifications or parts that might increase quality, speed up delivery, save money, and the like; (3) the most economical size of orders; and (4) the determination of decisions to purchase or make various parts. Thus purchasing sought to be consulted during the planning and decision-making process of other units before requests for purchase orders were drawn up.*

> **Interdependencies and Conflicts with Engineering**: *Purchasing was often expected to buy products based on specifications from the engineering department. If engineering specified a particular brand or wrote up its specifications too tightly, the purchasing department had little discretion in choosing among suppliers. This could reduce the status of purchasing internally and reduce its bargaining power with suppliers. Within organizations, the degree to which a group can exercise discretion or make significant decisions is often a key factor in determining its relative status. Purchasing sometimes contended that engineering put undue emphasis on quality and reliability and was somewhat indifferent to speedy delivery and low cost. Such issues were further aggravated where purchasing attempted to change specifications and the like after engineering considered these tasks to be completed.*

> **Interdependencies and Conflicts with Production Scheduling**: *Production scheduling usually takes the initiative in determining the size of orders and the dates on which they are to be delivered. A variety of interdependencies and conflicts between purchasing and production scheduling ensue: (1) purchasing may claim too short a notice is given and try to get production scheduling to revise its date of needed delivery; (2) purchasing may claim that production scheduling engages in sloppy planning with the result that purchasing has to choose from a limited number of suppliers, pay higher prices, and ask special favors of sales rep-*

resentatives for quick delivery (thus creating future obligations); and (3) production scheduling may claim that short delivery times are due to such factors as delays by engineering in the preparation of blueprints (plans) or the sales unit's acceptance of rush orders. Another source of interdependence and potential conflict becomes evident when purchasing disagrees with requested order sizes from production scheduling because of its failure to adequately consider inventory costs and/or savings from quantity discounts.

Tactics Used by Purchasing: A variety of tactics were used by purchasing units in dealing with other departments on problems that could not be easily routinized, programmed, or standardized. The tactics used by purchasing can be grouped into five general categories; rule-oriented; rule-evading; personal-political; educational; and organizational-interactional. Brief explanations and examples of these tactics are presented in Table 10–1. Not all these tactics are necessarily "right," "good," or "best." They are simply the ones found to be followed in various circumstances. It may well be that some tactics would be effective in the short run for purchasing but would increase intergroup conflicts and difficulties over the long term and/or not be in the interest of the organization as a whole.

Significance to Management.   Three major conclusions regarding task relations have significance well beyond the case study on purchasing. *First,* the types of tactics used by purchasing may also be employed by other departments in organizations. *Second,* groups such as purchasing, personnel, and quality control may exercise influence in the decision-making process well in excess of the advisory role implied in being formally identified as staff units. Staff units typically attempt to move from a dependent task relationship with other groups to at least an interdependent task relationship. Of course, this implies the potential for intergroup conflicts and the need to actively manage the interface between groups. *Third,* to understand intergroup relations, it is necessary to assess the work flow or task interdependencies between groups.

Resource Sharing

Resource sharing refers to the degree to which two or more groups must obtain needed goods or services from a common group and to the degree to which these goods or services are adequate to meet the needs of all groups.[14]

Case Application of Resource Sharing.   Two departments made use of the same typing pool for the preparation of most letters, mem-

TABLE 10–1.   Tactics Used by Purchasing in Relations with Other Groups

Classification of Tactics	Explanation and Example
Rule-oriented	1. Appeal to some common authority to direct that the requisition be revised or withdrawn.
	2. Refer to some rule (assuming one exists) which provides for longer lead times.
	3. Require the scheduling department to state in writing why quick delivery is required.
	4. Require the requisitioning department to consent to having its budget charged with the extra cost (such as air freight) required to get quick delivery.
Rule-evading	1. Go through the motions of complying with the request, but with no expectation of getting delivery on time.
	2. Exceed formal authority and ignore the requisitions altogether.
Personal-Political	1. Rely on friendships to induce the scheduling department to modify the requisition.
	2. Rely on favors, past and future, to accomplish the same result.
	3. Work through political allies in other departments.
Educational	1. Use direct persuasion, that is, try to persuade scheduling that its requisition is unreasonable.
	2. Use what might be called indirect persuasion to help scheduling see the problem from the purchasing department's point of view (in this case it might ask the scheduler to sit in and observe the agent's difficulty in trying to get the vendor to agree to quick delivery).
Organizational-Interactional	1. Seek to change the interaction pattern, for example, have the scheduling department check with the purchasing department as to the possibility of getting quick delivery before it makes a requisition.
	2. Seek to take over other departments, for example, to subordinate scheduling to purchasing in an integrated materials department.

Adapted and modified from Strauss, G., Tactics of lateral relationship: The purchasing agent, *Administrative Science Quarterly*, 1962, 7, pp. 161–186.

oranda, reports, and the like. Both departments lacked the skills and resources to perform this type of work themselves. If the typing pool has adequate resources (typists, typewriters, paper, reproduction equipment, and the like) to meet the demands of both departments, few, if any, problems should occur between the two departments over the sharing of the typing pool. Then each department expanded its workload and number of employees, but the typing pool's resources remained constant. This might even be a deliberate strategy by higher management if they feel that the typing pool is staffed to meet the peak demands from the other two departments with the consequences or underutilization much of the time. Higher management might feel that better planning and/or more realistic deadlines for the typing pool could enable it to produce much more with little added costs. Their belief could be reinforced by previous complaints from several workers in the typing pool of having to work frantically one day and being bored by inactivity the next day. Initially, the two departments may respond by pressuring the typing pool to the point that everything is urgent. The next step might be for each department to establish priorities on its own materials to be typed. If this does not solve the problem, representatives of the two departments and the typing pool might try to work out a set of priorities and understandings through group problem solving. The representative from the typing pool is likely to claim they have been "put in the middle too often for too long and what's been going on is upsetting the staff and lowering output." One understanding could be that if one department encounters a true emergency requiring the typing pool to set aside another department's work, there would be direct contact between the two departments to work out some accommodation.

Significance to Management.   The need for two or more groups to share a common pool of resources can result in competition or cooperation between them. The case application just presented assumed that the groups were initially competitive and became more cooperative when they confronted the problems. Management has special responsibilities to encourage collaborative problem solving between groups who are sharing in a scarce pool of resources or to set priorities to minimize unnecessary competition and destructive conflicts. Management is also in a unique position to influence the "attitudinal sets" of groups toward each other when they experience difficulties in sharing resources. The importance of attitudinal sets will become clear in the next section.

Attitudinal Sets

Attitudinal sets are the thoughts and feelings that two or more groups have of each other.[15] A group with a rigid and well-defined attitudinal set of another group is said to have a *stereotype* of that group.

Cause and Consequence.   The sets of attitudes that the members of a group hold toward another group can be both a *cause* and a *consequence* of the nature of their relationship. The dynamics might begin with the groups being trusting, cooperative, and open with each other. In this situation, the ways in which the other contingencies in group dynamics (goals, uncertainty absorption, substitutability, task relations, and resource sharing) are met are somewhat influenced as well. For example, if the groups trust each other, there is likely to be greater consideration of the other group's point of view, greater willingness to avoid blaming the other group when problems occur, and a greater tendency to check with each other before making decisions that might have a mutual impact. If the intergroup dynamics begin with attitudes of distrust, competitiveness, secrecy, and closed communications, just the opposite can be expected.

The attitudinal sets of groups toward one another can also be a consequence of the other contingencies in group dynamics. If an auditing group in an organization is evaluated solely on the basis of finding and reporting errors in other groups and reporting them to higher management, the other groups may have attitudes of distrust, competitiveness, and closed communications toward the auditing group. Of course, these attitudes are more likely to prevail if higher management uses the reports from auditing primarily as a means of punishing the other groups rather than as an aid to improvement. These other groups are quite likely to give the auditing group the appearance that they are being cooperative and open in their communications, although in fact they are not.[16]

Cooperative versus Competitive Attitudinal Sets.   The sets of attitudes that groups come to hold toward one another often form into stereotypes. *Stereotypes* are "standardized short-cut evaluations that reflect present or past relations between groups or a picture of these relations presented to the group."[17] A number of possible attitudinal and behavioral consequences have been identified if the groups basically stereotype their relationships as cooperative or competitive.[18]

Figure 10–2 summarizes some of these attitudinal and behavioral consequences. Each dimension is presented as varying along a continuum. In extremely competitive relationships, the groups are likely to be distrusting and unresponsive, to emphasize self-interests, to interact only when required, to resist influence or control from each other, and so on. On the other hand, a highly cooperative relationship is more likely to be characterized by trust, responsiveness, emphasis on mutual interests, easy and frequent interaction, acceptance of mutual influence or control, and the like. Intergroup dynamics are probably rarely at one or the other end of the continuum.

Intergroup problem solving and effectiveness are likely to be greater when relations are more indicative of the cooperative characteristics in Figure 10–2 than of the competitive characteristics. This may be especially true for intergroup relations within organizations and when the

FIGURE 10–2.   Some Attitudinal and Behavioral Consequences
of Dynamics between Groups

Under extreme conditions of cooperation	*Continuum*	Under extreme conditions of competition and conflict
Trusting		Distrusting
Flexible		Rigid
Open and authentic		Closed and deceptive
Responsive		Unresponsive
Mutual interests and goals		Self interests and goals
Friendly or neutral		Aggressive or enemies
Realistic		Unrealistic
High and necessary interactions		Low and sporadic interactions
Listening to each other		Listening to selves
Accepts mutual control		Resists control of each other
Pleasurable		Painful
Optimistic		Pessimistic
Achievement and/or affiliation		Power and coercion
Confronting and compromising		Forcing and avoiding
Satisfaction		Dissatisfaction

effectiveness criteria are based on what's desirable for the organization
as a whole. However, within the broader U.S. political and economic
arena, some evidence suggests that groups (such as business firms, industry groups, occupational groups, reform groups, and political groups)
that are characterized by some of the more competitive characteristics
may be more likely to attain their goals.[19] Thus we need to be careful not
to assume that there is only one set of desirable intergroup relations.
Desirability and the definition of effectiveness can be influenced by the
goals and the viewpoint of the involved groups.

   Case Study of Intergroup Competition and Conflict.   The following
case study, which summarizes the work of Rolf E. Rogers, illustrates attitudinal sets as both a cause and consequence of intergroup relations.[20]

   *The study is concerned with the Management Analysis Depart-
ment and Data Processing Department within the Weapon Sys-*

tems Division of a multidivisional aerospace firm located in a large West Coast city. Both departments had responsibilities for operating and developing a management system within the division. Management systems are activities designed to increase control of the operations in the division. The Management Analysis Department reported to the vice-president for administration and the Data Processing Department reported to the controller, who was the chief financial officer. These two executives, in turn, reported to the president of the division.

Formally, the Management Analysis Department would be given operating and management problems for analysis. A report was usually issued to the "client" describing the problem, assessing alternatives, and recommending a solution. If part of the solution required a data processing computer system and this recommendation was accepted by the "client," the report would be turned over to the Data Processing Department for more detailed computer systems design.

The conditions leading to the problems and dysfunctional stereotyping between the two departments developed over time. There had been a steady decline in profitability of the weapons division, which had been underbid by competitors a number of times and was consequently not obtaining new contracts. The president asked Dr. Robert Benson, manager of the Management Analysis Department, to have his unit develop a system for working up cost estimates. A major recommendation of the study was to develop a computer-based estimating system. It was intended that this system would take the accounting and production data already in the computer and integrate them for purposes of preparing cost estimates.

At a September staff meeting, the president directed Dr. Benson to submit the report to the Data Processing Department for design, programming, and implementation. The president also instructed Mr. Bowen, the controller, to direct Don Ludden, the director of data processing, to give his project high priority and to provide monthly progress reports.

Incidents: To develop a personal feel for the attitudinal sets that were forming, we will quote directly from samples of conversations that took place during the next month. At the next staff meeting (October 15) the following discussion took place:[21]

President:	Mr. Bowen, I have not received a progress report from your organization on the status of the new estimating system. Why not?
Mr. Bowen:	I don't know, sir, but I'll check on it immediately.
President:	Please do. (Mr. Bowen leaves the room to call Don Ludden, the director of data processing.)

Mr. Bowen:	(on the phone) Don, where is the progress report to the president on the new estimating system? I told you that this report is due every month in my office on the 10th and in the president's office on the 12th.
Don Ludden:	We are having problems making sense out of the system proposed by management analysis (department). I tried to reach Carl Abel (project leader in Management Analysis Department), but he is out of town.
Mr. Bowen:	O.K., but I want action on this project immediately. I'll talk to Dr. Benson about Abel. (Mr. Bowen returns to the staff meeting.)
President:	Well, Mr. Bowen?
Mr. Bowen:	My data processing people tell me that they can't make sense out of the management analysis report and they have not been able to reach the project chief, Carl Abel.
President:	Dr. Benson?
Dr. Benson:	Well, I don't know why there should be any problem in understanding the proposal. Mr. Abel is out of town on another assignment but they could have talked to Dr. Dolan or any one of the team members.
President:	I suggest that you two gentlemen get together on this and "get the show on the road." I should have been informed immediately of any problems, Mr. Bowen, instead of my having to bring the subject to your attention. I suggest that you personally keep track of this project from now on.
Mr. Bowen:	Yes sir.

On October 18, *a meeting was held with the following individuals: Benson, Dolan, and Abel from the Management Analysis Department; and Bowen, Ludden, Warick, and Sorensen from the Data Processing Department. The following conversation ensued:*[22]

Dr. Benson:	Well, what's the problem in your shop with getting this new system "off the ground"?
Mr. Bowen:	I'll let Sam (Warick) describe some of the initial problems.
Sam Warick:	Well, to begin with, your proposal is too vague for us to do any detail design work. None of my systems people can make sense out of the "interface" model in the system. Secondly, your proposal calls for the use of the XL–2 programming language; we have

	never used that language here and I don't have anyone who can program it.
Philip Sorensen:	Yes, that's right. The XL–2 is so new that nobody has had any experience with it. I called several computer manufacturers and none of them have used it; they are still testing whether the language can be used at all.
John Dolan:	To answer your first point, it is not our responsibility to do detail design work; that is your job and you are supposed to have people to do it. If you don't, that's your problem, not ours. Secondly, on the XL–2 language, I'll ask Carl to answer that.
Carl Abel:	I don't know who you have been talking to, Phil, but that language is used by the Computer Center at the State University and they tell me it's the best approach to the type of computation required in our proposed system.
Philip Sorensen:	That's just great. Who do you think we have for programmers here? Ph.D.'s in computer science? We are lucky if we can get people with Bachelor's degrees. If you people would check your "high-level" solutions with us practical people instead of writing all this theoretical _____, we wouldn't have half of the problems we have now.
Don Ludden:	That's right. We are handed the dirty work without being consulted and then told it's our problem.
Dr. Benson:	Now let's not get personal. It seems to me that we have two problems. First, there is some problem in understanding the proposed system; second, there is a problem with the programming language. Now I suggest that Carl, Sam, and Phil sit down together and work these problems out. We will meet again, as a group, one week from today at the same time to discuss what solutions you three have come up with. Is that O.K. with you Sam (Bowen)?
Mr. Bowen:	O.K.

During the next week, Carl, Sam, and Phil attempted to work out the design and programming language problems without success. Relations between the two departments were hostile and rigid and involved accusations of incompetency. Further meetings between the two groups were cancelled. On October 26, a meeting with the division president was called.[23] After little progress in this meeting, the president indicated he would think over this problem and let them know of his decision.

"Solutions": *At the November 15 meeting, the president announced he had retained an outside consulting firm to assess the current problems between the two departments. There was little interaction between the two departments during the period of the consultant's study. At a special staff meeting on January 14, the president announced the formation of the Management Systems Department, which would report directly to him. Basically, the new department consisted of the present Management Analysis Department and Data Processing Department. Mr. O'Connel from the Corporate Management Audit Staff was made the new director. He, along with the directors of personnel from the division and headquarters, was given the responsibility for the staffing and appointment of managers. Abel, Benson, and Dolan resigned; Bowen and Sorensen requested transfers; but there was no unusual turnover reaction in the lower levels of the two units. A follow-up six months later indicated that the new departmental arrangement was working quite effectively. The consultant's recommendation that "study teams" be established (so that all affected units would be represented right from the start of a project) was implemented.*

In this case, changes in organizational structure, task relations, and personnel were used to solve the conflict situation, negative attitudinal sets, and problems in task relations. But we have no way of second-guessing whether the changes represented the "best" solutions to the problems.

Significance to Management.   The importance of attitudinal sets in relation to this case study is not in how this organization "solved" the problems. Rather, the case study dramatically demonstrates the possible role of attitudinal sets, task relations, goals, and the like as contingencies that can influence the nature of intergroup dynamics. The case suggests that a number of the contingencies discussed are likely to be in effect simultaneously or at least interconnected in having an influence on intergroup dynamics. The attitudinal sets, whether cooperative or competitive, can have a significant influence on the ability and willingness of groups to work together to achieve organizational goals. If groups are interdependent, it is likely that competitive attitudinal sets will reduce goal accomplishment because of the high expenditure of time and energy on trying to "get one up" on the other group.

An overall implication of the case study is that the relative importance of the six contingencies discussed (goals, uncertainty absorption, substitutability, task relations, resource sharing, and attitudinal sets) cannot be generalized and may even be quite difficult to assess between two actual groups.

FORMAL MECHANISMS FOR MANAGING THE DYNAMICS BETWEEN LATERAL GROUPS

The section explains formal mechanisms for managing the dynamics between groups that are in a lateral relationship to each other. *Lateral relations* occur when two or more groups are interdependent, have the ability to influence each other, and are not in a hierarchical relationship with each other. Six major mechanisms are presented; hierarchy, plans, linking roles, task forces, integrating roles, and matrix organization. Of course, many of the behavior processes, issues, and mechanisms discussed in other chapters, such as those on individual styles, motivation, and leadership, can have major impacts on intergroup dynamics as well.

Factors Influencing Lateral Relations

Three major factors influence the extensiveness and sophistication of formal mechanisms needed to manage the dynamics between groups that are in a lateral relation with each other: the degree of *differentiation* between the groups; the degree of *integration* required between the groups; and the degree of *uncertainty* confronting the groups. As shown in Figure 10–3, each of these factors can vary on a continuum from high to low.

Differentiation. Differentiation is the degree to which organizational units differ from one another in terms of the extent of departmental structure (high to low), members' orientation toward time (short or long), members' orientation toward others (permissive to authoritarian), and members' orientation toward environmental sector (certain to uncertain).[24] Each of these components of differentiation has been discussed previously in this and prior chapters. Thus a few brief examples are sufficient here. Production units often have a high degree of departmental structure, in-

FIGURE 10–3.   Factors Influencing Lateral Relations between Groups

Factors	Continuum			Brief Explanations
Differentiation	High	Moderate	Low	Groups can vary in being substantially alike to being quite different
Integration	High	Moderate	Low	Groups can vary in needing to work closely together to having few contacts with each other
Uncertainty	High	Moderate	Low	Groups can vary in having to work together on tasks for which little knowledge exists to having well-defined ways for getting the job done

cluding many rules and procedures, tight supervisory control, and frequent and specific reviews of individual and departmental performance. The opposite situation is often found in research departments. With respect to members orientation toward others, research and sales personnel tend to prefer open, interpersonal relationships while those in production units tend to prefer more directive and structured relationship with coworkers. In terms of time orientation, sales and production have shorter time horizons and accordingly think more about immediate problems and profits, whereas research units tend to think several years into the future. In general, the greater the differences between groups, the greater the difficulty and problems in getting them to work together.

Integration.   Integration is the "degree of collaboration (cooperation) and mutual understanding actually achieved among the various organization units."[25] The need for integration (coordination and cooperation) is created by both the division of labor employed and the task interdependencies between groups.[26] The major purpose of this part of the chapter is to inform you of the major mechanisms for achieving integration between groups under various levels of differentiation and uncertainty.

Uncertainty.   As discussed earlier in this and other chapters, uncertainty is the degree to which there is a gap between what is known and what needs to be known to make correct decisions. A general idea of the degree of task uncertainties that are confronting two or more groups as they work together would be suggested by responses to the following types of questions:

1. To what extent is there a clearly defined body of knowledge or guidelines that can be used by the two groups as they work together?
2. How often do the two groups come across mutual problems that they do not know how to solve and the groups must take time to think the problems through before taking any action?
3. In general, how much actual "thinking" time must the two groups spend before trying to implement solutions to their mutual problems?
4. What percent of the time are the two groups generally sure of the results of their mutual and independent efforts?
5. On the average, how long is it before each group knows whether their work efforts have been effective?
6. To what extent do the people do about the same things in the same ways in dealing with issues within and between the groups?

Significance to Management.   Logic and research have suggested several significant implications regarding the combinations of the differentiation, integration, and uncertainty factors. *First,* the easiest intergroup situation to manage occurs under conditions of low uncertainty, low differentiation, and low integration requirements. In this situation, the departments are practically autonomous or independent of each other. An example would be custodial groups in different buildings on a college campus.

Second, increases in the degrees of uncertainty, differentiation, and desired integration need to be accompanied by increases in the expenditure of resources to obtain integration, increases in the variety of formal mechanisms to obtain integration, and increases in the use of certain behavioral processes or mechanisms to obtain integration.

Third, the most difficult intergroup relation to manage is likely to occur under conditions of high uncertainty, high differentiation, and high required integration. For example, the production of the first Boeing 747 jets was accompanied by all these conditions. The greatest expenditure of resources and greatest variety of formal and behavioral mechanisms are utilized to manage interunit relations under this set of conditions.

Organizations can err in trying to establish too much or too little integration between units. With too little integration, there is likely to be a lower quality of decisions and consequent underutilization or misutilization of resources. With too much integration, the costs associated with integration are likely to far exceed any possible benefits. Moreover, the two groups are likely to prove more obstructionist than helpful in achieving their tasks.

Overview of Formal Mechanisms

Figure 10–4 places the six formal managerial mechanisms that might be used to establish integration between two or more groups that are in an approximate lateral relationship with each other along a continuum. It is important to keep in mind that increases in, or higher levels of, uncertainty and differentiation are primarily important in the choice of formal mechanisms *only if* it is desirable or required that the groups be integrated. These mechanisms are placed along a single continuum to indicate the varying

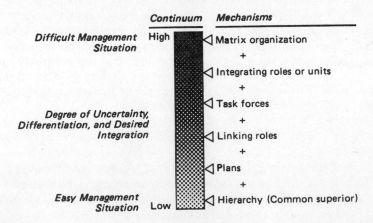

FIGURE 10–4.   Mechanisms for Managing Lateral Intergroup Dynamics under Varying Conditions

levels of sophistication and resource requirements associated with each mechanism. The continuum in Figure 10–4 represents a combination of the three factors presented in Figure 10–3. Thus the continuum ranges from low to high for uncertainty, differentiation, and desired integration. The types of mechanisms that may be most appropriate for varying levels of uncertainty, differentiation, and desired integration are shown to the right of the continuum. The plus sign (+) between each mechanism suggests there is likely to be a use of the prior identified mechanisms along with the new mechanism as one moves to higher intergroup relations on the continuum. For example, if linking roles are appropriate to help integrate two or more groups, some use of hierarchy and plans are likely to be appropriate as well.

Hierarchy

Hierarchy is a mechanism for obtaining integration between two groups through the use of a common superior. In the case involving the Management Analysis Department and Data Processing Department, the manager of the Management Analysis Department reported to the vice-president for administration and the manager of the Data Processing Department reported to the controller. In turn, the vice-president for administration and the controller reported to the president of the division. In this case, the problems and differences between the two units involved the active participation of the president. He represented the common superior between the two units. After consultation, he made several structural and personnel changes to resolve the interunit differences.

The use of hierarchy (common superior) to help integrate groups is based on the assumption that people at upper levels have more power and expertise than those at lower levels. However, the *exclusive* use of hierarchy to cope with integration between groups, as well as a number of other issues, is open to question on several grounds. While many of these have been presented previously, we will briefly review some of the major concerns resulting from undue emphasis on the use of hierarchy:

1. It might create or increase personal alienation, conflict, and frustration.
2. It might interfere with trained specialists, who may have more expertise in the problem area, preventing them from interacting as needed.
3. It might interfere with the flexibility needed to respond to uncertain and changing environments and technologies.
4. It might be inconsistent with the values of openness, participation, and self-control.
5. It might overload higher level managers, with the result that they spend too much time on less important issues.[27]

As suggested in Figure 10–4, the primary use of hierarchy to resolve intergroup problems and possible coordination issues may be especially appropriate under conditions of low uncertainty, few integration requirements, and minor differences between the groups. Of course, the use of hierarchy does not necessarily prevent representatives of the involved groups from sitting down with the common superior and working through the issues together or at least having an opportunity to influence and discuss the problem.

Plans

Plans and planning processes can be used in managing intergroup relations. In the broadest sense, planning has been defined as:

> The continuous process of making present entrepreneurial (risk-taking) decisions systematically and with the greatest knowledge of their futurity; organizing systematically the efforts needed to carry out these decisions against the expectations through organized systematic feedback.[28]

Through accepted or agreed upon plans, it is possible for two or more groups to act and make decisions on a day-to-day basis without constantly interacting with one another. Yet they could be quite integrated and interdependent in terms of their objectives. For example, two construction firms might start working on a section of highway many miles apart from one another. As long as both groups make their decisions in relation to the requirements or constraints of the plan (and the plan is accurate), we can be fairly sure the road surfaces being laid by each group will meet. Of course, this example involves virtually no uncertainty regarding the ability to measure accurately and to plot the path of the roadway. A less restricted view of plans and planning as mechanisms for integrating two or more groups is suggested in the following example of the planning at Babcock and Wilcox.[29] This example also demonstrates the role of hierarchy in achieving integration.

Planning at Babcock and Wilcox.   Babcock and Wilcox is a multidivisional firm operating in electrical power-generation equipment, tubular products, and nuclear materials. The firm has grown from $500 million in 1965 to over $1 billion in 1978. There are a number of ways in which integration is established or increased through their plans and planning autonomy. All plans must be coordinated and related to overall corporate objectives. This is a first step in obtaining integration between the corporation as a whole and its divisions. The basis and forms of integration between the corporation and divisions are explicitly presented in a Comprehensive Business Plan (CBP) prepared annually by each division. Through this process, top management may conclude that certain activities or programs in one division offer greater advantages to the organization's future than those in another and change priorities accordingly. The Comprehensive Business Plan also calls for "systematic feedback" of results within subunits of the divisions and between divisions and headquarters. This monthly reporting of the relation between planned performance and actual performance provides tangible feedback on developing problems.

Babcock and Wilcox claim that they do not view their plans as "straightjackets" on the divisions and their subunits. Their business plans are said to be dynamic, to change as conditions change, and to make reasonable allowance for contingencies. If all factors could be controlled and predicted, there would be virtually no uncertainty. The plans could be specified in great detail for extended time periods and provide the mechanism for tight integration. But this is rarely the case for organizations.

In sum, the Babcock and Wilcox case is an example of how plans and hierarchy can be used as a mechanism for achieving some degree of integration between units that are in a hierarchical and/or lateral relationship with each other. As uncertainty, differentiation, and desired integration increase, however, the ability to reply only on plans and/or hierarchy becomes more difficult, requiring the use of additional mechanisms.

Linking Roles

Linking roles are specialized positions in which people attempt to facilitate communications and problem solving between two or more interdependent groups. Such a role can be thought of as an incremental mechanism to facilitate integration when the exclusive use of hierarchy and/or plans becomes too slow or time-consuming. For example, if minor issues were continually referred up the hierarchy, the common superior might become overloaded and the response time might increase.

Under the topic of uncertainty absorption, a case study of the industrial relations and production units of a multicompany corporation were described. A key industrial relations representative was physically located in each manufacturing facility. This representative was also regarded as a member of the industrial relations department located at company headquarters. While the industrial relations representative helped serve the manufacturing department, he or she also was the primary link between the two functional departments.

Simple or Complex Roles. At the simplest level, the linking role may be little more than a convenient mechanism for systematically handling the flow of paperwork and following up on issues as required. In a more complex linking role, such as that of the industrial relations representative just mentioned, the linking individual may have expertise in such areas as:

1. Helping the linked groups develop a better understanding of each other's functions and responsibilities.

2. Assisting in interpreting to one group the terminology and semantics unique to the other.
3. Serving to reduce the tendency for differences in the average educational levels in two groups to create status differences that become barriers to problem solving.
4. Providing a continuous way of keeping each group aware of its interdependencies with other groups in day-to-day decision making.[30]

External Links.   Although the focus in this chapter is on linking roles between groups within an organization, specialized roles may be created to link an organization to external groups or other organizations. These roles, often called *boundary-spanning* roles, provide an essential mechanism for facilitating the flow of information and decision making between an organization and its environment.[31] For example, a safety manager might be in a boundary-spanning role between an organization and the Occupational Safety and Health Administration of the federal government with respect to safety and health issues.

Task Forces

Task forces are special groups that consist of one or more representatives from each of the interdependent groups and have the responsibility for working on specific problems that are of mutual concern. Task forces are usually formed to work on ad hoc issues or problems. Once the issue or problem is resolved, the task force is disbanded. Some members could be engaged in the task force on a full-time basis and others part time. Members may provide a linking role between their groups and the task force. It is usually assumed that the members can provide information and ideas regarding common problems, serve as transmitters of ideas and information between the task force and their group, and help assess the impact of decisions by the task force on their group.

Formal or Informal.   Task forces may develop on a formal or an informal basis. An informal task force may simply involve several people getting together to consider a mutual problem. A formal task force is one that higher management specifically recognizes and creates, usually in writing, through such means as stating the problem area to be of concern to the members. Once the objectives of the task force are attained, it is disbanded. Task forces, as well as the other integrating mechanisms discussed here, are used in both business and nonbusiness organizations. The following is an example of a task force in a nonbusiness setting.

External Affairs Task Force.   The dean of the College of Business Administration (CBA) of a major university created a "CBA External Affairs Task Force." Six faculty members from various departments and disciplines within the College were appointed by the Dean after consultation. The purpose of the task force was to develop "a recommended plan of action for CBA external affairs activities that would encompass a three- to five-year time horizon with special emphasis on year one." During the first six months, the task force engaged in such activities as holding brainstorming sessions; interviewing managers and executives; meeting with administrators in the university concerned with various aspects of external affairs, such as alumni and government relations; personally visiting and interviewing representatives from schools of business around the country; and seeking faculty ideas and attitudes through hearings and a questionnaire. Finally, a five-year strategic plan was approved at a faculty meeting some nine months after the creation of the task force. This document represented a series of recommendations regarding priorities, programs, and activities related to external affairs. Upon completion and acceptance of this plan, further considerations and implementation of the recommendations will occur through the established organizational channels.

Task forces are not always successful. You will recall in the earlier case involving the Management Analysis Department and the Data Processing Department that the president created a task force consisting of Carl, Sam, and Phil to work out the design and programming language problems. The task force obviously failed.

Integrating Roles

An *integrating* role is the permanent assignment of one or more individuals to assist two or more groups in their relationships with each other. As the need for integration and the amount of differentiation and uncertainty increase, intergroup difficulties and problems may occur with such frequency and/or be of such magnitude that more permanent, complex, and powerful integrating mechanisms are needed. Since integrating roles and specialized integrating groups can vary together in so many basic ways, they will be discussed together. An integrating role is filled by one person, whereas an integrating group has several people formally assigned to the task of facilitating integration between two or more other groups. Examples of roles and groups that often serve the integrating function (in addition to those previously discussed) are product or brand manager, program coordinator, project manager, group vice-president, group management committees, annual meetings between corporate and division general managers, and boards of directors.

Usually, the role of the integrating position or group consists of helping the resolution of nonroutine, unanticipated problems that develop between groups, particularly between functional areas such as marketing, production, and research. Integration issues often revolve around intergroup conflicts, major capital-investment decisions, numerous tactical decisions regarding service or product features, production levels or mix, schedules, cost estimates, and standards of quality.

When to Use.   The decision to use a position or a specialized group to achieve integration is likely to depend upon the contingencies in the situation. Obviously, a specialized group is likely to be a more costly integrating mechanism than a single role. There is a tendency to move toward integrating groups of increasing sophistication under the following types of circumstances: as the degree of differentiation between the groups needing integration increases; as the degree of needed integration increases; as the degree of uncertainty increases. In addition, a variable that has been found to influence the use of integrating mechanisms, particularly between headquarters and divisions in large-scale organizations, is top management's philosophy.[32] If top management has a philosophy of tight control and authoritarianism, there is more likely to be a greater number of integrating mechanisms, greater formal authority assigned to them, and greater emphasis on domination and uniformity than on shared decision making.

Degrees of Formal Authority.   The degree of formal authority granted to integrating roles or groups can vary widely. Figure 10–5 provided a general continuum of these varying degrees of formal authority. At the lowest level of formal authority, higher management simply recognizes a particular individual with expertise (specialized knowledge or interpersonal skills) that is relevant to the relations between two or more groups. This individual is assigned to assist in helping the groups with their relationships, but the groups can decide when and whether expertise is called for. However, it should not be concluded that expertise is a weak form of power. If the groups are receptive and recognize that they need the

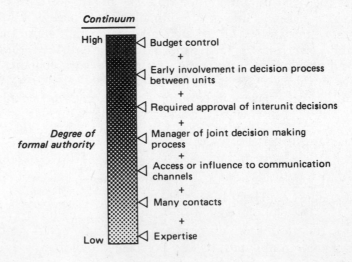

FIGURE 10–5.   Degrees of Formal Authority for Integrating Roles or Groups

Adapted and modified from J. Galbraith, *Designing Complex Organizations* (Reading, Mass.: Addison-Wesley, 1973), pp. 93–102. Used with permission.

expertise being made available, the expert may have a considerable impact.

As we move up the continuum in Figure 10–5, the examples represent increasing levels of formal authority with respect to obtaining integration between groups. The highest level of formal authority shown suggests that the integrating role or group would have a budget (financial control over certain resources in its decision-making area). The integrating manager or group would essentially purchase resources from other groups. The integrating role or group obviously would become more active and influential in the decision-making process, particularly in terms of planning and resource allocation. The next level of integration would likely lead to a matrix organization.

Matrix Organization

The *matrix organization* represents a balance between organizing resources around products, programs, or projects and around functional classifications, such as marketing, production, finance, personnel, and research.[33] Since matrix organization is discussed in Chapter 4, only some highlights are presented here. An organization may decide not to organize solely around products, programs, or projects because doing so might reduce desired functional specialization or create the need to duplicate too many resources. For example, Dow Corning Corporation uses a matrix form of organization in conjunction with product units such as rubber and sealants, resins and chemicals, fluids and compounds, specialty lubricants, and consumer products.[34]

Distinguishing Features. A matrix organization is characterized by duality in authority, information, and reporting relationships and systems. The integrating role or group has an authority, information, and reporting relationship with at least one functional (specialist) group and one project or product group. In turn, the integrating role or group is evaluated by both a project (or product unit) department and a functional department. The project and functional units (usually their managers) influence the chances for promotion and salary increases for those involved with integration. Ideally, this results in a power balance between the influence of the project (or product) groups and the functional group on the integrating group (or individuals).

A matrix organization is not without a hierarchy. But hierarchy in the matrix approach is often overlooked because of the attention given to lateral or diagonal relations, shared and dual authority, flexible decision making based upon expertise, and the like. The tendency to play down hierarchy probably occurs because it is not the distinguishing feature of the matrix organization.

The need for individuals to work with two superiors in the matrix form can create difficult, but not impossible, problems. If the two bosses cooperate, they can minimize the amount of conflicting pressures or demands they place on subordinates. An analogy can be drawn between matrix organization and the family unit.[35] Both mothers and fathers give directions to their children. The children experience healthy development as long as their parents are relatively consistent in the signals about what they expect. The same can be true for the subordinates in a matrix organization.

Potential Advantages.   While a matrix structure is a costly form of organization and the power balances are subtle and difficult to maintain, it may be superior to other organizational forms under conditions of high uncertainty, high differentiation, and high need for integration. Specific advantages claimed for the matrix form include:

1. It identifies a specific individual as the central point for all activities associated with a particular project.
2. It facilitates flexible use of individuals, because functional specialists can be obtained from the functional departments and shifted among projects as needed.
3. It provides a home base to which functional specialists, who assist in the development of expertise and knowledge, can "return" between projects.
4. It provides for built-in checks and balances between cost considerations, project considerations, and functional specialist (technical) considerations.

This section has evaluated the contingencies under which six different formal mechanisms can be used to assist in managing the dynamics between lateral groups. As indicated in Figure 10–4, these mechanisms are hierarchy, plans, linking roles, task forces, integrating roles or units, and matrix organization. One mechanism does not necessarily substitute for or preclude the use of other mechanisms.

FORMAL APPROACHES FOR MANAGING THE DYNAMICS BETWEEN WORKERS AND MANAGEMENT

Four formal approaches are frequently used to manage the dynamics between workers as a group and management as a group: hierarchical approach, joint-consultation approach, collective-bargaining approach, and workers' control approach. Since the hierarchical approach was presented previously in this and other chapters, it will not be discussed further here.

These four approaches can be differentiated on the basis of the amount of influence, participation, and/or control by workers in decision making. Figure 10–6 differentiates these approaches along a continuum of the amount of worker influence or control in the decision-making pro-

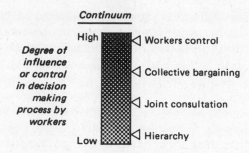

FIGURE 10–6.   Continuum of Workers' Influence with Various Formal Approaches

cess. As always, it must be kept clearly in mind that these formal approaches and how they are supposed to operate may differ substantially in practice. The classification and discussion in this section draw from the work of Strauss and Rosenstein.[36]

Joint Consultation

Joint consultation is an approach that permits workers and their representatives to be heard on various decision issues, but management usually retains the authority to make the final decisions. The Tennessee Valley Authority (TVA), a semiautonomous agency of the United States government, is a major example of an organization using the joint-consultation approach. Its 18,000 employees are primarily concerned with flood control, electric power generation, and agricultural and forest improvement in the Tennessee Valley area.

The TVA's Cooperative Committees.   The TVA joint-consultation program, called the cooperative program, provides for a formal system of consultation and joint decision making between employees and management representatives.[37] An underlying assumption of the cooperative program, and all joint-consultation approaches, is that there is a substantial commonality of interests or goals between management and the workers. The basic purpose of the formal cooperative program is to provide an additional outlet through which mutual goals can be realized. Since the TVA workers are also represented by a union, the regularly held meetings by employee and management representatives focus on the discussion of mutual problems outside the scope of collective bargaining. The size of each cooperative unit or committee is typically quite large, such as an engineering division or a power plant. The representatives of management normally include the top managers of each unit, while the workers are represented by eight to ten elected individuals chosen by employees in various subparts of the unit. The employee representatives are usually union members, but not union officers. The meetings, normally several hours long, are held once a month. The areas of discussion include issues of mutual concern such as improvements in working methods, safety, hospitalization plans, training, park facilities, and community fund drives. While decisions are often made by consensus rather than by voting, management retains the ultimate authority for accepting, rejecting, and implementing decisions.

The activities of the cooperative committee are communicated to workers through their representatives and printed summaries. Between major monthly meetings, various subcommittees work on issues and report back to the committee as a whole.

Importance of Management Attitude: The enthusiasm, strength, and perceived significance of the cooperative program vary widely among major units of the TVA. A key variable is the degree of support and enthusiasm for it from the management group in each unit. A lower level supervisor indicated that the management of his engineering division assigned little importance to the program in these words:

> Now these cooperative conferences don't impress us much here at _____ division. The things they do don't seem to get to us as much as in other parts of TVA. We don't seem to appreciate the benefits. We do get information, suggestions, and the committees are good, but there is no real enthusiasm for them here.[38]

On the other hand, an assistant unit operator in one steam plant commented:

> Yes, we have a cooperative committee here and if you have an idea you draw it up and submit it to the job steward, who goes to the monthly meeting. Then they take it and have a committee survey it. And if they think it will work, they'll OK it. I could show you numerous changes around here suggested by employees. I've got three or four changes out there myself.[39]

In sum, the joint-consultation approach, as illustrated through the TVA cooperative program, is a formal mechanism for bringing management and workers together. It provides a systematic basis for considering issues of mutual concern and for resolving these issues, whenever possible, in a mutually beneficial manner.

Collective Bargaining

Collective bargaining is the negotiation and implementation of an agreement between management and workers, usually through a designated union organization.

Features of Bargaining Relationships.   All bargaining relationships, whether they are between two or more individuals, departments, or organizations have certain basic features in common. The prominent characteristics or features of all bargaining relationships have been synthesized by Rubin and Brown as including the following:

1. At least two parties are involved.
2. The parties have a conflict of interest with respect to one or more different issues.
3. . . . the parties are at least temporarily joined together in a special kind of voluntary relationship (for bargaining to exist, the parties must believe they are participants by choice rather than compulsion).
4. The primary activity in the bargaining relationship concerns: (a) the division or exchange of one or more specific resources and/or (b) the resolution of one or more intangible issues among the parties or among those whom they represent.
5. The activity usually involves the presentation of demands or proposals by one party, evaluation of these by the other, followed by concessions and counterproposals. The activity is thus sequential rather than simultaneous.[40]

Somewhat in contrast with the joint-consultation approach, the collective-bargaining approach assumes that workers and management have some conflicting interests and some power struggles. Up to a point, these differences may be inevitable, necessary, and legitimate. Collective bargaining provides the formal structure and mechanisms through which various differences can be resolved.

At a fundamental level, collective bargaining as a negotiating process has been regarded as relatively unchanging. It has been suggested that if a five-thousand-year-old Babylonian were to sit opposite present-day management or worker representatives, his methods would be almost the same as those currently used.[41] Some individuals who call for the introduction of new processes for utilizing collective bargaining have identified various social and mechanical technologies for doing so.[42] In many parts of this book, concepts and approaches that are relevant to intergroup decision making and conflict are discussed. Thus, we will not deal with these issues here.

Bargaining Framework. A useful framework for considering the collective-bargaining approach has been developed by Walton and McKersie.[43] They identify four major subprocesses for collective bargaining: distributive bargaining, integrative bargaining, intraorganizational bargaining, and attitudinal structuring.

Distributive bargaining occurs in situations in which the goals of management and workers are considered to be in conflict. In the extreme, it is assumed that a zero-sum situation exists in which management's gain is a loss to the workers, or vice versa. A strike between union and management is one of the most visible signs of distributive bargaining in action.

Integrative bargaining occurs in situations in which the goals of each group are perceived as mutually reinforcing, or at least not in conflict with one another. Integrative bargaining requires attitudes and behaviors such as joint problem solving, joint fact gathering, joint exploration of problems, and mutual concern and interest in each other's welfare.[44] In contrast, distributive bargaining implies a continuous process of offensive and defensive positions being taken by each group. Distributive bargaining is probably more prevalent than integrative bargaining within the area of negotiating new union-management contracts.

Intraorganizational bargaining is the activities and bargaining that take place within the worker group (union) and within the management group about the positions to be taken by the representatives of each group in the actual collective-bargaining sessions. During the 1978 coal miners' strike, intraorganizational bargaining was a major problem within the United Mineworkers Union. Union President Arnold Miller and the bargaining representatives had their proposed contract rejected by the bargaining council. After renegotiation and approval by the bargaining council, the proposed contract was rejected by the field leadership and members. This whole process was characterized by intense conflict and bargaining within the union.

Attitudinal structuring refers to the types of attitudes and activities that change attitudes and relationships. (See Figure 10–2 for contrasting types of attitudes under conditions of cooperation and competition.) As you might expect, the attitudes two groups hold toward each other are likely to be relatively positive where there is an emphasis upon integrative bargaining and somewhat negative where the emphasis is on distributive bargaining. Attitudes and other noneconomic factors can influence the relationships between two groups, in addition to more traditional economic issues.[45] Of course, any given collective-bargaining relationship may consider some issue areas primarily in an integrative style, such as day-to-day administration of a collective-bargaining agreement, and other issue areas primarily in a distributive style, such as negotiation over a wage increase in a new contract.

Influence of Collective Bargaining on Organizational Change.   The conduct of collective bargaining can accentuate forces and factors such as goals, power, and conflict in management's attempts to change organizations. If outside consultants or behavioral scientists are to operate successfully in change efforts, they must accept and respect the appropriateness of the differences in goals between management, workers, and union organizations. Accordingly, change agents should seek to use change processes that recognize the needs and goals of each of these groups.[46] Chance processes and issues will be discussed in Part V.

Workers' Control

The *workers' control* approach is a system where the final decision-making authority rests in elected representatives of the workers. This is in contrast to the joint-consultation approach, where management has final decision-making authority. In theory, these worker representatives determine policy and employ management to implement it. The workers' control approach is most common in Yugoslavia, although other socialist countries have some versions of it. Some of the formally stated characteristics of the workers' control approach will be described by using the Yugoslav system as a case illustration.

Some research suggests that this approach does not always operate or function in reality as claimed on paper.[47] For example, management may have so much information, expertise, and education that in some areas the workers' representatives can do little more than go through the motions of approving management's recommendations.

Yugoslav System.   Yugoslav enterprises are socially owned, which means that ownership of the enterprise is by society as a whole.[48] The management of a firm is delegated (by the state) to a workers' collective consisting of those individuals who work within the firm. The only limitation on the workers' collective is that it is responsible for enhancing and maintaining the value of the firm. This system provides for direct and indirect participation by all workers. Direct participation can occur through meetings of the whole workers' collective (usually once or twice per year), meetings of the immediate work unit (once or more per month), and referenda (voting on issues, such as whether to merge with another enterprise). Indirect participation occurs through elected representatives.

Each enterprise has an elected Workers' Council consisting of ten to fifty members, depending upon the size of the enterprise. The council is the ultimate operating authority and is accountable to the collective as a whole. The council and subgroups of the council, created to handle particular decision areas, make decisions concerning issues such as approval of production plans, prices of products and services, investments, use of profit, distribution of salaries and wages, and hiring and firing of employees, particularly management and staff personnel. The Workers' Council also selects the top managers, normally for a four-year period. The top managers may be reelected after each term of office. However, public announcements are made regarding the expiring terms of managers and candidates are invited to apply.

The stated rationale of the Workers' Council approach in Yugoslavia is alleged to provide a mechanism for: (1) resolving class conflict by abolishing classes through the elimination of private property, and (2) humanizing work and creating conditions to assist in the development of the individual.

──────────────── **SUMMARY** ────────────────

This chapter opened with an incident describing some of the dynamics between two groups within the New York State court system—the judges and the Office of Court Administration. You should now be able to diagnose the key contingencies that play roles in the dynamics between these two groups and identify some formal mechanisms that might be used to improve their relationships. It is apparent that the following contingencies, in combination, play a role: goals, task relations, attitudinal sets, and, possibly, resource sharing. To work through the mutual problems between the judges and the Office of Court Administration, it appears that some combination of the following mechanisms and approaches will be needed: task forces (consisting of both judges and representatives of the Office of Court Administration); linking roles (to open up communication and increase trust between the conflicting groups); and collective bargaining (both parties are powerful and will probably need to compromise on some issues) so that plans can be developed to serve the public better. And, a strong dose of hierarchy is probably needed to get the parties on the path toward working out their differences while keeping the interests of the public on the table as being a relevant factor in their deliberations.

Our approach to considering the dynamics between groups has been a highly contingent one. Only after careful diagnosis can management draw conclusions as to the best mechanism or combination of mechanisms for managing intergroup dynamics. Management can err by doing too little or too much to manage the dynamics between groups. Too little management of the interfaces between groups can result in poor coordination, duplication of effort, and destructive conflicts. Too much management of intergroup dynamics can result in unnecessary paperwork and meetings, excessive expenditure of resources on management, and lack of a sense of accomplishment by any of the parties.

Although the dynamics between groups has been treated in a separate chapter, it should be apparent that a number of other chapters also bear directly on various aspects of the interfaces between groups. In particular, the chapters on organizational design, the communication process, leadership, and conflict illustrate how other factors play strong roles in managing the dynamics between groups.

DISCUSSION QUESTIONS

1. How serious a problem do you think goal incompatibility is between groups within organizations? Explain. Can you think of any personal examples where goal incompatibility occurred between a group in which you were a member and some other group? Describe the situation.

2. In what ways might a marketing research department absorb uncertainty for a sales department?

3. Are there any conditions under which a department should be able to substitute services provided by a firm outside the organization for those provided by another group within the organization? Explain.

4. Can there be interdependent task relations between two or more groups that are also characterized as being autonomous groups?

5. By utilizing the continua in Figure 10–2, how would you describe the intergroup dynamics between any two groups with which you have a personal familiarity? Does your diagnosis have any implications for the relative effectiveness or ineffectiveness of these groups? Explain.

6. Discuss and evaluate the following statement: "Hierarchy in organizations and society in general is nothing more than a mechanism to enable a few individuals at the top to control and suppress the many individuals at the bottom."

7. Discuss and evaluate the following statement: "The matrix form of organiza-

tion is one of those mechanisms advocated by the eggheads in the university. Its use within an organization would surely lead to confusion, with everyone being responsible for everything but no one accountable for anything."

8. Should there be a widespread utilization of formal joint-consultation programs between workers and management in business and nonbusiness organizations? Explain.

9. Do you think the use of the workers' control approach is likely to increase in the future within the United States? Explain.

MANAGERIAL PROBLEMS

INLAND DIVISION: GROUP AND INTERGROUP RELATIONS*

The Inland Division of General Motors Corporation, with sales estimated at more than $275 million a year, ranks as a big operation in its own right. But within GM, which Inland supplies with such equipment as steering wheels and padded dashboards, its size is hardly more than a speck on a windshield.

So, for nearly ten years, Thomas O. Mathues, Inland's general manager, has been running a participatory management system intended to keep the division's 600 line managers from getting lost in the corporate shuffle. Mathues insists—and most of his managers agree—that the system allows the division to respond more quickly to the dictates of annual model changes. More importantly, the division's managers get broader, more varied experience, and more opportunity to make key decisions than do executives at most companies.

Mathues' brand of team management includes these innovations:

Teams of 25 to 75 members operate internally as individual companies and are responsible for one or more of Inland's product lines, which range from foam seats to ball joints.

Rotating team chiefs, who are specialists in manufacturing, product engineering, or production engineering, serve as boss for four months each year when the product cycle is especially demanding of their talents.

A nine-member division staff acts as a "board of directors" for each of the teams, reviewing progress at quarterly "board" meetings at which up

* Reprinted from the October 25, 1976, issue of *Business Week* by special permission. Copyright © 1976 by McGraw-Hill, Inc.

to a dozen members of a single team may discuss problems such as quality control and manufacturing performance.

Mathues began deemphasizing the traditional vertical line-management organization at Dayton-based Inland, replacing it with his team concept almost as soon as he took over as general manager in 1966. "We were a sluggish giant," says fifty-three-year-old Mathues, a General Motors Institute graduate who began testing brake linings at Inland in 1947 and has spent his entire career there. "And the way to do this was to get decision making and the overall direction of the divsion down to lower levels. It gives people a sense of proprietorship."

Before Mathues took over, manufacture of all of the division's products was supervised by the division staff, and at times there was little cooperation or coordination among the engineering, manufacturing, sales, and other personnel.

In forming the teams, the first step was to bring together managers involved in engineering and manufacturing. Later the teams became more autonomous as salaried employees were added for such functions as purchasing, finance, and sales. Recently the teams have been trying, with mixed results, to bring hourly workers into the team effort as well.

No empires. The whole idea of the teams has been to tear down the little empires that develop within large organizations and that often work at cross-purposes. "Before the teams, a guy would say, 'I'm the quality control inspector and I don't give a damn about your production problems,'" says George Francis, manufacturing manager for hose assemblies who has worked under three general managers at Inland. "Now all of us are working on common problems." Adds Mathues: "If something isn't working right, they're all in the same boat."

The teams have wide latitude in operating as long as they get the job done. Some form subteams, for example. The instrument-panel pad team has six subteams, while the brake hose team has two subteams—all of which meet on their own.

All team members have access to information necessary for general management of the team, such as selling price, competitive position in the marketplace, and materials costs for their product. Based on the data, each team makes up its own annual operating budget, giving up—on paper —50 percent of its profits for taxes and 70 percent of its after-tax earnings to GM as "dividends." Whatever is left, plus depreciation, the teams may use for capital investment. Any remaining profit is "loaned" to the division at 9 percent interest. But, if the team's capital needs are unusually high, it can "borrow" from the division at the same rate of interest. Last year, for example, a bumper rub-strip team had to take out a substantial loan to buy a new $500,000 rubber mixing machine to replace one carried on the books at only $250,000.

Inland will not release sales or earning figures, but Mathues says there is clear evidence the system works. Since he began phasing the teams in, he says, sales in constant dollars (eliminating the effects of inflation) have increased 45 percent per employee, 35 percent per salaried employee, and 20 percent per square foot of plant space.

QUESTIONS

1. What concepts and mechanisms presented in this and the preceding chapter are illustrated in this case?
2. What human problems might you expect with this system?
3. What contingencies are illustrated in this case?

LINDELL-BILLINGS CORPORATION*

David R. Lindell and Lemuel K. Billings are, respectively, chairman and president of the Lindell-Billings Corporation, one of the most aggressive mini-conglomerates in the United States. The company, which manufactures rubber and woven hose products, was founded by Lindell's father about forty years ago. It has, in the past decade, acquired a small life insurance company (the Benjamin Rush Life Insurance Company of Hartford, Connecticut), a chain of eighteen quick-service restaurants (Chihuahua Tacos), twenty ultramodern gas stations located off interstate highways (Okla-Arkla Gasoline), and it is considering taking over the Ranchero Motel chain in the Southwest.

Lindell-Billings' top management consists of Lindell, a hard-driving fellow who progressed from a manufacturing position in the rubber-hose division of the business; Billings, a shrewd financier who was chairman of Benjamin Rush before moving to the parent corporation; Francis X. Mahoney, manager of the Rubber and Woven Hose Products Division; Harold P. Thayer, general manager of the Benjamin Rush Life Insurance Division; Dennis Gomez, general manager of the Chihuahua Tacos Division; Norman Jamieson, general manager of the Okla-Arkla Gasoline Division; and Lewis J. Diamond, executive vice-president of the staff group. This seven-man team works well together and is extremely entrepreneurial in its outlook. (Figure 10–7 shows the organization chart of the firm.)

Beneath the top-management team are managerial groups that direct the day-to-day operations of the various divisions. Lindell-Billings provides these managers with considerable autonomy but looks for inputs from Lew Diamond's staff group when it considers long-range business planning. Diamond's staff vice-presidents and managers have in-depth expertise in such fields as finance, personnel, engineering, marketing, purchasing, pub-

* From *The Worldly Philosophers.* Copyright © 1953, 1961, 1972 by Robert L. Heilbroner. Reprinted by permission of Simon & Schuster, a division of Gulf & Western Corporations.

LINDELL-BILLINGS CORPORATION ORGANIZATION CHART

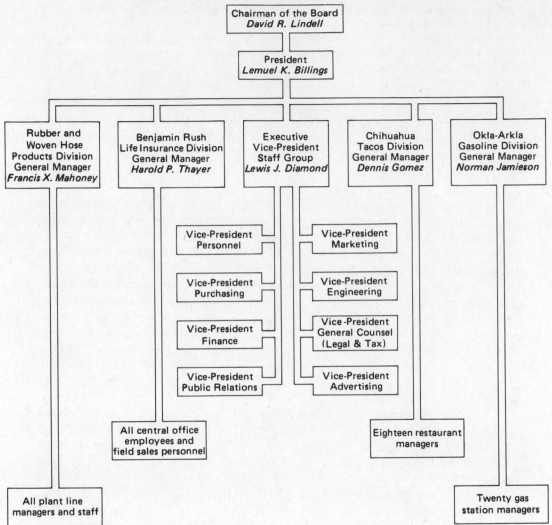

FIGURE 10–7.   Lindell-Billings Corporation Organization Chart

lic relations, advertising, and legal and tax affairs. It should be emphasized that the staff group reporting to Diamond contains a number of highly competent and highly paid executives who have approximately the same status as the divisional general managers.

Lindell and Billings have just pulled off a financial coup that has Diamond's staff upset and concerned. Several are threatening to resign, to report data to the Justice Department or the Securities and Exchange Commission, or otherwise to disrupt the business. On the other hand, the top-management group (including Diamond) stands solidly behind Lindell and Billings, who have hired an OD consultant to conduct a confrontation meeting with the staff group.

These are the issues that concern the staff group:

Lindell and Billings gave a check for $39 million to wheeler-dealer John J. LaVerne for the purchase of the Ishpeming Copper Company, on the condition that he would deposit it in the National City Bank and leave it untouched for a specific period. LaVerne has a controlling interest in the Ishpeming Copper Company and is answerable to virtually no one.

Lindell and Billings then set up a "paper" organization known as the LB Copper Corporation, with the names of certain members of the staff group as dummy directors, and had the LB Copper Corporation buy Ishpeming Copper—not for cash, but for $75 million in LB Copper stock which was conveniently printed for the purpose.

Lindell and Billings then borrowed $39 million from the National City Bank to cover the check they had given to LaVerne. As collateral for this loan they used the $75 million in LB Copper stock.

They then sold the LB Copper Corporation stock on the market (first having touted it through their brokers) for $75 million.

With the proceeds, Lindell and Billings retired the $39 million loan from the National City Bank and subsequently reported $36 million as the parent company's profit on the deal.

QUESTIONS

1. What intergroup problems exist in this case?
2. What concepts are illustrated in this case?
3. What mechanisms should have been used to avoid these problems?
4. What mechanisms can now be used?

KEY WORDS

Goals
Goal conflict
Uncertainty absorption
Power
Substitutability
Independent task relation
Interdependent task relation
Dependent task relation
Resource sharing
Attitudinal set
Stereotype
Lateral relations

Differentiation
Integration
Uncertainty
Hierarchy
Plans
Linking roles
Task forces
Integrating roles
Matrix organization
Joint consultation
Collective bargaining
Workers' control

REFERENCES

1. Morale of justices in New York is low, *The New York Times*, May 21, 1976, p. 1.

2. Schein, E., *Organizational Psychology* (Englewood Cliffs, N.J.: Prentice-Hall, 1965), pp. 80–81.

3. Mack, R., *Planning on Uncertainty: Decision-Making in Business and Government Administration* (New York: Wiley-Interscience, 1971); Galbraith, J. *Organization Design* (Reading, Mass.: Addison-Wesley, 1977), pp. 36–39.

4. Thompson, J., *Organizations in Action* (New York: McGraw-Hill, 1967).

5. Kaplan, D., Power in perspective, in Kahn, R., and E. Boulding (eds.) *Power and Conflict in Organizations* (London: Tavistock Publications, 1964), pp. 11–32.

6. Goldner, F., The division of labor: Process and power, in Zald, M. N. (ed.) *Power in Organizations* (Nashville, Tenn.: Vanderbilt University Press, 1970), pp. 97–143.

7. Ibid., p. 105.

8. Ibid., p. 127.

9. McNeil, K., Understanding organizational power: Building on the weberian legacy, *Administrative Science Quarterly*, 1978, 23, pp. 65–90.

10. Hickson, D., C. Hinnings, C. Lee, R. Schneck, and J. Pennings, A strategic contingencies theory of intraorganizational power, *Administrative Science Quarterly*, 1971, 16, pp. 216–229.

11. Duncan, W., *Organizational Behavior* (Boston: Houghton Mifflin, 1978), pp. 244–246.

12. Van de Ven, A., A panel study on the effects of task uncertainty, interdependence, and size on unit decision making, *Organization and Administrative Science*, 1977, 8, pp. 237–253.

13. Strauss, G., Tactics of lateral relationship: The purchasing agent, *Administrative Science Quarterly*, 1962, 7, pp. 161–186.

14. Tushman, M., A political approach to organizations: A review and rationale, *The Academy of Management Review*, 1977, 2, pp. 206–216; Butler, R., D. Hickson, D. Wilson, and R. Axelsson, Organizational power, politicking and paralysis, *Organization and Administrative Science*, 1977/1978, 8, pp. 45–49.

15. Hackman, J., Group influences on individuals, in Dunnette, M. (ed.), *Handbook of Industrial and Organizational Psychology* (Chicago: Rand McNally, 1976), pp. 1455–1525.

16. Sayles, L., *Managerial Behavior* (New York: McGraw-Hill, 1964).

17. Sherif, M., and C. Sherif, *Groups in Harmony and Tension: An Integration of Studies on Intergroup Relations* (New York: Octagon Books, 1966), p. 231.

18. Likert, R., and J. Likert, *New Ways of Managing Conflict* (New York: McGraw-Hill, 1976); Blake, R., A. Shepard, and J. Mouton, *Managing Intergroup Conflict in Industry* (Houston: Gulf Publishing, 1964).

19. Gamson, W., *The Strategy of Social Protest* (Homewood, Ill.: Dorsey Press, 1975).

20. Rogers, R., *The Political Process in Modern Organizations* (Jericho, N.Y.: Exposition Press, 1971), pp. 84–117. Used with author's permission.

21. Ibid., pp. 93–94.

22. Ibid., pp. 94–95.

23. Ibid.

24. Lorsch, J., and P. Lawrence, Organizing for product innovation, *Harvard Business Review*, 1965, 42, pp. 109–122.

25. Lorsch, J., and S. Allen, III, *Managing Diversity and Interdependence: An Organizational Study of Multidivisional Firms* (Cambridge: Harvard University, Graduate School of Business Administration, 1973); also see Lawrence, P., and J. Lorsch, *Organization and Environment: Managing Differentiation and Integration* (Homewood, Ill.: Richard D. Irwin, 1969).

26. Lorsch, J., J. Baughman, J. Reece, and H. Mintzberg, *Understanding Management* (New York: Harper and Row, 1978), pp. 82–86.

27. Tannenbaum, A., B. Kavcic, M. Rosner, M. Vianello, and G. Wieser, *Hier-*

archy in Organizations: An International Comparison (San Francisco: Jossey-Bass, 1974).

28. Drucker, P., Management: Tasks, Responsibilities, Practices (New York: Harper and Row, 1973), p. 125.

29. Allio, R., The corporate road-map planning at Babcock and Wilcox, Long-Range Planning, 1972, 5, pp. 9–15.

30. Tushman, M., Special boundary roles in the innovation process, Administrative Science Quarterly, 1977, 22, pp. 587–605; Edstrom, A., and J. Galbraith, Transfers of managers as a coordination and control strategy in multinational organizations, Administrative Science Quarterly, 1977, 22, pp. 248–262.

31. Keller, R., and W. Holland, Boundary-spanning roles in a research and development organization: An empirical examination, Academy of Management Journal, 1975, 18, pp. 388–393.

32. Vance, S., Managers in the Conglomerate Era (New York: Wiley-InterScience, 1971), esp. pp. 255–269.

33. Davis, S., and P. Lawrence, Matrix (Reading, Mass.: Addison-Wesley, 1977).

34. Goggin, W., How the multidimensional structure works at Dow Corning, Harvard Business Review, 1974, 52, pp. 54–56.

35. Lorsch, Baughman, Reece, and Mintzberg, Understanding Management, p. 87.

36. Strauss, G., and E. Rosenstein, Workers' participation: A critical view, Industrial Relations, 1970, 9, pp. 197–214.

37. Patchen, M., Participation, Achievement and Involvement on the Job (Englewood Cliffs, N.J.: Prentice-Hall, 1970); Sashkin, M., Changing towards participative management approaches: A model and

methods, The Academy of Management Review, 1976, 1, pp. 75–86.

38. Patchen, Involvement on the Job, p. 183.

39. Ibid., p. 184.

40. Rubin, J., and B. Brown, The Social Psychology of Bargaining and Negotiation (New York: Academic Press, 1975).

41. Karrass, C., The Negotiating Game (New York: World, 1970).

42. Balke, W., K. Hammond, and G. Meyer, An alternative approach to labor-management relations, Administrative Science Quarterly, 1973, 18, pp. 311–327.

43. Walton, R., and R. McKersie, A Behavioral Theory of Labor Negotiations: An Analysis of a Social Interaction System (New York: McGraw-Hill, 1965).

44. Drexler, V., Jr., and E. Lawler, III, A union-management cooperative project to improve the quality of work life, The Journal of Applied Behavioral Science, 1977, 13, pp. 373–387.

45. Tracy, L., The influence of noneconomic factors on negotiators, Industrial and Labor Relations Review, 1974, 27, pp. 204–215.

46. Kochan, T., and L. Dyer, A model of organizational change in the context of union-management relations, The Journal of Applied Behavioral Science, 1976, 12, pp. 59–78.

47. Obradovic, J., Workers' participation: Who participates? Industrial Relations, 1975, 14, pp. 132–144; also see Garson, G., The codetermination model of workers' participation: Where is it leading? Sloan Management Review, 1977, 18, pp. 63–78.

48. Tannenbaum, A., B. Kavčič, M. Rosner, M. Vianello, and G. Wieser, Hierarchy in Organization (San Francisco: Jossey-Bass, 1974), pp. 27–32.

PART V

INDIVIDUAL, GROUP, AND ORGANIZATIONAL PROCESSES

11

Motivation in Organizations

11

LEARNING OBJECTIVES

When you have finished reading and studying this chapter, you should be able to:
▲ Discuss motivation as a determinant of individual performance.
▲ Describe the motivational process.
▲ Describe four models of the motivation of behavior in organizations: need hierarchy, achievement motivation, two-factor theory, and expectancy theory.
▲ Describe individual differences in the motivation process.
▲ Examine the implications of motivation for managers.

THOUGHT STARTERS

▲ What motivates you?
▲ How can you motivate others?
▲ Are motivation and job satisfaction related?
▲ Are job satisfaction and job performance related?
▲ What can managers do to increase motivation?

OUTLINE

"Thank God it's Friday" is a statement widely heard in many organizations. TGIF individuals are expressing the feeling that their work is basically painful or an activity that is to be endured so that more important things—recreational activities, family life, community service—can be enjoyed. In contrast, "workaholics" perceive work as the main purpose in life; it is from their work that they derive recognition and self-fulfillment.

Why some people work harder than others is often difficult to understand. How would you analyze this person's behavior?

Until four years ago, John Ashley had been a corporate attorney. He then joined the prestigious law firm of Futterman, Hurvitz, Thomas, and Harrison. Most of the firm's clients are business organizations requesting help in matters such as contracts and taxes. Complaints about John's handling of client problems had never previously been brought to the attention of senior members of the firm. He was respected by clients for his competence about legal matters, but his method of relating to them was somewhat abrupt and cold. Few clients mentioned that they enjoyed working with John. Recently, John's performance for the firm was sufficiently below par to come to the attention of principals of the firm. John, for example, had made errors in interpreting tax regulations and he failed to notice a serious loophole in a labor-management contract. He had also been absent from the last two luncheon meetings of the firm.

Two principals of the firm met with John over a long lunch to delve into the reasons underlying his substandard job performance. Toward the end of a tense half hour, John was asked in several different ways whether or not he enjoyed working for the firm. It was further suggested that unless he could elevate his job performance, he perhaps should seek a position similar to his old job as a corporate attorney. John became visibly upset and retorted: "That's absolutely the last damn thing in this world I would ever do. I hate all the phoniness in big companies. And I hate working for this stuffed shirt, old-fashioned, creepy law firm. All we do around here is lick the boots of clients. Even this stupid luncheon meeting is a waste of time. I'm not lazy. I just hate what I'm doing. I'm leaving the firm."[1]

The partners of the law firm concluded the luncheon meeting and drove back to the office. During their drive, they tried to understand why John behaved as he did and arrived at several possible conclusions: (1) he was lazy and tired; (2) personal problems, such as family illness, marital difficulties, or alcoholism were adversely affecting his performance; (3) he was involved with a basic personality clash with the partners of the firm and could not work with them; (4) he was poorly placed in his present position; and (5) he just wasn't motivated any more. The partners analyzed each of these possibilities and concluded that John's lack of motivation was the real problem.

THE ROLE OF MOTIVATION

Motivation affects the kind of adjustment employees make to an organization. Productivity is affected by the particular motives employees have for working at a particular place on a particular job. In many respects, the job of management is the effective channeling of employee motives toward organizational goals. Over the desk of Jack Pascal, the head of IBM's New York City financial branch, reads a sign "New York Financial—The Difference Is People." What this sign means is how well the employees at IBM perform determines the overall effectiveness of this $16.3 billion industrial giant. Frank T. Carey, chairman of the four-man corporate management committee that runs IBM, estimates that the company spends $2.3 billion a year, about 14 percent of its 1976 gross revenues, to motivate people.[2] Why?

To begin with, managers have recently begun to direct more attention toward the behavioral requirements of the organization. Every organization should satisfy three behavioral requirements:[3]

1. People must be attracted not only to join the organization but also to remain in it.
2. People must perform the task for which they were hired.
3. People must go beyond routine performance and engage in creative and innovative behavior at work.

In other words, for an organization to be effective, it must come to grips with the motivational problems of stimulating both the decision to join the organization and the decision to produce at work.

First, to induce people to join the company and to remain with it, large corporations, such as IBM, provide generous pension plans, group life insurance, and excellent medical coverage. IBM operates three dollar-a-year country clubs for workers and their families, it rebates the tuitions of those who want to go back to school to broaden their educations, and it runs a vast network of schools and training centers where employees can learn everything from computer programming to international finance.

Second, to guarantee that employees are performing the tasks for which they were hired, applicants are carefully screened to determine if they have the skills the job requires. Once hired, they find their performances routinely evaluated. At IBM, employees who do not produce at work never get promoted and/or get transferred from the corporate power centers.[4] Of course, the least satisfactory workers will be dismissed. Given the ever tightening constraints placed on organizations by unions, government agencies, increased foreign and domestic competition, citizens action groups, and the like, management has to look for new ways to maintain and increase its effectiveness and efficiency. Much of the profits that organizations could depend upon in the past are disappearing in the face of these new constraints. At Georgia-Pacific Corporation, the rate of profit that it was able to make in the lumber and timber industry between 1945 and 1975 has been steadily declining because of increased foreign and domestic competition and government regulations. Given such circumstances, the company must demand the fullest from its employees.

Third, beyond top performance, companies faced with new problems require creative and innovative behavior from their employees. To renew its growth, Georgia-Pacific has begun to exploit minerals beneath the timber and is starting to explore the possibility of entering into the oil and petrochemical industries.[5] Such innovation requires executives ready and able to move into these new areas as they open up.

As technology increases the complexity of the production processes, machines alone cannot increase production. People too must increase production. Modern technology can no longer be considered synonymous with automation. The auto industry, which gave the world mass production, is pioneering in the dismantling of some of the system. In cooperation with the United Auto Workers, General Motors is encouraging projects aimed at "improving the quality of working life" for its 560,000 employees. At a GM assembly plant in Tarrytown, New York, a problem with breakage in the glass installation department led to special training in problem-solving techniques for the department's 60 employees. The training program has now been extended to all 3,400 workers, with a noticeable decline in grievances and rise in productivity. At GM, as well as in thousands of other firms, it becomes necessary for the organization to bring together workers to apply their skills and knowledge most productively for the success of the company.[6]

Organizations have long viewed their financial and physical resources from a long-term perspective. But only recently have they begun to apply this same perspective to their human resources. Many organizations are now beginning to pay more attention to developing their employees as future resources upon which they can draw and develop. Evidence for such concern can be seen in the recent growth of "assessment centers" and manpower planning programs. The assessment center provides a method of identifying employees who have the potential to be top managers. At the centers, managers from various departments make decisions under simulated conditions, lead group discussions, conduct performance appraisals, and give oral presentations. To the extent that the simulation exercises and procedures accurately assess the dimensions of managerial effectiveness, the centers yield relevant appraisals. At present, more than one hundred organizations, including Sears, General Electric, AT&T, and Penney's, are using assessment centers as aids in management development.

In summary, then, there appear to be several reasons why the topic of motivation is receiving greater attention by managers. It is now recognized that building on an understanding of employee motivation will help attract and keep the best workers and will encourage these workers to perform at their most skillful and creative levels.

THE MOTIVATIONAL PROCESS: BASIC CONSIDERATIONS

Motivation is a predisposition to act in a specific goal-directed manner. Although this definition of motivation is restricted to purposive or goal-directed behavior, it must be noted that some behavior, such as reflexes, is not goal-directed. Reflexes are determined by the reaction of various nerves to external stimuli, such as heat or cold, and will not be dealt with in this chapter. When managers discuss motivation in their organizations, they are concerned with: (1) what drives behavior; (2) what direction behavior takes; and (3) how this behavior is maintained.[7]

In theory, the motivational process begins with a person's needs as illustrated in Figure 11–1. The basic blocks in the model are: (1) needs, desires, or expectations; (2) behavior; (3) goals; and (4) feedback. People possess, in varying strengths, a multitude of needs, desires, and expectations. For example, some managers may have a high *need* for power, a strong *desire* for advancement, and an *expectation* that working long hours will lead to a promotion. These needs, desires, and expectations create tensions within the managers that they find uncomfortable. Believing that some specific behavior could reduce this feeling, a person behaves. The behavior is directed toward the goal of reducing this state of tension. The initiation of this behavior sets up cues that feed information back to the person concerning the impact of his/her behavior. For example, people who have a strong desire to manipulate others (have a high need for power) may attempt to increase their empire in the organization by acquiring big offices (behavior) in hopes of gaining more influence (goal) in the organization.

FIGURE 11–1.   The Basic Motivational Process

Adapted from R. Steers and L. Porter, *Motivation and Work Behavior* (New York: John Wiley & Sons, 1976), p. 7.

This general model of the motivational process is simple and straightforward. In the real world, of course, such is not the case. First, motives can only be inferred; they cannot be seen. Suppose as a supervisor you notice two carpenters building packing crates for several large generators that your organization manufactures and ships to customers. They work the same shift, have similar abilities, and build the crates to the same specifications. When a crate is completed, the carpenter places it on a conveyor belt and proceeds to gather materials to begin the construction of another crate. After watching these two carpenters working for a week or so, you notice that one carpenter has completed about twice as many crates as his fellow worker. What does this tell you about the two carpenters? You can conclude that performance equals motivation times ability, and since both carpenters have similar abilities, that the answer must lie in the motivations of each person. The difference in their work output strongly suggests that they have different motivations. But it will take more investigation to determine what motivates each carpenter.

A second complication of the general model centers around the dynamic nature of motives. At any one time, each of us has many needs, desires, and expectations. Not only do these motives change, but they may be in conflict with each other. A manager who puts in many extra hours at his office to fulfill his needs for accomplishment may find these extra hours in direct conflict with his needs for affiliation as expressed in his desire to be with his family.

Third, considerable differences exist among people in the way in which they select certain motives over others and the drive with which they pursue these motives. Just as organizations differ in the products they manufacture or services they render, people differ in what motivates them to work. Some people work primarily for money, others for companionship, others for the challenge their work offers them, and still others for a combination of reasons. Organizations have tried numerous methods to motivate employees on the job—giving employees interesting jobs, using participative management, using pay-incentive systems, exercising close supervision, and the like. None of these methods could possibly work for all employees.

MOTIVATION VERSUS JOB SATISFACTION

It is important to distinguish between motivation and job satisfaction, for too often these terms are confused one with the other. Most workers develop feelings toward various aspects of their work—the pay, supervision, promotional opportunities, and the like—that can be classified as attitudes. *Attitudes* are affective responses (feelings), cognitive responses (beliefs and thoughts), and behavioral acts. Attitudes most commonly refer to affective responses. A worker's attitudinal response to a questionnaire or some other research instrument that is designed to measure factors affecting a worker's job are often called "facets of job satisfaction." *Satisfaction* is an end-state resulting from the attainment of some goal. It is the worker's affective responses to (feelings about) aspects of the work situation.

Motivation is primarily concerned with the individual's desires and how they can be fulfilled in the work situation. The basic difference between motivation and satisfaction was recently illustrated in a columnist's analysis of the firing of Tommy Heinsohn, the head coach of the Boston Celtic's basketball team:

> "Explain to me about motivation," said the owner. "Does the coach provide motivation by telling the team to go out and win one for Max Zaslofsky? Does he say, Win this game and I'll let you all stay up and watch the Johnny Carson show the next time we're in Detroit?"
>
> "No," the GM said. "Motivation is a more subtle art. The coach has to make his players feel wanted. He has to make them feel they're contributing. He has to make them feel good."
>
> The owner thought that over.
>
> "The last time I looked at my books," he said, "I was paying about two and a half million dollars a season in salaries. Doesn't that make them feel wanted? Doesn't that make them feel good?"
>
> "It would me," said the general manager. "But times have changed. All that money simply makes our players self-satisfied. Big cash ties their legs together so they can't dive for loose balls, and turns their brains into fettucini so they can't figure out when to switch and when to play their own man."[8]

What the owner is saying is that the coach must be able to motivate the players to achieve the goal of the organization, winning basketball games. The winning of the basketball games will give the players, coach, and owner satisfaction.

Assessment of Job Satisfaction

Job satisfaction is a worker's feelings about various aspects of the work setting. Various formats have been developed to measure job satisfaction. Once such format asks the respondent to indicate a choice of "yes," "no," or "uncertain" in response to whether or not a statement or an adjective is descriptive of the job. This approach is illustrated in Figure 11–2. For example, consider a job that you have performed, and answer the questions in Figure 11–2. This technique does not ask you directly about your satisfaction with the five related job factors (work, pay, promotions, supervision, and coworkers), but it infers the level of satisfaction from the adjectives that you consider descriptive of the job. For

FIGURE 11–2.   A Measure of Job Satisfaction

Work	Yes	No	If you cannot decide		Pay	Yes	No	If you cannot decide
Fascinating	—	—	—		Income adequate for normal expenses	—	—	—
Routine	—	—	—		Barely live on income	—	—	—
Satisfying	—	—	—					
Boring	—	—	—		Bad	—	—	—
Good	—	—	—		Insecure	—	—	—
Creative	—	—	—		Underpaid	—	—	—
Respected	—	—	—					
					Supervision			
Promotions					Asks my advice	—	—	—
Good opportunity for advancement	—	—	—		Hard to please	—	—	—
Dead-end job	—	—	—		Impolite	—	—	—
Regular promotions	—	—	—		Tactful	—	—	—
Unfair promotion policy	—	—	—		Up-to-date	—	—	—
Coworkers								
Stimulating	—	—	—					
Lazy	—	—	—					
Slow	—	—	—					
Ambitious	—	—	—					
Stupid	—	—	—					
Fast	—	—	—					

Adapted from Smith, P., L. Kendall, and C. Hulin, *The Measurement of Satisfaction in Work and Retirement* (Chicago: Rand McNally, 1969), p. 83.

example, it is unlikely that you would be satisfied with your coworkers if you responded "yes" to the adjectives "lazy," "slow," and "stupid." On the surface, this technique simply asks you to describe the various aspects of your work. In describing your work, however, you do provide information that is used to infer a state of satisfaction or dissatisfaction. Most of the adjectives are evaluative (satisfying, good, bad). There is a clear attempt to avoid the use of needs, wants, or desires since these are aspects of motivation.

Assessment of Motivation

One way to answer the questions "What does a person do?" and "To what degree does he or she do it?" is to assess the meaning of work and what it can provide for the individual. Behavioral scientists have identified many worker desires: security, esteem, self-actualization, autonomy, prestige, and so on. Two methods are frequently used to assess the strength of these desires. First, questions pertaining to specific desires are formulated and employees are asked to indicate the presence or absence of these desires for them. The list of desires that could be generated is substantial. The problem with following this approach is that it does not enable the worker to respond according to the strength of each desire, nor does it take into account the influence of one desire on another.

A second procedure is to assume that each worker has a hierarchy of needs, some stronger than others, and that an individual will seek fulfillment of the strongest desires first. If we measure the relative strength of desires, we can compare groups and individuals with respect to differential fulfillment of desires. This approach provides information with respect to the absolute level of desire strength for a single employee and a comparison of desire strengths among employees.

Porter designed an instrument to assess the fulfillment of needs.[9] The first question asks how much of the desired characteristic is now in the workplace? The second asks how much of the desired characteristic should there be in the workplace? The respondent circles his/her answer on a scale from (1) minimum to (7) maximum. Fulfillment of needs can be assessed by subtracting the response to the first question from the response to the second. The smaller the difference, the more the fulfillment of that need in the work situation. For example, suppose that the following question was used to measure degree of fulfillment of the self-actualization need, and the responses were as circled:

What opportunity is there in your management position for participating in setting goals?

How much is there now?

Minimum   1   2   3   (4)   5   6   7   Maximum

How much should there be?

Minimum   1   2   3   4   5   (6)   7   Maximum

The difference (2) indicates some lack of fulfillment in this need. We would expect that management would take some action to try to decrease the discrepancy between what there is and what there should be. Discrepancy scores should be interpreted with some caution, however. One problem is that a deficiency score can be derived in many ways ($7 - 5 = 2$; $6 - 4 = 2$; $5 - 3 = 2$, and so on). You can even get a negative score ($5 - 7 = -2$, for example) if an employee felt that currently there was too much participation. Nonetheless, Porter's scale is widely used to tap the motivational desires of individuals.[10]

FIGURE 11-3.   Theories of Motivation: Three Basic Questions

1. What is it about the nature of individuals that causes goals to become desirable to them?
2. What general classes of goals do people find desirable or undesirable?
3. What factors influence the desirability of these goals?

THEORIES OF MOTIVATION

An adequate theory of motivation must deal with three separate but interrelated questions, which are listed in Figure 11-3. These questions will be returned to in the analysis of each theory of motivation. Unless the second and third questions are answered, it is impossible to predict the kind of behavior choices a person will make.

The two major theoretical approaches to motivation—content and process—are summarized in Table 11-1.

Content

Content theories of motivation focus on the question of what it is that arouses individuals' behavior; that is, what specific things motivate people? The answer to this question has been provided by various motivational theorists in their discussion of the needs and drives and the incen-

TABLE 11-1.   Approaches to Motivation

Approach	Characteristics	Theories	Managerial Examples
Content	Concerned with factors that start or arouse motivated behavior	1. Need hierarchy 2. Achievement motivation 3. Two-factor	Motivation by satisfying individual needs for money, status, achievement, and working conditions
Process	Concerned with not only things that start behavior, but also the choice of behaviors and factors that increase the likelihood that desired behavior will be repeated	1. Expectancy 2. Reinforcement (operant conditioning)	Motivation through clarifying the individual's perception of work inputs and by rewarding desired behavior

Adapted from *Organizational Behavior and Performance* by John Ivancevich, Andrew Szilagyi, and Marc Wallace, p. 104. Copyright © 1977 by Goodyear Publishing Co. Reprinted by permission.

tives that cause people to behave in a particular manner (for example, promotion, salary, recognition, fringe benefits, and friendly coworkers). A need or motive is considered to be an integral state of the individual. Hunger (need for food) or a steady job (the need for security) are seen as motivators that arouse people and may cause them to choose a specific behavior (eating or working in a financially sound industry). The three most popular content theories of motivation are Maslow's need hierarchy, McClelland's achievement motivation, and Herzberg's two-factor theory. These theories have received considerable attention in both research studies and managerial applications. However, there are controversies and concerns regarding each of these theories.

Process

The content theories of motivation provide managers with an understanding of the particular work-related factors that arouse employees. But these theories provide little insight into why people *choose* a particular behavioral pattern to accomplish work goals. This choice aspect is the objective of process theories. Process theories attempt to explain and describe the process of how behavior is energized, how it is directed, how it is sustained, and how it is stopped. A content theory may talk about different needs that are important for understanding motivation. A process theory discusses how these needs interact and influence one another to produce certain kinds of behavior. The simple statement that "individuals exert more effort to obtain rewards that satisfy important needs than to obtain rewards that do not" would be an example.

The two best known process models are expectancy and operant reinforcement. Both models have been developed to explain, predict, and influence behavior. There are differences between these models. In the expectancy model, motivation is determined by expectations about behavior and the satisfaction value that will be derived from the outcomes of behavior. Thus, it is future oriented. One's expectations about the future determine the effort one puts forth now to accomplish the task.

In the operant reinforcement model (see Chapter 6 for a complete discussion of this model) behavior persists because of what happens after the behavior occurs (reinforcements). The reinforcement schedule by which the person's behavior has been reinforced affects the tendency to repeat that behavior. According to the operant model, people are likely to exert high effort when they are in an environment in which performance has been previously reinforced. While these two process models suggest different strategies for managers, both involve the choice process.

CONTENT THEORIES OF MOTIVATION

Maslow's Need Hierarchy

The most widely used theory for the study of motivation in organizations is Maslow's need hierarchy.[11] Maslow proposed that people have a complex set of needs, which are arranged in a hierarchy of prepotency. There are four basic assumptions in this hierarchy:

1. A satisfied need is not a motivator. When a need is satisfied, another need emerges to take its place, so that people are always striving to satisfy some need.
2. The need network for most people is very complex, with a number of needs affecting the behavior of each person at any one time.
3. Lower level needs must be satisfied, in general, before higher level needs are activated sufficiently to drive behavior.
4. There are many more ways to satisfy higher level needs than there are for lower level needs.

Maslow's theory postulates five need categories: physiological, security, affiliation, esteem, and self-actualization. These five need categories are arranged in the hierarchical order shown in Figure 11–4.

Physiological Needs. The need for food, water, air, and shelter are all physiological needs. Such needs are at the lowest level in the hierarchy. People concentrate on satisfying these needs before turning to the higher order needs. When a person is very hungry, no other interests exist. That person is primarily motivated to obtain food. Sadly enough, even in today's society, there are many people who are deprived of the basic physiological needs.

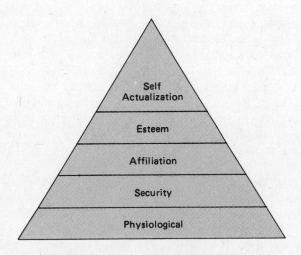

FIGURE 11–4.   Hierarchy of Needs

Managerial Implications.   To the extent that employees are motivated by physiological needs, they are really concerned with issues that are not centered on the work that they are doing. Any job that serves this need is acceptable. When managers focus on this need system to motivate subordinates, they are acting on the assumption that people work primarily for monetary rewards and are primarily concerned with comfort, avoidance of fatigue, and the like. Managers will try to motivate employees by offering wage increases, better working conditions, more leisure time, longer breaks, and better fringe benefits. But in organizational settings, managers usually encounter few employees whose physiological needs are not met. They turn their attention to security needs as the lowest level relevant to the analysis of work behavior.

Security Needs.   The need for safety, stability, and absence from pain, threat, or illness are all security needs. As in the case with physiological needs, when security needs are not satisfied, people become preoccupied with satisfying these needs. For many workers security needs are expressed in the desire for a safe and stable job and one with medical, unemployment, and retirement benefits. In the mid-1960s, many contractual agreements between labor and management focused on job retention for workers. Several industries, most notably airlines, newspapers, railroads, and shipping, have negotiated extensive provisions for workers whose jobs have been or may be eliminated by a change in technology. The Occupational Safety and Health Act of 1970 indicated that the federal government is trying to reduce the number of safety and health hazards in industry. And the Pension Act of 1974 was passed to assure workers that the monies they have invested in pension plans will be there upon retirement.

Managerial Implications.   Persons motivated primarily by security needs value their jobs mainly as a defense against the loss of basic need satisfactions. As with physiological needs, this need system involves issues that are not centered around the work itself. Any type of job that affords safety, security, and long-range protection against layoffs will be valued. If this is the most important need for employees, managers focus on this need system in their management style by emphasizing rules and regulations, job security, fringe benefits, and employee protection against automation. A manager whose subordinates have strong security needs will indicate little innovation in solving problems, risk taking will be avoided or not rewarded, and employees will behave as good bureaucrats.

Affiliation Needs.   The needs for friendship, love, and of belongingness are all affiliation needs. When the physiological needs and the security needs are satisfied, the affiliation needs emerge and serve to motivate people. This level in the hierarchy represents a clear-cut step above the first two (physical) needs. Nonfulfillment of these needs may affect the mental health of the employee. Examples of nonfulfillment of these needs can be evidenced in high absenteeism rates, poor productivity, low job satisfaction, and emotional breakdowns.

Managerial Implications. When affiliation needs are the primary source of motivation, people value their work as an opportunity for finding and establishing warm, harmonious interpersonal relationships. Jobs that afford opportunities for social interaction among coworkers are likely to be valued. Managers who perceive their subordinates as striving to satisfy this need system are likely to act in a particularly supportive and permissive way, placing much emphasis on being accepted by coworkers, extracurricular activities such as organized sports programs and company picnics, and following group norms. Managers will encourage a high level of employee satisfaction and loyalty, but this may be accompanied by a performance reduction since the employees' attention may be turned away from work to social relationships.

Esteem Needs. Esteem needs include both personal feelings of achievement or self-worth and recognition or respect from others. In affiliation needs, people want others to accept them for what they are. At the esteem level, people want to be perceived as competent and able. They are concerned about the achievement, prestige, status, and promotional opportunities that others will provide as recognition of their competence and capabilities. The desire for excellence, mastery of some problem or skills, and independence are internal or personal feelings that may be indicators of self-esteem. The desire for respect, prestige, increased responsibility, promotion, recognition, and appreciation by others are external indicators of one's status that can also fulfill the need for esteem. The fulfillment of esteem needs leads to feelings of worth, adequacy, and self-confidence. The inability to fulfill these needs may lead to a feeling of discouragement. There is a real danger to mental health when esteem is bestowed upon someone by others if it is based upon external celebrity or fame, rather than upon actual competence or capacity to perform the task.

Managerial Implications. Managers who focus on esteem needs in their attempts to motivate employees tend to emphasize public reward and recognition for services. Emphasis on the difficulty of the work and the skills required for success characterize managers' contacts with employees. Lapel pins, articles in the company paper, published performance lists, and the like may be used as a means of promoting pride in one's work. To the extent that this need system is dominant, managers may promote both high satisfaction and performance rates through job designs that capitalize on the need to excel coupled with effective means of providing status-serving rewards, and a lot of opportunity for independence and autonomous action.

Self-actualization Needs.   Self-fulfillment, or the realization of one's potential is the goal of self-actualization needs. A person who has attained self-actualization experiences acceptance of self and others, increased problem-solving ability, increased spontaneity, increased detachment, and a desire for privacy. To fulfill the need to become everything that one is capable of becoming requires that the individual has at some time partially fulfilled the other needs. However, self-actualizers may focus on the fulfillment of this highest need to such an extent that they consciously or unconsciously make sacrifices in the fulfillment of lower level needs. Figure 11–5 lists some behaviors that might be thought of as indicating self-actualization needs.

Managerial Implications.   When self-actualization needs are dominant, people are motivated to channel their most creative and constructive skills into their work. Managers who focus primarily on these needs recognize that every job has areas within it that allow innovation; creativity is not the sole possession of managers, but may be desired by anyone. Managers who emphasize self-actualization are likely to use techniques

FIGURE 11–5.   Some Symptoms of Self-Actualization

1. Self-actualization means experiencing fully, vividly, selflessly, with full concentration and total absorption.

2. Life can be thought of as a process of choices, one after another.

3. Talk of self-actualization implies that there is a self to be actualized.

4. When in doubt, be honest rather than not. Looking within oneself for many of the answers implies taking responsibility.

5. One cannot choose wisely for a life unless he dares to listen to himself—his own self—at each moment in life, and to say calmly, "No, I don't like such and such."

6. Self-actualization is not only an end-state but also the process of actualizing one's potentialities at any time, in any moment.

7. Peak experiences are transient moments of self-actualization. They are moments of ecstasy which cannot be bought, cannot be guaranteed, cannot even be sought.

8. Finding out who one is, what one is, what one likes, or doesn't like, what is good for him and what bad, where one is going and what one's mission is— opening up one's inner self—means the exposure of psychopathology. It means identifying defenses, and after defenses have been identified, it means finding the courage to give them up.

From Maslow, A. H., *The Farther Reaches of Human Nature* (New York: Viking Press, 1971), pp. 45–49.

for making work more meaningful. They may employ involvement strategies in planning job designs, make special assignments that capitalize on an employee's unique skills, or provide leeways to the employee group in designing work procedures and plans for implementation.

Summary of the Need Hierarchy. Maslow's theory of needs assumes that people are motivated to satisfy the need(s) that is (are) important at that point in their lives. Further, the strength of any particular need is determined by its position in the need hierarchy and by the degree to which it and all lower level needs have been satisfied. The theory predicts a dynamic, step-by-step, causal process of motivation, in which behavior is governed by a continuously changing set of "important" needs. Maslow did not propose that the hierarchy is rigidly fixed in only one set for all people. This is especially true for the middle-level needs (affiliation and esteem), where the order would probably vary from person to person. However, Maslow clearly indicates that the physiological needs are the most prepotent and the self-actualization needs are the least fulfilled.

Controversies Regarding the Need Hierarchy Theory. From the point of view of the three questions asked in Figure 11–3, the need hierarchy theory provides fairly complete answers to the last two questions. That is, Maslow's theory makes specific statements about what goals people will value and also suggests what type of behavior will influence the fulfillment of various needs. It provides less complete information as to *why* the needs originate. It does, however, imply that higher level needs are potentially present in most people. Moreover, these higher level needs will motivate most people if the demands of the situation do not block them from appearing.

The need hierarchy theory has received much attention from those interested in the study of behavior in organizations,[12] undoubtedly because the theory, if valid, would provide managers with a powerful tool for predicting behavior in their organizations. For example, the hierarchy suggests that when individuals are permitted to exercise more discretion in their jobs and their lower level needs have been satisfied, they will become more concerned with middle level and upper level need fulfillment. Unfortunately, the research evidence does not provide a clear indication that the hierarchy is a valid predictor of motivational desires. While it is beyond the scope of this book to examine all the criticisms of the theory, several relevant questions can be asked.

Is there a need hierarchy? Strong evidence supports the notion that unless basic needs are satisfied, none of the higher level needs can affect behavior. However, there is very little evidence to support the view that there are five specific levels of needs. Even if five levels exist, research indicates that most people are simultaneously motivated by needs at the same level, not motivated by needs at two different levels.[13] One person, for example, might be motivated by hunger and thirst needs, while another may be motivated by social and autonomy needs. However, it is less likely that a person would be motivated by physiological and esteem needs at the same time. The lower level needs would assume greater importance until they had been fulfilled. The person would engage in behavior (searching for food and water) that would be directed at fulfilling these prepotent needs.

Can outcomes fulfill more than one need? Considerable research evidence supports the contention that many outcomes are relevant to the fulfillment of more than one need. For example, adequate pay appears to satisfy not only physiological and security needs, but also esteem needs.[14] It is not difficult to see how pay can fulfill the need for food and other necessities by giving the employee money to buy articles that satisfy the lower level needs and also afford him or her a certain amount of esteem and respect in our society. Another example is the midmorning coffee break. It fulfills the workers' physiological hunger need and their affiliation need.

How important are different needs? Many researchers have tried to measure the importance of different employee needs. The data in Figure 11–6 are taken from a sample of over 1,900 managers. The figure clearly indicates that the higher level needs (in this case, autonomy and self-actualization) are the most important. Other studies show that the managers' lower level needs are easily fulfilled by the organization, but that most of the higher level needs are not fulfilled in the work setting.[15]

Studies have also shown that the fulfillment of needs differs according to such factors as the job a person performs in the organization, his or her age or race, the size of the company, and the cultural background of the employee.[16] Briefly, these studies have found:

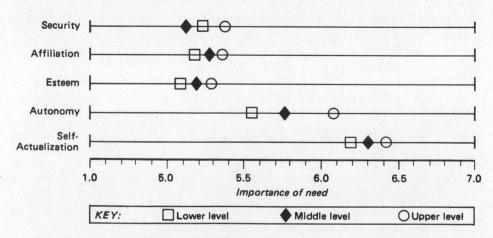

FIGURE 11–6.   Importance Attached to Five Needs by Managers from Three Organization Levels

1. Line managers perceive greater fulfillment than do staff managers in the areas of security, affiliation, esteem, and self-actualization needs. The largest differences between line and staff managers occur in esteem and self-actualization needs.
2. Young workers (twenty-five years old or less) have greater need deficiencies than do older workers (thirty-six years old or more) in esteem and self-actualization needs.
3. Black managers report a greater lack of need fulfillment in every need than do their nonblack counterparts.
4. At lower levels of management, small-company managers are less deficient in their needs than are managers who work for larger companies.
5. Workers in different cultures have different hierarchies from those of workers employed in U.S. firms.

There are *individual differences in need strength.* As implied in the previous section, there are large differences in the needs of individuals, and these differences are attributable to numerous factors. If we relate differences in need strength to personal characteristics, we might begin to understand some of these differences. For example, urban workers seem to be more alienated (estranged or separated) from their work and less concerned about fulfillment of their higher level needs on the job than are rural workers.[17] Similarly, workers in Mexico place a greater importance on the fulfillment of their needs in the work situation than do workers in the United States. An interesting profile of a worker for whom money is the only important work-related factor is:

> The employee is a male, probably in the twenties; his personality is characterized by low self-assurance and high neuroticism; he comes from a small town or farm background; he belongs to few clubs, and he owns his own home and is probably a Republican.[18]

The list of individual differences affecting the fulfillment of needs could go on and on. The important thing to note is that there are individual differences among employees and that these differences affect the importance of different needs and outcomes. This point has some interesting implications for managers. For example, it means that it is possible to identify those employees for whom a particular need is likely to be important. Moreover, it may suggest the desirability of tailoring the organization's environment and management systems to make them flexible enough to recognize need differences among people in the organization.

How changeable is the importance of needs? Evidence indicates that personal and organizational events can and do change the importance of needs. For example, the importance of needs can be shaped by parents in early childhood. Organizational practices can strongly influence the arousal and fulfillment of many higher level needs. Esteem needs can be aroused by a promotion based on past competence in a position. One study has found that as managers advance in the organization, their security needs tend to decrease, with a corresponding increase in their needs for affiliation, esteem, and self-actualization.[19]

The following statements summarize the major points regarding the hierarchy of needs.

1. Needs can be thought of as desires that individuals strive to fulfill.
2. The higher level needs will motivate the individual only when the lower level needs have been fulfilled.
3. All needs except self-actualization can be fulfilled and as they become fulfilled, they decrease in importance for the individual.
4. An individual can be motivated by more than one need at any given time; individual differences can affect the hierarchy of needs for any one individual; and the hierarchy of needs is changeable over time.

McClelland's Achievement Motivation

Achievement motivation has been extensively studied by McClelland, especially with regard to entrepreneurship.[20] *Achievement motivation* is the desire to perform in terms of a standard of excellence or a desire to be successful in competitive situations. While McClelland indicates that nearly everyone feels that he/she has an "achievement motive," probably only 10 percent of the U.S. population is strongly motivated for achievement. The amount of achievement motivation people have is dependent on childhood, personal and occupational experiences, and the type of organization a person is working for.

Motives are located mentally just below the level of full awareness in the preconscious mind—the borderland between the conscious and unconscious. This is the area of reverie, of daydreams, where people talk to themselves without quite being aware of it. But the pattern of these reveries can be tested, and people can be taught to change their motivation by changing these reveries.

Assessment of Achievement Motivation.   McClelland measures the strength of people's achievement motivation by using the projective method. In the projective method, a subject is presented with an unstructured stimuli, one that is capable of arousing many different kinds of reactions. Examples are an ink blot that can be perceived as many different objects, or a picture that can elicit a variety of stories. A major intent is to obtain the subject's own perception of the world. There are no right or wrong answers; nor is the subject faced with a limited set of alternatives. The emphasis is on the individual perception of the stimuli, the meaning each subject gives to it, and how each subject organizes the stimuli. The nature of the stimuli and the way in which it is presented do not clearly indicate the purpose of the researcher or the way in which the subject's responses will be interpreted. Although subjects are not asked to talk about themselves, according to McClelland, the responses are often interpreted as indicating each subject's own view of the world,

FIGURE 11–7.   Sample Picture Used in a Projective Test From David A. Kolb, Irwin M. Rubin, and James M. McIntyre, *Organizational Psychology: An Experiential Approach*, © 1971, p. 65. Reproduced by permission of Prentice-Hall, Inc., Englewood Cliffs, N.J.

personality structure, needs and feelings, and ways of interacting with others.

Look at the picture in Figure 11–7 for 10–15 seconds. Then write a short story about the picture, answering these questions:

1. What is going on in this picture?
2. What is the man thinking?
3. What has led up to this situation?

After writing your story, compare it with this story written by one manager. It is an example of a story showing a strong achievement motive.

The individual is a chief executive officer of a large corporation who wants to get a contract for his company. He knows that the competition will be tough because all the "big" boys are bidding on this contract. He is taking a moment to think how happy he will be if his company is awarded the large contract. It will mean stability for the entire company and probably a large raise for himself. He is smiling because he has just thought of a way to manufacture a critical part that will enable his company to bring in a low bid and complete the job with time to spare.

Does your story sound like this? If so, then you might fit McClelland's description of a high achiever.

Characteristics of High Achievers.   The major characteristics of the self-motivated high achiever have been identified as follows:

First, high achievers like to set their own goals. Seldom content just to drift aimlessly and let life "happen to them," they are nearly always trying to accomplish something. They are quite selective about the goals to which they become committed. For this reason, they are unlikely to accept automatically goals that other people—including their supervisors—select for them. They do not tend to seek advice or help, except from experts who can provide needed skills. High achievers prefer to be as fully responsible for the attainment of their goals as possible. If they win, they want the credit, and if they lose, they accept the blame. For example, assume that you are given a choice between rolling dice with one chance in three of winning and working on a problem with one chance in three of solving the problem in the time allotted. Which would you choose? A high achiever would choose to work on the problem, even though rolling the dice is obviously less work and the odds of winning are the same. High achievers prefer to work at a problem rather than leave the outcome to chance or to others.[21]

Second, high achievers tend to avoid the extremes of difficulty in selecting goals. They prefer moderate goals that are neither so easy that winning them would provide no satisfaction nor so difficult that winning or attaining them would be more a matter of luck than ability. They gauge what is possible and then select a goal that is as tough as they think they can make—the hardest practical challenge. An ordinary example of ring-tossing might illustrate this point. In most carnivals, there are ring-tossing games that require the participant to throw rings over a peg from some minimal distance, but no maximal distance. Imagine the same game, but you are allowed to stand at any distance you wish from the peg. Some of you will throw more or less randomly, standing now close, now far away. But those with a high achievement motive seem to calculate carefully where they should stand to be most likely to have a chance of winning a prize. These individuals seem to stand at a distance that is not so close as to make the task ridiculously easy and not so far away as to make it impossible. They set a distance that is moderately far away, but where ringing a peg is potentially achievable. In other words, they set challenges for themselves and tasks that will make them stretch themselves a little.

Third, high achievers prefer tasks that provide them with more or less immediate feedback. Because of the importance of the goal to them, they like to know how well they are doing. This is one reason why the high achiever often decides on a professional career or a career in sales or engages in entrepreneurial activities.[22] Golf is a sport that has characteristics that would appeal to most high achievers. Golfers can compare their scores to the par for the course or their own previous performance on the course. Performance is related to both feedback (golf score) and goal specificity (handicap).

McClelland points out that the effect of monetary incentive on high achievers is complex. On the one hand, high achievers usually have a high opinion of the value of their services and prefer to place a high price tag on themselves. High achievers have self-confidence, in that they are aware of what they're good at and what they're not good at, which gives them confidence when they choose to do a particular job. They are unlikely to remain for long in an organization that does not pay them well if they are performing well. On the other hand, it is questionable whether an incentive plan actually increases their performance, since they are normally working at peak efficiency anyway. Thus money is a strong symbol of their achievement and adequacy, but it may create dissatisfaction because of feelings that it is inadequate relative to their contribution.

When achievement motivation is operating, good job performance may become very attractive to people. However, achievement motivation does not operate when achievers are performing tasks that are routine or boring or where there is no competition.

Developing Achievement Motivation. How can you improve your achievement motivation? McClelland has suggested four ways. (1) *Arrange for some accomplishment feedback.* This is the art of designing tasks so that you succeed bit by bit, gaining a reward each time and thus strengthening your desire to achieve more. (This has worked for us. When we got bogged down in writing this book, we decided to publish articles and participate in executive development programs. The sense of accomplishment in these tasks kept us going.) (2) *Seek models of achievement.* If people around you succeed, it will stimulate your desire to succeed. (For example, Harry Truman came from a modest home, but he attributed the prominence he attained to the heroes he modeled himself after— the famous statesmen he had read about in books.) (3) *Modify your self-image.* People with high achievement motivation seek personal challenges and responsibilities and require continual feedback of success. These are experiences that they desire so much that they may be said to need them. McClelland believes that it is possible to develop such wants by reconceptualizing oneself as someone who requires these things. (As a first step, imagine yourself as a person who must have success, responsibility, challenge, and variety.) (4) *Control your reveries.* Just beyond the borderline of awareness, most of us are constantly talking to ourselves. Athletes, such as Billie Jean King, talk to themselves during matches, repeating words of encouragement. Conversely, negative ideas should be discouraged.

Summary of Achievement Motivation. Research on achievement motivation suggests that the theory provides answers to the second and third questions of Figure 11–3. But as with the need hierarchy theory, it falls short of explaining why the achievement motivation is desired. That is, McClelland's theory clearly indicates what types of job-related experiences high achievers desire from their work and some of the factors (feedback, pay, moderate goal setting) that influence the desirability of their work experiences. It is hard to see, however, how achievement could be classified as a primary drive in the sense of Maslow's lower level needs. Situational factors, such as child-rearing practices of parent, culture, and organizational practices affect the development of the achievement motive.

Herzberg's Two-Factor Theory

The Herzberg two-factor theory is the last theory to be discussed here that has as its primary focus an attempt to specify why certain job-related outcomes are valued by employees. Currently, this theory is one of the most controversial theories of motivation. Two aspects of the theory are unique and probably account for most of the attention it has received. First, it stresses that some job factors lead to satisfaction while others can only prevent dissatisfaction. Second, the theory states that job satisfaction and dissatisfaction do not exist on a single continuum.

In order to understand these major points, let's briefly look at the development of the theory. Herzberg and his associates examined the relationship between job satisfaction and productivity among a group of accountants and engineers.[23] Through the use of semistructured interviews, they accumulated data on various factors that these workers indicated affected their feelings toward their jobs. The result was the emergence of two different sets of factors.

Motivator and Hygiene Factors. The first factor, *motivators*, include the work itself, recognition, advancement, and responsibility. These factors are associated with positive feelings about the job and are related to the content of the job itself. These positive feelings are associated with the individual's having experienced achievement, recognition, and responsibility in the past. These positive feelings are predicated on lasting rather than temporary achievement in the work setting.

The second factor, *hygienes*, include company policy and administration, technical supervision, salary, working conditions, and interpersonal relations. These factors are associated with negative feelings about one's work and are related to the context or environment in which the job is performed. That is, these factors are *extrinsic* or external to the job or the work itself. In contrast, the motivators are related to the *intrinsic* or internal factors associated with the job.

Viewed somewhat differently, extrinsic outcomes are largely determined by the formal organization (salary, company policies and rules, and the like). Extrinsic outcomes serve as a reward for high performance only if the organization recognizes high performance. On the other hand, intrinsic outcomes, such as feelings of accomplishment after successful task performance, are largely administered internally by the individual. The organization's policies have only an indirect impact on them. For example, by stating what defines exceptional performance, the organization may be able to influence individuals to feel that they have performed their tasks exceptionally well.

Although motivators are usually associated with positive feelings toward one's job, they are sometimes associated with negative feelings. However, hygienes are almost never associated with positive feelings, but are associated with states of mental depression, quitting the organization, absenteeism, and the like.

Figure 11–8 illustrates the two-factor theory. It shows the frequency with which each factor was mentioned by the accountants and engineers in connection with high (satisfying) and low (dissatisfying) work experiences. As can be seen, achievement was present in more than 40 percent of the satisfying experiences and in less than 10 percent of the dissatisfying experiences.

The second major point of the theory is the concept that satisfaction and dissatisfaction are not on a single continuum, but are separate and distinct, as indicated in Figure 11–9. One of the most interesting things about these dual continua is that a person can be satisfied and dissatisfied at the same time. The dual continua also imply that hygiene factors, such as working conditions and salary, cannot increase or decrease job satisfaction; they can only affect the amount of job dissatisfaction.

Controversies Regarding the Two-factor Theory

The research designed to test Herzberg's theory has not provided clear-cut evidence either supporting or rejecting the theory. It is beyond the scope of this chapter to review these numerous studies.[24] However, we can consider some of the major criticisms levied against the theory.

A major criticism is that the procedure Herzberg used was *method-bound;* that is, the method used to measure the factors determined the results. Two key questions were asked: "Can you describe, in detail, when you felt exceptionally good about your job?" and "Can you describe, in detail, when you felt exceptionally bad about your job?" In response to such questions, people tend to give "socially desirable" answers, that is, answers that the respondents think the researcher wants to hear or that sound "reasonable." Also, people have a tendency to attribute good results from their job to their own efforts and to thrust reasons for their poor performance onto others.

A second major criticism questions whether satisfaction and dissatisfaction really are two dimensions, as indicated in Figure 11–9. Research

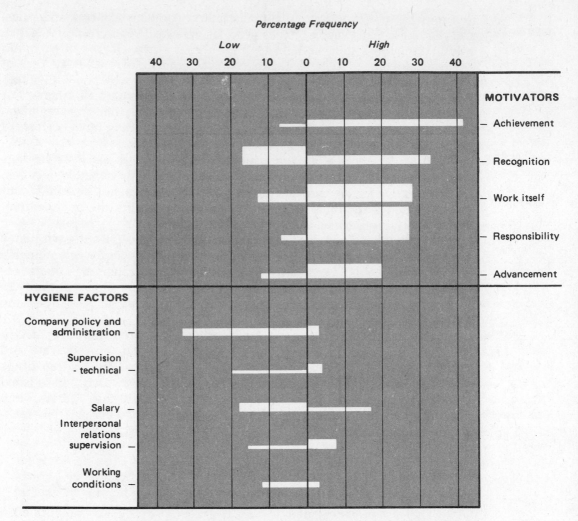

FIGURE 11–8.   Comparison of Motivator and Hygiene Factors

results are mixed. It has been found that some factors can contribute to both satisfaction and dissatisfaction, while other researchers have found that motivators can contribute to dissatisfaction and hygiene factors can contribute to satisfaction. Although these findings raise serious questions about the theory, the concept that satisfaction and dissatisfaction are two different continua has not been destroyed.

While a considerable amount of effort has been directed at resolving these two criticisms, few efforts have been directed toward answering the three questions posed in Figure 11–3. The evidence, although not strong, suggests the kinds of experiences that might lead to a strong motivation to perform well. For example, increasing job responsibility,

FIGURE 11–9.   Satisfaction Continua

challenge, and advancement opportunities have been linked to high performance. Unfortunately, Herzberg provides little theoretical basis for
these findings. Little attention has been paid to constructing a theory that
explains why certain job factors should affect performance positively or
negatively. Similarly, few attempts have been made to explain why certain outcomes are attractive to employees and why a person chooses a
certain type of behavior versus another in order to obtain a desired outcome. Thus, in terms of the three questions, the two-factor theory is not a
theory of motivation because it does not: (1) specify how outcomes become desirable for people, and (2) specify the factors that influence the
desirability of the goals. It does, however, explain the determinants of job
satisfaction and dissatisfaction, and it has pointed out important concepts
for those individuals concerned with job enrichment programs in industry.
These concepts will be dealt with in the next chapter.

Summary of Content Theories

The content theories of Maslow, McClelland, and Herzberg attempt to identify what it is that motivates people at work (self-actualization, need for achievement, or motivators). Each model attempts to explain
what motivates individuals from a slightly different perspective. None of
them should be accepted by the practicing manager as the sole basis for
understanding behavior of employees in organizations. As will be pointed
out, process motivational theorists are skeptical of attempting to explain
behavior solely on the basis of needs, desires, and satisfaction because
such approaches provide only a minimal understanding of what actions
people will choose so that their needs will be satisfied. Even so, people
have needs, various job factors do in fact result in differing degrees of job
satisfaction, and individual motives are real aspects in organizations.

PROCESS THEORY OF MOTIVATION

The content theories of Maslow, McClelland, and Herzberg provide
managers with an understanding of the particular work-related factors
that start the motivational process. However, these theories provide little
understanding of why people choose a particular behavior to accomplish

work-related goals. This *choice* aspect is the major focus of process theories.

Consider the following situation:

Cindy Nardoni has just reported to work in the management department at a large eastern university. Her new boss has chatted with her briefly about the nature of the department's work and introduced her to her coworkers and the department's faculty. Cindy thought that her coworkers were a likeable group, that they were having a good time even though the work load was heavy. This was important to Cindy because at her last job she had no chance to socialize with other workers.

Before leaving Cindy by herself, her supervisor took her aside and told her that her new job success will depend completely on how well she wants to do; she will be paid according to her productivity and her productivity will be taken into account when raises and promotions are discussed. Shortly after she started work, Cindy was told by her coworkers in no uncertain terms that if she wanted to get along she would produce the departmental "norm." No secretary produces more than this. The last secretary who produced more than the norm found life "lonely," and got the "silent treatment" from the rest of the secretaries.[25]

How will Cindy behave? Will she ignore the group's established "norm" and strive to meet her best productivity? Or, will she bow to the pressure, restrict her output, and gain acceptance by the group?

If we were to analyze this incident using Maslow's need hierarchy, we would start by considering whether belonging to the group (satisfaction of affiliation needs) or recognition from the department head (satisfaction of esteem needs) was more important to Cindy. According to Maslow's model, affiliation needs are more basic than esteem needs. Until they can be satisfied, they assume more importance than esteem needs. If we were analyzing this situation using McClelland's model, Cindy might be motivated to achieve high performance because of her achievement motive. High achievers are seldom content just to drift aimlessly around and let others tell them what to do. When the achievement motive is operating, good job performance becomes a very important goal. We might also analyze this situation using Herzberg's two-factor theory. Coworkers are a hygiene factor, whereas the challenge of the task and task-related factors are motivators. According to Herzberg's theory, only such aspects as a challenging job, recognition for doing a good job, and opportunities for advancement, personal growth, and promotion function to provide a situation for motivated behavior. If Cindy wants to obtain these job-related benefits, then she must ignore her coworkers' pressures and establish her own performance level.

Vroom's Expectancy Theory

Another way of looking at the situation is through the process model of motivation presented in Vroom's expectancy theory.[26] Vroom's theory departs from those of Maslow, McClelland, and Herzberg in that it shows a system of cognitive variables that reflects individual differences in work motivation. It does not attempt to describe what the content is or what the individual differences are. It does not provide specific suggestions on what motivates people. Expectancy theory relates to choice behavior. That is, people usually have several alternative behaviors from which to select. They choose one of them, based on their expectations about the alternatives. The key variables in Vroom's model besides choice are expectancy, valence, and instrumentality.

Expectancy. Expectancy is the belief that a particular behavioral act will be followed by a particular outcome. This belief can vary from complete lack of a relationship between the act and a given outcome and complete certainty that an act will result in a given outcome. For example, if Cindy found both outcomes (high productivity and low productivity) equally likely, then her decision would be most difficult. If she believed that her probability of being able to achieve high productivity was only 20 percent even if she were able to meet the requirements for outstanding performance, but she knew almost without a doubt (95 percent) that she could reach the output quota established by other secretaries, she would probably follow the group norm. In this situation, Cindy would be more motivated to follow the group norm than to attempt to achieve high productivity because she believes high productivity is not easily within her grasp.

Valence. Valence is a measure of the individual's feelings about a particular outcome. Valences, which can be positive or negative, depend upon what results can come from the outcome and how the individual feels about these. In Cindy's situation, we would expect such outcomes as pay, promotion, and recognition by coworkers to be positive valences; such outcomes as conflict with coworkers and reprimands from the department head are negative valences. Cindy will attempt to evaluate the value she places on the outcomes for each alternative. If she doesn't care about being accepted by the group (low valence), then she may be indifferent about the possible "silent" treatment that she would expect to receive from the other secretaries if she exceeded the group norm. In this situation, a pay raise and promotion would have a higher valence (preference) than would group acceptance.

Instrumentality. Instrumentality is the relationship between outcomes. Instrumentality can vary between $+1.0$ and -1.0. If Cindy's first-level outcome (high performance) always leads to a pay increase (second-level outcome), the instrumentality would always be $+1.0$. If there is no perceived relationship between first- and second-level outcomes, then instrumentality approaches zero. If Cindy believes that high performance would always result in a pay decrease, then instrumentality would be −1.0.

To complete the model, Vroom states that expectancy and valence combine multiplicatively to determine motivation. If valence and/or expectancy equals zero, motivation will be zero. If Cindy desires a promotion (high valence) but does not believe that she has the ability or necessary secretarial skills to achieve this level (low expectancy), the motivation for high performance will be low.

Vroom's model is illustrated in Figure 11–10. Using Cindy's situation, we might think of how she will handle the situation she is faced with. In order to gain group acceptance, she must first limit her production to the group's norm. She also knows that if she cannot meet the group's norms, she will be definitely kept out of the group. On the other hand, if Cindy were completely certain that she could meet the group's productivity level (expectancy would be 1.0), then she might feel that by limiting her productivity, she would gain full acceptance by the group. Even if she really wanted to get promoted and believed that high producers got promoted (instrumentality near +1.0), unless she had the ability to achieve this level (high expectancy), she would not strive for high productivity. A highly desired outcome with little chance of attaining it, in most cases, fails to motivate the person.

What if Cindy believes that both high and low performers receive the same outcomes, that pay, fringe benefits, and football tickets are not affected by performance but by tenure in the university? How will this affect her decision? In this case, being highly productive may be perceived as leading to nothing more than tiring oneself out. So why produce? In most organizations, people are forced to choose among a limited

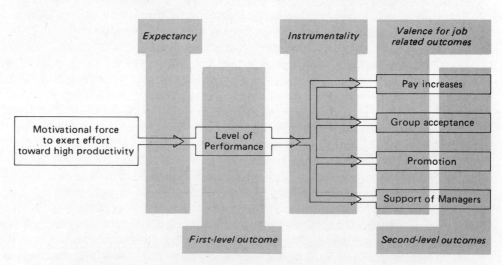

FIGURE 11–10.   Expectancy Model of Motivation

number of performance range choices. Vroom's theory predicts that the individual will choose that performance option that has the highest motivational force.

Research on Vroom's Model.   Numerous research studies have attempted to validate Vroom's expectancy model.[27] The various studies have indicated that a person's expectations about job-related outcomes can affect choice behavior. In a study of nursing school graduates, it was found that nurses choose hospitals that let them satisfy a variety of work-related outcomes (attractive working hours, pay, leisure, work in specialized fields of interest, and challenging work assignments). Hospitals that gave nurses opportunities to satisfy these outcomes were chosen by the nurses to a greater extent than hospitals that didn't give the nurses the opportunity to achieve these outcomes.[28] Similarly, incentive-paid workers with high expectations about their pay were found to be significantly more productive than workers with low expectations about the pay-performance relationships. Further developments and refinements with the model have indicated that personality variables (self-esteem and self-expectancy) appear to have an affect on an individual's expectancy formations and valence perceptions.

Although these research findings appear to be encouraging in comparison with the research conducted on the content theories of Maslow, McClelland, and Herzberg, a number of issues surrounding expectancy theory have been uncovered.[29] First, with the extensions and refinements of the basic model, the model has become too complex to measure. Each researcher has chosen to measure expectancy, instrumentality, and valence in different ways, thereby making comparisons between studies difficult. Closely related to this problem is that the complexity of the model makes it too difficult to test. Few studies have been reported that have tested all the variables within the model.[30] Several of the variables influencing individual expectations about affecting performance include past experience with other situations, ability, style of supervision, and the work environment. Finally, the research evidence does not support the multiplicative calculations required by the model before an individual is motivated to exert some effort. Whether these variables interact or act independently to affect a person's motivation is still questionable.

In summary, there is some support for Vroom's expectancy theory. It is a more valid indicator of a person's motivational process than are the content theories. The expectancy model answers the last two questions of Figure 11–3. It argues that both the attractiveness of the outcomes and the person's expectancies and instrumentalities influence the range of performance alternatives a person will try to obtain. The model also details how these alternatives will be sought. The choice of a behavior also implies that the individual has a choice of what behavior will be attempted. However, the theory does not address the question of how an individual develops expectancies and instrumentalities and what influences them.

Managerial Implications. Vroom's model departs from those of Maslow, McClelland, and Herzberg in that it shows a thought process of why individuals choose various outcomes and ignore others. It does not attempt to describe what outcomes are for every individual or what individual differences (personality, perception, learning) affect the motivational process. Therefore, while it does not provide specific suggestions on what motivates a person, it does indicate the determinants of motivation and how they are related. Expectancy theory is like marginal analysis in economics. Managers seldom calculate the point where marginal costs equal marginal revenues, but it is still regarded as a useful concept in the theory of the firm. The expectancy model recognizes the complexities of work motivation and seems to be heading in the right direction.

Four implications for managerial practices can be drawn using the expectancy theory. First, people make conscious evaluations with respect to the result of their efforts and the outcomes of their performance. Cindy was able to decide if high performance was obtainable and what the consequences were ("the silent treatment" by the group). Second, a manager can clarify and increase employees' perceptions of how to assure that effort will lead to effective performance through the use of guidance and coaching. If Cindy wanted to be a high-performing secretary but didn't have the needed secretarial skills (typing, shorthand, dictation), her supervisor might recommend that she learn these skills by taking courses offered in the evening school at the local high school. Third, rewards must be closely and clearly related to those behaviors that the organization desires. This has been stated in Chapter 6. A person's rewards must be contingent on her behavior. In Cindy's case, the department head made it very clear that Cindy's salary and promotion were tied directly to her secretarial performance. Finally, individuals place different importance on work outcomes. How important is pay to you? How important are attractive working conditions? Would you take a job that is challenging but has lower pay? These and many other questions should be analyzed by managers with the emphasis on matching the desires of the employees with the particular organizational reward. For example, pay has motivational power because:

1. It buys the means of satisfying physiological needs.
2. It helps ensure against possible financial disaster and satisfies security needs.
3. It can buy the means for socialization, such as membership in country clubs and food for parties.
4. It is frequently a symbol of a person's worth to an organization and to society. In this function, it is capable of satisfying a person's status, power, and self-esteem needs.
5. When pay is tied to performance, it serves as a measure of personal achievement (self-actualization).

If the employee values pay, the value of the manager's motivational plan will increase if it corresponds with the employee's pay preferences.

AN INTEGRATED MODEL OF MOTIVATION

Despite the considerable amount of research and the modifications and extensions of the models discussed in this chapter, there appears to be no one perfect model of the motivational process. The content theories assume that satisfaction of needs and work-related factors lead to improved performance and that dissatisfaction detracts from high performance. The two-factor model is really more of a theory of job satisfaction. And research has not shown any strong relationship between job satisfaction and performance.[31] The Vroom model does not look at the relationship of satisfaction and performance. Although satisfactions can be assumed under Vroom's concept of valences, it was not until Porter and Lawler refined and extended Vroom's model that the relationship between satisfaction and performance was dealt with directly by a motivational model.[32]

The Porter-Lawler Model

Porter and Lawler start with the assumption that motivation does not equal satisfaction or performance. Motivation, satisfaction, and performance are distinct concepts that relate in different ways from what has been traditionally assumed. In essence, they argue that satisfaction, rather than being a cause, is an effect of performance; that is, performance causes satisfaction. Differential performance determines rewards that, in turn, produce variations in employee satisfaction(s).

Figure 11–11 shows the basic model for understanding the relationship between motivation, satisfaction, and performance. The *value of reward* (box 1) is similar to Vroom's valence measure. That is, various rewards a person might hope to obtain—the friendship of coworkers, promotion, merit salary increases, a feeling of accomplishment—from the job can be desired in differing amounts. For Cindy, the friendship of coworkers might be highly desired; this reward would have a high positive valence for her. The value of reward reflects the individual's state of need satisfaction. A hungry person (physiological need) would value food more than a person who had just eaten dinner.

Perceived Effort-Reward.   The perceived effort-reward (box 2) refers to a person's expectations that given amounts of reward depend upon given amounts of effort. Suppose a manager desires a transfer from the northeast to the sunshine belt. The manager might feel that his chances of obtaining a transfer have very little to do with his level of performance because virtually no transfers are being made and when they are made, they depend on other things (luck, "pull," the state of the economy). Under these conditions, the manager would perceive a low effort-reward possibility.

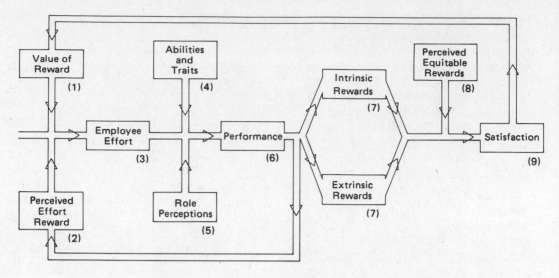

FIGURE 11–11.   Integrated Motivation Model

From Lyman W. Porter and Edward E. Lawler III, *Managerial Attitudes and Performance* (Homewood, Ill.: Richard D. Irwin, Inc., 1968), p. 165. Reprinted with permission of Richard D. Irwin.

Effort.   By effort (box 3) is meant the amount of energy a person exerts in any situation. That is, how hard is the person trying? In a baseball game, a move made by the shortstop to throw the runner out is an example of effort. Whether or not his throw resulted in an out would be a measure of performance. You may spend lots of time and energy (effort) studying for this course, yet your grade (performance) may be disappointing. The amount of effort depends upon the interaction between the value of the reward and the perceived effort-reward probability. This is equivalent to Vroom's use of the term *motivation*. Therefore, effort refers to the energy expended to perform a task, but not how successfully it is carried out.

Abilities and Traits.   According to Porter and Lawler, effort (motivation) does not directly lead to performance, but is mediated by individual abilities and role perceptions. Abilities and traits (box 4) refer to individual characteristics, such as intellectual capacity, manual skills, and personality traits that can affect the ability to perform a task. These are considered relatively independent of the situation. In Cindy's case, her typing, dictation, and shorthand skills were brought by her to her new job. Although these abilities could be learned or sharpened on the job with practice, for the most part, they are learned before the individual starts the job.

Role Perceptions.   Role perceptions (box 5) refer to the kind of activities that people believe they should perform if they want to perform a job successfully. At the Standard Steel Corporation, many middle-level managers believe that the best way to perform well on their job (in order to get a promotion and raise) is to become highly knowledgeable in their field, such as metallurgy, finance, melting, marketing, or accounting. If a manager can prove to his boss that he is proficient, then his efforts to improve himself in this function should pay off. If, however, top management at Standard Steel considers broad administrative capabilities as a prime requirement for advancement, then a manager who puts effort into developing technical skills might actually be engaging in an activity that will not lead to promotion. To summarize, role perceptions deal with the way in which people define their jobs and the types of efforts that they believe are essential to effective performance.

Performance.   The combination of value of rewards and perceived effort-reward form expectations about performance (box 6). Performance comes after effort (or motivation) has been exerted. Performance depends not only on the amount of effort exerted by people, but also on their abilities and the way they perceive the role they should take. In other words, even though employees exert a great amount of effort, if they have little ability and/or an inaccurate assessment of what it takes to succeed in the organization, their resulting performance might be low.

Consider the following incident:

Stanley Rikovski has just returned from an important meeting between representatives from the finance and manufacturing departments. Based on some encouraging projections of increased sales, the manufacturing representatives requested funds for plant expansion. Prior to the meeting, the finance department had determined that the company could not afford plant expansion. During the meeting, Rikovski made a persuasive appeal for the financial point of view. He said to his secretary: "We sure nailed those manufacturing guys to the wall. You should have seen the expression on their faces when I pointed out the holes in the marketing report. They know that from now on they will have to play ball with us first before anything gets done."

The denial of the manufacturing group's desire to expand their facilities occurred in spite of the amount of effort that they exerted to develop their ideas of plant expansion. Because these executives had misperceived the role of the finance department in a plant expansion decision, their effort did not result in a plant expansion decision.

Rewards.   Desirable outcomes are rewards (box 7—note that there are two). Initially, Porter and Lawler included only a single reward variable in their model. However, empirical testing showed that this category should be more accurately divided into *extrinsic rewards* and *intrinsic rewards.* Extrinsic rewards are given by the organization. They include such job-related rewards as supervision, working conditions, salary, status, job security, and fringe benefits. Extrinsic rewards are what Herzberg called hygiene factors. Intrinsic rewards are administered by the individual himself and include things such as achievement, self-recognition for a job well done, work itself, responsibility, and personal growth. Intrinsic rewards are what Herzberg called motivators. As used in Porter and Lawler's model, both intrinsic and extrinsic rewards are desirable. However, research has indicated that intrinsic rewards are much more likely to produce higher job satisfaction than are extrinsic rewards.[33]

Intrinsic rewards can be increased by the organization through job redesign. If the design of a job provides sufficient variety, feedback, autonomy, and challenge so that the employees feel they have performed well, they can reward themselves. If the design of the job does not involve these characteristics, then there would be little relationship between good performance and intrinsic rewards. Thus, the relationship between performance and intrinsic rewards is dependent on the makeup of the job duties. Chapter 12 will discuss job redesign in much more detail.

Perceived Equitable Rewards.   The amount of rewards that people feel they should receive as the result of a given level of performance are the perceived equitable rewards (box 8). In most jobs, people have an implicit notion concerning the amount of rewards that ought to be available for a person performing the type of work required in such a job. These might include a personal secretary, private office, reserved parking place, car, country club privileges, challenging job assignments, recognition, windows and carpeting in office, year-end bonuses. Such notions are based on the individual's perception of the requirements of the job, the demands that the job makes on the individual, and the contributions that the individual makes to the company. In essence, these reflect a fair level of rewards that the individual feels should be granted for high performance in a particular job.

Satisfaction.   As was noted early in this chapter, satisfaction is not the same thing as motivation. Satisfaction (box 9) is an attitude, an individual's internal state. To the degree that valued rewards exceed actual rewards, the person is dissatisfied. At Hershey Foods Company, all employees are paid on an hourly rate, regardless of their productivity. A group of workers packaging lasagna found a way to increase their productivity from 500 to 750 packages per hour. At the end of the year, all employees in the plant were given the same hourly increase. This created a general state of dissatisfaction among the lasagna packers because their actual rewards were below what they perceived to be valued rewards.

Satisfaction is important for two reasons. *First*, the model indicates that satisfaction is only partially determined by the actual rewards received. It depends also on what people feel the organization should reward them for a given level of performance. *Second,* the model recognizes that satisfaction is more dependent on performance than performance is on satisfaction. Only through a feedback loop (to value of reward) will satisfaction affect performance.

Managerial Implications.   Although it is clear that both employee satisfaction and performance are the result of complex processes that have not yet been agreed upon by practitioners and researchers, it is fairly well established that rewards can produce variance in job satisfaction. For the manager who wants to enhance the job satisfaction of subordinates, the appropriateness of the reward is important. In other words, there must be consistency between the reward and what the individual needs or wants if the manager wants to increase job satisfaction. However, a manager must recognize that there are often significant differences among individuals in what they consider rewarding. A 7 or 8 percent salary increase may satisfy one person but have little or no positive effect on another person at the same salary level. Furthermore, a sizeable reward in one situation might be considered small by the same individual in a different set of circumstances. Generally speaking, extrinsic rewards have their greatest value when the individual is most strongly motivated to satisfy what Maslow has referred to as lower level needs—physiological needs and security needs and those higher-level needs that can be linked to status. Pay, for example, may be valued by an individual because of the belief that it is a determinant of social position within the organization or community because it constitutes a means for acquiring status symbols.[34]

The potency of pay notwithstanding, there are other rewards potentially under the control of the manager. Intrinsic rewards are more likely to be valued by employees after lower level needs have been satisfied. This is not, however, a sufficient condition for using intrinsic rewards. In other words, most managers realize that there must be an adequate level of satisfaction with extrinsic rewards before intrinsic rewards can be effectively used. For many employees the manager needs to provide meaningful work assignments, that is, work with which the subordinate can identify and become personally involved. Challenging yet attainable goals can be established, or in some cases, it may be more advantageous to create conditions that greatly enhance the likelihood that the employee will succeed. The manager may also consider such things as delegation of authority or forms of job enlargement for extending the scope and depth of the jobs of subordinates shown to be motivated by high-level needs.

In summary, managers should match the rewards at their disposal, both intrinsic and extrinsic, with what the subordinate indicates a desire for. As indicated in Chapter 6, by varying the magnitude and timing of the rewards, this could help establish clearly in the subordinate's mind the desired relationships between effort and performance.

While granting differential rewards may cause subordinates to express varying degrees of satisfaction or dissatisfaction, the relationship between performance and rewards is often not so simple. Other causes of performance may have a greater impact. The work environment, previous job experience, technology, and group processes might all be significant causal variables. Where the work group adheres to norms of restricting performance, for example, the subordinate will similarly restrict performance to the extent that identification with the group is important.

SUMMARY

This chapter discussed the dynamics of motivation. The assumption that satisfaction, motivation, and performance are related were shown to be inadequate for managers and researchers. Satisfaction and motivation are different things that relate to performance in different ways. The modern approach to motivation can be divided into content and process theories. The Maslow, Herzberg, and McClelland models attempt to identify specific content factors that motivate employees. For Maslow, it is the satisfaction of five hierarchical needs; for McClelland, it is the building of an achievement motive; for Herzberg, it is the work environment and the work itself. Although these approaches are logical and easy to understand, research evidence points out some definite limitations. Little research supports the theoretical underpinning for these models. Although each of these theories provides outcomes that people find desirable, and managers can generate a series of actions that can influence the desirability of these outcomes, none can answer why these outcomes are desirable. The trade-off for simplicity sacrifices true understanding of the complexity of the work motivation process. On the positive side, the content models have given emphasis to important factors, and the Herzberg model is a useful explanation for job satisfaction.

The process model provides a more complete theoretical explanation of motivation than the content models. The expectancy theory of Vroom and the refinements by Porter and Lawler help explain the important cognitive variables that affect motivation. Both models attempt to answer the question "Why do outcomes become desirable?" The Porter and Lawler model also addresses the important relationship between satisfaction and performance. However, these models are relatively complex in comparison with the content models because each individual's motivational basis may be unique. The more directly the worker perceives that a given performance level is directly related to a desired goal or reward, the more highly motivated that worker is.

DISCUSSION QUESTIONS

1. Explain the sequence by which needs are translated into action in a work situation.

2. Explain how the same need or motive can cause different behavior (a) among different people and (b) by the same person at different times.

3. How does performance relate to satisfaction?

4. Exactly how might rewards, such as pay, promotion, and positive feedback affect the determination of job satisfaction? How might they affect performance?

5. Why has Maslow's theory of motivation been so popular among managers and organizational researchers?

6. If high achievers tend to be superior performers, why could a manager not increase organizational performance simply by hiring only high achievers?

7. What is the basic difference between motivators and hygienes? Which are more important in work motivation? Why?

8. Explain the differences between Vroom's expectancy theory and McClelland's achievement motivation theory.

9. In your own words, briefly explain the Porter and Lawler model of motivation.

10. Of what practical value is the expectancy model for managers? What can managers learn from the model that could improve their effectiveness on the job?

MANAGERIAL PROBLEMS

PAUL ARCHIBALD

Paul Archibald, forty-three years old, began working at Standard Steel Corporation in the Metallurgical Department as a quality control inspector eighteen years ago. After spending five years in this position, Paul progressed to be head of the quality control program. After he had spent six years as head of this program, Paul advanced to head of the melting control program. He has been working on that job for the last seven years.

Paul was able to move upward in the Metallurgical Department much faster than most people his age, bypassing several managerial positions and individuals. Paul possesses above average intelligence and potential and had been identified in high school and college as very talented. Of the heads of program in the Metallurgy Department, he is the youngest and lowest in seniority. Paul's next possible advancement would be chief of the Metallurgical Department.

Each major shop in the steel mill—the melting department, rolling department, ring department, and the like—has one senior metallurgist assigned to it. Each metallurgist has supervisory responsibilities for quality control, the training of observers, and the conduct of safety meetings in the department. Weekly and monthly quality-control reports and other observations are given to the chief metallurgist.

Each metallurgist has one or more observers reporting to him.

These individuals are responsible for making routine quality-control checks. Their job description has a very detailed set of instructions outlining the procedures to follow. For example, the observer in the rolling ring mill has a job description that includes activities such as checking the weights of the rings, the interior and exterior diameters, hardness results, and surface defects.

Paul apparently did an outstanding job during his first years at Standard, as evidenced by his rapid movement upward in the department. However, during the past few years, Paul's performance has deteriorated, according to the chief metallurgist and some of the subordinates reporting to Paul. Some of the complaints are: (1) lack of technical detail in the melting process reports; (2) lack of job interest; (3) absence at safety meetings; (4) late reports; and (5) loss of confidence in subordinates.

With the shortages of natural resources in mid-1974 and the loss of three major government contracts, the company was forced to make some production cutbacks. As a result of these economic conditions, Paul was asked to return to his previous job as head of the quality control program. Although Paul had not worked on this job the last seven years, the chief metallurgist thought that he should have no problem. However, during the first month on the job, Paul was absent for three safety meetings and made some errors in a report concerning the hardness of a finished ring for the government. Whether it was a deliberate attempt to falsify the report or a slip-up, Paul was laid off for one week.

In late 1975, as business improved to its pre-1974 condition, Paul was advised by the chief metallurgist that his recent poor performance would no longer be tolerated. In early spring 1976 Paul was called in by the chief metallurgist and was again disciplined for these continued behaviors. This time, Paul was laid off for two weeks and was advised that he was subject to discharge for his performance if it did not come up to that of other program heads immediately.

The chief metallurgist did not know that in his spare time and on weekends, Paul was a housing contractor. While he subcontracted most of the work to others, this activity took a lot of his time. Business had been profitable for several years. These profits were invested in a restaurant with another partner. However, during 1974 the interest rate on mortgages was high and most contractors in the area found that they could not sell homes that they had erected.

QUESTIONS

1. Explain Paul's motivation problem in terms of the content models of Maslow and Herzberg. What are the things that Paul is looking for in his job?
2. Explain how Paul's motivation affected his performance.
3. If you were the chief metallurgist, what would you do?

CLAIRE SHEEHAN

Claire Sheehan is an accountant in a large insurance company. She comes from a small farming community in which her family had low income and followed strict rules for proper behavior. In order to achieve her college degree, she worked on numerous odd jobs.

Claire is an intelligent and capable worker. Her main fault is that she does not want to take any risks. She hesitates to make decisions for herself, often referring small or routine decisions to her supervisor or to other accountants for a decision. Whenever she does a major audit, she brings it in rough draft to her supervisor for approval before she completes it.

Since Claire is a capable accountant, her supervisor wants to motivate her to be more independent in her work. The supervisor believes that this approach will improve Claire's performance, relieve the supervisor from extra routine, and give Claire more self-confidence. However, the supervisor is not sure how to go about motivating Claire to improve her performance.

QUESTIONS

1. In the role of the supervisor, how would you motivate Claire? Give reasons.

KEY WORDS

Motivation
Attitude
Satisfaction
Needs
Content theories
Process theories
Need hierarchy
Achievement motivation
Projective method
Two-factor theory

Motivators
Hygienes
Extrinsic factors
Intrinsic factors
Method-bound
Expectancy theory
Expectancy
Valence
Instrumentality

REFERENCES

1.   Adapted from DuBrin, A., *Fundamentals of Organizational Behavior* (New York: Pergamon Press, 1974), pp. 60–61.

2.   Mayer, A., and M. Rudy, One firm's family, *Newsweek,* November 21, 1977, p. 83.

3.   Katz, D., and R. Kahn, *The Social Psychology of Organizations,* 2d ed. (New York: John Wiley and Sons), 1978.

4.   Mayor and Rudy, One firm's family.

5.   Morgan, D., Timber and paper: A story of growth, *The Washington Post,* October 30, 1977, p. A14.

6.   Dewar, H., GM pioneers in putting brains to work: Humanizing life on the assembly line, *The Washington Post,* November 13, 1977, p. A-1.

7.   Steers, R., and L. Porter, *Motivation and Work Behavior* (New York: John Wiley and Sons, 1975), p. 6.

8.   Courtesy of *The Boston Globe.*

9.   Instrument reported in Porter, L. and E. Lawler, *Managerial Attitudes and Performance* (Homewood, Ill.: Richard D. Irwin and Dorsey Press, 1968).

10.   Sheridan, J., and J. Slocum, The direction of the causal relationship between job satisfaction and work performance, *Organizational Behavior and Human Performance,* 1975, 14, pp. 159–172. For an excellent review, see Locke, E., The nature and causes of job satisfaction, in Dunnette, M. (ed.), *Handbook of Industrial Organizational Psychology* (Chicago: Rand McNally Publishing, 1976), pp. 1297–1350.

11.   Maslow, A., A theory of human motivation, *Psychological Review,* 1943, 80, pp. 370–396; *Motivation and Personality,* rev. ed. (New York: Harper and Row, 1970).

12.   For a review, see Pinder, C., Concerning the application of human motivation theories in organizational settings, *Academy of Management Review,* 1977, 2, pp. 384–397; Wahba, M., and L. Bridwell, Maslow reconsidered: A review of research on the need hierarchy theory, *Organizational Behavior and Human Performance,* 1976, 15, pp. 212–240; Chung, K., *Motivational Theories and Practices* (Columbus,

Ohio: Grid, 1977), pp. 37–58; Wanous, J., and A. Zwany, A cross-sectional test of need hierarchy theory, *Organizational Behavior and Human Performance,* 1977, 18, pp. 78–97.

13.   Salancik, G., and J. Pfeffer, An examination of need-satisfaction models of job satisfaction and job attitudes, *Administrative Science Quarterly,* 1977, 22, pp. 427–456.

14.   Lawler, E., and L. Porter, Perceptions regarding management compensation, *Industrial Relations,* 1963, 3, pp. 47–49; Lawler, E., *Pay and Organizational Effectiveness: A Psychological View* (New York: McGraw-Hill, 1971).

15.   Cummings, L., and C. Berger, Organization structure: How does it influence attitudes and performance? *Organizational Dynamics,* 1976, 5, no. 2, pp. 34–49.

16.   For references in this section, see Porter, L., Job attitudes in management: II. Perceived importance of needs as a function of job level, *Journal of Applied Psychology,* 1963, 47, pp. 141–148; Altimus, C., and R. Tersine, Chronological age and job satisfaction: The young blue-collar worker, *Academy of Management Journal,* 1973, 11, pp. 53–66; Slocum, J. and R. Strawser, Racial differences in job attitudes, *Journal of Applied Psychology,* 1972, 56, pp. 28–33; Porter, L., Job attitudes in management: IV. Perceived deficiencies in need fulfillment as a function of size of the company, *Journal of Applied Psychology,* 1963, 47, pp. 386–397; Slocum, J., P. Topichak, and D. Kuhn, A cross-cultural study of need satisfaction and need importance for operative employees, *Personnel Psychology,* 1971, 24, pp. 435–445.

17.   Robey, D., Task design, work values and worker response: An experimental test, *Organizational Behavior and Human Performance,* 1974, 12, pp. 264–273.

18.   Lawler, *Pay and Organizational Effectiveness,* p. 51.

19.   Hall, D., and K. Nougaim, An examination of Maslow's need hierarchy in an organizational setting, *Organizational Be-*

havior and Human Performance, 1968, 3, pp. 12–35.

20. McClelland, D., *The Achieving Society* (Princeton: Van Nostrand Reinhold, 1961.

21. Adapted from McClelland, D., *Assessing Human Motivation* (Morristown, N.J.: General Learning Press, 1971), p. 12; also see McClelland, D., and D. Burnham, Power is the great motivator, *Harvard Business Review,* 1976, 54, no. 2, pp. 100–111.

22. Steers, R., Task-goal attributes in achievement and supervisory performance, *Organizational Behavior and Human Performance,* 1975, 13, pp. 392–403; Durand, D., Effects of achievement motivation and skill training on the entrepreneurial behavior of black businessmen, *Organizational Behavior and Human Performance,* 1975, 14, pp. 76–90.

23. Herzberg, F., B. Mausner, and B. Snyderman, *The Motivation to Work* (New York: John Wiley and Sons, 1959).

24. For excellent reviews, see Kerr, S., A. Harlan, and R. Stogdill, Preference for motivator and hygiene factors in a hypothetical interview situation, *Personnel Psychology,* 1974, 25, pp. 109–124; House, R. and L. Widgor, Herzberg's dual-factor theory of job satisfaction and motivation: A review of the evidence and criticism, *Personnel Psychology,* 1968, 20, pp. 369–389; Dunnette, M., D. Campbell, and M. Hakel, Factors contributing to job satisfaction and dissatisfaction in six occupational groups, *Organizational Behavior and Human Performance,* 1967, 2, pp. 143–174; Gardner, G., The higher-order needs of London bus crews: A two-factor analysis, *Human Relations,* 1977, 30, pp. 767–785.

25. Adapted from Herbert, T., *Dimensions of Organizational Behavior* (New York: Macmillan, 1976), p. 225.

26. Vroom, V., *Work and Motivation* (New York: John Wiley and Sons, 1964).

27. For critical reviews, see House, R., H. Shapiro, and M. Wahba, Expectancy theory as a predictor of work behavior and attitude: A re-evaluation of empirical evidence, *Decision Sciences,* 1974, 5, pp. 481–506; Mitchell, T., Expectancy models of job satisfaction, occupational preference and effort: A theoretical, methodological, and empirical appraisal, *Psychological Bulletin,* 1974, 81, pp. 1053–1077.

28. Sheridan, J., J. Slocum, and M. Richards, A comparative analysis of expectancy and heuristic models of decision behavior, *Journal of Applied Psychology,* 1975, 60, pp. 361–368.

29. Connolly, T., Some conceptual and methodological issues in expectancy models of work performance motivation, *Academy of Management Review,* 1977, 1, pp. 37–47.

30. Peters, L., Cognitive models of motivation: Expectancy theory and effort: An analysis and empirical test, *Organizational Behavior and Human Performance,* 1977, 20, pp. 129–148; Staw, B., Motivation in organizations: Toward synthesis and reduction, in Staw, B. and G. Salancik, (eds.), *New Directions in Organizational Behavior* (Chicago: St. Clair Press, 1977), pp. 55–96.

31. For an excellent review, see Greene, C., and R. Craft, The satisfaction-performance controversy revisited, in Downey, K., D. Hellriegel, and J. Slocum, *Organizational Behavior: A Reader* (St. Paul, Minn.: West Publishing, 1077), pp. 187–201.

32. Porter, L., and E. Lawler, *Managerial Attitudes and Performance* (Homewood, Ill.: Richard D. Irwin, 1968).

33. Dyer, L., and D. Parker, Classifying outcomes in work motivation research: An examination of intrinsic-extrinsic dichotomy, *Journal of Applied Psychology,* 1975, 60, pp. 455–458; Farr, J., R. Vance, and R. McIntyre, Further examinations of the relationship between reward contingency and intrinsic motivation, *Organizational Behavior and Human Performance,* 1977, 20, pp. 31–53.

34. Cummings, L., and D. Schwab, *Performance in Organizations: Determinants and Appraisal* (Glenview, Ill.: Scott, Foresman, 1972).

12

Job Design

This Chapter Contributed by
DENIS UMSTOT
Air Force Institute of Technology

12

LEARNING OBJECTIVES

When you have finished reading and studying this chapter, you should be able to:

▲ Understand the importance of the job design process.

▲ Describe the different approaches to job design.

▲ Explain the psychological processes that make jobs motivating.

▲ Understand how to diagnose job design problems.

▲ Describe the techniques for enriching jobs.

▲ Explain the benefits and drawbacks of different job design strategies.

▲ Demonstrate the relationship between social aspects of the job and technology.

THOUGHT STARTERS

▲ What makes the difference between a good job and a bad job?

▲ Are you satisfied with your job (or your role as a student)? Why or why not?

▲ Does everyone want a challenging job?

▲ Could an auto assembly line be humanized?

▲ Are American workers dissatisfied with their jobs?

OUTLINE

WHAT IS JOB DESIGN?
EFFICIENCY THROUGH JOB ENGINEERING
    The Benefits and Problems of Job Engineering
ADDING VARIETY TO JOBS: JOB ENLARGEMENT AND JOB ROTATION
JOB ENRICHMENT CONCEPTS
    Herzberg's Definition
    The Hackman-Oldham Model
DIAGNOSING JOB ENRICHMENT PROBLEMS
    Applying the Hackman-Oldham Model
    Structural Clues
    The Job Diagnostic Survey
INGREDIENTS OF ENRICHED JOBS
THE SUCCESS OF JOB ENRICHMENT
    Why Job Enrichment May Fail
BENEFITS OF JOB ENRICHMENT
    Performance
    Satisfaction
GOAL-SETTING APPROACH
SOCIOTECHNICAL APPROACH
    Volvo's Kalmar Plant
    Sociotechnical Model
    Applications of the Sociotechnical Approach
WHICH APPROACH TO USE?
SUMMARY
DISCUSSION QUESTIONS
MANAGERIAL PROBLEMS
    Keypunch Operation
    McGuire Industry
KEY WORDS
REFERENCES

Now that several approaches to explaining motivation have been studied, it is time to see how this knowledge is put to work in designing motivating jobs. Every time a manager assigns work, gives instructions, or checks to make sure a job is being done, job redesign is taking place. Consciously or unconsciously, managers are constantly changing the jobs of their subordinates. Since this type of change is inevitable, it makes sense to plan the structure of jobs deliberately so that they are as motivating as possible. That is what this chapter is about—the systematic redesigning of jobs as part of the basic managerial task.

With rising educational levels and the resultant increase in expectations of American workers, the gap between what people want in their jobs and what they actually have is widening. A report of the Special Task Force to the secretary of health, education and welfare stated that: "Significant numbers of American workers are dissatisfied with the quality of their working lives. Dull, repetitive, seemingly meaningless tasks, offering little challenge or autonomy, are causing discontent among workers at all occupational levels."[1] The results of employee dissatisfaction and alienation affect both the individual employee and the organization. The employee becomes bored, frustrated, apathetic, and even mentally ill; the organization pays high costs in terms of absenteeism, turnover, and poor product quality. Job design is the primary method for improving the job itself and is thus a crucial aspect of the quality of working life.

WHAT IS JOB DESIGN?

Job design is the deliberate, purposeful planning of the job including all its structural and social aspects and their effect on the employee. Job design is a broad concept that can refer to any part or combination of parts of the job. For example, job engineering and job enrichment are both job design approaches. Figure 12–1 provides an overview of the dimensions of job design. It highlights their overlapping, interconnecting nature. It also indicates that many factors affect job design, such as managerial style, unions, working conditions, and technology. While this chapter focuses on the central core of job design, the impact of the total system must be considered for a full understanding of the process.

EFFICIENCY THROUGH JOB ENGINEERING

Late in the nineteenth century, Frederick W. Taylor established the foundation for modern industrial engineering, or job engineering. An interesting example of Taylor's approach to the scientific management of job

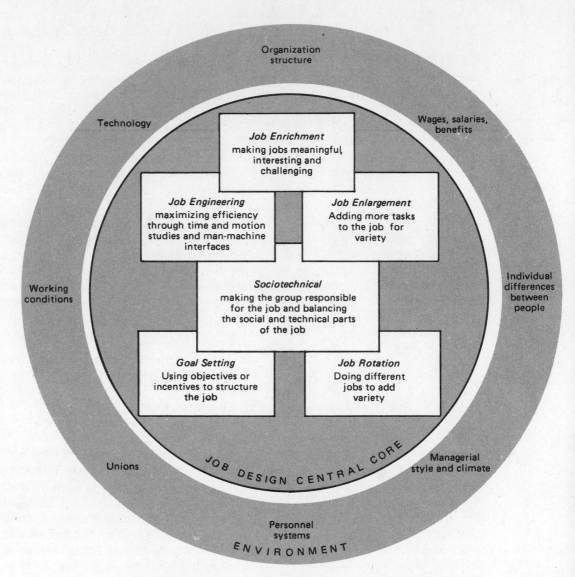

FIGURE 12–1.   The Dimensions of Job Design

engineering is his description of the application of his principles at a Bethlehem steel plant:

> The Bethlehem Steel Company had five blast furnaces, the product of
> which had been handled by a pig-iron gang for many years. This gang,
> at this time, consisted of about 75 men. They were good, average pig-iron
> handlers, were under an excellent foreman who himself had been a pig-
> iron handler, and the work was done, on the whole, about as fast and as
> cheaply as it was anywhere else at that time.

We found that this gang were loading on the average about 12½ long tons per man per day. We were surprised to find, after studying the matter, that a first-class pig-iron handler ought to handle between 47½ and 48 long tons per day, instead of 12½ tons.

Once we were sure that 47 tons was a proper day's work for a first-class pig-iron handler, the task which faced us as managers under the modern scientific plan was clearly before us. It was our duty to see that the 80,000 tons of pig-iron was loaded on to the cars at the rate of 47 tons per man per day, in place of 12½ tons, at which rate the work was then being done. And it was further our duty to see that this work was done without bringing on a strike among the men, without any quarrel with the men, and to see that the men were happier and better contented when loading at the new rate of 47 tons than they were when loading at the old rate of 12½ tons.

We selected Schmidt as the most likely man to start with. He was a little Pennsylvania Dutchman who had been observed to trot back home for a mile or so after his work in the evening about as fresh as he was when he came trotting down to work in the morning.

Schmidt started to work, and all day long, and at regular intervals, was told by the man who stood over him with a watch, "Now pick up a pig and walk. Now sit down and rest. Now walk—now rest," etc. He worked when he was told to work, and rested when he was told to rest, and at half-past five in the afternoon had his 47½ tons loaded on the car. And he practically never failed to work at this pace and do the task that was set him during the three years that the writer was at Bethlehem. One man after another was picked out and trained to handle pig iron at the rate of 47½ tons per day until all of the pig-iron was handled at this rate, and the men were receiving 60 per cent more wages than other workmen around them.[2]

Modern job engineering is concerned with product design, process design, tool design, plant layout, work measurement, and operator methods. Design of the job is mainly concerned with what tasks are to be performed, the methods to be used, the work flow between workers, the layout of the workplace, performance standards, and the interface between people and machines (human factors). Often these design strategies are combined under the heading "time-and-motion studies" because of the central focus on the time to do each subtask and the efficiency of motion needed to perform the task.[3] Figure 12–2 shows an example of the use of time-and-motion studies.

Specialization is a cornerstone of job engineering because it (1) allows workers to learn the task rapidly, (2) permits short work cycles so performance can be almost automatic with little or no mental direction, (3) makes hiring easier since lower skilled people can be easily trained and paid relatively low wages, and (4) needs less supervision because of simplified jobs and standardization. Thus the job engineering approach concentrates on maximizing the efficiency of workers.

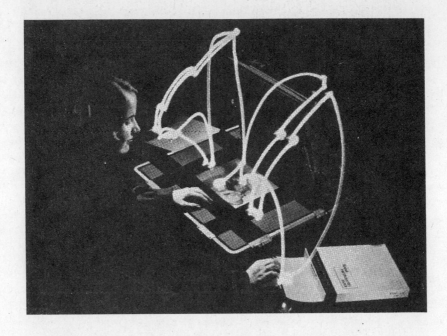

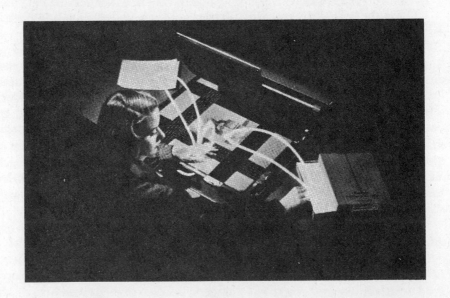

FIGURE 12–2.   Results of a Motion and Time Study

From R. M. Barnes, *Motion and Time Study: Design and Measurement of Work*, 5th ed. (New York: John Wiley & Sons, 1964), p. 132.

The Benefits and Problems of Job Engineering

Even though managers and industrial engineers have recognized that job engineering has created fractionalized, boring jobs, it remains the dominant job design strategy. One reason for this is that the immediate cost savings generated by time-and-motion studies are easier to measure and visualize than the more illusive benefits in improved quality, decreased absenteeism, and decreased turnover that result from other job design strategies. However, with the changing nature of the work force, employees and unions are demanding that the quality of work life be improved. Thus the challenge to managers is to create jobs that are both satisfying to the employees and more efficient and productive.

ADDING VARIETY TO JOBS: JOB ENLARGEMENT AND JOB ROTATION

Although the terms job enlargement and job enrichment are often used interchangeably, here they will be described separately.

Job Enlargement

Doing a wide number of different tasks enlarges the job. For example, an auto assembly-line worker's job was enlarged from installing just one tail light to installing both tail lights and the trunk. In another example, an auto mechanic switched from just changing oil to changing oil, greasing, and changing transmission fluid. The objective of job enlargement is to add more tasks to the job so that it will have more variety and hence be more interesting. Although this strategy often works, it is sometimes resisted on two counts: (1) the enlargement is seen as just adding more routine, boring tasks to the job, and (2) the advantage that the job can be done almost automatically is eliminated. Some employees may value their opportunity to daydream about their big date tonight, their vacation next month, or they may simply prefer to spend their time socializing with nearby workers. If the enlarged job requires greater attention and concentration, then the enlarged tasks must be interesting to the employee or the job may actually be worse after job enlargement.

Job Rotation

Job rotation is closely related to job enlargement. Instead of giving the worker more tasks to do, the worker is rotated between different tasks. Both strategies focus on adding variety to the job to reduce boredom. If all tasks are similar and routine, the same problems noted for job enlargement are likely to occur with job rotation. However, if job rotation is used to place people in more challenging jobs *and* they are left in that job long enough to gain competence and show their ability to perform, then the strategy may be effective for improving job satisfaction.

JOB ENRICHMENT CONCEPTS

Job enrichment began in the 1940s at IBM.[4] The 1950s saw a slow growth in the number of companies interested in job enrichment. Several important studies were done under the supervision of Louis Davis of the Industrial Engineering Department of the University of California at Los Angeles. The impetus that really made job enrichment popular was Herzberg's two-factor (motivator-hygiene) theory (discussed in Chapter 11).[5] Herzberg's theory provided a relatively simple, intuitively appealing approach to looking at the job itself. Successful and widely publicized experiments using Herzberg's model at American Telephone and Telegraph Company,[6] Texas Instruments,[7] and Imperial Chemical Industries[8] led to an increasing awareness and interest in job enrichment.

Herzberg's Definition

Herzberg defined job enrichment (which he now prefers to call "orthodox job enrichment") as the improvement of the motivator factors —especially achievement, recognition, responsibility, advancement, and opportunity for growth—of an individual's job.[9] Although these factors sound very promising, it is often difficult to go from theory to practice (for example, how does one improve achievement or growth in a job?).

The Hackman-Oldham Model

Another popular approach to job enrichment, recently developed by Hackman and Oldham,[10] is shown in Figure 12–3. Their approach defines job enrichment as the inclusion of, or increasing the amounts of, certain core job dimensions—skill variety, task identity, task significance, autonomy, and feedback—so the employee will experience a sense of meaningfulness and responsibility in the job and how well or poorly it is accomplished. The model shows that the core job dimensions, or job characteristics, lead to three psychological states that in turn lead to a number of positive personal and work related outcomes. (This framework is closely linked with the materials presented in Chapter 6 on learning theory.) People experience positive feelings toward jobs to the extent that they learn (knowledge of

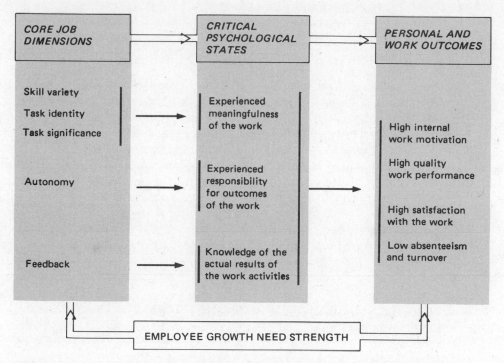

FIGURE 12–3.   The Relationships Among the Core Job Dimensions, the Critical Psychological States, and Expectancy Outcomes

Adapted from: J. Hackman and G. Oldham, "Development of the Job Diagnostic Survey," *Journal of Applied Psychology*, 1975, 60, p. 161. Copyright 1975 by the American Psychological Association. Reprinted by permission.

results) that they have personally performed well (experienced responsibility) on a task that they care about (experienced meaningfulness). If all three psychological states are present, a self-perpetuating cycle of positive work motivation based on self-generated rewards is activated. All three states must be present for motivation to occur. A job without meaningfulness or responsibility or feedback is incomplete and thus does not fully motivate.

Now let's define the specific characteristics that make up a motivating job. Try to get these terms firmly in mind because these characteristics are important for understanding the remainder of this chapter.

Skill variety: Doing different things; using different skills, abilities, and talents.

Task identity: Doing a job from beginning to end; the whole job rather than bits and pieces.

Task significance: The degree that the job has a meaningful impact on others in the organization; the importance of the job.

Autonomy: Freedom to do the work; discretion in scheduling, decision making, and means for accomplishing a job.

Feedback: Clear and direct information about job outcomes and performances.

An Enriched Job: The Surgeon.   One job that is high on all the core job dimensions is the surgeon. There is a constant opportunity for using highly varied skills, abilities, and talents in diagnosing and treating illnesses. There is plenty of task identity since the same surgeon normally does the diagnosis, performs the operation, and monitors the convalescence. Task significance is also very high since much of the surgeon's work will be a matter of life or death to the patient. Autonomy is quite high since the physician is the final authority on the procedures and techniques of the job (perhaps malpractice suits are causing a lower sense of autonomy than surgeons once had). Finally, the feedback from the job is excellent because the surgeon can tell almost immediately if the operation was successful.

DIAGNOSING JOB ENRICHMENT PROBLEMS

Several methods can be used for diagnosing job enrichment problems, including such clinical approaches as applying the Hackman-Oldham model and using Whitsett's list of structural clues or by using the survey approach, such as the Job Diagnostic Survey.

Applying the Hackman-Oldham Model

By applying the Hackman-Oldham model, a manager can evaluate a given job by observations, interviews, and work flow analysis. For example, let's look at the job of a typist in a large word processing center (a modern day equivalent of a typing pool using more sophisticated technology) in a large insurance company.

Skill variety: Moderately low. Once the machines are mastered, the job is basically just different forms of a single skill—typing. Thus there is little skill variety or challenge.

Task identity: Virtually nonexistent. Jobs are assigned to keep a continuous work load rather than to provide whole, identifiable jobs.

Task significance: Low, because the employees do not see the importance of the seemingly endless flow of paperwork.

Autonomy: None. Employees punch in and out on time clocks and breaks are rigidly controlled. The managers arrange and direct the daily tasks. Quality control and proofreading are done by a separate department.

Feedback: Very low. Once the product is sent back to the using department, there is no contact with the typist concerning the quality or acceptability of the product. If retyping or corrections are needed, they are given to the first available typist rather than to the person who originally typed the product.

A clinical evaluation of the typist job would be that it is very unenriched with particularly bad problems in the areas of task identity, autonomy, and feedback.

Structural Clues

Another clinical approach to diagnosing job design problems is to look for certain types of jobs or situations that are often associated with poor jobs. David Whitsett has developed a list of structural clues that may indicate job design deficiencies.[11] Although all of them won't be discussed, several that are particularly important are described here.

Inspectors or Checkers. When people do not inspect their own work, autonomy is usually much lower. Feedback is also less direct and does not come from the job itself.

Trouble-shooters. Existence of this function usually means that all the exciting, challenging parts of a job have been given to someone else. The worker does not experience a sense of responsibility for work outcomes. Task identity, autonomy, and feedback are usually poor.

Communication and Customer Relations Sections. These functions usually serve to cut the link between the person who does the job and the customer or client. Thus feedback and task identity are degraded.

Labor Pools. Pools of typists, engineers, computer programmers, and so forth look appealing because they offer the potential of efficiency and ability to meet erratic workloads. However, pools almost always destroy "ownership" and thus task identity. As we saw in the example of the word processing center, pools may adversely affect all job characteristics.

Narrow Span of Control. When a boss only has a few subordinates (say 1 to 3), it is more likely that the boss will become involved in details of the day-to-day operation. Centralization of decision making and overcontrol is often a result of too narrow a span of control. Thus, autonomy may be seriously affected.

The Job Diagnostic Survey

An easier and more systematic way of analyzing jobs than a clinical approach is to use a questionnaire. One carefully developed and tested instrument is the Job Diagnostic Survey (JDS), which was constructed by Hackman and Oldham to measure the job characteristics in their model and the outcomes that may result from job redesign.[12] Before proceeding with this discussion, develop your own job profile by answering the questions in Figure 12–4 taken from the JDS.

FIGURE 12–4.   Selected Questions from the Job Diagnostic Survey

Please describe your job as objectively as you can.

1. How much *variety* is there in your job? That is, to what extent does the job require you to do many different things at work, using a variety of your skills and talents?

1--------2--------3--------4--------5--------6--------7

| Very little; the job requires me to do the same routine things over and over again. | Moderate variety | Very much; the job requires me to do many different things, using a number of different skills and talents. |

2. To what extent does your job involve doing a *"whole" and identifiable piece of work*? That is, is the job a complete piece of work that has an obvious beginning and end? Or is it only a small part of the overall piece of work, which is finished by other people or by automatic machines?

1--------2--------3--------4--------5--------6--------7

| My job is only a tiny part of the overall piece of work; the results of my activities cannot be seen in the final product of service. | My job is a moderate-sized "chunk" of the overall piece of work; my own contribution can be seen in the final outcome. | My job involves doing the whole piece of work, from start to finish; the results of my activities are easily seen in the final product or service. |

3. In general, how *significant or important* is your job? That is, are the results of your work likely to significantly affect the lives or well-being of other people?

1--------2--------3--------4--------5--------6--------7

| Not very significant; the outcomes of my work are *not* likely to have important effects on other people. | Moderately significant | Highly significant; the outcomes of my work can affect other people in very important ways. |

4. How much *autonomy* is there in your job? That is, to what extent does your job permit you to decide *on your own* how to go about doing the work?

1--------2--------3--------4--------5--------6--------7

Very little; the job gives me almost no personal "say" about how and when the work is done.

Moderate autonomy; many things are standardized and not under my control, but I can make some decisions about the work.

Very much; the job gives me almost complete responsibility for deciding how and when the work is done.

5. To what extent does *doing the job itself* provide you with information about your work performance? That is, does the actual *work itself* provide clues about how well you are doing—aside from any "feedback" coworkers or supervisors may provide?

1--------2--------3--------4--------5--------6--------7

Very little; the job itself is set up so I could work forever without finding out how well I am doing.

Moderately; sometimes doing the job provides "feedback" to me; sometimes it does not.

Very much; the job is set up so that I get almost constant "feedback" as I work about how well I am doing.

The five questions in Figure 12–4 measure perceived skill variety, task identity, task significance, autonomy, and feedback from the job. The complete JDS uses several questions to measure each dimension so that the answers are considerably more reliable and valid than those derived from the abbreviated version used for illustration in Figure 12–4.

Using your scores (1 to 7) for each job dimension, you can calculate an overall measure of job enrichment called the *motivating potential score* (*MPS*). MPS is computed as follows:

$$\text{MPS} = \left(\frac{\text{Skill variety} + \text{task identity} + \text{task significance}}{3}\right) \times \text{Autonomy} \times \text{Feedback}$$

The way the MPS formula is constructed is based on the assumption that skill variety, task identity, and task significance when combined are equal in importance to autonomy and feedback. It also indicates that since skill variety, task identity, and task significance are additive, if one of them is missing the others can partially offset the deficiency. Try substituting zeros and sevens for the variables in the equation to help understand this process. For example, if there was no skill variety (0) and high task identity (7) and high task significance (7), the meaningfulness part of the equation would still be moderately high at 4.67 [(0 + 7 +7)/3 = 4.67]. However, if autonomy or feedback from the job were missing (0), the MPS score would be zero regardless of what the other scores were because the model assumes multiplicative relationships.

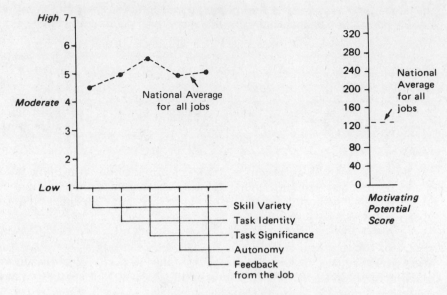

FIGURE 12–5.   The JDS Profile .

Plot your job profile and MPS score on the graphs in Figure 12–5, which show the national averages for all jobs. Do you score higher or lower than the national average?

INGREDIENTS OF ENRICHED JOBS

Although the techniques used for enriching jobs are often specific to the job being redesigned, there are some common implementing concepts that are applicable to a wide variety of jobs.[13]

Client Relationships.   One of the most important approaches is to get the worker in touch with the user of his or her output. Too often employees wind up working for the boss rather than the customer or client. In the word processing center example, certain operators could be assigned to specific clients or groups of clients, such as sales or engineering, so that when problems arise or peculiarities are present the operator would work directly with the client.

Schedule Own Work.   Most employees are fully capable of scheduling their own work. Deadlines or goals may be set by the supervisor; within that broad guidance, the individual worker should be allowed to set the pace for meeting the deadline. Another form of scheduling that is becoming very common is *flextime*, which allows the employee, within certain limits, to vary arrival and departure times to suit individual needs and desires.[14] Flextime facilitates self-work scheduling, since the supervisor cannot always be there to breathe down the employee's neck.

Ownership of the Whole Product.   An employee who builds an entire television set, or assembles an entire washing machine, or types a whole report can feel more identification with the finished product. Allowing employees to perform a whole or complete task cycle helps create a sense of pride and achievement. Another version of this concept is to assign drivers their own vehicle so that they can take pride in its upkeep and repair. Ownership can also be created by assigning people total responsibility for a certain geographical area. The Indiana Bell Company found substantial improvements in performance and satisfaction when telephone directory compliers were assigned a city or part of a city of their very own.[15]

Direct Feedback Structures.   Most feedback is filtered through the boss, and it often has a negative connotation. This job design strategy focuses attention on getting feedback *directly* back to the worker without management filtering. It may be a simple matter of routing reports or computer outputs directly to the employees instead of to their manager. An often used technique is to let people check their own work so they catch their own errors. Obviously this technique also increases autonomy. Direct communications with others may be another way of greasing feedback channels. If people in different divisions or companies are allowed to communicate directly by phone and letter, distortions and delays in feedback may be eliminated.

THE SUCCESS OF JOB ENRICHMENT

Major successes with job enrichment include the pioneering work of Ford at AT&T,[6, 15] Myers at Texas Instruments,[7] and Paul and Robertson at ICI.[8] A wide variety of jobs were enriched including clerical, manufacturing, service, sales, and engineering. Consulting firms such as Roy Walters Inc. and Drake-Beam & Associates, Inc. have engaged in full time job enrichment consulting with favorable results.[16] More recently, Herzberg and others have been conducting extensive job enrichment efforts in the public sector with consistently positive results. Recent reviews of the literature provide generally positive support for job redesign—although methodological problems abound.[17]

But Richard Hackman, in an article entitled "Is Job Enrichment Just a Fad?"[18] claims that: "Despite the recent fervor, job enrichment seems to be failing at least as often as it is succeeding." We don't really know if Hackman's statement is true since most failures are not reported. However, many job enrichment experts agree that most failures are really "nonsuccesses" in that they usually leave the organization in about the same state —as far as job design is concerned—as before job enrichment.

Why Job Enrichment May Fail

Managerial Resistance.   Perhaps the major reason for job enrichment failures is overt or covert resistance of the first line managers. Often managers volunteer for job enrichment because it is the "thing to do." However, once they get deeply involved, the enrichment process becomes threatening since the manager must usually relinquish some control and planning to the workers. The manager may be afraid to do this—what will be left for him or her to do after job enrichment? How will the manager's job be enriched?

No Real Change.   Sometimes, job enrichment gets only lip-service—there is a lot of publicity and emotional wing flapping, but in the end nothing really changes. Using the JDS before and after a job enrichment effort will check for this problem. If really meaningful changes in the core job dimensions are not made, no improvements can be expected.

Individual Differences.   So far, individual differences have been ignored; we have assumed that everyone wants an enriched job. But this may not be true. There is considerable evidence that some people respond more favorably to job enrichment than do others. Researchers have been examining many possible factors that may affect workers' reactions to job enrichment. The most widely, although not universally, accepted moderator is individual *growth need strength* (GNS), defined as the desire for growth, personal accomplishment, and learning. If GNS is high, individuals will respond positively to enriched jobs; performance and satisfaction will increase. If GNS is low, individuals will usually be unimpressed by enrichment. They will probably grumble but still do the job. Little change in motivation or satisfaction usually occurs. We should emphasize that, so far, research has not shown job enrichment to be negatively related to satisfaction or performance for low GNS individuals. Thus, except in exceptional cases, it seems probable that people respond from neutral to positive to an enriched job. Other individual differences, such as need for achievement and social need strength, are possible moderators, but little evidence exists to support or refute them.

Technological Constraints.   Some jobs are just too costly to redesign. For example, there is little that can be done with automobile assembly-line jobs without eliminating the line itself. Such a major technological change would be extremely costly and risky; most managers would not want to take the chance. (Later in this chapter we will discuss Volvo, which did eliminate their assembly line at one new plant.) Returning to the word processing center, an ideal job would be to locate the typists with the users. However, the expensive computerized typewriting equipment makes this option extremely costly and inefficient. Thus, we must often work within the constraints of technology. A third example of a job with limited enrichment potential is that of an Air Force security police guard protecting a B-52 strategic bomber. Unless a new technology, such as special infrared sensors and TV surveillance is developed, the guards will have to continue their boring, lonely vigil. Thus, many jobs have technological constraints that limit the applicability of job enrichment. However, even the worst jobs can usually be improved somewhat by systematically applying job enrichment concepts.

Organizational Climate.   The last barrier to job enrichment is nebulous but important. Organizational climate is the degree of trust, communications, and supportiveness that exists in the organization. A favorable climate can really facilitate the job enrichment process; a poor climate can stop it in its tracks. Job enrichment, if properly implemented, almost forces a more favorable climate. However, if the manager is an authoritarian, unchangeable individual, it is unlikely that enrichment would succeed.

BENEFITS OF JOB ENRICHMENT

Job enrichment can lead to improvements in both job performance and job satisfaction.

Performance

Seldom does job enrichment result in increased effort or individual productivity gains. However, this does not mean that major performance gains don't accrue. For example, one common theme of job enrichment is to get rid of inspectors or checkers. This frees more people for direct production. Also, employees working in an enriched job are much more interested in the quality of their work. This can result in fewer rejects, lower parts consumption, less wastage, and improved customer satisfaction.

Satisfaction

Job enrichment consistently results in improved job attitudes. Enhanced quality of working life has not only social benefits but also bottom-line benefits to the organization. People who are satisfied are more likely to come to work (absenteeism declines) and they are more likely to stay in the job (lower turnover rates). Both of these outcomes have major impacts on organizational costs. There are also many less tangible benefits, such as employee goodwill, family support and happiness, and even improved employee health.

GOAL-SETTING APPROACH

Closely related to both job engineering and job enrichment is the use of a goal-setting strategy of job design. *Goal setting* is the process of developing, negotiating, and formalizing targets or objectives that an employee is responsible for accomplishing. Even the most casual observation will reveal that people with indefinite goals often work slowly, perform poorly, lack interest, and accomplish little. On the other hand, people with clearly defined goals appear to be more energetic and more productive—they get things done within a specified time period and move on to other activities (and goals). Goals may be implicit or explicit, vague or clearly defined, self-imposed or externally imposed; but whatever their form, they serve to structure time and activities for people.

Three elements seem particularly important in the goal-setting approach:

1. *Goal clarity.* Goals must be clear if they are to be useful for directing effort. If they are clear and specific, the employee will have clear knowledge of the expectations of the boss.
2. *Goal difficulty.* Goals should be moderately challenging. If they are too easy, the employee may procrastinate or attack the goal lackadaisically. If the goals are too difficult, the employee may not accept the goal and thus will not try to meet it. Goal difficulty is related to job challenge, which in turn is related to job enrichment.
3. *Goal acceptance.* If goals are not accepted, then they do not energize behavior and are worthless. Acceptance is a complicated issue that seems to be related to goal difficulty and whether or not the employee participated in setting the goals. Participation enhances the chances for acceptance and commitment to the goals.

Figure 12–6 places the three elements in the goal-setting approach within the framework of Figure 12–3, the Hackman-Oldham model of job enrichment.

A goal-setting strategy of job design would use goals, objectives, and incentives to structure the job.[19] The goals provide the boundaries or structure for work activities and serve to channel and direct effort. Although goal-setting strategies may be used as the sole job design approach, an integration of goal setting with other job design strategies—such as job enrichment or autonomous work groups—seems more fruitful. The goal-setting process shown in Figure 12–6 may be combined with the job enrichment process shown in Figure 12–3 to provide an integrated model of job design.[20]

SOCIOTECHNICAL APPROACH

We noted earlier that technology can sometimes be a constraint on the job enrichment process. The sociotechnical approach overcomes this

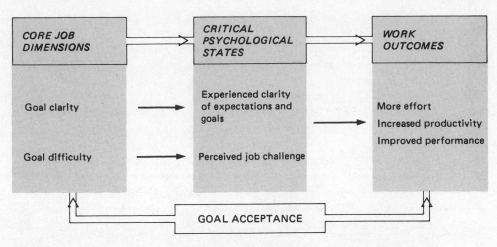

FIGURE 12–6.   Job Design through Goal Setting

constraint by deliberately designing jobs so as to optimize the relationship between the technological system and the social system. This approach is often centered around creating self-managing or autonomous work groups to perform a job that was once done on an assembly line. Since it is difficult and costly to change technology in an ongoing plant, sociotechnical approaches work best when an entirely new plant is being designed.

Volvo's Kalmar Plant

One of the most famous examples of sociotechnical job design is the new plant built by Volvo in Sweden.[21] When Pehr Gyllenhammar became Volvo's president in 1971, he saw that a new era was emerging—employees were demanding more meaningful work, job security, pay, and participation. When these demands were not fulfilled, people left their jobs and went to work elsewhere. Turnover at Volvo for 1969 was 52 percent; and absenteeism was also a serious problem. To overcome these problems, which were very costly to Volvo, Gyllenhammar decided on a risky course—to completely redesign their new Kalmar plant. His goal was to make it possible for an employee to see a Volvo driving down the street and say: "I made that car." To accomplish the job redesign, the conventional auto assembly line that moved through a warehouse had to be changed so that the work remained stationary and the materials were brought to the working station. To accomplish this goal, it was necessary to develop a special carrier so that an entire car could be transported and positioned for assembly (see Figure 12–7). These carriers move around on an electric tape track. They can be removed or held in place while assembly is performed.

(a)

(b)

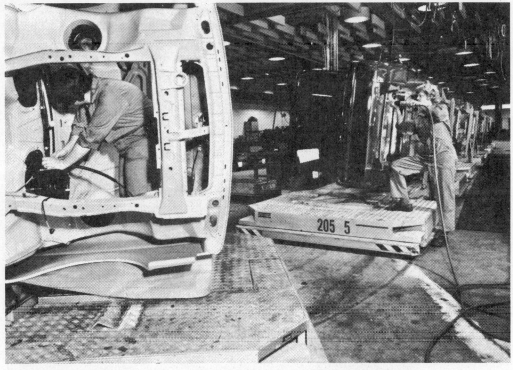

(c)

FIGURE 12–7.   Application of the Sociotechnical Approach
left: (a) A traditional assembly line at Volvo
(b) Volvo's new patented car carrier
above: (c) Volvo's car carriers in action

Reprinted from *People at Work* by Pehr G. Gyllenhammar, copyright © 1977, by Addison-Wesley Publishing Company, Inc., Reading, Mass. All rights reserved.

The Work Group.   The basis of sociotechnical approaches is not only technology, such as new carriers and plant layouts, but also work groups organized so as to optimize the social aspects of the system. The Kalmar plant has approximately 25 twenty-person work groups organized to perform all the work on certain subsystems, such as electrical systems, instrumentation, steering and controls, and interiors. Each team has its own area of the shop floor and its own rest area. Each team organizes itself. Responsibilities and work procedures are not dictated by management. Teams may elect to organize so that each member specializes in an individual job or they may organize into subteams to do parts of the job, or they may devise rotation schemes. The opportunities for self-control are substantial. Teams contract with management to deliver a certain number of finished doors, brake systems, interiors, etc., per day. The pace of work and break times are determined by the groups. Teams conduct their own inspections and a special computer-based quality control system flashes the results directly back to the work stations on TV.

Sociotechnical Model

Figure 12–8 is a sociotechnical model of job design.[22] It consists of three major elements: the social system, the technological system, and moderators.

Social System Characteristics.   The social system can be built on an individual or a group approach to job design. A college professor is an example of the individual approach, while the crew aboard an aircraft is an example of the group approach. The job characteristics of Hackman and Oldham can then be superimposed over the individual or group approach. For example, returning to the Volvo example, look at the job characteristics of the work teams. Almost all of Hackman and Oldham's characteristics are present. Another important element, especially when designing jobs for groups, is the interpersonal relations among the members. Do people get along well? Is there mutual trust and cooperation? Is there conflict and "back stabbing"? If interpersonal relations are poor, it may be difficult to design jobs for self-managing work groups.

Technological System Characteristics.   The type of production process (assembly line, process, batch, or unit) is a very important element in the sociotechnical model. In a process-technology organization, such as an oil refinery, most work is automated and workers spend most of their time monitoring dials. The process industries tend to be very capital intensive. Small unit technologies, such as plumbing, TV repair, sales, and investment brokers, tend to be very labor intensive. Obviously, differing production processes require different approaches to job design. A second technical characteristic is the physical work setting (light, temperature, noise, pollution, geographical isolation, and orderliness). Volvo went to considerable expense to make the work setting conducive for self-managing work teams. Complexity of the production process is a third technological issue. It may be quite easy for a person to learn to build an entire toaster, but it is unlikely that a single person could build even a major subsystem of a complex jet aircraft. Other technological characteristics that are important are the nature of the raw material used in production and the time pressure inherent in the process.

Moderators in the Sociotechnical Balance.   Work roles provide a set of behaviors or functions appropriate for a person holding a particular position in a given situation. For example, the student role involves attending classes, preparing assignments, taking examinations, preparing for graduation, and so on. Work roles help to define the relationships between people who perform tasks and the technological requirements of the task. Roles help to stabilize work relationships and provide the glue that binds the sociotechnical system together. Work goals also tend to facilitate sociotechnical integration. For example, within Volvo, work teams are responsible

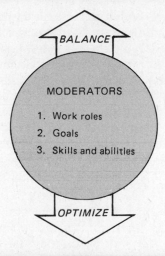

FIGURE 12–8.   A Sociotechnical Model of Job Design

for producing so many subassemblies or cars per day. The goals actually allow them to be autonomous because they can structure the work any way they want, as long as the goal is met. A final moderator includes the skills and abilities of the employees. If you have a highly skilled, educated workforce, such as you might have in Sweden, a different sociotechnical mix would be possible than for an underdeveloped country where skill levels and educational levels were quite low.

The sociotechnical model involves designing and implementing work rules that optimally integrate people with technology. The joint sociotechnical optimization is not only a work design strategy but a basic function of management.

Applications of the Sociotechnical Approach

Although the Volvo experience is the best known and to date most extensive sociotechnical project, numerous other projects have been implemented in Europe and the United States.[23] Firms that have been involved in sociotechnical approaches include General Foods, General Motors, Wyerhauser, TRW, Rushton Mining, and TVA.

WHICH APPROACH TO USE?

The contingencies associated with job design are complex and varied. Perhaps the most basic issue is management philosophy and values. If you are interested in improving the quality of work life, then the job enrichment or sociotechnical approach is appropriate. If you want to maximize production and efficiency, then concentrate on job engineering and goal setting. However, things may not be this simple. Employees and unions may not stand for the job engineering approach unless it meets the needs and desires of the employees. Strikes, absenteeism, turnover, and low product quality can all lead to failure just as quickly as task inefficiency can. Technology is another major variable. Some jobs cannot be enriched without redesigning the whole plant. When it is impossible to change a job, other techniques (such as flextime, rewards, job rotation) may soften the effects of a bad job. Leadership style and organizational climate are important because many job design approaches call for increased employee or work group autonomy. In an autocratically managed company it may be hard to change this style.

Perhaps the best strategy for the manager is to understand the various approaches to job design discussed in this chapter and to use the strategy that best fits his or her organization. Such a strategy would probably call for a combination of approaches. Job enrichment might be combined with goal setting or work simplification. Autonomous work groups might employ job rotation. Nor should a training approach to changing jobs be ignored. Perhaps the best way for organizations to improve both performance and the quality of work life is for every manager in the organization to thoroughly understand job design, so that day-to-day managerial tasks can be done based on an internal motivation model (such as the Hackman-Oldham model in Figure 12–3).

SUMMARY

Job design is a continuous managerial task. With the changing nature of the workforce it is no longer possible to ignore quality-of-working-life issues. Jobs must be designed so that they are both efficient and satisfying to the employee. Job design includes many different approaches such as job engineering, job enlargement, job rotation, job enrichment, goal setting, and sociotechnical. Job engineering includes traditional industrial engineering techniques that simplify the job to make it more efficient. Job enlargement and rotation both seek to make boring jobs more interesting by adding variety. Job enrichment seeks to make jobs more meaningful and challenging. Job design problems can be diagnosed by using clinical approaches or survey approaches. Jobs can be enriched through many techniques, including establishing client relationships, allowing employees to schedule their own work, providing a sense of ownership of the whole product, and providing direct feedback structures.

If jobs are properly designed, there is considerable evidence that employees are more satisfied and perform better. However, one must keep individual differences in mind when redesigning jobs—some people may not want enriched jobs or may not want to work in groups. Also, some organizational or technological situations may not permit job enrichment. The sociotechnical and goal-setting approaches provide alternative ways of harnessing the motivation of individuals and groups. Setting clear, moderately difficult goals will result in increased effort and performance providing they are accepted. The sociotechnical approach welds technology and social relationships together to form an optimum way to do the job. It seems to work best in new plants. Job design strategies and decisions, like other managerial decisions, contain many contingencies. Perhaps the best way to understand and balance the contingencies is through a thorough knowledge of the process and approaches of job design.

DISCUSSION QUESTIONS

1. Why should managers be concerned with the quality of working life?

2. What characteristics make up an enriched job?

3. Why can there be adverse reactions to the job engineering approach to job design?

4. Does job enlargement or job rotation result in enriched jobs?

5. Graph your estimate of the job characteristics present in a professional baseball player's job with a cook's job in a fast-food restaurant. Which one has the highest motivating potential?

6. What clues might you look for to see if a job needs redesign?

7. Why does job enrichment sometimes fail?

8. Why does goal setting increase performance?

9. How does the sociotechnical approach to job design differ from job enrichment?

===================== MANAGERIAL PROBLEMS =====================

KEYPUNCH OPERATION

The function of the keypunch division is to transfer written or typed insurance documents on to computer cards.[24] The division consists of 98 keypunch operators and verifiers (both have the same job classification), seven assignment clerks and seven supervisors. There are two keypunch supervisors (each with about 25 keypunch operators), two verification supervisors (again with about 25 verifiers each), and an assignment supervisor (with all seven assignment clerks). All the supervisors report to an assistant manager who then reports to the keypunch division manager.

The size of the jobs vary from just a few cards to as many as 2,500 cards. Some jobs are prescheduled while others come in with due dates— often in the form of crash projects that need to be done "right now." All jobs are received by the assignment branch where they are checked for obvious errors, omissions, and legibility. Any problems found are reported to the supervisor who contacts the user department to resolve the problem. If the departmental input is satisfactory, the assignment clerk divides up the work into batches that will take about one hour to complete so that each operator will have an equal workload. These batches are sent to the keypunching branches with the instructions to "Punch only what you see. Don't correct errors, no matter how obvious they look." Operators have no freedom to arrange their schedules or tasks. They also have little knowledge concerning the meaning and use of the data they are punching.

Because of the high cost of computer time, all keypunching is 100 percent verified. The verification process is done by having another operator completely repunch the data to see if the two inputs match. Thus, it takes just as long to verify as it does to punch the data in the first place. After verification, the cards are sent to the supervisor. If errors are detected, they are sent to the first available operator for correction. Next, the cards are sent to the computer division where they are checked for accuracy using a computer program. The cards and the computer output are sent directly to the originating department, which checks the cards and output and returns the cards to the supervisor if any errors are found.

Many motivational problems exist. There are numerous grievances from the operators. Employees frequently display apathy or outright hostility toward their jobs. Rates of work output are low and schedules are frequently missed. Absenteeism is much higher than average, especially on Mondays and Fridays. Supervisors spend most of their time controlling the work and resolving crisis situations. In short, the performance of the keypunch division is marginal at best.

QUESTIONS

1. Draw a JDS profile similar to the one shown in Figure 12–5 for the job of keypunch operator. Estimate what you think their job characteristics and motivating potential scores might look like.
2. How would you enrich the jobs in the keypunch division?
3. What outcomes would you predict if the jobs were enriched?
4. Is there another approach to job redesign that might be appropriate?

MCGUIRE INDUSTRY

In spite of a modern $30 million facility for overhauling engines, a Department of Defense industrial facility is having trouble meeting its production quotas. The morale of the civilian employees also seems to be at a low ebb—absenteeism and tardiness are major problems. The plant is located in the southwestern United States. Approximately 70 percent of the 2,000 employees are Mexican-Americans; however, only a few of them are supervisors. The engine facility is directed by a colonel who has had extensive management experience in military units but has never directed an industrial organization.

The engine facility was designed to utilize the latest technology in engine overhaul. Engines enter at one end of the half-mile-long plant where they are disassembled and placed on conveyor lines to the areas that specialize in repairing, replacing, and cleaning various components, such as turbine wheels and fuel controls. Work groups are highly specialized. They consist of 10–15 workers and a foreman. Their workload is determined by the pace of incoming components. After they have cleaned and repaired the item, it is sent to a testing group and then on to the next group for combining with other parts into a subassembly. When the subassemblies finally arrive at the other end of the building, the engine is assembled and sent to the testing department for an operational run-up. Problems, if any, are corrected by trouble-shooting teams. Finally, the engines are packed for shipment to the using organization.

Employees are tightly controlled. They punch time clocks and take breaks only when the buzzer sounds. Their mobility is quite limited. Even the rest rooms are tightly controlled; they may only use shop rest rooms. Supervisors and white-collar workers have their own separate rest rooms.

QUESTIONS

1. Is the sociotechnical system balanced?
2. How could these jobs be enriched?
3. How could goal setting be used to improve the jobs?
4. How would you improve performance and morale?

KEY WORDS

Job design	*Feedback*
Job engineering	*Job Diagnostic Survey*
Job enlargement	*Motivating potential score*
Job rotation	*Flextime*
Job enrichment	*Growth need strength*
Hackman-Oldham model	*Goal setting*
Skill variety	*Goal clarity*
Task identity	*Goal difficulty*
Task significance	*Goal acceptance*
Autonomy	*Sociotechnical systems*

REFERENCES

1. *Work in America,* report of a special task force to the Secretary of Health, Education and Welfare (Cambridge: MIT Press, 1973), p. xv.

2. Taylor, F. W., *The Principles of Scientific Management* (New York: W. W. Norton, 1911), pp. 42–47.

3. Barnes, R. M., *Motion and Time Study: Design and Measurement of Work,* 5th ed. (New York: Wiley, 1964).

4. Walker, C. R., The problem of the repetitive job, *Harvard Business Review,* 1950, 28 (May–June), pp. 54–58.

5. Herzberg, F., B. Mausner, and B. B. Snyderman, *The Motivation to Work* (New York: John Wiley and Sons, 1959).

6. Ford, R. N., *Motivation through the Work Itself* (New York: American Management Association, 1969).

7. Myers, M. S., *Every Employee a Manager* (New York: McGraw-Hill, 1970).

8. Paul, W. J., K. B. Robertson, and F. Herzberg, Job enrichment pays off, *Harvard Business Review,* 1969, 47 (March–April), pp. 61–78.

9. Herzberg, F. The wise old Turk, *Harvard Business Review,* 1974, 52 (Sept.–Oct.), pp. 70–80.

10. Hackman, J. R., G. R. Oldham, R. Janson, and K. Purdy, A new strategy for job enrichment, *California Management Review,* 1975, 17, pp. 57–71.

11. Whitsett, D. S., Where are your enriched jobs? *Harvard Business Review,* 1975, 53 (Jan.–Feb), pp. 74–80.

12. Hackman, J. R., and G. R. Oldham, Development of the job diagnostic survey, *Journal of Applied Psychology,* 1975, 60, pp. 159–170.

13. For more information on this topic, see Herzberg, The wise old Turk; Hackman et al., Strategy for job enrichment.

14.   There are many possibilities in flexible scheduling such as a flexible lunch hour, earlier or later starting times, more core time. The figure at the bottom of the page gives an example of one flextime approach. For more information on flextime, see Ebling, A. O., H. Gadon, and J. R. M. Gordon, Flexible working hours: It's about time, *Harvard Business Review*, 1974, 52 (Jan.–Feb.), pp. 18–33; Ebling, A. O., H. Gadon, and J. R. M. Gordon, Flexible working hours: The missing link, *California Management Review*, 1975, 17, no. 3, pp. 50–57.

15.   Ford, R. N., Job enrichment lessons from AT&T, *Harvard Business Review*, 1973, 51 (Jan.–Feb.), pp. 96–106.

16.   Herzberg, F. I., and E. A. Rafalko, Efficiency in the military: Cutting costs with orthodox job enrichment, *Personnel*, 1975, 52, (Nov.–Dec.), pp. 38–43.

17.   For reviews of job redesign literature see Pierce, J. L., and R. B. Dunham, Task design: A literature review, *Academy of Management Review*, 1976, 1, pp. 83–97; Cummings, T. G., and E. S. Malloy, and R. Glen, A methodological critique of fifty-eight selected work experiments, *Human Relations*, 1977, 30, pp. 675–708; and Dunham, R., Job design, in S. Kerr (ed.), *Organizational Behavior* (Columbus, Ohio: Grid Publishing, 1979).

18.   Hackman, J. R., Is job enrichment just a fad? *Harvard Business Review*, 1975, 53 (Sept.–Oct.), pp. 129–138.

19.   For reviews of the effects of goal setting see Steers, R. M., and L. W. Porter, The role of task-goal attributes in employee performance, *Psychological Bulletin*, 1974, 81, pp. 434–452; Latham, G. P., and G. A. Yukl, A review of research on the application of goal setting in organizations, *Academy of Management Journal*, 1975, 18, pp. 824–845.

20.   For more information about the integration of job enrichment and goal setting, see Umstot, D. D., C. H. Bell, and T. R. Mitchell, Effects of job enrichment and task goals on satisfaction and productivity: Implications for job design, *Journal of Applied Psychology*, 1976, 61, pp. 379–394.

21.   Gyllenhammar, P. G., *People at Work* (Reading, Mass.: Addison-Wesley, 1977).

22.   Based in part on the model of sociotechnical systems presented in Cummings, T. G., and S. Srivasta, *Management of Work: A Socio-technical Systems Approach* (Kent, Ohio: Kent State University Press, 1977); also see Susman, G., *Autonomy at Work: A Sociotechnical Analysis of Participative Management* (New York: Praeger Publishers, 1976); Cummings, T., Self-regulating work groups: A socio-technical synthesis, *Academy of Management Review*, 1978, 3, 625–634.

23.   Perhaps the most widely publicized sociotechnical approach in the United States is reported in Walton, R. E., How to counter alienation in the plant, *Harvard Business Review*, 1972, 50 (Nov.–Dec.), pp. 70–81; for a follow-up see Walton, R., Work innovations at Topeka: After six years, *Journal of Applied Behavioral Science*, 1977, 13, pp. 422–433.

24.   This managerial problem is adapted from an example given in Hackman et al., Strategy for job enrichment.

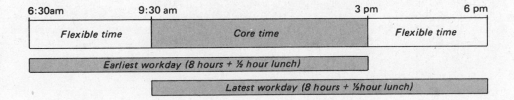

13

The Leadership Process

13

LEARNING OBJECTIVES

When you have finished reading and studying this chapter, you should be able to:
▲ Describe the leadership process.
▲ Describe how people exercise influence over others.
▲ Describe the effects of certain leadership behaviors on the performance and satisfactions of subordinates.
▲ Discuss five models of leadership.

THOUGHT STARTERS

▲ What is leadership?
▲ Why do people follow leaders?
▲ How do you influence others?
▲ Why are some people more successful leaders than others?
▲ What are some of the important things that leaders should consider before attempting to lead others?

OUTLINE

The previous chapters on motivation, job design, and group processes described and illustrated many factors that influence the behavior and attitudes of employees working in organizations. While many different management practices, rules, and regulations are potentially important in determining the behavior of employees, managers exercise great influence over what factors are considered important by their employees. In spite of this, very little is known about the effectiveness of leadership styles. Read the following case and decide what you would do.

> *You are a manager in a large chemical plant. The company has recently installed new machines and simplified the work system, but to the surprise of everyone, the expected increase in productivity has not been achieved. You have checked out the new machines yourself and realize that nothing has been installed improperly. You have also called other companies who have installed similar machines from the same manufacturer and they report no problems with the machines. You suspect that some parts of the new work system may be responsible for the decrease in productivity, but this view is not widely shared by the first-line foremen and other production people. These individuals attribute the drop in production to poor training of operators, lack of adequate financial incentives, and poor morale.*
>
> *This morning you received a phone call from your division manager. She has just received your productivity figures for the last six months and was calling to express her concern. She indicated that the problem was yours to solve in any way you thought best, but would like to know what you intended to do about the problem within the next seven days.*[1]

Even for the most experienced managers, deciding what style of leadership is the most appropriate is not an easy task. In their day-to-day work, they are continually faced with issues described in this case—responsibility and authority delegation, control, performance evaluation, team building, resolving conflict, and negotiating with customers. From their experiences come a host of questions about the process of leadership. How can I get the job done most effectively? What is the "best" leadership style? When should I listen to my subordinates and when should I give orders? If I become too friendly with my subordinates, will I lose their respect? How should I use my power to reward and punish people?

Although managers confidently discuss the characteristics of successful managers, and many managers think that they can select good leaders on the basis of personal experience, the need to develop more effective leaders remains a problem. Peter Drucker points out that leaders are the basic and the scarcest resource of any business enterprise.[2] Most business failures can be attributed to ineffective leadership. Most organizations face a continuous search for persons who have the necessary ability to lead effectively. Just look at the help wanted sections of the *New York Times, Washington Post,* or *Wall Street Journal* and you will find hundreds of companies looking for persons who are dynamic and effective leaders.

Each of us has a theory of leadership. We can all recall instances where we thought that the leadership was good, and other instances where we thought the leadership was poor. What are your ideas about leadership? Before reading this chapter, take a few minutes to write down your impressions of effective leadership.

My impressions about effective leadership are: _____

_____

_____

_____

Hundreds and hundreds of managers have attempted to answer this question in the search for understanding the leadership process. No single answer is correct. One point of departure for understanding leadership is to study the behavior of individual leaders in different organizations—business, government, military, civil rights, and religious. This strategy might focus on the study of celebrated leaders such as Andrew Carnegie, Winston Churchill, Mahatma Gandhi, Golda Meir, George Patton, Martin Luther King, and Billy Graham. Much can be learned about leadership through the biographies of such outstanding, charismatic people, but most of the evidence bearing on the leadership process stems from numerous studies conducted in factories, offices, college laboratories, military units, and voluntary organizations. While a thorough understanding of all the leadership studies is beyond the scope of this book, this chapter attempts to provide an understanding of the dynamics involved in the leadership process.

NATURE OF THE LEADERSHIP PROCESS

What is the difference between "leadership" and the "leader"? A popular definition of a leader is a person who draws other people to himself. A leader in this sense is someone whom others want to follow, who commands their trust and their loyalty. However, most of the work in an organization is accomplished by individuals who are not so inspiring. These are managers of insurance offices, teachers, line supervisors at local mills, bank vice-presidents, and newspaper editors. A *leader* in an organization is someone who plans, organizes, controls, communicates, delegates, and accepts the responsibility to reach the organization's goals. In other words, the leader is an individual appointed to a job with authority, responsibility, and accountability to accomplish the goals and objectives of the organization. The manager of a local insurance company, for example, has the responsibility and authority to write insurance policies, train secretaries and other agents, handle client insurance claims, process changes in insurance policies, and investigate claims. The manager usually accomplishes these tasks through the exercise of leadership.

Leadership is the process of influencing group activities toward the achievement of goals.[3] This simple statement captures the essence of what we mean by leadership. There are two important threads in this definition. *First*, leadership is a relationship between two or more people in which influence and power are unevenly distributed. Whenever two or more people join together to achieve a goal, a group structure develops. Part of the structure deals with the way in which members influence one another while trying to reach the group's goals. Because all group members will at times influence other group members, each group member will at times exert leadership. In this definition of leadership, there is a difference between being the *designated leader* of a group—the one person who is in charge of the group and has been given the authority to exert influence on it—and engaging in leadership behavior while being a member in a group. For example, the director of industrial relations may be the person designated by management to settle grievances that have been brought against the company by employees. But a shop steward who is a member of the grievance committee may have more influence in reaching settlements that are mutually acceptable to management and the employees.

Second, leaders do not exist in isolation. If you want to know whether or not you are exercising leadership, look behind you. Is anyone following you? In most instances, you cannot coerce people into behaving in certain ways. Therefore, leadership implies that followers must give their consent to be influenced. In accepting an individual as a leader, the followers voluntarily give up some of their freedom to make decisions in order to achieve a goal. An individual who finds it difficult to give up some decision-making freedom will not be a satisfied group member, just as an individual who finds it hard to make decisions for others will not find leadership very rewarding. In effect, followers must suspend their judgments and allow another individual to make certain decisions in specific situations. This leader-member relationship involves a psychological or economic exchange.[4]

A leader is considered to be valuable by subordinates and to be an integral part of the group or team only after proving his or her value as a leader to his or her subordinates. For example, Tom Landry, football coach of the Dallas Cowboys, has demonstrated his leadership abilities on the gridiron—he has led the Cowboys to the Superbowl several times and won it twice. The football players follow his advice on the football field and suspend their own decision-making judgments because of Landry's ability to bring extra economic and psychic rewards to the players. Psychic rewards include a sense of achievement when the group reaches desired goals, as when the Cowboys won the Superbowl in January 1978.

The emotional relationship is by no means one-sided. A leader also becomes involved with subordinates, and their feelings toward him or her are important. Whether a leader is perceived as fair or unfair, liked or disliked, friendly or unfriendly, all are integral parts in determining whether the leader has the support of the group.

A position of leadership provides economic and psychic rewards for the holder. In many organizations, people at the top of the organization may be paid ten to twenty times as much as the lowest paid employees. Notwithstanding the possibility that people may not be worth that much, it is clear that somebody thinks so. However, leadership is sought even when economic rewards are absent. The captain of a collegiate football team, union steward, chairperson of a civic or church committee, and PTA chairperson are not paid positions, but persons holding these positions usually exercise leadership. Why? Leadership gives one influence or power over others, and with this power comes satisfaction in the knowledge that one can influence, to some extent, the well-being of others and can affect one's own destiny.

The leader receives his or her authority from the group because the group has accepted that individual as a leader. To maintain a leadership position, a person must enable the members to gain satisfactions that are otherwise outside their reach. In return, the group satisfies the leader's need for power and prominence, as well as giving the leader the power necessary to reach the organization's goals.

Sources of Leader Influence

Not all leaders derive their sources of influence from their role in the organization. Five distinct sources of power available to a leader have been identified: legitimate, reward, coercion, referent, and expert.[5]

Legitimate.   Legitimate power is vested in a manager's position in the organizational hierarchy. Each manager has authority to make decisions in a specific area. For example, a rank-and-file worker who has been promoted to a foreman's position has legitimate power over other rank-and-file workers in his efforts to achieve the company's goals. If the new foreman has been accepted by the coworkers, his or her influence is likely to be great.

Reward.   The influence of reward stems from the capability of the leader to specify rewards that are valued by subordinates. A subordinate who complies with the leader's requests does so with the expectation that this behavior will lead to positive rewards, either psychological or economic. Therefore, this type of influence derives from the ability of the leader to provide desired outcomes for others, in exchange for compliance.

Coercion.   Coercion is based on fear. A subordinate perceives that failure to comply with orders from a superior can lead to punishment or some other outcomes that are undesired (for example, an official reprimand for not following orders, poor work assignments, and/or stricter enforcement of all work rules). Unfortunately, the effect of this type of power on the worker's behavior is uncertain. As indicated in Chapter 6, negative reinforcement does not necessarily encourage desired behavior. The worker who receives an official reprimand for shoddy work, for example, may find other ways to avoid the punishment, such as not performing the task at all, falsification of performance reports, and absenteeism.

Referent.   Referent power is based on the follower's identification with the leader. This identification may be based upon a personal liking of the leader. Usually, this identification includes a desire on the part of the follower to "be like" the person with referent power. Referent power is usually associated with individuals who possess admired personality characteristics, charisma, or a "good" reputation.

Expert.   Expert power stems from the perceived and demonstrated competence of the leader to implement, analyze, evaluate, and control the task that the group has been assigned to complete. Street gangs usually assess and ascribe expert power to those who can fight the best; academicians, to those colleagues who write journal articles and books and advance new theories. Expert power is narrow in scope; we tend to be influenced by another person only within the individual's area of expertise.

A leader can possess varying amounts of these sources of power. The areas of legitimate, reward, and coercion power are largely specified by the hierarchical structure of the organization. For example, the first-line foreman is at a lower level in the organization's hierarchy than the vice-president for manufacturing. Consequently, the foreman's bases of legitimate, reward, and coercion power are less than the vice-president's. On the other hand, some supervisors may possess personal characteristics that increase their referent or expert power, regardless of their position in the organization's hierarchy.

MODELS OF LEADERSHIP BEHAVIOR

Many people believe that they possess the intuitive ability to identify outstanding leaders. A personnel director may believe that people with pleasing personalities will be highly successful managers. Imbued with this belief, the personnel director recommends as managers people who have a great deal of personal charm, rather than basing the choices on merit or effort. Why does this happen? One answer is that it is difficult, in most managerial situations, to determine how well a leader has performed. Getting a manager to evaluate a subordinate's leadership style is almost impossible. The manager will tell you what the individual does, how much time is spent doing various tasks, and the like. However, because a manager performs many tasks, trying to single out good performance criteria is extremely difficult. A second answer is that the personnel manager would not have been in that position unless somebody else spotted certain personal qualities in him. Therefore, the personnel manager thinks "If these qualities enabled me to get this position and carry out my responsibilities successfully, I will pick others who have qualities similar to my own, so they can also be successful." This statement means that an individual's leadership success may depend on a manager's personality. If a subordinate has a manager with similar personal qualities, the chances of the subordinate's getting a high recommendation are greater than if the subordinate has a manager with dissimilar personal qualities. While it may be true that some managers have an ability to select individuals who become good leaders, it is equally true that most managers do not possess this ability. In an attempt to understand the leadership process, five basic models of leadership will be presented: trait, behavioral, Fiedler's contingency, path-goal, and leader reward. The complexity and multidimensional character of leadership should keep you from jumping prematurely to conclusions about leadership.

Trait Model

The *trait model* attempts to isolate the attributes of successful and unsuccessful leaders and, using this list of traits, predict the success or failure of potential leaders. While there is considerable support for the notion that effective leaders have different interest patterns, different abilities, and, perhaps, different personality traits than do less effective managers, most researchers have come to regard the trait approach as somewhat ineffective in predicting successful leadership.[6] Why?

First, although over a hundred personality attributes of successful leaders have been identified, no consistent pattern(s) has been found. For example, successful sales managers are optimistic, enthusiastic, and dominant, whereas successful production managers are progressive, have a genuine respect for people, are introverts, and are cooperative. The problem with studying personalities is that the list of traits is unending, and researchers often disagree over which traits are the most important for the effective leader.

Despite these difficulties, one researcher has pulled together four traits shared by most successful leaders.[7] Not all leaders have them, and they are more likely to be present in middle and upper level managers than in those who hold supervisory positions. Given these limitations, these four traits are:

Intelligence. Leaders tend to have somewhat higher intelligence than their followers.
Social maturity and breadth. Leaders have a tendency to be emotionally mature and to have a broad range of interests.

Inner motivation and achievement drives. Leaders want to accomplish things; when they achieve one goal, they seek out another. They are not primarily dependent on others for their motivation to achieve goals.

Human relations attitudes. Leaders are able to work effectively with other persons in a variety of situations. They respect other individuals and realize that to accomplish tasks they must be considerate of others.

Individual personality cannot be left out of the leadership picture. Individual differences affect the social perceptions of individuals and, consequently, play an important part in determining individual behavior.

Second, physical and constitutional factors have also been related to effective leadership. Height, weight, appearance, physique, energy, health, and intelligence have all been related to successful leadership. However, most of these factors are also correlated with many other situational factors that, in some cases, significantly affect a leader's effectiveness. For example, in the military or police force, members must have a certain minimal height and weight in order to perform their tasks effectively. While these attributes may assist an individual to rise to a leadership position, the number of inches of height or the number of pounds of weight do not relate highly to performance. In other organizations (e.g., educational or business), height and weight requirements are not requisites for rising to a leadership position.

Third, leadership skills vary by the type of work the person performs in the organization. Leaders may be required to use three different types of skills at different levels in the organization: technical skills, human skills, and conceptual skills.[8] The amount of these skills that a leader uses varies at different organizational levels, as shown in Figure 13–1.

Technical skills are the most important at lower, or first-line, managerial levels where the products or services of the organization are actually produced. These skills involve methods, procedures, and techniques. It is easy to visualize the technical skills of design engineers, market researchers,

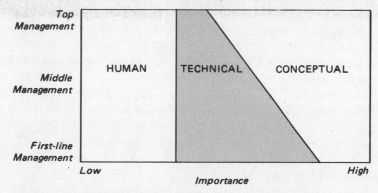

FIGURE 13–1.   Managerial Skills

Adapted from D. Hellriegel, and J. Slocum, *Management: Contingency Approaches* (Reading, Mass.: Addison-Wesley, 1978), p. 11.

accountants, and computer programmers. Of the three skills, the technical skill is the most concrete and is most often emphasized in educational institutions and in on-the-job training programs. As a manager moves up the organization's hierarchy, the importance of technical knowledge decreases and the job begins to require increasing amounts of other skills. When this happens, the manager must rely more and more on the technical skills of subordinates.

Human skills maintain a high degree of importance throughout all management levels. They are concerned with the interpersonal relations between the manager and those with whom the manager comes in contact. Human skills relate to the ability to lead, motivate, manage conflict, and instill teamwork.

Conceptual skills are most important at top-management levels where long-term planning and broad thinking are required. They involve the ability to see the organization as a whole, its relationship to the external environment, and to understand how the various departments of the entire company rely on each other to produce the organization's products and/or services. As managers move to higher positions in the organization, they must increasingly develop and utilize these skills. Not all managers are able to do so. For example, someone who is effective as a salesperson may be unable to trade these technical skills for conceptual skills and turn out to be a poor district sales manager.

Fourth, personality description and measurement themselves may be inadequate. Leadership researchers may not have investigated the really significant aspects of a leader's personality. That is, most of the traits are measured by pencil-and-paper questionnaires that were designed to be valid indicators of other behaviors, such as stability, anxiety, achievement, and dependency. Trait theorists assumed that these questionnaires would also be valid indicators of leadership ability.

Fifth, leadership itself is known to be a complex and probably not a consistent pattern of individual roles. There could be a relation between personality and taking of particular roles, which is not reflected in a study relating personality to a measure of effectiveness. For example, one study found that high earners (a measure of success) in small firms were more ascendant, tended to have interests similar to those of personnel managers, were more open-minded, and described themselves as more considerate than low earners. In such firms, each individual is required to perform numerous roles. Those individuals who are predisposed to performing a multiplicity of roles will seek out small firms that permit them to do so.[9]

Behavioral Models

Because of the failure of the trait model to predict successful leadership behavior, researchers turned to an examination of the structure and functions of groups. The emphasis turned from identifying what traits are important in the leadership process to the study of what leaders actually do and how they do it. Effective leaders perform the tasks of assisting the group in achieving certain task goals by being task-centered in their relations with subordinates. To assist the members to achieve certain personal goals, such as work satisfaction, promotions, and recognition, leaders are also viewed as being considerate or supportive. Examples of task behavior include focusing attention on production or reviewing the quality and quantity of work accomplished. Examples of supportive leadership behavior include settling disputes, keeping the group happy, providing encouragement, and giving positive reinforcements.

Continuum of Leadership Behaviors.   A variety of styles of leadership behavior exists between being task-oriented and supportive. One way to look at these styles is depicted as a continuum (illustrated in Figure 13–2). Leaders whose behavior is observed to be task-directed and who use their formal authority to influence their subordinates, appear on the left side of the figure. Leaders whose behavior appears to be considerate or supportive of the needs of subordinates, thus giving them more freedom in their work, are located on the right side. The continuum illustrates that a manager can choose a large number of styles and can shift styles. A manager who has capable and talented subordinates might prefer a more democratic or relations-oriented approach, as opposed to the manager who perceives subordinates as incapable of self-judgment and control. Managers who have more confidence in their own capabilities than in those of their

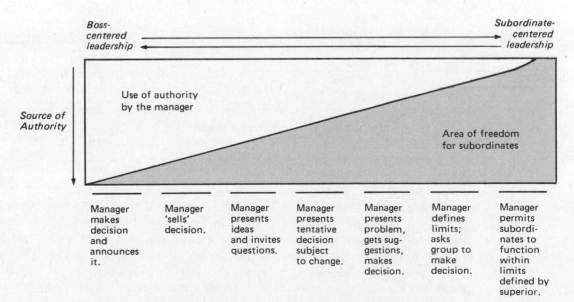

FIGURE 13–2.   Styles of Leadership Behavior

From R. Tannenbaum and W. Schmidt, "How to Choose a Leadership Pattern," *Harvard Business Review,* 1973, 51, p. 164. Reproduced with permission, *Harvard Business Review.*

subordinates will not delegate many decision-making functions to subordinates. Managers' value systems will also determine their particular style of leadership. How strongly do managers feel that individuals should have a share in the decisions that affect them? The strength of convictions on questions such as this will tend to move managers from one end of the continuum to the other. The last factor facing managers is the situation. Managers who delegates decision-making functions to subordinates reduce the predictability of the decision to some extent. Some managers with a lower tolerance for ambiguity than others have a greater need to know the outcome of the decision.

Before deciding how to lead, managers should consider a number of factors affecting subordinates' behavior. For example, do the subordinates have a need for independence? Are they ready to assume the responsibility for decisions? Do they understand the goals and objectives of the company? Generally speaking, if a manager can answer yes to these questions, that manager can permit subordinates greater freedom.

In addition to forces in both manager and subordinates, certain general characteristics of the situation will also affect the manager's behavior. Among the more critical situational circumstances are those that stem from the organization, the work group, the nature and scope of the problem, and the pressures of time.

These, then, are the critical forces that affect a manager's leadership style at any one instance and tend to determine his or her behavior in relation to subordinates. As the manager works on problems that arise day by day, the most effective leadership will change. Thus, a leader has a continuum of styles to choose from, as indicated in Figure 13–2.

Leaders whose behavior is observed to be at the authoritarian end of the continuum tend to be task-oriented and use their legitimate and coercive power to influence their followers; leaders whose behavior appears to be at the democratic end tend to be group-oriented and thus give their followers considerable freedom to carry out their assignments. Often, this continuum is extended beyond democratic behavior to include laissez-faire style. This behavioral style permits subordinates to do whatever they want to do. No policies or procedures are established by the leader. Table 13–1 outlines the basic behavioral leadership styles of autocratic, democratic, and laissez-faire leaders.

During the 1930s, two researchers conducted a study with small children to determine the effect of these three styles of leadership behavior on performance.[10] The findings indicated that although the quantity of work produced was greatest in the autocratic groups, the quality of work was at its best in the democratic groups. Also, when the autocratic leader left the production area, the children almost stopped working (a sign of job dissatisfaction), whereas performance under the democratic leader decreased only slightly. In general, the laissez-faire style was ineffective in stimulating performance. Less work was done under the laissez-faire leader and the work that was done was of poorer quality than in either the democratic or autocratic groups.

TABLE 13-1. Three Leadership Styles

Autocratic	Democratic	Laissez-faire
1. All determination of policy by the leader.	1. All policies a matter of group discussion and decision, encouraged and assisted by the leader.	1. Complete freedom for group or individual decision, with a minimum of leader participation.
2. Techniques and activity steps dictated by the authority, one at a time, so that future steps were always uncertain to a large degree.	2. Activity perspective gained during discussion period. General steps to group goal sketched, and where technical advice is needed, the leader suggests two or more alternative procedures from which choice can be made.	2. Various materials supplied by the leader who makes it clear that he or she would supply information when asked. Takes little part in work discussion.
3. The leader usually dictates the particular work task and work companion of each member.	3. The members are free to work with whomever they choose, and the division of tasks is left up to the group.	3. Little participation of the leader in determining tasks and companions.
4. The leader tends to be "personal" in praise and criticism of the work of each member; remains aloof from active group participation except when demonstrating.	4. The leader is "objective" or "fact-minded" in praise and criticism, and tries to be a regular group member in spirit without doing too much of the work.	4. Infrequent spontaneous comments on member activities unless questioned, and little attempt to appraise or regulate the course of events.

Ohio State Leadership Studies. The leadership studies initiated in the late 1940s by the Bureau of Business Research at Ohio State University attempted to identify dimensions of leadership behavior.[11] This effort resulted in the specification of two dimensions of leadership behavior: consideration and initiating structure.

Consideration is the extent to which a leader is likely to have job relationships characterized by mutual trust, two-way communication, respect for subordinates' ideas, and consideration of their feelings. This style emphasizes the needs of the individual. Some typical statements used to indicate this style of leadership behavior are:

"The leader finds time to listen to group members."
"The leader is willing to make changes."
"The leader looks out for the personal welfare of group members."
"The leader is friendly and approachable."

A high consideration score indicates psychological closeness between the leader and subordinates; a low score indicates a more psychologically distant and impersonal stand on the part of the leader.[12]

Initiating structure is the extent to which a leader is likely to define and structure his or her role, and those of subordinates, toward accomplishing the group's goal. This style emphasizes directing group activities through planning, communicating information, scheduling group members to tasks, emphasizing deadlines, and giving directions. Some typical statements used to indicate this style of leadership behavior are:

"The leader schedules the work to be done."
"The leader assigns particular employees to the task."
"The leader maintains definite standards of performance."
"The leader asks the group members to follow standard rules and regulations."

In short, a leader who scores high on initiating structure is one who is concerned with getting the task accomplished by following directions.

Figure 13–3 illustrates the basic relationship between these two leadership behaviors. Leader consideration appears to be a reliable indicator of subordinate satisfaction and the behavioral consequences of job satisfaction or dissatisfaction, such as group harmony and cohesion. Leaders who

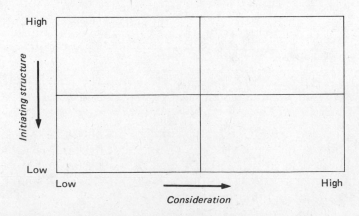

FIGURE 13–3. Ohio State Leadership Grid

were rated high on initiating structure by their subordinates were generally rated high by their superiors in terms of productivity. However, when the leader was very high on initiating structure, the number of grievances and turnover were also high.

The underlying assumption made by the researchers at Ohio State was that leadership behavior was related not only to indirect measures of performance, such as absenteeism, grievances, and turnover, but also to direct measures of performance, such as the number of units produced. In one review, the author concluded that little is known about how these styles affect work group performance. While this comment may appear harsh, many studies have failed to find a significant relationship between these dimensions of leadership behavior and performance.[13] Some reasons for these findings are that individual productivity is influenced by other factors such as:

1. Individual social status within the group.
2. Type of technological process employed.
3. Individual expectations of a certain style of supervision.
4. Individual psychological rewards from working with a particular type of leader.

When is consideration effective? The underlying belief of managers using consideration is that participation by subordinates in the decision-making process will improve the process because it is through the participative process that subordinate knowledge and expertise can be brought to bear on problems. Further, if the decisions require that subordinates accept and implement the decision, participation will increase the likelihood of acceptance. Therefore, the most positive effects on productivity and satisfaction occur when:

1. The task is routine and denies the individual any job satisfaction.
2. Subordinates are predisposed toward participative leadership.
3. Subordinates must learn something new.
4. Subordinates feel that their involvement in the decision-making process is legitimate and will affect their job performance.
5. Few status differences exist between the leader and followers.

When is initiating structure effective? The use of initiating structure leadership behaviors is contingent on several factors.[14] Its most positive effects on productivity and satisfaction occur when:

1. There is high degree of pressure for output due to demands imposed on sources other than the leader's.
2. The task is satisfying to the subordinate.
3. Subordinates are dependent on the leaders for information and direction on how to complete the task.
4. Subordinates are psychologically predisposed toward being told what to do and how to do it.

5. The leader has more than twelve people reporting to him.
6. The task is nonroutine.

Summary of Leadership Research

This first part of the chapter summarized research conducted over the past three decades. The findings are seen to be neither consistent nor very definite. A conclusion reached in one study is easily refuted in another. The major conclusion that can be reached is that leadership style is situationally dependent. That is, there is no one best style; there is no style that is appropriate for all situations. This conclusion helps make sense of the conflicting research; however, it is of little help to the practicing manager or aspiring manager who is left with unanswered questions.

CONTINGENCY MODELS

Research on the leadership process done prior to the mid-1960s indicated no consistent relationship between leadership style and various measures of performance, group processes, and job satisfaction. Although much of the research concluded that the environment within which a leader functions plays a significant role in the determination of the leader's effectiveness, very little work was undertaken to identify key situational variables. Contingency leadership theorists, in contrast, direct their research toward discovering the situational variables that permit leader behaviors and characteristics to be effective in a given situation. For example, contingency theorists would hypothesize that substantially different characteristics would be effective for head nurses and drill sergeants.

Diagnosis of situational variables requires that managers examine four factors: (1) their own characteristics, (2) their subordinates' characteristics, (3) group characteristics, and (4) organizational structure.[15] Figure 13–4 diagrams interrelationships between these four factors.

Leader Characteristics

Those characteristics that the leader brings to the situation are the leader characteristics. Leader characteristics may be important or unimportant depending on the situation.[16] Some important variables of leadership characteristics are:

1. *Personality dimensions.* How much aggressiveness does the leader have? Does the leader possess the intellectual abilities to be a capable leader? Is the personality of the leader stable or unstable in the situation?

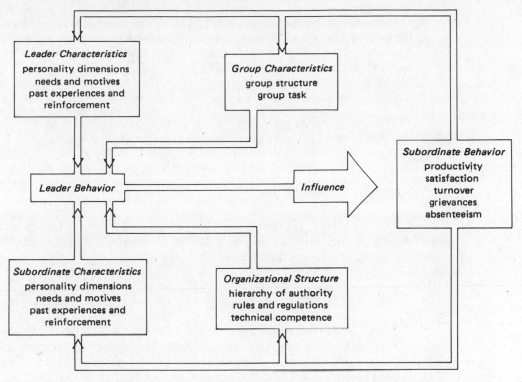

FIGURE 13–4.   Contingencies Affecting Leader Behavior

Adapted from *Organizational Behavior and Performance* by John Ivancevich, Andrew Szilagyi, and Marc Wallace, p. 283. Copyright © 1977 by Goodyear Publishing Co. Reprinted by permission.

2. *Needs and motives.* What particular needs are motivating the leader in this situation? What are the motivator factors in the situation? What are the hygiene factors?

3. *Past experiences and reinforcement.* Has the leader received positive reinforcements from using a particular style of leadership in the past? Has the leader had previous experience in a similar situation?

Subordinate Characteristics

Before a leader decides on a particular style of leadership, he or she should consider the characteristics of the subordinates. Subordinates, like the manager, have certain needs, motives, and expectations that are operating in the situation to affect their behavior. Among these are:

1. *Personality dimensions.* The personalities of subordinates will affect how they will react to the leader's behavior(s). Will a highly democratic subordinate accept the leadership style of a highly initiating structure leader? How does a passive leader react to aggressive subordinates?

2. *Needs and motives.* As with the leader, what kinds of needs are operating within the subordinate's motivational system? Is this situation one in which the subordinate's higher order needs are going to be satisfied? What are the chances of experiencing intrinsic satisfactions from performing the task well?

3. *Past experiences and reinforcement.* What kinds of behaviors in the past have led to successful task completion? For example, if I really do a great job, what is the probability that I will receive some reward (monetary or psychological)? If no rewards are received for participating in a program, then why participate in the program?

Group Characteristics

Chapters 9 and 10 discussed how groups operate in organizations, with Chapter 9 emphasizing the description of group characteristics. Some important group characteristics affecting leadership are:

1. *Group structure.* Are the group's norms in agreement with the organization's? If the group is highly cohesive, what style of leadership will keep members highly attracted to their work group and at the same time permit them to complete the job? Do the members of the group all get along or are there cliques within the group? What kind of communication network exists within the group?

2. *Group task.* Does the task require cooperation of all members? What kinds of decisions can the group make? Is the task better suited for a nominal or interacting group?

Organizational Structure

Chapter 4 discussed the properties of organizations and how these relate to effectiveness. Organizational structure is the formal system of communication, authority, and responsibility that operate within the organization. Some important characteristics of organizational structure for a leader to consider are:

1. *Hierarchy of authority.* What are the bases for the leader's power? What kinds of rewards and punishments does the leader control because of his or her position within the hierarchy? For example, if all decisions are centralized and referred up to higher managers, what types of decisions can this manager really make?

2. *Rules and regulations.* To what extent do formal, written statements specify acceptable and unacceptable decisions and behaviors? For example, if numerous rules and regulations govern the behaviors of employees in the organization, as in the Civil Service or the Seven-Eleven food chain, what leeway does the leader have to deviate from these?

3. *Technical competence.* Highly trained professionals may rely more on their own expertise than on the leader's, thus limiting the ability of

the leader to influence them. For example, if a head nurse wants to improve patient care, should she try to be more considerate or use more initiating structure?

No list of important situational factors could be inclusive. What we want to point out is that the leadership process is very complex and that simple prescriptions, such as "democratic leaders have more satisfied workers than autocratic leaders," just do not work. The next sections discuss three situational theories of leadership: Fiedler's contingency model, House's path-goal model, and the leader-reward model. These theories have provided at least a partial explanation of how situational variables affect the leadership process.

Fiedler's Contingency Model

The first contingency model of the leadership process was developed by Fred Fiedler and his associates.[17] This model is a departure from the trait and behavioral models of leadership in that it specifies that performance of a group is contingent upon both the motivational system of the leader and the degree to which the leader has control and influence in a mance of a group is contingent upon both the motivational system of the interaction of the leader's behavior with three situational variables: group atmosphere, task structure, and leader's position power. Let's briefly look at these variables.

Group Atmosphere.   The group atmosphere variable measures the leader's feelings of being accepted by the group. The leader's authority partly depends on his or her acceptance by the group. If others are going to follow the leader because of her referent power, for example, they are following the leader because of the leader's personality, trustworthiness, and the like. Also, they are likely to accept the person as their leader. Many of the factors influencing this were discussed at length in Chapter 9.

Task Structure.   Task structure is a measure of the extent to which the task performed by subordinates is simple or routine, can be done only one way or numerous ways, and is highly specific or vague. If the task is routine, it is likely to have clearly defined goals and only a few steps or work procedures, be verifiable, and have a correct solution. An axle assembler in an auto plant who secures front and rear assemblies to chassis springs is performing a highly structured task because the goals are clearly spelled out, the method to accomplish the task is detailed and specific, and whether the task was correctly performed is verifiable. Managing subordinates who perform such structured tasks is relatively easy.

At the other extreme is the task that is completely nonroutine. In this condition, the leader may possess no more knowledge than the subordinates. The goals are unclear, the paths to achieve the goals are multiple, and the task cannot be done by the "numbers." Tasks performed by detectives, policy makers, and marketing researchers are examples of unstructured tasks that are difficult to manage.

Position Power.   Position power is the extent to which the leader possesses reward, coercion, and legitimate power bases. Typical questions asked to determine the leader's position power are: Does the leader have the right to promote or demote a subordinate? Can the leader instruct subordinates concerning task goals? In most business organizations, foremen, supervisors, and managers have high position power. In most voluntary organizations, committees, and other social organizations, leaders tend to have low position power.

In sum, the higher each of these variables is—the more pleasant the relations, the more structured the task, and the greater the power—the more favorable the situation is for the leader.

Assessing Leadership Style.   Fiedler's contingency model measures the leadership style of a person by using an instrument called "esteem for least preferred coworker" (LPC). The respondent is asked to think of all coworkers one has ever had, and then to describe the person with whom he or she could work least well, the "least preferred coworker." The description is made by rating that person on a simple bipolar scale, examples of which are shown in Figure 13–5. Each bipolar scale is scored from one to eight, with eight indicating the most favorable perception of one's least

FIGURE 13–5.   Leadership Style: LPC

Think of the person with whom you can work least well. He may be someone you work with now, he may be someone you knew in the past. He does not have to be the person you like least well, but should be the person with whom you have the most difficulty in getting a job done. Describe this person as he appears to you. The farther you go from the middle of each scale toward the end, the stronger the person has the quality described.

Friendly	: 8 : 7 : 6 : 5	4 : 3 : 2 : 1 :	Unfriendly
Rejecting	: 1 : 2 : 3 : 4	5 : 6 : 7 : 8 :	Accepting
Helpful	: 8 : 7 : 6 : 5	4 : 3 : 2 : 1 :	Frustrating
Unenthusiastic	: 1 : 2 : 3 : 4	5 : 6 : 7 : 8 :	Enthusiastic
Tense	: 1 : 2 : 3 : 4	5 : 6 : 7 : 8 :	Relaxed
Distant	: 1 : 2 : 3 : 4	5 : 6 : 7 : 8 :	Close
Cold	: 1 : 2 : 3 : 4	5 : 6 : 7 : 8 :	Warm
Cooperative	: 8 : 7 : 6 : 5	4 : 3 : 2 : 1 :	Uncooperative
Supportive	: 8 : 7 : 6 : 5	4 : 3 : 2 : 1 :	Hostile
Boring	: 1 : 2 : 3 : 4	5 : 6 : 7 : 8 :	Interesting

Adapted from F. Fiedler and M. Chemers, *Leadership and Effective Management* (Glenview, Ill.: Scott, Foresman, 1974), p. 75.

preferred coworker. The LPC score is obtained by totaling up point values for all the items. A low score indicates the degree to which an individual is ready to reject those with whom he or she cannot work. This attitude is reflected by describing in negative terms coworkers' attributes that are not directly related to their work. The lower the LPC score, the greater the task orientation of the leader. A more positive score indicates a willingness to perceive even the worst coworker as having some reasonably positive attributes. A high LPC person sees both good and bad points in his least preferred coworker and is more motivated to use a relations-oriented leadership style.

Fiedler interprets a leader LPC score to be an index of a motivational hierarchy, or of behavioral preferences. The high LPC person, who perceives his or her least preferred coworker in a more favorable light, has as his basic goal the desire to be related with others—to work in a positive group atmosphere. If the leader reaches this goal, he or she will want to reach the secondary goals of status and esteem. In return, the leader wants the subordinates to show admiration and recognition.

The low LPC person has a different motivational system. This person's basic goal is task accomplishment. Self-esteem is gained through achievement of task-related goals. However, so long as accomplishing the task presents no problems, this person also tends to be friendly and pleasant in relations with subordinates. It is only when task accomplishment is threatened that good interpersonal relations assume secondary importance to accomplishing the task.

Figure 13–6 plots the three basic variables on a continuum. The eight octants, which represent combinations of the three variables, are arranged in order of leader favorableness from most favorable to least favorable. The model assumes that a leader will have the most control and influence in groups that fall into octant 1, that is, in which group atmosphere is high, position power is strong, and subordinates perform structured tasks. The leader will have somewhat less control and influence in octant 2, where group atmosphere is high and tasks are structured but position power is weak. As we proceed along the continuum to groups in octant 8, the leader's control and influence will be very small. In this situation, group atmosphere

	Most favorable							Least favorable
Group atmosphere	Good	Good	Good	Good	Poor	Poor	Poor	Poor
Task structure	Structured		Unstructured		Structured		Unstructured	
Leader position power	Strong	Weak	Strong	Weak	Strong	Weak	Strong	Weak
	1	2	3	4	5	6	7	8

FIGURE 13–6.   Continuum of the Three Basic Variables of Leadership

Adapted from: Fiedler, F., "Engineer the Job to Fit the Manager," *Harvard Buiness Review,* 1965, 45, p. 118. Reproduced with permission, *Harvard Business Review.*

is poor, the group is performing unstructured tasks, and the leader has little position power.

Some typical groups that might be placed in these various octants are: octants 1 and 5, telephone offices, craft shops, meat departments, grocery departments; octants 2 and 6, basketball and football teams, surveying parties; octants 3 and 7, general foremen, ROTC groups, research chemists, military planning groups; and octants 4 and 8, disaster groups, church groups, and mental health groups. The critical question is "What kind of leadership style is most effective in each of the different group situations?"

Findings: The average results of the various studies conducted by Fiedler and his associates are plotted in Figure 13–7, the basic contingency model. The horizontal axis of this figure is the continuum of Figure 13–6. The vertical axis plots the leader's LPC score. Above the midline, the solid line on the graph indicates a positive relationship between LPC and group performance. That is, high-LPC leaders performed better than low-LPC leaders. Below the midline, the solid line indicates that low-LPC leaders performed better than did high-LPC leaders. The solid line represents the best predictions between a leader's LPC score and work group effectiveness.

As Figure 13–7 shows, task-motivated (low-LPC) leaders performed most effectively in the most favorable situations, octants 1, 2, and 3, and in the least favorable situation, octant 8. Low-LPC leaders are basically motivated by task accomplishments. In favorable situations in which their group

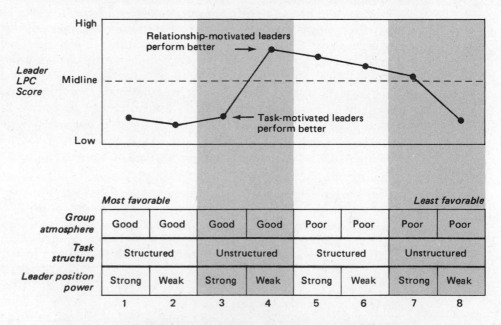

FIGURE 13–7.   Basic Contingency Model

Adapted from: Fiedler, F., "Engineer the Job to Fit the Manager," *Harvard Business Review,* 1965, 45, p. 118. Reproduced with permission, *Harvard Business Review.*

supports them, their power position is high, and the task is structured, they will strive to develop pleasant work relations by directing subordinates. Their behavior will seem friendly and considerate toward coworkers. In the unfavorable situation (octant 8), in which the task is unstructured, they lack group support, and their position power is low, they will devote their energies to achieving the primary goal of the group.

Figure 13–7 also indicates situations in which a high-LPC leader is most likely to perform better. High-LPC leaders obtain best group efficiency under conditions of moderate or intermediate favorableness, octants 4, 5, 6, and 7. Octants 4 and 5 describe situations in which (1) the task is structured but the leader is disliked and must demonstrate concern for the emotions of subordinates, or (2) the leader is liked, but the group has an unstructured task, and the leader must depend upon the willingness and creativity of the group's members to accomplish the goals.

Implications: Several important implications can be drawn from this model. *First*, both relationship-motivated and task-motivated leaders perform well under certain situations but not under others. An outstanding manager at one level who gets promoted to another level may fail at higher levels because his or her motivational base does not match the demands of the situation. The practice of a company's taking its most successful floor supervisor and promoting that individual to production manager is such a case. The contingency model suggests that the supervisor's failure in the new position may not indicate a lack of intellectual ability, but rather a change in leadership situation to one in which the individual is no longer able to function at his or her best. The task has probably changed from a relatively structured one to a less structured task situation. Assuming that this person's position power and ability to get along with the group didn't change, the contingency model would predict two different leadership styles as being effective. That is, the supervisor may move from a situation requiring a task-motivated style to a situation requiring a more human-relations style.

Second, it is not totally accurate to speak of a good or poor leader. Rather, one must think of a leader who performs well in one situation but not in another. The example of the supervisor promoted to production manager illustrates this point.

Third, the performance of a leader depends upon both the leader's motivational bases and the situation. Therefore, the organization can change leadership effectiveness by changing the motivational states of the leader or by modifying the favorableness of the leader's situation.

Validity of Model: Studies to determine the validity of this model in a wide variety of groups, teams, and organizations (e.g., research teams, department stores, military units, basketball teams, hospital wards) have raised several important issues.[18]

First, what does LPC mean? Early in his research, Fiedler assumed it was a measure of the leader's personality. His most recent interpretation is that it reflects an individual's motivational structure with respect to need gratification from groups. Despite the fact that the interpretation of a leader's LPC score is cloudy, it does seem to reflect a leader's underlying motivational bases and not a leader's cognitive ability or basic personality and it has been highly related to group productivity.

Second, the reliability of a leader's LPC score over time is open to question. The lack of reliability of the LPC score seriously limits the validity of the research supporting the model. It seems hardly worthwhile to change a work situation on the basis of a leader's LPC score if there is probability that the leader's LPC score will change within a short period of time and will vary according to group performance. That is, high performance of a group can increase a leader's LPC score, while low performance can cause a decrease. While it is true that changes in the LPC score occur as a result of changes in an individual's life and the leader's success or nonsuccess, the job cannot be engineered to fit the manager if the manager's motivational bases are constantly changing.

Third, the model does not take into account the fact that the leader can influence the task structure because of his or her knowledge of the situation. That is, a leader can take a nonroutine task and provide some structure to it before assigning it to subordinates. They, in turn, perceive the task to be more structured than unstructured. The leader can also affect the group's atmosphere through a particular style of behavior. A leader who is approachable, friendly, and supportive may facilitate the development of group harmony and high group cohesiveness. On the other hand, a leader who is aloof, unapproachable, and unfriendly may create hostility and resentment in the work group.

Fourth, since LPC is a unidimensional concept, it implies that if an individual is highly motivated toward task accomplishment, he or she must be completely unconcerned with relations among group members, or oriented away from social concerns, and vice versa. But it is possible for an individual to be both task- and relations-motivated. Thus, a leader's orientation with respect to one dimension should not completely determine the orientation on the other. The leader may well be motivated by both task and relational concerns.

In summary, Fiedler's contingency model stresses that both relations-oriented and task-oriented leaders can perform well, but under different conditions. Task-motivated leaders perform best in situations in which their power and influence are either very high or low, as well as in situations in which their task is highly structured and there are good leader-member relations. Relations-motivated leaders perform best under conditions of moderate favorableness, in which the power and influence they have are mixed, leader-member relations are low, and the structure is either high or low.

House's Path-Goal Model

Puzzled by the contradictory findings in the leadership area, Robert J. House developed a model that is based on Vroom's theory of motivation (see Chapter 11). House's model of leadership effectiveness does not indicate the "one best way" to lead, but suggests that a leader must select a style most appropriate to the particular situation.[19]

The basic idea of House's model is that one function of a leader is to enhance the psychological states of subordinates so that the result is motivation to perform a task or satisfaction with the job. The leader's function is to increase the personal satisfactions of subordinates for goal attainment and to make the path to these satisfactions easier to obtain. This is accomplished by clarifying the nature of the task, by reducing the road blocks from successful task completion, and by increasing the opportunities for subordinates to obtain personal satisfactions. The model states that, to the extent the leader accomplishes these functions, the motivation of subordinates will increase. Subordinates are satisfied with their jobs to the extent that performance leads to things that they highly value. The function of the leader is to help subordinates reach these highly valued job-related goals. The specific style of leadership behavior is determined by two situational variables: characteristics of subordinates and task structure.

Characteristics of Subordinates.   With respect to subordinates' characteristics, the model states that leader behavior will be viewed acceptable to subordinates to the extent that the subordinates see such behavior as either an immediate source of satisfaction or as needed for future satisfaction. For example, if subordinates have a high need for esteem and affiliation, supportive leader behavior may serve as an immediate source of need satisfaction. On the other hand, subordinates with high needs for autonomy, responsibility, and self-actualization are more likely to be motivated by leaders who are directive rather than supportive. Similarly, individuals who are internally oriented (believe they can control their own behavior) as opposed to externally oriented (believe that their behavior is controlled by fate) prefer leaders who demonstrate more supportive behavior than those low on this dimension.

Supportive leadership is demonstrated by a friendly and approachable leader who shows concern for the status, well-being, and needs of subordinates. Such a leader does little things to make the work more pleasant, treats members as equals, and is friendly and approachable. Where subordinates perceive themselves as having the ability to perform the task, a leader who demonstrates constant coaching and directiveness is likely to be perceived unfavorably. Directive leadership is characterized by a leader who lets subordinates know what is expected of them, gives specific guidance as to what should be done and how it should be done, maintains definite standards of performance, and asks that group members follow standard rules and regulations.

Task Structure.   The second major variable in the path-goal model is the task structure. Where path-goal relationships are apparent because of the routine nature of the task, attempts by the leader to further clarify path-goal relaionships will be perceived by subordinates as unnecessarily close control. While such close control may increase performance by preventing "goofing off," it will also result in decreased job satisfaction. For example, axle assemblers in an auto plant probably cannot derive any intrinsic satisfactions (i.e., esteem, self-actualization) from the performance of this highly structured and repetitive task. Directive leadership style is likely to be perceived by the assemblers as redundant and excessive and directed at keeping them working on unsatisfying tasks. Within this task structure, a leader who is supportive is likely to have more satisfied employees than one who is directive. A supportive leadership style is likely to increase the worker's extrinsic satisfaction (e.g., satisfaction within supervising company and the like) on a job that provides little intrinsic satisfaction.

On the other hand, when tasks are highly unstructured, a more directive leadership style is appropriate to the extent that it helps subordinates cope with task uncertainty and clarifies the paths leading to highly valued goals. For example, the manager of an industrial relations team who gives subordinates guidance and direction on how to process a grievance for arbitration is attempting to clarify the direction of the subordinates for the attainment of an organizational goal. This style of leadership is not perceived as excessive and redundant since it helps the subordinates reach their goals, a source of intrinsic job satisfaction.

Figure 13–8 illustrates the effect of task structure on leadership behavior and subordinates' job satisfaction. On the horizontal axis is a leader's directive behavior, ranging from high to low. On the vertical axis is job satisfaction, ranging from low to high. Task structure moderates the relationship between leader behavior and subordinate job satisfaction. When the task is highly structured, the leader who does not give direction and excessive coaching is likely to have highly satisfied subordinates. On the other hand, when the task is unstructured, a directive leadership style is likely to increase subordinate's job satisfaction. Several other variables (e.g., performance, supervisor satisfaction, promotion satisfaction) could replace job satisfaction, but the relationships in the figure would not change.

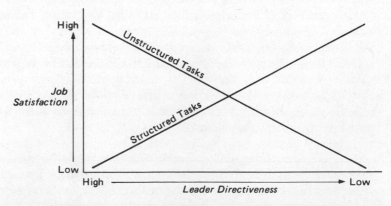

FIGURE 13–8.   A Path-Goal Leadership Model

Findings: It is too early to make anything but a preliminary assessment of House's path-goal theory of leadership because there is so little research data to go on. However, early research findings have been encouraging. Workers performing highly structured tasks have reported high job satisfaction when their immediate supervisor uses a supportive (as opposed to directive) leadership style. On the other hand, managers performing in unstructured task environments are more productive when their immediate supervisor uses a more directive leadership style. However, this style does not always lead to high job satisfactions.[20]

Implications: The implications of these findings for managers indicate that the kind of leadership style needed varies according to the situation. The findings support the notion that while shop-floor personnel prefer a supportive leader, to gain some intrinsic satisfaction from performing routine and often boring tasks, middle level and professional employees work better with a more directive leadership style. At these levels, job descriptions are usually written without much specification, and a directive leader can clarify the task(s) and the goal(s) for the subordinates. It does not seem unreasonable that different leadership styles will be required for different occupational groupings and levels of the organization's hierarchy.

Contingent Leader Reward Behavior

Very recently, a new approach to the study of leadership, with operant or reinforcement theory (see Chapter 6) as an underlying theoretical framework, has emerged. According to this approach, the manager is particularly important in structuring contingencies of reinforcement that influence the behavior of subordinates.[21] The manager is assumed to act as a leader by providing environmental cues (discriminative stimuli) that indicate expected behavior on the part of subordinates and also by providing rewards (reinforcers) to subordinates that are contingent upon the behavior of the subordinates.

A leader who provides environmental cues establishes expectations that are intended to guide subordinate behavior *before* the behavior occurs. This is similar to the concept of initiating structure, because the manager "initiates structure" for the subordinate's task *prior to* the performance of the task. In this respect, this operant approach is fairly consistent with the Ohio State leadership studies and with Fiedler's concept of a task-oriented leader.

However, the operant approach provides an additional viewpoint that appears to be missing from the Ohio State leadership studies, Fiedler's contingency theory, and House's path-goal theory. The operant viewpoint attempts to provide an answer to the question: What does the manager do *after* the performance of the subordinate? None of the other approaches deal with this question. In answering the question, the operant viewpoint considers two dimensions: contingent positive leader reward behavior and contingent punitive leader behavior.

Contingent positive leader reward behavior is the degree to which the leader administers rewards that are contingent upon the desirable performance of subordinates. That is, if a leader practices contingent positive leader reward behavior, then rewards are administered only when subordinate performance meets some desirable level. Conversely, *contingent punitive leader behavior* is the degree to which the leader administers punishment (especially oral reprimands) that are contingent upon undesirable subordinate behavior. In general, the operant approach theorizes that subordinate performance is predominantly related to contingent positive leader reward behavior. That is, when leaders provide rewards to subordinates that are contingent upon subordinate performance, future subordinate performance is likely to improve.

For the most part, the leader reward approach focuses on the superior-subordinate relationship and does not directly consider the environment surrounding this relationship (e.g., organizational structure, group processes). However, the approach can be considered as a contingency theory because the prescription of effective leader behavior is contingent upon subordinate behavior. The effective leader is generally considered to be one who provides rewards that are somehow contingent upon the performance-related behavior of subordinates.

An effective leader is one who is skilled at pinpointing critical performance-related work behaviors and then structuring contingencies of reinforcement to increase (or decrease in the case of undesirable behaviors) that behavior. The critical factor is the viewpoint that the reward behavior of the leader is made contingent upon the performance-related behavior of subordinates. In general, the leader reward approach can be considered an *internal contingency theory* because it considers only the superior-subordinate relationship, while other contingency theories, such as Fiedler's and House's, are *external contingency theories* because they consider factors in the surrounding environment (group, task, and power).

Pat, the production superintendent, was discussing his foremen with Mack Bronsky, the personnel training consultant from corporate staff. They were talking about what it took to be a good leader if you were a foreman. As usual, Pat was in high spirits and he didn't hesitate to share his opinion with Mack.

"Yep," said Pat, "I've never been to college, but I've been around here long enough to know what it takes to be a good leader. I've got two young foremen now, and they are about as opposite as can be in terms of leadership effectiveness."

"Sam is the best leader of all the young foremen. First, he lets his crew know what he expects. That doesn't mean that he doesn't listen to his crew, but he is always clear about what kind of performance he expects from them. Next, if his crew is successful in achieving its performance levels then Sam is very good at telling them how pleased he is. Sam's crew knows that Sam

will give appropriate recognition when it's deserved. Last, Sam isn't afraid to let his crew know he's displeased if their performance isn't up to par. But he's not an extremist on this. When he lets one of the crew know he's unhappy, it's usually because he has just cause and it's usually taken seriously."

"I'm afraid Joe just isn't an effective leader at all. First, he tried to be buddy-buddy with his crew, thinking that if he's nice to them that they will perform well. Frankly, that doesn't seem to have much effect, and when their performance drops, he gets on their back with a ferocity that's almost obscene. When his crew doesn't do well, Joe has trouble controlling his own temper. I'm afraid Joe just hasn't developed as a leader at all. If he doesn't get any better within the next three or four months, I'll have to get rid of him."

Research on Leader Reward Behavior.   The leader reward behavior approach was originated in the early 1970s.[22] Since then, several studies have investigated the question of whether leader contingent positive reward behavior is related to subordinate performance. In single-time studies, researchers found that positive reward behavior was positively related to performance.[23] In longitudinal studies, researchers have found that leader positive reward behavior was positively related to performance.[24] Positive reward behavior tends to cause subordinate performance rather than subordinate performance tending to cause positive reward behavior. Although these studies have been few in number, they have provided consistent results from a diversity of samples. The leader reward behavior research is backed up by a growing number of laboratory studies that have generally shown positive relationships between contingent rewards and performance. Most of this laboratory research is not directly associated with leadership research, but the general conclusion remains: Rewards that are administered contingent upon performance do improve subsequent performance.

In addition, a few of these studies have compared leader contingent reward behavior with the more traditional leadership dimension of consideration, which could be called noncontingent reward behavior. In all studies, contingent reward behavior was found to have stronger relationships to subordinate performance than consideration.

Undoubtedly, the viewpoint that leadership is a process of reinforcement remains in the emergent stages, but the early empirical results appear promising. Replication of research in more diverse samples is required. Most importantly, a complete theoretical viewpoint that will consider the impact of contingencies that are both external and internal to the leader-subordinate relationship are required.

LEADERSHIP IN COMPLEX SITUATIONS

In the most fundamental sense, the leader's role is to mobilize human and material resources in the accomplishment of a task. This activity is usually considered as the exercise of leadership. Based on what people feel they know about leadership, individuals make decisions about how a manager *ought* to act toward subordinates in particular situations. Turning back to the opening of this chapter, how did you decide to resolve the problem facing the manager of the chemical plant? Also, recall how you defined leadership. Do you want to change your definition? If so, how?

Clearly, we are a long way from being able to offer leaders prescriptions about how to behave. The hundreds and hundreds of leadership studies are filled with contradictory results and often leave one confused. It has become apparent that one style of supervision might be effective within a given situation, but the same style might lead to low performance in a different situation. This realization has culminated in the situational or contingency approach to leadership. The contingency approach argues that appropriate leadership behavior is a function of many different factors, among them the characteristics of the leader, the characteristics of subordinates, the nature of the task, the organization's structure, and the group processes.

Several factors affecting the leadership process will be discussed in this section. This should help you to understand the complexity of the leadership situation. The list, although not exhaustive, does identify important factors that should be considered and evaluated by managers.[25] Because of the interactive and multiplicative relationships between the variables, it must be remembered that although they are discussed separately, they do not act separately from one another.

Nature of the Work Task.   In simple, highly routine, and structured tasks, a considerate or supportive leadership style may be more closely related to subordinates' high job satisfaction and performance than a more directive leadership style. In many instances, workers find highly routine jobs unrewarding and boring. Where a supervisor is in frequent contact with the workers, this contact is likely to be perceived as a source of harassment. Under these conditions, workers do not need much supervision and therefore prefer a leader who is not continually looking over their shoulders. For example, warehouse workers and secretaries seem to prefer a more considerate leader (as opposed to autocratic) in order to compensate for the routine working conditions and frequent interactions with their boss.

On the other hand, in less structured tasks, subordinates appreciate more direction by their immediate supervisor. In these tasks, the supervisor who can contribute to the subordinates' effective and satisfying work experience by giving them direction and guidance is perceived as exercising the most effective leadership style. A leader's behavior can affect subordinates' perceptions of the structuredness of the task. A sales manager can help subordinates make a sale by instructing them who to see, how the person likes to be treated, and what proper promotional pitch to use to close the sale.

Organizational Level.   Different leadership styles are often needed at different levels in the organization. Most high-level executives are implicitly asked to operate at two organizational levels; an executive may be in charge of other executives (peers) or subordinates or both. For example, in a nursing unit the head nurse is in charge of other nurses, licensed practical nurses, orderlies, and nurses' aides. The head nurse's leadership style may be directly related to the performance or satisfaction of nurses' aides, orderlies, and other nurses. Higher level supervisors may also compensate for lower level supervisor behavior. The head nurse's considerate style of leadership behavior may compensate for the ward nurse's directive style with aides and orderlies.

Supervisor's Upward Influence.   The degree to which subordinates perceive their supervisor as a means of securing valued work-related goals from higher management may also determine the effectiveness of the leaders. Supervisors who are advocates of their subordinates' positions to higher management—who "go to bat" for their subordinates—may be able to bring to their subordinates payoffs that they perceive as desirable. Thus the considerate, upwardly influential supervisor can act as a facilitator to higher management for subordinates and, by doing so, satisfy employees' needs. The time spent with top management may be more important for subordinates than the time that the supervisor actually spends directing their activities.

Work-group Homogeneity.   The degree of homogeneity in the work group (the similarity of the members) and how the leader relates to it affect the performance and satisfaction of the work group. This is especially true for groups whose members are dependent upon each other for successful accomplishment. In a football team, the team's score depends on the coordination of each of the individual's efforts on offense and defense. If the team is highly cohesive, a considerate style of leadership behavior may be appropriate to motivate team members for task accomplishment. If the team is torn by strife, the leader may choose to use a more directive style. Similarly, in the waning seconds of a close football game, the coach may become more directive in his leadership style. This increase in leader directiveness will be tolerated by the team so that they may win the game. Group cohesiveness will not decline under these conditions because the players need additional direction to win.

Work-group Size.   As pointed out in Chapter 9, work-group size affects member satisfaction, level of decision making, communication channels, and leadership style. In small work groups, leaders tend to perform much like social specialists, emphasizing interpersonal functions. In larger groups, where individual members are relatively autonomous, leaders tend to emphasize task-goal accomplishment and resolution of conflict between the individual members of the group. One reason for this is that in small groups members can often best achieve success and satisfaction by working together. In large groups, success is less dependent upon group cohesiveness.

Reward Systems.   One of the easiest ways to motivate many employees toward task accomplishment is to demonstrate to them that there is a direct relationship between performance and rewards. For example, where organizational pay policies make this relationship specific, the leader's behavior can play an important role in determining subordinate pay. Where organizational policies make this impossible, such as for an assembly-line worker or workers whose pay is determined by time in the system, supervisor efforts to increase performance may be to no avail. It is important for the leader to control the rewards (salary, promotions, etc.) that subordinates deem desirable.

Subordinate Values.   As indicated in Chapters 11 and 12, there are movements to increase the humanization of work. The subordinates' attainment of challenging and responsible jobs is a task for supervisors at all levels where workers are seeking advancement. Supportive leader behavior provides a means for employees to satisfy their ego and social needs. Supportive leadership style gives employees greater opportunities for regulating and controlling their own activities and has been found to increase the degree to which individuals can express their various and diverse needs. Directive or task-centered leader behavior reduces the degree to which social needs can be satisfied through the accomplishment of a task. Therefore, subordinates seeking to satisfy social needs on the job will find greater opportunity to satisfy their needs with supportive leadership styles, and less opportunity with directive leadership styles.

Organizational Climate.   The organizational climate is the set of attributes that workers perceive about their organization.[26] An organization having many rules and regulations and a formal organizational hierarchy to make all decisions would elicit expression of one set of attributes about the organization, whereas an organization that did not use these mechanisms would elicit different responses from its employees. The significant fact to note is that the organization's climate can be partially created by the leader's behavior. If employees perceive both the organization and their leaders as autocratic, the employees are likely to have low job satisfaction, negative attitudes toward the company, low innovation and productivity. If the organization is perceived as achievement-oriented and the leaders are considerate, the employees are likely to respond by exhibiting high levels of achievement, high job satisfaction, positive attitudes toward the company, and high performance.

=============================== **SUMMARY** ===============================

The basic purpose of this chapter was to discuss the leadership process. Leadership was distinguished from the leader in that it is a process in which one individual influences others toward achieving a goal. How a leader attempts to influence others depends on the power available to the leader. Five types of power were discussed—legitimate, reward, coercive, referent, and expert.

First, the trait model of leadership was examined. The trait model assumes that successful leaders possess certain personality traits that distinguish them from unsuccessful leaders. While a number of specific traits were identified—most importantly, intelligence, social maturity and breadth, human relations attitudes, and inner motivation and achievement drives—no specific traits were found to be common to successful leaders across various situations. Because this approach did not lead to an adequate understanding of the leadership process, researchers turned to studying the behaviors of leaders. Two styles of leadership behavior were discussed—consideration and initiating structure. Once again, it was found that no one particular style was effective in all situations.

Contingency theories do not seek to identify universal traits or behaviors, but rather focus on the situational factors facing the leader. The theories of Fiedler, House, and the operant conditioning group were examined. Fiedler focuses on the effective diagnosis of the situation in which the leader will operate. Thus the emphasis is on understanding the nature of the situation and then matching the correct leadership style of the individual to that situation. Three elements are identified in the situation: group atmosphere, task structure, and the leader's power position. Each leader has a motivational system (LPC) that indicates under what combinations of these situations that style is likely to be effective.

House's path-goal model sees leadership behavior as contingent on the characteristics of the subordinates and the nature of the task. The goal of the leader is to reduce the stumbling blocks that hinder employees from reaching their goals. If the task is routine, then a leader who is more considerate of employees will more likely be in charge of satisfied and productive employees than a leader who is not as considerate.

The leader reward behavior model studies the impact of rewards and punishment on subordinate behavior. Positive rewards, such as recognition for a job well done, pay increases, and promotion serve to strengthen and increase the individual's motivation and performance. The administration of punishment, such as an oral reprimand from a manager, acts to discourage or extinguish undesired behaviors on the part of the employee.

The last section of the chapter presented a representative list of factors important to an understanding of the complexity of the leadership process.

DISCUSSION QUESTIONS

1. What is the difference between a leader and the leadership process?

2. What functions does a leader have to exercise in most work groups?

3. Why has the trait approach to leadership failed? Why, then, do managers still employ the trait approach?

4. Describe situations under which "consideration" and "initiating structure" leadership behaviors are most likely to be successful.

5. Describe Fiedler's contingency model.

6. What background factors (personality motives) do you think affect whether or not a person is a high-LPC or a low-LPC leader?

7. What sources of power do leaders have at their command to influence subordinates' behaviors?

8. Should leadership style be rigid or flexible?

9. Is it feasible to alter the job to fit the particular style of the leader in order that the leader be more effective? If so, what things might you change in the job of a foreman, a sales manager, of an R & D researcher?

MANAGERIAL PROBLEMS

BUDGET MOTORS, INC.

Plant Y was the largest and oldest of six assembly plants of Econocar division, a subsidiary of Budget Motors Inc. It had close to 10,000 employees and was managed by Mr. Wickstrom. During the last few years, it fell behind all the others in performance. Not unexpectedly, headquarter management (HQM) started showing some uneasiness as there were signs that things would not improve in the foreseeable future. In its attempt to straighten things out, it has exerted steady pressure and issued specific directions for local plant management to follow.

Mr. Wickstrom was a respected and competent manager. He was not new to the responsibility of running a large plant. After all, he came up the hard way through the ranks, and was well known for his ambition, technical competence, human relations skills, and hard work. Moreover, he was a no-nonsense manager, well-liked by his subordinates. Under his leadership, plant Y had performed adequately well until the energy and environmental crises teamed up to hit the auto industry really hard in the early 1970's. At that time, in all six plants, there was a hysteria to fill the demand for little compacts that are economically cheap to run and environmentally safe to use. The speed of the lines was stepped up, three-shift operations were begun, and workers were hired (mostly immigrants), and a large number of managers had to be placed in new jobs.

Although all the plants of the Econocars division had their share of the stress and strains inherent in the sudden changeover from bigger to smaller cars, the managers of these plants adapted themselves differently to this new development in the market situation. Instead of comparing Mr. Wickstrom's adaptive behaviour with that of his counterparts in other plants, we would rather concentrate on contrasting his own style with that of Mr. Rhenman, his successor in the same plant. Following are some examples that illustrate how Mr. Wickstrom tried to cope with this crisis atmosphere:

1. One day, while doing his regular plant tour, he personally ordered the foreman of a given section to change the sequence of assembling the instrument panels. He thought this change would speed up the operation. When his production manager, Mr. Aberg, found out about the new system, he got upset because it disturbed the schedule. He went to see Mr. Wickstrom in his office and to make a new suggestion about the sequencing—one that coordinates Mr. Wickstrom's plan with his own. Much to Mr. Aberg's surprise, Mr. Wickstrom reacted in a rude manner and told Mr. Aberg that things would remain the way he had ordered.

2. When Mr. Wickstrom read the weekly performance record of the body assembly line, he flew into a terrific temper and called in the foreman of this line, Mr. Jorgen, to his office and threatened to fire him if the production was not speeded up. This tactic shook up Mr. Jorgen who instantly thought of the incident two weeks before when his colleague, Mr. Ulf, had indeed been fired. He tried to justify the slowness of production by complaining that he was operating against overwhelming handicaps: antiquated and rundown equipment, inexperienced workforce and, uninteresting and noninvolving job structure. Unfortunately, nobody cared to listen to him.

3. One day, the supply of electric power for the plant was reduced and the next day it was shut off completely. This was due to a break-down in the power station outside the plant. It was not Mr. Wickstrom's policy to run the plant by committee meetings, but faced with this crisis at hand, he summoned a meeting of the production managers and the foremen. It was clear that the electric company would need at least a week to repair its network. The upshot of the meeting was a decision to shut down production and to seek union's support for a half pay for the workers in exchange for two days of the paid holidays. Upon submitting the minutes of this meeting to the HQM, his decisions were immediately vetoed. The HQM argued that since economical compacts sell almost as fast as they can be rolled off lines, production should not stop and that a mobile auxiliary power unit be brought in, no matter what its cost would be. This proved to be a very expensive proposition and it also meant a lot of trouble for workers and managers alike. For no sooner than Mr. Wickstrom called in his second meeting to inform his top aides as to the feedback he received

from the HQM, than some of his managers angrily protested this high-handed interference in their "domestic affairs." Here again, they said, is one more example of the H.Q. boys telling us how to run our show. Other plant managers, equally concerned, blamed their boss, Mr. Wickstrom, for his inability to stand by his guns, fight his case back with the HQM and challenge its excessive domination like other plant managers do. They felt that they were put at the order-receiving side by the HQM which has no real feeling for what was going on in the plant. Some plant managers further complained that carrying out daily instructions from HQM had become Mr. Wickstrom's chief preoccupation. Managers in such staff services as accounting, quality control, material control and personnel also complained that they themselves were receiving too many specific orders from HQM. Like their line counterparts, they generally resented this contracting behavior on the part of the HQM. They complained that they were no longer allowed to run their own departments or stations, or to manage within their sphere of competence. This in turn, left them no choice but to withdraw legitimate authority from their immediate subordinates and interfere in the handling of their own affairs, thereby compounding the felany throughout the hierarchy.

In responding to the voices from below, HQM argued that the trouble with plant Y lies in Mr. Wickstrom's lack of control rather than in bad equipment, boring jobs and inexperienced personnel.

With the intensification of the energy crisis caused by the sudden outbreak of the Mideast War of October, 1973, the demand for little cars far outstripped the available supply. Being dissatisfied with plant Y's performance, HQM decided to replace Mr. Wickstrom by Mr. Rhenman. The latter accepted the job on condition that he should have a "carte blanche" in running his own show for a reasonable period of time. This he got from HQM which also assured him that there would be no interference and that he was free to proceed in any manner he saw fit.

At the outset, Rhenman indicated that although HQM thought that dead wood should be removed from the staff, he disagreed and would give everyone ample opportunity to prove his worth. (It developed, in fact, that only a handful of people in an organization of 10,000 were dismissed during his regime). He asked for money from HQM to modernize the plant, starting first with the cafeteria and washrooms used by blue-collar workers. He also went to the cafeteria himself during lunch hours, mingled with workers, foremen and the lower level managers. He not only listened to their complaints, but also secured their cooperation and suggestions. He encouraged groups to meet regularly to solve common problems and, more important, to engage his long-range planning and consultation to prevent daily crisis. His foremen often met informally, thereby increasing lateral communication. He structured an ongoing problem-solving dialogue between his staff and line personnel. Through this dialogue, staff personnel had learned how irrelevant or self-defensive their services had been in the line. He inspired confidence and loyalty and erased the fear and crisis syndrome that had prevailed. He did not change the formal organization structure of the plant. He expected his managers to set goals for their units and be responsible for their achievements. He delegated to them the requisite authority, and left them alone to perform their jobs.

Now, after about six months in his job, plant Y has started heading towards a rebound. Its performance record shows marked improvements. Mr. Rhenman is promoted to a top executive job at the H.Q. Interestingly enough, plant Y is performing well without him. On the other hand, Mr. Wickstrom was given an early retirement.

QUESTIONS

1. Compare and contrast the leadership style of
    a. Wickstrom and Rhenman
    b. Napoleon and Gutexkov
2. Who is to blame for Wickstrom's failure? Why did he lose his magic touch?
3. What caused plant Y to become an outstanding success?
4. Does it really make sense to talk about choosing your own leadership style as some academics lead us to believe?
5. What lessons have you learned from that case?

BUDGET MOTORS CASE—Evaluation Matrix

Analysis: *Balanced versus Imbalanced*	*Scholarship:* *Ability to use OB concepts and tools*	*Organization and Coherence*

PART A
1. Comparing leadership styles of Wickstrom and Rhenman.
   a. Differences
      orientation: task vs. people
      sources of power
      motivational assumption
      in means of reaching management goals
   b. Parallels
      both accept management goals
      both interested in results
2. What caused plant Y to become an outstanding success?
   a. Rhenman administrative strategy. What did he do?
   b. Rhenman initial position. What did he inherit from his predecessor?

    c. Rhenman chosen strategy.
3. What has become of Wickstrom?
   Why did he lose his magic touch?
    a. Sudden changes in environ-
      ment
    b. Headquarter's interference:
      Withdrawing legitimate au-
      thority from him, while giving
      it back to Rhenman.
4. Choosing leadership style
   Evaluation of theories of leadership
   The case for contingency theory
   The overexaggerated role of
   leadership.

PART B
5. Lesson Learned
    a. The notion of self-fulfilling
      prophecy
    b. The paradox of control
    c. Situational leadership: Contin-
      gency theory
    d. The factory as a socio-technical
      system
   Overall Evaluation
    a. Ability to tie the 3 OB modules
      together: breadth
    b. Ability to diagnose Plant Y
      situation accurately: depth
    c. Coherence of analysis.

TACK FREIGHT COMPANY

The Tack Freight Company is a small, independent hauler that operates in the northeastern section of Pennsylvania. The company delivers
freight from Youngstown, Ohio, to New York City and adjacent points between. During the past several years, the company has grown to where it has
45 tractors, 100 trailers, and more than 50 drivers. Mechanics, maintenance
personnel, and office staff together add about 75 more employees. Because
of this size, the president of the company, Randy Harrison, decided that he
could not personnally keep in touch with all aspects of the company and
that some new organizational structure was needed. After an extensive
study conducted by the consulting firm of Straka and Bowersox, Randy
decided on a new structure. The company was reorganized into three divisions: maintenance and heavy equipment repairs, personnel, and marketing. As a result of this reorganization, three new managerial positions were
created.

When Stephen Millman was appointed as manager of the personnel division, there was much skepticism among the drivers. Steve had been in the office for most of his career, and, according to one driver, "couldn't find a tire wrench if his life depended on it." After Steve had been on the job only a short time, he noticed that absenteeism and lateness among the drivers was increasing and the quality of their driving had slackened considerably. After some investigation by Steve, he found out that the person most of the drivers thought should have gotten his new position was Chuck Snow. Chuck had been the dispatcher for the past five years and had been doing a good job handling the drivers. Steve also learned that Chuck had applied for the job he got and that after Steve was appointed by Randy, Chuck went to Randy and complained.

QUESTIONS

1. What are the major situational factors facing Steve?
2. What style of leadership should Steve use?
3. How should Randy handle Chuck Snow?

KEY WORDS

Leader
Leadership
Designated leader
Trait model
Technical skills
Human skills
Conceptual skills
Autocratic leader
Democratic leader
Laissez-faire leader
Consideration
Initiating structure

Fiedler's contingency model
Group atmosphere
Task structure
Power position
LPC
Path-goal model
Contingent positive leader reward
    behavior
Contingent punitive leader
    behavior
Internal contingency theory
External contingency theory

REFERENCES

1. This case was adapted from Vroom, V., A new look at managerial decision-making, *Organizational Dynamics*, 1973, 1, pp. 72–73.

2. Drucker, P., *Management: Tasks, Responsibilities, and Practices* (New York: Harper and Row, 1974).

3. Stogdill, R., Definitions of leadership,

Handbook of Leadership (New York: Free Press, 1974), pp. 7–16.

4. Jacobs, T., *Leadership and Exchange in Formal Organizations* (Alexandria, Va.: Human Resources Research Organization, 1971).

5. French, J., and B. Raven, The bases of social power, in Cartwright, D. (ed.), *Studies in Social Power* (Ann Arbor: Institute for Social Research, 1959), pp. 150–167.

6. Sank, L., Effective and ineffective managerial traits obtained as naturalistic descriptions from executive members of a supercorporation, *Personnel Psychology*, 1974, 27, pp. 423–434.

7. Ghiselli, E., *Explorations in Managerial Talent* (Pacific Palisades, Calif.: Goodyear Publishing, 1971).

8. Katz, R., Skills of an effective administrator, *Harvard Business Review*, 1974, 52, pp. 90–101.

9. Harrell, T., *Managers' Performance and Personality* (Cincinnati: Southwestern Publishing, 1961).

10. Lippitt, R., An experimental study of the effectiveness of democratic and authoritarian group atmosphere, *University of Iowa Studies in Child Welfare*, 1940, 16, pp. 43–195.

11. Stogdill, R., and A. Coons (eds.), *Leadership Behavior: Its Description and Measurement* (Columbus: Bureau of Business Research, Ohio State University, 1957).

12. For an excellent review of this literature, see Schriesheim, C. and S. Kerr, Theories and measures of leadership: A critical appraisal of current and future directions, in Hunt, J., and L. Larson (eds.), *Leadership: The Cutting Edge* (Carbondale: Southern Illinois University Press, 1977), pp. 9–45.

13. Korman, A., Consideration, initiating structure, and organizational criteria: A review, *Personnel Psychology*, 1966, 19, pp. 345–362; Kerr, S., and C. Schriesheim, Consideration, initiating, and organizational criteria: An update of Korman's 1966 review, *Personnel Psychology*, 1974, 27, pp. 555–568.

14. Kerr, S., C. Schriesheim, C. Murphy, and R. Stogdill, Toward a contingency theory of leadership based upon the consideration and initiating structure literature, *Organizational Behavior and Human Performance*, 1974, 12, pp. 62–82.

15. Tannenbaum, R., and W. Schmidt, How to choose a leadership pattern, *Harvard Business Review*, 1958, 36, pp. 95–102; McCall, M., Leaders and leadership: Of substance and shadow, in Hackman, R., E. Lawler, and L. Porter (eds.), *Perspectives on Behavior in Organizations* (New York: McGraw-Hill, 1977), pp. 375–386.

16. Most of this section draws heavily on the work published by Ivancevich, J., A. Szilagyi, and H. Wallace, *Organizational Behavior and Human Performance* (Santa Monica, Calif.: Goodyear Publishing, 1977), pp. 282–284.

17. Fiedler, F., *A Theory of Leadership Effectiveness* (New York: McGraw-Hill, 1967); Fiedler, F. and M. Chemers, *Leadership and Effective Management* (Glenview, Ill.: Scott, Foresman, 1974); Fiedler, F., Personality, motivational systems, and behavior of high and low LPC persons, *Human Relations*, 1972, 25, pp. 391–412.

18. For an excellent review, see Vecchio, R., An empirical examination of the validity of Fiedler's model of leadership effectiveness, *Organizational Behavior and Human Performance*, 1977, 19, pp. 180–206; also see Schriesheim, C., and S. Kerr, Theories and measures of leadership: A critical appraisal of current and future directions, in Hunt, J. and L. Larson (eds.), *Leadership: The Cutting Edge* (Carbondale: Southern Illinois University Press, 1977), pp. 22–27.

19. House, R., A path-goal theory of leadership, *Administrative Science Quarterly*, 1971, 16, pp. 321–338; Some effects of leader behavior on self-esteem, perceived outcomes, goal characteristics, and valences of subordinates: An extension of the path-goal theory of leadership, unpublished working paper (Faculty of Management Studies, University of Toronto, Canada, 1976).

20. Schriesheim, C., and M. VonGlinow, The path-goal theory of leadership: A theoretical and empirical analysis, *Academy of*

Management Journal, 1977, 20, pp. 398–405; Downey, H., J. Sheridan, and J. Slocum, The path-goal theory of leadership: A longitudinal analysis, *Organizational Behavior and Human Performance*, 1976, 16, pp. 156–176; Schriesheim, J. and C. Schriesheim, A test of the path-goal theory of leadership across multiple occupational levels in a large public utility, unpublished manuscript (College of Business Administration, Kent State University, Ohio, 1978).

21.   For summaries of this approach, see Mawhinney, T. and J. Ford, The path-goal theory of leader effectiveness: An operant interpretation, *Academy of Management Review*, 1977, 2, pp. 398–411; Sims, H., The leader as a manager of reinforcement contingencies: An empirical example and a model, in Hunt, J., and L. Larson (eds.), *Leadership: The Cutting Edge* (Carbondale: Southern Illinois University Press, 1977), pp. 121–137; Keller, R., and A. Szilagyi, A longitudinal study of leader reward behavior, subordinate expectancies, and satisfaction, *Personnel Psychology*, 1978, 31, pp. 119–129.

22.   For an excellent overview, see Scott, W., Leadership: A functional analysis, in Hunt, J., and L. Larson (eds.), *Leadership: The Cutting Edge* (Carbondale: Southern Illinois University Press, 1977), pp. 84–93.

23.   Oldham, G., The motivational strategies used by supervisors: Relationships to effectiveness indicators, *Organizational Behavior and Human Performance*, 1976, 15, pp. 66–86; Sims, H., and A. Szilagyi, Leader reward behavior and subordinate satisfaction and performance, *Organizational Behavior and Human Performance*, 1975, 14, pp. 426–438.

24.   Greene, C., A longitudinal investigation of performance reinforcing leader behavior and subordinate satisfaction and performance, paper presented at the Midwest Academy of Management, St. Louis, Missouri, May 1976.

25.   These are adapted from a list suggested by Ritchie, J., Supervision, in Strauss, G., R. Miles, C. Snow, and A. Tannenbaum (eds.), *Organizational Behavior: Research and Issues* (Belmont, Calif.: Wadsworth Publishing, 1976), pp. 66–71.

26.   Joyce, W., and J. Slocum, Organizational climates, in Kerr, S. (ed.), *Organizational Behavior* (Columbus, Ohio: Grid Publishing, 1979).

14

Conflict Processes

This Chapter Contributed by
THOMAS L. RUBLE & RICHARD A. COSIER
Indiana University

14

LEARNING OBJECTIVES

When you have finished reading and studying this chapter you should be able to:

▲ Define conflict and distinguish between conflict and competition.

▲ Identify different levels of conflict within organizations.

▲ Describe different conflict-handling styles and identify their probable effects.

▲ Explain the difference between vertical conflict and horizontal conflict within organizations.

▲ Describe the causes and effects of role conflict.

▲ Identify some basic strategies for managing conflict.

THOUGHT STARTERS

▲ What does conflict mean to you?

▲ In what type of situations should conflict be avoided?

▲ Is conflict ever desirable?

OUTLINE

CONFLICT DEFINED
POSITIVE AND NEGATIVE ASPECTS OF CONFLICT
  Conflict as a Positive Force
  Conflict as a Negative Force
LEVELS OF CONFLICT
  Intrapersonal Conflict
  Interpersonal Conflict
    Conflict-handling Styles
    Research on Conflict-handling Styles
  Intragroup Conflict
    Effects of Intragroup Conflict on Group Process
    Effects of Group Process on Intragroup Conflict
  Intergroup Conflict
  Intraorganizational Conflict
MANAGING CONFLICT
  Structural Methods to Reduce Conflict
    Dominance through Position
    Decoupling
    Buffering with Inventory
    Buffering with a Linking Pin
    Buffering with an Integration Department
  Confrontation
    Negotiation
    Third-party Consultation
  Promoting Cognitive Conflict
    Dialectical Inquiry
    Devil's Advocate Method
SUMMARY
DISCUSSION QUESTIONS
MANAGERIAL PROBLEM
  Acme Aerospace
KEY WORDS
REFERENCES

PEACE TALKS BREAK DOWN
MINE WORKERS ON STRIKE
STUDENTS PROTEST AGAINST TUITION HIKE

Newspapers, radio, and television constantly remind us that conflict is a common occurrence in modern life. Conflict occurs at all levels of social interaction—from international conflict to interpersonal conflict. Moreover, conflict is usually newsworthy because of its frequent destructiveness. It is not surprising, therefore, that there has been a widespread concern for devising means for resolving conflict.

The basic concern of this chapter is the effective management of conflict. However, the chapter will not simply focus on specific techniques for managing conflict. Because the ability to understand and correctly diagnose conflict is a prerequisite to its management, most of this chapter is directed toward achieving a better understanding of conflict processes within organizations.

CONFLICT DEFINED

Conflict is difficult to define because it occurs in many different settings. However, across the diverse settings the essence of conflict seems to be disagreement, contradiction, or incompatibility. Thus, *conflict* is defined as any situation in which there are incompatible goals, cognitions, or emotions within or between individuals or groups and that leads to opposition or antagonistic interaction. This definition recognizes three basic types of conflict:

1. *Goal conflict,* which occurs when desired end-states or preferred outcomes appear to be incompatible.
2. *Cognitive conflict,* which occurs when individuals become aware that their ideas or thoughts are inconsistent.
3. *Affective conflict,* which occurs when feelings or emotions are incompatible, i.e., people literally become "mad" at each other.

One problem in defining and studying conflict has been the tendency to equate conflict and competition. However, conflict is not synonymous with competition. *Competition* involves actions taken by one person to attain his or her preferred goal which may result in the other person not attaining his or her goal. For example, two pole vaulters may compete to achieve the highest vault. Since their is little interaction or interdependency between them, it is unlikely that they will engage in conflict. Of course, competition may produce conflict, but not all conflict involves competition. For example, two managers who agree to pursue the same goal, such as increased sales, are not necessarily competing. But, if they openly disagree on the best sales policy to attain their shared goal, they are in conflict. The distinction between conflict and competition is not made merely to split hairs.[1] Conflict exists in many different forms besides that which may result from competition.

Given our concern with the management of conflict, it is important to understand the different ways in which conflict emerges and is resolved. The processes of conflict resolution are likely to be strongly influenced by the setting of the conflict. Thus, conflict will be examined from a variety of viewpoints. First, we will look at both the positive and negative aspects of conflict. Second, we will discuss the different levels of conflict that can occur within organizations. Finally, we will identify some of the basic strategies for managing conflict.

POSITIVE AND NEGATIVE ASPECTS OF CONFLICT

The likelihood of conflict is high in organizational settings. However, this is not necessarily a negative feature. Often the resolution of conflict leads to constructive problem solving.

Conflict as a Positive Force

The need to resolve conflict may lead to a search for ways to change the current way of doing things. Thus the conflict resolution process can stimulate positive change within the organization. Moreover, the search for ways to resolve conflict may not only lead to innovation and change, but may make change more acceptable, even desirable.[2] Sears provides an example of an organization that benefited from effective conflict resolution. In 1925 Sears established retail stores to sell directly to the public. This was a marked deviation from the previous exclusive focus on catalog sales. The new sales strategy was accompanied with substantial conflict. Sears had a highly centralized decision-making structure that had at least an implicit goal of limiting decision-making discretion at the retail store level. This was in direct conflict with the goal for each retail store to serve its customers' needs. The retail store management needed more autonomy. The search to resolve this conflict led to a new, decentralized structure at Sears in the early 1940s. The decentralized structure apparently contributed to Sears' success in retailing.[3] However, it appears that Sears is now trying to recentralize some of their activities to achieve better integration.

The intentional introduction of conflict into the decision-making process may be beneficial. For example, in group decision making a problem occurs when a cohesive group's desire for agreement interferes with its consideration of alternative solutions. As discussed in Chapter 9, this problem, called *groupthink*,[4] may be reduced if the introduction of conflict takes the form of one or more dissenting opinions. Several famous fiascos (e.g., the Bay of Pigs) serve as examples of group decisions that lacked adequate consideration of conflicting opinions.

Competition that leads to conflict over one or more goals may also have some beneficial effects. Employees who perceive a competitive atmosphere among fellow workers with respect to performance may be motivated to put forth greater effort to come out ahead in such competition.[5] Empirical evidence suggests that competition enhances the quantity of product produced per time period.[6] If an organization's primary goal is to produce a large number of units in a given time period, a competitive atmosphere may be advisable. For example, the employee responsible for the most units produced may be given a bonus.

Conflict as a Negative Force

Conflict can have serious negative effects. One serious problem is the propensity for conflict to divert efforts from goal attainment. Instead of organizational resources being directed primarily toward reaching prescribed goals, resources may be depleted in the attempt to resolve conflict. Time and money are two important resources that are frequently diverted to conflict resolution.

Conflict may also take its toll on the psychological well-being of employees. Several studies have shown exposure to conflicting opinions results in "hard feelings," tension, and anxiety.[7] These hard feelings appear to be a result of conflict threatening important personal goals and beliefs. Over an extended period of time, conflict conditions may make it difficult to establish supportive and trusting relationships.[8]

Finally, competition that requires interaction between the parties appears to have a negative effect on product quality.[9] For example, pressure for results tends to emphasize immediate and measurable goals, such as product quantity, at the expense of product quality. When high product quality is a primary organizational goal, competition may be ill advised.

LEVELS OF CONFLICT

Figure 14–1 illustrates the five levels of conflict that will be examined in this chapter. As indicated in the figure, conflict can be *intrapersonal* (within an individual), *interpersonal* (between individuals), *intragroup* (within a group), or *intergroup* (between groups). Moreover, all these levels of conflict can occur within organizations, resulting in *intraorganizational* conflict. Conflict can also occur between organizations (*interorganizational* conflict), but this level of conflict is beyond the scope of this chapter.

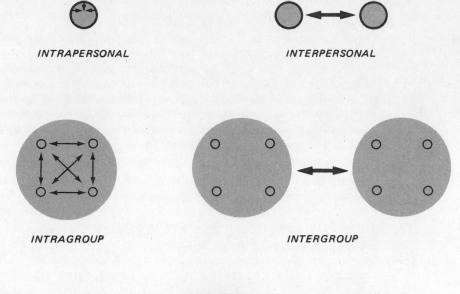

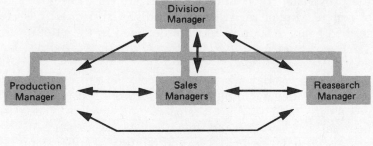

FIGURE 14–1.   Levels of Conflict

Intrapersonal Conflict

In defining conflict, we distinguished between goal conflict and cognitive conflict. This distinction is useful when considering intrapersonal conflict. Goal conflict exists for an individual when that individual's behavior will result in outcomes that (1) are mutually exclusive or (2) have incompatible elements (both positive and negative outcomes). For example, college graduates might have to decide whether to take jobs in business or in government (mutually exclusive outcomes). Further, if they take jobs in business, they might make more money but be involved in less interesting work (incompatible elements). Because goal conflict involves an interplay of positive and negative outcomes, we can identify three basic types:

1. *Approach-approach* conflict occurs when a person has a choice between two or more alternatives with positive outcomes. For example, choosing between two jobs that appear to be equally attractive.

2. *Avoidance-avoidance* conflict occurs when a person has to choose between two or more alternatives with negative consequences. For example, when employees are threatened with punishment (a demotion) unless they do something they dislike (e.g., travel a lot on their job).

3. *Approach-avoidance* conflict occurs when a person must decide whether to do something that has both positive and negative consequences. For example, being offered a good job in a poor location.

Most decisions we make in our day-to-day activities involve the resolution of goal conflict—particularly approach-avoidance conflict. At times, these conflicts can be very intense. The intensity will increase as (1) the number of alternatives increases, (2) the alternatives tend toward equality in their positive and negative consequences, and (3) the issue increases in importance for the decision maker. As the conflict becomes more intense, we experience tension, and choice becomes difficult.

Cognitive conflict at the intrapersonal level exists when individuals recognize inconsistencies in the relations between pairs of elements in their thoughts. The elements include the beliefs people hold about themselves, their behavior, and their environment. According to Leon Festinger's *Theory of Cognitive Dissonance*,[10] the existence of inconsistent beliefs or thoughts is psychologically uncomfortable. Individuals experiencing this discomfort are usually motivated to reduce the inconsistency (dissonance) and achieve a state of equilibrium (consonance). To achieve consonance, there are two basic alternatives: (1) change one's beliefs, and (2) obtain more information about the issue causing dissonance. Suppose, for example, that a group of salespersons consider themselves to be very effective at selling. If they fail to achieve their sales quotas, they may experience cognitive dissonance. This dissonance could be reduced in a number of ways. Some individuals might change their beliefs about themselves—"I guess I am not really very good at selling." Some individuals might change their beliefs about others—"I guess the customer didn't recognize a good deal." Other individuals might change their beliefs about what they have to do—"I guess I had better work harder next time to make the sale." Finally, some individuals may realize that the product doesn't match the competition—"From our market research, I now realize that we need to make some improvements in this product, rather than in our sales efforts."

For many personal decisions, both goal conflict and cognitive conflict are present. We experience approach-avoidance conflict over many decisions (for example, accepting a job offer). It has been suggested that the greater the goal conflict before the decision, the greater the cognitive dissonance following the decision. The postdecision dissonance occurs because we know that the alternative accepted has negative (avoidance) elements while the alternative rejected has positive (approach) elements. Thus, the more difficulty in arriving at the original decision, the more the need to justify the decision afterward.

Interpersonal Conflict

Interpersonal conflict involves two parties rather than one individual. A distinguishing feature of interpersonal conflict is the need to recognize the joint outcomes of the parties as well as the individual outcomes of each party. Consider the following situation:

> *Two suspects are taken into custody and separated. The district attorney is certain that they are guilty of a specific crime, but he does not have adequate evidence to convict them at a trial. He points out each prisoner's alternative to him: to confess to the crime that the police are sure they have committed or not to confess. If they both do not confess, then the district attorney states he will book them on some very minor but trumped-up charge such as petty larceny and illegal possession of a weapon for which they would both receive minor punishments; if they both confess they will be prosecuted, but he will recommend less than the most severe sentence; but if one confesses and the other does not, then the confessor will receive lenient treatment for turning state's evidence, whereas the latter will get "the book" slapped at him.*[11]

An important part of this situation is that each prisoner must decide what to do without knowing the other's decision.

The possible outcomes for this situation are presented in Figure 14–2. If both prisoners confess, they will each be sentenced to six years in jail. If they both remain silent, they will each receive sentences for three years. If one confesses while the other remains silent, the confessor will get off with only a year while the nonconfessor will receive ten years in jail.

This type of situation, called a *prisoner's dilemma* (PD), includes many features of interpersonal conflict. First, the dilemma is based on the interdependencies and contingencies present in the payoff matrix. The outcomes for each person depend on what the other does. Second, the dilemma emphasizes the distinction between individual outcomes and joint outcomes. For each person, the best individual outcome results from confessing. However, the best joint outcome results from both remaining silent. Third, the dilemma involves the role of trust. Assume the district attorney allows the two prisoners to meet before they reach their separate decisions. Assume further that the prisoners agree to remain silent. When they return to their separate cells and reconsider the payoff matrix,

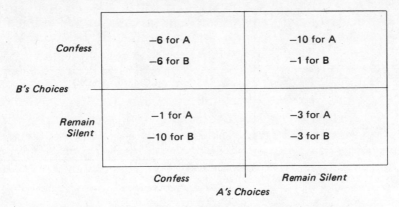

FIGURE 14–2.   Prisoner's Dilemma Payoff Matrix

it is still in their best individual interest to confess. Can one trust the other? What would you do?

The Prisoner's Dilemma (PD) has been a popular model for research on interpersonal conflict because it captures interesting aspects of conflict in a relatively simple format. The two alternatives—confess or remain silent—are considered to represent *competitive* versus *cooperative* responses to conflict. Confession is a competitive response because one party attempts to achieve its best outcome at the expense of the other.

Reviews of research on the PD indicate that the level of cooperation between two parties is affected by a number of factors.[12] For example, research shows that:

1. When the situation involves a series of decisions (a number of "trials"), cooperation tends to be low or decline at first and then shows a rise.
2. People respond more to changes in the other's strategy compared to fixed strategies. For example, a person is more likely to cooperate if the other person shifts from competition to cooperation than if the other had been consistently cooperative from the start.
3. Opportunities for feedback and communication usually increase the probability of cooperation. However, since communication can be used to deceive, the effects of communication must be considered in the broader context of the player's intent.

Conflict-handling Styles.   Although the PD format is useful for studying some aspects of conflict, it tends to oversimplify the possible responses available in a conflict situation. That is, the PD format allows only two possible responses that are considered to represent competitive or cooperative behavior. However, other responses may be possible in a real-world conflict situation. To expand our view of possible responses to conflict, consider Figure 14–3, which is a model that recognizes five different conflict-handling styles.[13]

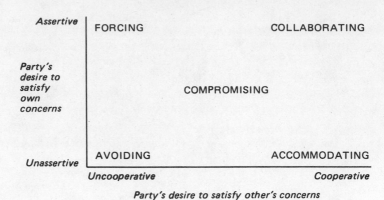

FIGURE 14–3.   Model of Conflict-handling Styles

Source: Adapted from Thomas, K. W., "Conflict and Conflict Management." In M. D. Dun-nette, ed., *Handbook of Industrial and Organizational Psychology* (Chicago: Rand McNally, 1970), p. 900. Used with permission.

The five conflict-handling styles are identified according to their location along two dimensions. The two dimensions are based on the distinction between a person's desire to satisfy his or her own concerns and the desire to satisfy the concerns of the other party. The "desire to satisfy one's own concerns" refers to the extent to which a person is *assertive* in pursuing personal goals. The "desire to satisfy the other's concerns" refers to the extent to which a person exhibits a *cooperative* orientation. Thus, the five conflict-handling styles represent different combinations of assertiveness and cooperativeness.

Behavior that is unassertive and uncooperative reflects an *avoidance* of conflict. A person using this style would try to stay out of conflicts, ignore disagreements, or remain neutral. This approach might reflect a decision to "let the conflict work itself out" or it might reflect the person's aversion to tension and frustration. Sometimes avoiding may be useful in order to minimize the possibility of escalating the conflict. However, avoiding an issue is often frustrating to the other party. People who consistently use this conflict-handling style are evaluated unfavorably by others.

Behavior that is assertive and uncooperative reflects a win-lose approach to conflict. Persons using this style would try to achieve their own goals without concern for others. Thus, the *forcing* style often involves an element of power and dominance. The forcing person feels that one must win and, by necessity, one must lose. This orientation may be useful in assisting people to achieve their individual goals, but this style—like avoiding—tends to result in unfavorable evaluations by others.

An *accommodative* response reflects a cooperative orientation and a lack of assertiveness concerning one's own outcomes. Accommodation could represent an altruistic action, a strategy to induce cooperation by the other, or a submission to the wishes of the other. In most cases, a person who accommodates is evaluated favorably but may also be perceived as being weak.

A *collaborative* style is reflected in behavior that is both cooperative and assertive. The collaborative style represents a desire to maximize the joint outcomes of the two parties. Filley[14] has identified the following characteristics of a person employing a collaborative style:

1. Sees conflict as natural and helpful, even leading to a more creative solution if handled properly.
2. Evidences trust and candidness with others and recognizes the legitimacy of feelings in arriving at decisions.
3. Feels that the attitudes and positions of everyone need to be aired and recognizes that when conflict is resolved to the satisfaction of all, commitment to the solution is likely.
4. Sees everyone as having an equal role in resolving the conflict, views the opinions of everyone as equally legitimate.
5. Does not sacrifice anyone simply for the good of the group.

People using the collaborative style tend to be perceived as dynamic individuals and are evaluated favorably by others.

A *compromising* style is reflected in behavior that is intermediate in both assertiveness and cooperation. This style is based on a process of give-and-take and may involve negotiation and a series of concessions. The emphasis is on "splitting the difference." Compromise is commonly used and widely accepted as a means of resolving conflict. People who compromise with others tend to be evaluated favorably. Compared with a collaborative style, compromising would not be expected to generate the potential for maximizing joint satisfaction. Rather, compromise is viewed as a means of achieving moderate, but only partial, satisfaction for each party.

To better appreciate the difference between compromise and collaboration, it is useful to mention again the difference between distributive bargaining and integrative bargaining (see Chapter 10). *Distributive bargaining* is behavior intended to allocate limited resources between two parties. In contrast, *integrative bargaining* is behavior intended to solve problems in such a way that the parties increase the resources available for allocation. Distributive bargaining assumes a fixed amount of resources; integrative bargaining assumes that the resources are flexible and may be increased. For example, assume that two people work together on a project and earn $500. If they decide immediately to divide the income, they are engaged in distributive bargaining. Since one person's gain is the other person's loss under distributive bargaining, an extreme outcome would be for one person to take the entire $500. Less extreme outcomes might include an even split, since a compromise is one form of distributive bargaining. The two people could decide to invest their $500 to earn a return of $600. In this case, they have engaged in collaboration, a form of integrative bargaining. Thus, compromise differs from collaboration as distributive bargaining differs from integrative bargaining.

Most conflict situations involve elements of both integrative and distributive bargaining. Thus a particular conflict episode may find a person engaging in more than one of the possible styles. If we reconsider the example of the $500 income, eventually the two parties will have to decide how to allocate the income earned. Even if they initially engage in collaboration to increase the amount of money, they ultimately will need to adopt a distributive bargaining orientation (possibly compromise) to decide how to divide the money.

Research on Conflict-handling Styles.   A number of studies have been conducted on the use of the different conflict-handling styles.[15] These studies indicate that people tend to describe themselves as using collaboration more often than the other styles. This result is encouraging, because collaboration tends to be characteristic of (1) more successful managers compared with less successful managers and (2) higher performing organizations compared with medium and lower performing organizations. In addition, collaboration tends to be perceived as being associated with the constructive use of conflict. Finally, the use of collaboration seems to evoke positive feelings from others as well as favorable evaluations of one's performance and abilities.

In contrast with the constructive effects of collaboration, forcing and avoiding apparently have a number of negative consequences. Forcing and avoiding tend to be associated with decreases in the constructive use of conflict, negative feelings from others, and unfavorable evaluations of one's performance and abilities.

The effects of using accommodation and compromise appear to be mixed. In one study, the use of accommodation seemed to bring forth positive feelings from others but did not lead to favorable evaluations of performance and abilities. Finally, one study found no significant effects of compromise, but another study found that compromise was followed by positive feelings from others.

Intragroup Conflict

A group can be considered as something greater than and different from the simple sum of its individual parts. Likewise, intragroup conflict is viewed as something beyond a simple sum of intrapersonal and interpersonal conflict. Conflict within a group may involve the group as a whole as well as the individual members. Thus we would expect intragroup conflict to have an effect on the group's processes and output. In addition, the task and social processes within a group should influence the instigation or resolution of intragroup conflict.

Effects of Intragroup Conflict on Group Process.   A classic study by Deutsch investigated the effects of cooperation and competition on group process and productivity.[16] As part of a course requirement, fifty college students were divided into ten teams. The teams were assigned problems each week and graded on their performance. The method of grading allowed the researcher to create two very different social situations. Five of the groups were assigned to a "cooperative" situation, while the remaining five groups were assigned to a "competitive" situation. In the cooperative social situation, the groups were graded as a unit. That is, the group as a whole received a grade depending on how well they did compared with the other groups. In the competitive social situation, the individuals were graded as individuals. Within each group, the person who contributed the most was given the highest grade. Moreover, the grade was based on a ranking system so that the individual contributing most received a "1," the next highest contribution received a "2," and so on down to a "5" for the person contributing the least. Thus, in the cooperative situation the group members shared a common goal (maximize the group's grade) while in the competitive situation the goals were not shared (maximize an individual's grade).

By the end of the study (five weeks), it was clear that the two grading systems had different effects on the groups' processes and output. Compared with groups in the competitive situation, groups in the cooperative situation showed the following characteristics: (1) greater coordination of effort, (2) better understanding of communications, (3) greater friendliness, (4) more favorable evaluations of the group, (5) greater productivity per unit time, and (6) higher quality solutions.

From the results of this study, Deutsch concluded that intragroup cooperation facilitates positive group processes (e.g., coordination, communication) while also improving the quantity and quality of group output. However, Deutsch's conclusions have been criticized because his situation of *intra*group cooperation also included *inter*group competition. Thus, in part, the element of competition between groups may have stimulated each group to try better.

Another study examined the effects of intragroup cooperation without intergroup competition.[17] In this study, some groups were graded as a unit without being in competition with other groups (this was called a situation of pure cooperation). The results showed that the pure cooperative groups had lower productivity with lower quality compared with the other types of grading systems. However, measures of group process indicated that the groups under pure cooperation developed consistently more favorable interpersonal relations within their teams. Thus, intragroup cooperation does seem to have a positive effect on group process, with or without the element of intergroup competition. However, intergroup competition seemed to stimulate productivity. Apparently, competition facilitates performance on some tasks.

Effects of Group Process on Intragroup Conflict. If a group is experiencing intragroup conflict, the conflict may eventually be resolved, allowing the group to reach a consensus. Or, the conflict may not be resolved and the group discussion ends in disagreement among the members. Can we identify some of the conditions that lead to (1) a successful resolution of the conflict (consensus) or (2) a failure to resolve the conflict (disagreement)? This question prompted a study of a large number of groups engaged in business and governmental decision making.[18] It became apparent in this study that conflict within the groups was not a simple, single phenomenon. Rather, the intragroup conflict seemed to fall in two distinct categories: (1) substantive conflict and (2) affective conflict. *Substantive* conflict is conflict based on the nature of the task or "content" issues. Substantive conflict is associated with intellectual disagreements among the group members. In contrast, *affective conflict* derives primarily from the group's interpersonal relations. Affective conflict is associated with emotional responses aroused during interpersonal clashes.

The researchers' analysis of conflict resolution indicated that certain elements of group process apparently helped the resolution of both substantive and affective conflict. Other elements of group process were associated with the resolution of one type of conflict but not the other type. Table 14–1 summarizes the elements of group process associated

TABLE 14–1.   Conflict Resolution within Groups

Type of Conflict Resolved	*Elements of Group Process Associated with Successful Conflict Resolution Within Groups*
Substantive only	1. When facts were available and used.
	2. When the chairperson, through much solution proposing, aided the group in penetrating its agenda problems.
	3. When the participants felt friendly toward each other.
Affective only	1. When the group considered only the discrete, simpler agenda items and postponed other more difficult issues.
	2. When the participants had little interest in what was being discussed and withdrew from the problem solving.
	3. When the participants withdrew from interpersonal contact.
Both Substantive and Affective	1. When there was little expression of self-oriented needs.
	2. When there was a generally pleasant atmosphere and the participants recognized the need for unified action.
	3. When the group's problem-solving activity was orderly, understandable, and focused on one issue at a time.

Adapted from Guetzkow, H., and J. Gyr, An analysis of conflict in decision-making groups, *Human Relations*, 1954, 7, pp. 367–381.

with the successful resolution of intragroup conflict. The summary reveals an interesting difference in the way substantive conflict is resolved compared with the resolution of affective conflict. A group experiencing substantive conflict tends to achieve consensus by emphasizing the factors that promote consensus (accentuate the positive). In contrast, a group in affective conflict tends to achieve consensus by reducing the forces that promote disagreement (eliminate the negative). The reduction of negative forces is basically a result of withdrawing from the conflict.

The results of this research suggest that intragroup conflict does not automatically lead to negative consequences. That is, certain aspects of a group's process may work to overcome the conflict and promote consensus. However, since one form of intragroup conflict (competition) seems to have a negative effect on interpersonal relations, a group experiencing conflict may have to work very hard to achieve constructive outcomes.

Intergroup Conflict

The discussion of intragroup conflict noted that intergroup competition may stimulate groups to perform better. This section considers this issue further and identifies some of the possible costs and benefits of intergroup conflict.

The effects of intergroup competition were identified in a study conducted as part of a management training program.[19] The participating managers were assigned to groups to work on a number of managerial "dilemmas." After the groups had been working together for awhile (12 to 14 hours), they were given a problem that supposedly measured their effectiveness in group problem solving. The problem was presented so that each group was competing with another group to come up with the best solution. Thus one group would be a "winner" and the other group would be a "loser." Once the problem was assigned, the element of competition began to affect behavior within each group as well as relations between the groups.

Behavior within Groups.   As work on the problem got underway, a group became closer and a sense of group loyalty developed. The group experienced a rapid increase in cohesion. Associated with the increased cohesiveness was pressure toward conformity (the groupthink phenomenon) and a suppression of interpersonal conflict. The group was primarily concerned with task goals. Members became more willing to follow autocratic leaders. The net result of all these trends was for group members to feel satisfied with the group and rate the group in very positive terms. The researchers referred to the members' high rating of their group as a natural "superiority complex." That is, group members tended to regard their group as superior to other groups.

Relations between Groups.   An attitude of hostility developed between the groups. The other group was viewed as an "enemy." Perceptions of the other group tended to be distorted; inaccurate stereotypes developed. These distorted and inaccurate perceptions were maintained as interaction and communication between the groups tended to decrease. The hostility, misperceptions, and reduced communication seemed to be reinforcing. The intensity of the conflict escalated.

Reactions to the Choice of a Winner.   When a neutral judge chose the "best" solution, the two groups' reactions were, predictably, different. The winning group considered the decision to be fair and impartial. After the decision, the winning group became even more cohesive. Winning had validated their positive views of the group. The leaders became even more established in their positions. Group members became self-satisfied and engaged in playful tension release—they become "fat and happy." This feeling of self-satisfaction led to a complacent attitude in future competition. As a result of such complacency, a winning group may not improve much over its past performance.

In contrast, the losing group considered the judge's decision to be unfair and biased. After hearing that they had lost, the group tended to become disorganized. Unresolved intragroup conflict began to surface. The group looked for something or someone to blame for their defeat. Often the leaders were considered responsible for the loss and a new leadership structure emerged.

If further competition is scheduled, the losing group is likely to reorganize and become more cohesive. If they find valid reasons for their previous failure, they may learn valuable lessons from the loss. Thus they may well improve their performance in later problem-solving situations. Of course, the intragroup dissension following the loss may also cause the group to become demoralized. The group could adopt a defeatist attitude. Moreover, the group may miss valuable learning opportunities if they simply try to shift the blame for their loss. Of course, winning groups may also ignore the opportunity to learn as a result of the "fat and happy state" that sometimes follows success.

In a business game involving intergroup competition, the losing groups reacted quite differently from the winning groups.[20] Compared to the winning groups, the losing groups rated the exercise as having less learning value. The losing groups failed to see the learning opportunities that came from making poor decisions. In summary, intergroup conflict may have a number of negative side effects, and these negative effects may persist long after the competition is over. It seems that intergroup conflict should be minimized if possible and managed with great care when it is present.

Intraorganizational Conflict

When looking at conflict from an intraorganizational perspective, four types of conflict are apparent: (1) vertical conflict, (2) horizontal conflict, (3) line-staff conflict, and (4) role conflict. Although these types of conflict may overlap, especially with role conflict, each has distinctive characteristics.

Vertical Conflict. Superior-subordinate conflict is an example of vertical conflict. Any conflict between levels in the organization is vertical conflict. Vertical conflicts usually arise because superiors attempt to control subordinates and subordinates tend to resist.[21] Employees may resist because they believe the control is an infringement on their personal freedom. In addition to the potential reaction against a loss of freedom, vertical conflict may arise because of inadequate communications, conflicts of interest (goal conflict), or lack of consensus concerning perceptions of information and values (cognitive conflict).[22]

Horizontal Conflict. Conflict between employees or departments at the same hierarchical level is horizontal (lateral) conflict. A fundamental cause of horizontal conflict is the pressure for suboptimization in most organizations.[23] Each department may suboptimize by independently striving for its own departmental goals. These goals may be incompatible between departments, causing goal conflict; or the perceptions of the importance of the goals may differ between departments, causing cognitive conflict. Differences in the education, experience, and training of employees between departments also may lead to conflict.[24] Opportunities for horizontal conflict increase the higher the functional interdependence between departments, the fewer buffers (i.e., inventories) there are between departments, or the greater the dependence on common resources between departments.[25]

Thompson provides examples of three types of functional interdependence.[26] These are depicted in Figure 14-4. Two departments representing *pooled interdependence* operate with relative independence of each other. They are interdependent only in the sense that both departments are integral parts of the same organization. *Sequential interdependence* has a higher propensity for conflict than pooled interdependence. The outputs from one department become the inputs for another department. Thus the receiving department is dependent on the sending department. Finally, reciprocal interdependence occurs when the outputs from one department become the inputs of another department, and vice-versa. Thus, both departments are highly dependent on each other.

Lawrence and Lorsch did an extensive study of six organizations selected from each of three industries—plastics, containers, and food.[27] To analyze the effects of horizontal conflict, they examined the degree of differentiation and integration that existed within each firm. You may recall from Chapter 10 that differentiation was defined as the difference in

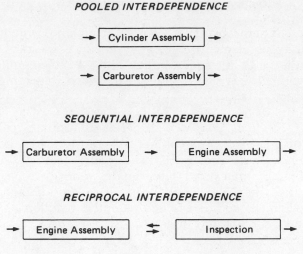

FIGURE 14–4.   Three Types of Interdependence

cognitive and emotional orientation among managers in different functional departments. The more managers are different in their attitudes, behaviors, knowledge, and departmental segmentation, the higher the differentiation. *Integration* was defined as the quality of the state of collaboration that exists among departments that are required to achieve unity of effort by the demands of the environment. In Chapter 10, we described formal integration mechanisms such as linking roles, task forces, and integrating roles or departments.

The three industries were said to exist in different environments. The plastics industry faced a complex and dynamic environment—primarily characterized by high competition, uncertain markets, and rapidly advancing scientific knowledge. The container industry faced a relatively certain and stable environment, and the food industry operated in an environment that fell between the plastics and container industries in degree of uncertainty.

The firms in each industry that were most effective in handling horizontal conflict used differentiation and integration techniques that were appropriate for their respective environments. Functional departments in the successful plastics and food industries were highly differentiated. This high degree of differentiation tended to cause many departmental conflicts. To handle the conflict, the successful plastics firm had a special integration department that functioned to coordinate the efforts of the various departments. The successful food firm had an individual formally assigned to an integration role. In contrast, the container industry tended to experience fewer and more predictable conflicts. The successful container firm therefore relied on formal hierarchical means to integrate departmental efforts—rules, regulations, and authority related to functional position.

Line-Staff Conflict.   Most organizations have staff units to assist the line departments. While the line managers are normally responsible for some process that creates a part (or all) of the firm's product, the staff managers are expected to serve an advisory function that requires their technical knowledge.

The line-staff relationship frequently involves conflict. Staff managers and line managers typically have different personal characteristics. Staff employees tend to have a higher level of education, come from different backgrounds, and are younger than line employees.[28] These different personal characteristics are frequently associated with different values and beliefs. The surfacing of these different values tends to create conflict situations.

Line managers may feel staff managers are infringing on their areas of legitimate authority. In many instances, staff people specify the methodologies and control the resources used in the manufacturing processes. For example, many manufacturing organizations have staff engineers who specify how each product should be made and what materials should be used. At the same time, line managers are responsible for supervising the production workers and are held responsible for the output. Understandably, line managers may perceive conflict when the engineers are seen to be directing the activities of the production people. Line managers reason that their authority to direct the workers is lessened but that their responsibility for the output remains unchanged. Perceived authority is less than perceived responsibility due to staff involvement.

Role Conflict.   An employee's role is the group of activities that others expect the individual to perform in his or her position in the organization. Since a role frequently involves conflict, it is useful to consider some of the factors involved in role behavior. Figure 14–5 presents a model of a role episode. Prior to a message being sent, people in role sender positions have expectations, perceptions, and evaluations of the focal person's activities. These prior experiences then influence the actual messages that are transmitted. The reception of these messages may then lead to role conflict if the messages are incompatible. Finally, the focal person will respond with coping behaviors that serve as inputs to the role sender's experiences.

The group of role senders form the focal person's *role set.* A role set usually includes a person's manager, perhaps the manager's immediate supervisor, subordinates, and other employees with whom the person works closely. Four types of role conflict can result from incompatible messages and pressures from the role set:[29]

1. *Intrasender* conflict: different messages and pressures from a single member of the role set may be incompatible.
2. *Intersender* conflict: messages and pressures from one role sender oppose messages and pressures from one or more other senders.

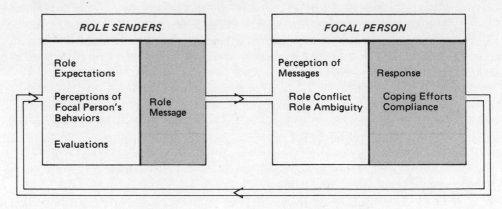

FIGURE 14–5.   A Role Episode Model

Source: Adapted from Kahn, R. L., Wolfe, Donald M., Quinn, Robert P., Snoek, F. D., and Rosenthal, R. A. *Organizational Stress: Studies in Role Conflict and Ambiguity* (New York: John Wiley & Sons, 1964), p. 26.

3. *Interrole* conflict: role pressures associated with membership in one group are in conflict with pressures stemming from membership in other groups.
4. *Person-role* conflict: role requirements may violate moral or ethical values.

In addition to being "caught in the middle" because of one or more of the four types of role conflict, employees can experience conflict due to role ambiguity. *Role ambiguity* is the lack of clear, consistent information about the required activities on the job. As is the case for role conflict, role ambiguity tends to cause stress and subsequent coping behaviors. Three possible coping behaviors are (1) aggressive action and hostile communication, (2) withdrawal, and (3) approaching the role sender(s) in order to attempt joint problem solving.[30]

Even though stress may be a common reaction to role conflict, there is evidence that some role conflict is inevitable. In some cases role conflict may be functional. One study found that role conflict was viewed as acceptable in some dynamic and flexible organizations and helped to achieve some organizational goals.[31] Another study found widespread use of dual supervision in some successful small-batch and continuous-process production firms.[32]

MANAGING CONFLICT

A wide range of tactics have been suggested for managing conflict. This section summarizes some of the major approaches under three headings: (1) structural methods, (2) confrontation approaches, and (3) promoting conflict. In general, the structural and confrontation approaches assume that conflict is already present and requires management. However, they differ in that the structural approaches tend to minimize the direct expression of conflict by separating the parties, while the confrontation approaches try to surface the conflict by bringing the parties together. In contrast to the assumption in the structural and confrontation approaches that conflict is already present, the promotion of conflict is based on the assumption that "adequate" conflict is lacking.

Structural Methods to Reduce Conflict

The structure of the organization provides several opportunities to reduce conflict. Formal authority can be given to managers that allows them to issue directives in order to manage conflict. Thus conflict can be reduced through positional authority. Another option is to design the organization to promote effective conflict resolution.

Dominance through Position.   If conflict reduction authority exists at all levels of the organization, managers may attempt to resolve conflict within their departments by issuing a directive. This directive may specify the course of action that subordinates are expected to follow, or it may serve to reduce ambiguity. For example, two vice-presidents in the same firm may be working on the organizational strategy. One vice-president may advocate a strategy based on growth and the other may desire a strategy that requires authority to be concentrated at the top levels of the organization. In this case, the growth objective may be in direct conflict with the centralized authority objective. The president may exercise authority to specify which objective should be operational.

Positional authority also can be used to settle conflicts within or between departments. Within a department, the supervisor may issue a directive to resolve the conflict. Between departments, the issue is carried up the hierarchy until a common supervisor is located for both departments. This common supervisor renders a decision intended to resolve the conflict.

Sometimes the use of the hierarchical authority is ineffective at resolving interdepartmental conflict. It may be unrealistic for a vice-president to resolve some conflict issues that may arise between lower level operational units. Furthermore, the dominance approach does little to prevent conflict from occurring. It primarily serves to remedy conflict after it has occurred.

Fortunately, there are other steps that can be taken to promote cooperation and the integration of activities within the firm. Decoupling and buffering are two basic options for managing conflict through organizational design.

Decoupling. An organization may be designed to directly reduce interdependence between departments. Providing departments with resources and inventories that are independent of those provided for other departments should "decouple" those departments and reduce the propensity for interdepartmental conflict. However, the costs of providing independence should be considered against the benefits. Many times independence will require a duplication of efforts between departments. Moving to the product form of organization, as discussed in Chapter 4, is a structural way of decoupling.

Buffering with Inventory. If it is too costly to completely decouple departments (make them totally independent), it may be possible to buffer the work flow between departments with inventory. Thus if department A produces a product that serves as input to department B, an inventory between the departments could prevent department B from being severely affected by a temporary shutdown or slowdown in department A.

Buffering with a Linking-pin. Likert has suggested that linking pins be incorporated into the organization structure.[33] A *linking pin* is an individual assigned to departments which have overlapping activities. This individual is expected to understand the operations of both departments and thus be able to coordinate both sets of departmental activities.

Buffering with an Integration Department. We noted earlier that Lawrence and Lorsch identified the need for formal integration departments to coordinate the activities of other departments. According to their research, integration departments were useful for firms that experienced uncertain environments.

Confrontation

Confrontation has diverse meanings. Some people see confrontation as refering to win-lose conflicts that involve antagonistic interactions. However, we will use the term to describe constructive approaches to managing conflict. In this sense, *confrontation* is a process by which parties in conflict directly engage each other, openly exchange information on the issues, and try to work out the differences between themselves to reach a mutually desirable outcome. The underlying assumption is that both sides may be able to gain something (a win-win situation). Thus, confrontation is a more complete version of the collaborative interpersonal style discussed earlier in the chapter.

Confrontation, as defined here, does not automatically occur when two parties directly engage each other. If the parties adopt win-lose strategies, the interaction is better described as forcing rather than as confrontation. Thus, the attitudes and goals of the parties are crucial to the confrontation of conflict. The assumption that both sides may win is the important characteristic of confrontation that distinguishes it from other responses to conflict. Confrontation may be enhanced through the use of negotiation and third-party consultation.

Negotiation. When two parties disagree about something but want to reach an agreement, they can engage in negotiation.[34] *Negotiation* is a process in which two parties try to reach an agreement that determines what each party gives and receives in a transaction. Like bargaining, negotiation has both distributive and integrative elements. If the parties see only the distributive (win-lose) elements, negotiation may not result in confrontation. However, if the parties work at recognizing integrative (win-win) elements, negotiation offers an opportunity for confronting conflict.

Some of the differences between win-lose and win-win strategies of negotiation are presented in Table 14–2. To achieve a confrontation approach, one needs to communicate openly, seek mutual goals, remain flexible, and avoid the use of threats. However, this strategy cannot be

TABLE 14–2.   Negotiation Strategies

Win-Win Strategy	*Win-Lose Strategy*
1. Define the conflict as a mutual problem.	1. Define the conflict as a win-lose situation.
2. Pursue joint outcomes.	2. Pursue individual outcomes.
3. Find creative agreements that satisfy both parties.	3. Force the other party into submission.
4. Try to equalize power by emphasizing mutual interdependence.	4. Try to increase one's power over the other by emphasizing one's own independence and the other's dependence.
5. Use open, honest, and accurate communication of one's needs, goals, and proposals.	5. Use deceitful, inaccurate, and misleading communication of one's needs, goals, and proposals.
6. Avoid threats (to reduce the other's defensiveness).	6. Use threats (to force submission).
7. Communicate flexibility of position.	7. Communicate high commitment (rigidity) regarding one's position.

David W. Johnson, Frank P. Johnson, *Joining Together: Group Theory and Group Skills,* © 1975, pp. 182–183. Adapted by permission of Prentice-Hall, Inc., Englewood Cliffs, N.J.

taken without risks. Sometimes individuals who adopt win-win strategies leave themselves open to exploitation by others who adopt win-lose strategies. Thus, negotiation can pose dilemmas for individuals—dilemmas of openness, honesty, and trust. Confrontation is not an easy approach to the management of conflict.

Third-party Consultation.   Most confrontation occurs in the form of negotiation between parties. However, there is an increasing awareness of the value of a neutral person, a third-party consultant, to help parties resolve their conflicts.[35] Strategic functions of a third-party include the following:

1. *Ensure mutual motivation.* Both parties should have incentives for resolving the conflict.
2. *Achieve a balance in situational power.* If power is not approximately equal, it may be difficult to establish trust and maintain open lines of communication.
3. *Synchronize confrontation efforts.* It is important to coordinate one party's positive overtures with the other party's readiness to reciprocate. A failure to coordinate positive initiatives and readiness to respond may undermine future efforts to work out differences.
4. *Promote openness in dialogue.* The third-party can help establish norms of openness, provide reassurance and support, and decrease the risks of being open with the other party.
5. *Maintain an "optimum" level of tension.* If threat and tension are too low, the incentive for change (or a solution) is minimal. However, if threat and tension are too high, the parties may be unable to process information and see creative alternatives. The parties may begin to polarize and take rigid positions.

It is quite easy for one to assume the role of a third-party. However, it is not at all easy to be effective in the role. To be an effective third-party consultant, a person needs a number of conceptual and behavioral skills. First, a third-party must be able to diagnose the conflict. Substantive conflict needs to be approached differently than affective conflict. Substantive conflict requires problem-solving skills, while affective conflict requires the ability to work through negative feelings. Second, a third-party must be skilled in breaking deadlocks and interrupting interaction at the "right" time. Finally, a third-party needs to evidence mutual acceptance and have the personal capacity to provide emotional support and reassurance. Thus the style of the consultant must instill confidence and acceptance by the parties in conflict.

Usually a third-party consultant tries to facilitate conflict resolution without providing a specific set of procedures for the parties to follow. However, occasionally it is useful for the third-party to provide a relatively structured context for the parties' confrontation to ensure that they concentrate on the appropriate issues and direct their efforts to these issues. One example of such a structured approach is the intergroup confrontation technique.[36] The procedure for such a confrontation is as follows:

Step 1:   Each group meets in a separate room and develops two lists. On one list they indicate how they see themselves as a group, particularly in their relationship to the other group.
On the second list they indicate how they see the other group.

Step 2:   The two groups come together and share perceptions. The third-party consultant helps them clarify their views and, it is hoped, develop better understandings of themselves and the other group.

Step 3:   The groups return to their separate rooms to look deeper into the issues and diagnose their current problems. What does each group contribute to the conflict?

Step 4:   The groups meet together again to share their new insights. They are urged to identify common issues and plan the next stages for seeking solutions.

As in most approaches to confrontation, the intergroup confrontation technique does not guarantee successful resolution of conflict. Rather, this procedure provides a vehicle for parties in conflict to begin exploring their differences. A skillful third-party consultant can use such an opportunity to get the parties started toward an effective confrontation of their conflict.

Promoting Cognitive Conflict

We noted earlier that cognitive conflict might be beneficial if it served to avoid the groupthink phenomenon. Hence, it is useful to consider alternatives that serve to create functional cognitive conflict.

Dialectical Inquiry.   One approach to introducing cognitive conflict into the decision-making process is the dialectical inquiry (DI). The DI involves the development and recommendation of a course of action by one advocate (or group of advocates), and development and recommendation of a contradictory course of action by another advocate (or group of advocates). The decision maker considers the recommendations of both groups before choosing one alternative, or a composite alternative. Since the two recommended courses of action are based on opposing viewpoints of the same situation, cognitive conflict should occur when both recommendations are considered by the decision maker. By resolving this type of conflict, management might reach a decision that reflects a synthesis of the two conflicting viewpoints. For example, in a case study of a West Coast manufacturing firm, top executives felt a DI was helpful in their planning decisions.[37]

Devil's Advocate Method.   Another approach to introducing cognitive conflict into the decision-making process is the devil's advocate (DA) method. The DA method involves a critique of a recommended course of action. Unlike the DI, there is no second course of action offered. The criticism alone should promote cognitive conflict for the decision maker. The need to resolve the cognitive conflict may lead to a better understanding of the problem and, thus, a better decision. There is evidence that in some situations the DA leads to better decisions than the DI.[38] The DA method may be effective in causing the decision maker not to take the recommendations from any one person or group as a given, hence the decision maker may be sensitive to data confirming or disconfirming the recommended course of action.

SUMMARY

Conflict is an inevitable fact of organizational life. But it is not inevitable for conflict to result in destructive consequences for the organization. Depending on how the conflict is managed, the negative effects may be minimized and there also may be positive effects.

The effective management of conflict is based, in part, on a better understanding of the different ways by which conflict emerges and is resolved. Conflict was examined at five different levels within organizations. Intrapersonal conflict occurs when individuals experience goal conflict or cognitive conflict within themselves. Conflict at this level may lead to personal stress, anxiety, and tension. Interpersonal conflict occurs between two parties. Depending on the conflict-handling styles of the parties, the outcomes of interpersonal conflict may represent integrative solutions (win-win outcomes) or distributive solutions (win-lose outcomes). A collaborative style that is both assertive and cooperative is generally considered the best way to achieve integrative solutions.

Minimizing intragroup conflict seems to promote more favorable interpersonal relations within groups. But, it is not clear that such conditions are sufficient to produce increased quantity and quality of output. In some cases, intergroup conflict (competition) seems to lead to better productivity. However, intergroup competition seems to have a number of negative side effects including hostility, misperception, and reduced communication between groups. It was concluded that intergroup conflict should be managed carefully.

Four types of organizational conflict were identified: (1) vertical, (2) horizontal, (3) line-staff, and (4) role. These conflicts are based, in part, on the interdependencies inherent in organizations. While the interdependencies cannot be totally eliminated, organizational conflicts can be managed by structural methods such as positional dominance, decoupling, and buffering. Other approaches to managing conflict include negotiation and third-party consultation.

Finally, it may be useful to promote conflict in some instances. The dialectical inquiry and devil's advocate method are used to enhance decision making through the intentional introduction of conflicting points of view.

DISCUSSION QUESTIONS

1. What are some of the differences between conflict, competition, and cooperation?

2. Conflict is often considered to be a negative feature in organizations. What are some of the positive features of conflict? Provide an example from your personal experience where conflict was beneficial.

3. If you were involved in a PD (prisoner's dilemma) situation, what would you do to encourage a cooperative response from the other party? If you had a guarantee from the other party that they would cooperate, what would you do? Why?

4. Identify the five different conflict-handling styles. Give examples of situations when each style would be appropriate. What criteria did you use to decide what is appropriate behavior?

5. What are the possible advantages and problems associated with intergroup conflict? As a manager, would you promote this type of conflict? Why or why not?

6. What were the major findings of the Lawrence and Lorsch study of horizontal organizational conflict? When would a formal integration department be desirable or undesirable?

7. What are the different types of role conflict? What are the options for coping with role conflict?

8. What is meant by decoupling to manage conflict? What is a buffer in an organization? How do these methods of organizational design lead to lower propensities for conflict?

9. Compare and contrast the DI (dialectical inquiry) and DA (devil's advocate) methods for promoting conflict. Why might these methods lead to better decision making?

MANAGERIAL PROBLEM

ACME AEROSPACE

Before 1976, Acme Aerospace, Inc., manufactured jet engine parts. Acme's business was usually gained by bidding on jobs offered by the major airplane manufacturers. Major manufacturers would receive contracts for new jets and then would subcontract part of the job (such as the turbines) to Acme or one of Acme's competitors.

In January 1976, the president of Acme, Rick Alpin, decided to enter a new product area. The Air Force was soliciting bids for an engine to be used in the "Pluto Project." The firm that received the job was to construct an entire nuclear rocket engine to power the "Pluto-Rover" spacecraft. The job was open to competitive bidding and the competition was expected to be stiff.

In February 1976, Alpin hired Art Disney, a rocket expert, to provide advice on the nuclear engine. Disney was given a staff position at the vice-president level. Due almost exclusively to Disney's efforts, Acme landed the Pluto-Rover nuclear engine contract.

Acme found itself faced with a monumental challenge. A prototype of the engine had to be completed by December 1977. Alpin hired a personnel staff specialist, Bernice Hutton, to organize Acme to meet the deadline. She too was appointed a vice-president.

After studying the situation, Hutton recommended a matrix structure for Acme. This involved the establishment of two project teams within Acme. The personnel for the project teams were to be drawn from the three functional departments that had existed within Acme ever since the company was founded in 1960 (see Figure 14–6).

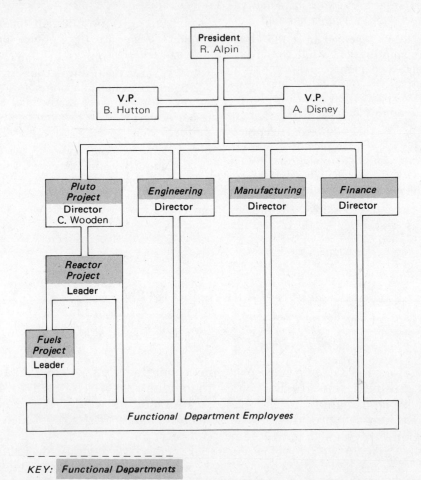

FIGURE 14–6.   Organization at Acme Aerospace, Inc.

Cal Wooden was hired in March 1976 by Alpin out of a large midwestern university to be the Pluto project director. Wooden (age thirty-six) had his MBA in finance and a bachelor's in aeronautical engineering. The three functional department directors had been with Acme since 1960.

At the close of August 1977, Alpin faced severe difficulties. The engineering and manufacturing directors were threatening to resign. They claimed that they could not work with Wooden or Disney. The reactor project was designing a unit that was incompatible with the fuel system that was being designed by the fuels project. Several employees assigned to the project teams were complaining that they were receiving incompatible directives from their project team leaders and their functional directors.

Alpin was perplexed. He called a meeting with Hutton, Disney, Wooden, the project team leaders, and the functional directors. Alpin needed to diagnose Acme's difficulties and implement corrective action.

QUESTIONS

1. What types of conflict may have occurred at Acme?
2. What structural changes may be needed at Acme?

KEY WORDS

Conflict
Goal conflict
Cognitive conflict
Affective conflict
Competition
Groupthink
Approach-approach conflict
Avoidance-avoidance conflict
Approach-avoidance conflict
Cognitive dissonance
Prisoner's dilemma
Avoiding
Competing
Accommodating
Collaborating
Compromising
Distributive bargaining

Integrative bargaining
Substantive conflict
Vertical conflict
Horizontal conflict
Pooled interdependence
Sequential interdependence
Reciprocal interdependence
Role conflict
Role set
Role ambiguity
Decoupling
Buffering
Negotiation
Intergroup confrontation technique
Dialectical inquiry
Devil's advocate

REFERENCES

1. Deutsch, M., Conflicts: Productive and destructive, *Journal of Social Issues*, 1969, 25, no. 1, pp. 7–41.

2. Litterer, J. A., Conflict in organizations: A re-examination, *Academy of Management Journal*, 1966, 9, pp. 178–186.

3. Brown, K. H., and J. W. Slocum, An application of systems concepts in diagnosing organizational strategies, in Hellriegel, D., and J. W. Slocum, Jr. (eds.), *Management in the World Today: A Book of Readings* (Reading, Mass.: Addison-Wesley, 1975), pp. 54–70.

4. Janis, I. L., *Victims of Groupthink* (Boston: Houghton Mifflin, 1972).

5. Steers, R. M., and L. W. Porter, Task-goal attributes in performance, *Psychological Bulletin*, 1974, 81, pp. 434–452.

6. Cosier, R. A., and G. L. Rose, Cognitive conflict and goal conflict effects on task performance, *Organizational Behavior and Human Performance*, 1977, 19, pp. 378–391.

7. Maier, N. R. F., Assets and liabilities in group problem solving: The need for an integrative function, *Psychological Review*, 1967, 74, pp. 239–249; Maier, N. R. F., and L. R. Hoffman, Acceptance and quality of solutions as related to leaders' attitudes toward disagreement in group problem solving, *The Journal of Applied Behavioral Science*, 1965, 1, pp. 373–386.

8. Bennis, W. G., K. D. Benne, R. Chin, and K. E. Corey, *The Planning of Change* (New York: Holt, Rinehart and Winston, 1976).

9. Cosier and Rose, Cognitive and goal conflict effects.

10. Festinger, L., *A Theory of Cognitive Dissonance* (Evanston, Ill.: Row, Peterson, 1957).

11. Luce, R. D., and H. Raiffa, *Games and Decisions* (New York: McGraw-Hill, 1957), p. 95.

12. Vinacke, W. E., Variables in experimental games: Toward a field theory, *Psychological Bulletin*, 1969, 71, pp. 293–318.

13. Thomas, K. W., Conflict and conflict management, in Dunnette, M. D. (ed.), *Handbook of Industrial and Organizational Psychology* (Chicago: Rand McNally, 1976), pp. 889–935. Thomas' model is derived from Blake, R. R., and J. S. Mouton, *The Managerial Grid* (Houston: Gulf Publishing, 1964). Research on the reactions to different conflict-handling styles is reported in Ruble, T. L., and K. W. Thomas, Support for a two-dimensional model of conflict behavior, *Organizational Behavior and Human Performance*, 1976, 16, pp. 143–155.

14. Filley, A. C., *Interpersonal conflict Resolution* (Glenview, Ill.: Scott, Foresman, 1975), p. 52.

15. Blake and Mouton, *Managerial Grid*; Burke, R. J., Methods of resolving superior-subordinate conflict: The constructive use of subordinate differences and disagreement, *Organizational Behavior and Human Performance*, 1970, 5, pp. 393–411; Lawrence, P. R., and J. W. Lorsch, *Organization and Environment* (Homewood, Ill.: Richard D. Irwin, 1969); Ruble and Thomas, Two-dimensional model; Thomas, K. W., Conflict-handling modes in interdepartmental relations, doctoral dissertation, Purdue University, 1971.

16. Deutsch, M., A theory of cooperation and competition, *Human Relations*, 1949, 2, pp. 129–152. Deutsch, M., An experimental study of the effects of cooperation and competition on group process, *Human Relations*, 1949, 2, pp. 199–232.

17. Julian, J. W., and F. A. Perry, Cooperation contrasted with intra-group and inter-group competition, *Sociometry*, 1967, 30, pp. 79–90.

18. Guetzkow, H., and J. Gyr, An analysis of conflict in decision-making groups, *Human Relations*, 1954, 7, pp. 367–381.

19. Blake, R. R., and J. S. Mouton, Reactions to intergroup competition under win-lose conditions, *Management Science*, 1961, 4, pp. 420–425.

20. Ruble, T. L., Locus of control and performance in a management simulation,

Proceedings of the Fifth Annual Meeting of the Association for Business Simulation and Experiential Learning (Denver, 1978).

21.   Pondy, L. R., Organizational conflict: Concept and models, *Administrative Science Quarterly*, 1967, 12, pp. 296–320.

22.   Smith, C. G., A comprehensive analysis of some conditions and consequences of intra-organizational conflict, *Administrative Science Quarterly*, 1966, 10, pp. 504–529.

23.   Pondy, Organizational conflict.

24.   Lawrence and Lorsch, *Organization and Environment.*

25.   Pondy.

26.   Thompson, J. D., *Organizations in Action* (New York: McGraw-Hill, 1967).

27.   Lawrence and Lorsch, *Organization and Environment.*

28.   Dalton, M., Conflict between staff and line managerial officers, *American Sociological Review*, 1966, 15, pp. 3–5.

29.   Kahn, R. L., D. M. Wolfe, R. P. Quinn, J. D. Snoek, and R. A. Rosenthal, *Organizational Stress: Studies in Role Conflict and Role Ambiguity* (New York: John Wiley, 1964).

30.   Ibid.

31.   Burns, T., and G. M. Stalker, *The Management of Innovation* (London: Tavistock Publications, 1961).

32.   Woodward, J., *Industrial Organization: Theory and Practice* (London: Oxford Press, 1965).

33.   Likert, R., *New Patterns of Management* (New York: McGraw-Hill, 1961).

34.   This section draws from Johnson, D. W., and F. P. Johnson, *Joining Together: Group Theory and Group Skills* (Englewood Cliffs, N.J.: Prentice-Hall, 1975).

35.   This section is based on Walton, R. E., *Interpersonal Peacemaking: Confrontations and Third-Party Consultation* (Reading, Mass.: Addison-Wesley, 1969).

36.   Blake, R. R., H. A. Shepard, and J. S. Mouton, *Managing Intergroup Conflict in Industry* (Houston: Gulf Publishing, 1964).

37.   Mason, R. O., A dialectical approach to strategic planning, *Management Science*, 1969, 15, pp. B403–B414.

38.   Cosier, R. A., The effects of three potential aids for making strategic decisions on prediction accuracy, unpublished manuscript, Indiana University, 1978; Cosier, R. A., T. L. Ruble, and J. C. Aplin, An evaluation of the effectiveness of dialectical inquiry systems, unpublished manuscript, Indiana University, 1978.

PART VI

ORGANIZATIONAL CHANGE

15

The Nature of Planned Organizational Change

15

LEARNING OBJECTIVES

When you have finished reading and studying this chapter, you should be able to:

▲ Discuss the objectives of planned organizational change.

▲ Discuss the pressures being exerted upon organizations to change.

▲ Discuss the resistances to change.

▲ Present a general model of change.

▲ Identify characteristics of successful and unsuccessful change efforts.

▲ Identify various types of change agents and their behaviors.

▲ Discuss the ethical considerations involved in change.

THOUGHT STARTERS

▲ Can change really be managed?

▲ Why do organizations and individuals often resist change?

▲ How does change start and by whom is it started?

▲ What makes change successful in some instances and unsuccessful in others?

▲ Do you think that it is ethical for an organization to change an employee's behavior even though it might be against the employee's own personal values?

OUTLINE

OBJECTIVES OF PLANNED ORGANIZATIONAL CHANGE
  Organizational Adaptation
  Individual Adaptation
PRESSURES TO CHANGE
  Changing Technology
  Knowledge Explosion
  Rapid Product Obsolescence
  Changing Nature of the Work Force
  Quality of Work Life
  Life-Style
RESISTANCES TO CHANGE
  Resistances by Individuals
  Resistances by Organizations
GENERAL PROCESS MODEL OF CHANGE
  Strategy for Change
  Major System Variables
PATTERNS OF SUCCESSFUL AND UNSUCCESSFUL CHANGE
  Conditions Required for Successful Change
  Pitfalls to Avoid
TYPES OF CHANGE AGENTS
  People-change Technology (PCT)
  Analysis-from-the-Top (AFT)
  Organization Development (OD)
  Internal and External Change Agents
  Basic Qualification of Change Agents
ETHICAL CONSIDERATIONS
  Power
  Freedom
SUMMARY
DISCUSSION QUESTIONS
MANAGERIAL PROBLEMS
  Macungie Corporation
  Weis Market
KEY WORDS
REFERENCES

We hear and read much about the demands on management in a rapidly changing world:

The mass media have heightened public awareness of consumer products.

The rate of technological change is accelerating.

Peoples' knowledge can become obsolete even before they have begun careers for which they have been trained.

Competitive threats come not only more rapidly, but from unexpected sources.

Certainly the speed and complexity of change test the capability of management. The ability to adapt quickly is the critical requirement for acceptable progress. The sheer speed with which change is rushing toward us can be overwhelming unless we are prepared for it both emotionally and intellectually.

Managers must be trained not only to survive in an environment of change but also to:'

Lead.

Capitalize responsibly on the values and opportunities in change.

Thrive on uncertainties created by forces that threaten the status quo.

Manage people in organizing the disorder of change.

Bring new order into being that breathes renewed vitality into our basic values.

The forces of change are not limited to the business sector. Nonbusiness organizations, such as educational institutions, hospitals, governments, and religious institutions, are also faced with change. The proliferation of social demands together with costs seemingly out of proportion to available revenues require that organizations be more effective than ever.

Many organizations are faced with ferment and flux. In increasing instances the bureaucratic model, with its emphasis on rigid structure; functional specialization; hierarchy of authority; fixed systems of rights, duties, and procedures; and impersonal human relationships, is responding inadequately to the demands placed upon it from within and outside of an organization. There is increasing need for experimentation, for learning from experience, for flexibility and adaptability, and for personal growth.

To solve these problems, many organizations, including General Electric, Equitable Life Assurance, TRW Systems, Citicorp, Dow Corning, and Shell Oil, have turned to a matrix management structure. Discussed in Chapter 4, the basic idea of the matrix structure is to push decision making down to more people, use teamwork, and restore the flexibility of a small company to large and complex organizations. Dow Corning, for example, found that by using a matrix management structure the company could handle more information and respond more quickly to changes in technology, market conditions, and governmental regulations, while at the same time relieving some senior executives of some of their decision-making burdens. William Goggin, former chairperson and architect of the company's matrix system, notes that sales have risen an average of 15 percent per year, from a bit more than $100 million in 1967 to $355 million in 1976, while net earnings have done even better, quadrupling from $10.2 million to about $43 million during the same period.[1]

Not just organizations are in flux. People, perhaps to an extent greater than ever before, are ceasing to be objects used by the organizations, are increasingly asserting themselves, and are involving themselves in complex and important problems. The reasons why people are now getting involved are numerous and complex. They include higher levels of educational attainment; increased availability of technology that both frees people from the burdens of physical and routine labor and makes them more dependent on society; an increasing rate of change affecting their environment, which threatens and challenges them; and higher levels of affluence that open up opportunities for a variety of experiences never before so generally available.

The evidences of this trend are many. They are found in the seeking within many religions for more viable modes and values. They are found in the demand for equality by minorities and in the challenges of youths, who question established values. And they are found in the involvement of so many people in self-expression activities in the arts and leisure activities.

To design modified or new organizations, employee roles, and interpersonal processes and to bring them into reality is the domain of organizational change and development. Even if it were possible for a single individual or small group to develop a master blueprint for introducing organizational change, it is doubtful whether the organizational members who are affected would readily accept the change or have the required skills for implementing the change. For these reasons, it is critical that change agents—whether they be managers, consultants, or employees with ideas—be as competent in deciding *how to introduce* change as they are in diagnosing *what needs to be changed*.

OBJECTIVES OF PLANNED ORGANIZATIONAL CHANGE

The most difficult issue in studying change is to define it. Most things are in a continual state of change. Certainly most people change their behavior over time. Given that behavior is always changing, what determines change from the status quo? *Planned organizational change is the intentional or purposive attempt by an organization to influence the status quo of itself or any other organization.* Because the management of an organization cannot completely control its environment, it continually has to introduce internal organizational changes that allow it to cope more effectively with new challenges presented by employees and from the outside by increased competition, advances in technology, new governmental legislation, and pressing social demands. Most frequently, organizational changes are introduced in *reaction* to these environmental pressures. In some cases, however, changes are made in *anticipation* of future problems (e.g., impending governmental regulations, new products being introduced on the market by a competitor).

If planned organizational change is purposeful, then what are the goals of planned change? Goals listed by executives include higher productivity, acceptance of new technology, greater motivation of employees, more innovative behavior, and greater share of the market. These goals, and a host of others, have two underlying objectives: (1) change the organization's way of adapting to changes in its environment, and (2) change employee attitudes, means of communication, and ways of relating within the organization.[2]

Organizational Adaptation

If most planned organizational changes are introduced in reaction to or in anticipation of changes in the firm's external environment, it is essential that the firm obtain information from its environment to maintain and increase its effectiveness. Companies such as General Motors, DuPont, Scott Paper, Lever Brothers, Monsanto, and Honeywell Corporation have established permanent corporate staffs charged with the responsibility of monitoring the multiple environments of the corporation and alerting management to developing trends that could affect the organization's effectiveness. These staffs maintain contacts with a wide variety of organizations, including government agencies, future-research centers, planning staffs of other companies, professional societies, and universities.

How does General Motors, for example, adapt to changes in the automobile industry?[3] Clear evidence of GM's effective response to that challenge is the transformation of its product line to meet the demands of the marketplace and the federal government for better gas mileage. When the Arab oil embargo hit at the end of 1973, GM had the worst average gas mileage among U.S. automakers, about 12 miles per gallon. As buyers turned away from the gas-guzzlers in panic during 1974, GM's share of the U.S. new-car market fell to 42 percent, the lowest since 1952. Just three years later, in the 1977-model year, the average mileage of GM cars was 17.8, the best among the big three. Largely as a result, the company's market share rebounded to about 55 percent and profits were up 14 percent from 1976.

At the center of this product revolution was GM's downsizing strategy, which went into production in 1977. GM gambled that it could redefine the meaning of "big" from its traditional exterior bulk to a more functional, European style definition based on interior space and driving quality. The gamble succeeded. But how did it happen? In 1974, a committee reporting to the chief executive officer recommended that GM reorganize itself. Complicated in its details, basically the reorganization upgraded the responsibilities of the vice-presidents and brought in new executives in key managerial areas. GM also adopted a project center management system that enabled the company to coordinate the decisions of the five automobile divisions more effectively. GM adopted the project center idea in order to meet the special demands created by the downsizing decision. The project center is not composed of a permanent group of executives. Every time a new effort is planned, say a body changeover, a project center is formed, and it operates for the duration of that project. Project centers work on parts and engineering problems common to all divisions, such as frames, electrical systems, steering gears, and brakes.

The project center was probably GM's single most important managerial tool in carrying out the decision to downsize its cars. It has eliminated much redundant effort and speeded numerous new technologies into production. The costs of adapting to the environment have been enormous. GM's research and development expenditures are running at an annual rate well over $1 billion, which is equivalent to more than a third of 1976 net income ($2.9 billion, on revenues of $47 billion). The company estimates that by 1980 capital expenditures for the decade will have amounted to more than $25 billion, most of which will go to meet the demands for emission controls, safety, and downsizing. And some managerial decisions have been costly too. For example, in early 1978 the company was selling Chevettes at a loss because it felt that it must pay that price to establish itself more securely in the low end of the price market.

What happens to organizations that cannot or do not adapt to changes in their environment? Eventually they will die. Penn Central, W. T. Grant, Robert Hall, and the *Pennsylvania Mirror* are only several of the companies that have recently ceased operations. What happened at the *Pennsylvania Mirror*? The *Pennsylvania Mirror* was born on December 11, 1968, as a daily newspaper in central Pennsylvania and died on December 31, 1977.[4] Unanticipated and increasing expenses were given as the reasons for forcing the *Mirror* to shut down its presses. Through its nine-plus years, the *Mirror* had won more than thirty newspaper awards. It was judged best newspaper in its class (dailies with circulation under 15,000) on three separate occasions by the Pennsylvania Newspaper Publishers Association. Because of its nearness to a large university, top-notch journalism students were easy to attract.

However, there were several things that forced the *Mirror* to close down. First, it could not hold on to its best reporters. It served as a training ground for other newspapers that would then reap the benefits of the experience that these young college graduates had received at the *Mirror*. Second, the newspaper failed to attract sufficient advertising from local merchants. Only three of the ten largest groceries were placing ads in the

Mirror. Many of the grocers believed that they could be better served by putting their advertising dollar in the other local daily newspaper, or on radio, television, or billboards. One reporter on the *Mirror* staff commented, "Most intelligent people will buy advertising if they think it will do something for them; we could never convince them of that." Since the *Mirror* was a morning newspaper, it was always considered as an afterthought by local merchants who believed that the evening paper was a better place to put their ads. Third, the geographical area served by the paper didn't grow as fast as expected. The editor attributed this slow growth to the stalled Appalachian Thruway and the slow-to-be-completed Keystone Shortway. Fourth, the *Mirror* lacked consistent and evenly balanced news coverage of the local area. According to one former employee, "We wanted to play cowboy today, and then fireman, and then a jet pilot. We had no marketing strategy." Several people on the paper thought that it should have been a regional newspaper, but it lacked a sufficient number of reporters to cover the region. Millions of dollars were spent on the physical plant, but the paper was constantly understaffed. This caused lapses in coverage that impaired the paper's credibility with the readers.

Individual Adaptation

The second objective of planned organizational change is to achieve changes in the attitudes, styles, and behavioral patterns of individuals within the organization. An organization may not be able to change its adaptation strategy for reacting to its relevant environment unless the members in the organization behave differently in their relationships to one another and to their jobs. Organizations survive, grow, decline, or fail because people make decisions. If GM had not been able to change the behavior of managers to work in project centers instead of their own division, the changes would have been less successful. Every organization has its unique decision-making process. At GM, decentralization of decision making is rewarded, whereas in McDonalds, decision making is highly centralized.

Any organizational change, whether it is introduced through a new structural design or a company training program, is basically trying to get employees to change their behavior. In a frequently changing environment, such as the aerospace, electronics, and pharmaceutical industries, a rigid authority hierarchy may restrict the channels of communication and thus reduce the amount of information needed by the organization's top managers to make effective decisions. Even if the structure of the organization shifts to a more decentralized one, there is a high probability that unless the employees' behavioral patterns are changed, the new structure will have little impact on the effectiveness of the organization. In order for organization-wide effects to be felt, new employee behavior consistent with the demands of the organization's environment must emerge. Chapters 16 and

17 examine strategies that focus on changing the attitudes, styles, and behaviors of employees.

PRESSURES TO CHANGE

A striking feature of the U.S. economy is the way in which it constantly changes. A hundred years ago the country's biggest industry was agriculture; a few decades later, manufacturing engaged the largest number of people; today, more than six out of every ten workers are involved not in producing goods but in delivering services. Automation and the increasing use of computers are certain to accelerate this trend. Some experts predict that by the year 2000, more than 90 percent of the labor force could be employed in the services industry. Managers operating in this changing environment are in demand to diagnose the important changing factors that affect their organization. This section discusses the major pressures facing organizations in the 1970s and early 1980s, when most of you will be practicing managers.

Changing Technology

The rate of technological change is greater today than it has been at any time in the past. In *The Two Cultures* C. P. Snow commented that during all human history until this century, the rate of social and technological change had been very slow—so slow that it could pass unnoticed in one person's lifetime. That is no longer possible.[5] The rate of technological change is a keynote feature in Alvin Toffler's *Future Shock*.[6] Toffler's central thesis is that our society's inability to adapt to the increasing *rate* of change—not its content or direction—is the most critical problem of our time. During the last hundred years, the speed of communications has increased by a factor of 10^7, the speed of handling data 10^6, the speed of travel by 10^2.

During the next decade or so, electronic transfer of funds will be commonplace. Cash will continue to exist, but checks will be replaced by bank cards. Electronic funds transfer will reach about 50 percent substitution of paper. It is expected that 40 percent of U.S. households will be able to purchase merchandise at home via their TV. Products will be displayed on the screen and the viewer will order merchandise by keying in on a 12-key phone pad or other type of keyboard. Two-way television systems will be found in many homes. With the use of lasers in communications, the use of picturephone and two-way cable video service will rapidly expand.

A sophisticated communications network will make it possible to move managerial functions from the central office to the home. A switched network will provide audiovideo and hard-copy services, utilizing the technologies of picturephone, rapid facsimile transmission, cable television, and satellite communications. The greatest problems will involve software, personnel reorganization, the cost, and managers' disinclination to supervise at-home personnel.[7]

At National Cash Register Company at Dayton, Ohio, the impact of new technology has been felt in several ways.[8] NCR has reduced its Dayton work force from about 20,000 to 5,000 and, at the same time, has shrunk its worldwide work force from 103,000 to about 65,000. How could this happen in a company that had sales of $2.3 billion in 1977 and a $95.6 million profit after taxes? The invention of a tiny silicon chip that replaced many mechanical parts has radically changed the technology of making cash registers. The traditional cash register, with 5,000 parts, has been replaced by an electronic machine with only a few hundred parts. The microcircuit's system means that fewer workers are needed to make and assemble parts. NCR can also purchase parts on the open market from mass producers who can make them more cheaply than NCR. At one assembly line in Dayton, where 350 to 500 employees were required per shift, the work force has been reduced to 15 to 20. The jobs that have been retained are also simpler than the old jobs. Workers have to master only a few tasks that can be learned in several days.

Technology will change the nature of jobs being performed at all levels. Fewer employees will be needed for purely repetitive work in conventional factories. Many industries will require less direct labor input. A single worker will be able to operate a large hydroelectric plant, oil refinery, or cement plant with the assistance of automated machinery directed by the computer. People will still be required to operate and service the highly complex automatic equipment, but far fewer people will be needed.

Many middle management positions will either be eliminated or dropped to a lower rung in the organization as machines take over more and more of the routine tasks commonly undertaken by middle managers. Those middle managers' jobs that remain will be relatively unstructured, providing communication links between work groups. It will be the middle manager's job to promote high levels of cooperation between technically trained personnel and to provide them with a work environment conducive to group collaboration. They will also search for better decision rules that will require managers to study the relationship between their areas of responsibility and the rest of the organization. Future middle managers will spend most of their time *managing by exception:* When an unexpected problem baffles the computer, when a change in rules is needed, or when a computer breaks down, the middle manager will take over. As middle management positions become less structured, innovation and creativity will become more important managerial skills.

As information technology develops, top management will come to rely less on middle managers and will be able to focus more attention on determining organization goals, establishing long-range planning, and facilitating organizational relations with the external environment. To accomplish this, the traditional management practice of a single chief executive officer will be impractical. In order to make complex decisions, chief executives will either have to expand their staffs greatly to include a variety of diverse specialists or allow the decision-making process to flow through an executive team. Some organizations, such as Caterpillar Tractor, already use the executive team approach. Other organizations can be expected to develop similar approaches to top-management problems.

Knowledge Explosion

The rate at which society has been storing useful information about itself has been spiraling upward at an increasing rate. Today, for example, the number of scientific journals and articles is doubling about every fifteen years, and the number of book titles produced each day has been estimated at 1,000. As a result, knowledge in a particular field quickly becomes obsolete. In addition, organizations that depend on highly sophisticated knowledge bases can easily become obsolete unless planned change efforts are continuous. For example, Bowmar, the manufacturer of the first pocket calculator in 1971, lost its dominance in the market in 1975. This occurred because, as the technology to make calculators became simpler and cheaper, competitors moved into the market, prices fell, and Bowmar couldn't adapt. Industry sales of pocket calculators made quantum jumps —from an estimated 4 million sold in 1972 to 28 million in 1975—but Bowmar mismanaged the knowledge explosion in terms of consumer wants and needs. Left with outdated equipment and large overhead expenses, Bowmar's management could not adapt its technology to compete with other firms in the industry.[9]

Rapid Product Obsolescence

Fast-shifting consumer preferences, combined with frequent technological changes, have shortened the life cycle of many products and services. Every consumer has had the experience of trying to buy certain items in the supermarket only to find that the product was impossible to locate or that the brand no longer existed. Approximately 55 percent of the items sold today did not exist ten years ago, and of the products sold then, about 40 percent have been taken off the shelf. In the volatile pharmaceutical and electronics fields, a product is often obsolete in as short a period as six months. As the pace accelerates, managers may well create products with the knowledge that they will remain on the market for only a matter of months. When Bowmar introduced the pocket calculator in 1971, it sold for $247. In 1978, it appeared that almost every month a new, less expensive but more complex instrument was introduced to the market, rendering older ones obsolete, to some extent.

When product life cycles are shortened, organizations must be able to shorten their lead times to get into production. Thus flexible organizations, or at least flexible subsystems, are likely to be required for continued viability in the future. These temporary or flexible organizations will permit managers to assemble small groups of personnel for the purposes of developing strategies and analyzing decisions. Aside from its value in permitting flexibility and adaptation for the corporation, this type of structure enables the corporation to react quickly to information gathered by an early warning system, facilitates transitions to new forms of operations, encourages broadly based and participative decision making, and provides a multitude of situations in which potential future leadership can be observed and developed.

Changing Nature of the Work Force

Major changes in the nature of the work force include shifts in the age of workers, the ratio of male to female workers, and the educational level of workers. In 1957, 18.5 percent of the work force was twenty-four years old or younger. By 1974, the share of the work force held by young persons had risen to 24.9 percent. In 1978, this percentage was roughly the same. In 1974–1978, the percentage of workers fifty-five and older was declining. Female workers rose from 31.2 percent of the total work force in 1957, to 37.9 percent in 1974, to 40.1 percent in 1978. The educational level of workers has climbed substantially. A U.S. Department of Labor survey indicated that less than 30 percent of the labor force held college degrees in 1969; by 1973, the college educated had increased their share to 36 percent, and by 1978, the figure had risen to 39 percent. This younger, less male-dominated, and better educated work force has already questioned some traditional management styles and practices. Women will further increase their share of the work force in the early 1980s. Even more importantly, their status within the work force will improve. And the educational level of workers is expected to continue to rise. But the percentage of young workers will level off or decrease, because of the lower birthrate in the 1960s.

Not only will the composition of the work force change, but there also will be more interorganizational mobility. Occupational mobility will be aided by pension plans that enable workers' pension plans to move with them from company to company. If an organization cannot meet a worker's need for vocational or personal development, the worker will simply leave. Workers will become more cosmopolitan and less loyal to an individual employer or company. They will maintain their strongest ties to their profession or skill rather than to the organization. Workers may, however, be forced to change their occupation several times during their work life in order to adjust to changing occupational needs. As a result, people will commonly have several different careers during their lifetimes.

Managers will need to be more broadly and intensively educated as work becomes increasingly intellectual and the level of education in the general population increases. Managers will need an education that provides them with skills and tools for a lifetime of career moves. Businesses and government will make large-scale provisions for the continual reeducation of the work force. Many organizations, such as IBM, Xerox, General Electric, Westinghouse, B. F. Goodrich, and Exxon have established their own educational centers. Using advanced educational and technological systems, these companies offer materials that range from basic educational and vocational training to programs for executive development.

Quality of Work Life

The quality of work life has become a major issue in the labor force, not only in the United States but throughout the Western industrial society. *Quality of work life* is the degree to which members of a work organization are able to satisfy important personal needs through their experiences in the organization.[10] Management, organized labor, and even government are interested in participating in the design of organizational change activities aimed at improving the quality of work life.

Little data speak directly to the seriousness or the scope of the quality-of-work-life problem. Those who argue that it is important generally contend:

1. Worker alienation and job dissatisfaction are increasing, primarily as a result of meaningless jobs and autocratic managers.
2. The productivity of American workers is declining while counterproductive behaviors (such as turnover, sabotage, union militancy, theft, drug abuse, alcoholism) at work are increasing.
3. Confidence in big business is eroding.

The quality of an individual's work life has been linked to many on-the-job and off-the-job behaviors. Improvements in quality of work life might, for example, lead to more positive feelings toward oneself (greater self-esteem), toward one's job (improved job satisfaction and involvement), and toward the organization (stronger commitment to organization goals). Improved physical and psychological health, fewer mental health problems and less drug abuse, and greater growth and development of the individual as a person and a productive member of the organization might result from improvements in quality of work life. Finally, a higher quality of work life may lead to decreased absenteeism and turnover, fewer industrial accidents, and higher quality and quantity of outputs of goods and services.

Life-Style

Life-style is the outward evidence of one's values, beliefs, and perspectives. A person's life style affects and is effected by organizationally related issues.[11] Three dimensions of a person's life-style are important for managers: formalistic, interpersonal, and personalistic. Each person's life-style contains a certain proportion of each of these three dimensions, as indicated in Table 15–1.

The table presents nine basic values or behaviors and how these interrelate with the three dimensions of a person's life-style. The *formalistic* life-style dimension reflects the value that a person places on having his or her actions guided by directives from formal authorities. Control over individual behavior comes from rules, regulations, policies, and standard

TABLE 15–1.   The Values and Behaviors of Three Major Life-styles.

Value/Behavior	Formalistic	Interpersonal	Personalistic
Direction from	Authorities and those responsible	Discussion, agreement with others who are close	Within individual
Guidance from	Precedent and policy	Close relationships with others	Self-knowledge of what one wants to do
Desired condition	Clear pathways for advancement and reward	Friends and colleagues who are committed	Freedom to choose how one lives
Basis for growth and progress	Learning from and following the established order	Learning from and sharing with others	Learning from one's own experience, acting on one's own awareness
Faith in	Rules, laws, policies, orders	Group norms, what close friends say and advise	One's own sense of justice
Strives for desired state	Advancement and prestige, compliance, respect	Intimacy and acceptance, collaboration, agreement, consensus	Freedom and independence, self-determination and realization
Incentive	Security and comfort	Intimate relationships and shared values	Experimentation and self-discovery
Responsible to	Those in positions of higher responsibility	Those with whom one has close personal relationships	Self
Feelings and emotions	To be channeled and made rational	To be shared with others who are close	To be totally experienced

From Friedlander, F., Emergent and contemporary life styles: An intergenerational issue, *Human Relations*, 1975, 28, pp. 329–347.

operating procedures. Direction comes from the top positions in the organization. The individual grows and develops by following an established order set forth by the organization. The traditional bureaucratic organization, characterized by a detailed list of rules, policies, and regulations, closely follows this life-style. Communications are mostly downward; decisions are made at the top and are implemented by individuals down the organization's hierarchy.

The major value dimensions in the *interpersonal* life-style are developed through interaction with others. The values are derived from accepted group norms and serve as a basis of control of individual behavior. The individual grows and develops through interaction with others. The informal work group is the organization's parallel to this life-style. In a work group, authority is vested in the standards and norms developed by the group. Decisions are made by consensus. Communication is, for the most part, carried on between members of the group, and conflict is resolved through consensus.

The third major value dimension is the *personalistic* style. This style emphasizes that an individual's actions are guided by his or her own personal experience and feelings. Growth and awareness development result from increased self-awareness. The individual strives for freedom, independence, and the development of a sense of values. In many organizations, this dimension can be seen in the use of temporary systems, such as project management, committees, and task forces. In these systems, two or more people come together because they share some common concern, and they stay together because of it. Each individual decides what he or she wants to do and directs himself or herself toward achieving that goal. Communication is mostly within each individual in terms of ideas, reactions, and feelings, and progress toward goal achievement. Conflict between members is dealt with openly and resolved by the persons involved.

People with a formalistic life-style welcome rigid directions from top management. They find satisfaction in carrying out the rules and procedures of the organization. People with an interpersonal life-style may tolerate this direction from above as long as the internal operation of their department is based on staff involvement and cooperation. But people with a personalistic life-style chafe at directives from above and are not appeased by departmental interaction. They need to be able to work independently. In order to achieve maximum performance and high job satisfaction for each employee, managers must, as much as is possible, match each employee's life-style with positions in the organization that complement that life-style.

RESISTANCES TO CHANGE

Most managers today are deeply concerned with the problem of developing strategies appropriate to the changing conditions of their environment. The changes through which our organizations and society are going are not independent of one another. They reflect some of the basic changes noted in the previous section. Successful managers are continually seeking to develop flexible organizations that can change with the requirements of the environment and can also anticipate and be active in influencing the environment. It is not enough to carry out piecemeal efforts to patch up a problem here, redesign a job there, or rewrite a rule. There is an increasing need for systematic, planned change efforts that coordinate the ways of work, relationships, and communication systems with the predictable and unpredictable requirements of the future.

Why do individuals and organizations resist change? Resistance to change is one of the most baffling problems that managers face because it can take so many forms. Overt resistance may take the form of strikes, reduction in productivity, and shoddy workmanship. Implicit resistance may be manifested in increased absenteeism, requests for transfer, resignations, loss of motivation to work, "mental errors," and lateness in arriving at work. The effects of resistance, either overt or implicit, may be subtle and cumulative. That is, minimal reactions to a small change (for example, a change in location of an office machine or a change in office routine) can take place without a manager being aware of employee resistance. In contrast, a major overt indicator of resistance may be a wildcat strike or work slowdown.

Resistances by Individuals

This section focuses on resistance as it operates within the individual. The list of resistances is somewhat arbitrary and many of the individual and organizational resistances interact.[12]

Selective Attention and Retention.   Once an attitude has been established, a person responds to others' suggestions within the framework that has been established. Situations may be perceived as reinforcing the original attitude when they actually do not. People resist the possible impact of change on their lives by reading or listening to only what agrees with their present views, by conveniently forgetting any learning that could lead to opposite viewpoints, and by misunderstanding communications that, if correctly perceived, would not be congruent with preestablished attitudes. For example, managers enrolled in executive training programs are exposed to different managerial philosophies. They may do very well at discussing and answering questions about these philosophies, but they may carefully segregate in their minds the new approaches that "of course, would not work in my job" and those that they are already practicing.

Let's look at another example where selective attention is used to resist a change:

Sally Hillyard was a supervisor in a dairy plant in Pine Grove Mills, Pennsylvania. The company installed an automatic ice cream machine, which when fully operational would reduce the number of personnel by half. Sally resented this change because it took away from her responsibilities and authority. Several days after the new machinery had been installed, a group of corporate executives from Hawk Run, Pennsylvania, were visiting the plant to see the new machinery in operation. During their visit, something went wrong with the new machinery. Ice cream was flowing all over the floor and piled up several inches by the time the visiting executives reached the room. Horrified, the plant superintendent (who served as a tour guide for the visiting executives) demanded an explanation from Sally. Sally stated, "What was I supposed to do? Nobody gave me instructions on how to stop the machine from making ice cream."

Habit.   Unless a situation changes noticeably, individuals continue to respond to stimuli in their accustomed way. Once a habit is established, it may become a source of satisfaction for the individual. If an organization were suddenly to announce that every employee was immediately to receive a 20 percent pay raise, few would object. However, if the company were suddenly to announce that every employee was immediately to receive a 20 percent pay cut, many would object. In the latter case, many habits— taking vacations, buying new cars every three years, shopping for convenience foods—would have to be changed because of the inability to finance these activities. In the recession of 1974–1975, individual buying habits changed slowly and only under severe economic conditions (after unemployment benefits were exhausted).

Dependence.   All human beings begin life dependent upon adults. Parents sustain life in the helpless infant and provide major satisfactions. The inevitable outcome is that children tend to incorporate the values, attitudes, and beliefs of their parents. Dependency on others can be a resistance to change if people have not developed a sense of self-esteem. People who are highly dependent on others and lack self-esteem are likely to resist changes until those they are dependent on endorse the changes and incorporate them into their behavioral activities. A worker who is highly dependent on his or her boss for feedback on performance will probably not incorporate any new techniques or methods unless the boss personally okays the decision and indicates to the employee how these changes will improve performance.

Let's look at one incident:

A junior executive at Standard Steel was told by a colleague that the United Fund was looking for volunteer workers and that she

> *thought that he could qualify and do a great job. Six months later, during a performance appraisal, the junior executive was asked by his boss why he had not contributed his time to community affairs. He replied, "I didn't know of any suitable openings or that the company would give me time off."*

Working for the United Fund was of low interest to this manager because he thought only other junior level managers became involved. During the next United Fund campaign, he was a very active fundraiser now that he was aware that the boss thought it was a good idea.

Fear of the Unknown.   Confronting the unknown makes most people anxious. Each major change in the work situation carries with it an element of uncertainty. A woman who is starting a second career after raising her family might be anxious about how she will fit in with other workers after a long absence from work. A sales manager may wonder: "What might happen if I relocate to company headquarters in Texas? Will my family like it? Can I find friends? Suppose I say no? What will the company think of me?" Uncertainty in this situation arises not from the change itself, but from the consequences surrounding the change. To avoid making decisions and the fear of the unknown, some managers refuse promotions if it means moving.

Economic Reasons.   Money weighs heavily in people's considerations. Changes that pose the possibility of lowering a person's income directly or indirectly will usually be resisted. Development in recent years of the "do-it-yourself divorce kits" that provide the purchaser with a flow chart of activities that enable a person to obtain a divorce without paying an attorney have been fought by lawyers. Lawyers have also voiced their concern over no-fault automobile insurance because this does away with the need for trial lawyers. While one may argue that these resistances represent a genuine desire to protect the public's interest, much of this resistance appears to be economically based.

Security and Regression.   Another obstacle to change is the tendency of some people to seek security by regressing into the past. When life becomes frustrating, people think about the happy days of the past. The irony is that this frustration-regression sequence usually occurs just when old ways no longer produce the desired outcome and experimentation with new approaches is most needed. Even under these conditions, people with a high degree of insecurity are apt to cling even more desperately to old, unproductive behavior patterns. The manager who does not recognize the effects of equal-opportunity legislation on his policy of hiring only white males seeks somehow to find a road back to the old days when he ran the shop according to his personal likes.

Resistances by Organizations

Most organizations have been designed so that they resist innovation. Like fully automated factories, most organizations have been designed to do a narrowly prescribed assortment of things and to do them reliably. To ensure reliability of prescribed operations, the organization may create strong defenses against change. Moreover, change often runs counter to vested interests and probably violates certain territorial rights or decision-making prerogatives that have been established and accepted over time.

Threats to Power and Influence.   Change may be seen as a threat to the power or influence of various persons in an organization. One source of power in organizations is the control of something that other people need, such as information, money, or jobs. If people ranking higher than you need your cooperation, then you can use your power to bargain for favors, freedom, assignments, and even raises and promotions. Once your power position in the organization has been established, a change that may be seen as reducing your power and authority will be resisted. In a large midwestern school district, teachers were encouraged to make recommendations to principals and district personnnel regarding possible solutions to school-related problems. Some of the strongest resistance to this change problem came from the principals. A typical response by a principal is the following:

> I have a real problem with this program. What you are really doing is giving teachers an input into the decision process. By doing this, you are increasing their power. Now I have to check things with them before making decisions. That really takes away my authority.[13]

This response clearly identifies the feeling that the change poses a threat to the principal's authority, and thus it becomes a resistance to achieving change.

Organizational Structure.   To assure predictability, the typical bureaucratic organization narrowly defines jobs; clearly spells out lines of authority, responsibility, and accountability; and stresses the flow of information from the top to the bottom. A strict emphasis on the hierarchy of authority is likely to cause employees to adhere only to specific channels of communication and to feed back only positive information regarding their jobs. They neglect any negative feedback that might actually help the organization better identify both the need and means for change. The more bureaucratic the organization, the more channels of communication through which the idea must travel. This then increases the probability that any new idea will be screened out because it violates the status quo in the organization.

Power in most organizations comes to the individual with access to vital information. Having access to such information, the politically smart manager controls others by manipulating this information. Robert Townsend, in his satirical yet insightful book *Up the Organization,* cautions managers about disrupting the status quo in organizations.

> If you discovered how to eliminate air pollution for $1.50 per state, the worst way to accomplish it would be to announce your discovery. You'd be amazed how many people would oppose your plan. The best way, if you could stay along and out of jail, would be just to start eliminating it, state by state.[14]

Townsend is saying that novel ideas and the new use of resources may disrupt the power relationships within organizations and therefore will often be resisted.

The reward structure of an organization can also be a factor in resistance to change. If managers are asked to learn skills to use on their job, they are likely to be resistant if they feel that they are not going to be rewarded for it. This elementary principle is frequently violated in organizations.

> *A large corporation issued a policy statement that the corporation would place more emphasis on participative management. To demonstrate the seriousness of this intent, a product committee was established with representatives from all key functional areas of the business. A stated purpose of this committee was "to assist top management in making decisions about new ventures which could shape the destiny of the organization." Three months later it was announced that the corporation was negotiating to acquire a large electronics firm.*

No one on the product committee was asked his/her opinion about the desirability of such a course of action. The members of the product committee perceived that they were not rewarded for participating in the decision process and soon stopped showing up for meetings. Future policy statements by the corporation were met with considerable skepticism by employees.

The goals of an organization can also act as a resistant to change. The conservative financial policy of Montgomery Ward immediately after World War II assured Ward of great organizational stability. But since the retail environment was changing, this drive for economic stability was a major factor in Ward's decline in the merchandising field. On the other hand, Sears assumed that risk taking, in terms of opening new stores in suburban areas and adding new lines of merchandise, was needed to gain prominence in the market. As a result of these different strategies, Sears' sales in 1977 were 210 percent of Ward's.

Resource Limitations.   While some companies want to maintain the status quo, others would change if they had the available resources to do so. The problems of the American steel industry are hardly a secret: formidable competition from abroad, slack demand, high labor costs, aging mills, rigorous antipollution laws that require huge investments in nonproductive equipment. In Ohio's Mahoning Valley, the once booming steel plants are dying.[15] Bethlehem Steel Corporation, the nation's second largest producer, announced during the summer of 1977 that it was laying off 3,500 workers in Lackawanna, New York, an industrial neighbor of Buffalo with a population of only 28,000, and another 3,500 in Johnstown, Pennsylvania. Bethlehem also decided to abandon the construction of a multimillion dollar oxygen furnace at Johnstown because it lacks the resources to recover from the flood of July 1977 and complete the furnace. Bethlehem does not have the profit margin (slack resources) available to introduce planned change in facilities; long-term returns from such an investment may be in doubt.

Those who earn their livelihood by selling to the steelworkers are feeling the impact also. The unemployed steelworkers are gradually reducing their standard of living. Tony Risi, the owner of a store in Conshohocken, Pennsylvania, says that he would like to sell his store, but he doesn't have enough cash to fix it up. In good times the place might have been worth $150,000, but the most recent offer he had was only $80,000.

Sunk Costs.   Resource limitations are not confined to organizations lacking assets. Rich organizations may find themselves as hard put because of *sunk costs*—the investment of much of their capital in fixed assets (equipment, building, land, etc.). The plight of many central business districts may serve to illustrate this resistance. Most of our larger cities evolved in the era before automobiles; they can hardly begin to handle today's motor traffic. Therefore, these cities have had an increasingly difficult time meeting the competition of suburban shopping centers. Sunk costs are not always limited to physical things. They can also be expressed in terms of people. What happens to an employee who is no longer making a significant contribution to the organization but has enough seniority to maintain his or her job? Unless the employee can be motivated to higher task performance, he or she will likely stay with the company until retirement. Fringe benefits, salary, and the like are payments to the individual for past services and represent sunk costs for the company.

Interorganizational Agreements.   Agreements between organizations usually impose obligations on people that can act as restraints on their behavior.[16] Labor contracts are the most pertinent examples because some things that were once considered major prerogatives of management (right to hire and fire, assignment of personnel to tasks, promotions, etc.) now have become subjects of negotiation. But labor contracts are not the only kinds of contracts that restrain management. Proponents of change in an organization's structure may also find their plan delayed by arrangements with competitors, commitments to suppliers, pledges to public officials in return for licenses or permits, promises to contractors, and the like.

While agreements can be ignored or violated, potential legal costs may be expensive, lost customers might be hesitant to buy the product again, and credit-rating declines can be disastrous.

Does it follow, therefore, that managers must be forever saddled with the task of trying to achieve change in organizations or individuals that resist change? Our answer is no. Resistance to change will probably never cease completely, but managers can learn to succeed and to minimize the resistance by planning the change. The next section of this chapter identifies a model that managers can use to understand the process of change.

GENERAL PROCESS MODEL OF CHANGE

One difficulty that managers often encounter in situations involving change is that they find it difficult to get a handle on the situation. The problem sometimes becomes quite complex because of the variety of inter-relationships.[17] The expectations of people within the organization or of customers buying its products or services, the organizational structure used to make decisions, and the demands of the technology used to manufacture the product must all be examined.

Kurt Lewin, a pioneering social psychologist, developed a way of looking at change that has proved to be highly useful to action-oriented managers.[18] Lewin saw change not as an event, but as a dynamic balance of forces working in opposite directions. Any situation can be considered in a state of equilibrium resulting from a balance of forces constantly pushing against each other. For example, a manager may wish to delegate decision-making authority to subordinates more effectively.[19] There are certain forces in the situation—the resistances to change—that tend to maintain the status quo, to resist more delegation. At the same time, acting opposite to these forces, pushing for change, are the pressures to change. The combined effect of these two sets of forces results in the situation illustrated in Figure 15–1. Resistances to change and pressures to change are categorized as discussed in the previous sections of this chapter. Note that you don't have to have an equal number of resistances and pressures to change. If you identify five pressures to change, there is no reason why you must also identify five resistances to change. Often one resistance may offset the effects of several pressures to change.

Strategy for Change

To initiate change, a manager must take some action to modify the current equilibrium of forces. In other words, the current equilibrium must be "unfrozen." The manager can do this by:

1. Increasing the strength of the pressures for change.
2. Reducing the strength of the resisting forces or removing them completely.
3. Changing the direction of a force; that is, make a resistance into a pressure for change.

Figure 15–2 shows the resistances to change and the pressures to change confronting a manager who wants to delegate responsibility more effectively.

After a diagnosis of the resistances and pressures to change, the manager is then faced with the task of determining what action to take to effect the situation. For example, although we identified six resistances, two or three may have relatively greater impact on the organization than the others. These resistances, if modified, will have a greater impact on the proposed change than will less powerful resistances. Of course, the same situation may exist with regard to the pressures for change. Some are stronger than others and are more important in the current situation. Thus the process of planned change is one of altering the forces that support a particular level of equilibrium so that one set of forces replaces another.

This model for understanding the processes of change has several benefits. It requires that the change agent get a specific picture of the current situation. By becoming skillful at diagnosing forces pressing for change and the resistances to change, the manager should have an idea of

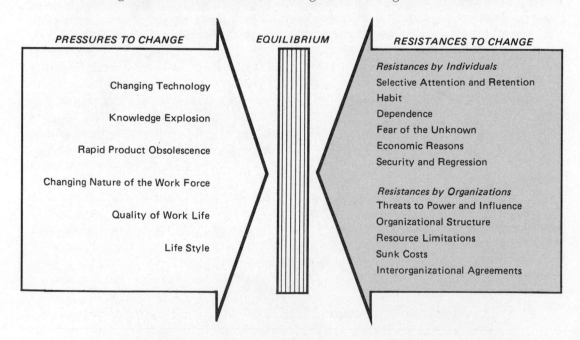

FIGURE 15–1.   Forces Supporting and Resisting Changes in Organizations

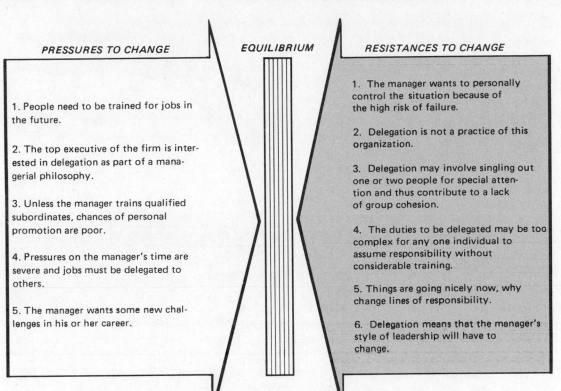

PRESSURES TO CHANGE

1. People need to be trained for jobs in the future.

2. The top executive of the firm is interested in delegation as part of a managerial philosophy.

3. Unless the manager trains qualified subordinates, chances of personal promotion are poor.

4. Pressures on the manager's time are severe and jobs must be delegated to others.

5. The manager wants some new challenges in his or her career.

EQUILIBRIUM

RESISTANCES TO CHANGE

1. The manager wants to personally control the situation because of the high risk of failure.

2. Delegation is not a practice of this organization.

3. Delegation may involve singling out one or two people for special attention and thus contribute to a lack of group cohesion.

4. The duties to be delegated may be too complex for any one individual to assume responsibility without considerable training.

5. Things are going nicely now, why change lines of responsibility.

6. Delegation means that the manager's style of leadership will have to change.

FIGURE 15–2.   Pressures and Resistances to Change

the relevant forces under consideration. In addition, the concept of equilibrium provides the manager with some kind of useful framework to analyze a complex situation. Finally, the model serves to highlight those factors that can be changed and those that cannot. Too many managers spend a great deal of time considering actions related to forces over which they have little control. When the manager directs attention to those forces over which he or she has some control, the likelihood is increased that the options chosen will have the most impact.

To carry through on the previous example, let's assume that the manager has decided to delegate more decision-making responsibility and authority to qualified subordinates. The manager's first task is to unfreeze the attitudes, beliefs, and personal styles of subordinates. As indicated in Figure 15–3, when this occurs, the subordinates' performance is likely to decrease, in the short run. In this example, the subordinates' performance of 100 units per day is assumed to decrease fairly quickly to 60 units per day. During this time period, indicated on the horizontal axis, subordinates must develop new attitudes, skills, and techniques to handle their enlarged decision-making responsibilities. This transition period is the *moving stage*,

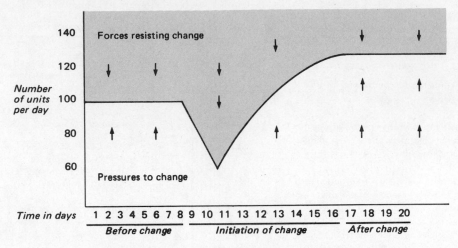

FIGURE 15–3.   Forces Influencing Change

when attitudes or beliefs are changing. The equilibrium of the situation has been disturbed and the forces resisting the change are greater than the pressures supporting the change. During the moving period, days 8 through 16, the manager should attempt to reduce some of the resistances. For example, the manager's own leadership style might be changed to be more compatible with the philosophy of delegation of decision making. Similarly, the manager's superiors must provide him or her with the necessary psychological and financial support, in case a subordinate fails to complete the task as desired. As the manager and subordinates gradually overcome these resistances to change, the forces pressing for the change increase. When the change process has been completed, the performance may be 20 units higher than before the change was initiated (i.e., 120 versus 100 units per day). At that point, the manager and subordinates must *refreeze* this newly established equilibrium—that is, rearrange the forces in the situation to maintain the higher level of productivity.

While this example illustrates the benefits of a change in decision making, many managers are unsuccessful in creating meaningful change. One reason is that some managers have a strong tendency to increase the pressures to change in order to produce the desired change. This will, of course, disrupt the balance and result in short-run changes. Unfortunately, an increase in the pressures to change also has negative effects on the stability of the system. This was illustrated in Figure 15–3 when production dropped from 100 to 60 units per day. However, increasing the forces toward change can often have the effect of stimulating new forces of resistance or reawakening or strengthening existing forces of resistance. This process is much like inflating a balloon. As you increase the air on the inside, you also decrease the strength of the balloon, and at some point the balloon explodes because it cannot absorb any more pressure. What is needed is an understanding of resistances to change and how these resistances and pressures to change interact, so that the system will be able to remain stable and not reach the breaking point over the long run.[20]

Major System Variables

Before leaving the general model of planned change, it is important to review some of the major variables that can be changed. Harold Leavitt lists four interacting variables in an organization—task, structure, people, and technology.[21] The *task* refers to whether the job is simple or complex, novel or repetitive, standardized or unique. Some tasks, such as the placement of a bumper on an automobile, are highly standardized, repetitive, and simple, whereas the design of a new safety bumper would be unique, novel, and complex. The task's nature can also create independent, interdependent, or dependent relations among departments in an organization. The *structure* is the systems of communication, authority, and responsibility. Each organization has its own structure that specifies power relations among individuals in it. The *people* variable is those individuals working within the organization. This includes their attitudes, personal styles, and motivations to work in the organization. Finally, the *technology* variable is the problem-solving methods or techniques, such as computers, typewriters, and drill presses. As indicated in Figure 15–4, these four variables are highly interdependent. A change in any one usually results in a change in one or more of the others. For example, a structural change toward de-

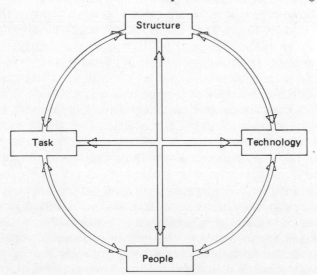

FIGURE 15–4.   Variables in Organization Change

From Leavitt, H., "Applied Organizational Change in Industry: Structural Technological and Humanistic Approaches." In *Handbook of Organizations*, March, J., ed. (Chicago: Rand McNally & Co., 1965), p. 1145.

centralization of decision making should result in assignment of different people to certain organizational tasks. But decentralization of decision making will also probably change the technology for performing the tasks, as well as the attitudes and values of the people performing the task. The introduction of computers (technology change) in insurance companies in the mid-1950s caused changes in the structure (communication channels, number of hierarchical levels, locus of decision making), changes in people (their numbers, skills, motivations), and changes in the performance of tasks (the ability to use complex operation-research models to solve unique and novel problems).

Organizational change can be introduced through alteration of these variables, singly or in combination. Obviously, organization members need to decide "what is to be changed" before undertaking a planned change effort. Leavitt's framework provides an opportunity to examine some change approaches. While specific approaches to change will be spelled out in detail in Chapters 16 and 17, an overview is presented in the following section.

Task.   The task approach focuses on the job performed by the worker. Examples of task approaches include job enrichment, job rotation, and behavioral modification. Emery Air Freight put a few behavioral modification techniques (such as providing feedback and reinforcements) to the practical test of modifying on-the-job behavior and succeeded. Under the general direction of Edward Feeney, Emery was able to save $2 million over a three-year period by identifying performance-related behaviors and strengthening them with positive reinforcement.[22]

Structure.   The structural approach involves changing the internal structure of the organization, that is, the role responsibilities and relationships of organization members and their centers, coordinative mechanisms within the organization, span of control, number of hierarchical levels, and the like. An example of a structural change is decentralization of decision-making authority and responsibility. One reason for decentralization is that it reduces the need for coordination between departments and also increases a manager's control over the departments. That is, each department is given more decision-making discretion and autonomy.[23]

People.   The people approach attempts to change organizations by modifying the attitudes, values, styles, behavior, and interpersonal processes of organization members. It assumes that people are the major force pressing for or resisting change. One common thread in this approach is the redistribution of power among organization members. This redistribution of power can be accomplished by encouraging independent decision making by subordinates and by opening communication channels.

One example of this approach is the Scanlon Plan, a union-management plan used by many companies, which focuses on (1) money bonuses to all members of the organization in proportion to their base rates for all improvements in the firm's efficiency, and (2) a system of work-improvement committees that crosses organizational levels. The plan has had a great impact on the nature of the interpersonal relations between managers and workers and among the workers themselves. In general, the plan has fostered a greater acceptance of responsibility by lower level personnel and a sharing with lower level groups in the hierarchy.[24] This approach, along with others, such as T-group training, grid training, and transactional analysis, focuses on the forces affecting an individual's behavior in the organization.

Technology.   The technological approach focuses mainly on problem-solving mechanisms and the processes by which new problem-solving methods are generated and adopted by the organization. Historically, this approach has its bases in the pioneering work of Frederick Taylor and the scientific-management movement. Out of Taylorism emerged a group of individuals (industrial engineers) who were primarily trained in planning and measuring units of production. Since Taylor, the technological approach has been expanded to include not only measurement of specific jobs but also work flow among departments, information systems, and the like. For example, Volvo's redesign of the car manufacturing process is an example of a technological change. For half a century, it has been argued that the economics and technology of making cars left no alternative but the assembly line. However, Volvo has redesigned this process to emphasize team work and job enrichment.

It should be pointed out that all these variables are usually present in a change process. A systems approach to change requires that all these variables be understood before one variable is disturbed. For example, a redesign of jobs to permit more decision-making authority by employees should probably be accompanied by more participative supervision, by a pay system that recognizes and rewards performance, and by a communication system that encourages open channels of communication.

PATTERNS OF SUCCESSFUL AND UNSUCCESSFUL CHANGE

To increase the probability that change will be in the direction desired by the organization, we must know more about how successful changes take place. With such knowledge, the change agent can more effectively plan actions and programs that will result in desired permanent changes. Too often, lack of such knowledge has caused substantial waste in time, money, and resources. What appears to be a good means to create change may (1) trigger no change at all, (2) create change that is only temporary, or (3) trigger change that has unplanned and often undesirable organizational effects.

Conditions Required for
Successful Change

Listed here are conditions that have to exist before changes can get started and become permanent in organizations.[25]

1. *People in the organization must feel pressure in order to be ready for change.* High rates of absenteeism, turnover, grievances, and sabotage can create internal pressures to change. External pressures include poor productivity that makes the firm less competitive, pressure for change from community interest groups, or pressures to change from government regulations enforceable by laws. These pressures often result in changes of leaders or leadership patterns by the organization's chief executive officers, which in turn cause a reexamination of past practices and current problems. At the Northrop Corporation, a consistently profitable aerospace corporation, stockholders brought suit against the corporation because its executives had made illegal campaign contributions to the Richard Nixon reelection campaign. A federal judge eventually agreed to their complaint and required a restructuring of the board of directors, bringing in four new independent members and requiring that in the future 60 percent of the company's directors be genuine outsiders not connected with the company. Their responsibility was to sort out management's improprieties and their possible liabilities and to prevent future political secret funds from being created and used contrary to the law.

2. *Participation and involvement of people in reexamining problems and practices are needed to build commitment for the change.* Participative practices help management learn about the needs of employees and allow these needs to be reflected in the final solution. This suggests that employees who might be affected by changes should be involved in the planning process. This is not to say that change cannot or should not occur through unilateral directives. Sometimes this is the only feasible solution. However, such an approach does not result in the same high level of commitment and therefore requires tighter managerial control to assure continuation of the change.

3. *Some new ideas or concepts must be brought in from the outside to help people in the organization find new approaches that will improve the organization's effectiveness.* Organizations should have alternatives successfully used by other organizations at at their fingertips.

4. *To ensure early success and prevent major failures that can slow down the momentum of the change, early innovations leading to improvements should be limited in scope.* Not until the change has been demonstrated to be feasible and lessons have been learned from small-scale trial-and-error projects should changes be widely spread throughout the organization.

5. *A skilled leader or change agent is often needed to bring in new ideas and support individuals in the process of improving the organization's effectiveness.* The leader serves as sponsor of the change and can help people learn and move through the change. Even when the change is trig-

gered by external pressures, a change agent is often needed within the organization to translate these pressures into a feasible change program for the organization.

Pitfalls to Avoid

It is also necessary to discuss some of the pitfalls that change efforts can encounter. You should be aware of these potential problems when considering the analysis of various change strategies that follow in Chapters 16 and 17. The list of pitfalls is not meant to be comprehensive, but represents some of the key problems in organizational change.[26]

1. *Change attempts are often characterized by poorly defined goals.* In fact, it is often the case that there is ambiguity about the objective beyond that of simply "changing things." For example, an organization may decide to implement a training program for supervisors to make these supervisors more aware of their subordinates' problems. What is the goal here? It it to change the attitudes of supervisors or change the behavior of the supervisors toward subordinates? The exact goal is important because it should affect how the training program is implemented and evaluated.

Another problem with poorly defined change goals is that they are likely to create uncertainty and anxiety for those who are going to be affected by the change. Research has indicated that when people are informed and understand the change goals and have some participation in the change process, they are more receptive to the change itself.[27]

2. *Change attempts are often characterized by poorly defined problems.* Too often symptoms are mistaken for causes of problems. This results in misdirected change efforts. It is not uncommon to find tunnel vision among people responsible for the diagnosis of the problems. Community development leaders see the lack of government cooperation as the reason why modernization occurs slowly, whereas family planners see the problem as one of overpopulation. The role of the change agent in defining the problem is discussed in the next section of this chapter.

3. *Change attempts are often misled by the assumption that people behave in a vacuum and are not influenced by those around them in the organization.*[28] Initiators of change programs geared to changing the attitudes and behavior of the individual often forget that the individual's behavior is affected quite dramatically by those around him. If a person is asked to change behavior that is not supported or reinforced significantly by others, behavioral change is unlikely to occur, or at least unlikely to be maintained. Thus change strategies that neglect the social and physical context of the situation in which the change takes place are missing some of the important causes of behavior. It may be important that certain key individuals in the system change, but in order for change to affect the entire organization, this change must be supported throughout the system.

4. *Change attempts are often misled by the belief that all the change agent has to do is present the change program to management and then*

management will implement it on its own. Such a belief neglects the need for a strategy for implementing the change and the fact that the management system undergoing the change may need some assistance in actually implementing the change. Since change usually results in shifts in the power, status, and other formal organizational relationships, it may be necessary for the change agent to work with management as it moves through this process. In adopting a new computer-based management information system, for example, it is useful if the change agents are still present in the organization after the new system is in operation. Their job is to work with the managers and get them comfortable with the equipment. Also, the presence of the change agents is important in reducing anxiety and misunderstanding among managers involved in the change process.

TYPES OF CHANGE AGENTS

Managers frequently differ as to who should initiate an organizational change, what type of person this should be, and what methods this person should use. If you hired ten outside consultants for the same job and provided them with the same organizational data, would you expect their initial organizational diagnosis to be the same? Probably not. As was pointed out in Chapters 5 and 6, what managers perceive determines their behavior. If a change agent diagnoses the problem in terms of personal and interpersonal dimensions, then the change strategy chosen will reflect these personal biases. Because organizational diagnosis plays such a vital role in determining what methods will be used to achieve change, and since the change agent is usually the key person in the diagnostic situation, you should know something about the types of persons attempting to achieve change in organizations.

Who are change agents? *Change agents* are individuals who influence organizations to make decisions affecting change deemed desirable by the individual or the organization. Change agents may be regular employees of the organization performing their duties as marketing managers, manufacturing managers, accountants, controllers, and the like. Or they may be external agents hired by the organization to effect change. Consulting firms, such as the Boston Consulting Group; Booz, Allen & Hamilton; and national CPA firms can be used by organizations to create planned change.

The change agent's organization model determines what information is collected for diagnosing an organization's problems. The most important things examined during diagnosis also tend to be the things that are worked on most often to create change in the organization. The relationship between diagnosis and change approaches has been proposed by Noel Tichy, who studied ninety-one types of change agents.[29] Figure 15–5 is a model designed by Tichy for studying the role of change agents.

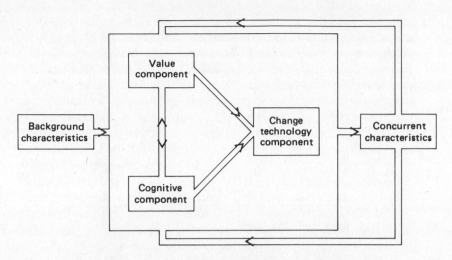

FIGURE 15–5.   Framework for Change Agent's Role

Reprinted from "Agents of Planned Social Change: Congruence of Values, Cognitions, and Actions," by Noel M. Tichy. Published in *Administrative Science Quarterly,* vol. 19, no. 2 by permission of the *Administrative Science Quarterly.* Copyright 1974. Reproduced by permission.

There are five basic components to the model, all of which interact with each other. First are the *background characteristics* of the change agent. These typically include the agent's educational training, income, religion, age, sex, relationships to clients, and so forth. The second part of the model is the *value component.* This is the agent's evaluative orientation toward change, such as his or her attitudes toward important social changes, political orientation (liberal, moderate, conservative), his or her own social-change goals (increased range of individual freedom and choice, improved satisfaction of members, equalization of power between organization members, and so forth), and the goals he or she feels change agents should have. This component represents behavior expected of a change agent. The third basic component is the agent's *cognitive component*—concepts about means of affecting change. Tactics such as shifting organizational power and authority, changing the selection system, management training, and job redesign represent different means for affecting change. The relative emphasis placed on the four variables—task, structure, people, technology—discussed earlier in this chapter are still other examples of cognitive components. The fourth basic component is the agent's *technology component.* This refers to the tools and skills the change agent used to effect social change. To make use of his or her other knowledge (cognitive component) and to act on his or her other values (value component), each change agent has a set of techniques, such as sensitivity training, operations research, survey feedback, and team development that can be applied to a situation. Finally, the *concurrent characteristics* refer to the actual behavior of the change agent. The relationship among the five components of the model assumes that stress exists in the change agent when the value component and concurrent characteristics or the cognitive component and actions are not in agreement with each other. For example, an agent whose values are openness and trust will most likely use tactics such as transactional analysis or T-group training, which reflect these values, and not operations-research techniques, to understand an organizational problem and bring about a planned change.

Based on consistent differences in the patterns of these five components of the model in Figure 15–5, four different types of change agents have been identified. These are (1) people-change technology (PCT), (2) analysis-from-the-top (AFT), (3) organization development (OD), and (4) outside pressure (OP). Since the outside-pressure type (e.g., Ralph Nader, Betty Furness) is rarely used by managers to bring about changes, only the three other types of change agents will be discussed. Table 15–2 outlines the change tactics likely to be used by each type of change agent and the frequency with which they are used. Many of the change tactics listed in this figure will be discussed in Chapters 16 and 17.

People-change Technology (PCT)

Change agents who use people-change technology work to achieve change in the way employees behave. These agents are concerned with

TABLE 15–2.   Percentage of Different Change Tactics Used by Change Agents

Change tactic	People-change technology (PCT)	Analysis-from-the-top (AFT)	Organization development (OD)
Confrontation meetings	47	39	95
Survey feedback	46	38	50
Job training	65	75	22
Sensitivity training	41	21	79
Team development	65	31	100
Technological innovation	71	89	63
Change in reward structure	82	71	58
Change in decision-making structure	76	96	94
Role clarification	100	95	100

Reprinted from "Agents of Planned Social Change: Congruence of Values, Cognitions, and Actions," by Noel M. Tichy. Published in *Administrative Science Quarterly*, vol. 19, no. 2. By permission of the *Administrative Science Quarterly*. Copyright 1974.

improving motivation, job satisfaction, and productivity. One PCT agent described her role as:

> To help individuals and organizations focus on goals, obstacles which stand in the way of goal attainment, individual motivation patterns and requirements of the task, organizational goal attainment, emphasis on individual and organizational self-development.

Tactics favored by the PCT change agent, as listed in Table 15–2, are role clarification, change in reward structure, change in decision-making structure, technological innovation, job training, and team development. Use of these tactics should lead to job enrichment, behavioral modification, need-achievement training, management by objectives, and the like. The basic assumption of PCT change agents is that if individuals change their behavior, the organization, too, will change, especially if enough (or the right) individuals in the organization change.

The data gathered by Tichy indicate that PCT change agents usually hold academic positions with doctorates, range in age from thirty-five to forty, and have median incomes ranging from $20,000 to $30,000. Their political orientation is liberal, and they express a moderate degree of social criticism. The linkages between political orientation and values indicate that their primary value is to improve system efficiency, increase output, and to equalize the power and responsibility within the organization.

Analysis-from-the-Top (AFT)

Change agents who use the analysis-from-the-top approach rely primarily on the operations-research model. These agents work on improving decision making and maintaining and controlling employee performance. One AFT agent described his role as:

> To work with groups concerned with problems of design and operation of system, in order to aid in resolving their problems. Normally the work involves technological remodeling and analysis.

Tactics favored by the AFT change agent, as listed in Table 15–2, are change in decision-making structure, role clarification, technological innovation, job training, and change in reward structure. Use of these tactics should lead to changes in the decision-making structure of the organization, technological innovations, and job training in areas such as computerized information processing systems and development of new tasks. AFT change agents assume that if the organization's impersonal technical and structural processes are changed, the organization's efficiency will increase.

AFT change agents are likely to be older than the PCT change agents (ranging in age from forty to fifty), have a median income over $40,000, are not associated with an academic institution, and do not have a doctorate. They are moderates in political orientation and are not critical of society.

Organization Development (OD)

Change agents who use organization-development techniques work to improve the organization's problem-solving capabilities by helping people learn to help themselves. This involves assisting members of the organization to work out their interpersonal problems and communications, conflicts of interest, career plans, and the like. As indicated in Table 15–2, OD change agents rely on team development, role clarification, confrontation meetings, change in decision-making structure, and sensitivity training to achieve their goals. A basic goal of the OD change agent is to increase democratic participation in decision making by all members. In this way, the organization can develop problem-solving mechanisms so that key executives can work with each other.

The background characteristics of the OD change include a median age of forty to fifty, primarily Protestant religious beliefs, a high proportion holding degrees, and a median income of $30,000 to $40,000. Their political affiliation tends to be liberal to moderate. They do not advocate radical changes in organizations to achieve their objectives.

Summary of Types of Change Agents

This typology of change agents suggests that each type of change agent has somewhat different goals and tactics for bringing about organizational change. The PCT change agent's goals, however, seem to be closely aligned with the goals of the OD agent, which are the improvement of organizational problem solving, while the AFT change agent's primary goal is to increase organizational output and the organization's efficiency. In addition to these different goals, the tactics used by each change agent are different. OD change agents emphasize team development and confrontation meetings. The PCTs focus more on individually oriented tactics, such as role clarification and job training, whereas the AFTs rely more on impersonal technical and structural tactics to achieve their goals.

The data in Table 15–2 illustrate the relative emphasis on tactics used by these three types of change agents. However, you should notice that all three types of change agents, depending on the situation and their individual values and philosophy, can rely on similar tactics to bring about planned change. For example, all three types of change agents report they use tactics such as confrontation meetings, survey feedback, job training, and role clarification to varying degrees. In other words, although the values and cognitions may differ among the three types of change agents, the change tactics may be quite similar, with major differences being those of relative emphasis and focus.

The establishment of the three types of change agents can be linked to Leavitt's system variables—task, structure, people, and technology. The OD change agent is more likely to examine people as forces either supporting or resisting change; the PCT agent is more likely to examine both people and structure, and the AFT change agent is more likely to examine the technological forces. Change agents' selection of forces is influenced by their own goals and sometimes by those of the organization.

Internal and External Change Agents

As has been noted, change agents can be members of the organization or outsiders. Many large organizations, including General Electric, Corning Glass Works, TRW Systems, Imperial Chemical Industries Limited, and Shell Oil Corporation, employ full-time change agents. These organizations often set up a department in the corporate headquarters, usually reporting either to the vice-president of industrial relations or of human resources, called an organization development or organization improvement department. This department frequently functions as an internal consulting organization available to various departments of the organization to help them with diagnosis, planning of changes, and conducting training programs. Most smaller firms cannot sufficiently utilize such personnel to warrant the cost associated with a full-time staff. These firms usually rely on external consultants for assistance.

There are several differences between internal and external change agents. In general, the roles of internal and external change agents cannot be interchanged.[30] The role of the external change agent is more clear-cut than that of the internal consultant, who may have more difficulty in explaining his or her role to members of the organization. Further, internal change agents are more likely to accept the system as given and try to accommodate their change tactics to the needs of the organization. Thus internal change agents are more likely to focus on such tactics as team building and improving the quality of meetings. By accepting the norms of the organization, these change agents spent little time in helping the organization move toward self-renewal, growth, and change. In contrast, the external consultants appear to be freer to examine the organization from a total systems viewpoint and are much less affected by organizational norms. And external consultants are likely to have easier access to top managers, since they are usually the people who initiate contact with the external agents.

Basic Qualifications of Change Agents

Selecting a change agent is a crucial element in the process of organizing for planned change. The capabilities and performance of this person have often been critical factors in the success or failure of many organizational changes. A conference on change agent training held at the University of Michigan suggested a number of characteristics change agents should have to be successful. The specific characteristics are presented in Table 15–3. These characteristics are far from exhaustive.[31] At the same time, it is a rare case in which a single individual can be found who possesses all these characteristics.

Looking through these characteristics, we can distinguish at least three basic skills: technical, administrative, and interpersonal.

Technical Competence.   Of the three skills, *technical competence* in the specific tasks of the change project is most important. Dangers exist in bringing in a person from an unrelated or only marginally related field to run the change program. A PCT change agent focuses on how people feel about their job and uses change tactics of job enrichment and changes in the performance-reward system. This type of change agent is usually not skilled to handle problems related to group processes and how teams function within the organization. On the other hand, an OD change agent focuses on having the employees learn to help themselves and assists organizational members with interpersonal problems. A commonly used tactic is sensitivity training. This type of change agent is usually not trained in job enrichment and operations-research techniques; the agent should not attempt to create change in these fields because of a lack of technical competence to assist the organization in these areas. A related problem is the change agent's ability to adapt and apply his/her skills to problems that are simple and ordinary in nature. There is the danger of imposing complicated solutions on simple problems needing only simple solutions. This is sometimes a danger when external consultants are brought in to assist in solving simple problems.

Administrative Ability.   Willingness to allocate time to relatively detailed matters is an important element of administrative ability. For example, the failure to check on whether the printing of the training manuals for a group of executives was on schedule resulted in the postponement of a one-month training program for nearly a year. The printing was three weeks behind schedule, and approximately ten months passed before all the executives scheduled for the training program could be reassembled at the same time. Another administrative skill is planning. Particularly important is the ability to plan for the unexpected by allowing flexibility through alternative or contingency planning. Although a change agent should be able to perform effectively during periods of crisis, when crises repeatedly arise and require attention, there is good reason to believe that there was inadquate planning.

Interpersonal Relations.   The third important trait for a change agent is to be able to establish good interpersonal relations. This refers to

TABLE 15–3.   Characteristics of Successful Change Agents

1. The Change Agent Should Have These Attitudes and Values:
    Primary concern for the benefit of the ultimate user.
    Respect for strongly held values of others.
    Belief that change should provide the greatest good to the greatest number.
    Belief that employees have a need and a right to understand why changes
    are being made (rationale) and to participate in choosing among alterna-
    tive change means and ends.
    A strong sense of his or her own identity and own power to help others.
    A strong concern for helping without hurting, for helping with minimum
    jeopardy to the long- or short-term well being of society as a whole and/or
    specific individuals within it.

2. The Change Agent Should Know These Things:
    That individuals, groups, and societies are open interrelating systems.
    How the change agent's role fits into a larger picture of the organization's
    goals.
    Present role and potential role in the future.
    How others will see the role.
    The range of human needs and their interrelationships.
    The resources of the organization and the means of access to them.
    The value bases of different individuals in the organization.
    The motivational bases of different individuals in the organization.
    Why people and systems change and resist change.
    How people and systems change and resist change.
    The knowledge, attitudes, and skills required of a change agent.
    The knowledge, attitudes, and skills required of an effective user of re-
    sources.

3. The Change Agent Should Possess These Skills:
    How to build and maintain change project relationships with others.
    How to bring people to think of their needs in relation to needs of others.
    How to resolve misunderstandings and conflict.
    How to convey to others a feeling of power to bring about change.
    How to build collaborative teams for change.
    How to organize and execute successful change projects.
    How to convey to others the knowledge, values, and skills he/she possesses.
    How to bring people to a realization of their own resource-giving potential.
    How to work collaboratively with other departments in the organization.
    How to relate effectively to powerful individuals and groups.
    How to make systemic diagnoses of client systems, and how to generate
    self-diagnosis by clients.

Adapted and modified from Zaltman, G., and R. Duncan, *Strategies for Planned Change*
(New York: Wiley-Interscience, 1977), pp. 188–189.

the agent's ability to identify with others—to share their perspectives and feelings with others. An ability to empathize with others is often needed in change programs because the people undergoing the change often express fears about "what's going to happen to us." The ability of the change agent to communicate his/her concern and understanding of the employees' anxiety can help reduce their feelings of threat and fear.

ETHICAL CONSIDERATIONS

The knowledge about the control and manipulation of human behavior that the consultant is capable of applying is beset with enormous ethical ambiguities. The change agent must accept the responsibility for the social consequences of the application of this knowledge.[32] The change agent must be concerned with the question of how this knowledge is likely to be used by the organization and at the same time be concerned with choosing an approach that will facilitate the organization's reaching its goal(s). For people who are concerned with the individual's fundamental freedom of choice, any manipulation of the behavior of others constitutes a violation of this basic "right." This would be true regardless of the tactics used by the change agent. However, some degree of manipulation and control of individual behavior is an inherent part of every planned change. An implicit imposition of the change agent's values, cognitions, and technology on the organization he or she is trying to influence is accepted by the organization that hires the agent. In attempting to provide answers to these questions, the ethical considerations can be grouped into two major categories: power and freedom.[33] Although these categories are tightly interwoven, they will be treated separately.

Power

Two important questions are raised in regard to power. The first is one of justice. Is it fair for those who already possess power and control over others to exert influence over the change process? This question is especially important because many of the tactics used by change agents will likely change or reinforce the balance of power, influence, and authority in the organization. For example, an OD tactic of team development depends on the willingness of members to look at the way in which they interact with each other. The result often is changes in behavioral patterns that strengthen the influence of some members relative to others.

The second question related to power centers on the degree of openness regarding the power implications of a change effort. Important issues are:

1. What is to be defined as a problem?
2. How can the change be brought about with maximum benefit and minimum damage?
3. Who will evaluate the effectiveness of the change?
4. How will the information be gathered?

Typically, information is collected in an atmosphere of trust, where no one will be harmed by his or her honesty, but trust and openness have their limits in organizations where power and status differences exist.

Freedom

Critical issues in a planned change effort lie in the area of personal freedom and the related value of individual welfare. The essential points of freedom are: (1) informed consent; (2) manipulation; and (3) misuse of information.

Informed Consent. Informed consent is the awareness of options for choice, knowledge of the consequences for each option, and the ability to act upon a decision. Many employees have only the vaguest notion of what the change will mean to them personally at the time they agree to participate or are persuaded to participate. "The boss thinks this is a good idea" is too often used as the rationale for enlisting employees in a change effort. While there is no easy solution to this problem, guidelines have been suggested by practicing change agents. First, the change agent should clearly articulate the tactics likely to be used in the change effort. Second, the results of the change effort are likely to be more effective when participation is voluntary and the participants have had a voice in whether or not the change should be undertaken.

A study conducted by Coch and French in a clothing factory illustrates the benefits of participation and informed consent.[34] The change agents (PCT type) introduced changes in work methods by varying the amount of participation in the change process. This set up a "field experiment" research design (see Chapter 2 for a detailed description of this). Members of the first group, "no-participation," were told that there was a need for a minor methods change in their work procedures and were given instructions on how to perform their work in accordance with the new method. In the second group, "participation-through-representation," the workers were given the problem facing the company. After they had reached agreement about the need for change, the group was asked to name workers who would be given the needed specialized training. In the third and fourth groups, "total-participation," all workers were introduced to the work change on a total participation basis and were asked to discuss how existing work methods could be improved and unnecessary operations eliminated. The results clearly indicate the effects of varying amounts of participation. The output of the first group dropped immediately to about two-thirds of its previous output. There were marked expressions of hostility—deliberate restrictions of output, conflict with the methods engineers —and a 17 percent quit rate. In contrast, the productivity rate of the total-participation group exceeded the previous rate and there were no signs of hostility and conflict. The results of the second group were intermediate between the first group and the third and fourth groups.

Manipulation.   Manipulation is the deliberate attempt to change the structure of people's personal, social or physical environment without their knowledge. Some change agents encourage participants to "open up" and reveal their true feelings and thoughts. That is, they place the individual in situations that may involve an invasion of privacy; through group pressure they force the individual to respond.

Misuse of Information.   A basic component in many change tactics is an honest expression of problems and the expression of negative feelings. Unfortunately, these revelations by employees can sometimes be used against them by their superiors. For example, in the U.S. Foreign Service, where status differences are accentuated, promotions depend heavily on the favorable impressions of superiors, and transfer to other organizations in the same career line is difficult. Thus, the effects of honesty could be devastating to career development for certain organizational members. Differences in power and authority could give some members of the organization the opportunity to retaliate for unpleasant revelations. However, change agents are usually in a "doctor-patient" relationship where norms of confidentiality have been formed and are usually adhered to.

SUMMARY

A rapidly changing world places many demands on managers, including how to control and direct change effectively. Planned organizational change is the intentional attempt to influence the status quo of an organization. Organizational change requires adaptation by the organization as a whole and by individuals in the organization, who must alter their attitudes, styles, and behaviors.

Change may be effected by internal (staff) or external (consulting) change agents. Pressures to change include changing technology, the knowledge explosion, rapid product obsolescence, the changing nature of the work force, the quality of working life, and the life-styles of workers and change agents. Life-styles fall into three basic patterns: formalistic, interpersonal, and personalistic. Change agents must work with these different life-styles, not against them, as much as is feasible.

Individuals may resist change through selective attention and retention or through the effects of habit, dependence, and fear of the unknown. Economic reasons and the need for security, which may result in regression, also act as individual resistances to change. Organization resistances to change can be caused by the threat to power and influence, the organizational structure itself, resource limitations or sunk costs, and interorganizational agreements.

The general process model of change indicates how pressures for change and resistances to change must be balanced. Pressures for change must be encouraged; resistances to change must be discouraged or converted into pressures for change. The change process passes through three stages: unfreezing, moving, and refreezing. The major system variables in the change process are task, structure, people, and technology.

Patterns of successful and unsuccessful change were presented as a model for studying change agents. The five basic components of the model are background characteristics, value component, cognitive component, change technology, and concurrent characteristics.

Three techniques change agents often use are people-change technology, analysis-from-the-top, and organization development. Each technique sets different priorities on what needs to be changed and how to go about it. A detailed list of basic qualifications of change agents was given. These qualifications group into the general areas of technical competence, administrative ability, and interpersonal relations. Finally, the ethical considerations in change were discussed under the two categories of power and freedom. Power is important because a change usually affects the authority relationships that have been established by the company. Those who are in powerful positions may see the change as a threat to their position and therefore, try to sabotage the effort. Freedom is concerned with informed consent, manipulation, and misuse of information.

DISCUSSION QUESTIONS

1. Identify some internal and external sources of pressure for change within the college or university you are attending.

2. How might an individual resist change?

3. Why are organizations often referred to as "innovation-resisting" by many change agents?

4. Identify some of the characteristics usually found with successful organizational change.

5. How does Lewin's process model deal with resistance to change?

6. What are the four major system vari- ables affecting an organization's ability to achieve change? How are they interrelated?

7. What are the differences between PCT, AFT, and OD change agents?

8. Discuss some of the general qualifications of successful change agents.

9. Are there differences between an internal and external change agent? Under what conditions might one be more effective than another?

10. What are some of the ethical considerations facing managers who attempt to achieve change in their organizations?

MANAGERIAL PROBLEMS

MACUNGIE CORPORATION

The manufacturing operations at the Phelps plant of the Macungie Corporation consist of fabricating and assembling trucks—over-the-road, fire engines, and panel trucks. Traditionally, the manufacturing systems have been designed and built around an assembly line operation.

As general production manager of the Phelps plant, Emil Schaadt, who has developed through the management ranks largely by following the basic principles of management, must give final approval to all system changes that will affect the operations of this plant. A new design for an engine of the over-the-road truck has been completed by product engineering. In turn, it has been released to manufacturing engineering for implementation into the assembly line system.

The manufacturing engineering group recently studied the available research relative to the advantages of job enrichment and how it compares with the traditional method of an assembly line, in terms of providing the workers with more challenging tasks, relief from boredom, and greater responsibility for the product. Management realized that job satisfaction and motivation continued to be a problem on assembly-line work. A system that included job enrichment was developed to assemble the new components of the engine along with the traditional conveyor-paced system. After the systems had been in operation for six months, the results of each system were presented to Schaadt for his approval. The manufacturing engineering group recommended that he adopt the job enrichment system because it relieved workers from performing dull, meaningless, and repetitive tasks. Schaadt, being aware of the perceived monotony and boredom of the assembly line, decided to accept the recommendation from the manufacturing engineering group.

As the production date arrived, the facilities were completed and a number of operators moved from the assembly-line process to new jobs. They, in turn, were told to assemble the engine completely and stamp their work with a personalized identification stamp that Macungie had provided.

Output and quality during the first week were 10 percent below that expected. During the next few weeks very little improvement was shown. In fact, the output was significantly below that of similar engine work at an adjacent conveyor-paced system.

Schaadt's boss was upset, since efficiency was low and excessive overtime was necessary to meet the heavy demands for trucks. Schaadt, realizing that he is responsible for the production at the Phelps plant, is trying to determine what happened and what course of action to take.

QUESTIONS

1. What should Schaadt do?
2. What factors should Schaadt consider changing?

WEIS MARKET

In 1977, the management of Weis Market, located in Sunbury, Pennsylvania, realized that demand for grocery products was increasing in the central Pennsylvania region. Expansion of existing facilities and a wider diversity of products carrying the Weis label were necessary if this demand was to be met and the market position of the firm maintained. As a result, Weis expanded its retail stores, constructed warehouses, and purchased several food-processing plants in central Pennsylvania.

One of the retail outlets affected by this expansion plan was located in the university town of State College. Having served the university community for more than fifteen years, it was still the kind of store where clerks waited on each individual customer. According to the central headquarters in Sunbury, the location was above average in sales potential because the university's enrollment was increasing, light industry was locating in the town, and customers were on friendly terms with the employees of the store.

In addition to the store manager, there were five clerks working in the grocery department, one clerk in the produce department, and five butchers. All the employees were friendly with one another because most had gone to the same high school. They often stopped to chat or joke with each other about the "good old days." Horace Cannon, the store manager, was a very efficient and cordial person. He insisted on certain work standards, but seldom interfered with the work of his subordinates. All the employees, including Cannon, had been working for Weis Markets for at least ten years. Consequently, it was understood and evident that each individual knew his particular job.

The congenial relations that existed among the employees may be exemplified further. Certain informal customs existed. Mathews, Wilson, Bither, Dolich, and Olson—the five grocery clerks—were equally capable workers. When they had nothing to do, they often loaded the grocery bags of customers for the checkers, unloaded deliveries, or helped the produce clerk. Mitchell, the produce clerk, generally had enough work to keep himself busy, and when he couldn't handle all the work, Olson gave him a hand. Besides helping each other with their jobs, vacations were mutually scheduled so that more than one clerk could be absent at a time. All belonged to the Elks and played on the store's softball team.

This was the situation in 1978 when the division manager went to the State College store to acquaint Cannon with the plan for Weis expansion. He stated that the company's directors had decided to open a new supermarket in State College to replace the old store because of the increase in sales in the area and the opening of a new shopping center with a large K-Mart. Cannon was told that the new store would be ready within ten months and that all employees, except himself, would become part of the staff of the new store. Cannon was to report to the main office in Sunbury as part of the staff there. The employees received the news enthusiastically, realizing the advantages of the new store and feeling that their experience and seniority would provide them with opportunity for better jobs.

Ten months later, the new Weis store was completed, and the eleven employees of the old store reported to the supermarket for their assignments. All the grocery clerks were assigned to their usual job with no pay increases; Homan, the meat manager in the old store, was made assistant meat manager in the new store at $20 per week more; the other four butchers from the old store were given meat-cutting jobs with no raise; Mitchell, the produce clerk, was transferred to the dairy department with no salary adjustment.

During the next several months the old employees found that routines in the new supermarket were quite different from the old. Within a short time they found that work assignments were received from the various department heads at the beginning of each day, and there was little time for fraternizing. In addition, they found that the new store manager, Mr. Kelley, had little to do with the employees directly. Once when Olson asked for a day off, he was told by Kelley to go through proper channels.

The butchers from the old store had even greater problems. Homan, the assistant meat manager, had fifteen years of experience with the company but reported to a meat manager who had just recently graduated from the local university. The latter, a Ms. Straka, placed most of the work load on Homan and gave him great freedom in running the department. When other managers were around, however, Straka took most of the credit for running the department, something that Homan resented.

Even worse, the other four butchers found that they now had to cater to a group of packers, who packaged the meat when cut, and distributed it to the self-serve boxes in the store. Often the packers blamed the butcher for any shortage in supply, even if he had nothing to do with the situation.

As time passed, tremendous pressure was put on all employees because the ratio of sales to labor was declining. Contact between employees was almost nonexistent. When Mathews, Wilson, Bither, and Dolich learned that two better jobs in the store had been filled by new employees, they all quit Weis and found employment at Dean's Market in State College. Within two months after this, Homan asked for a transfer to another store in the Weis chain, and Olson quit.

QUESTIONS

1. What type of change strategy was used by Weis management?
2. Assuming you are Mr. Cannon, what would you recommend to remedy the situation?

KEY WORDS

Planned organizational change
Organizational adaptation
Individual adaptation
Future shock
Managing by exception
Quality of work life
Life-style
Formalistic life-style
Interpersonal life-style
Personalistic life-style
Pressures to change
Selective attention

Resistances to change
Sunk costs
Unfreezing stage
Moving stage
Refreezing stage
Change agent
People-change technology
Analysis-from-the-top
Organization development
Informed consent
Manipulation

REFERENCES

1. How to stop the buck short of the top, *Business Week*, January 16, 1978, pp. 82–83; also see Davis, S., and P. Lawrence, *Matrix* (Reading, Mass.: Addison-Wesley, 1977).

2. Greiner, L., and L. Barnes, Organization change and development, in Dalton, G., P. Lawrence, and L. Greiner (eds.), *Organizational Change and Development* (Homewood, Ill.: Richard D. Irwin and Dorsey Press, 1970), p. 2.

3. Burck, C., How G. M. turned itself around, *Fortune*, January 16, 1978, p. 87.

4. Dalton, T., The Pennsylvania Mirror: What happened? *Center Daily Times*, State College, Pa., January 10, 1978, p. 5.

5. Snow, C. P., *The Two Cultures: A Second Look* (New York: Mentor Books, 1964).

6. Toffler, A., *Future Shock* (New York: Random House, 1970); also see Toffler, A., *Learning for Tomorrow* (New York: Random House, 1974).

7. Dillon, C., In the search of the year 2000, *Administrative Management*, 1977, 38, 1, pp. 32–34.

8. McInnis, D., How technology altered NCR and Dayton, *Washington Post*, January 8, 1978, F–2.

9. Langway, L., Corporations: Brain drain, *Newsweek*, March 24, 1975, pp. 76.

10. Hackman, J., and J. Suttle, *Improving Life at Work: Behavioral Sciences Approaches to Organizational Change* (Santa Monica, Calif.: Goodyear Publishing, 1977), p. 4.

11. DiMarco, N., and S. Norton, Life style, organization structure, congruity, and job satisfaction, *Personnel Psychology*, 1974, 27, pp. 581–591.

12. For an extended list of individual and organizational resistances to planned change, see Zaltman, G., and R. Duncan, *Strategies for Planned Change* (New York: Wiley-Interscience, 1977).

13. Ibid., p. 76.

14. Townsend, R., *Up the Organization* (New York: Alfred Knopf, 1970), p. 55.

15. Smith, L., Hard times come to steeltown, *Fortune*, 1977, 96, 6, p. 87.

16. Shepard, H., Innovation-resisting and innovation-producing organizations, *Journal of Business*, 1967, 40, pp. 470–477.

17. For a description of these interrelationships, see Sashkin, M., W. Morris, and L. Herst, A comparison of social and organizational change models, *Psychological Review*, 1973, 80, pp. 510–526.

18. Lewin, K., Frontiers in group dynamics, *Human Relations*, 1947, 1, pp. 5–41.

19. The example used draws upon the work of Knudson, H., R. Woodworth, and C. Bell, *Management: An Experiential Approach* (New York: McGraw-Hill, 1973), pp. 341–356.

20. For other illustrations, see Beckhard, R., and R. Harris, *Organizational Transitions: Managing Complex Change* (Reading, Mass.: Addison-Wesley, 1977).

21. Leavitt, H., Applied organizational change in industry: Structural technological and humanistic approaches, in March, J. (ed.), *Handbook of Organizations* (Chicago, Ill.: Rand McNally, 1973), pp. 1144–1170.

22. Feeney, J., At Emery Air Freight: Positive reinforcement boosts performance, *Organizational Dynamics*, 1973, 1, pp. 41–50; also see Chapter 6 for many other examples of the positive benefits associated with behavioral modification.

23. Luke, R., P. Block, J. Davey, and V. Averch, A structural approach to organizational change, *Journal of Applied Behavioral Science*, 1973, 5, pp. 611–636.

24. Frost, C., J. Wakeley, and R. Ruh, *The Scanlon Plan for Organization Development: Identity, Participation and Equity* (East Lansing: Michigan State University Press, 1974).

25. These were condensed from a list provided by Beckhard, R., *Organization Development: Strategies and Models* (Reading, Mass.: Addison-Wesley, 1973).

26. Bennis, W., *Changing Organizations* (New York: McGraw-Hill, 1966); Argyris, C., *Management and Organizational Development* (New York: McGraw-Hill, 1971).

27. Marrow, A., D. Bowers, and S. Seashore, *Management by Participation* (New York: Harper and Row, 1967).

28. Katz, D., and D. Kahn, *The Social Psychology of Organizations*, 2nd ed. (New York: John Wiley and Sons, 1978).

29. Tichy, N., How different types of change agents diagnose organizations, *Human Relations*, 1975, 28, pp. 771–779; Tichy, N., and J. Nisberg, Change agent bias: What they view determines what they do, *Group and Organization Studies*, 1976, 1, pp. 286–301.

30. Beer, M., The technology of organization development, in Dunnette, M. (ed.), *Handbook of Industrial and Organizational Psychology* (Chicago: Rand McNally, 1976), pp. 937–994.

31. Havelock, R., and M. Havelock, *Training for Change Agents* (Ann Arbor: Institute for Social Research, University of Michigan, 1973).

32. Steele, F., *Consulting for Organizational Change* (Amherst: University of Massachusetts Press, 1974); Kelman, H., Manipulation of human behavior: An ethical dilemma for the social scientists, *Journal of Social Issues*, 1965, 21, pp. 31–46.

33. Walton, R., and D. Warwick, The ethics of organization development, *Journal of Applied Behavioral Science*, 1973, 9, pp. 681–689; Bowers, D., Organizational development: Promises, performances, and possibilities, *Organizational Dynamics*, 1976, 4, no. 4, pp. 50–62.

34. Coch, L., and J. French, Overcoming resistance to change, *Human Relations*, 1948, 1, pp. 512–532.

16

People-focused Approaches to Organizational Change

16

LEARNING OBJECTIVES

When you have finished reading and studying this chapter, you should be able to:

▲ Explain and illustrate several specific people-focused approaches for changing an organization, one of its units, or its employees.

▲ Identify some of the key contingencies that should influence the choice of a particular change approach.

▲ Diagnose when certain people-focused change approaches are likely to be more effective than others.

▲ Respond more effectively to various types of change efforts.

THOUGHT STARTERS

▲ Why might an organization want to use a people-focused approach to organizational change?

▲ What do you think would be some of the characteristics of a people-focused approach?

OUTLINE

Innovation has probably done more than anything else to shape the quality of the economy and life in advanced industrial societies. Innovation creates jobs, boosts productivity, and contributes to a rising quality of life. Jerry Wasserman, senior consultant with Arthur D. Little, Inc., notes:

> For 25 years after World War II, we saw some of the most dramatic commercial innovations in our history. There was television, computers, the transistor and integrated circuit, containerized shipping, microwave ovens, Polaroid "instant" cameras, Xerox copiers, automatic transmissions—things that changed our basic way of life. Now most so-called innovations build on existing technologies and simply extend the state of the art. This is true whether you're talking pocket calculators, digital watches, or whatever.[1]

There is a growing concern that increasing numbers of American managers have slowly and subtly turned into supercautious, no-risk managers who have become unwilling to gamble on anything short of a sure thing. The various resistances to individual and organizational changes were spelled out in Chapter 15, as were the existing pressures and needs for further change. This chapter and Chapter 17 discuss approaches available to managers for bringing about various types of changes in organizations and their employees. Each of these approaches may be valuable under certain contingencies because it may assist directly or indirectly in increasing innovation, creativity, and productivity. This is not to suggest that the hows of innovating and adapting are simple and easy. But the choice for management over the long run is clear-cut—innovate and adapt or stagnate and die.[2]

Considerable controversy exists over the best approach for changing an organization or its employees. No claim is made to resolving such controversy within this chapter. From the pragmatic view of "Does it work?" a number of different approaches have been successfully utilized in organizational change efforts. But an approach to organizational change that was a success in one organization might be a failure in another organization. Because there are numerous potential explanations for such conflicting results, this chapter emphasizes the contingency perspective. In terms of organizational change, the contingency perspective suggests that there is not a single best approach to change—no one approach is likely to be equally effective under all circumstances. Accordingly, this chapter presents an overview and comparison of four major people-focused approaches to organizational change, together with a discussion of a sample of specific change strategies within each of the four approaches.

OVERVIEW OF APPROACHES

This and the next chapter are, to some extent, organized as if each approach discussed is independent and mutually exclusive of the others.

Nothing could be further from the truth. The decision to present each approach somewhat independently is based on the following two considerations. (1) An understanding of the various approaches that are commonly used and referred to within organizations is improved. (2) The desire to avoid becoming excessively complex forces us to avoid focusing on detailed similarities and differences in the approaches.

Interdependence of Change Approaches

The change approaches discussed here are often quite interdependent. There is not a zero-sum or win-lose relationship between the approaches. They can be used with each other in an overall change program. Corning Glass Works Corporation is a good example of a firm that applies several change approaches simultaneously. Corning "doesn't believe that it's possible to label any one intervention strategy (approach) as the most effective strategy, equally appropriate to all circumstances and adequate for all problems."[3]

A key contingency that influences the choice of approach or combination of approaches applied at Corning is the nature of the problem the company is trying to resolve. For example, an approach that emphasizes the development of group problem-solving for production workers who are dissatisfied and frustrated with highly controlled, boring, and routine jobs could easily increase the problem. The opportunity for the production workers to discuss openly and explicitly the nature of their work, without the opportunity to make any changes in the ways in which the tasks are performed, may well increase their dissatisfaction and frustration. The key approach to change would probably focus on the nature of the production workers' jobs and opportunities to enrich the tasks performed. Group problem-solving sessions with the production workers might be a supplementary approach used to gain their assistance and embrace their ideas in redesigning the tasks to be included in the jobs.

Corning's Medfield Operation.   The Medfield operation of Corning, which produces various types of electrodes, provides a concrete example of a change program involving the combined use of several approaches. At the time of intervention, Medfield was new and small, with about 120 employees. The operation was nonunion and had a technology that permitted major changes in the task factor. The redesign of tasks was supplemented with approaches emphasizing people and structure factors. A major change program is likely to have an impact on task, structure, technology, and people and may require a combination of approaches to bring about change in each of these variables. At the Medfield operation of Corning, the variety of changes included:

1. Widespread introduction of job enlargement, particularly at the level of production workers, that enabled employees to be responsible, indi-

vidually or as an autonomous group, for the production of substantial components.
2. Monthly group meetings at every organizational level.
3. Weekly meetings between the plant manager and representatives of production and clerical employees.
4. Special meetings to consider technical and productivity issues or problems.
5. Creation of autonomous groups in some departments with responsibility for scheduling, assembly, training, and some quality issues.
6. Involvement of hourly workers in influencing their own productivity goals in relation to overall plant goals.
7. Redesign of pay systems to make them consistent and as a means of reinforcing these other changes, such as more use of group versus individual pay incentives.

The many positive effects of these changes were shown within six months of introduction and have been retained during the following years. The qualitative and quantitative indicators improved substantially. Michael Beer, the director of organization development at Corning Glass when this change program was completed, summarized the results this way.

> Voluntary turnover among hourly employees has consistently been below that for the area; productivity and quality have improved as changes have been made in department after department. The plant handles more volume with less supervision and indirect labor, management is able to introduce new and highly complex products without drops in productivity.[4]

Implications: One implication that can be drawn from the experience at Corning and other organizations is that successful major change programs are likely to require the use of a variety of approaches. Of course, there are also many minor change efforts frequently underway in organizations that can be successfully implemented through a limited application of these approaches.

When the tasks to be performed are routine, structured, and involve little uncertainty, some suggest it may be best to start with one or more approaches that emphasize the structural factor and are followed by one or more approaches that emphasize the people factor. Structural changes in such situations may be more readily used to "unfreeze" the organization, especially since decision making, power, and information are more likely to exist at the highest management levels. In contrast, where the tasks are nonroutine, unstructured, and involve considerable uncertainty, it may be best to start with one or more approaches that emphasize the people factor. In such a set of circumstances, it is assumed that relevant information and knowledge are spread throughout the organization. Moreover, crucial technical competencies may be greatest at the lowest organizational levels.[5] While the logic and empirical evidence for these guidelines are appealing, the area of organizational change is too new and has been inadequately investigated to date to justify a hard conclusion on this question.

DIAGNOSING CHOICE OF APPROACHES

No ready-made or agreed-upon formula for determining the approach or combination of approaches to utilize in changing an organization exists. One key factor should be the nature of the problem the organizational members are attempting to resolve. However, as was noted in the earlier discussion of types of change agents and individual problem-solving styles, individuals may be predisposed to perceive problems in particular ways and to choose particular change approaches.

Richard Beckhard has suggested some guidelines for choosing an approach or combination of approaches. It is assumed that the approach chosen provides the greatest and most effective leverage to begin the change process. Beckhard identifies four issues that should be diagnosed:

1. Definition of the change problem.
2. Determination of the readiness and capability for change.
3. Identification of the change agent's own resources and motivations for the change.
4. Determination of the intermediate change strategy and goals.[6]

Defining the Change Problem

Although widespread agreement may exist among organizational members as to the need for change, organizational members may have different perceptions as to the change approaches that should be used and/or where they should be implemented. To increase accuracy in defining the change problem, there should be a systematic attempt to determine whether the primary initial focus requires a change (1) of attitudes; if so, whose? (2) of behavior; if so, by whom and to what? (3) of knowledge and understanding; if so, where? (4) of organizational procedures; if so, where and to what? (5) of practices and ways of work; if so, whose? The initial approaches or interventions that are most likely appropriate can be partially determined by rank ordering the relative importance of these questions.

Determining the Readiness and Capability for Change

The second issue focuses on assessing the attitude and motivational levels concerning the change, as well as the physical, financial and organizational capacity to make the change. Approaches that require massive commitment of personal energies and organizational commitment are likely to be doomed if there is not a corresponding level of readiness and capacity. In such circumstances, it may be best to start with more moderate, less demanding approaches and then increase the depth and breadth of the change approaches as the organization develops the necessary capacity and commitment. If the organization is in a state of crisis, the luxury of staged interventions over a long time span may not be a viable option. Given this situation, there may be a tendency to do whatever is felt to be necessary. The prevailing attitude may be, "After all, if you're at the bottom, there is no way to go but up."

Identifying the Change Agent's Resources and Motivations

The third issue consists of two components: self-awareness by the change agents and openness with the client system. Change agents should know themselves before dealing with others. This will reduce the tendency of a change agent to promote "solutions" that fit their own personal philosophy and style rather than meet the needs of the client. Second, change agents should be open with the client about the knowledge and skills they lack.

Determining the Intermediate Change Strategy and Goals

The fourth issue concerns the use of intermediate approaches and goals to move toward the ultimate goals and approaches. This is illustrated by the earlier discussion of possibly starting with some structural approach and then moving to a people approach, or vice versa.

A conscientious consideration of each of the issues should increase the probability of appropriate judgments in the development of a change program.

COMPARISON OF APPROACHES

The approaches to change considered in this and the next chapter are intended to be a representative, rather than an exhaustive, inventory. Some of the approaches to change that have been woven into previous chapters, such as job enrichment and behavioral modification, will not be discussed at length here.

Relative Emphasis on Major System Variables

Table 16–1 provides an overview of the change approaches to be discussed in this and the next chapter, the focus of each approach, and the relative direct impact of each approach on four major system variables: people, task, technology, and structure.

In Table 16–1, each approach is characterized in terms of whether it usually has a high, moderate, or low *direct* impact on each of the four major system variables. For those approaches that can often vary in their degree of direct impact on a particular system variable, a range is indicated. For example, the management-by-objective change approach may vary between a moderate to a high direct impact on the people variable. As you review the matrix in Table 16–1, a word of caution as to interpretation is in order. Any one of the change approaches could ultimately have a substantial impact on all four of the major system variables. Our interpretation of *direct* impact is based on the typical nature, focus, and orientation of each change approach, rather than on its unanticipated, indirect, or ultimate impacts. It will become evident that the nature of some of these approaches has certain common and overlapping char-

TABLE 16–1.   Comparison in Relative Direct Impact of Selected Change Approaches on Major System Variables.

Change approaches	Relative direct impact on major system variables			
	People	Task	Technology	Structure
People focus				
Survey feedback	High	Low to moderate	Low	Low to moderate
Grid organization development	High	Low to high	Low	Low to high
Transactional analysis	High	Low	Low	Low
Sensitivity training	High	Low	Low	Low
Task focus				
Behavior modification	Moderate to high	High	Low	Low to moderate
Autonomous groups	Moderate to high	Very high	Low to moderate	Moderate to high
Job enrichment	Moderate to high	Very high	Low to moderate	Low to moderate
Management by objectives	Moderate to high	High	Low	Low
Technology focus				
Mass Production	Low	Moderate to high	Very high	Low to high
Automation	Low	Moderate to high	Very high	Low to high
Structure Focus				
Bureaucracy	Low	Moderate to high	Low	Very high
Matrix	Low to moderate	High	Low	Very high

acteristics. For example, the autonomous groups approach and the job enrichment approach have several elements in common.

Since the objective of this book is to give special emphasis to people and the tasks they perform, a corresponding concentration on change approaches with a people and task focus is presented in these two chapters. Thus, the fact that only two approaches each are mentioned under those that have a technology and structure focus should not be interpreted as meaning that these are of minor importance in organizational change programs.

It is our judgment, based on the literature on organizational change, that approaches with a people focus are more likely to be effective if preceded, accompanied, or followed by one or more approaches with a task, technology, and/or structural focus.

Relative Emphasis on Other Dimensions

A second set of comparisons for assessing change approaches is shown in Table 16–2. This table suggests the typical relative emphasis of

TABLE 16–2.   Comparisons along Four Dimensions of Selected Change Approaches

Change Approaches	Dimensions			
	Types Change Agents	Cognitive Emphasis	Affective/ Emotional Emphasis	Need for Trusting Behaviors
People focus				
Survey feedback	OD	Moderate	Low to moderate	Moderate
Grid organization development	OD	High	Moderate to high	Moderate to high
Transactional analysis	OD	Moderate to high	Moderate to high	Moderate to high
Sensitivity training	OD	Low to moderate	High	High
Task focus				
Behavior modification	PCT	High	Low	Low
Autonomous groups	PCT, OD	High	Low to moderate	High
Job enrichment	PCT, OD	High	Low	Moderate
Management by objectives	AFT, PCT, OD	High	Low to moderate	Low to moderate
Technology focus				
Mass production	AFT	High	Low	Low to moderate
Automation	AFT	High	Low	Low to moderate
Structure focus				
Bureaucracy	AFT	High	Low	Low
Matrix	AFT, PCT, OD	High	Low to moderate	High

OD = organizational development type; PCT = people-change technology type; AFT = analysis-from-the-top type.

each approach in terms of four dimensions: (1) types of change agents most likely to utilize each approach (see Chapter 15 for an explanation of each); (2) degree of cognitive emphasis; (3) degree of affective/emotional emphasis; and (4) degree of need for trusting behaviors.[7] Each approach is characterized as high, moderate, or low in relation to three of the four dimensions. If an approach can often vary in terms of these dimensions as a result of different forms of application, the typical range is indicated.

In Table 16–2, note that several types of change agents may utilize the same change approach. However, the style used by the different change agents for implementing a particular approach can vary substantially. For example, the organizational development (OD) change agent tends to consider changes in structure by involving the individuals who are likely to be affected by the changes, whenever possible. The analysis-from-the-top (AFT) change agent is also likely to use various structural approaches, but would not, to any great extent, involve members at lower organizational levels who might be affected by the changes. Another example is the difference between the people-change technology (PCT) type and the organizational development (OD) type in their use of the management-by-objectives approach. The PCT type is more likely to focus on individual objectives and overt behavior. The OD type is more likely to employ a management-by-objectives approach by first considering group attitudes, norms, and objectives.

The *cognitive emphasis* in a change approach is the extent to which the change approach focuses on observable and overt aspects of the organization, as well as task-related knowledge and skills of individuals. The *affective/emotional emphasis* in a change approach is the extent to which the change approach focuses on the values, attitudes, sentiments, and personal styles of members. The *trusting behavior dimension* is the extent to which the change approach requires actions that increase one's vulnerability.[8] The ranking of an approach as requiring low trusting behavior by those directly affected by the change should not be dependent on a high-trust relationship. Any of the change approaches would be met with hesitation, skepticism, and resistance if there exists a high degree of distrust.

PEOPLE-FOCUSED APPROACHES

This chapter explains and assesses four change approaches that are roughly classified as people-focused. These approaches are survey feedback, grid organization development, transactional analysis, and sensitivity training. The key contingencies that are likely to be associated with the successful application of each approach are also examined. The next chapter discusses task-, technology-, and structural-focused approaches to change.

Survey Feedback Approach

Although this discussion of the survey feedback approach draws from a number of sources, Mann and other members of the Institute for Social Research at the University of Michigan have been the most heavily involved in the development of the survey feedback approach.[9] The primary objective of the survey feedback approach is not to introduce a specific change (such as a new computer system) but to improve the relationships among the members of each organizational group and between organizational groups through their discussion of common problems. An organizational group consists of the managers at any hierarchical level plus the employees reporting directly to them.

The survey feedback approach involves a number of interrelated elements.[10] Typically, the process starts by obtaining commitment and endorsement from top management. Members of the whole organization or of a particular group, such as a plant or department, complete a standardized questionnaire. Generally it is preferable to survey members of the whole organization or at least all the members in a particular chain of command, such as from the vice-president of marketing on down through all members in the marketing group. The questionnaire is answered anonymously. It usually asks for members' perceptions and attitudes on a wide range of areas including communication processes; motivational conditions; decision-making practices; coordination between departments; and satisfaction with company, supervisor, job, and work group. Figure 16–1 is a sample of items included on one questionnaire that provided the data for a survey feedback program.

A survey feedback questionnaire may include standardized items that can be completed by all employees in many organizations; it may also include specially developed items for a particular organization or department. The questionnaire normally contains items that focus on the respondent's group as well as on processes that may characterize the organization as a whole. Top management may only want to use questionnaire items that relate to practices and processes they are willing and able to change. Since this approach requires the feedback of data from the completed questionnaires to all respondents, there should be concern about not raising expectations of lower level members toward areas of change that top management has no intention of modifying.

The data from the questionnaire are usually prepared in a format that breaks out a summary of the responses for each organization, department, or unit. At a minimum, all members of an organizational group are given a report that tabulates their responses, as well as those obtained from all other parts of the organization.

Group-discussion and problem-solving meetings are then held by organizational groups to discuss the data being fed back. Under ideal conditions, these group sessions move from discussing the tabulated perceptions and attitudes to identifying possible implications, concluding with commitments to various action steps. A single group session may deal

FIGURE 16–1.   Sample Questions in Feedback Program

Instructions: To indicate how descriptive each statement is (or should be) of your situation, write a number in the blank beside each statement, based on the following scale.

1	2	3	4	5
To a very little extent	To a little extent	To some extent	To a great extent	To a very great extent

_____   1.   To what extent is this organization generally quick to use improved work methods?

_____   2.   To what extent does this organization have a real interest in the welfare and happiness of those who work here?

_____   3.   How much does this organization try to improve working conditions?

_____   4.   To what extent does this organization have clear-cut, reasonable goals and objectives?

_____   5.   To what extent are work activities sensibly organized in this organization?

_____   6.   In this organization to what extent are decisions made at those levels where the most adequate and accurate information is available?

_____   7.   When decisions are being made, to what extent are the persons affected asked for their ideas?

_____   8.   People at all levels of an organization usually have know-how that could be of use to decision-makers. To what extent is information widely shared in this organization so that those who make decisions have access to all available know-how?

_____   9.   To what extent do different units or departments plan together and coordinate their efforts?

How friendly and easy to approach are the persons in your work group?

_____   10.   This is how it is *now*.

_____   11.   This is how I'd *like* it to be.

When you talk with persons in your work group, to what extent do they pay attention to what you're saying?

_____   12.   This is how it is *now*.

_____   13.   This is how I'd *like* it to be.

To what extent are persons in your work group willing to listen to your problems?

_____   14.   This is how it is *now*.

_____ 15.   This is how I'd *like* it to be.

To what extent does your supervisor offer new ideas for solving job-related problems?

_____ 16.   This is how it is *now*.

_____ 17.   This is how I'd *like* it to be.

To what extent does your supervisor encourage the persons who work for him to work as a team?

_____ 18.   This is how it is *now*.

_____ 19.   This is how I'd *like* it to be.

Adapted from Taylor, J. C., and D. G. Bowers, *Survey of Organizations: A Machine-scored Standardized Questionnaire Instrument* (Ann Arbor: Institute for Social Research, The University of Michigan Press, 1972). Used with permission.

only with particular parts of the data fed back. The organizational group may have several meetings over a period of time to process these data fully. In any event, these meetings are conducted in a task-oriented and problem-solving manner that consciously tries to avoid focusing on personalities.

Prior to conducting these meetings, an external agent often counsels the immediate superior in each organizational group as to the nature of the responses; the basis and meaning of the questionnaire measures; suggestions regarding the interpretation and use of the data; and guidelines for conducting the group problem-solving sessions. There are two basic ways of timing the feedback of the data: Everyone gets the data (1) almost simultaneously or (2) in a "waterfall" pattern, in which group meetings are held at the highest organizational levels first, followed by group meetings at each succeeding lower level.

Conditions for Success with the Survey Feedback Approach.   Several conditions should exist if the survey feedback approach is to have maximum impact. The first condition has already been mentioned: the sessions need to be conducted in a factual, task-oriented environment. Second, each organizational group must have sufficient discretion to consider and take positive action, or at least recommend changes, based on its findings and analysis for its own group. A pattern of usage involving only the measurement of perceptions and discussion of them without the opportunity to determine or strongly influence corrective actions may actually be counterproductive. Under such conditions, participants are likely to sense that they were deceived, manipulated, and misrepresented. A third condition that enhances the effectiveness of the survey feedback approach is the practice of reporting up the line the results of the problem-solving meetings from the immediate lower organizational group. This serves several purposes. Higher management is more likely to become rapidly involved in recommendations requiring some action on its part. And there is more likely to be a recognition at all levels that this process is important and not mere window dressing. Thus the commitment by all parties may be greater if there is a belief that their efforts could make a difference.

Assessment of the Survey Feedback Approach. It has been suggested that the effectiveness of the survey feedback approach "in comparison to traditional training courses, is that it deals with the system of human relationships as a whole (superior and subordinate can change together) and that it deals with each manager, supervisor, and employee in the context of his own job, his own problems, and his own work relationships."[11]

A strength, but also a limitation, of this approach is that it relies upon, and might actually reinforce, the existing organizational structure. This can occur because of the emphasis on improving working relationships and two-way communications between the various organizational levels within the present structure. Another impact of the survey feedback approach can be to increase the influence of lower level units with respect to higher organizational levels. But higher levels may also have greater influence with lower levels because their policies are better understood and the competencies and knowledge throughout the organization are brought to bear on organizationally related issues. Fundamental structural changes, such as a shift from a functional to a matrix form of organization, are not usually a direct part of the survey feedback approach. But the survey feedback approach may be quite useful in surfacing problems and clarifying issues that serve to indicate the need for a major structural change.

A major study of the relative long-term effectiveness of the survey feedback approach was launched in 1966 and covered a five-year time span.[12] The survey feedback approach was used in five organizations and involved about 5,700 respondents. The respondents and organizations included blue-collar and white-collar workers in varying technologies and functions. The assessment of the effectiveness of the survey feedback was limited to repeated administrations, usually one year apart, of a standardized questionnaire, which focused on 18 scales or indices including decision-making practices, leadership, work-group support, and job satisfaction.

The results of this assessment process indicated that the survey feedback approach was associated with a significant frequency of improvement. The effectiveness of this approach was substantially attributed to: (1) the broad coverage of the process to include virtually all members; (2) the amount of unfreezing that the approach stimulated; and (3) the members' tendency to perceive the data generated and the process as being directly relevant to the problems and goals of the organization and its units.

In sum, the survey feedback approach can be effective in meeting both organizational goals and individual needs.[13] However, it is not a radical approach in the sense of bringing about fundamental changes in the structure, task design, or technology of the organization.

Grid Organizational Development

Blake and Mouton advanced the Grid approach in 1964 and since that time have been enthusiastically involved in writing and consulting on the approach.[14] The following discussion is primarily drawn from their writings.

Grid organization development tends to be a more encompassing change approach than is survey feedback. It specifically addresses cognitive as well as affective/emotional issues that may be unexplored in the survey feedback model. The Grid approach covers a wide range of organizational and behavioral issues, concepts, and skill areas. As will become evident, discussions of many of these have been presented in earlier chapters.

The Grid approach to change in a large organization is claimed to take three to five years for complete implementation. It requires a highly systematic approach, consisting of six phases that are designed to be logically connected and to build upon each other. All six phases of the Grid organization development approach rest on the assumption that there is a potential win-win relationship between the people side and production side of organizations. Each of the phases can become quite complex, and efforts to implement them may be time-consuming. It should therefore be recognized that the following represents a skeleton description of each phase.

Phase I—Orientation.   Phase I is essentially a seminar for the involved supervisors and managers. Normally it is conducted outside the organization. Lasting about a week, it consists of all-day sessions, including evening assignments. The participants study reading materials, listen to short lectures, and, most importantly, diagnose their personal styles and approaches to management. This is accomplished through completion of questionnaires and small-group (team) processes and assessments of the organization's norms, past practices, and organizational climate.

Phase II—Work-Team Development.   Phase II focuses on assisting the members of all work teams in the organization, such as managers and their subordinate supervisors, to apply what they learned in Phase I directly to their specific situation. This process usually starts with the top executives and individuals reporting directly to them and then moves downward to work groups at succeedingly lower levels. The work-team development phase encourages: (1) diagnosis and resolution of barriers interfering with the effectiveness of the work team; (2) development of agreement on how the members want to operate; (3) setting of objectives, with a timetable, for improving team functioning; and (4) creation of skills and a climate for introspecting and critiquing their own patterns of operation.

Phase III—Intergroup Development.   The objective of the intergroup development phase is to improve working and problem-solving relationships between groups (work teams) requiring closer integration. Interventions in the intergroup development phase focus principally on the representatives from each group who are primarily responsible and who are involved in actual and direct contact with each other. These individuals are often assigned the tasks of: (1) developing an ideal model of what their relationships should be like; (2) comparing and exchanging group images of each other; (3) identifying problems and blockages in moving toward this ideal; and (4) developing an action plan for progress. An internal or external change agent is normally quite influential in sequencing the flows of activities and preventing sessions from degenerating into name calling, scapegoating, or blame placing.

Phase IV—Developing an Organization Blueprint.   Phase IV focuses on designing an ideal model of what the organization should *become,* with a decreased emphasis on what it *is.* As may be expected, the organization blueprint phase requires a particularly heavy commitment of time and energy by the top executives. This phase is also intended to move down through the lower levels, at least through all management and professional classifications. The output of this phase should include statements and understandings of changes in organizational strategies, objectives, structures, and policies. If the organization blueprint phase is seriously implemented, there should be fundamental changes in the people, task, and structural system variables. However, this phase of grid organization development does not generally consider the technology variable directly.

Phase V—Blueprint Implementation.   Phase V is designed to bridge the gap from "what is" to "what should be." This phase requires the greatest period of time, possibly two or three years. Although there is no simplistic formula for the blueprint-implementation phase, a common recommendation is to create planning teams for logical parts or subsystems of the organization. These teams often have the tasks of conducting conversion studies of how they are to change and what specific changes they need to make. It is recommended that an overall planning team of top executives be actively engaged in the tasks of taking initiatives that don't naturally fall within the scope of other planning teams. This executive team also facilitates and reviews the progress and outputs of the other planning teams.

Phase VI—Stabilization.   This final phase involves an overall critique and evaluation of the organization's progress and the development of insights about the need for new changes and replanning. There is concern for reinforcing the new patterns developed from Phase I through Phase V, and making them "standard practice." The stabilization phase may require administering questionnaires, interviewing individuals, reviewing performance data, and the like, to assess the degree of change and to identify weaknesses and plan ways of eliminating them.

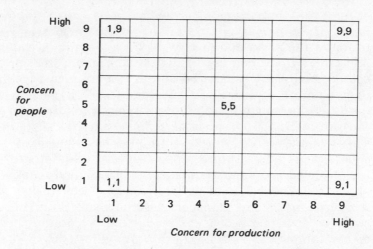

FIGURE 16–2.   The Basic Managerial Grid

Basic Grid Model.   The basic model underlying the concepts, attitudes and skills of all six phases in the Grid change approach is the Managerial Grid. Figure 16–2 shows the basic Managerial Grid. The Grid serves as a framework for describing different ways of managing, as well as prescribing how one ought to manage. As shown in Figure 16–2, the Managerial Grid consists of two dimensions, each of which can vary along a nine-point continuum. The vertical axis plots the managers' degree of concern for people, particularly their subordinates. This is shown as ranging from 1, low concern for people, to 9, high concern for people. The horizontal axis plots the managers' degree of concern for production, especially by their subordinates. Again, this is shown as ranging from 1, low concern for production, to 9, high concern for production. Concern for production is used in the broadest sense to include number and quality of outputs, ideas developed, quality of decisions, and activities performed.

Since the basic Managerial Grid (as shown in Figure 16–2) is a 9 by 9 grid, there are 81 possible combinations between concern for people and concern for production. As a practical matter, the focus is on the five critical combinations (four extreme and one central). Blake and Mouton use questionnaires to assess various aspects of managers' styles and behaviors. The scoring process for these questionnaires enable managers to plot where they fit on the 81-cell grid. There is nothing sacred about this 9 by 9 grid. It could just as easily have been developed as a 7 by 7 grid, an 11 by 11 grid, or on some other numerical scaling.

Five Managerial Styles.   Let's briefly consider the five managerial styles noted in Figure 16–2. Blake and Mouton suggest that managers are likely to have a dominant style, such as 9,9, and a backup or secondary style, such as 5,5. No natural link is inferred between a particular dominant style and its backup style. The combination will depend on the situation and individual.

The 1,1 managerial style has been called *impoverished manage-ment*. These managers tend to put people on jobs and then avoid them, to follow the rules, and to serve as little more than conduits for messages and orders from their superiors. The 1,9 managerial style has been called *country-club management* because of the exclusive emphasis on the feel-ings, comfort, and needs of subordinates. The concern is with obtaining loyalty from subordinates that will motivate them to produce without pressure. The 9,1 managerial style has been called *task management*. These managers do the planning and push to get the work out, since subordinates are assumed to be lazy and indifferent. The subordinates are expected to follow the manager's rules, instructions, procedures, and schedules. The 5,5 managerial style has been called *middle-of-the-road management*. These managers assume there is an inherent conflict be-tween concerns for people and production. Accordingly, there is an attempt to compromise and balance these two dimensions. The 9,9 managerial style has been called *team management*. It is regarded as the ideal style and the one that managers and the organization are encouraged to adopt. This style focuses on people's higher order needs. It involves subordinates in decision making and assumes that the objectives of the organization and the subordinates are compatible.

Assessment of Grid Organization Development.   The Grid approach is potentially the most comprehensive of the people-focused approaches to organizational change discussed in this chapter. It emphasizes the point that specific change approaches may well call for alterations in two or more of the four basic variables: people, task, technology, and structure.

It is difficult to draw hard conclusions about Grid organization development because studies on the Grid do not make clear that: (1) the processes were always implemented as prescribed; (2) the full range of phases was implemented; and (3) the research design permitted sufficient opportunity for drawing inferences about change.

The Grid appears to be based on the assumption that there is one best way to manage and change organizations. This is certainly not con-sistent with some of the other research discussed in this and other chap-ters, nor with the overall approach of this book. It is our judgment that the Grid approach can be effective particularly where: (1) the managerial value system approaches quality-of-life management (see Chapter 3 for a detailed explanation); (2) the external environment (such as govern-mental regulations or customer demands) does not tightly mandate in-ternal processes; and (3) the technology can be modified or does not tightly control people. Unfortunately, the best we can conclude is that the research suggests that the Grid approach has had successes, failures, and mixed results.[15]

Transactional Analysis

As of this writing, transactional analysis has somewhat the status of a fad in terms of its use within organizations and the current level of public attention. Sensitivity training, discussed in the next section, went through the same process of simplistic attention and reached its peak as a fad about 1971. Like many ideas or things that develop into fads, there is a tendency for people who are attempting to exploit the fad to make excessive and misleading claims about what can be accomplished, as well as presenting desired objectives as guaranteed promises. Yet numerous qualified and competent change agents are capable of effectively utilizing transactional analysis and sensitivity training. It is unfortunate that these professional change agents are sometimes faced with a need to overcome the disillusionment or embitterment created by such misrepresentation by other sources.

Although the processes of transactional analysis and sensitivity training differ considerably, their objectives, particularly when utilized for organizational purposes, are quite similar. In an organizational change program, both approaches are often intended to help the organization members:

1. Improve interpersonal communications.
2. Develop improved ways and styles for managing interpersonal conflict.
3. Gain self-insight by becoming more aware of their own behavior and obtaining feedback from others.
4. Develop diagnostic skills, particularly as related to the individual and small groups.
5. Acquire an understanding of the factors that interfere with or facilitate group functioning.
6. Reduce self-defeating attitudes and behaviors.

Both approaches strongly focus on the people variable, especially in terms of individual and small-group processes. Compared with the other approaches already discussed, there tends to be: (1) relatively (and absolutely) little direct emphasis on the task, technology, and structural variables (see Table 16–1); (2) relatively high affective/emotional emphasis; and (3) relatively high need for trusting behaviors (see Table 16–2). As explained by Bowen and Nath, the careful application of transactional analysis or sensitivity training can be an effective initial approach to unfreezing the organization's members for consideration of other changes.[16]

Basic Transactional Analysis Model. Transactional analysis was first formally developed by Eric Berne in 1961 and was elaborated upon by him in a number of succeeding books.[17] As shown in Figure 16–3, the basic model of transactional analysis consists of seven interdependent

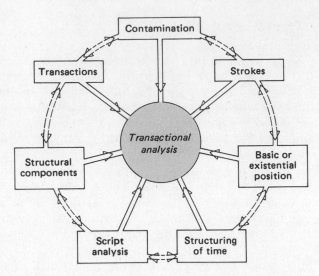

FIGURE 16–3.   Basic Elements in Transactional Analysis Model

Adapted from Anderson, J. P., "A Transactional Analysis Primer," in Pfeiffer, J., and Jones, J., *The 1973 Annual Handbook for Group Facilitators* (Iowa City: University Associates, 1973), pp. 145–157.

elements: structural components, transactions, contamination, strokes, basic or existential position, structuring of time, and script analysis.

Structural Components: The structural components of the transactional analysis model are three ego states: Parent, Adult, and Child. An *ego state* is the typical way of feeling, thinking, and reacting. Each of us is capable of displaying these three ego states.

The *Parent ego state* is the feelings, thoughts, and reactions in each of us that are similar to those perceived by us in our mothers, fathers, or other important individuals who might have reared us. The Parent in us assumes numerous functions, including setting limits, giving advice, disciplining, guiding, protecting, making rules and regulations about how life should be (the musts, shoulds, always, nevers, goods, bads, etc.), teaching how to's, keeping traditions, nurturing, judging, and criticizing. In themselves, the parental functions, like those of the other ego states, are not necessarily to be regarded as good or bad. One of the objectives of the transactional analysis change approach is to assist us in becoming more aware of the Parent ego state and then to help each of us determine for ourselves what forms and parts of it are relevant or irrelevant to our current lives. This is to help us live our own lives and not those of our parents. The ways in which parents or significant others use and communicate these functions strongly determines how children view parents, authority, and society.

The *Adult ego state* is the part that computes, stores experiences, and uses facts to make decisions. The Adult ego state is the unemotional cognitive part of us. In the transactional analysis model, the Adult ego state is not intended to mean or suggest maturity. The Adult functions include data gathering on all three ego states, identifying and assessing alternatives, setting objectives and determining how to attain them, and all components of ordered planning and the decision-making process. The manner of functioning of the Adult ego state varies among individuals, as well as in the extent to which it includes all these functions.

The *Child ego state* is what we were in our younger years. There could be a number of "children" in us from the past. The Child in us could range from angry, rebellious, frightened, or conforming, to creative, carefree, fun loving, adventurous, and trusting.

All three of these ego states (Parent, Adult, and Child) exist within us, and all are important. It is desirable to have our Adult operating at all times so that it can keep us aware of the Parent and the Child and the situation, as well as help us with our decisions. Thus, latitude of choice and freedom to be ourselves is increased.

Transactions: Transactions are interactions we have with others and with our internal selves. Transactions include verbal and nonverbal communications that can vary from an exchange of compliments to a brawl. The three basic forms of interpersonal transactions are parallel, crossed, and ulterior. These transactions occur between the three ego states of one person and the three ego states of another person. In the examples given here, the following notation is used: P = Parent, A = Adult, and C = Child.

Transactions are parallel when the lines of communication between two individuals are complementary, such as Parent to and from Parent, Parent to and from Child, and Parent to and from Adult. The following examples of parallel transactions were suggested by Luchsinger and Luchsinger:[18]

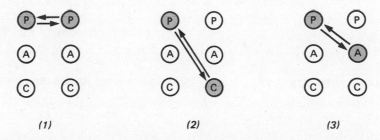

(1)   *(2)*   *(3)*

1. *Parent-Parent Transaction*
   Manager: An effective maintenance repair program always reduces costs.

   Employee: I always say that a stitch in time saves nine.

2. *Parent-Child Transactions*
   Manager: An effective maintenance repair program always reduces costs.

Employee: Yes, sir.

3. *Parent-Adult Transaction*
   Manager: An effective maintenance repair program always reduces costs.

   Employee: The problem is the new supplier. Maintenance and production records show that his parts don't last as do the
   parts from Acme Company.

In these three examples, the employees are acting in the perceived
expected ego states.

A crossed (noncomplementary) transaction occurs when the interactions do not have common origination and terminal ego states. Difficulties in communication and arguments often arise from crossed transactions, as the following illustrates:

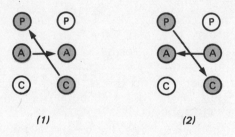

(1)   *(2)*

---

1. *Crossed Transaction*
   Joe: Do you know how long it takes (the bus) to get to Philadelphia?

   Jack: I wish we could stop for a milkshake.

2. *Crossed Transaction*
   Doting Mother: You can never trust a man. They're just no good.

   Sally: You can't judge a man you haven't met.

Ulterior transactions occur when one individual attempts to create the
impression of relating to one ego state when, in fact, he or she is responding to another. Ulterior transactions are attempts to be dishonest, manipulate, or engage in unconscious "game playing." Ulterior transactions involve
the simultaneous activity of more than two ego states and are the basis
for psychological games, as in the following example:

1. *Ulterior Transaction*

Sue Supersales:	You'd get a better vacuum for another $30.00, but, I don't think you can afford it.
Patsy:	I'll take it.

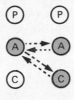

(1)

Here, the salesperson addressed Patsy Adult-Adult on the social level, but Adult-Child on the psychological level. This is done in the hope of hooking the Child into responding "Yes, I'll take it." A wary Adult would realize the financial irresponsibility and squash the offer.

Contamination: Contamination is the Child's acceptance in us of our parents' or significant others' prejudices, opinions, and feelings as our own. Thus, we may be prone not to use our Adult to check out the "facts" for ourselves. Contamination may be conveyed and illustrated as follows.

1. *Contamination Transaction*

Father:	Joe, let me warn you that you can never trust managers; they are no good and only try to exploit you.
Grandfather:	That's right, Joe. This family is proud of its tradition of fighting management by sticking together.
Joe:	O.K.

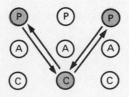

(1)

Strokes: Strokes are the positive or negative ways in which we recognize the existence of others. This occurs through verbal and nonverbal means. Positive strokes would include expressions of love, respect, friendship, and recognition. Negative strokes would be characterized by the opposite expressions.

Basic or Existential Position: The Child in each of us has its own basic way of experiencing itself and perceiving others. The general intrapersonal and interpersonal view taken by the Child is called the basic or existential position. Individuals may differ by taking one of four different basic positions. These positions, as described here, are pure types; individuals fall along a continuum from one extreme to the other. The four pure existential positions are:

1. *I'm O.K.: You're O.K.* This is the healthy position that is the ultimate change objective in transactional analysis.
2. *I'm O.K.: You're not O.K.* This is a position of distrust in which the Child in us is suspicious of other people.
3. *I'm not O.K.: You're O.K.* In this position, the Child in us has a negative self-concept and is likely to feel low or depressed.
4. *I'm not O.K.: You're not O.K.* In this position, the Child in us feels that other people, itself, and life in general "just aren't any good." At the extremes of this position, the Child could sense total helplessness or rage and possibly engage in suicide or homicide.

Structuring of Time: Our particular basic (existential) position will strongly influence how we structure our time. Six types of time structuring are expressed through transactions: withdrawal, rituals, activities, pastimes, games, and intimacy. *Withdrawal* is the psychological removal of ourselves from the people around us, as, for example, by constantly daydreaming. *Rituals* are transactions that are socially agreed upon ways of behaving toward each other. *Activities* are spontaneous transactions between or among individuals, such as eating, playing tennis, and working. *Pastimes* are transactions that serve to fill time with others, such as, bull sessions, discussing Saturday's football game, and gossiping. *Games* are "recurring set(s) of transactions, often repetitious, superficially plausible, with a concealed motivation, or . . . gimmick."[19] Games always have an ulterior motive and are designed to obtain a payoff for one of the individuals, which was the real reason for playing the game. Over ninety games have been described, including such types as "Yes, But," "Ain't it Awful (about them)," "See What You Made Me Do," and "Now I've Got You, You S.O.B." *Intimacy* involves transactions concerned with the mutuality of two people in a shared identity. Mutuality occurs through giving, sharing, taking risks, and trusting one another.

Script Analysis: Our script is the life plan we feel compelled to act out. It is closely related to our basic position and our way of structuring time. A script is thought to be a subconscious life-plan formed within our Child by about the age of seven. Although decisions have been made about our script at one point in time, it can be redecided. Individuals with problems often have scripts with unfavorable outcomes (sickness, failure, insanity). One of the aims of transactional analysis is to assist us in freeing ourselves from these scripts.

Many other aspects of transactional analysis could be considered, but to do so would take us well beyond our limited objectives.

Assessment of Transactional Analysis.   Because of the recency in applications of transactional analysis within organizational settings, most of the reports assessing its effectiveness are based on single-time attitude surveys and case study reports from those using it. Among the larger organizations making some use of transactional analysis are Bank of America, American Airlines, Mountain Bell Telephone Co., and the Data Processing Division of IBM.[20] The applications of transactional analysis by these firms are mostly in a training format, where individuals are expected to attend a certain number of sessions. In a few cases, there have been attempts to apply the transactional approach to entire work teams. We have not uncovered any reports of efforts to apply the transactional-analysis change approach along with other approaches.

Sensitivity Training

Sensitivity training, which is also called T-group or laboratory training, is an experience-based approach that focuses on individual and small-group development and change. Sensitivity training sessions are often conducted in group settings of about eight to fifteen individuals. The duration of the sessions can vary widely, with most groups meeting from a total of ten to forty hours. The sessions can be continuous, as in a marathon weekend T-group; conducted over one to two weeks, as in a live-in program; or spread out over a year, as in a college program.

T-groups may be used as part of a larger change approach usually referred to as laboratory education. Laboratory education may also involve the use of case studies; a wide variety of structured exercises, often involving role playing; lectures on cognitive material relevant to interpersonal relations; and other instruments or questionnaires.

Basic Sensitivity Training Model.   While the nature of sensitivity training can vary widely, it usually contains the following elements: here-and-now focus; unstructured group; self-disclosure; intense interpersonal feedback; creation of ambiguity, dilemmas, and anxiety; and generalizations from direct experience.[21] Sensitivity training should not be, although it commonly is, confused with some forms of the "let it all hang out" encounter groups.

Trainers of T-groups may start the process by defining their role and forming an environment to bring about "unfreezing" by creating ambiguity, dilemmas, and anxiety within the members. The following statement is an example of how trainers might start.

This group will meet for many hours and will serve as a kind of laboratory where each individual can increase his understanding of the forces that influence individual behavior and the performance of groups and organizations. The data for learning will be our own behavior, feelings, and reactions. We begin with no definite structure or organization, no agreed-upon procedures, and no specific agenda. It will be up to us to fill the vacuum created by the lack of these familiar elements and to study our group as we evolve. My role will be to help the group to learn from its own experience, but not to act as a traditional chairman or to suggest how we should organize, what our procedure should be, or exactly what our agenda will include. With these few comments, I think we are ready to begin in whatever way you feel will be most helpful.[22]

In such an ambiguous situation, members may try to organize the group by selecting a chairperson, selecting a topic for discussion, withdrawing and waiting in silence, getting the trainer to take a more active role, and so forth.

Regardless of what takes place, the here-and-now focus means that the members should eventually start discussing why they responded as they did, how they felt personally, how they felt about the actions of others. In other words, the basic focus for the interactions is on what is happening and being experienced in the group, not on something that happened a year ago or in some other place. The emphasis on the here and now is contrary to most of our previous learning experiences and consequently may generate considerable frustration and anxiety.

The process of making more of oneself known to the other members is *disclosure*. Random and wide-open disclosure may suggest personal difficulties. Sensitivity training usually encourages disclosure and operates on the position that we tend to conceal too much of our feelings and self-reactions for maximum psychological adjustment.

Feedback is the other face of disclosure in sensitivity training. Feedback enables us to know how we are perceived by others and what impact we are having on others. Through feedback, we can gain insight as to our tendency to be evaluative or descriptive, and we learn how to give helpful (instead of hurtful) feedback. This insight can occur through feedback on whether others perceive our communications as based on inferences or observations and on how they experienced our communications. Throughout sensitivity training, there are likely to be segments of time devoted to drawing inferences, generalizations, and conclusions from the group members' here-and-now experiences. Rather than imposing a concept or model on the group, trainers may intervene by asking members to reflect and introspect on the meaning of what has just taken place.

Assessment of Sensitivity Training.   Individuals may experience the same T-group quite differently, and they may vary in their experiences of different T-groups. Table 16–3 summarizes some possible effects of T-groups and the consequences for individual members.

Two key factors that appear to influence the effects of sensitivity

TABLE 16–3.   Possible Effects of T-Groups on Individuals

| | Diverse consequences for individuals | |
Possible group effects	Positive	Negative
1. Achieving and maintaining group cohesiveness	Feeling a part of the group, experiencing a sense of belonging	Giving up autonomy in order to belong, losing oneself in the group
2. Conforming to group norms	Awareness of participating in creating group norms	Feeling pressured to abide by group norms
3. Validating personal perceptions through group consensus	Reality testing and correcting personal distortions	Sharing illusions of the group
4. Expression of affective feelings	Free expression of feelings	Feeling inadequate unless expressing group approved emotions
5. Group perception of problems	Unblocked thinking	Forced to share problems with groups
6. Potency of group	Chance to feel influential	Feeling manipulated
7. Role differentiation	Achieving role flexibility	Type-cast in a role
8. Self-disclosure	Insight into personal blind spots	Becoming shaken in belief in self

Adapted from Lakin, M., *Experimental Groups: The Uses of Interpersonal Encounter, Psychotherapy Groups, and Sensitivity Training* (Morristown, N.J.: General Learning Press, 1972), p. 11.

training are the trainer and each member's personality. *First,* some data suggests that T-group trainers who provide excessive stimulation and give too much attention to the control function are associated with negative outcomes for the members.[23] Excessive stimulation is illustrated by behaviors that emphasize revealing feelings, challenging, confrontation, revelation of personal values, and frequent participation. The control function is revealed in behaviors emphasizing suggestion of rules, setting limits, managing time, and sequencing activities.

Second, the personalities of T-group members are likely to determine whether the reactions to the sensitivity training process are basically positive or negative. Some data suggests that individuals strongly characterized by introversion, sensation, or thinking orientations (especially when two of these are combined in a single person) are more likely to reject and have unfavorable experiences from standard T-groups.[24] Recall from Chapter 7 that:

1. Introvert types like quiet for concentration, have some problems communicating, work contentedly alone.
2. Thinking types are unemotional, are uninterested in people's feelings, like analysis and putting things into logical order.

3. Sensation types dislike new problems unless there are standard ways to solve them, such as an established routine.

Since the processes and requirements of sensitivity training are so contrary to the introvert, thinking, and sensation types, it also seems logical that individuals with these characteristics would be less receptive to this type of experience.

Sensitivity training is probably the most controversial of the various change approaches, particularly when utilized as part of an organizational change program. One issue concerns possible harm to the individual and invasion of privacy, especially when the T-groups consist of members from the same organization.[25] A second issue concerns its effectiveness as a change approach. While well-conducted sensitivity training can bring about change in the individual in the work situation (in terms of increased flexibility, more openness, better listening skills, etc.), the effect on individual role performance and overall organizational change remains a debatable question.[26]

Comparison of Transactional Analysis and Sensitivity Training

Transactional analysis differs from sensitivity training in several aspects:

1. It is a relatively nonthreatening approach to self-evaluation.
2. It places more emphasis on examining ourselves.
3. It requires less self-disclosure between individuals.
4. It requires less risk taking by participants.
5. It places greater emphasis on individuals controlling and consciously deciding upon the types and the depth of personal change they would like to achieve.

Because these factors offer the potential for accomplishing many of the same objectives as does sensitivity training, we feel that the transactional analysis approach is more readily usable with many types of organizations and individuals.

SUMMARY

A major goal of this chapter has been the development of your conceptual skill for diagnosing when to use various approaches to organizational change. Tables 16–1 and 16–2 provide a framework for comparing the approaches discussed in this and the next chapter as well as the key contingencies that should be evaluated in making your choice. While this chapter discussed four people-focused approaches to organizational change —survey feedback, Grid organization development, transactional analysis, and sensitivity training—the next chapter will discuss approaches to change that focus on the system variables of task, technology, and structure.

Each of the people-focused approaches has the potential for creating positive outcomes. With the possible exception of Grid organization development, however, they do not strongly and directly address the task, technology, and structure variables in organizations. It may often be desirable to utilize one or more people-focused approaches as part of a change program that is oriented to approaches that focus more on the task, technology, or structure variables.

DISCUSSION QUESTIONS

1. Evaluate this statement: "The survey feedback approach should be effective in any type of organization with virtually every class of employee."

2. Is Grid organization development consistent with a contingency approach to management? Explain.

3. Should an organization require its employees to attend a sensitivity training program? Explain.

4. What are two of the basic differences between sensitivity training and transactional analysis?

5. Of the four people-focused approaches discussed, which is the most comprehensive? Discuss.

MANAGERIAL PROBLEMS

INTERVIEW WITH MINTZBERG

The following is excerpted from an interview with Henry Mintzberg, a management theorist.[27] It brings out some of his positions on the nature of managerial work, organizational power, and change.

Interviewer: How are you approaching the study of power?

Mintzberg: My orientation is quite different from most works on power. I'm not concerned with individual power. Individual motivation, need for achievement, group dynamics and the like are treated as a given. But when you assume that there are people inside and outside an organization attempting to obtain power through and over the organization, a number of fascinating questions arise. How do they get power? What do they do with it when they have it? What kind of alliances or power configurations do they form? All fascinating questions.

Interviewer: You use the phrase power in and around organizations. Could you explain that in more detail?

Mintzberg: Let's consider two kinds of influences on an organization. Outside the organization there are the owners, the customers, unions, government, special interest groups and so on. Inside the organization you have the chief executive officer, other line managers, the technocratic or analytic staff, the support staff, and the workers. Each of these has a greater or lesser influence on the organization, on the decision-making process. Basically, what people are after is to control either the decisions or the actions the organization takes. Where to build a factory, what products to market, what services to provide are the decisions people seek to influence.

Interviewer: How does a group achieve greater rather than lesser influence over the decisions of an organization?

Mintzberg: Let's consider that question in terms of coalitions. Broadly, there is the External Coalition and the Internal Coalition. There are a number of means that each can use to gain influence or power. One external means of influence is to attempt to gain membership or representation on the board of directors. In Europe, there is a strong movement to place workers on the board of directors. Here, there are movements for special interest representation, consumer advocates, minority representatives and the like. Candidly, I think that's not a good forum for influence. A board of directors is a bit like a bee—it only has a single stinger. Its only real power is to change the chief executive officer and it can't do that every three weeks. Two powerful ways external forces can gain influence are through "Pressure Campaigns," the Ralph Nader vs. General Motors type campaign, and the "Specific Constraints" or get-a-law passed approach.

By the way, there are three different kinds of external coalitions. I call one the "Dominated External Coalition." This is where one person or group share the same goals and control the organization. The best example is the closely held business corporation where the owners are all well defined and known.

The second external coalition is the "Divided External Coalition." Here we are dealing with highly politicized groups. Typical of this is the university where there is competition for control between student groups, faculty groups, government, and trustees.

The third is the "Passive External Coalition." Most typical is the classic case of the widely held business. Shareholders become so widespread that they have no power. Management has all the power. Those are the three major external coalitions.

Interviewer: And the internal coalitions?

Mintzberg: The process of internal power is pretty complex. There are power systems to look at before looking at the internal coalitions. The first two are control systems. The "Personal Control System" is just control exerted by giving orders and watching directly over people.

   The second I call the "Bureaucratic Control System." This is the formalized control system where management by objectives, management information systems, and the like are in place and viewed as important.

   Let's see, the third system is the "Political Control System" which is operationalized by people trying to block the other two control systems. They replace the goals of the manager or management by some other goals, perhaps their private ones.

   The fourth system, and the one I find most fascinating and most ignored, is the "System of Ideology." This is the system of norms, beliefs, and traditions the corporation operates under. Belief in the organization, belief in the founder, belief in the corporate strategy are strong possible influences on decision making. When we talk about climate or culture or atmosphere or character of an organization, I believe we are talking about this system of ideology. There isn't much research on ideology of organizations but what there is tends to talk about famous or critical events in the history of an organization or a charismatic leader.

Interviewer: What would be an example?

Mintzberg: Take Mercedes Benz. They make cars and GM makes cars. But Mercedes has this ideology, this great belief in quality. Polaroid is another example. Everything there has been geared to the fulfillment of Land's obsession with perfecting that one camera. The early AT&T image of providing everyone in America with cheap telephone service is another case in point.

   The whole area is virtually unexplored. Most researchers are uncomfortable with things they can't immediately operationalize. You walk into IBM and you know you're in IBM. You can't describe it easily. You can't necessarily measure it, but you sense it. It's real.

Interviewer: And these power systems somehow form the internal coalitions?

Mintzberg: Yes, just as I described three external coalitions, there are five internal coalitions. One is the "Autocratic Internal Coalition." That one's based largely on personal control systems. The second is the "Bureaucratic Internal Coalition" based on the bureaucratic controls. A third is the "Ideological Internal Coalition" based on those nebulous myths and ideologies. A fourth is something I call a "Meritocratic Internal Coalition." This is a coalition based on the power of knowledge and expertise. The fifth is the "Politicized Internal Coalition." Ideology or control or expertise aren't important, just the political alliances.

Interviewer: We have to ask you a "so what" question. So what if you know about all of these coalitions and systems?

Mintzberg: The "so what" as you call it is that you can develop a set of power configurations when you understand all the forces. This helps you understand how things work, how to get things done in a given organization.

QUESTIONS

1. Based on this interview, how do you think Mintzberg would feel about the approaches to organizational change discussed in this chapter?
2. What similarities or differences do you see between the positions taken in this interview with those in the chapter?
3. What do you think Mintzberg would emphasize in attempting to change an organization?

GEORGIA RAMO COMPANY

Since its beginnings in 1950, Georgia Ramo Company (GRC) like most U.S. firms, has used a policy of "last hired—first fired." This means that when GRC cannot support all its workers, the first people to be fired are those who were the last to be hired. This policy was originally adopted to protect the seniority and to reward the loyalty of long-time personnel at GRC.

During the past three years of economic difficulty, GRC has managed to retain most of its employees, although it has hired only enough new people to meet the minority quota requirements established by the Department of Labor. Now, however, due to the recession, GRC must fire 5 percent of its employees—eighty-four people.

If GRC follows its "last hired—first fired" policy, among those released would be twenty-two black men, twelve black women, eighteen Caucasian women, two Chinese men, and four Vietnam veterans. Firing so many minority workers would create major legal problems. GRC is committed to nondiscrimination; however, it feels a moral responsibility to those workers who have been with the company for longer periods of time.

QUESTIONS

1. Could any of the change approaches discussed in this chapter be helpful in dealing with or preventing the changes facing GRC? Explain.
2. Assume your group has been asked to consider this problem and to make recommendations to GRC. The president of GRC has indicated that if GRC decides to protect long-standing workers and fire fifty-eight minority people, he is willing to face the legal battles. He simply wants to come up with the fairest policy for all. What would you do?

KEY WORDS

Cognitive emphasis
Affective/emotional emphasis
Trusting behavior dimension
Survey feedback
Grid organization development
Impoverished management
Country-club management
Task management
Middle-of-the-road management

Team management
Transactional analysis
Ego state
Transactions
Contamination
Strokes
Sensitivity training
Disclosure

REFERENCES

1. The breakdown of U.S. innovation, *Business Week*, February 16, 1976, pp. 56–68.

2. Beckhard, R., and R. Harris, *Organizational Transitions: Managing Complex Change* (Reading, Mass.: Addison-Wesley, 1977).

3. Dowling, W., To move an organization: The Corning approach to organization development, *Organizational Dynamics*, 1975, 3, pp. 16–34.

4. Ibid.

5. Tushman, M., *Organizational Change: An Exploratory Study and Case History*, ILR paperback no. 15 (Ithaca: New York State School of Industrial and Labor Relations, Cornell University, 1974);

Guest, R., *Organizational Change: The Effects of Successful Leadership* (Homewood, Ill.: Richard D. Irwin and Dorsey Press, 1962).

6. Beckhard, R., Strategies for large system change, *Sloan Management Review*, 1975, 16, pp. 43–55.

7. Harrison, R., Choosing the depth of organizational intervention, *Journal of Applied Behavioral Science*, 1970, 6, pp. 181–202; Selfridge, R., and S. Sokolik, A comprehensive view of organization development, *MSU Business Topics*, 1975, 23, pp. 46–61; Zand, D., Trust and managerial problem solving, *Administrative Science Quarterly*, 1972, 17, pp. 229–239.

8. Zand, D., D. Kegan, and A. Ruben-

stein, Trust, effectiveness and organization development: A field study in R&D, *The Journal of Applied Behavioral Science*, 1973, 9, pp. 498–513.

9. Baumgartel, H., Using employee questionnaire results for improving organizations: The "survey" feedback experiment, *Kansas Business Review*, 1950, 12, pp. 2–6; Bass, B., A systems survey research feedback for management and organizational development, *The Journal of Applied Behavioral Science*, 1976, 12, pp. 215–229; Mann, F., Studying and creating change: A means to understanding social organization, in *Research in Industrial Human Relations* (Madison, Wis.: Industrial Relations Research Association, no. 17, 1957), pp. 146–157; Taylor, J., and D. Bowers, *Survey of Organizations: A Machine-Scored Standardized Questionnaire Instrument*, Ann Arbor: University of Michigan Press, 1972).

10. Nadler, D., *Feedback and Organization Development: Using Data-Based Methods* (Reading, Mass.: Addison-Wesley, 1977).

11. Taylor and Bowers, *Survey of Organizations;* Baumgartel, Survey feedback experiment.

12. Bowers, D., and D. Hausser, Work group types and intervention effects in organizational development, *Administrative Science Quarterly*, 1977, 22, pp. 76–96.

13. Huse, E., *Organizational Development and Change* (St. Paul, Minn.: West Publishing, 1975), pp. 163–174.

14. Blake, R., and J. Mouton, *The Managerial Grid* (Houston: Gulf Publishing, 1964); Blake, R., and J. Mouton, *Building A Dynamic Corporation through Grid Organization Development* (Reading, Mass.: Addison-Wesley, 1969). Blake R., and J. Mouton, An overview of the grid, *Training and Development Journal*, 1975, 29, pp. 29–36.

15. Beer, M., and S. Kleisath, The effects of the managerial grid on organizational and leadership dimensions, in Zalkind, S. (ed.), *Research on the Impact of Using Different Laboratory Methods for Interpersonal and Organizational Change*, paper presented at the American Psychological Association, Washington, D.C., 1967, Blake, R., J. Mouton, L. Barnes, and L. Greiners, Breakthrough in organization development, *Harvard Business Review*, 1964, 42, pp. 133–155; Kreinick, P., and N. Colarelli, Managerial grid human relations training for mental hospital personnel, *Human Relations*, 1971, 24, pp. 21–104; Using the managerial grid to ensure MBO, *Organization Dynamics*, 1974, 2, pp. 54–65.

16. Bowen, D., and R. Nath, Transactional analysis in OD: Applications within the NTL model, *The Academy of Management Review*, 1978, 3, pp. 79–89.

17. Berne, E., *Transactional Analysis in Psychotherapy* (New York: Grove Press, 1961); Berne, E., *The Structure and Dynamics of Organizations and Groups* (Philadelphia: Lippincott, 1963); Berne, E., *Games People Play* (New York: Grove Press, 1964); Berne, E., *Principles of Group Treatment* (New York: Oxford University Press, 1966); Berne, E., *What Do You Say after You Say Hello?* (New York: Grove Press, 1972).

18. Luchsinger, V., and L. Luchsinger, Transactional analysis for managers, or How to be more OK with OK organizations, *MSU Business Topics*, 1974, 22, pp. 5–12.

19. Berne, *Games People Play*, p. 22.

20. Jongeward, D., and contributors, *Everybody Wins: Transactional Analysis Applied to Organizations* (Reading, Mass.: Addison-Wesley, 1973); also see James, M., and D. Jongeward, *Born to Win: Transactional Analysis with Gestalt Experiments* (Reading, Mass.: Addison-Wesley, 1971); Harris, T., *I'm OK—You're OK* (New York: Harper and Row, 1967); Meininger, J., *Success through Transactional Analysis* (New York: Grosset & Dunlap, 1973).

21. Buchanan, P., Innovative organizations—a study in organization development, in *Applying Behavioral Science Research in Industry* (New York: Industrial Relations Counselors, 1964); Back, K., *Beyond Words: The Story of Sensitivity Training and the Encounter Movement* (New York: Russell Sage Foundation, 1972); Golembiewski, R., and A. Blumberg (eds.), *Sensitivity Training and the Laboratory Approach: Readings*

about Concepts and Applications, 3rd ed., (Itasca, Ill.: F. E. Peacock, 1977); Schein, E., and W. Bennis, (eds.), *Personal and Organizational Change through Group Methods: The Laboratory Approach* (New York John Wiley, 1965).

22. Seashore, C., What is sensitivity training? *NTL Institute News and Reports* 1968, 2, pp. 1–2.

23. Lieberman, M., L. Yalom, and M. Miles, *Encounter Groups: First Facts* (New York: Basic Books, 1973); Lundgren, D. C., Trainer-member influence in T-groups: One-way or two-way? *Human Relations*, 1974, 27, pp. 756–766.

24. Kilmann, R., and V. Taylor, A contingency approach to laboratory learning: Psychological types versus experiential norms, *Human Relations*, 1974, 27, pp. 891–909; Melnick, J., and M. Wood, Analysis of group composition research and theory for psychotherapeutic and growth oriented groups, *The Journal of Applied Behavioral Science*, 1976, 12, pp. 493–512; Steele, F., Personality and laboratory style, *Journal of Applied Behavioral Science*, 1968, 4, pp. 25–45.

25. Scott, W., Schmidt is alive and enrolled in a sensitivity training program, *Public Administration Review*, 1970, 30, pp. 621–625.

26. Buchanan, P., Laboratory training and organization development, *Administrative Science Quarterly*, 1969, 14, pp. 466–480; Dunnette, M., J., Campbell, C. Argyris, A symposium: Laboratory training, *Industrial Relations*, 1968, 8, pp. 1–45; House, R., T-group education and leadership effectiveness: A review of the emperic literature and a critical evaluation, *Personnel Psychology*, 1967, 20, pp. 1–32.

27. Adapted and excerpted from Power in and around your organization, *Training HRD*, 1977, 14, pp. 35–38.

17

Task-, Technology-, and Structure-focused Approaches to Organizational Change

17

LEARNING OBJECTIVES

When you have finished reading and studying this chapter, you should be able to:

▲ Explain and illustrate several task-, technology-, and structure-focused approaches for changing an organization or any of its units.

▲ Identify several of the key contingencies that influence when each of these approaches to change is likely to be effective.

▲ Diagnose when to use task-, technology-, and structure-focused approaches to change.

THOUGHT STARTERS

▲ How do you think task, technology, and structure approaches to organizational change differ from people-focused approaches?

▲ Why do you think there are so many different approaches to organizational change?

OUTLINE

TASK-FOCUSED APPROACHES
  Basic Task-focused Model
  Autonomous Groups
    Application of Autonomous Groups
    Assessment of Autonomous Groups
  Management by Objectives
    Relation to Managerial Value Systems
  Individual-oriented MBO Model

  Objective Setting
  Subordinate Participation
  Implementation
  Review and Feedback
  Criticism of Individual-oriented MBO
  Team-oriented MBO Model
    Success Requirements of Team-oriented MBO Model
  Assessment of Management by Objectives
TECHNOLOGY-FOCUSED APPROACHES
  Mass Production Technology
    Application of Mass Production Technology
  Automation
    Application of Automation
  Assessment of Technology-focused Approaches
STRUCTURE-FOCUSED APPROACHES
  Bureaucracy
    Application of Bureaucracy: U.S. Postal Service
  Matrix Organization
    Application of Matrix Organization: TRW Systems Group
  Assessment of Structure-focused Approaches
SUMMARY
DISCUSSION QUESTIONS
MANAGERIAL PROBLEMS
  Philippine Consulting Corporation
  Job Objective Scoring Key
KEY WORDS
REFERENCES

This chapter is a continuation of the discussion of approaches to organizational change. Chapter 16 covered people-focused approaches. This chapter zeros in on task-, technology-, and structure-focused approaches. As in the previous chapter, it must be emphasized that there is no one best way to change an organization or any of its units. No one approach to change is likely to be equally effective in all circumstances. A key need is to know how to diagnose the change problem so that the right choices will be made. This chapter should increase your ability to do this by briefly assessing the conditions under which each approach is likely to be effective.

TASK-FOCUSED APPROACHES

Task-focused approaches are sometimes classified under structure or technology. While there are close relationships with these two variables and a degree of overlap, the task approach focuses on making changes in the activities (or tasks) each person or work group does—when, where, with whom, how long, how often. The change process normally begins with an analysis of the nature and flow of tasks that are performed at the lowest organizational levels. That is, changes in tasks are developed from the "bottom up." However, this "bottom-up" style does not necessarily mean that employees at the lowest organizational levels are heavily involved in the redesign of the tasks performed and work flow employed.

Basic Task-focused Model

From a change perspective, the task-focused approach basically involves increasing or decreasing the task difficulty and task variability in a position or work unit. *Task difficulty* is the degree to which the work itself is easily understandable with well-defined procedures or steps for performing tasks.[1] *Task variability*, on the other hand, is the degree to which exceptional or nonroutine problems are experienced that require different or new procedures and steps for doing the work. A security guard who has to punch clocks at predetermined intervals would have both low job difficulty and low job variability. In contrast, most physicians experience both high job difficulty and high job variability. Managers can experience high or low job difficulty and job variability. They can routinely carry out company procedures (low difficulty, low variability) or they can innovatively approach changing conditions (high difficulty, high variability). Conceivably, they could approach a routine job innovatively (low difficulty, high variability) or approach a complex job with routine responses (high difficulty, low variability). You should be careful not to confuse task variability with task variety. Task variety could simply refer to the number of different kinds of activities being performed, with the possibility of none of them being nonroutine, novel, or difficult.

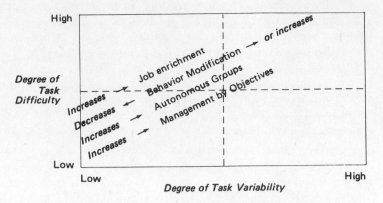

FIGURE 17–1.   Simplified Model of Task Structure

Task difficulty and variability are independent dimensions varying along separate continua. Figure 17–1 is a model for assessing the task structure of a position or work group. The vertical axis shows the degree of task difficulty ranging from low to high. The horizontal axis shows the degree of task variability also ranging from low to high.

The change strategies of job enrichment, autonomous groups, and management by objectives usually involve increasing the *amount* of task variability and task difficulty handled by individuals and groups as well as improving their ability to deal with variable and difficult tasks. The use of the behavior modification approach on the other hand, could result in changes that had either to be increased or decreased in the variability or difficulty of tasks being performed by individuals or groups.

The behavior modification approach was discussed in depth in Chapter 6; the job enrichment approach was covered in Chapter 12. You may want to refer back to these chapters to refresh yourself on these approaches. This chapter discusses the nature and use of autonomous groups and management by objectives as task-focused change approaches.

Autonomous Groups

In the *autonomous group* approach to organizational change, work groups are redesigned so that they contain virtually all the resources and skills needed to produce a specific output and/or to serve a particular geographic area of clientele. Two features distinguish autonomous groups from more traditional ways of organizing tasks and controlling employees: (1) the focus is on the grouping of interdependent tasks into relatively small groups of from seven to twenty-five individuals; and (2) there is much greater control of the tasks within the autonomous work group. Thus, individuals in autonomous groups participate extensively in task-related decision making and often have their higher level esteem and self-actualization needs met. From the standpoint of the organization, productivity is usually equal or better and the human-side of the organization is often vastly improved in terms of such factors as labor-management relations, absenteeism, turnover, cooperation among workers.[2]

The small groupings permit face-to-face meetings for decision making and coordination. Tasks typically performed by separate departments are often made a part of the responsibilities of the autonomous group. For example, the group may be much more responsible for its own maintenance, quality control, custodianship, industrial engineering, and personnel (such as screening job applicants and training). This typically leads to an increase in the interdependences between members within the group. Group members are required to develop and use mental abilities to perform such tasks as planning, diagnosing problems, considering alternatives. An attempt is made to develop all members so that they can perform all jobs within the group. Pay increases are usually based on the mastery of an increasing number of jobs within the group. Normally, no limit is placed on how many members of the group can qualify for the highest pay brackets.

With the autonomous group approach, the traditional supervisor role is changed. The supervisor becomes more of a group leader who has the responsibility for helping the group develop and make decisions.[3] Instead of giving orders, the supervisor or manager places greater emphasis on listening, collaborating (seeking win-win solutions to conflicts), motivating, and compromising. Although this process takes time, the long-term results may be better than for conventional groupings because once decisions are made they may be accepted and implemented more rapidly.

The introduction of autonomous groups has several important organizational effects, including:

1. Fewer decision problems are referred up the hierarchy.
2. Less integration is needed between different groups because almost all the resources required to create a given output are located within one group.
3. The members of the group usually have clearly defined goals, can readily perceive these goals, and are subject to less division of labor.

Application of Autonomous Groups.   The most dramatic example of a firm that has substituted the autonomous strategy for the bureaucratic strategy is the Kalmar plant of Volvo discussed in Chapter 12.[4] The 600 employees who had been performing a few simple repeated tasks along a conveyor belt are now divided into autonomous groups of fifteen to twenty-five workers. Each group, working in a separate, self-contained area, is responsible for assembling a complete part of the car.

Within the limits of being able to complete their assigned parts of the assembled car, the groups can decide for themselves how the work will be done, including who will do which jobs. To increase familiarity with each operation in a group, members are encouraged to rotate jobs. While the groups are responsible for attaining output goals (such as twenty electrical systems of acceptable quality assembled per day), they have some control over the pace at which they work. This is possible because the area between each group is used for storing inventory. As long as a group has at least three completed units in inventory ready for the next group, the group can vary its work rate as it pleases.

Volvo has also implemented the autonomous group approach in the higher managerial levels. In stages, Volvo has gone from a functional to a divisional structure while also pushing decentralization. Headquarters personnel consist of ten staff units reporting directly to a five-person executive committee, for a total of about 100 individuals. This contrasts with the 1,700 individuals at headquarters before the changes, most of whom were reassigned within the divisions. Profit centers have been established within Volvo's four divisions, with a high degree of independence for attaining specific objectives.

Assessment of Autonomous Groups.   Autonomous groups, along with job enrichment (see Chapter 12) are often employed with the idea of increasing employee satisfaction, work motivation, democratization, and humanization of work. Whereas job enrichment reduces the amount of interaction and communication flowing between individuals, autonomous groups do the same thing between departments and levels in the organization. Both strategies are intended to increase employees' desire to achieve, particularly by providing greater discretion in decision making and identifiable goals.

Autonomous groups and job enrichment have both been successfully employed. But such factors as technology, costs, and attitudes and norms might limit their usefulness.[5] Even in the Volvo plant, where management was willing to make substantial changes in the technology, the work groups have no choice in the selection of parts to be installed and, of course, the parts must be assembled in a given sequence. Often, the economic costs and benefits of alternative technologies may be the crucial deciding factor. Limits on autonomous groups and job enrichment may also be imposed by the skills and educational levels of employees. Finally, while these two strategies are intended to improve workers' attitudes and norms toward work, negative attitudes and norms of workers may resist the introduction of such changes. This has apparently been particularly true with some types of unionized craft groups, which frequently try to protect job security by maintaining jurisdiction and control over a well-defined set of tasks.

Management by Objectives

In the *management-by-objectives* (MBO) approach to organizational change, managers meet with workers to jointly work out realistic change objectives for the workers. At specified future times, the success of the employees in attaining the objectives is evaluated. MBO is a widely used approach to change and management. Generally recognized in the business world since about 1965, MBO is gaining considerable attention and enthusiasm in the public sector as well. Although MBO goes under a single label, there are major differences between the ways in which it is prescribed in its ideal form and the ways in which it is practiced. The better known model of MBO emphasizes the individual. The other, less frequently discussed, model emphasizes the work team and interdependent groups.

Relation to Managerial Value Systems.   Several different managerial value systems underlie the different forms of application of the management-by-objective approach. Chapter 3 presented three models of managerial values: profit-maximizing management, trusteeship management, and quality-of-life management. A key element in the management-by-objectives approach is the degree to which subordinates are involved in the process of setting objectives or goals. The prevailing managerial value system may play a crucial role in determining whether objectives are set by higher management and handed down to each lower level, or whether an interaction process takes place between superiors and subordinates in the objective-setting process. Figure 17–2 suggests the general relationship likely to be found between the level of subordinate involvement in goal setting and the three managerial value systems.

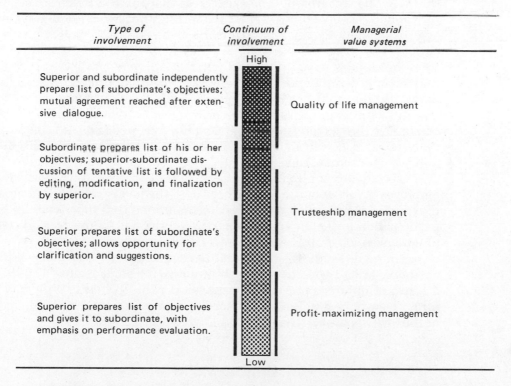

FIGURE 17–2.   Relationship between Subordinate Involvement and Managerial Value System

Adapted from French, W. I., and Hollman, R. W., "Management by Objectives: The Team Approach," *California Management Review*, 1975, 16, pp. 13–22.

In the profit-maximizing management value system, objectives for the immediate lower level are established and tightly controlled by each higher level of management. Higher management is likely to emphasize the use of MBO as a tool for tighter performance evaluation. The important value for the organization is to maximize profits; all other decisions and actions are directed toward this singular end. A recent study of the largest firms in the United States found a number of cases where MBO was used in an authoritarian manner with minimal subordinate involvement in objective setting.[6] This represents a difference often found between the prescribed approach to MBO and the way it may actually be practiced. While there are some notable exceptions, MBO is usually prescribed as an approach that should have a moderate to high level of subordinate involvement in the objective-setting process.

In the trusteeship management value system, a strong sense of organizational self-interest and the need to earn certain targeted profit levels are stressed. But there is also likely to be a recognition of the value of some group and individual participation in decision making. Organizational members are viewed as both a means and an end and should have certain rights that must be recognized. Consistent with this value system, employees will probably be involved in the objective-setting process. Subordinates may be able to actually negotiate and formulate certain objectives with their superiors, but there are likely to be other job-related objectives over which the subordinates have little influence. For example, production supervisors may have little influence over the number of units to be produced by their plant. But they may be able to negotiate with the plant manager so that the quantity objectives are established on a weekly rather than daily basis. This could give the supervisors more flexibility in planning and coping with unanticipated contingencies, such as machine breakdowns, absenteeism, and set ups for new runs.

The quality-of-life management value system is consistent with high employee involvement in establishing both the levels and types of objectives they are to pursue. This value system maintains that individual and group participation in the organizing, planning, and controlling of work relevant to employee job domains is necessary and desirable.

In sum, as an organizational change approach and process of management, MBO is practiced in substantially different forms. This is partly a result of different prevailing managerial value systems. With this recognition clearly in mind, the next section focuses on one prescriptive model of the MBO approach that has an individual orientation.

Individual-oriented MBO Model

The individual-oriented MBO model has four basic elements, each of which consists of a number of dimensions. As shown in Figure 17–3, these elements are objective setting, subordinate participation, implementation, and review and feedback. The arrows in Figure 17–3 indicate that all the elements should be operating simultaneously to make the MBO process effective and that a high degree of linkage exists among the elements.

Objective setting.   MBO tries to get subordinates and superiors to define and focus on the objectives of jobs, rather than on rules, activities, and procedures. (Objectives is used synonomously with goals, outputs, results, ends, or standards of performance.) The objective-setting process includes identifying specific areas of responsibility for jobs, the standards of performance in each area, and, possibly, a work plan for achieving the desired results. Table 17–1 provides a hypothetical example of selected task-related responsibility areas and possible specific objectives for a salesperson.

Over time, the responsibility areas in a particular job are likely to change less dramatically and frequently than the specific objectives associated with each responsibility area. Thus, in Table 17–1, the salesperson is surely going to have sales volume as a responsibility area on a continuing basis, but the specific level and changes in sales volume could vary dramatically. These changes might be due to general economic conditions, changed market acceptance, greater or less opportunities in one's sales territory, and the like.

In setting objectives, two obvious recommendations should be heeded: (1) objectives should not be stated in such broad and general terms that they have little personal significance to the employee, such as stating that the job objective is to maximize the welfare of the firm and society; (2) objectives should not be stated in such narrow and detailed terms that the employee is expected to concentrate on dozens of different objectives.

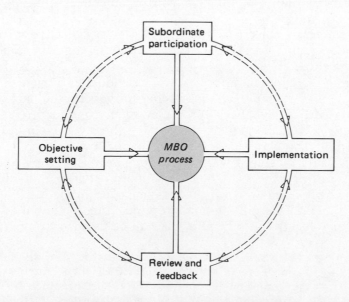

FIGURE 17–3.   Individual MBO Model

TABLE 17–1.   Hypothetical Responsibility Areas and Objectives
for a Salesperson

Selected Responsibility Areas	Specific Objectives
Sales Volume	Increase sales volume by 10 percent
Gross margin of goods sold	Keep average gross margin on goods sold at 40 percent
Number of calls per day	Increase the average number of calls per day to 8
Order-call ratio	Increase order-call ratio to 25 percent
Average order size	Increase average order size to 200 dollars
New accounts	Generate 20 new accounts

Adapted from Jackson, D. W., and R. J. Aldag, Managing the sales force by objectives, *MSU Business Topics,* 1974, 22, pp. 53–59.

An analysis of what the various writers in the area of MBO regard as criteria or indicators of a "good" formulation of objectives identified nine criteria often prescribed as indicators of a "good" set of objectives.[7] Table 17–2 lists these criteria. In the right-hand column, the percentage of MBO writers who agree on the inclusion of each criterion is indicated. These criteria might serve as useful guidelines for both developing statements of objectives and assessing an established MBO process. Many additional guidelines and criteria have also been prescribed for formulating objectives.

Throughout this discussion, several limitations on the seemingly clear-cut nature of management by objectives must be kept in mind. As Steers and Porter conclude in their analysis of numerous studies on management by objectives and the process of objective setting, "performance under goal- (objective-) setting conditions appears to be a function of at least three important variables: the nature of tasks goals, additional situational-environmental factors, and individual differences."[8]

For example, one researcher found that the performance of individuals with a high need for achievement significantly increased when objectives were made more specific and there was clear-cut feedback on their efforts. The performance of individuals low in need for achievement significantly increased with greater opportunities to participate in the objective-setting process.[9] Thus, differences between individuals can influence how, why, and even whether they respond to the MBO approach.

With these limitations in mind, three potential advantages in developing objectives for certain jobs can be listed.[10]

1. *Increased knowledge of expectations.* MBO should increase employee knowledge of what is expected of them. Such knowledge is often a precondition for improved work performance because the employees have better information about priorities, methods by which results will be assessed, resources available, and the outputs expected. More-

TABLE 17–2.   Criteria Prescribed for Developing Statements of Objectives

Criteria	Percentage of Agreement by MBO Writers
Statements of objectives for a job should:	
be defined in terms of measurable results	100
include the indicators or methods of measuring the attainment of the objectives	94
specify the time period for accomplishing the objectives	88
be in writing	82
be reviewed two to four times a year	73
include both routine and new developmental objectives	73
have priorities or weights assigned to each objective	67
include personal developmental objectives	55
include a plan of action for accomplishing the objectives	55

Adapted and modified from Kirchoff, B. A., MBO: Understanding what the experts are saying, *MSU Business Topics,* 1974, 22, 53–59.

over, there should be greater clarification and understanding of inevitable types of role conflict and ambiguity between superiors and subordinates. Of course, objectives as standards of performance may be difficult to define. For example, is a 15 percent increase in sales for a sales representative a fair, achievable, and challenging objective? However, there is some research that suggests many people will perform better than when no objectives are set, regardless of whether they participated in setting them.

2. *Reduction in goal displacement.* MBO should reduce the tendency for goals or objectives to be displaced because of an undue emphasis on rules, conformist behavior, and rigid behavior in light of changed or special job circumstances. This tendency for goal displacement may be exaggerated to the point where primary concern with conformity to rules interferes with the purpose of the organization (or job).[11] Since the underpinning of MBO requires a conscious and systematic consideration and modification of job-related objectives, there should be less possibility for serious cases of goal displacement.

3. *Systematic linking of jobs to departmental and organizational objectives.* MBO should have the potential merit of linking the objectives of jobs to those of the employees' department, which are, in turn, linked to a higher organizational unit such as a whole function or division.

Figure 17–4 is a job objectives questionnaire. If you complete this questionnaire, you should find it easier to understand and relate to the dis-

FIGURE 17–4.   Job Objectives Questionnaire.

As employees, each of us has certain objectives that are part of our work. Sometimes, these objectives are spelled out in detail; other times, the objectives are simply intuitively "understood." The following statements refer to your job, and to the objectives that are associated with your job. Read each statement, then circle the number indicating *how untrue* or *how true* you believe each statement to be. (If you prefer, you can think about a job you've had with some organization in the past.) You may want to use a separate sheet of paper to record your responses.

		Definitely Not True	Not True	Slightly Not True	Uncertain	Slightly True	True	Definitely True
1.	Management encourages employees to define job objectives.	−3	−2	−1	0	1	2	3
2.	If I achieve my objectives, I receive adequate recognition from my supervisor.	−3	−2	−1	0	1	2	3
3.	My objectives are clearly stated with respect to the results expected.	−3	−2	−1	0	1	2	3
4.	I have the support I need to accomplish my objectives.	−3	−2	−1	0	1	2	3
5.	Achieving my objectives increases my chances for promotion.	−3	−2	−1	0	1	2	3
6.	My supervisor dictates my job objectives to me.	3	2	1	0	−1	−2	−3
7.	I need more feedback on whether I'm achieving my objectives or not.	3	2	1	0	−1	−2	−3
8.	My supervisor will "get on my back" if I fail to achieve my objectives.	−3	−2	−1	0	1	2	3
9.	My job objectives are very challenging.	−3	−2	−1	0	1	2	3
10.	Management wants to know whether I set objectives for my job or not.	−3	−2	−1	0	1	2	3
11.	My supervisor will compliment me if I achieve my job objectives.	−3	−2	−1	0	1	2	3

12.	My objectives are very ambiguous and unclear.	3	2	1	0	−1	−2	−3
13.	I lack the authority to accomplish my objectives.	3	2	1	0	−1	−2	−3
14.	Achievement of objectives is rewarded with higher pay here.	−3	−2	−1	0	1	2	3
15.	My supervisor encourages me to establish my own objectives.	−3	−2	−1	0	1	2	3
16.	I always have knowledge of my progress toward my objectives.	−3	−2	−1	0	1	2	3
17.	My supervisor will reprimand me if I'm not making progress toward my objectives.	−3	−2	−1	0	1	2	3
18.	My objectives seldom require my full interest and effort.	3	2	1	0	−1	−2	−3
19.	Management makes it clear that defining job objectives is favorably regarded.	−3	−2	−1	0	1	2	3
20.	My supervisor gives me more recognition when I achieve my objectives.	−3	−2	−1	0	1	2	3
21.	My objectives are very concrete.	−3	−2	−1	0	1	2	3
22.	I have sufficient resources to achieve my objectives.	−3	−2	−1	0	1	2	3
23.	My pay is more likely to be increased if I achieve my objectives.	−3	−2	−1	0	1	2	3
24.	My supervisor has more influence than I do in setting my objectives.	3	2	1	0	−1	−2	−3
25.	I wish I had better knowledge of whether I'm achieving my objectives.	3	2	1	0	−1	−2	−3
26.	If I fail to meet my objectives, my supervisor will reprimand me.	−3	−2	−1	0	1	2	3
27.	Attaining my objectives requires all my skill and know-how.	−3	−2	−1	0	1	2	3

From Sims, H., and E. Slusher, Attributes of job objectives: A multivariate approach, in Allen, W. R., and P. Weissenberg (eds.), *Proceedings of the Eastern Academy of Management*, 1977, pp. 25–30. Used with permission.

cussion of management by objectives. The key for scoring your responses is presented toward the end of the chapter under the section entitled "Managerial Problems." This key will provide scores for most of the dimensions of MBO being discussed here.

Subordinate Participation.   Some aspects of the amount of subordinate participation in the MBO process were previously discussed and summarized in Figure 17–2. While there is no uniformity of agreement on the issue, it is frequently contended that there should be a moderate to high level of participation by subordinates in the objective-setting process. But, before there can be any significant participation by subordinates, discretionary content in the job must already exist (or an increase be planned). Discretionary content enables employees to perform planning and controlling tasks in addition to "doing" tasks.

MBO, in and of itself, requires increasing or stimulating planning and control tasks on the part of subordinates. Highly routinized and programmed jobs are likely to require enrichment and redesign before considering the utilization of the MBO approach.

Black and Decker, a firm with an MBO program, has the following stated objectives for its program, which includes a high level of subordinate participation:

1. To help individuals improve their knowledge and skill.
2. To assure continuing two-way communications between the employees and their immediate supervisor.
3. To convert Black and Decker's goals into targets for employees.
4. To realistically appraise the performance of employees.[12]

The ways in which subordinate involvement has been systematized is expressed in their overall performance worksheet. The general instructions for the procedures to be followed in establishing objectives at Black and Decker are as follows:

1. The managers of each division, department, or section should meet with their subordinates in a briefing session to discuss how the group's targets can be converted to targets for each individual.
2. After the briefing session, employees should review the group's targets and determine what their own targets should be to help the group achieve its overall targets. Then the employees should prepare the first three elements of the work sheet concerning personal development, principal job responsibilities, and specific objectives. All managers should do the same for each individual reporting to them.
3. Finally, the employees should again meet with their manager and mutually agree on the personal and job targets and principal job responsibilities for next year.
4. Both the managers and the subordinates will have a copy of the worksheets. The employee's copy is the working copy to be used throughout the year. The managers' copies are their working copy and becomes the permanent file copy at the end of the year.[13]

The Black and Decker example departs from the individual MBO model because there is some degree of group problem solving and consideration of the objectives for the unit as a whole. There could also be more than one meeting between the superiors and subordinates in developing the statements of objectives and working through of differences. A number of the group problem-solving skills, communication skills, conflict management skills, and the like discussed in previous chapters could be instrumental in making these sessions a constructive experience for both the superiors and subordinates. But if the parties have a low level of interpersonal competence or if there are unresolved political issues, numerous difficulties in these objective-setting sessions can be anticipated. In this regard, George Odiorne has noted:

> One of the major reasons for the failure of MBO in many organizations is that those in charge fail to recognize the political character of the implementation process. MBO is indeed logical and systematic but it must also deal with a number of factors, including power and authority, the organization form, and the values and expectations of people.[14]

After the objective-setting sessions are completed, subordinates should also engage in behaviors such as personally reviewing progress toward objectives on a regular basis, renegotiating objectives when major changes occur, taking the initiative in letting their superior know when progress is lagging, and informing the superior when they feel there is lack of coordination with others or lack of resources that require action.[15]

Previous chapters in this book addressed the potential advantages and limitations of subordinate participation in decision making. For the most part, these findings hold with respect to participation in the objective-setting process. While recognizing the potential limitations to participation, some of the advantages might include higher and better performance levels, greater job satisfaction, greater acceptance of objectives, lower turnover and absenteeism, improved understanding and communication between superior and subordinate. On the other hand, participation may be time-consuming, result in unnecessary emotional conflicts, and not always result in the best ideas being implemented.

Implementation.   Implementation is translation of the outcomes from the objective-setting process into new day-to-day behaviors that will ultimately lead to the attainment of the desired objectives. This phase is often accompanied by action planning that focuses on *how* objectives are to be achieved. For superiors, implementation often means they must give greater latitude and choice to subordinates. Accordingly, superiors might need to discontinue managing the hour-by-hour and day-to-day activities of subordinates. A key behavior and attitude of superiors is to be available to coach and counsel the subordinates as needed. Superiors assume somewhat less of a judgmental role and more of a helping or facilitating role. At Black and Decker, superiors are expected to hold periodic meetings during the year with subordinates to review progress, discuss any assistance or help needed, and to make any changes in objectives if they are necessary. This last point needs special emphasis. It is generally considered desirable to change or modify objectives as needed. This serves to keep MBO from being perceived as a rigid system and encourages major new problems or changes to be addressed as they occur.

In sum, to increase the probability that MBO will be a successful change approach, implementation requires a conscientious consideration of the types of behaviors the superiors and subordinates need to engage in on a day-to-day basis.

Review and Feedback.   Subordinates develop a clear understanding of their progress through review and feedback. Feedback is a key element of MBO because it provides knowledge of the correspondence between the employees' objectives and their degree of attainment. The *knowledge of results* of behavior is often essential to changes in job performance and personal development in the form of new skills, attitudes, and/or knowledge.

Unlike some other approaches, MBO places heavy emphasis on the subordinates' evaluating their own performance. By knowing their own objectives and the measures of indicators of achievement of these objectives, and having information available regarding these areas, subordinates should be able to gain substantial insight into their performances and the possible need for modified behaviors. For example, two objectives for the salesperson illustrated in Table 17–1 were an increased sales volume of 10 percent and the maintenance of average gross margin on goods sold at 40 percent. As long as the salesperson has information fed back regarding these areas, it is possible for him or her to have a concrete self-understanding of his or her results in relation to the objectives.

Unfortunately, the review process is often not so simple. In the case of the salesperson, there may be factors, other than the salesperson's own behavior, influencing possible gaps between the stated objectives and actual results. Second, significant parts of many jobs may not lend themselves to the development of indicators of performance that are based on "objective" measures.[16] As might be expected, an objective evaluated on the basis of judgment can result in a variety of different perceptions. Thus, the problem of determining whether or not the objective was achieved exists even before getting to questions of why it was or was not attained.

While MBO does not recommend a passive role for superiors in review and feedback, it does require superiors to shift from a judgmental and critical role to more of a helping and mutual problem-solving role. At times, individuals have interpreted this element and the whole MBO process as "soft." Quite to the contrary! Individuals can be demoted and dismissed under this system. This is because the rationale and basis for such actions should be readily apparent, so it should be easier for the superiors to confront the necessity of making such decisions. On the other hand, the MBO process is intended to reduce and prevent the need for such decisions.

Under ideal conditions, what might the review and feedback sessions between superiors and subordinates look like? Carroll and Tosi have summarized the relevant literature on the common guidelines often suggested for reviewing performance. They are quick to recognize that the day-to-day relations between the superiors and subordinates are most likely to be the major influence in setting the tone and quality of the interviews.[17] Their guidelines for review and feedback sessions include the following:

1. Meet on "neutral grounds" such as a conference room rather than the superiors' office. This is to reduce the possibility of superiors being perceived as sitting in the "judge's" chairs or actually behaving in such a manner.
2. Before the meeting, the superiors and subordinates should review progress during the designated time period (such as three months, six months, a year), bring data they regard as relevant, and prepare a list of items they want to discuss.
3. The superiors should create an atmosphere of a mutual problem-solving session.
4. The superiors should listen attentively.
5. The superiors should use reflective summaries to make sure there is an understanding of the subordinate's perceptions and feelings about a particular situation.
6. The superiors should remain quiet if it appears that the subordinates are resisting discussion of a certain issue.
7. Superiors should encourage and accept self-insight and criticism by subordinates, especially through nonverbal communications such as smiling and nodding.
8. Superiors should give direct, rather than evasive, answers to the subordinates' questions.
9. Superiors should minimize, but not necessarily eliminate, criticism of subordinates. If there is criticism, it should be oriented toward the problem rather than the person. Whenever possible, descriptive and nonevaluative feedback is preferred.
10. Superiors should allow subordinates to release frustration through an open expression of their feelings without being criticized or attacked for doing so.
11. Superiors should use probing questions to encourage subordinates to consider causes of problems and possible solutions.
12. Superiors should encourage the confrontation and resolution of disagreements before the review session is ended. If not, the disagreements should be openly acknowledged.

These guidelines are not intended to be exhaustive or to be a mechanistic, cookbook approach. Guidelines such as these, which are easy to state but difficult to put into practice, are primarily valid under conditions of a high level of subordinate involvement and participation in the MBO process.

Criticism of Individual-oriented MBO.   While the previous discussion assumed a positive posture supportive of the individual-oriented MBO process, a number of concerns have been expressed about it, particularly in terms of how it is actually applied in organizations. Criticisms of the MBO process concern how individuals actually use it, rather than how it is supposed to be used. A sampling of the criticisms of individual-oriented MBO includes:

1. Too much emphasis develops on a reward-punishment psychology (i.e., you are rewarded for accomplishing objectives and punished for not doing so).
2. An excessive amount of paperwork and red tape develops—the very thing MBO is intended to reduce.
3. The process is really controlled and imposed from the top, allowing little opportunity for real participation.
4. The process turns into a zero-sum (win-lose) game between superiors and subordinates.
5. Aspects of jobs that can be assessed quantitatively, rather than qualitatively, receive undue emphasis.
6. Too much emphasis on individual objectives and performance drives out recognition of the need for collaborative teamwork and group objectives. Individuals may optimize their own objectives at the cost of overall objectives.[18]

This last criticism is considered in the following discussion of the team-oriented MBO model.

Team-oriented MBO Model

The team-oriented MBO model is fundamentally consistent with the key elements of the individual-oriented MBO model. But a key difference is that the process includes entire work groups or teams, as well as individual jobs. The team-oriented model attempts to overcome two major deficiencies in the individual-oriented MBO model. First, the team model explicitly recognizes the interdependencies between jobs, especially those at the supervisory and managerial levels. Second, it encourages coordination of objectives between the individuals occupying the interdependent jobs, rather than placing the entire responsibility for integration upon the common superior.

As with the individual MBO model, the degree of participation and influence in setting objectives by work groups can vary widely in the team MBO model. French and Hollman have developed a nine-phase approach to the team MBO model that incorporates a number of aspects of the managerial Grid.[19] Since the Grid was discussed in the last chapter as a people-focused approach to organizational change, we will merely highlight here the distinguishing aspects of the team MBO model.

1. Overall organization objectives to be achieved within a certain time period are developed in team meetings of the top executives, primarily

on the basis of consensus. Of course, prior to this, it is assumed that there would have been inputs and interaction from lower levels.
2. Departmental or unit objectives to facilitate the attainment of overall organizational objectives are again developed in team or group sessions, primarily through a consensus process.
3. Individual objectives are developed within this framework. However, a major difference with the individual MBO model in this phase is that team members may discuss each other's objectives, make suggestions for change, and openly discuss the interdependent nature of their responsibilities.
4. While performance reviews will take place between superiors and subordinates, matters of concern to the team are discussed in regularly scheduled meetings.

Success Requirements of Team-oriented MBO Model. The team MBO model is likely to have the greatest potential for success only if certain contingencies exist. First, there must be a real need for integration among individuals. Second, the top management group must cooperate and offer mutual assistance, rather than engage in political power struggles. Third, the participants must have some degree of skill in group processes and interpersonal relations.

Assessment of Management by Objectives

Throughout this discussion of MBO, a number of comments involving an assessment of the MBO model based on personal observations, case studies, or one-time attitudinal measures have been made. Very few studies report objective performance measures before and after the implementation of an MBO program. Even worse, it is difficult to determine from these studies how fully the MBO model was actually implemented.

One of the more recent and complete studies of changes in performance due to the implementation of an MBO program has been presented by Ivancevich.[20] The following is an outline of his study.

1. Involved were 181 supervisors in the production and marketing departments of three of the six similar plants of a manufacturing firm that had about 5,000 employees.
2. Objective performance data were collected at five points in time over a thirty-six-month period.
3. Two plants had MBO introduced (experimental plants) and one plant was used as a comparison unit (control).
4. One of the MBO plants had a reinforcement schedule introduced thirty months after the program was initiated. The reinforcement schedule consisted of letters, memos, meetings, and telephone discussions from higher management to (and between) lower levels of management. These reinforcements emphasized expression from higher management of appreciation of implementing the MBO program, support for the program, and encouragement to keep at it.

Although the results from this study were quite involved and there were some differences between marketing and product, it appeared that: (1) the MBO program generally had a positive impact on performance; (2) the introduction of the positive reinforcement schedule in the plant was followed by significant improvements in performance; and (3) the MBO program didn't seem to have much, if any, impact on one of the two production departments.

This and other studies suggest that the MBO approach to planned change can be effective, but its introduction is not a guarantee of instant success.[21]

TECHNOLOGY-FOCUSED APPROACHES

The technological approach is probably the most widespread and common explanation for changes in organizations, changes in society and its institutions, changes in people (by wiping out certain types of jobs and creating new ones), creation of new organizations, elimination of established organizations, and growth in large-scale and multinational organizations.[22] While recognizing that it is not the only source of change, Toffler characterizes technology as "that great, growling engine of change."[23] Of course, the organizational, cultural, or social setting in which technological changes are introduced can have much to do with whether these changes are experienced as benefits or problems.

Definitions of technology have ranged from a narrow perspective including only machines, to an extremely broad definition that equates it with rationality. For our purposes, technology is defined as:

> Tools in a general sense, including machines, but also including such intellectual tools as computer languages and contemporary analytical and mathematical techniques. That is, we define technology as the organization of knowledge for the achievement of practical purposes.[24]

There is almost an infinite variety of specific technological developments. The concern here is only to highlight two general technological approaches that have been extensively used by many organizations to bring about change—mass production and automation. Our limited treatment of the technological approach should not be interpreted as implying that it is unimportant. Rather, the objective and focus of this book is simply intended to emphasize the human side of organizations.

Mass Production Technology

Mass production technology is the manufacture of large volumes of identical or similar goods, usually through the use of assembly-line paced work. Jobs are usually highly specialized, with employees performing a limited number of tasks many times over during the work day. The production of automobiles, baby food, and toothpaste illustrate mass production technology.[25] The pace of work is strongly influenced by the speed of the assembly line and the use of numerous rules and regulations that define in great detail who should do what, when, how, and where. Mass production technology is often cited as creating dehumanizing and boring jobs. But it has frequently been implemented because of its efficiency in reducing per unit costs of production and its ability to use relatively unskilled workers. Since mass production technology is generally stereotyped as being "bad," a brief case example of a recently successful application is useful.

Application of Mass Production Technology.   The dietary department of a large metropolitan hospital had the responsibility for planning, preparing, and delivering the meals to hospital patients, employees, and visitors.[26] The technology change in one of the units of this department mainly affected the assembly and delivery of meals. Before the change, patient meals were assembled and delivered by a single diet aide with the use of a large delivery cart. The diet aide assembled each meal from various places in the kitchen according to the prescribed menu.

The felt need for change came from the difficulty and expense of repairing or replacing the elaborate carts as well as the frustration in the workers caused by frequent breakdowns in the carts. At the suggestion of an outside consultant, a new technology was suggested that revolved around the use of a fifty-foot-long conveyor belt. Trays were fed onto the moving belt with patient orders attached. Diet aides stood at various stations along the belt and placed the appropriate food item on each tray as it passed them. At the end of the line, the tray was double-checked and loaded on a less elaborate cart for immediate delivery to the appropriate floor.

The planning for this change took place over several months. While the workers were not directly consulted about the change, they were kept informed and assured of their job security. This change led to more routine work for 129 diet aides and increased the rigidity of the work flow and task interdependence. In general, the change solved the problems of assembling and delivering meals and did not lead to a deterioration in the human side of the organization.

Automation

Automation is a production process that utilizes the "automatic" or feedback principle. A control mechanism triggers an operation after taking into consideration what has happened before. The most extreme form of automation occurs when there is no human interference from the time the raw materials enter the production process until after they have been transformed into the finished product.[27] Oil and chemical refineries approach this stage of automation.

Automation is virtually synonomous with the developments in various information technologies, especially computers. Information technology evolved over three stages of increasing sophistication:

1. The first stage involved devices that mechanized communications, enabling the transmission of symbols. Examples are the telephone, telegraph, radio, and television.
2. The second stage involved devices that can observe, record, generate, and remember symbols (data). Examples are the thermometer, speedometer, and radar.
3. The third stage, which appeared in the 1940s, involved devices that can generate symbols, store, transmit, and manipulate them to make decisions. The computer and its various software are the best illustration of this phase.[28]

Machines have long been used as a substitute for human labor in the performance of physical and routine tasks. The bulk of computer applications appear to be oriented toward tasks that are highly routine and must be performed repeatedly. However, computer information technology, especially since 1955, has made possible increasing numbers of applications where planning, control, and decision-making activities are automatically performed in place of individuals, including managers.

Application of Automation.   Automation can have major effects on an organization, especially at lower levels. Insurance companies are only one example of an industry that has massively introduced automation, especially through the use of computers.

In one long-term study of nineteen insurance companies, the widescale introduction of automation appeared to lead to changes in many aspects of these organizations. Some of these effects included:

1. Increased managerial productivity by improving the ability to control and coordinate complex activities.
2. Increased employee productivity, by performing tasks previously undertaken by humans and accomplishing the same (or more) objectives (outputs) with fewer employees.
3. Reduced the number of organizational levels, particularly at the lower levels where routine tasks were performed.
4. Changed the pattern of departmentalization and size of some departments because certain previously separated information-handling tasks were moved into a computer center.
5. Shifted to a greater degree of centralization of control and decision-making.
6. Shifted the control of certain organizational activities from individuals to the computers so that computers participate in the managerial control function.

7. Increased task interdependency between lower-level workers and decreased individual discretion.
8. Changed job requirements and skill levels.[29]

Automation is not always a source of such widespread changes in organizations. Some studies suggest that this technology can be consistent with "decentralization" and may actually make possible increased decentralization. It appears that the applications and the effects of automation, especially computer information technology, can vary somewhat as a function of the prevailing managerial philosophy and the degree of uncertainty in decision making within the organization.[30]

Assessment of Technology-focused Approaches

Mass production and automation technologies will continue to have a major effect on society and organizations. Table 17–3 outlines the major impacts of technology on society and organizations along seven dimensions: goal accomplishment, unintended effects, knowledge of effects, alternatives, new needs and goals, tools, and self-knowledge. Although technology is clearly a major approach to change, there can be considerable variations in the nature of its effects on an organization's members, structure, and task design.

STRUCTURE-FOCUSED APPROACHES

Structural approaches focus on changing organizations by changing position (role) definitions, relationships between positions, and the expected behavior of people in positions through modifications of variables or forces external to them.

Structure-focused approaches have long been utilized to change organizations. At times, structural changes may be made to accommodate changes brought on by new technologies, such as the introduction of computers. At other times, structural changes may be made to better serve or cope with environmental pressures (competitors, customers, government, and the like).[31] For example, a petroleum refiner, which ranks about thirtieth in the United States, had two employees assigned to handling Federal Energy Administration matters for the company in 1976. By 1978, the company had seventy-two people assigned to dealing with the newly created Department of Energy.[32] At still other times, structural changes may be made to accommodate varying managerial, work force, or societal values. For example, increased decision-making discretion at lower levels, increased participation by those from lower levels in decisions normally made at the top of the organization, fewer organization levels, and the like, are often

TABLE 17–3.   Selected Impacts of Technology on Society and Organizations

Dimensions	Explanations
1. Goal accomplishment	Enhances our abilities to accomplish individual and collective goals (e.g., to produce an adequate supply of food).
2. Unintended effects	Often produces unintended and unwanted side effects, typically proportional in magnitude to its intended effects (e.g., the amount of sulfur oxides vented to the atmosphere grows proportionally with the production of energy).
3. Knowledge of effects	Provides knowledge about these same side effects, which might otherwise go undetected, so that we can take account of them in our decisions to use or eschew the use of particular technologies (e.g., chromatography, an example of advanced technology, enables us to detect trace quantities of possibly noxious substances in air or water or food).
4. Alternatives	Provides alternative routes among which we may choose in pursuing our goals (e.g., planes, trains, and cars as alternative modes of transportation).
5. New needs and goals	Makes us aware of new needs, and sets new goals (e.g., technology taught us that we need adequate quantities of vitamins in our diets).
6. Tools	Provides tools for analyzing and understanding complex systems (e.g., the standard tools of management science which may then be applied to the decision processes for selecting technologies).
7. Self-knowledge	Provides knowledge of ourselves, helping to define the terms of the human condition (e.g., it instructs us about how human aspiration levels are determined, and how human beings manage frequently to redefine the situations in which they find themselves as zero-sum games).

Adapted and modified from Simon, H., Technology and environment, *Management Science*, 1973, 19, p. 111.

regarded as structural changes that may democratize and humanize the workplace.

Table 17–4 summarizes some of the elements and dimensions often regarded as part of the structural approaches to change.

Structural approaches can be employed along a collaborative-unilateral continuum. At the collaborative end of the continuum, people to be affected by the changes are heavily involved in defining what the changes

TABLE 17–4.   Elements Often Included in Structural
Approaches to Change

Rules	Number of organizational levels
Procedures	Committees
Formal reward systems	Staff-line
Reporting requirements	Performance criteria
Plans	Formal decision-making authority
Basis of departmentation	Promotion criteria
Span of control	Selection criteria
Matrix structure	Project groups
Schedules	Budgets
Communication systems	Formal training
Task teams	Chain of command

should be and how they should be implemented. At the unilateral end of the continuum, top management or some other group (such as the federal government whose action may break up a company into several independent firms) defines the changes and implements them. The structural approach has probably most frequently been employed along the unilateral end of the continuum, especially when the structural changes focus on use of (1) profit centers; (2) functional, product, or geographic departmentation (or some combination); (3) matrix structures and project groups; (4) more or fewer organization levels; (5) wider or narrower spans of control; (6) levels of formal authority in positions (such as changing the amount of money a manager can authorize, without prior higher level approval, from $100 to $500); (7) formal reward systems (such as implementing an individual or group incentive system); and (8) changes in certain types of formal rules (e.g., requiring receipts to accompany all requests for reimbursement of travel expenses) and dimensions often regarded as part of the structural approach. Structural approaches to change are often more obvious and dramatic than other approaches in the sense that manipulations by management are relatively clear-cut. For example, it is highly visible when management adds a rule, changes spans of control, or adds a department. Since major structural changes aren't easily reversible in the short run, they should be well planned for before implementation.

Changes made by R. H. Jones when he became chairperson and chief executive officer of General Electric illustrate the use of the structural approach at the top of an organization. Jones redefined the role of his job and those of several other top GE officers. Prior to Jones, GE's chief executive had three vice-chairpersons who served as a corporate executive staff, with responsibility for policy development, but without direct financial accountability for the operations they watched over and reviewed. Now the three vice-chairpersons are financially accountable for the operating groups reporting to them and are more involved with line operations. Jones also gave up the direct review function he had over the power generation and power delivery groups, stating: "I want to give myself a little more time to step back from the operating responsibility I had, to work on the general thrust of the corporation." [33]

This section will highlight two structural approaches to change— bureaucracy and matrix organization.

Bureaucracy

The bureaucratic approach is probably the most common structural strategy being used today in attempts to change organizations. Chapter 4 provides a detailed discussion of this form of organization. The bureaucratic approach usually attempts to change organizations through the increased use and reliance on hierarchy of authority, division of labor, rules, procedural specifications, impersonality, and technical competence. In theory, bureaucracy is supposed to provide better services and goods at lower prices. In practice, this is often not the case.

Bureaucracy works best under the following contingencies: (1) the tasks to be performed are routine and not changing rapidly; (2) the external task environment is relatively simple and unchanging; and (3) employees and managers have values and attitudes that are compatible with the requirements of the bureaucratic model. Unfortunately, this change approach is often used under the wrong conditions, especially when the external environment is complex and rapidly changing.

Application of Bureaucracy: U.S. Postal Service.   As clearly demonstrated by the 1971 reorganization of the U.S. Post Office Department into the U.S. Postal Service, there is no guarantee that further bureaucratization of an organization will automatically lead to success as defined by its own members or those external to it.[34] A key factor in influencing the potential effectiveness of this or any other change approach is the political (power) system that exists internal and external to the organization.[35] In the case of the postal service, the reorganization stimulated internal and external groups to protest or to consolidate their interests. It is premature to judge whether bureaucratic changes implemented by the postal service will be effective or ineffective over the long run. As of this writing, the push for efficiency and economy led various groups to pressure Congress to eliminate or reduce the "autonomy" of the postal service. Major structural changes, such as those implemented by the postal service, serve to emphasize that change is not just a rational and logical process of finding the best means to achieve organizational objectives. Different groups within or external to an organization compete for the control and allocation of its resources and often want the organization to pursue competing objectives. This is often a relatively greater problem with public than with private organizations.

Matrix Organization

Matrix organization represents a balance between organizing resources around products, programs, or projects and around functional classifications such as marketing, production, finance, personnel, and research. It operates on concepts quite different from those governing bureaucracy. An organization may decide not to organize solely around products, programs, or projects because it might reduce desired functional specialization or create the need to duplicate too many resources.

As discussed in Chapter 4, the distinguishing feature of a matrix organization is the existence of at least dual authority, information, and authority relationship with at least one functional (specialist) and one project or product group. In terms of authority relations, the integrating role or department is evaluated by both a project (or product unit) and a functional department. The project and functional units (usually their managers) affect the chances for promotion and salary increases for those involved with integration and their performance goals. Ideally, this results in a power balance between the influence of the project (or product) department and the functional unit on the integrating department (or individuals).

The matrix form of organization has been successfully introduced into manufacturing organizations such as aerospace, chemicals, electronics, pharmaceuticals, heavy equipment; service organizations such as banking, construction, insurance, and retailing; and research and development or consulting organizations.

While the matrix structure is a costly form of organization and the power balances are subtle and difficult to maintain, it may be superior to other organizational forms under conditions of instability, complexity, and high needs for integration.[36] An increasing number of organizations are selectively introducing the matrix structure. For example, a General Electric planning document states:

> We've highlighted matrix organization . . . not because it's a bandwagon that we want you all to jump on, but rather that it's a complex, difficult and sometimes frustrating form of organization to live with. It's also, however, a bellwether of things to come. But, when implemented well, it does offer much of the best of both worlds. And all of us are going to have to learn how to utilize organization to prepare managers to increasingly deal with high levels of complexity ambiguity in situations where they have to get results from people and components not under their direct control. . . . Successful preparation for an individual to run a huge diversified institution like General Electric—where so many complex, conflicting interests must be balanced—than the product and functional modes which have been our hallmark over the past twenty years.[37]

Application of Matrix Organization: TRW Systems Group. TRW Systems is an example of an organization that moved from a functional to a matrix form of organization. It is a high technology company in the areas of space vehicles, electronic systems, power systems, and the like. Without going into the details of TRW's matrix organization, you might like to get a feel for the complexities of managing in a matrix where people have two bosses. Jim Dunlop, who was the director of industrial relations at TRW Systems at the time the matrix was introduced, states:

> The decisions of priority on where a man should spend his time are made by the president because he is the only common boss. But, of course, you try to get them to resolve it at a lower level. You just have to learn to live with ambiguity. It's not a structured situation. It just can't be.
>
> You have to understand the needs of Systems to understand why we need the matrix organization. There are some good reasons why we use a matrix. Because R&D type programs are finite programs—you create them, they live and then they die—they have to die or overhead is out of line. Also there are several stages in any project. You don't necessarily need the same people on the project all the time. In fact, you waste the creative people if they work until the end finishing it up. The matrix is flexible. We can shift creative people around and bring in the people who are needed at various stages in the project. The creative people in the functions are professionals and are leaders in their technical disciplines. So the functional relationship helps them to continue to improve their professional expertise. Also, there is a responsiveness to all kinds of crises that come up. You sometimes have 30 days to answer a proposal —so you can put together a team with guys from everywhere. We're used to temporary systems; that's the way we live.
>
> Often an engineer will work on two or three projects at a time and he just emphasizes one more than others. He's part of two systems at the same time.
>
> The key word in the matrix organization is interdependency. Matrix means multiple interdependencies. We're continually setting up temporary systems. For example, we set up a project manager for the Saturn project with twenty people under him. Then he would call on people in systems engineering to get things started on the project. Next he might call in people from the Electronics Division, and after they finish their work the project would go to FIT (Fabrication, Integration and Testing) where it would be manufactured. So what's involved is a lot of people coming in and then leaving the project.
>
> There is a large gap between authority and responsibility and we plan it that way. We give a man more responsibility than he has authority and the only way he can do his job is to collaborate with other people. The effect is that the system is flexible and adaptive, but it's hard to live with. An example of this is that the project manager has no authority over people working on the project from the functional areas. He can't decide on their pay, promotion, or even how much time they'll spend on his project as opposed to some other project. He has to work with the functional heads on these problems. We purposely set up this imbalance between authority and responsibility. We design a situation so that it's ambiguous. That way people have to collaborate and be flexible. You just can't rely on bureaucracy or power to solve your problems.[38]

Assessment of Structure-focused Approaches

The structural approach is potentially powerful as a change strategy. From the standpoint of enabling or enhancing the achievement of organizational goals, structural changes have ranged from smashing successes to dismal failures, even being blamed as a cause of organizational death. While there may be many reasons for the failure of a structural intervention, one common theme seems to reoccur—lack of consideration of the people variable.

This raises the point introduced earlier in the chapter. While a change program may have a particular emphasis and/or begin with a particular focus, it may ultimately have to include approaches with other focuses in order to increase and enhance effectiveness.

SUMMARY

Besides the people-focused approaches to organizational change discussed in Chapter 16, there are task-focused, technology-focused, and structure-focused approaches. Task-focused approaches are concerned with changing task difficulty and task variability. Besides job enrichment, discussed in Chapter 12, the use of autonomous groups and management by objectives are important task-focused approaches to organizational change. Management by objectives may concentrate on individual change or on team change. MBO has four basic elements: objective setting, subordinate participation, implementation, and review and feedback. The two technology approaches discussed were mass production and automation, and the two structure approaches discussed were bureaucracy and matrix organization.

This and the previous chapter stressed that no single approach to organizational change can be completely successful without drawing upon some aspects of several, if not all, of the four variables: people, task, technology, and structure. Accordingly, major organizational change programs may need to incorporate a combination of approaches to maximize the positive and minimize adverse consequences. Organizational change is not simply a rational process that involves choosing the right approach and implementing it. The system of power relationships both within and external to the organization will play a crucial role in determining the degree of change and which change approach or combination of approaches will be feasible.

DISCUSSION QUESTIONS

1.   How would you describe the values that seem to be implicit or explicit in each of the change approaches discussed in this chapter and Chapter 16?

2.   What difficulties, if any, do differences in formal power between individuals create in the implementation of a management by objectives system? Explain.

3.   Is it always possible for employees (including managers) to have a high level of involvement in the object-setting process?

4.   Can an organization simultaneously utilize the individual MBO model and the team MBO model? Explain.

5.   What are the similarities and differences between grid organization development and management by objectives?

6.   What are some of the limitations that an organization's technology may place on task-focused approaches to change?

MANAGERIAL PROBLEMS

PHILIPPINE CONSULTING CORPORATION*

In 1964, the Philippine Consulting Corp. (PCC) was organized to "accelerate the development of the economy by providing professionalized management services to industry and government." In spite of the entry of various firms into the industry, the PCC had consistently ranked second in terms of industry sales. In addition to its traditional business services, the firm was noted for having pioneered in the areas of management development and industrial research.

In December, 1969, Mr. Celestino Rivera was appointed Chief Executive Officer of the company. He announced that his management style would be "participatory," in contrast to what was viewed as a highly "authoritative" style of his predecessor. This was interpreted by many consultants to mean that they would be allowed to participate in important policy matters, particularly those related to performance evaluation and salary scales. As the former Chief Executive officer hardly consulted anyone in making a decision, the announcement made by Mr. Rivera was very well received and was considered by employees to facilitate their goal of becoming number one in industry sales.

Six months later, the organization was in a state of "crisis." Two vice-presidents and several top consultants had resigned. As a result of this unfavorable publicity, sales had started to decline and clients were reported to have sent out "feelers" for new consultants. Internally, the atmosphere was quite tense—in the words of one consultant, "things were run under conditions of martial law."

* This case incident was prepared by Gerardo R. Ungson, assistant professor, University of Oregon, with the assistance of Professors John Slocum and Lawrence Hrebiniak. Used by permission.

PART ONE: THE PCC—MANAGEMENT AND ORGANIZATION

At the time of Mr. Rivera's appointment, the PCC was organized in three main departments: Management Consultancy, Management Training and Development, and Industrial Research. Each department was headed by a vice-president and was considered a profit center of the firm (see Figure 17–5).

The departments were organized on a "project-management" basis. After the review of the project contracts by the vice-president, these were assigned to senior consultants who were responsible for organizing their project teams. At this point, all liaison with clients became the responsibility of the senior consultant and the project team. As a final "quality-control" measure, the senior consultant, the project team, and the vice-president reviewed the project report before it was submitted to the client.

Mr. Celestino Rivera was appointed Chief Executive Officer to replace Mr. Jaime Casas. For a long time, the staff resented the latter's "authoritative" style; he had made decisions without conferring with the staff and was highly secretive about the firm's salary structure.

As second-in-command (Vice President, Consulting), Mr. Rivera had been the "sounding board" for all these complaints. Following his appointment, he immediately initiated new policies and procedures: (1) He announced that his style would be "participative," commencing with a management-by-objectives program for the company that would be started by external consultants. (2) A directive was issued that all senior consultants should discuss performance ratings with their subordinates. These were well received by the staff.

MBO PROGRAM—JANUARY 1970

In general, expectations of the MBO were high. Prior to the program, one Associate Consultant had remarked:

> The program will serve as a good forum to discuss our performance-appraisal system. Consulting is quite difficult; it takes several years to build up your reputation and one lousy project to bring you down. Our present system seems to emphasize these drawbacks. Moreover, a lot of evaluation is subjective: I want to be judged on results . . .

The behavior of Mr. Rivera at the MBO seminar came as a complete surprise. He "lorded it" over the experiential exercises and "pulled rank" in the formulation of operational objectives. Finally, he capped the seminar by presenting his Five-Year Plan for the PCC. Ostensibly, he had attached very little importance to an area perceived as critical by the staff: the performance appraisal system.

The tenor of comments made during and after the seminar was quite disturbing. One associate consultant said:

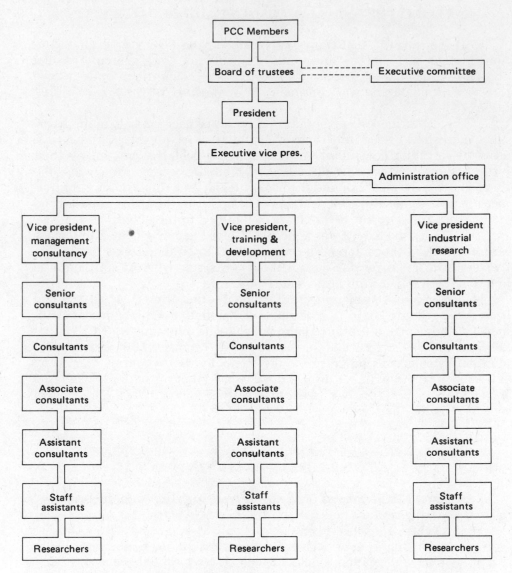

FIGURE 17–5.   Organization of the Philippine Consulting Corporation

I thought the MBO was supposed to be a joint formulation of objectives
. . . all I heard was his Five-Year Plan . . .

The MBO Director had the following comments:

The success of any MBO depends on the attitude of top management. Mr.
Rivera seemed to be more concerned with presenting his plans . . . in
fact, he de-emphasized the other important aspects of MBO—that of allowing the staff to participate in the formulation of evaluation standards.

In defense of his position, Mr. Rivera said:

You cannot redesign a program in days! I am working on the appraisal system now . . . To have discussed it during the seminar would have resulted in our getting bogged down on some details . . . I know the sentiments of the staff . . . I intend to incorporate all suggestions in the new system.

POST-MBO POLICIES

A few weeks after the seminar, PCC made the local headlines when one of its major clients complained about what it considered "substandard quality services." Following this fiasco, Mr. Rivera announced that he would be sitting in on all project meetings for "quality-control" reasons. The move was resented by many consultants:

I agree that there should be quality control. But he (Rivera) is overdoing it . . . I meet with client and we agree on basic study premises . . . suddenly, he "sits in" and suggests sweeping changes which I feel are totally irrelevant to the project . . . let us have some control but let us not overdo it . . .

Mr. Rivera, however, had justified his actions as follows:

Being new in my position, I cannot afford "early" mistakes . . . I have been a consultant for ten years and made no major mistakes . . . I know this is hard on the staff but after the XYZ project I cannot take another fiasco.

By March, 1970, he had presented the revised performance appraisal system: each department was given corporate "target quotas" based on its budget. Following the MBO method, they had full options of developing their own programs to meet their objectives. Many consultants were quick to point out some deficiencies but Mr. Rivera simply snapped:

What are you complaining about? Under Casas, you did not even see your rating . . . now you can develop your own programs to meet your objectives and you will be evaluated on this basis . . . I repeat: every man will be evaluated on the basis of performance . . . is this not in keeping with MBO which all of you wanted?

In May, 1970, the two vice-presidents and three senior consultants announced their resignations. The papers extensively covered all these events and PCC clientèle were alarmed. To curb off the "exodus," Mr. Rivera was meeting every staff member individually. His response was a bit philosophical:

I knew I was well liked when I became EVP . . . I have provided opportunities which Casas did not even want to discuss. How could this happen to me, when I was so sincere?

QUESTION

Prepare a five-to-seven-page report covering a diagnosis and your recommendations for the Philippine Consulting Corporation. In your diagnosis, make sure to include a discussion of both structural changes and motivational factors, realizing, of course, that the two may be interrelated. Moreover, develop both short-range (immediate) and long-range (policy orientations) recommendations for the corporation.

JOB OBJECTIVES SCORING KEY

This scoring key is to be used with the Job Objectives Questionnaire that was presented in Figure 17–4. You may score your responses to this questionnaire as follows. For each of the nine "scales" (A through I), compute a total score by summing the answers to the appropriate questions. Be sure to subtract "minus" scores.

Question Number			Question Number			Question Number		
1.	+	( )	3.	+	( )	6.	+	( )
10.	+	( )	12.	+	( )	15.	+	( )
19.	+	( )	21.	+	( )	24.	+	( )
Total score			Total score			Total score		
	A			B			C	

Question Number			Question Number			Question Number		
4.	+	( )	7.	+	( )	9.	+	( )
13.	+	( )	16.	+	( )	18.	+	( )
22.	+	( )	25.	+	( )	27.	+	( )
Total score			Total score			Total score		
	D			E			F	

Question Number			Question Number			Question Number		
5.	+	( )	2.	+	( )	8.	+	( )
14.	+	( )	11.	+	( )	17.	+	( )
23.	+	( )	20.	+	( )	26.	+	( )
Total score			Total score			Total score		
	G			H			I	

Next, on the following graphs, write in a large "X" to indicate the total score for each scale.

A   MANAGEMENT EMPHASIS
       ON OBJECTIVES   −9 −7 −5 −3 −1   1   3   5   7   9

B   CLARITY OF OBJECTIVES   −9 −7 −5 −3 −1   1   3   5   7   9

C   PARTICIPATION IN
       SETTING OBJECTIVES   −9 −7 −5 −3 −1   1   3   5   7   9

D   CONTROL OVER
       RESOURCES   −9 −7 −5 −3 −1   1   3   5   7   9

E   KNOWLEDGE OF
       RESULTS   −9 −7 −5 −3 −1   1   3   5   7   9

F   CHALLENGE OF
       OBJECTIVES   −9 −7 −5 −3 −1   1   3   5   7   9

G   CONTINGENT MATERIAL
       REWARD   −9 −7 −5 −3 −1   1   3   5   7   9

H   CONTINGENT PERSONAL
       REWARD   −9 −7 −5 −3 −1   1   3   5   7   9

I   CONTINGENT PERSONAL
       PUNISHMENT   −9 −7 −5 −3 −1   1   3   5   7   9

KEY WORDS

Task difficulty
Task variability
Autonomous group approach
Management by objectives
Individual-oriented MBO model
Team-oriented MBO model
Implementation

Technology
Mass production technology
Automation
Closed system
Structural approach
Matrix organization

REFERENCES

1. Van de Ven, A., and A. Delbecq, A task contingent model of work-unit structure, *Administrative Science Quarterly*, 1974, 19, pp. 183–197; also see Steers, R., and R. Mowday, The motivational properties of tasks, *The Academy of Management Review*, 1972, 2, pp. 645–658.

2. Cummings, T., and E. Molloy, *Improving Productivity and the Quality of Life* (New York: Praeger Publishers, 1977).

3. Walton, R., Work innovations at Topeka: After six years, *The Journal of Applied Behavioral Science*, 1977, 13, pp. 422–433.

4. Gyllenhammar, P. G., How Volvo adapts work to people, *Harvard Business Review*, 1977, 55, pp. 102–113; Willott, N., Volvo versus Ford, *Management Today*, January 1973, pp. 44–48.

5. Fein, M., Job enrichment: A reevaluation, *Sloan Management Review*, 1974, 15, pp. 69–88; Lammers, C., Self-management and participation: Two concepts of democratization in organizations, *Organization and Administrative Sciences*, 1975, 5, pp. 17–33; Miller, E., Socio-technical systems in weaving, 1953–1970: A follow-up study, *Human Relations*, 1975, 28, pp. 349–386; Sashkin, M., Changing toward participative management approaches: A model and methods, *Academy of Management Review*, 1976, 1, pp. 75–86; Susman, G., *Autonomy at work: A sociotechnical analysis of participative management* (New York: Praeger Publishers, 1976).

6. Schuster, F., and A. Kendall, Management by objectives: Where we stand—a survey of the Fortune 500, *Human Resource Management*, 1974, 13, pp. 8–11.

7. Kirchoff, B., MBO: Understanding what the experts are saying, *MSU Business Topics*, 1974, 22, pp. 17–22; also see Kleber, T., Forty common goal-setting errors, *Human Resource Management*, 1972, 11, pp. 10–13.

8. Steers, R., and L. Porter, The role of task-goal attributes in employee performance, *Psychological Bulletin*, 1974, 81, pp. 434–452.

9. Steers, R., Task-goal attributes, N achievement, and supervisory performance, *Organizational Behavior and Human Performance*, 1975, 13, pp. 392–403.

10. Huse, E., Putting in a management development program that works, *California Management Review*, 1966, 9, pp. 73–80; Odiorne, G., Management by objectives and the phenomenon of goal displacement, *Human Resource Management*, 1974, 13, pp. 2–7.

11. Merton, R., Bureaucratic structures and personality, *Social Forces*, 1940, 18, pp. 560–568.

12. Carroll, S., and H. Tosi, *Management by Objectives: Applications and Research* (New York: Macmillan, 1973).

13. Ibid.

14. Odiorne, G., The politics of implementing MBO, *Business Horizons*, 1974, 17, pp. 13–21.

15. Slusher, E., and H. Sims, Commitment through MBO interviews, *Business Horizons*, 1975, 18, pp. 5–12; also see Raia, A., *Managing by objectives* (Glenview, Ill.: Scott, Foresman, 1974).

16. Jamieson, B., Behavioral problems with management by objectives, *Academy of Management Journal*, 1973, 16, pp. 496–505.

17. Carroll, Tosi, *Management by Objectives*.

18. Jamieson, Problems with management by objectives; Levinson, H., Management by whose objectives? *Harvard Business Review*, 1970, 48, pp. 125–134; Kerr, S., Some modifications in MBO as an OD strategy, *Proceedings, 1972 Annual Meeting*, Academy of Management, 1973, pp. 39–42; Thompson, P., and G. Dalton, Performance appraisal: Managers beware, *Harvard Business Review*, 1970, 48, pp. 149–157; Wickens, J., Management by objectives: An appraisal, *Journal of Management Studies*, 1968, 5, pp. 365–379.

19. French, W., and R. Hollman, "Management by objectives: The team approach," *California Management Review*, 1975, 16, pp. 13–22.

20. Ivancevich, J., Changes in performance in a management-by-objectives program, *Administrative Science Quarterly*, 1974, 19, pp. 563–574; Ivancevich, J., Different goal setting treatments and their effects on performance and satisfaction, *Academy of Management Journal*, 1977, 20, pp. 406–419.

21. Tosi, H., R. Hunter, R. Chesser, J. Tarter, and S. Carroll, How real are changes induced by management by objectives, *Administrative Science Quarterly*, 1976, 21, pp. 276–306; Rose, R., Implementation and evaporation: The record of MBO, *Public Administration Review*, 1977, 37, pp. 64–71.

22. Ellul, J., *The Technological Society* (New York: Vintage Books, 1964); Galbraith, J., *The New Industrial State* (Boston: Houghton Mifflin, 1967); Kheel, T., *Technological Change and Human Development: An International Conference* (Ithaca, N.Y.: Cornell University Press, 1970); Sanders, D. (ed.), *Computers and Management in a Changing Society*, 2nd ed. (New York: McGraw-Hill, 1974); Whisler, T., *Information Technology and Organizational Change* (Belmont, Calif.: Wadsworth Publishing, 1970).

23. Toffler, A., *Future Shock* (New York: Bantam Books, 1970).

24. Mesthene, E., *Technological Change: Its Impact on Man and Society* (Cambridge: Harvard University Press, 1970).

25. Hellriegel, D., and J. W. Slocum, Jr., *Management: Contingency Approaches*, 2nd ed. (Reading: Addison-Wesley, 1978).

26. Billings, R., R. Klimoski, J. Breaugh, The impact of a change in technology on job characteristics: A quasi experiment, *Administrative Science Quarterly*, 1977, 22, pp. 318–339.

27. Joffe, A. and J. Froomkin, *Technology and Jobs: Automation in Perspective* (New York: Praeger Publishers, 1968).

28. Ackoff, R., *Redesigning the Future: A Systems Approach to Societal Problems* (New York: Wiley-Interscience, 1974).

29. Whisler, *Technology and Organizational Change*; Myers, C. (ed.), *The Impact of Computers on Management*, (Cambridge: MIT Press, 1967).

30. Robey, D., Computers and organization structure: A review and appraisal of empirical studies, paper presented at annual meeting of the National Academy of Management, 1974; Stewart, R., *How Computers Affect Management* (London: Macmillan Press, 1971).

31. Pfeffer, J., and G. Salancik, *The External Control of Organizations: A Resource Dependence Perspective* (New York: Harper and Row, 1978).

32. Collins, A., FEA demands increase oil company staffs, *Houston Chronicle*, February 5, 1978, section 5, p. 8.

33. G. E.'s Jones restructures his top team, *Business Week*, June 30, 1973, pp. 38–39.

34. Biggart, N., The creative destructive process of organizational change: The case of the post office, *Administrative Science Quarterly*, 1977, 22, pp. 410–426.

35. Hummel, R., *The bureaucratic experience* (New York: St. Martin's Press, 1977).

36. Davis, S., and P. Lawrence, *Matrix*, (Reading, Mass.: Addison-Wesley, 1977).

37. General Electric, *Organization Planning Bulletin*, 1976.

38. Davis and Lawrence, *Matrix*, pp. 100–101.

Cases

HOW HIGH THE DOC?*

Ms. Barret was Head Nurse of the operating room at Mountain View Hospital. She was experiencing some difficulties in scheduling scrub technicians and circulating R.N.'s to certain surgery rooms. People who had been doing fine during one surgery had come to the nursing station during clearance of the operating room to ask to be relieved of their next surgery. They complained of feeling dizzy or just in need of a break. This often put the R.N. at the desk on the spot as she had difficulty in replacing personnel in the middle of the day. Requests were always granted and the employees would break for fifteen minutes to an hour, and then ask to be reassigned.

After about two weeks of this, the problem was brought to Ms. Barret's attention and she told the nurses to send all relief requests to her personally. Gary, a Certified O.R. Technician who had been with the hospital for two years, was the first to come to her with a request.

Barret:	Gary, what seems to be the problem?
Gary:	Well, Ms. Barrett, I just don't feel very good and I'd just like to lie down for a while.
Barret:	If you don't feel good you'd better take the rest of the day off.
Gary:	I don't think I need to do that.
Barret:	Gary, can you tell me what's going on around here?
Gary:	Well, most people just don't like to work for Dr. Collins. He's pretty slow and seems to be out of it most of the time.
Barret:	Have you talked to Ms. Johnston the circulating R.N. about this?
Gary:	I've talked to her and Dr. Martin. Ms. Johnston gave me a hard time as usual. She says I am getting too big for my britches and if I don't like the situation I can ask for a transfer. Dr. Martin says that he's with Dr. Collins most of the time and he looks fine to him.
Barret:	Thank you Gary, this will be kept confidential.

Ms. Barret went to ask Ms. Johnston to come in to see her. After four days without seeing her, Ms. Barret went to find her.

Barret:	Ms. Johnston I'd like to ask you some questions. I asked to see you four days ago.
Johnston:	I have been trying to find time to see you.
Barret:	I have some questions to ask you about Dr. Collins. Do you feel he's competent in surgery?

* This case was prepared by Professor Richard B. Chase, for the University of Arizona, as a basis for class discussion.

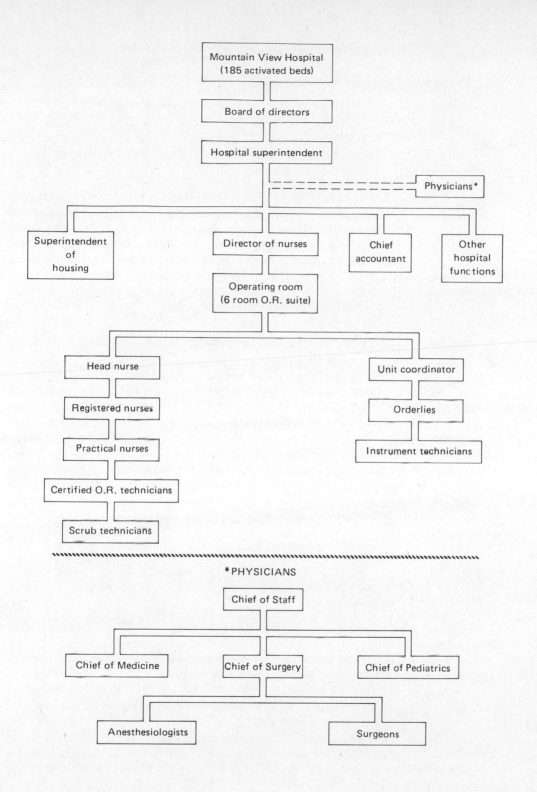

Johnston:	As far as I know.
Barret:	Have you ever seen him overly tired or not feeling well?
Johnston:	Well, he did come in last week hung over but that was an emergency. He was on call and had just been to a cocktail party the night before. That's what those techs are complaining about isn't it?
Barret:	How many times has this happened?
Johnston:	Well, I don't know. But if Dr. Collins has any problems, Dr. Martin is always there to take over. I always circulate for him and I know my business. The techs are complaining because they don't like to be told what to do. They just can't take orders and Dr. Collins gives it to them when they don't. They think just because they have been through a few cholesectomies they can start questioning the doctors and R.N.'s orders.
Barret:	Thank you Ms. Johnston that is all the questions I have.

Two days later Gary gave his notice and quit working three weeks later. Relief requests stopped coming in but two other O.R. techs gave their notice. Absenteeism rose.

Ms. Barret scheduled Ms. Johnston to work under another doctor and assigned Ms. McEvers to circulate for Dr. Collins. Later that day Ms. Barret went to visit the O.R. room where Dr. Collins was working. There she found Dr. Collins, head anesthesiologist, Dr. Martin assisting, and Ms. Johnston circulating as usual. She inquired into where Ms. McEvers was as she was scheduled for this surgery. She was informed by Dr. Martin that this operation could involve complication and they needed an experienced circulator.

Barret:	Dr. Martin you have every right to request certain circulators. I would appreciate some notice before you tamper with room scheduling.
Martin:	I am giving you notice that I would like to have Ms. Johnston circulate for me and Dr. Collins.
Barret:	Due to some difficulties in scheduling Ms. McEvers will circulate for you for the rest of the week. After that if I have your request in writing I will have no choice but to assign Ms. Johnston to you scheduling problems or not.

Ms. McEvers worked out the week under the two doctors and at the end of the week Ms. Barret asked to see her in her office to inquire into Dr. Collins' competence.

| McEvers: | I refuse to make waves here so I want this confidential. Dr. Collins often looks hung over in the morning when he does |

his patient's pre-op. I wouldn't stand up in court and swear he had been drinking but he sometimes smells of alcohol.

Barret: Have you ever inquired into his behavior?

McEvers: I asked Dr. Martin about it. He always has some story of Dr. Collins just being called in or not feeling up to par.

Later that week, Ms. Barret confronted Dr. Martin with this information.

Martin: Those are pretty serious charges you're leveling at Dr. Collins.

Barret: No one is accusing anybody of anything at this point.

Martin: What you're saying could have serious repercussions around here. If anyone got wind of this it could look very bad, not only for us but for the profession and the hospital.

Barret: I am concerned here with the patient's safety.

Martin: No one is in danger. Ms. Johnston and I are always with him.

Barret: That isn't the point.

Martin: Take it to the Chief of Staff then but let me give you some advice. You need some hard facts to make anything stick. You need the testimony of at least four nurses and under the circumstances that might be hard to get. You might like to know Dr. Collins is retiring next year.

JACK DOBBINS' PROBLEM*

Jack Dobbins left the vice president's office feeling elated as well as concerned about the responsibilities he was about to assume. Ralph Barnes, State College's vice president and comptroller, had just told Jack of the Executive Committee's decision to appoint him Superintendent of Buildings. Jack was concerned because Mr. Barnes had gone into considerably more detail about the many management and morale problems among the College's custodial workers and their supervisors than in any previous interviews.

* This case was prepared by Assistant Professor David R. Kenerson, University of South Florida, as a basis for class discussion. Distributed by the Intercollegiate Case Clearing House, Soldiers Field, Boston, Mass., 02163. All rights reserved to the contributors. Printed in the U.S.A.

The Situation

State College was located in a suburban area just outside of a major southern metropolitan area. It was one of several universities run by the state and was less than 10 years old. In this short time it had grown rapidly to 9500 students, the majority of whom lived off campus and commuted to school each day.

The Superintendent's major function was to plan, organize, direct and control the activities of about 80 employees and supervisors involved in keeping all college buildings (except for dormitories) in clean and orderly condition. There were 10 major buildings, ranging in size from 24,000 square feet to 137,000 square feet. Total square footage under the jurisdiction of the Superintendent amounted to 1,025,000. This space included classrooms, faculty offices, administration and library buildings, student center, etc.

Of the 80 employees in the department, 16 were women, 64 were men, including the 4 supervisors who reported to the Superintendent. Starting wages for maids had just been raised to $2580 per year from $2300. By some quirk of the state's budgeting system, starting wages for male janitors had just been lowered to $2700 per year from $2900. Employees could receive only one raise per year, usually on July 1st at the beginning of the fiscal year. It was within the Superintendent's authority to grant raises up to a maximum of 10% the first year, 7½% the second year, and 5% the third year. In order to qualify for the maximum, however, employees had to receive a rating of "outstanding." The work week was 40 hours. Vacation leave of 10 working days was allowed while sick leave was accrued at the rate of one day per month to a maximum of thirty days. Group life and health insurance was available by payroll deduction at employee expense. State employees were not covered under Social Security but did participate in the state retirement system under which both the State and the employee contributed. The total budget for the department amounted to about $280,-000, with $250,000 for wages and salaries and $30,000 for supplies and materials.

Turnover among employees was unusually high. In July and August of 1967, turnover amounted to 15% and 20%. Typically in this type of work in universities, turnover normally runs 100% per year. Most of the employees were Negroes, and the majority of them were holding down other full time jobs outside of the College.

Departmental Work Organization

There was no organization chart for the department, but Jack Dobbins felt it would look pretty much like the chart shown in Exhibit 1.

Work was organized on the basis of special tasks. Although supervisors were assigned responsibility for different buildings, work was spe-

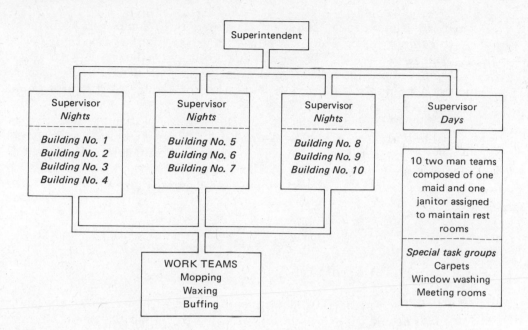

cialized into floor mopping crews, followed up by waxing and buffing crews. Supervisors decided when particular floors were mopped, waxed, and buffed and coordinated and scheduled the different crews in proper sequence. The day crews worked largely on restroom detail in all buildings with special groups assigned for carpet cleaning, window washing, and straightening and cleaning up meeting rooms before and after meetings.

Jack Dobbins' Background

Jack Dobbins was a retired military man with 20 years service in various posts as management analyst and operations and training officer. On resigning from the military, he had enrolled as a student in the College of Business Administration in order to earn a degree in management and business administration. At 45 he was looking forward to a new career in a new environment in a field where he felt his experience, knowledge and training could be most effectively used.

During the last hour and one-half in his talk with Mr. Barnes, he had learned much about the current problems of the department. Harry Kraft, the man he was replacing, had come to State College when the first students were admitted. He was about 50 years old, of limited education, and with a varied background as foreman or supervisor in construction firms. When the College was small with only a few buildings and few employees, he was reasonably successful. However, four months previously, Harry had fired one of the supervisors with rather disastrous results. Rank and file employees were indignant and had sent a petition all the way to the state capital in an attempt to get Harry's decision reversed. Some were threatening not to come to work. Morale was low, turnover high, and top officials of the College as well as the department itself, were being deluged with complaints about the lack of good housekeeping in all buildings. Toilets were not adequately serviced, classrooms and offices frequently went untouched for a week at a time.

Although Jack was concerned, he was not dismayed because he felt strongly that his recent exposure to a wide variety of management courses would make it relatively easy to show substantial improvements in this department, even despite the fact that no raises could be given to any employees before the next fiscal year 11 months away.

CENTER CITY ENGINEERING DEPARTMENT*

The Engineering Department of Center City employed approximately 1,000 people, all of whom worked under the provisions of the Civil Service System. Of these employees, about 100 worked in the Design Division. Parker Nolton, an Associate Engineer, had been employed in the Design Division for 19 years and was known personally by virtually everyone in the division, if not in Center City itself. Nolton had held the position of Associate Engineering for seven years on a provisional basis only, for he had never been able to pass the required civil service examinations to gain permanent appointment to this grade, although he had taken them often. Many of his co-workers felt that his lack of formal engineering education prevented him from passing the examinations, but Nolton felt that his failures were the result of his tendency to "tighten up" when taking an examination. Off the job, Nolton was extremely active in civic affairs and city sponsored recreational programs. During the past year, for example, he had been president of the High School Parent Teacher's Association, captain of the bowling team sponsored by the Engineering Department in the Municipal Bowling League and a member of the Managing Committee of the Center City Little League.

As Center City grew and the activities of the Engineering Department expanded to keep pace with this growth, younger men were hired into the Department in relatively large numbers. Among those hired were Ralph Boyer and Doug Worth. Both of these young men were graduate engineers, and had accepted the positions with the Engineering Department after fulfilling their military obligations. Ralph Boyer had been an officer in the Army Corps of Engineers. In order to give the new men opportunities to achieve permanent status in the Civil Service System, examinations were scheduled with greater frequency than they had been in the past. Nolton's

* Prepared by Professor H. R. Knudson, Jr., College of Business Administration, University of Washington, Seattle, Washington. Appeared in *Human Elements of Administration;* 1964. © Holt, Rinehart & Winston, New York. Reprinted by permission.

performance on the examinations continued to be unsatisfactory. The new men, however, passed the exams for successively higher positions with flying colors. Ralph Boyer in particular experienced marked success in these examinations and advanced rapidly. Three years after his initial employment he was in charge of a design group within the design division. Parker Nolton, in the meantime, had been shifted from the position of a project engineer to that of the purchase order coordinator. The position of purchase order coordinator was more limited in scope than that of a project engineer, although the responsibilities of the position were great. He continued to be classified as an Associate Engineer, however.

Ralph Boyer continued his successful career and soon qualified for the position of Senior Engineer. A new administrative group that had been created to meet the problems that arose in the Design Division because of the expanding activities of the Engineering Department was placed under his direction. Doug Worth, too, was successful in his examinations and was shortly promoted to the grade of Associate Engineer and transferred into the administrative group headed by Ralph Boyer.

One of the functions under the new administrative group was that of purchase order coordination. This relationship required that Parker Nolton report to Ralph Boyer. Nolton, however, chose to ignore the new organizational structure and dealt directly with the Chief Engineer, an arrangement which received the latter's tacit approval. Nolton was given a semi-private office and the services of a Junior Engineer to assist him in his activities. His assistant, John Palmer, soon requested a transfer on the grounds that he had nothing to do and there was no need for anyone in this position. Nolton, on the other hand, always appeared to be extremely busy and was continually requesting additional manpower and assistance to help him with the coordination of purchase orders.

Some four months after the organizational changes noted above had taken place, the Chief Engineer left the Company and his replacement, Stan Matson, was appointed from within the division. Matson was the logical successor to the position; his appointment came as no surprise and was well received by all the employees. His appointment was shortly followed by the assignment of Ralph Boyer to a special position which took him completely out of the Design Division. Doug Worth was assigned to the position thus vacated, Supervisor of the Administrative Group and consequently inherited the supervision of Parker Nolton's activities. This assignment, initially made on a provisional basis, was soon made permanent when Worth passed the required examinations and was awarded the grade of Senior Engineer. Doug Worth had never worked closely with Parker Nolton but had been on cordial terms with him since his arrival in the Engineering Department. He had had contact with Nolton in several recreational activities in which they both had participated.

During the months which followed, Parker Nolton continued his direct reporting relationship with the Chief Engineer, now in the person of Stan Matson, and never consulted or advised Doug Worth regarding the progress of his activities as purchase order coordinator. His former assistant, John Palmer, has been transferred and had been replaced by an engineering aide. Both the aide and Nolton appeared to be busy most of the time, and Nolton was still requesting more manpower for his activity through formal channels. When occasions arose which required that Doug Worth check on Nolton's activities, he was always forced to go to Nolton's office for information. Nolton always claimed to be too busy to leave his own office. During the conversations which occurred when Worth visited Nolton, Nolton frequently gave the impression that he regarded Worth's activities and interest as superfluous. Several times he suggested that in future situations Worth just send the inquiring party directly to him if questions arose about his activities. He often made the comment that he knew everyone in he department and often it was better to handle many situations informally rather than through channels.

Doug Worth was concerned with Nolton's attitude, for he did not feel that he could effectively carry out his responsibilities as Supervisor of the Administrative Group if he did not know the current status of activities in all of the functions under his control. Consequently, he attempted to gain more cooperation from Nolton by approaching the subject at times when the two men were engaged in common off-hours recreational activities. These attempts were uniformly unsuccessful. Nolton always quickly brought the conversation around to the standing of the bowling team, the progress of the P.T.A., or any other unrelated subject close at hand.

After several attempts to talk with Nolton in a friendly way off the job, Worth concluded that the situation as it currently stood was intolerable. While he realized he must do something, Worth felt he understood Nolton's attitude and reactions and was sympathetic. After all, Nolton had been in the department for years and had been relatively successful. He knew all the "ropes" and had many friends. Worth reflected that it must be a blow to a man like Nolton to have to report to young, relatively inexperienced men. Worth had faced similar problems during his military career, when he had had more experienced men many years his senior under his command. After much thought, he decided his best approach would be to appeal to Nolton in a very direct manner for a greater degree of cooperation. Thus, Worth approached Nolton on the job and suggested that they have a talk in his private office where they would not be disturbed by all the activity in Nolton's office. Nolton protested that he could not take time away from his duties. Worth was firm, however, and Nolton reluctantly agreed to come to Worth's office, protesting all the way that he really could not spare the time.

During his opening remarks to what Worth had planned as a sympathetic discussion of the situation, Worth referred to "the normal relationship between a man and his superior." Nolton's reaction was violent. He stated that he didn't regard any young upstart as a "superior," especially his. He told Worth to run his own office and to let him, Nolton, run his. He concluded by stating "if you haven't anything more to say I would like to get back to my office where important work is being neglected." Worth, realizing that nothing more could be accomplished in the atmosphere which prevailed, watched in silence as Nolton left.

Doug Worth subsequently reported his latest conversation with Nolton to Stan Matson, the Chief Engineer. He also related the events which had led to this conversation. In concluding his remarks, he stated that he could no longer take responsibility for Nolton's actions because Nolton would neither accept his guidance, nor advise him of the state of his work. Matson's reply to his last statement was "yes, I know." This was the only comment Matson made during the interview, although he listened intently to Worth's analysis of the situation.

At the next meeting of the Supervisory Staff of which Worth was a member but Nolton was not, Worth proposed that Nolton be transferred to the position of Design Drafting Engineer, in effect a demotion. As Worth was explaining the reasons for his proposed action regarding Nolton, one of the other members of the Supervisory Staff interrupted to proclaim very heatedly that Nolton was "one of the pillars of the entire Engineering Department" and that he would be violently opposed to the demotion of "so fine a man." Following this interruption, a very heated, emotional discussion ensued concerning the desirability of demoting Nolton.

During this discussion Stan Matson remained silent; yet he reflected that he should probably take some action during the meeting regarding the Nolton situation.

PARTS DISTRIBUTION DEPARTMENT*

Corporate Personnel representative Bruce Pritchard has spent the afternoon observing operational characteristics of Parts Distribution Department and interviewing its manager, Bob Warren. Parts Distribution, together with Marketing and Warehousing, comprise the Operations section of Midwest Sales, a division of an electrical parts manufacturing corporation. A relatively small department of thirty people, Parts Distribution is responsible for coordinating the stock of primary parts/inventory for the corporation's warehouse and distributor operations throughout the United States.

Pritchard's visit from corporate headquarters was made at the request of Charlie Elsley, Operations Director. Elsley is perturbed with continuing signs of poor morale in Parts Distribution as well as with its failing reputation among the sister departments of Operations.

* This case was prepared by Larry J. Bossman, Jr., of University of Detroit as a basis for class discussion rather than to illustrate either effective or ineffective handling of an administrative situation. Presented at the Northwestern University Case Workshop of the Intercollegiate Case Clearing House, October 28–30, 1973. Copyright © 1973 by Larry J. Bossman, Jr. Distributed by the Intercollegiate Case Clearing House. Soldiers Field, Boston, Mass. 02163. All rights reserved to the contributors. Printed in the U.S.A.

Before starting his afternoon of observations, Pritchard was made aware of Bob Warren's past history with Parts Distribution: Warren has been its manager for the past twelve years, having risen through the ranks of the department over a thirteen-year period. He now anticipates Charlie Elsley's retirement. With Charlie's retirement—certain within the next two years—Warren believes that he could become new Operations Director.

According to Warren, Parts Distribution has achieved an optimal organizational structure under his direction. The department's newest structure, he relates, allows him to make the most of the personnel who have "accumulated" over the years. "I've never been particularly happy with the supervisors; I've got to keep on their backs. But what do you do? They were the only ones available at the times we needed new supervisors." To compensate for individual weaknesses among the supervisors, he has reallocated certain tasks among them so that each might concentrate on those activities at which he is best.

Each supervisor typically oversees the work of two or three schedulers. The scheduler's job is core to the functioning of Parts Distribution. A scheduler (1) conducts a monthly survey on the inventory status of his assigned parts-line, (2) determines what should be purchased by part number, (3) executes purchase orders, (4) maintains warehouse contact by phone, message, or teletype, as well as supplier relations by telephone contact, expediting, and follow-up by phone. In addition, the scheduler maintains upgraded record sheets. This task accounts for over thirty percent of the scheduler's time. It is accomplished by hand-recording computer print-out data of end-of-month part stocks in the scheduler's book of monthly stock records.

Each scheduler receives from his supervisor a monthly-turnover estimate which represents the number of times a parts-line is expected to be restocked to full inventory in an average month's time.

The monthly-turnover estimate, also used by the supervisor in his yearly estimate of each part-line's projected annual volume, originates from Bob Warren's office. Warren and his assistant, Harold Frain, compute the monthly-turnover figures, using market forecasts received from Marketing and inventory open-order data received from Warehousing.

Employment turnover among schedulers is a growing problem. Some seek transfers to the "more glamorous" Marketing Department. Others quit. Of the sixteen schedulers, nine are the college graduates of the department. In-fighting has occurred among some scheduler groups.

Warren's former strategy for promoting interest and morale among the department's personnel was to upgrade the job classifications, and thus the salary ranges, of both schedulers and supervisors. However, corporate Personnel Activity has not approved Warren's last four requests for higher classifications. In turn, Warren has implemented several organizational changes in the department. He believes that he has arrived at an optimal structure because greater promotional opportunities are provided for his people. He has assigned one of the younger schedulers to "Systems," a one-man operation, to debug computer errors in end-of-month inventory print-outs; he has created two "general supervisor" positions for Dave Wilson and Sid Ladimere such that the six remaining supervisors report to them; he has appointed Harold Frain, his right-hand man, as "assistant manager" to whom Wilson and Ladimere report.

In addition to their direct line involvement, Wilson and Ladimere are responsible for all plant visitations. They visit the operations of seventy suppliers—both within and without the corporation—to improve plant shipment times and order clearances.

Warren is proud of his reorganization design. In addition to rewarding some of his key men with higher positions, he has focused plant visitation responsibilities on two men who can handle themselves well in the field. As Warren related to Bruce Pritchard, "Plant visitations used to be the responsibility of each supervisor for his part-lines. But some of them were so damned lousy at it, I just couldn't trust them anymore."

Over dinner cocktails that evening, Bruce listens to Charlie Elsley reiterate his concern for the Parts Distribution schedulers. He admits that his own prior attempts to persuade Warren to reshape the department's activities have led to little, if any, improvements. Parts Distribution continues to carry its "Operation Ostrich" reputation among other divisional departments.

At one point, Charlie turns his thoughts to the topic of a brochure which corporate Personnel Activity had recently issued to the Divisions. Charlie states that he was impressed with the concepts of job enrichment described in the brochure, and saw their direct application to the Parts Distribution situation. After admitting that an enrichment project could "gain much . . . but lose little for that department," Charlie asks for Bruce's opinion.

After a pause, Bruce questions whether Bob Warren would accept an enrichment project. He is immediately assured by Charlie: "I've already bounced the idea off Bob, and he'll be willing to give it a try. That's why I've called you in, Bruce."

THE CASE OF THE CHANGING CAGE*

Part 1

The voucher-check filing unit was a work unit in the home office of the Atlantic Insurance Company. The assigned task of the unit was to file checks and vouchers written by the company as they were cashed and returned. This filing was the necessary foundation for the main function

* The following case was taken from "Topography and Culture, The Case of the Changing Cage," *Human Organization*, 1957, 16,(1), by C. B. Richards and H. F. Dobyns. Reproduced by permission of the Society for Applied Anthropology from *Human Organization*, 1957, 16(1).

of the unit: locating any particular check for examination upon demand. There were usually eight to ten requests for specific checks from as many different departments during the day. One of the most frequent reasons checks were requested from the unit was to determine whether checks in payment of claims against the company had been cashed. Thus efficiency in the unit directly affected customer satisfaction with the company. Complaints or inquiries about payments could not be answered with the accuracy and speed conducive to client satisfaction unless the unit could supply the necessary document immediately.

Toward the end of 1952, nine workers manned this unit. There was an assistant (a position equivalent to a foreman in a factory) named Miss Dunn, five other full-time employees and three part-time workers.

The work area of the unit was well defined. Walls bounded the unit on three sides. The one exterior wall was pierced by light-admitting north windows. The west interior partition was blank. A door opening into a corridor pierced the south interior partition. The east side of the work area was enclosed by a steel mesh reaching from wall to wall and floor to ceiling. This open metal barrier gave rise to the customary name of the unit —"The Voucher Cage." A sliding door through this mesh gave access from the unit's territory to the work area of the rest of the company's agency audit division, of which it was a part, located on the same floor.

The unit's territory was kept closed by locks on both doors, fastened at all times. No one not working within the cage was permitted inside unless his name appeared on a special list in the custody of Miss Dunn. The door through the steel mesh was used generally for departmental business. Messengers and runners from other departments usually came to the corridor door and pressed a buzzer for service.

The steel mesh front was reinforced by a rank of metal filing cases where the checks were filed. Lined up just inside the barrier, they hid the unit's workers from the view of workers outside their territory, including the section head responsible for over-all supervision of this unit according to the company's formal plan of operation.

Part 2

On top of the cabinets which were backed against the steel mesh, one of the male employees in the unit neatly stacked pasteboard boxes in which checks were transported to the cage. They were later reused to hold older checks sent into storage. His intention was less getting these boxes out of the way than increasing the effective height of the sight barrier so the section head could not see into the cage "even when he stood up."

The girls stood at the door of the cage which led into the corridor and talked to the messenger boys. Out this door also the workers slipped unnoticed to bring in their customary afternoon snack. Inside the cage, the workers sometimes engaged in a good-natured game of rubber band "sniping."

Workers in the cage possessed good capacity to work together consistently and workers outside the cage often expressed envy of those in it because of the "nice people" and friendly atmosphere there. The unit had no apparent difficulty keeping up with its work load.

Part 3

For some time prior to 1952 the controller's department of the company had not been able to meet its own standards of efficient service to clients. Company officials felt the primary cause to be spatial. Various divisions of the controller's department were scattered over the entire 22-story company building. Communication between them required phone calls, messengers, or personal visits, all costing time. The spatial separation had not seemed very important when the company's business volume was smaller prior to World War II. But business had grown tremendously since then and spatial separation appeared increasingly inefficient.

Finally in November of 1952 company officials began to consolidate the controller's department by relocating two divisions together on one floor. One was the agency audit division which included the voucher-check filing unit. As soon as the decision to move was made, lower level supervisors were called in to help with planning. Line workers were not consulted but were kept informed by the assistants of planning progress. Company officials were concerned about the problem of transporting many tons of equipment and some 200 workers from two locations to another single location without disrupting work flow. So the move was planned to occur over a single weekend, using the most efficient resources available. Assistants were kept busy planning positions for files and desks in the new location.

Desks, files, chairs, and even wastebaskets were numbered prior to the move, and relocated according to a master chart checked on the spot by the assistant. Employees were briefed as to where the new location was and which elevators they should take to reach it. The company successfully transported the paraphernalia of the voucher-check filing unit from one floor to another over one weekend. Workers in the cage quit Friday afternoon at the old stand, reported back Monday at the new.

The exterior boundaries of the new cage were still three building walls and the steel mesh, but the new cage possessed only one door—the sliding door through the steel mesh into the work area of the rest of the agency audit division. The territory of the cage had also been reduced in size. An entire bank of filing cabinets had to be left behind in the old location to be taken over by the unit moving there. The new cage was arranged so that there was no longer a row of metal filing cabinets lined up inside the steel mesh obstructing the view into the cage.

Part 4

When the workers in the cage inquired about the removal of the filing cabinets from along the steel mesh fencing, they found that Mr. Burke had insisted that these cabinets be rearranged so his view into the cage would not be obstructed by them. Miss Dunn had tried to retain the cabinets in their prior position, but her efforts had been overridden.

Mr. Burke disapproved of conversation. Since he could see workers conversing in the new cage, he "requested" Miss Dunn to put a stop to all unnecessary talk. Attempts by female clerks to talk to messenger boys brought the wrath of her superior down on Miss Dunn, who was then forced to reprimand the girls.

Mr. Burke also disapproved of a untidy working area, and any boxes or papers which were in sight were a source of annoyance to him. He did not exert supervision directly, but would "request" Miss Dunn to "do something about those boxes." In the new cage, desks had to be completely cleared at the end of the day, in contrast to the work-in-progress piles left out in the old cage. Boxes could not accumulate on top of filing cases.

The custom of afternoon snacking also ran into trouble. Lacking a corridor door, the food bringers had to venture forth and pack back their snack tray through the work area of the rest of their section, bringing this hitherto unique custom to the attention of workers outside the cage. The latter promptly recognized the desirability of afternoon snacks and began agitation for the same privilege. This annoyed the section head, who forbade workers in the cage from continuing this custom.

Part 5

Mr. Burke later made a rule which permitted one worker to leave the new cage at a set time every afternoon to bring up food for the rest. This rigidity irked cage personnel, accustomed to a snack when the mood struck, or none at all. Having made his concession to the cage force, Mr. Burke was unable to prevent workers outside the cage from doing the same thing. What had once been unique to the workers in the cage was now common practice in the section.

Although Miss Dunn never outwardly expressed anything but compliance and approval of her superior's directives, she exhibited definite signs of anxiety. All the cage workers reacted against Burke's increased domination. When he imposed his decisions upon the voucher-check filing unit, he became "Old Grandma" to its personnel. The cage workers sneered at him and ridiculed him behind his back. Workers who formerly had obeyed company policy as a matter of course began to find reasons for loafing and obstructing work in the new cage. One of the changes that took place in the behavior of the workers had to do with their game of rubber band sniping. All knew that Mr. Burke would disapprove of this game. It became highly clandestine and fraught with danger. Yet shooting the rubber bands *increased*.

Newly arrived checks were put out of sight as soon as possible, filed or not. Workers hid unfiled checks, generally stuffing them into desk drawers or unused file drawers. Since boxes were forbidden, there were fewer unused file drawers than there had been in the old cage. So the day's work was sometimes undone when several clerks hastily shoved vouchers and checks indiscriminately into the same file drawer at the end of the day.

Before a worker in the cage filed incoming checks, she measured with her ruler the thickness in inches of each bundle she filed. At the end of each day she totaled her input and reported it to Miss Dunn. All incoming checks were measured upon arrival. Thus Miss Dunn had a rough estimate of unit intake compared with file input. Theoretically she was able to tell at any time how much unfiled material she had on hand and how well the unit was keeping up with its task. Despite this running check, when the annual inventory of unfiled checks on hand in the cage was taken at the beginning of the calendar year 1953, a seriously large backlog of unfiled checks was found. To the surprise and dismay of Miss Dunn, the inventory showed the unit to be far behind schedule, filing much more slowly than before the relocation of the cage.

SUSSEX OIL COMPANY*

The Sussex Oil Company was a relatively small, rapidly growing regional distributor of gasoline, lubricating oils, and other petroleum products. Throughout several contiguous seaboard states the produces distributed under the Sussex company's own brand names had enjoyed increasing consumer acceptance. The company had built or purchased a number of gasoline stations to distribute its products. Growth had also been achieved through what the company regarded as advantageous contracts with bulk-station operators and independently owned chains of gasoline stations. The success of the company was generally attributed in part to technically competent buying, but more especially to unusual skill in negotiations with refiners, customers, and bankers, and to a continuing, dynamic, "all-out" advertising program. The company had achieved some fame in local trade circles for its willingness to spend freely on promotional activities. Over the years, profits of the company had also grown, but by no means in proportion to the expanding scale of operations.

While the company paid salaries, wages, and commissions in line with those of competitors, it had attracted many of its employees, including even district managers, away from them. Employees of the company regarded a job with Sussex as very desirable and as carrying with it considerable prestige. Employee turnover at all levels was low, and few people left the company of their own accord. While the company was not ruthless in its handling of inept employees, "people took care to see to it that their work was satisfactory," as one executive phrased it.

The men who had founded the company still retained positions in its top management in the winter of 1940. The seven district managers who worked directly under this home-office group, as well as others throughout the entire organization, frequently commented on the founders' enthusiasm and energy. People in the organization sometimes said that this infectious aggressiveness had even permeated the managements of some of the company's customers.

The top-management group determined major policies, managed the company's finances, and negotiated contracts with suppliers and with some few of the more important customers. They delegated considerable authority in the actual operations of the company to the district managers, and gave some weight to their managers' views on broad policy matters.

During the year he had been with the company, Richard Hicks, manager of the company's Botany Bay district, attended many conferences and "pep meetings" at the home office, and scarcely a week went by that he did not receive a personal visit from some top official from the head office. These contacts generally amounted to pressure for increasing volume and injunctions—progressively urgent—to keep expenses down. Hicks responded in a negative way to this pressure to cut costs and expressed himself openly, both to his superiors and to his own office staff. Sussex, he asserted, was getting to be as bad as the large national refiner and distributor with which he had formerly been employed.

The Botany Bay district offices had been located in one of the newest office buildings in the center of the city, in the vicinity of the better hotels, shops, and theaters. The rental of this suite of offices amounted to about $25,000 a year, and renewal of the lease, which was about to expire, would raise the amount to at least $30,000. In addition to this cost the office paid monthly not inconsiderable sums for several direct telephone lines to the company's bulk-storage terminal. This plant, which consisted of large storage tanks and pumping facilities for unloading ocean-going tankers and for loading railroad tankcars and trucks, was located in a general area of docks and shipyards, warehouses, factories, and other oil terminals, all rather closely grouped together along the waterfront.

The top officials of the company had stated on a number of occasions that they thought Richard Hicks should move his district office from the central downtown location to a frame building located at the storage terminal in order to reduce costs. Hicks had been emphatic in his opposition to moving the offices, and the management, in accordance with its practice of giving authority to its district managers and respecting their judgment, had been reluctant to force the issue. On a recent visit, however, the president had indicated what Hicks thought were strong feelings on the subject. Hicks therefore had agreed to move.

The frame building at the plant had once housed the district office; but after the latter had been moved to the city location, it had remained largely vacant. It was, however, in a good state of repair; but in anticipation of the move it was painted, soundproofed, and otherwise renovated. In March of 1941 the 30-odd employees, including Richard Hicks, established themselves in their new quarters.

Within several weeks after the move to the plant, a noticeable unrest, which caused Hicks serious concern, developed among the office employees. This new atmosphere, in which strained relations, repressed spirits, and lack of enthusiasm about the work were outstanding characteristics, was totally different from that which he had known during the previous year. Even his immediate assistants stiffened in their relations with him; the banter and kidding in which almost the whole force used to engage disappeared; the performance of the whole group seemed somehow lethargic and lackluster. For example, the stock-records man frequently complained about being swamped and seemed always behind in his records. The bookkeepers and credit department workers found it hard to keep up with their work and of their own volition began to cut their lunch periods short to resume their duties before the period was up. All in all, the work of the office was far behind the par of promptness which had prevailed in the past. The attitude of the workers was apparently reflected not only in the results of their work, but also members of the office continually complained about the time they wasted driving to work, about the noise and the dirt and the inconvenience of having to remain around the plant during the lunch period to eat at nearby lunch counters. They were used to eating at the better restaurants uptown, where they did not mingle with factory laborers, truck drivers and other industrial workers. Although no one on the force had actually quit, many had requested higher wages or talked about finding better jobs.

Richard Hicks turned over in his mind these facts and others in the situation at considerable length. He discounted many of the complaints. He had made no changes in the organization's structure or its personnel. All procedures and systems were as before. The jobs performed were all substantially the same as before. In fact, several had been simplified by the proximity of office and plant. Members of the office force could now take up many problems directly and personally with the plant personnel, whereas formerly they had had to spend much time on lengthy and inconvenient telephone conversations and on visits down to the plant.

Hicks was sure the new offices, because of the soundproofing, were in fact not nearly so noisy as the old. He himself was glad to get away from the street noise which used to well up from the busy intersection which his office had overlooked. While there were, to be sure, some additional transportation problems, all workers now had free parking space on the grounds of the plant; before they had had to pay up to $10 a month for space several blocks from the office. To avoid the congestion of transportation facilities at rush hours, the office of the Sussex Oil Company opened and closed one-half hour earlier than the main shift at the shipyards. Hicks estimated that with this early closing time his people had at least an hour to shop and do errands in the city before the stores closed. Along with the entire staff, Hicks had his lunch at "Mammy's" where the food was excellent and well served, although the clatter of dishes, the babble of voices, and the music of a jukebox contrasted with some of the mid-town restaurants.

Nevertheless the pressure for wage and salary increases continued. This Hicks resisted for two or three months because the company not only paid competitive scales but, indeed, paid better than many types of business. Further, he was much concerned lest the savings of the move be offset by increased salary costs. On the other hand, he felt he could not possibly risk having to replace efficient people of long experience with the company at a time when the general demand for competent personnel far exceeded the supply, a condition which promised to become even more acute. As the pressure increased and the morale of the organization continued to deteriorate, Hicks eventually concluded there was no alternative to increasing wages and salaries of the office force. Because, it seemed to Hicks, the company could not raise the wages of the office force without raising those of the plant workers, he proposed to the home office that an increase be extended to the whole district organization. After some discussion and delay, the company accepted Hicks's proposal.

After the increase, there was much less talk about wages and salaries, but the office force seemed to devote an increasing portion of the working day to complaining about working conditions and about "the company." Several weeks later, after the morale of the organization had continued to degenerate, Hicks felt something positive and immediate had to be done. The breakdown was spreading to the plant workers, who had previously been a loyal and efficient group. The plant manager reported this development to Hicks and stated that while his men had made no specific complaints, they talked about the company "going to the dogs," and losing its spirit of competitive aggressiveness. Hicks was surprised to get this reaction from the plant workers. He was inclined to share their sentiment, even though he knew, as a matter of fact, that the company's sales and profits in the preceding year had reached the highest levels in its history. His own earnings were the largest of his career. The "penny-pinching" attitude of the home office, however, disturbed him more and more. One of his best salesmen had commented, "The company is on the downgrade; we are no longer pushing ahead; it's all 'retrenchment.' "

Hicks was thoroughly perplexed. It seemed clear to him that he could not move the office back to the city. The company, he thought, having just raised wages, would almost certainly not raise them again; in any event, he somehow thought that higher wages would not solve the problem. Yet, he felt, something had to be done if the situation were not to get completely out of hand.

JOSEPH LONGMAN*

Joseph Longman was hired in the spring 1938 as a tank operator on the night shift of the anodizing department at the Mallard Airplane Company. He was placed in this kind of work with a promise from the personnel department that he would be transferred to another job when the opportunity arose. Before working at the Mallard Airplane Company he had been employed as an arc welder. Almost all the welding in airplane production was done by acetylene torches and electric spot-welding machines. Longman was not qualified along these lines. He was, however, a good mechanic.

Longman was a red-haired Scotchman about 38 years of age. He was married and had a 13-year-old daughter of whom he was very proud. He had attended high school in California, and frequently referred to the fact that Robert Young was in the same school. Raising silver foxes was his hobby, and he hoped some day to have sufficient money and time to own a large fox farm. The small farm he owned, however, netted him an average income of $500 a year, an amount almost large enough to feed his family and keep up his house which was located in the country.

In the anodizing department where Longman worked, the duraluminum parts used in airplane construction were given a protective coating to increase their resistance to corrosion. The parts to be anodized were suspended by duraluminum clamps in tanks of chromic acid solution (dirty brown in color) and then charged with an electric current. There were two principal jobs in the department: tank operating and drying. Tanking operators loaded and unloaded the tanks and washed the acid from the parts, once they had been removed from the tanks. During the 20-minute period when the electrolytic process was going on, they prepared the next tank load by tying parts together with aluminum wire. Dryers wiped and counted the parts and placed them on racks to be sent to the next department.

At first sight, working conditions in the anodizing department seemed both arduous and repulsive, especially for the tank operators. They wore rubber boots, rubber coveralls, and rubber gloves, and were required by law to wear masks to keep the acid from their lungs. The heat from the acid and their nonporous rubber clothing caused them to sweat profusely. The department was generally known as the "tank hole," and the men who worked there were referred to as "those dirty tank men." The tank men, however, were congenial and enjoyed working together. By speeding up the preparation of a load for the tanks, they could have a few minutes to loaf and gossip before it was time to pull out the parts already in the anodizing bath. The department supervisor made no objection to their practice of talking with one another between loads as long as they got the required amount of work done.

There were approximately 20 workers in the department. Since it was the company policy to hire young men for the department, most of the workers were from 19 to 23 years of age. The work did not require previous training and could be learned in four to six weeks. Wage rates in the department were about average for the company. Stephen Gifford was the supervisor of the department. He was attending college during the day at this time.

The morale of the night shift in the anodizing department was very high. A number of the men, as well as Gifford, attended college in the daytime. They planned many social functions together. In the winter months they attended the college ice hockey games and cheered for their supervisor, who played on one of the teams. During the summer, when college students were not in school, the group frequently took their lunches to the beach and played volley ball before coming to work. Once in a while they had a steak fry at a nearby lake to which they took girl friends or wives.

Longman did not participate in playing volley ball on the beach because his fair complexion could not stand the sunshine. He was, however, active in other group activities. He enjoyed helping to plan parties, and his wife was congenial and eager to purchase the hot dogs and rolls or to bake a cake. In fact, one night Mrs. Longman sent a cake which was passed around the department at midnight. This cake-eating at midnight became a habit thereafter, each man taking turns buying or having his mother, wife, or best girl bake a cake.

In addition to helping load and unload the tanks, Longman was in charge of running the electric current through the acid in one of the tanks. It was a position with some responsibility. He also instructed and oriented new men, a task which he enjoyed, and he always went out of his way to help people with a problem. He was well liked and respected by the rest of the men. However, there were no opportunities for advancement within the department.

An opportunity for Longman's transfer to another job did not arise until he had been in the anodizing department for two years. It would not have arisen then except that Gifford knew that it had been promised to him at the first opportunity. Gifford thought highly of Longman and wanted to see him promoted. Consequently, he was glad to arrange the transfer. A position was open in the sheet metal department, and Longman was assigned there to operate a punch press. There were over 200 men in this department, all of whom worked on individual machines. They had higher wages, cleaner working conditions, and more chance for advancement than the men in the anodizing department. They were not free to talk to each other, however, for each one had to be busy with his own machine. Moreover, the sheet metal supervisor seldom spoke to his men but stared at them with his hands on his hips when they were not working at their machines.

The quality of Longman's work was satisfactory from the start, and his weekly earnings would have increased as soon as his transfer had been made permanent, which would have taken two weeks. Nevertheless, before this time had elapsed, Longman requested that he be transferred back to the anodizing department, and the request was granted.

After Stephen Gifford finished college in the spring of 1940, he transferred to the company's personnel department where he was concerned with employee relations. Late in 1941 he visited the plant and had the following conversation with Longman.

Gifford:	Hello, Joe.
Longman:	Well, it's a long time since I've seen you. How are you?
Gifford:	Good. How are you?
Longman:	Okay.
Gifford:	How are those foxes coming along?
Longman:	Better than ever. I've got some good pelts on foot this season —46 of them. With this war raising prices I ought to do okay. I'm going to make up a coat for Ruth. She's my daughter, you know.
Gifford:	How's Ruth?
Longman:	Mighty fine. She's a junior in high school now and doing mighty fine work. We got a letter from the principal telling us how fine Ruth was doing in her subjects. She wants to go to college, wants to be a school teacher some day. I guess college is pretty expensive, isn't it?
Gifford:	A great deal depends upon which college she attends.
Longman:	I've got to start putting some money away for Ruth's college education. After this war is over this airplane business isn't going to be so hot! In fact, it isn't so hot right now.
Gifford:	What do you mean by that?
Longman:	Oh, I don't mean we haven't got enough work. As far as a lot of the boys are concerned, we've got too damn much work. I guess the company has got a backlog of orders for the next two years, at least. What gripes me is all the changes that are being made around here.
Gifford:	I can see there have been a number of changes.
Longman:	You said it! A fellow just doesn't know where he stands these days. I used to help set up a load for the tanks, put the parts in the tank, and operate the generator. Now the generator is automatic. Since the two new tanks have been added and since the new conveyor system has been put in, the only thing I do is tie up the parts for each load. It keeps

seven or eight of us busy just doing that. I don't like it around here the way I used to. No steak fries, no parties, no talking with the guys—just work and plenty of it. I don't get to know any of the other guys in the department. There's twice as many now as there used to be. We've got over 40 now, mostly all new kids.

Gifford: Do you still help to break them in?

Longman: Our new foreman has changed things a lot. With all the expansion we each do just one job. You might say we're specialists. I don't think my foreman likes me. When I would try to help a new fellow with his job, the foreman would say, "Mind your own business, Longman. You do too much talking for your own good. You just take care of your own job." All I was ever trying to do was to help the new guys get straightened out on their new assignments. It's not easy when you're new around here, and I think they appreciate your helping them. But the foreman, he's just jealous or afraid that I'll show him up in front of the other guys. He's not as smart as he thinks he is. See that new conveyor belt up there on the ceiling? It breaks down quite frequently and instead of fixing it ourselves, the foreman runs to the maintenance department. Once I offered to arc-weld a part of the track, and he told me to get back on my job and stay put. Personally, I don't think he knew what arc-welding was.

Gifford: Did the maintenance men fix it?

Longman: Sure they did. They arc-welded it! And it works fine now. You ought to see us turn out the orders with the new setup around here. With the two additional tanks and the new conveyor system we really pour out the work. You see each guy does just one thing, over and over again. Sort of a line production with each of us specializing. It's really okay. Our output has about tripled since you were here.

Gifford: That's good.

Longman: Of course we're working six days a week, and that makes quite a difference. Sure helps the old pay check with time and a half for Saturday work. That strike we had really helped out.

Gifford: What do you mean?

Longman: We got a raise in pay, and it also gave us seniority rights.

Gifford: What does that mean?

Longman: Well, any layoff within a department or section must be made according to seniority. It's a pretty good deal for us older fellows.

BETTY RANDALL*

On March 15, 1949, Betty Randall came in to talk over a problem with Mr. Robbins. Betty was a production worker doing hand assembly work in a modern branch plant, which employed approximately 600 people in a large eastern city. Mr. Robbins was the Personnel Director for the plant. After Betty had told Mr. Robbins her story, he asked Betty to write out her description of the situation. The resulting written statement is reproduced below.

I consider this case not unusual nor typical, but as having happened to me and to a few others. As I am not equipped to do the work, it offers little or no solution to the problem at hand. I wouldn't be writing this report if I had not remembered the advice given by Mr. Robbins of Personnel. He told a group that should we have a problem, to please consult him before walking out. However, I will mention here that I have seen a few very conscientious workers walk out without "fighting the case."

When I was first hired, Mr. Lipton, the foreman, introduced me to the young lady who taught me the process of soldering lead wires. I asked her how much production I would be expected to turn in daily, and she secured this information for me from the other girls. This seemed at the moment like a fantastic sum, but she assured me that after a few days I would become quite efficient, which I soon did. I'm not one to "bite the hand that feeds me," so I began working and finally developed the system into sort of a game. A few weeks later one of the girls asked me how I was doing, and I told her that I was doing fine. She looked at my production sheet and swore. She was astonished to see how much I was producing each hour. She bitterly reminded me that girls that had been here for several months or even years were not producing what I had accomplished in a few weeks. I laughed that off as somewhat of a compliment. That was my big mistake as far as cooperating with the company or satisfying my gregarious tendencies was concerned. I was immediately and severely ostracized.

During the weeks that ensued I noticed I was not completely alone, there were a few others who were also "friendless." However, it was soon apparent that ostracism was not satisfying the desires of their fiendish little plan. Threats were to follow, and follow they did. Having worked in the violent ward of a psychopathic hospital, I was not the least bit nervous because of these threats, but others were. I noticed a few things about the character, temperament, and education of those who were apparently "bossing." They were usually the "oldtimers" and loafers. Girls with a great deal of confidence and little reason for it. Sometimes their reasons for fighting the enormous business organization, which represents their security, were quite convincing. Your work is never appreciated. They'll always want more and more. You haven't got a chance to get a merit wage increase unless you go out with the boss and. . . . After this general talking to the poor girls began to wonder; some of them stayed a few days and then didn't turn up for work. The clique had scored again.

I sat and wondered as I worked. What to do? I was assured I had the bosses on my side, but then. . . . The long dead silence and the vulgar, stupid remarks of the other girls soon began to get under my skin. I worked quite a while at the psychopathic hospital and "they" never bothered me, but those stupid little people and their moronic remarks soon began to annoy me something terrible. Because my production was high I was asked to work Saturdays. This brought a violent counterthrust from the rebels.

Soon their campaign began to affect me exactly as they had planned. (Or am I giving them too much credit?) My production was dropping. The assistant foreman, Bert, asked me if I was ill. When I told him my troubles, he advised me to see Mr. Lipton, which I did. Mr. Lipton listened attentively, asked the names of the rebels, which I readily gave, not feeling at all like an informer. He then assured me, though stammering, that justice would prevail. I noticed little change.

The little minds had other desires than to keep their jobs secure; they wanted to jeopardize the position of their immediate superiors. Bert, who had advised me to talk to Mr. Lipton, commonly held the reputation of a communist, nailed on him by "my rebels." I have always maintained in my philosophy that if one cannot become great by one's own methods of accomplishment, then one will probably pull everyone else down below them, until by comparison they are above the mob, hence great. This is commonly known as scapegoatism. These girls carry this farther than I ever dreamed would be done. Scapegoating is a common activity of the uneducated. Education of the population, while not the solution, will greatly aid in the eventual solution of this problem.

However, back to the practical aspects of the problem at hand. I had convinced myself that most of the girls were not the kind I would care to associate with anyway, so my scope of activity was not ruptured too severely. As they ignored me, I ignored them. As they cursed me, I ignored them. However, something happened that I had not counted on. I became physically ill from the entire situation. Having had a few lectures on psychosomatic diseases, I knew I had not incorrectly diagnosed the case.

My relief came in the form of a temporary transfer to another department. I knew it would take some time before the girls would become acquainted with my case, and the rest was welcome. I was shocked to find that no one was interested in my "reputation." I was further shocked when I began to notice that harmony, tranquility, and cooperation prevailed in this department. It is my opinion that part of the cause for such cooperation in this department may be attributed to the fact of one boss, and a capable, understanding man at that.

Then I was told to return to my former department, where I was greeted by my boss with, "Enjoy your vacation?" This does not strike me as being very complimentary to one who has been conscientious from the beginning.

I had been taught to report all inferior grade materials, and this particular morning I found the wire defective. After reeling yards of red tape from a few of my bosses, I finally was sent to Mr. Lipton. Again Mr. Lipton was glad to see me. "I want you to get back to your machine, sit down, and mind your own business. Your production is failing. Why?" This I was told before I had a chance to speak. Here I explained about the strain I was under and about the inferior materials. He then told me to work as best I could with the inferior materials as he didn't want to send any of the girls home. I then told him I had thought of leaving. He sarcastically mentioned that perhaps it was for the best. This shock drove me to Mr. Robbins of Personnel and to standing here in my living room dictating this to my husband, the typist of the family.

ROLAND-OLIVER, S.A.*

"We've just a real fight in my group. I think I've got things straightened out now. But for a time I was worried."

The speaker was Dr. Andre Dupas, a section head in the Sounds System Laboratory of Roland-Oliver, S.A., a medium-sized producer of electronic signalling systems. Dr. Dupas went on to explain to the casewriter how the conflict had arisen.

My group received this project. Potentially it had a large payoff—100 million francs or more. My boss, Dr. Menez, considered it top priority and it looked to both of us like an outstanding opportunity to make a breakthrough. We put three of our senior associates on the project, and right away they were fighting.

I won't confuse you with technical details but we were working with transducers which had to have very low breakdown voltages. I called together the three associates, Dr. Pierre Boyer, Dr. Jean Rault, and M. Kurt Kalcheck. Almost right away Dr. Boyer objected to the project on grounds that it was theoretically doubtful, if not impossible. Dr. Boyer is only about 26 years old. He received an advanced degree last year and demonstrated his first device three years ago. Frankly, I think he's brilliant. He's going to move up in this organization rapidly.

The rest of us were rather surprised by the speed and certainty with which Dr. Boyer responded. I'm not sure what Dr. Rault would have said if Dr. Boyer hadn't been so positive. At any rate Dr. Rault was lukewarm at best. However, I received immediate support from M. Kalcheck. He is much older than the other two, who are close friends. M. Kalcheck must be in his fifties. He has very little advanced mathematics and a background in engineering. He's one of the very few senior associates without an advanced degree. But M. Kalcheck is very loyal, diligent, practical and reliable and he'll work tremendously hard. We get along very well. M. Kalcheck said he would set up an experiment and see what happened.

It was agreed that the three of them should meet together and plan a preliminary investigation to decide whether the project should proceed. I remember thinking at the time that Dr. Boyer wasn't going to do any collaborating with anyone and I was right.

At 9:30 the next morning, Dr. Menez received an elaborate theoretical report, which demonstrated the mathematical impossibility of the project's objective. There was a forceful summary to the effect that we would be wasting our time proceeding any further. Dr. Boyer must have stayed up half the night to complete it. Both Dr. Menez and I were impressed by Dr. Boyer's speed and thoroughness. It was typical of him.

It was going to take time for us to evaluate the report and Dr. Menez was very busy that week. I was wondering whether to call M. Kalcheck off the project when some five days after Dr. Boyer's report had been submitted, M. Kalcheck came to see me. He had assembled the transducers and they worked. He'd done it! I was tremendously excited and so was Dr. Menez. Many people were congratulating M. Kalcheck. Dr. Boyer and Dr. Rault were called in and told the news. Dr. Boyer said nothing about having been wrong but began to examine M. Kalcheck's setup minutely.

A couple of hours later I received a call from Dr. Menez. Dr. Boyer was in his office complaining that M. Kalcheck refused to share information with him. I said I would handle it and I called Dr. Boyer, Dr. Rault and M. Kalcheck into my office. I said that this was M. Kalcheck's discovery and that no one must deprive him of the full credit for it. Probably Dr. Boyer could write a better article for the professional journals but M. Kalcheck must be permitted to exploit his work. I sympathized with M. Kalcheck's fear that his ideas would be taken over.

Dr. Boyer shrugged this off. He denied that he had the smallest intention of depriving M. Kalcheck of any credit. He merely wished to build on M. Kalcheck's work, for which he required information. Shared information was the basis of science.

That fight was two weeks ago and I think I resolved it. In a way M. Kalcheck was acting out of character. He isn't *expected* to discover new things. In fact Dr. Rault has announced that M. Kalcheck was only following my orders, which isn't true. M. Kalcheck is expected to be the practical one.

But you know something, I think M. Kalcheck has a lot of talent, if only he and others would start to believe it.

The casewriter asked to speak to Kurt Kalcheck. M. Kalcheck was a thin, balding man with glasses. He had a polite but earnest style of speaking and a distinct Polish accent. He was asked about his background and his life up to the present.

M. Kalcheck: I was born in Poland and educated in Munich, Germany. I studied engineering in France on a scholarship. After obtaining a degree, I accepted a job here at Roland-Oliver. At the time, it did not seem necessary to go on for an advanced degree. I had been here only a few months when the war broke out in 1939 and I was fired as a security risk. It was my Munich background and the fact that Poland was occupied.

It was a pretty bad time to be a security risk or to speak with any sort of mid-European accent. During the war I could not afford to return to the university and had to take temporary jobs. After the war the company re-hired me and I did some really important work on vacuum tubes. Thousands of systems used the miniature tubes I had developed. Then, quite suddenly the technology changed over to solid state devices and I was given only routine assignments on tubes. The creative work was no longer coming my way and hundreds of young men with advanced degrees just out of the university were way ahead of me.

Have you ever stopped to think what happens to people in these technical upheavals? I often wonder what it must have been like to be an expert on propeller-driven airplanes and then suddenly find oneself at the bottom, nobody wanting all your knowledge. Industry makes these studies on how to use waste products and it never stops to think of the human beings it consigns to the scrap pile. Management says it's "up to the individual." There's all these orientation programs for newcomers but what about *reorientation* for some of us?

Sometimes I think of all the brilliant people we have here and yet most of us are alone. Just a few yards away behind a wall there are probably a dozen men from whom we could learn so much. And yet there are high walls everywhere with many noncommunicating people duplicating each other's efforts. We do *emphasize* "team work" but we work so much as individuals that we just don't notice each other. People here are strongly opinionated and individualistic. They like to work by themselves. Maybe they fear others will steal their ideas.

I'll give an example of the quite needless rivalry that goes on here. One of the production division's development groups has been sent over here—to the research laboratory. The idea is to "facilitate" the production of our ideas. They'll come in and take your idea and five days later they'll be developing it in an unfinished state before we've even evaluated it ourselves. And since this new pressure on us to do application work is intensifying —we are converging with this fiercely competitive marketing-oriented group, who seem intent on rushing everything through. This is duplication and it's hurting the company. Why doesn't management give us clearer assignments, which don't overlap? We're doing some work on defense systems as you may know. Now what happens when the government receives competitive bids from different parts of this company? Because that's going to happen any day now. I've complained several times about this. The other day the marketing manager of this manufacturing division which has invaded us was in here. He told me, "Don't cry about it. Get in quickly—that's life!" He wants all our information. I must confess I've always found it difficult to push in front of people. We spend hours laying down a list of priorities, then all of a sudden it turns into a game of how to get around them. It seems so destructive to me. Beyond a certain point competition becomes detrimental to the organization. While I'm waiting my turn—as I promised to do—someone else comes in and grabs the needed equipment. It gets so that my civilized behavior is just exploited. There has to be a better way!

It's bad enough when this fighting goes on between departments but when it's *inside* the very group you are working with, when you cannot even trust your closest associates, then things are really falling apart.

Casewriter: I understand that there has recently been a dispute between you and Dr. Boyer. Is that what you were referring to?

M. Kalcheck: Well, that was typical, although more unpleasant than usual because it was so close to us all. We were called into Dr. Menez's office to discuss the development of very low-frequency transducers. There was a definite application in mind. We all agreed to explore it but after the meeting Dr. Boyer walked off by himself and began writing a paper. He likes to show how quickly he can respond. He didn't consult us, of course, and the paper virtually told us "That's my conclusion, and that settles it."

Well, Dr. Boyer has a good brain—but it doesn't matter how brilliant you are, it's always dangerous to say that something can't be done and even more dangerous to put it into writing. I couldn't follow Dr. Boyer's theoretical arguments very closely and he didn't seem inclined to explain them to me. Dr. Dupas had told me to go ahead and so I did.

I went to the manufacturing division and succeeded in getting some low-frequency devices from them, which they had recently developed. It was difficult getting them and they made me promise not to let anyone else use them. That's the sort of suspicion we have around here! I set up some experiments and within eight days I'd achieved 20% efficiency, which Dr. Boyer had argued couldn't be done.

Well, you never saw a faster change of attitude from anyone than Dr. Boyer's. Instead of offering to work with me he began taking notes and a couple of hours after my first demonstration he was setting up a duplicate experiment on his own. Every few minutes he would come down from his laboratory and look at what I had done. It was quite clear that he was imitating my setup. I didn't protest until his lab technician came into the room, went over to my setup and without asking me picked up a couple of filters. I said, "I'm using those!" He said, "You're not. They were on the table." I explained that I borrowed the equipment from many different people. I'd waited my turn until it was ready and that I would need all the filters I had. "Why can't you wait your turn," I said, "and why duplicate this setup? Aren't we supposed to be working together?" "That's what *I* thought," he said. "All right, keep your filters!" and he threw them down hard onto the table and walked out. Why did he have to do that? We've been friends for ten years. We used to sit together at lunch—now he won't speak to me. And it's all so silly and unnecessary. I'm really ashamed to discuss it.

Well, a few moments later Dr. Boyer comes into the room. He says, "I understand you obtained some special devices from the product division. Can I have some of them or at least their specifications?" I said I was sorry but the information was confidential. If he went to the product division they might help him but I had been made to promise that I would keep the devices to myself. He didn't argue but went straight to Dr. Dupas, who followed him back into this room. He said, "Dr. Dupas, tell M. Kalcheck that he must share information or I'll go straight to Dr. Menez." I said, "The information is confidential." As Dr. Dupas hesitated for a moment, Dr. Boyer left the room, heading straight for Dr. Menez's office.

I repeated my story to Dr. Menez who said if the information was confidential that was that. A promise was a promise. I told Dr. Boyer he could have all my measurements but not the product division's specifications. I said, "Dr. Boyer, we can go on fighting but people do get hurt in these fights. No one really comes out ahead."

He said he could do nothing without the specifications and I knew it. Last I heard, he was trying to order a duplicate set of devices from the division. And I've got all we need already!

People like Dr. Boyer don't realize that one *has* to work with other people. The equipment we use is expensive and we have to borrow back and forth all the time. No one can afford to be an island in this place. If you don't cooperate with other people, then they are not going to help you when you're in trouble and need equipment. There's no point appealing upstairs to Dr. Menez. He can't tell us how to cooperate. We have to learn.

The casewriter next tried to meet Dr. Boyer. After a series of delays he eventually managed to speak to him. Dr. Boyer was very cautious, would pause some time before answering, and chose his words carefully. Of the many persons interviewed in this company he expressed the most concern that his opinions could get him into trouble.

Dr. Boyer: Yes, I'd say I was satisfied with my job. Very satisfied on the whole, although there are always exceptions. I've sought employment elsewhere from time to time. Complaints? Well, it's a loose organization—too loose in my opinion. We don't always get cooperation from the other divisions and from each other. I feel we should be apprised of what other people are doing and have access to their work. People upstairs should take tighter control, insure better cooperation and that we get the equipment we need. It's a false economy being as short of equipment as we are. My technician takes a week to get equipment together. It shouldn't take that long. There isn't enough attention to doing what is best for the company. That has been my chief objective.

Casewriter: I've been talking with M. Kalcheck. That's his chief objective too.

Dr. Boyer: Well, of course you have to have some trust of people and he hasn't. It is in his make-up, his personality. He thinks someone is going to take something away from him. He's an extreme case as far as I'm concerned. I've never come across such distrust. . . . But I don't see how you're going to disguise all this I'm saying. It's bound to get out, isn't it? As far as I'm concerned this incident is closed. Who's going to read this case?

Casewriter: Well, I'm not sure how to reassure you. My experience has been that by the time these cases are typed up, disguised, and presented to the company for clearance, the incidents described have been forgotten. I've talked to about a dozen people. They have all expressed several opinions which were more negative than any expressed by you.

Dr. Boyer: Hm-m . . . all right. Well I assured M. Kalcheck that my motives were entirely honorable. I had no intention at all of depriving him of credit. All I wanted was to set up some more advanced experiments. There was a good opportunity for collaboration between us. He had made an interesting discovery. I could have come up with a model and proposed a further series of experiments.

Of course I do move a great deal faster than most other people. I realize, even if they don't, that a relatively small laboratory like this has some running to do. I attend professional conferences and I know what's going on. One of our competitors has ten people on a project similar to ours. I suspect that another competitor has thirty. We have the advantage of flexibility and concentration on one area provided we react fast. M. Kalcheck doesn't realize that I chose him to work with us. I'm all for cooperation. When you're working by yourself, just one small mistake can put you weeks behind. M. Kalcheck is thorough and he checks things. I've worked by myself here for five years and I felt the need for collaboration. That's the only way we're going to beat our competitors. Every time I work on a project I think will they beat me to it? We're up against tough competition make no mistake about it.

I've got a good record so far. A number of awards from the company and a couple from the industry. I'm seeking a reputation as an inventor and an original theorist. Most of my friends are professionals and the people I want to impress are fellow theoreticians and people at home. There was an article about me in the local newspaper last week.

Casewriter: Dr. Dupas feels that he helped to resolve the dispute between you and M. Kalcheck.

Dr. Boyer: Dr. Dupas didn't solve anything. I solved it. I solved it by keeping right away from M. Kalcheck. It's the only thing to do. I can work with Dr. Rault but not with M. Kalcheck. He wants to keep everything secret. Dr. Dupas gets very enthusiastic and so does M. Kalcheck, but we need to inject some realism into our work. But I'd rather not say anything more. . . .

Glossary of Key Words

Accommodating.   A conflict-handling style that is unassertive and cooperative. The attempt to help another person achieve their goals without concern for one's own goals.

Achievement Motivation.   A motive that causes people to prefer tasks that involve a moderate amount of risk and clear feedback on performance.

Activities.   The things that members of a group do, such as working on the physical environment with implements and with other persons.

Affective Conflict.   A situation in which feelings or emotions are incompatible.

After-Only Measurement.   This type of research design measures individuals only after a treatment has been administered.

Antecedent.   An environmental event that precedes an employee's behavior.

Approach-Approach Conflict.   Occurs when a person has a choice between two or more alternatives, each with positive outcomes.

Approach-Avoidance Conflict.   Occurs when a person has to choose whether to do something that has both positive and negative consequences.

Attitudes.   Affective responses, cognitive responses, and behaviors toward some object.

Attribution.   A tendency to judge a person's current behavior whether or not that behavior reflects the true person, what the person is really like, or what the person really feels.

Automation.   The production process that utilizes control mechanisms that trigger an operation after taking into consideration what has happened before without human intervention.

Autonomous Group Approach.   A change approach in which work groups are redesigned so that they contain virtually all of the resources and skills needed to produce a specific output.

Autonomy.   Freedom to do the work without much supervision. A core dimension in the Hackman-Oldham job enrichment model.

Avoidance.   Any behavior by an employee that prevents an aversive event from occurring.

Avoidance-Avoidance Conflict.   Occurs when a person has a choice between two or more alternatives each with negative consequences.

Avoiding.   A conflict-handling style that is unassertive and uncooperative. The attempt to stay out of conflicts or ignore disagreement.

Baseline.   A period of time where a behavior is observed and recorded, usually immediately prior to an intervention treatment.

Before-After Measurement.   This type of research design measures individuals before the treatment is given to the experimental group and after the treatment has been concluded.

Behavior.   Any observable and measurable response or act of an individual.

Behavioral Sciences.   The body of knowledge from sociology, psychology, economics, and anthropology pertaining to why and how people behave as they do.

Behavioral Contingency Management. The management of employee behavior through the systematic control of the antecedents and the consequences of that behavior.

Behavior Modification. The technology that describes practical techniques for producing changes in behaviors by the control of environmental events.

Buffering. The use of inventory, an integration department, or a linking-pin department to reduce their interdependence.

Bureaucratic Model. A form of organization that places heavy emphasis upon rules, procedural specifications, impersonality, division of labor, and hierarchy.

Case Study. The examination of numerous characteristics of a person, group or organization over an extended period of time. A useful research design when the experimenter wants to understand the object under study before making any hypotheses about relationships.

Centralization. The pattern of authority in which all major and possibly many minor decisions are made only at the top levels of the organization.

Change Agent. The individual or group which influences the organization to make decisions affecting the change deemed desirable.

Channels. The means by which messages travel from a sender to a receiver in interpersonal communication.

Charting. The use of a chart or graph to monitor behavior over time. The chart typically consists of the frequency or the intensity of a behavior recorded over a number of time periods.

Classical Conditioning. The use of stimulus events associated with reflexive behavior. Since virtually all employee behavior in organizations is operant (voluntary) behavior, classical conditioning is rare in organizational settings.

Cliché. A standard, routine, or habitual way of responding in interpersonal communications.

Closed System. A system which is programmed to receive predetermined instructions and achieve predetermined outputs without regard to environmental forces beyond the control of the system.

Closure. The perceptual process by which one tends to complete an object so that it is perceived as a constant overall form.

Coacting Group. A type of group where the members can perform their jobs relatively independently, in the short run, of each other.

Coercive Power. A form of power based on the leader's ability to obtain compliance on the basis of fear.

Cognitive Conflict. A situation in which individuals become aware that their beliefs are inconsistent.

Cohesiveness. The strength of the members' desires to remain in the group and their commitment to the group.

Collaborating. A conflict-handling style that is both assertive and cooperative. A concern for one's own and others' goals.

Competing.   A conflict-handling style that is assertive and uncooperative. The attempt to achieve one's own goals without concern for a counterpart.

Competition.   Actions taken by one person to attain his or her preferred goal while simultaneously blocking attainment of a counterpart's goal.

Complex-Dynamic Environment.   An environment which is constantly changing and difficult to manage.

Complex-Static Environment.   A highly complex environment in which there are few changes.

Compliance.   A type of conformity in which the behavior of an individual becomes or remains similar to the groups wishes because of real or imagined group pressure.

Compromising.   A conflict-handling style that is intermediate in both assertiveness and cooperation. An attempt to "split the difference" in terms of achieving outcomes.

Conflict.   Any situation in which there are incompatible goals, cognitions, or emotions within or between individuals or groups.

Conformity.   The tendency of individuals to hold similar norms, and possibly express similar types of behavior.

Confrontation.   A process in which parties in conflict directly engage each other, openly exchange information on the issues, and try to work out the differences between themselves.

Consequence.   An environmental event that follows an employee behavior. If the consequence increases the frequency of the behavior, then the consequence is reinforcing.

Consideration.   A leadership style characterized by mutual trust, two-way communications, and respect for a subordinate's ideas by the leader. A major variable in the Ohio State leadership studies.

Contamination.   The concept in transactional analysis that refers acceptance by the Child in us of our parents' or significant others' prejudices, opinions, and feelings as our own.

Content Theories of Motivation.   Theories that focus on the factors within the person that start, arouse or stop behavior. Maslow, McClelland, and Herzberg represent this approach.

Contingency Approach.   An approach to management that states that effective structure, leadership, motivation, design, etc., depends upon situational factors. If the environment is stable, then a bureaucratic structure is likely to be more effective than a flexible structure. The words *if* and *then* are critical in the logic.

Contingency of Reinforcement.   The sequence of events and behaviors consisting of environmental antecedent events, then employee behavior, and then environmental consequence event.

Contingent Delivery of a Reinforcer.   A reinforcing event that is administered to an employee only when the specified target behavior has been performed.

Continuity.   The perception process of perceiving objects as continuous patterns.

Continuous Reinforcement.   A procedure where a reinforcing event is administered after every desired behavior.

Contrast.   A principle in perception which states that external factors that stand out against the background or that are not what people are expecting are the most likely to be perceived.

Control Group.   The group in an experiment that is not exposed to or given a treatment.

Counteracting Group.   A group whose members interact to resolve some type of conflict, usually through negotiation and compromise.

Decoding.   The translation of received messages (signals) into interpreted meanings in interpersonal communications.

Decoupling.   A method to create independence between departments in order to reduce the propensity for conflict.

Degree of Change.   The dimension referring to the extent to which environmental factors considered by an individual or group are in a constant process of flux or remain basically the same over time.

Degree of Complexity.   The dimension referring to the extent to which an individual or group in an organizational unit must deal with few or many factors that are similar or dissimilar to one another.

Departmentation.   The process of forming organizational units, usually on the basis of function, process, or geographic location.

Dependent Variable.   An end result factor that is caused by an independent variable.

Deprivation.   How recently a person has had a reinforcer—the less recently, the more effective the reinforcer. Satiation is the opposite of deprivation.

Designated Leader.   The person appointed by management to lead a group.

Devil's Advocate.   A decision-making method involving a proposed course of action and a critique of the proposal. Intended to cause cognitive conflict for the decision maker.

Dialectical Inquiry.   A decision-making method involving a proposed course of action and a contradictory second course of action. Intended to cause cognitive conflict for the decision maker.

Differential Reinforcement.   A procedure where a desired behavior is reinforced while other undesirable behaviors are extinguished.

Disclosure.   The process of making more of oneself known to other individuals.

Discriminative Stimulus.   A stimulus which indicates a specific behavior. In organizations, a discriminative stimulus would cue an employee as to what behaviors will be reinforced.

Distributive Bargaining.   Bargaining behavior intended to allocate limited resources between two or more parties.

Division of Labor.   The dividing up of tasks that have to be performed to permit standardization and specialization.

Drive.   A need or motive that energizes and maintains behavior.

Ego.   The conscious mind that consists of feelings, thoughts, perceptions, and memories of which we are aware and can express to ourselves and others.

Ego State.   The individual's typical state of feeling, thinking, and reacting.

Effectiveness.   The extent to which organizations choose the proper goals and achieve them efficiently within constraints and limited resources.

Efficiency.   Output divided by input or the extent to which the result produced was at the least cost.

Encoding.   The sender's translation of messages into meaning that can be transmitted as part of interpersonal communications.

End-states of Existence.   The terminal or ultimate values attained or held by an individual.

Environment.   The external setting in which the organization operates. Of special importance are such factors as consumers, suppliers, competitors, etc., that may have a large impact on the organization's success.

Escape.   Any behavior by an employee that terminates an aversive event.

Event Recording.   The measurement of a behavior by counting the number of times a behavioral event occurs.

Expectancy.   The perceived probability that a particular act will be followed by a particular outcome, e.g., studying hard facts is highly related to receiving a good grade (outcome).

Expectancy Theory.   A process motivation theory which states that an individual will select an outcome based on how this choice is related to second-level outcomes (rewards).

Experimental Group.   The group that receives a treatment, or is exposed to the independent variable.

Expert Power.   A person's perception that another person has greater knowledge or expertise in an area and, therefore, the person's orders should be followed.

Expression Ability.   The skill to say what we mean or to express what we feel.

External Environment.   The conditions and facts that are not substantially controlled by the work group and represent "givens" for the members.

External Factors.   In terms of the perceptual process, those stimuli outside the individual that effect the perceptual process, such as size, intensity, contrast, motion, repetition, and novelty and familiarity.

Extinction.   The procedure of stopping an environmental event that has followed a behavior in the past, often causing a decrease in the future frequency of the behavior.

Extrinsic Rewards.   Rewards that a person receives from sources other than the job itself. They include pay, supervision, promotion, vacations, and friendships.

Extroversion.   The personality characteristic that may be described as an outgoing, candid, and accommodating nature that adapts itself easily to a given situation, quickly forms attachments, and will often venture forth with confidence into unknown situations.

Feedback. The response by the receiver to the sender's message in interpersonal communications. May also refer to providing information to individuals about the quality or quantity of their performance.

Feeling Type Individual. An individual who is aware of other people and their feelings, likes harmony, needs occasional praise, dislikes telling people unpleasant things, tends to be sympathetic, and relates well to most people.

Fiedler's Contingency Model. A model of leadership specifying that performance of a group is dependent upon both motivational system of the leader (LPC) and the characteristics of the situation.

Field Experiment. A research design that enables the manipulation of one or more independent variables in an ongoing organization.

Field Survey. A research design that measures the characteristics of a large group of individuals, usually at one point in time. Normally used to measure current problems, attitudes, or events.

Figure-ground. A principle stating that we tend to perceive the factor we are most attentive to as standing out against a background.

Fixed Interval Reinforcement. A reinforcer that is administered after a desired behavior and after a fixed period of time has elapsed.

Fixed Ratio Reinforcement. A reinforcer that is administered when an employee completes a fixed number of behaviors.

Flextime. A way of scheduling work so that an employee must be present during certain "core" hours of the day, but can begin and end work any time before and after these core hours.

Formal Structure. The structure that indicates to whom each person in the hierarchy reports; frequently diagrammed in an organization chart.

Formalistic Life-style. The value that individuals place on having their actions guided by directives from formal authorities.

Friendship Group. A group that serves the primary purpose of meeting the members' personal needs of security, esteem, and the like.

Fringe Benefits. Rewards given to an employee over and above a salary. They include vacations, pension plan contributions, insurance policies, and other nonsalary rewards.

Functional Analysis. An attempt to identify the events that support and maintain a particular employee behavior. In particular, the antecedents of the behavior and the reinforcing consequences are identified.

Functional Division of Labor. The various ways of dividing up tasks that have to be performed; such as on the basis of engineering, manufacturing, shipping, sales, and finance.

Future Shock. A term coined by Alvin Toffler to refer to society's inability to adapt to the increasing rate of change.

Goal Conflict. A situation in which desired end-states or preferred outcomes appear to be incompatible.

Goal Setting. The process of developing, negotiating, and formalizing objectives that an employee is responsible for accomplishing.

Group.   A number of persons who communicate with one another often over a span of time, and who are few enough so that each person is able to communicate on a face-to-face basis.

Group Atmosphere.   A variable in Fiedler's leadership model that refers to the negative or positive relationship between the leader and group members.

Group Goals.   The objectives or states desired by the group as a whole, not just the objectives desired by each individual member.

Group Properties.   The processes, such as communication networks, norms, cohesiveness, member composition, that influence the effectiveness of the group.

Groupthink.   A type of highly cohesive and conforming group with certain characteristics that can hinder the effectiveness of group decision making.

Growth Need Strength.   An attribute of individuals that refers to a desire for growth, personal accomplishment, and learning on the job. If growth need strength is high, individuals will probably react positively to job enrichment programs.

Hackman-Oldham Model.   A strategy for enriching jobs by increasing the core dimensions of the job—skill variety, task identity, task significance, autonomy, and feedback.

Halo Effect.   The process in which an impression, either favorable or unfavorable, is used to evaluate a person on other dimensions. This rating error is found in performance appraisals.

Horizontal Conflict.   Conflict occurring between employees or departments at the same hierarchical level in an organization.

Hygiene Factors.   Factors in Herzberg's motivation theory which can only prevent job dissatisfaction but cannot lead to job satisfaction. Typical hygiene factors are pay, working conditions, interpersonal relations, and so forth.

Hypothesis.   A statement about the relationship between two or more variables. It asserts that a particular characteristic of one of the factors (independent variable) determines the characteristic of another factor (dependent variable).

Impersonality.   The treatment of organizational members as well as outsiders without regard to certain individual qualities such as race, sex, and religion.

Incentive.   A type of motive that focuses on an outcome that is attractive to an individual.

Independent Variable.   A causal factor in a hypothesis.

Individual Adaptation.   The process individuals use to change their behaviors to meet the demands of the organization.

Individual Differences.   Those aspects, such as personality, perception, and communication styles, that are uniquely identified to an individual.

Individual-oriented MBO Model.   The change approach in which the interaction between management and lower levels is on a one-to-one basis and consists of the elements of objective setting, subordinate participation, implementation, and review and feedback.

Informal Leader.   The individual in a group who emerges over time with relatively high influence as compared with other group members.

Initiating Structure.   The extent to which leaders are likely to define and structure their roles, and those of subordinates toward accomplishing the group's goal. This leadership style emphasizes directing group activities through planning, communicating, information, and giving directions.

Instrumentality.   The relationship between first and second level outcomes, e.g., relationship between getting an A and gaining admittance into graduate school.

Integrated Group Problem Solving.   A six-phase approach that diagnoses the process and content of group problem solving and was developed by Morris and Sashkin.

Integrative Bargaining.   Behavior intended to solve problems in such a way that two or more parties increase the resources available to all of them.

Intensity.   A principle in perception stating that the more important the external factor, the more it is likely to be perceived.

Interacting Group.   A group that cannot perform a task until all members have completed their share of the task because of mutual interdependencies.

Interactions.   The patterns of communication that occur between group members.

Intermittent Reinforcement.   A procedure where a reinforcing event is administered after a behavior only at certain times.

Internal Factor.   Those aspects of the perceiver that influence the perceptual process. Two factors are learning and motivation.

Interpersonal Communication.   The transmission and reception of ideas, feelings, and attitudes—verbally and nonverbally—which produce a response.

Interpersonal Communication Network.   Those interconnected individuals who are linked by patterned interactions to other individuals.

Interpersonal Life-style.   A life-style developed through communications with others that reflects the group's norms and serves as a basis for controlling one's behavior in organizations.

Intervention.   The deliberate introduction of an antecedent or consequent event in an attempt to change the behavior of an employee.

Intrinsic Rewards.   Rewards that are associated with the job itself, such as the opportunity to perform meaningful work, receive feedback on results, and see finished parts.

Introversion.   A personality trait characterized by a hesitant, reflective, retiring nature that keeps to itself and shrinks from objects.

Intuition-Feeling Style.   An individual problem-solving style which primarily relies on intuition for purposes of gathering information and feeling for purposes of evaluating information.

Intuition-Thinking Style.   An individual problem-solving style which relies primarily on intuition for purposes of gathering information and thinking for purposes of evaluating information.

Intuitive Type Individual.   An individual who likes solving new problems, dislikes doing the same thing over and over again, jumps to conclusions, is impatient with routine details, and dislikes taking time for precision.

Job.   A set of work activities, the completion of which serves to increase or maintain the organization's effectiveness.

Job Design.   The deliberate, purposeful planning of the job including all its structural and social aspects and their effect on the employee.

Job Diagnostic Survey.   An instrument developed by Hackman and Oldham that analyzes the core dimensions of a job and the outcomes that may result from job redesign.

Job Engineering.   The application of the scientific method to the design of a job. The goal is to maximize the efficiency of the worker by studying the worker's behavior through time and motion techniques.

Job Enlargement.   A job design strategy that involves expanding job range of the individual by giving the person more tasks to complete.

Job Enrichment.   A job design strategy that seeks to improve performance and satisfaction of workers, by providing them with more challenging tasks, responsibility, authority, feedback, and autonomy.

Job Rotation.   A job design strategy that involves moving the worker from task to task over a period of time to reduce boredom.

Laboratory Experiment.   A research design conducted in a laboratory that is specifically created to study some variables. The essence of the laboratory experiment is to observe the effects of manipulating an independent variable on a dependent variable.

Law of Contingent Punishment.   A punishing event will be more effective if it is delivered only when the particular behavior to be punished occurs.

Law of Contingent Reinforcement.   A reinforcer will be at maximum effectiveness if it is administered only when the desired behavior has occurred.

Law of Immediate Reinforcement.   A reinforcer will be at maximum effectiveness the more immediately the reinforcer is administered after the target behavior.

Law of Reinforcement Size.   The larger the amount of any given reinforcer, the more effective that reinforcer.

Law of Reinforcer Deprivation.   The more deprived a person is of a certain reinforcing event, the more effective that reinforcer will be.

Leader.   The person who is in charge of the planning, organizing, and controlling in a group.

Leadership.   The ability of one person to influence the behavior of another.

Learning.   A relatively permanent change in behavior that results from reinforced practice or experience.

Least Preferred Coworker (LPC).   An integral part of Fiedler's leadership model that refers to the motivational system or behavioral preferences of the leader. High LPC leaders are relations-oriented; low LPC leaders, task-oriented.

Legitimate Power.   The belief by one person or group that it is rightful or desirable for another person or group to influence their actions within specific areas.

Life-style.   The outward evidence of a person's values and beliefs.

Line Activities.   The functional activities directly influencing the principal work flow in the organizations, such as engineering, stamping, assembly, and the like in a manufacturing organization.

Listening.   An intellectual and emotional process that integrates physical, emotional, and intellectual inputs in a search for meaning and understanding.

Management by Objectives.   An approach to organizational change where managers meet with workers to establish realistic change objectives and identify the general means for achieving them. The nature of MBO can vary tremendously depending upon the prevailing managerial value system.

Mass Production Technology.   The manufacture of large volumes of identical or similar goods, usually through the use of assembly-line paced work.

Matching.   A selection process used by the researcher where all subjects are matched on a number of predetermined factors such as age, sex, and educational experience.

Matrix Organization.   The organization form in which dual authority, information, and reporting relationships exist.

Meaning.   The ideas, thoughts, images, feelings, or facts that exist within us as a result of receiving messages from others. It may or may not be the same as the meaning intended by the sender.

Method-bound.   A problem in research where a particular method used by the researcher leads to certain results.

Model.   A simplified replication of a problem situation that can be manipulated to explore the range and quality of solutions to the problem.

Modes of Conduct.   The means for the attainment or achievement of one's ultimate values.

Motion.   The principle in perception which states that a moving factor (stimuli) is more likely to be perceived than a stationary one.

Motivating Potential Score.   The total score on all five core job dimensions in the Hackman-Oldham model. A high score indicates that the job has skill variety, task significance, task identity, autonomy, and feedback.

Motivation.   A predisposition to act in a specific goal-directed manner.

Motivators.   The part of Herzberg's motivation theory that is associated with positive feelings about work. Typical motivators include the work itself, challenging job, personal recognition, and responsibility.

Moving Stage.   A stage in the change process that occurs after the organization has broken existing habits and before the new habits are learned and reinforced.

Need Hierarchy Theory.   Because people are motivated by needs, when a need is present, it serves as a motivator of behavior.

Need Profile.   The unique configuration of needs for an individual.

Needs.   The deficiencies a person feels at a point in time.

Negative Feedback.   The communication from the receiver that informs the sender that the intended meaning of a message was not achieved.

Negative Reinforcer.   An aversive event that, when terminated or prevented by an employee's behavior, increases the frequency of that behavior. Avoidance and escape are both forms of negative reinforcement.

Negotiation.   A process by which two or more parties try to reach an agreement that determines what each party gives and receives in a transaction.

Noise.   Any interference in the channel other than the intended message in the process of interpersonal communication.

Nonverbal Communication.   All behavior expressed consciously or unconsciously, done in the presence of another (or others) and perceived either consciously or unconsciously.

Norm.   The generally agreed upon standards of member and group behavior that have emerged as a result of member interaction over time.

Novelty and Familiarity.   The principle which states that either a novel or familiar factor in the external environment can serve as an attention getter, thereby affecting a person's perception.

Objectives.   The levels of results to be attained within a specific period of time.

Operant Behavior.   The voluntary behavior of an employee. In contrast, respondent behavior deals with reflexes. Virtually all employee behavior of interest to management is operant behavior.

Operant Conditioning.   The management (changing) of an employee's target behavior primarily through the alteration of the environmental events (the reinforcing consequences) that follow the behavior.

Organization Chart.   The pictorial presentation of the formal organization.

Organizational Adaptation.   The process the organization uses to align itself with the environment in which it is operating.

Organizational Behavior.   A systematic attempt to study, understand, and influence the behavior of people in organizations.

Organizational Climate.   A set of properties in the work environment that are perceived by employees. These are descriptions of the work environment that affect employees' satisfactions and performance.

Organizational Design.   The formal system of communication, authority, and responsibility that is created by management to aid in achieving organizational goals.

Outputs.   The achievement of tasks and other goals by group members.

Overt Behavior.   Behavior that is publicly observable and measurable.

Participative Decision Making.   A form of decision making in which individuals have an opportunity to define problems, consider alternatives and influence solutions.

Participative Management.   An approach that emphasizes involving all of the concerned parties to the decision.

Path-Goal Leadership.   A model developed by Robert House that emphasizes the influence of leadership on subordinate goals and paths to achieve these goals.

Perceived Environment.   How individuals or groups interpret and evaluate their environment.

Perceptual Defense.   The tendency to protect oneself against objects or situations that are perceptually threatening. The major categories of perceptual defense are stereotyping, halo effect, projection, and attribution.

Perceptual Grouping.   The tendency to form individual stimuli into a meaningful pattern by means of continuity, closure, proximity, or similarity.

Perceptual Organization.   The process by which we group environmental stimuli into recognizable patterns.

Perceptual Processes.   The process by which individuals attend to incoming data, organize these data into recognizable factors, and give a response.

Perceptual Selection.   The process by which individuals filter out most stimuli so that they can deal with the more important stimuli.

Performance.   The actual results obtained.

Personal Acceptance Conformity.   A type of conformity in which the person's behavior, attitudes, or beliefs are consistent with the group's norms and wishes.

Personalistic Life-style.   A life-style in which individuals' actions are guided by their own personal experience and feeling.

Personality.   A broad concept defining how individuals affect others, how they understand and view themselves, and their pattern of inner and outer measurable traits and behaviors.

Personal Unconscious.   The experiences, feelings, thoughts, and wishes that exist below the level of consciousness.

Planned Organizational Change.   The intentional attempt by an organization to change the status quo.

Pluralism.   The concept that the power and the right to influence an organization is spread among a number of groups with conflicting values and goals.

Pooled Interdependence.   An organizational situation which involves two or more departments that are relatively autonomous and independent of each other.

Positive Feedback.   The communication by the receiver which informs the sender that the intended meaning of a message was achieved.

Positive Reinforcement.   The administration of a pleasant event after a behavior has occurred, which has the result of increasing the frequency of that behavior.

Power.   The ability of one person to obtain compliance from another person.

Practicality.   This refers to how useful the information obtained in the research design is to the organization under study.

Premack Principle.   The pairing of an unpreferred (nonreinforcing) employee behavior with a preferred (reinforcing) employee behavior, in order to achieve the unpreferred behavior.

Principal of Compensation.   A concept which states that, for the normal personality, one personality subsystem may compensate for the weakness of another personality subsystem.

Proactive Orientation.   The tendency to take action as a result of ideas, goals, or perceived opportunities that are created by the individual, group, or organization.

Procedural Specifications.   The written predetermined sequence of steps an employee must follow in performing tasks and dealing with problems.

Process Motivation Theories.   Theories that describe how and why people choose a particular behavioral pattern to accomplish work goals. Expectancy and reinforcement theories are two examples of process motivational theories.

Product Form of Organization.   The grouping together of activities that are necessary to create each of the outputs (products or services) of the organization.

Profit-maximizing Management.   The managerial value system in which primary emphasis is given to making decisions and taking actions which serve the sole purpose of achieving the highest possible level of long-run profits.

Projection.   A tendency to see in other persons traits that you possess.

Projective Method.   A research technique in which a subject is presented with an unstructured stimuli that is capable of arousing many different kinds of reactions.

Proximity.   A principle stating that a group of objects be perceived as related because of their nearness to each other.

Pseudoquestion.   A communication presented in the form of a question that is actually intended to present an opinion or make a statement.

Punisher.   Any aversive event following an employee's behavior that has the effect of decreasing the frequency of that behavior. A punisher can also be the withdrawal of a pleasing event after an employee's behavior that decreases the frequency of that behavior.

Quality-of-Life Management.   The management value system in which there is a recognized need for profit but which rationalizes profits in terms of social benefits and accepts the need for being concerned with people both within and outside the organization.

Quality-of-Work Life.   The degree to which organizational members are able to satisfy important personal needs through their experiences within the organization.

Random Selection.   A process whereby each individual has an equal chance of being selected.

Reactive Orientation.   The tendency to take action as a result of being influenced by some external event or force.

Reciprocal Interdependence.   An organization situation which involves the output from one department becoming the input to a second department, and vice versa. Thus, both departments share a mutual dependence on each other in accomplishing their objectives.

Reinforcer.   Any event following a behavior which increases the frequency of that behavior.

Referent Power.   Leadership power based on attractiveness or charismatic qualities. That is, the leader's orders are obeyed because of some personal qualities with which the followers closely identify.

Refreezing Change.   The last stage in the change process. It is the end result of the change strategy undertaken by management.

Relations-oriented Role.   The type of group member role that builds group-centered activities, sentiments, and viewpoints.

Reliability.   A measurement quality that refers to the consistency of the data obtained. Reliability is a necessary condition for validity.

Repetition.   A principle in perception stating that a repeated factor is more likely to be perceived by an individual than is a single factor.

Research Design.   A plan, structure, and strategy of investigation developed to obtain answers to one or more research questions.

Reward.   A subjectively pleasant environmental event. A reward becomes a reinforcer if it has the power to increase the frequency of the target behavior.

Reward Power.   A person's or group's perception that another person or group has the ability to provide varying amounts and types of rewards (promotions, salary increases, etc.).

Role Conflict.   Conflict that arises when a person in an organization receives incompatible messages regarding desired role behavior.

Rules.   The formal written statements specifying the acceptable and unacceptable behaviors and decisions by organization members.

Satisfaction.   An end-state that results from the attainment of some goal.

Scalar Chain of Command.   The idea that authority and responsibility are arranged hierarchically.

Scientific Approach.   A process for seeking out and analyzing information in a systematic and unbiased manner. The three basic elements in this approach include observation, measurement, and prediction.

Self-actualizing Communication Style.   An interpersonal communication style referring to individuals who spontaneously provide the appropriate amount of information about themselves, ask for feedback, and provide feedback in a constructive and nondefensive manner.

Self-administered Reinforcer.   A consequence that employees administer to themselves. Self-administered reinforcers are important to the concept of self-control.

Self-bargaining Communication Style.   An interpersonal communication style that refers to individuals who are willing to give feedback and open up to others in direct relation to the same process taking place with others in the interaction.

Self-concept.   How individuals see themselves and how they feel about what they see.

Self-denying Communication Style.   An interpersonal communication style that refers to individuals who are isolated from others and very withdrawn.

Self-disclosure.   Any information individuals consciously communicate, verbally or nonverbally, about themselves to one or more other individuals.

Self-exposing Communication Style.   An interpersonal communication style in which individuals attempt to get others to focus on themselves by constantly asking for reactions to their behavior.

Self-oriented Role.   A type of group role whereby individuals focus only on their own needs, often at the expense of the group.

Self-protecting Communication Style.   An interpersonal communication style that refers to individuals who probe others or make comments to others without revealing very much of themselves.

Sensation-Feeling Style.   The problem-solving style in which the individual relys primarily on sensing for purposes of gathering information and on feeling for purposes of evaluating information.

Sensation-Thinking Style.   The individual problem-solving style that relies primarily on sensing for gathering information and thinking for evaluating information.

Sensation Type Individual.   The type of individual who dislikes new problems unless there are standard ways to solve them, likes an established routine, must use the work all the way through to reach a conclusion, shows patience with routine details, and tends to be good at precise work.

Sensitivity Training.   An experience-based change approach that focuses on the individual and small group development.

Sentiments.   The feelings and attitudes that are held by group members toward their group.

Sequential Interdependence.   An organizational situation which involves the output from one department becoming the input to a second department. Thus, the second department is dependent on the first department.

Shaping.   The systematic reinforcement of successive approximations of a behavior until the ultimate behavior is achieved.

Simple-Dynamic Environment.   An environment that is noncomplex but is constantly changing.

Single-time Measurement.   Data are collected about the subject or object on only one occasion.

Size.   A principle in perception which states that larger external factors are more likely to be perceived than smaller ones.

Simple-Static Environment.   An environment in which there are few changes and little complexity.

Skill Variety.   The extent to which the worker is required to use different skills. A significant part of job enrichment.

Social Reinforcers.   The reinforcers which result from interpersonal interaction, such as attention, praise, approval, smiles, nods, and physical contact.

Sociotechnical Approach.   A strategy of designing work to optimize the relationship between the technical system and the social system in the organization.

Span of Control.   The number of persons supervised by a given manager.

Staff Activities.   The ancillary activities that provide service and advice to line personnel.

Stereotyping.   A tendency to assign attributes to someone solely on the basis of a category to which the person belongs, such as race, sex, or religion.

Stimulus.   Any event in the employee's environment that is related to the employee's behavior.

Strokes.   A concept in transactional analysis that refers to the positive or negative ways in which we recognize the existence of others.

Structural Approach.   A change approach that emphasizes modifications or alterations in position definitions, relationships between positions, hierarchical arrangements, and the expected behavior of people in positions through modification of variables or forces external to them.

Structure.   The formal arrangement of processes and functions within the organization.

Suboptimizing.   The concept that optimizing the work of one department or unit may be less than optimum for the organization as a whole.

Substantive Conflict.   Conflict based on the content of a task.

Systems Approach.   An approach to the analysis of organizational behavior which emphasizes the necessity for maintaining the basic elements of input-process-output and for adapting to the larger environment that supports the organization.

Target Behaviors.   A specific employee behavior that an organization or a manager desires to manage (modify).

Task Difficulty.   The degree to which the work that must be performed is easily understandable with well-defined procedures or steps for performing the tasks.

Task Group.   A group that interacts for the primary purpose of accomplishing organizationally defined goals.

Task Identity.   Permitting the worker to complete an entire task rather than doing just bits and pieces. A core dimension of the Hackman-Oldham job enrichment model.

Task-oriented Role.   The type of role group members may undertake that serve to facilitate and coordinate problem-solving activities.

Task Significance.   The degree to which the job has a meaningful impact on others in the organization. A core dimension in the Hackman-Oldham job enrichment model.

Task Variability.   The degree to which exceptionable or nonroutine problems are experienced that require different or new procedures and steps for doing the work.

Team-oriented MBO Model.   The management-by-objectives process which puts substantial emphasis on entire work groups or teams in the establishment of performance objectives.

Technical Competence.   The standards of individual skill and performance used in the selection, retention, demotion, dismissal, or advancement of employees.

Technology.   The organization of knowledge for the achievement of practical purposes with substantial emphasis on tools, machines, and intellectual tools such as computer languages and contemporary mathematical techniques.

Theory X.   The managerial assumption that employees are lazy, avoid responsibility, need direction, and must be coerced to work.

Theory Y.   The managerial assumption that employees seek responsibility, like work, do not want to be controlled and threatened, and want to satisfy their esteem and self-actualization needs on the job.

Thinking Type Individual.   The type of individual who is unemotional, uninterested in people's feelings, likes analysis and putting things into logical order, is able to reprimand people or fire them when necessary, may seem hard-hearted, and tends to relate well to other thinking types.

Time-and-Motion Studies.   Methods first promoted by the scientific management school. They include the study of physical work using stopwatches in order to break a task into smaller segments.

Traditional Management Approach.   The first identifiable school of management thought. It stressed the logical properties of the organization and how employees ought to behave.

Trait Model.   A leadership model that seeks to identify a limited set of leader traits that can distinguish effective and noneffective leaders.

Transactions.   The interactions that we have with others and with our internal selves. This is a key concept in transactional analysis.

Trusteeship Management.   The value system in which the managers recognize the responsibility to meet the goals of various groups that have an interest in the actions of the organization.

Two-Factor Theory.   A content theory developed by Herzberg that states that two different factors affect people's attitudes toward work: hygienes and motivators.

Unfreezing Stage.   The first stage in a change model that refers to the ability of the organization to break down old habits and open itself to new ideas.

Unity of Command.   The idea that no subordinate should receive orders from more than one superior.

Valence.   The strength placed by an individual on a particular reward.

Validity.   The degree to which a data collection method or instrument actually measures what it claims to measure.

Value.   An enduring belief that a specific mode of conduct or end state of existence is personally or socially preferable to an opposite mode of conduct or end state of existence.

Value System.   An enduring organization of beliefs concerning preferable modes of conduct and end states of existence.

Variable Interval Reinforcement.   When a reinforcer is administered after an employee behavior and after a variable period of time has elasped.

Variable Ratio Reinforcement.   When a reinforcer is administered after an employee completes a variable number of behaviors.

Vertical Conflict.   Conflict occurring between hierarchical levels in an organization.

Author Index

Subject Index